Sensors Expo and Conference 2023

Santa Clara, California, USA
20-22 June 2023

ISBN: 979-8-3313-0064-7

Printed from e-media with permission by:

Curran Associates, Inc.
57 Morehouse Lane
Red Hook, NY 12571

Questex Media Group, Inc.
275 Grove Street, Suite 2-130
Newton, Massachusetts 02466
USA

Phone: (617) 219-8300

info@questex.com

Additional copies of this publication are available from:

Curran Associates, Inc.
57 Morehouse Lane
Red Hook, NY 12571 USA
Phone: 845-758-0400
Fax: 845-758-2633
Email: curran@proceedings.com
Web: www.proceedings.com

TABLE OF CONTENTS

3D Printing Enables Complex Manufacturing Processes for Sensors

Doug Sparks
M2N Technologies LLC
June 20, 2023

Sensors Converge

website: https://m2ntechnologies.org/ email:dsparks@m2ntechnologies.org

Outline

- 3D Printing Background & Rebranding- Ink Jet Printing & Ni LIGA on CMOS
- DMLS (Direct Metal Laser Sintering) Metal MEMS Wafers
- Adding Circuits onto 3D MEMS wafers

© M2N Technologies LLC
website: https://m2ntechnologies.org/ email:dsparks@m2ntechnologies.org

Advantages of Additive Manufacturing- 3D Printing

Resonant Sensors

Material scrap is lower since it is a direct print additive process versus a subtractive machining or etching process – Think Micromachining.

By printing a single piece instead of using assembly steps, the manufacturing process can be simplified – large sensor or MEMS wafer

Unique features like weight reducing internal lattices can also be formed using AM (Additive Manufacturing) techniques.

AM is already used in Aerospace, Racing, Orthopedics, Dental- Low Volume, High Margins and for support of Remote Locations- naval ships, space stations...

website: https://m2ntechnologies.org/ email:dsparks@m2ntechnologies.org

AM Problems- Cracking & Warpage

Full MEMS wafer printing can encounter these issues

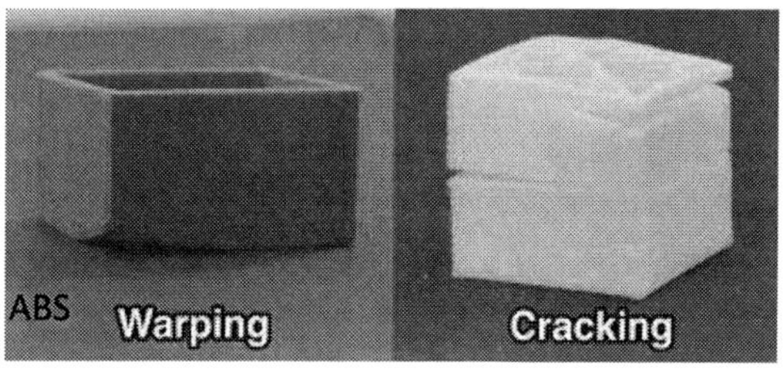

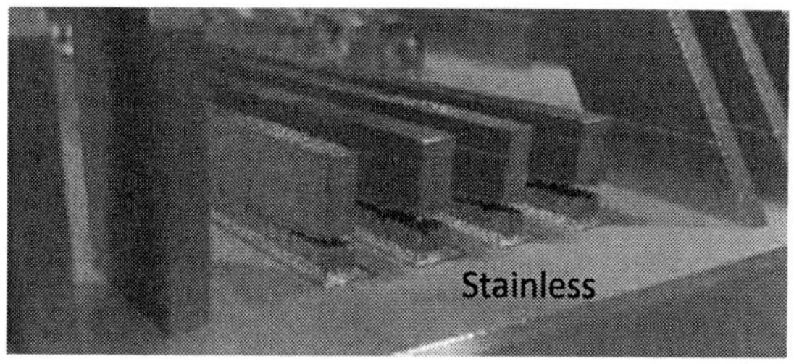

Cracked Metal

BRIDGES

Minimum allowable unsupported bridge distance is small (~2 mm/0.080 in.)

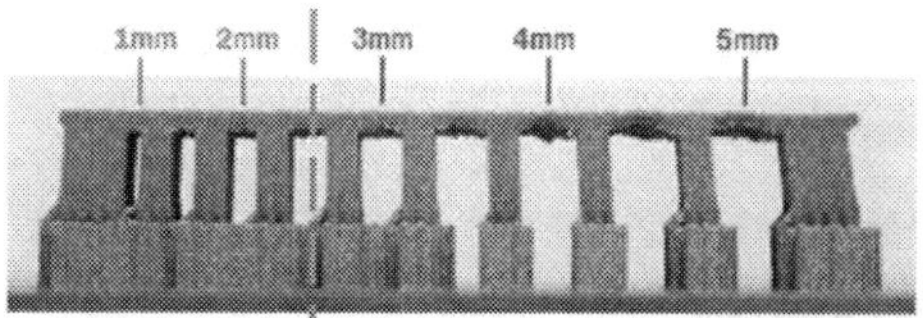

CHANNELS AND HOLES

As the diameter increases, the overhangs increase

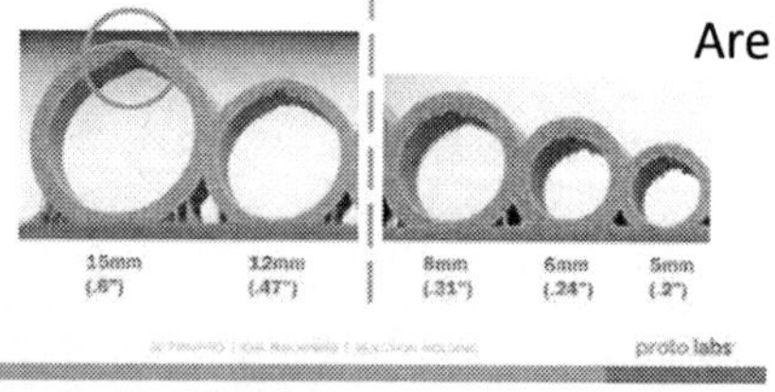

Design Rules Are Needed

ProtoLabs Design Rules for Metal AM

Supports & Orientation During Printing

Temporary supports are key for structural stability & the prevention of wafer warpage during printed

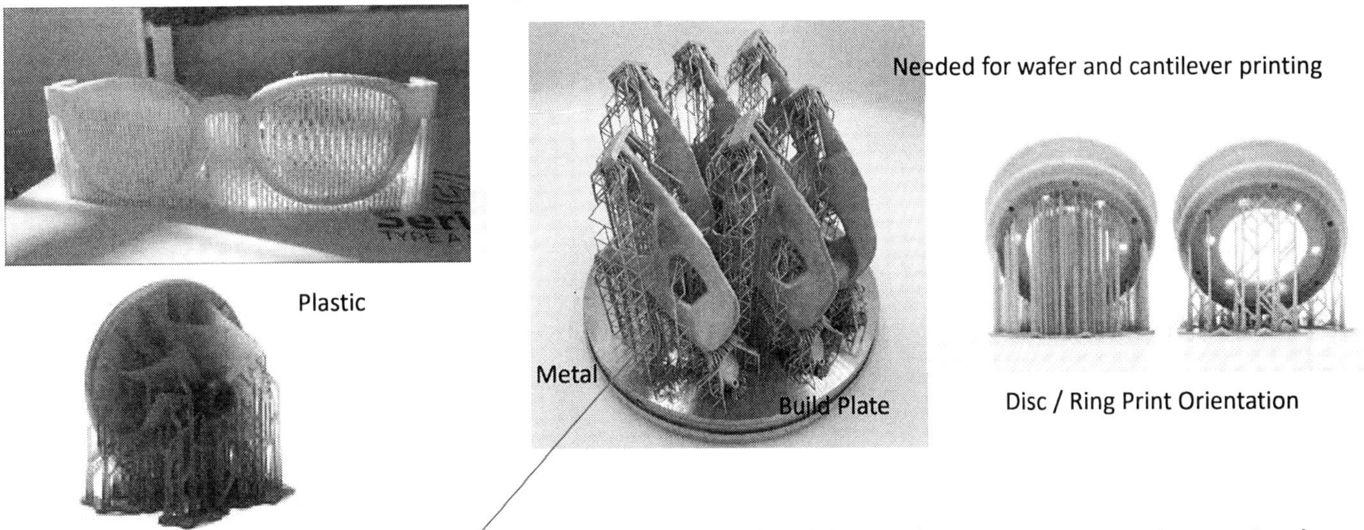

After printing these thin supports must be removed & additional post processing is required

AM Supports Release- Sacrificial Etch

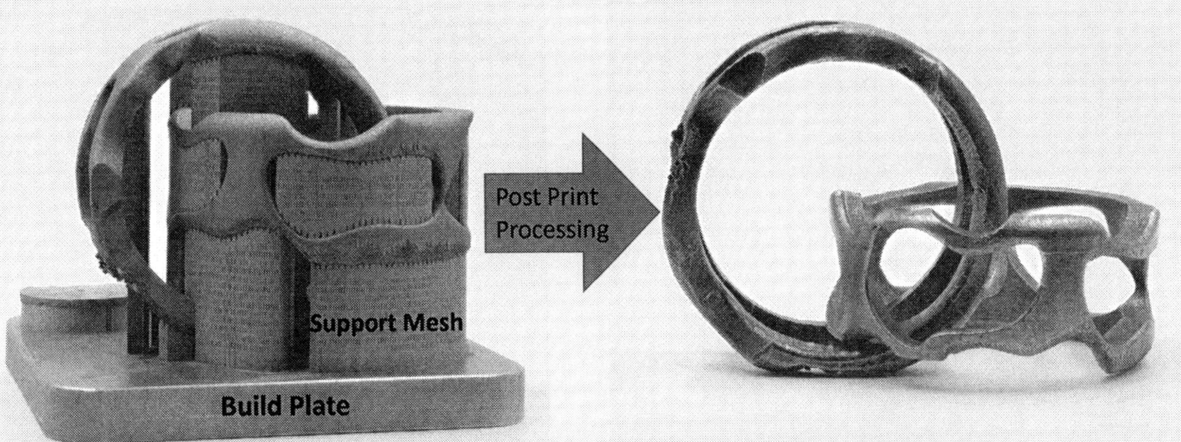

Supports are removed mechanically & chemically- wet etching, plasma etching, solvent vapor

The MEMS Wafer Processing Equivalent of the sacrificial etch- using vapor HF, XeF_2, Plasma O2, SF_6 or Wafer Dicing

website: https://m2ntechnologies.org/ email:dsparks@m2ntechnologies.org

First AM Applications for Sensors: Packaging

- Good for plastic cavity packages -- out of date/manufacture parts, after market, low volumes
- Can also help startups

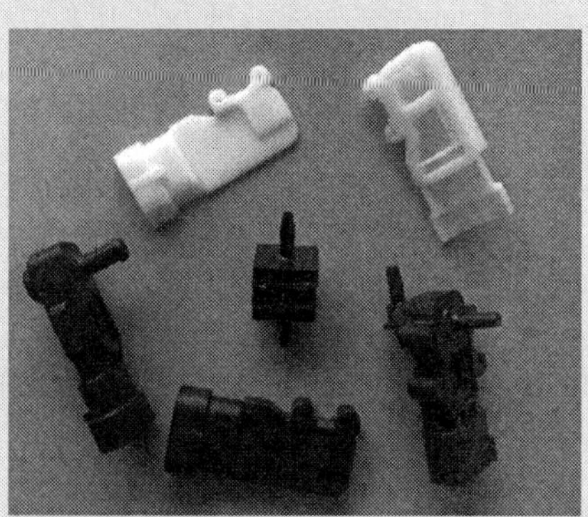

Pressure & Flow Sensor Packages

MAP Packages

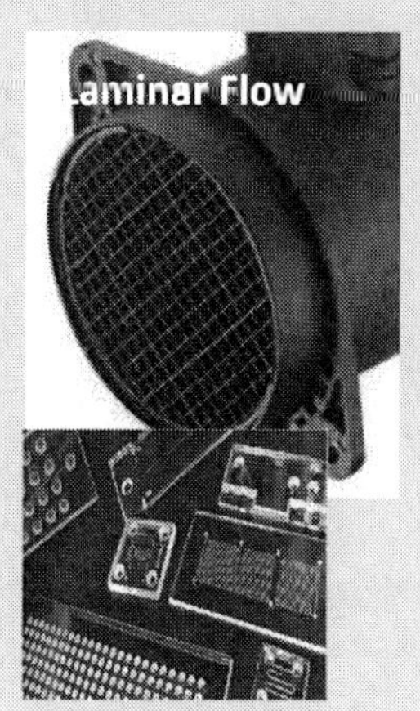

Microfluidics

Medical MEMS Sensor

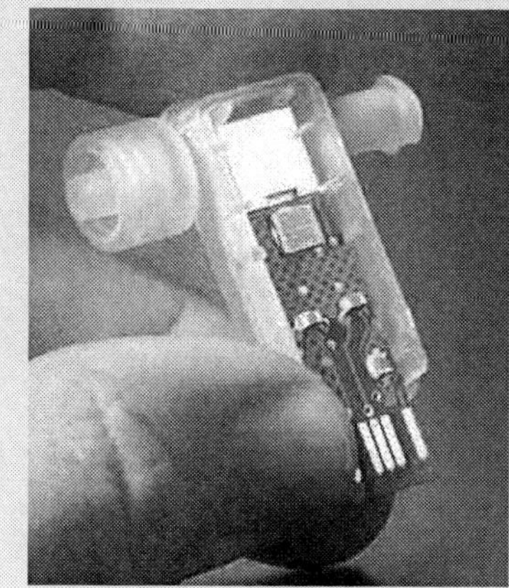

Cavity Package PCB Drop-in- 2004

3D Printed Plastic with Hot Pressed Metal Inserts

website: https://m2ntechnologies.org/ email:dsparks@m2ntechnologies.org

Micro 3D Printing: Polymers, Metals, Ceramics, Glass < 10mm Feature Sizes

BMF

Femtika

Mimotec

Incus

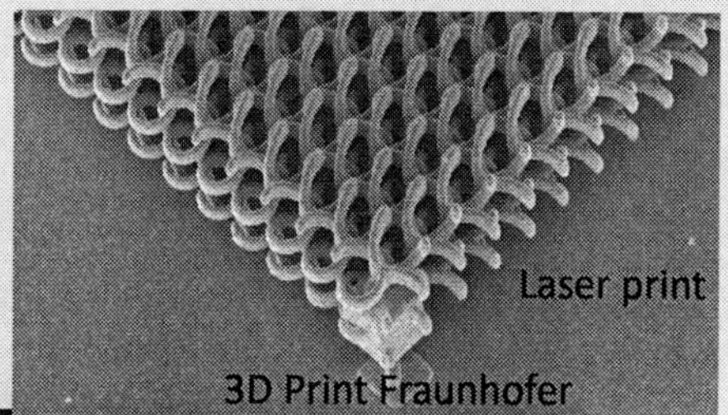

Upnano

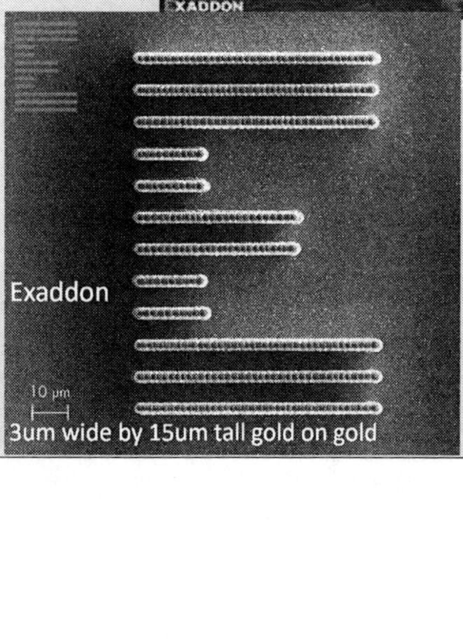

Mesoline

ATLANT 3D – ALD Printing

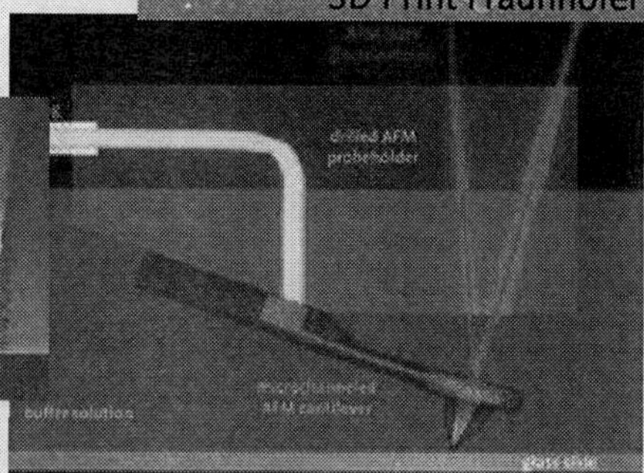

AFM-Like Metal Electroprinting

Microfabrica

Micromaker3D

website: https://m2ntechnologies.org/ email:dsparks@m2ntechnologies.org

AM Micro Feature Size Competitive Space in 2023

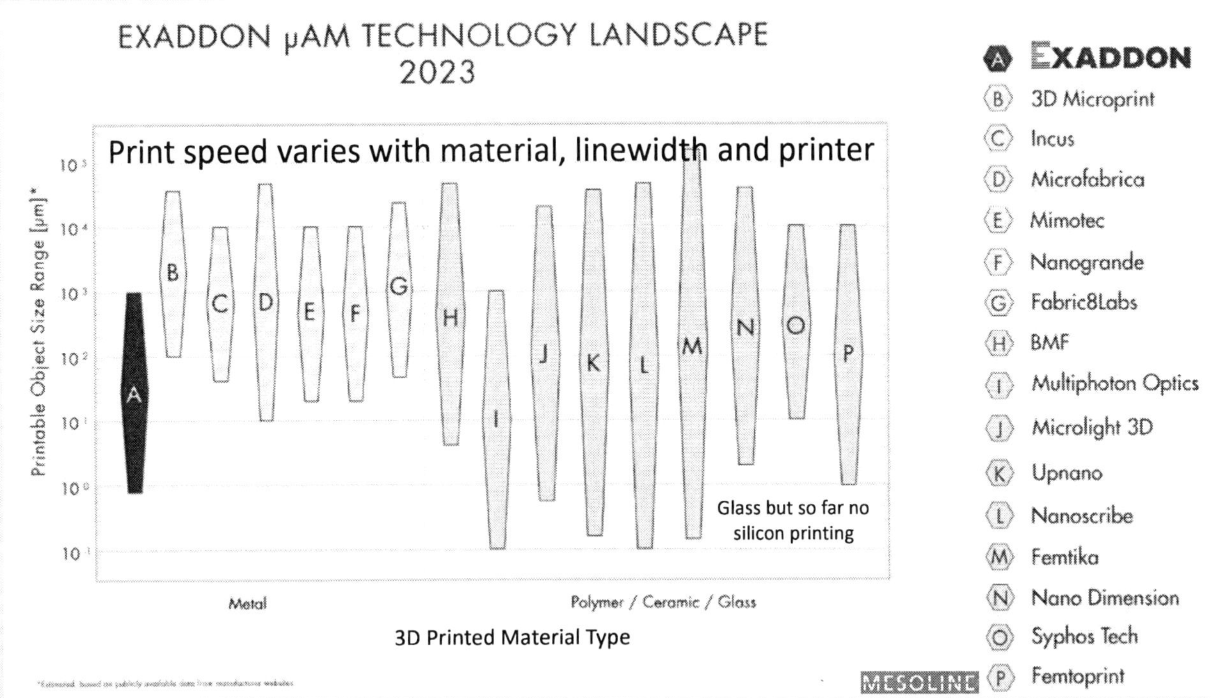

Rebranding- *Ink Jet Printing as 3D Printing*

Ink jet printing (2D) for metal and dielectric layers was applied to metal hybrid PCBs in the late 1970's-1990's, as well as for passivation coating of PCBs using silicones and acrylics

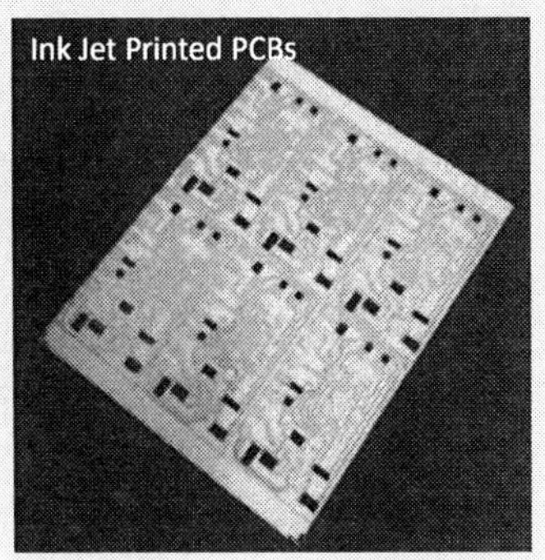

We see the similarities in NanoDimension's Dragonfly PCB 3D Printer
Its very similar to ink jet printed hybrid circuits

Materials, nozzles and X-Y controls have improved

3D Printed PCB
Larger Metal Trace
Dimensions (>0.1 mm)

website: https://m2ntechnologies.org/ email:dsparks@m2ntechnologies.org

Rebranding- LIGA as Wafer Level 3D Printing
3D Electro-Printing: Lessons Learned from LIGA

LIGA = Lithographie, Galvanoformung, Abformung

SEM Close-Up of LIGA Resonator on CMOS circa 1999-2001

- Plated, softer metals that easily plastically deform
- LIGA printed on a CMOS silicon wafer
- Drop Test and Shock Failures
- Work hardening & cyclic fatigue of micro-resonators
- Alloying for increased hardness
- Ferromagnetic? May need Mu metal shielding

UV-LIGA is offered at 3D printing by Mimotec

See: Sparks, Transducers 1997

website: https://m2ntechnologies.org/ email:dsparks@m2ntechnologies.org

3D Ni LIGA on CMOS Wafer Process Flow

- Deposit the sacrificial layer on the CMOS wafer- Polyimide, Aluminum… This includes a plating seed layer, electrically tied to the CMOS circuits
- Spin or spray the thick photoresist mold, UV expose and develop
- Electroplate the nickel alloy
- Remove the resist mold and sacrificial layer

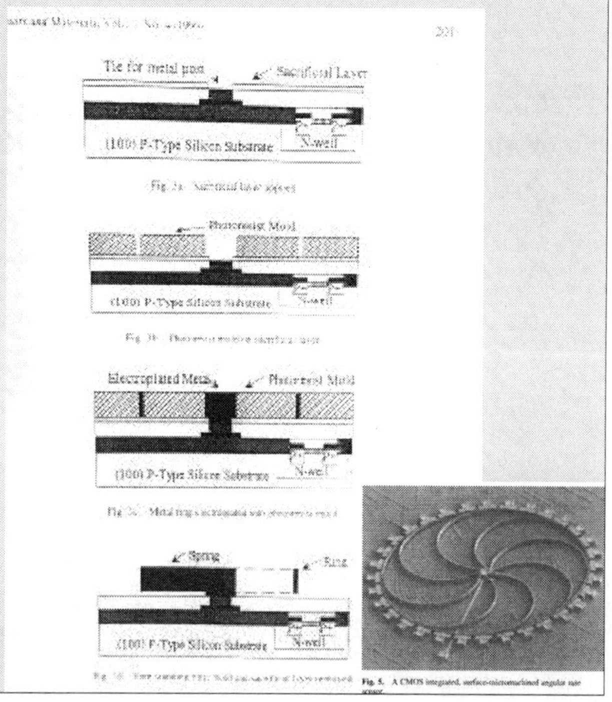

Examples of 3D Printing on Wafers

ATLANT 3D Nanosystems
ALD 3D Printing- Runners

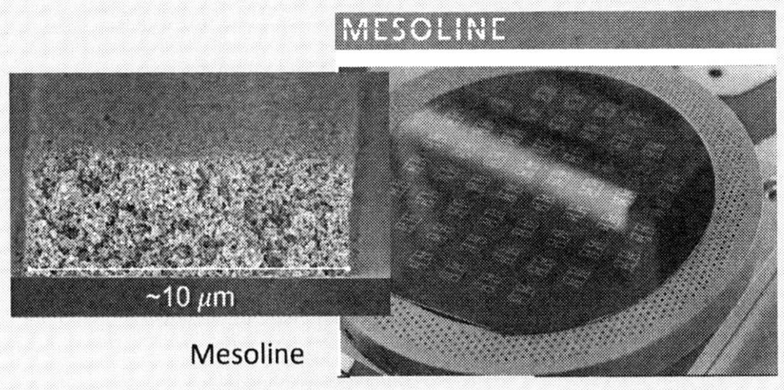

Mesoline

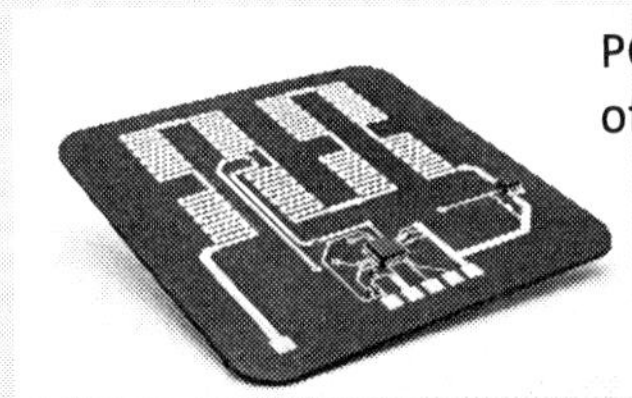

PCB circuit printing
of nanoparticles

Northeastern University

Sciperio

NanoDimensions

Outline

- 3D Printing Background & Rebranding- Ink Jet Printing & Ni LIGA on CMOS
- DMLS (Direct Metal Laser Sintering) Metal MEMS Wafers
- Adding Circuits onto 3D MEMS wafers

website: https://m2ntechnologies.org/ email:dsparks@m2ntechnologies.org

DMLS (Direct Metal Laser Sintering) of the Entire MEMS Wafers

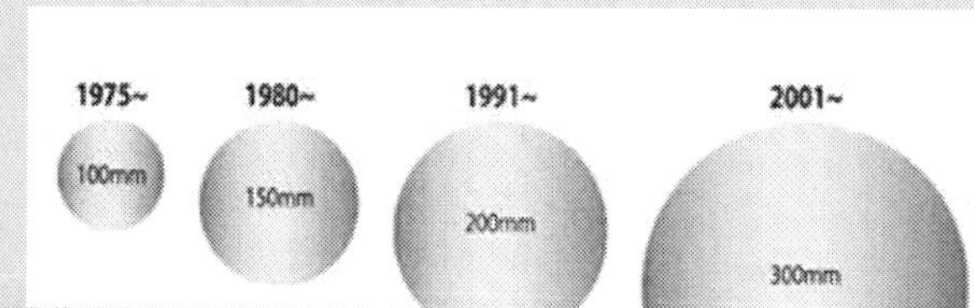

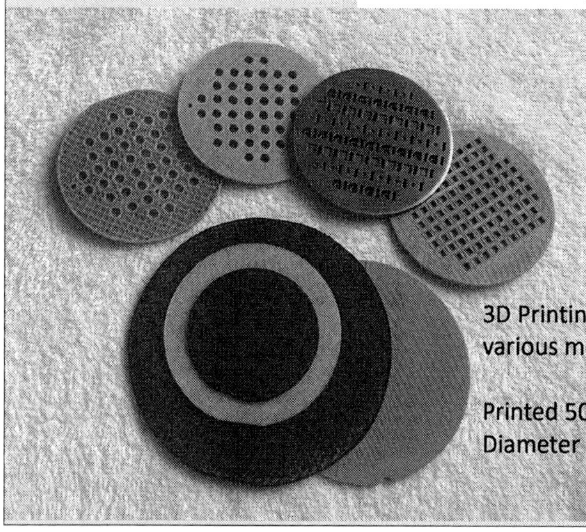

Si MEMS wafers are typically 100 to 200mm in diameter

3D Printing micromachined wafers using various metals & plastics

Printed 50, 75, 100, 125, 150mm Diameter Wafers

website: https://m2ntechnologies.org/ *email:*dsparks@m2ntechnologies.org

All these MEMS structures can simultaneously fabricated in one print

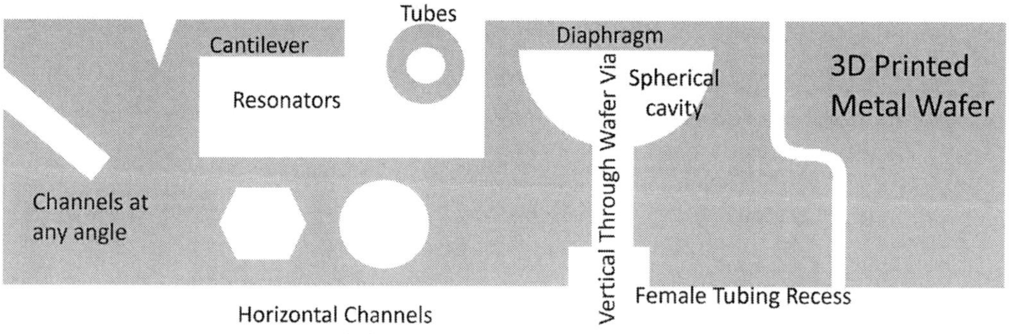

With a much wider variety of materials.

No DRIE, etch or bond development needed

Reduce MEMS wafer processing by 100's of steps

DLMS 3D Printed MEMS Wafer Cross-Section

website: https://m2ntechnologies.org/ *email:*dsparks@m2ntechnologies.org

AM+MEMS Expands the Material Spectrum for MEMS and Microfluidics

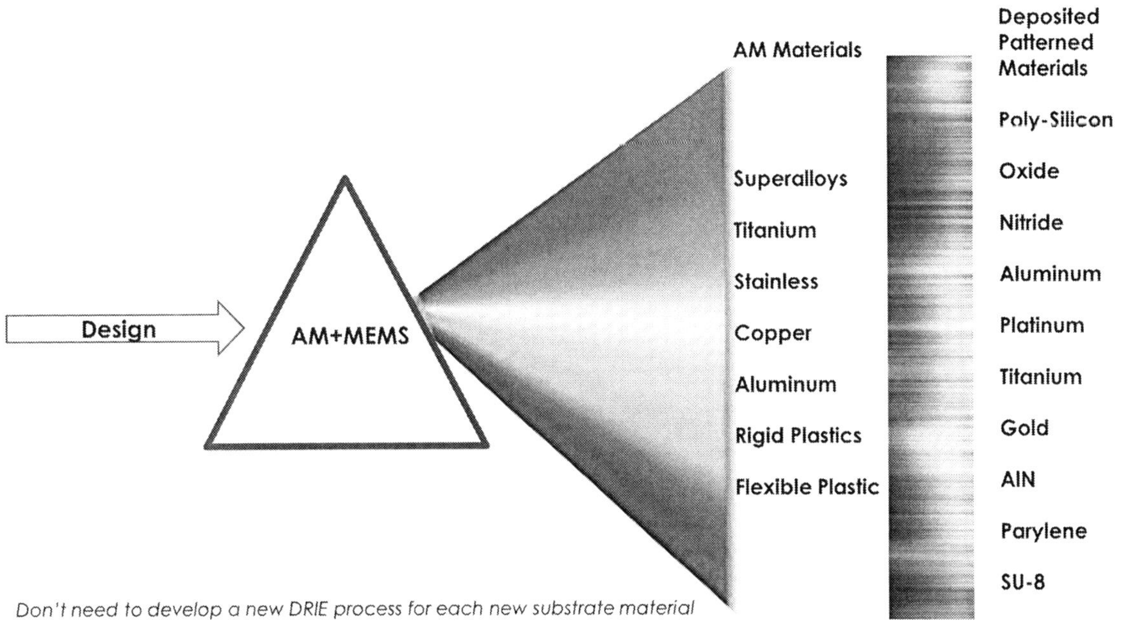

Example: Si MEMS Versus AM Microtube Process

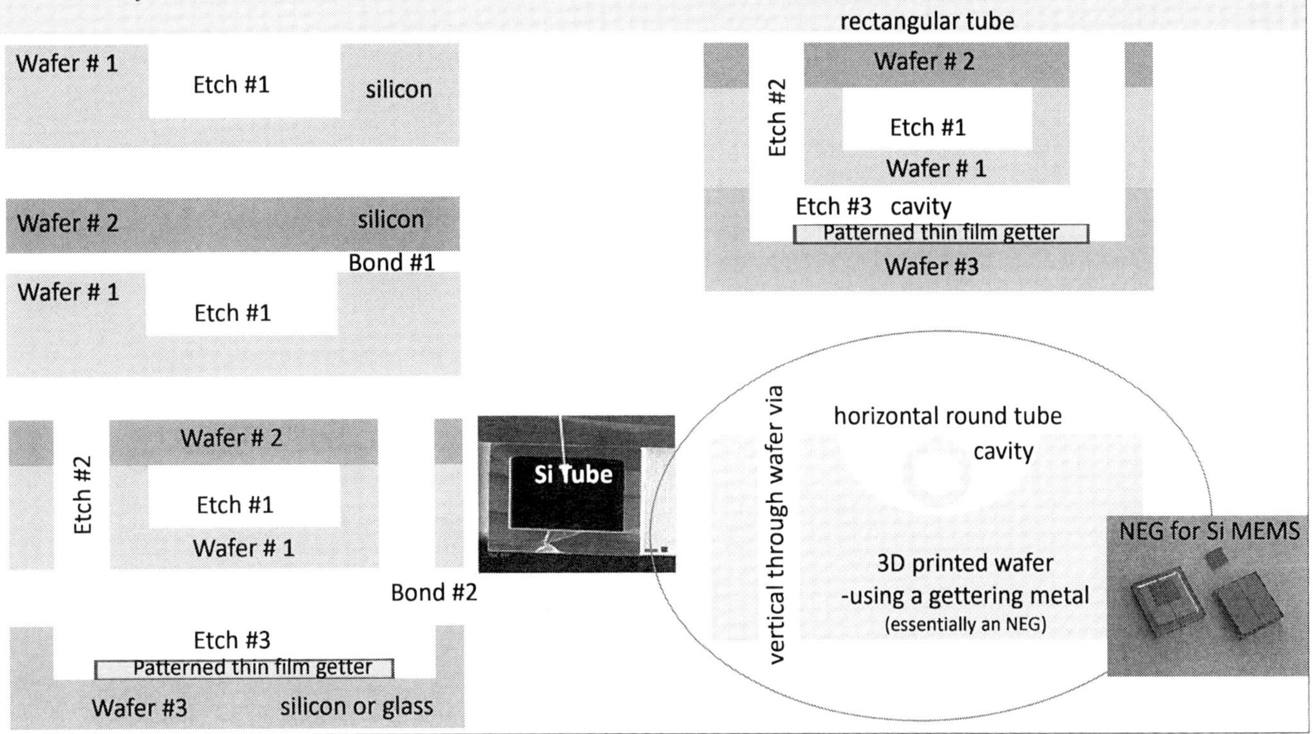

Silicon microfluidic failure modes can be avoided with Additive Manufacturing

Silicon Diaphragm Rupture

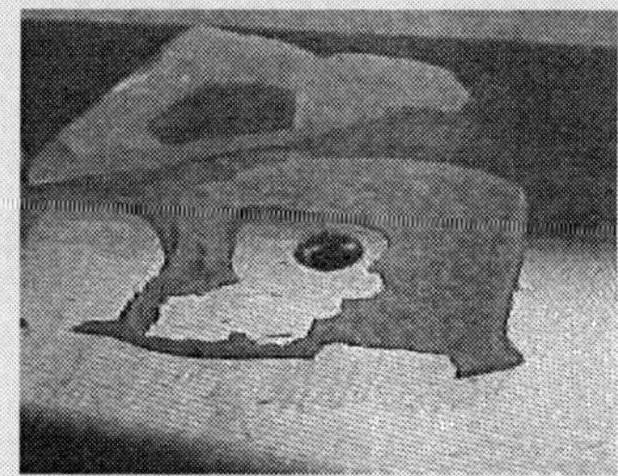

Epoxy Adhesion Failure

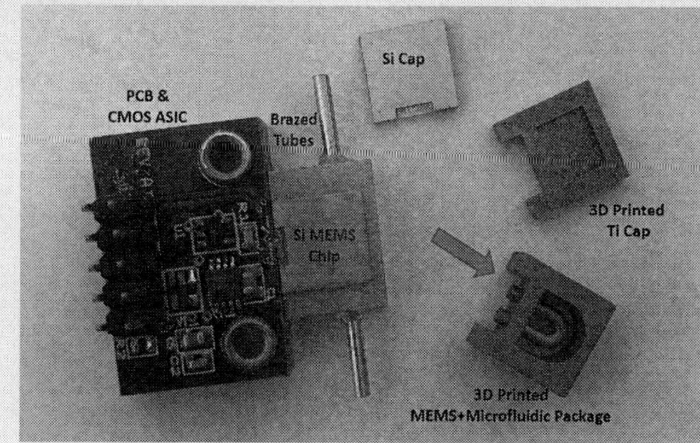

Titanium and stainless have superior fracture toughness to silicon

Combining the sensor chip and microfluidic interface eliminates weak epoxy or silicone die attachment

Helium leaks through most wafer bonding interfaces

website: https://m2ntechnologies.org/ email:dsparks@m2ntechnologies.org

Typical Si MEMS Pressure Sensor Failure Mode Solutions

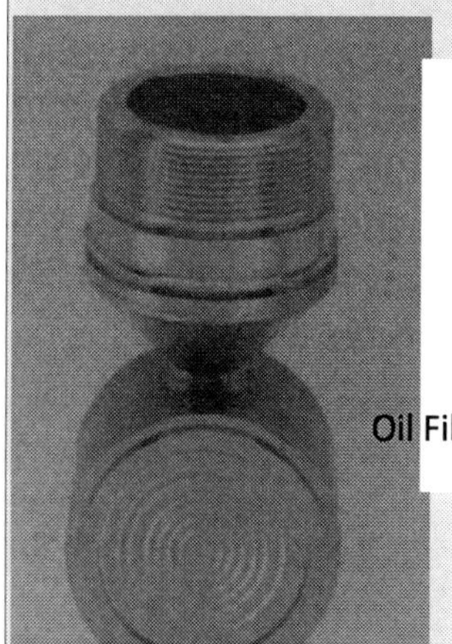

Industrial MEMS Pressure Sensors

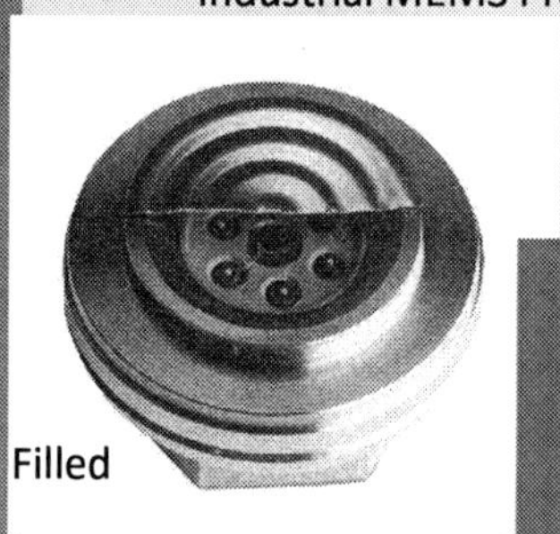

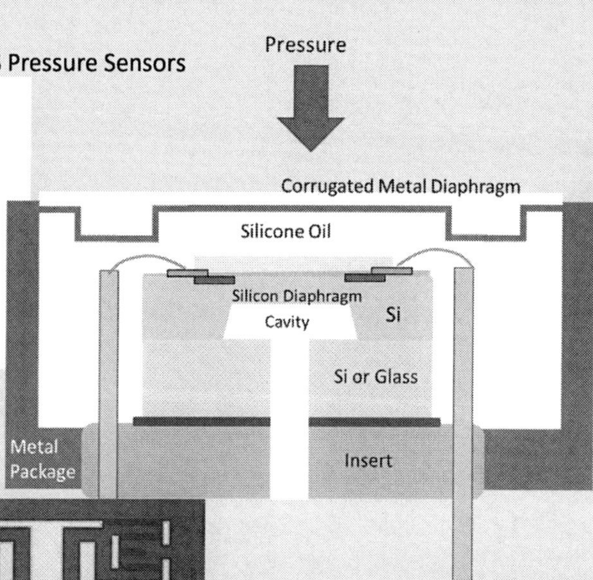

Pressure Snubbers

Corrosive fluid only touches the metal diaphragm, not the silicon chip

Backside Sense- Si Strain Gauge Glass Bonded to a machined metal diaphragm- laser assembled

website: https://m2ntechnologies.org/ email:dsparks@m2ntechnologies.org

AM Supports and Internal Lattices Applied to MEMS Wafers

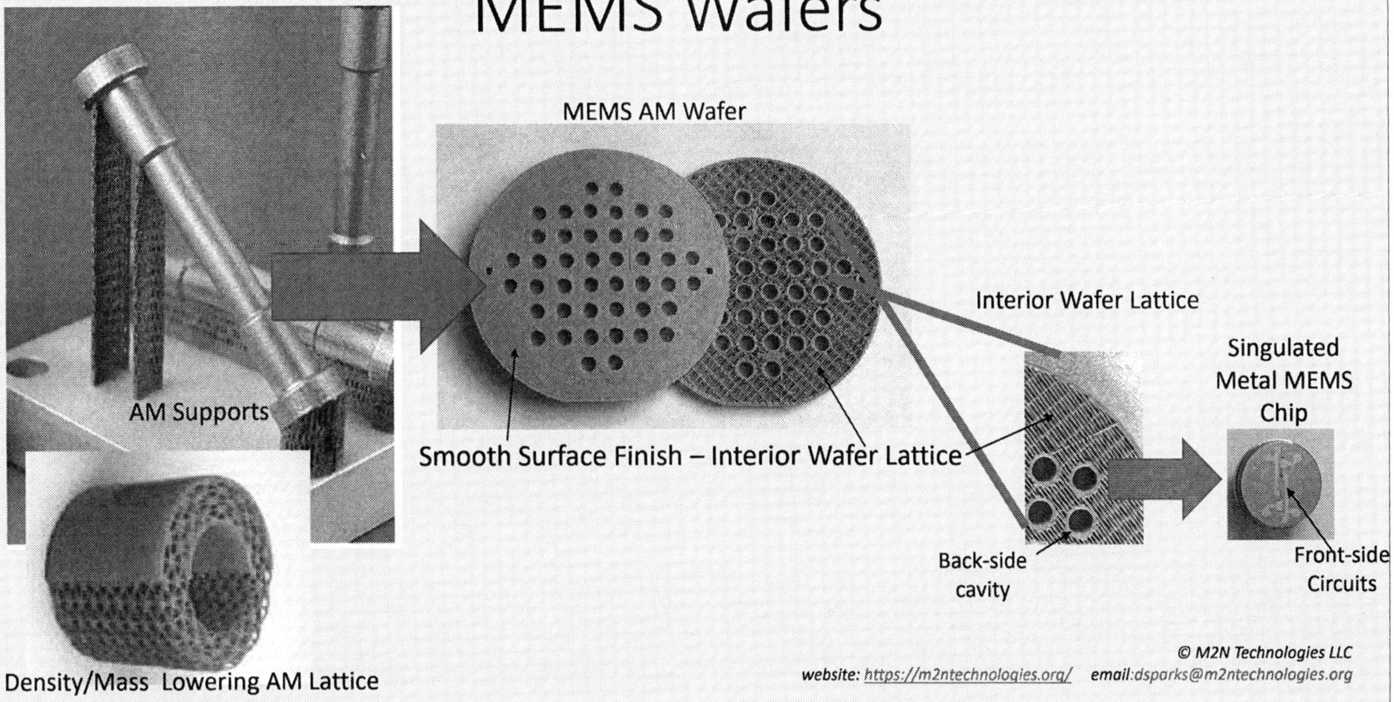

website: https://m2ntechnologies.org/ email:dsparks@m2ntechnologies.org

Challenges for DLMS MEMS AM Wafer Fabrication

- Reducing minimum printed feature size below 50 microns
- Thin wafer warpage
- Support structure removal and associated surface roughness

© M2N Technologies LLC
website: https://m2ntechnologies.org/ email:dsparks@m2ntechnologies.org

Outline

- 3D Printing Background & Rebranding- Ink Jet Printing & Ni LIGA on CMOS
- DMLS (Direct Metal Laser Sintering) Metal MEMS Wafers
- Adding Circuits onto 3D MEMS wafers

Circuit Options: 3D Printed Circuits versus Circuit formed with Traditional Fab Lithography on AM+MEMS wafers

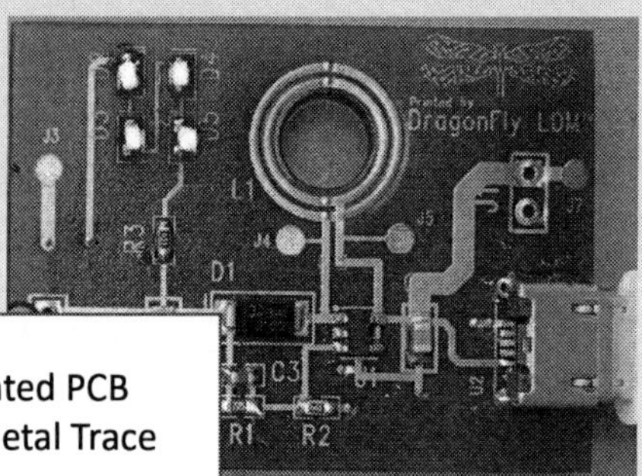

3D Printed PCB
Larger Metal Trace

NanoDimension's PCB 3D Printer
Dimensions are >0.1mm (100 microns)

or

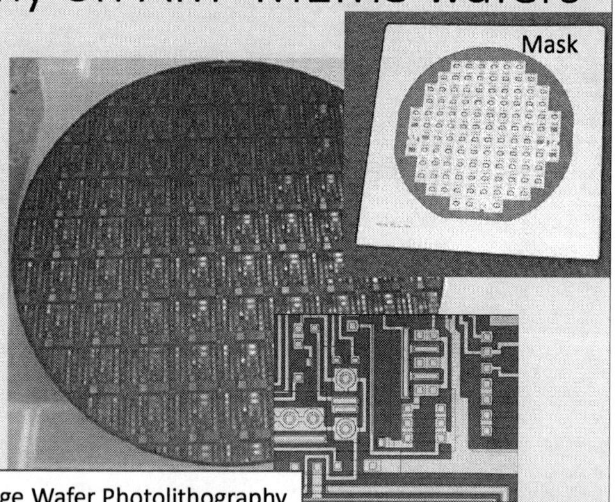

Leverage Wafer Photolithography for micron or nanometer-linewidths on the AM+MEMS® wafer

AM+MEMS Can Leverage Moore's Law on the 3D Printed Wafer Surface - *Convergence*

AM minimum 3D print linewidth varies with print method and material and has also been shrinking over the last 5 years.

Currently AM linewidths varies from > 100 microns down to < 1 micron

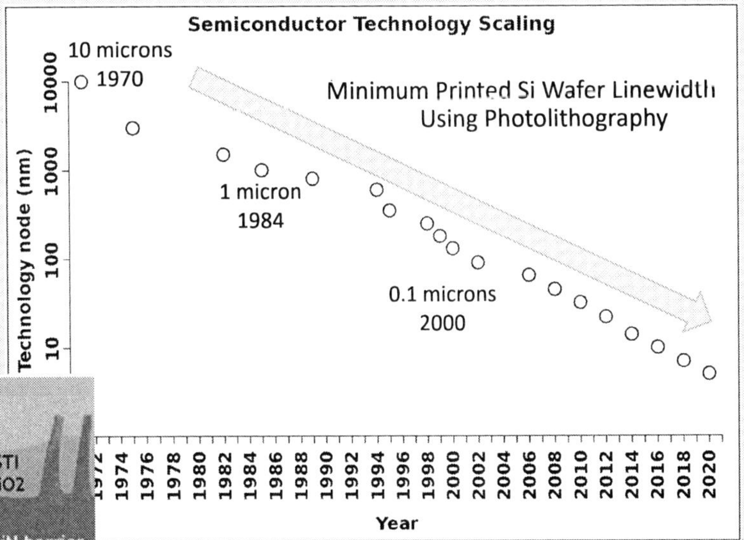

EUV Photolithography is already below 3 nm

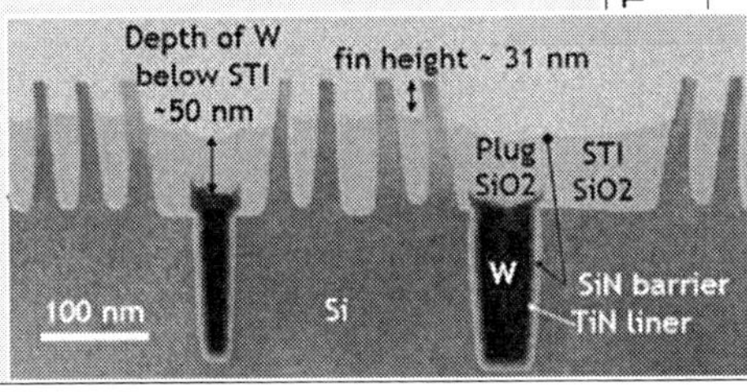

Forbidden BiCMOS Front End Fab Materials

- Transition metals (Fe, Ti, Sc, Co, Cu, Au…) can cause diode leakage, emitter-collector pipes, lower minority carrier lifetimes and gate oxide defects in BiCMOS devices.
- Frontend BiCMOS fabs will not allow these metals near high temperature fab tools- furnaces, RTP, CVD
- Dedicated MEMS fabs, without CMOS frontend processing can safely process these 3D printed materials

Transition Metals

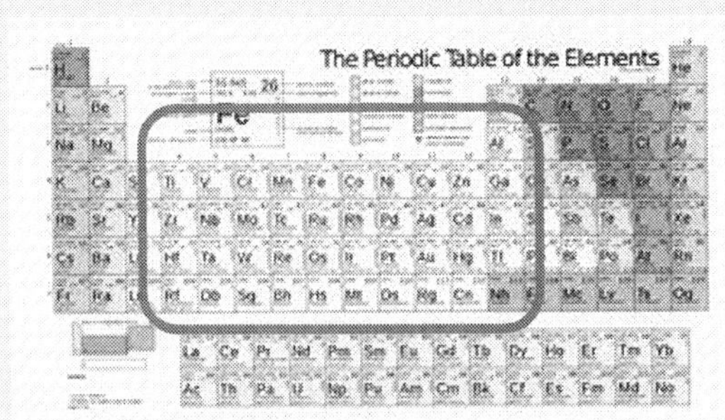

Modular Foundry for 3D Printed MEMS Wafer: InchFab

InchFab has developed a modular MEMS foundry system that lowers the CAPEX and material cost fabricating wafers.

Smaller diameter wafers are used to lower the cost of wafer processing.

This is ideal for adding circuits to 3D printed MEMS wafers

2" Silicon, GaN or AM Metal Wafer

website: https://m2ntechnologies.org/ email:dsparks@m2ntechnologies.org

Planar Photolithography on Additive Micro Machined Wafers

Retain one planar wafer surface for photolithography steps with spin or spray on resist

Thin Films On Steel Top Surface

Deposited & Patterned Thin Films Leveraging 2nm to 1+ µm Photolithography

Side View

Incorporate existing and future nanometer lithography availability for 200 and 300mm silicon wafers

Pattern thin films- conductive, dielectrics, piezoelectrics, thin film transistors, resistors, etc.

Vacuum processing on polymer AM wafers is a challenge due to outgassing

website: https://m2ntechnologies.org/ email:dsparks@m2ntechnologies.org

Pressure Sensors & Strain Gauges on 3D Printed Metal Wafers

CVD Wheatstone Bridge on Metal

MEMS on Metal Wafer Process

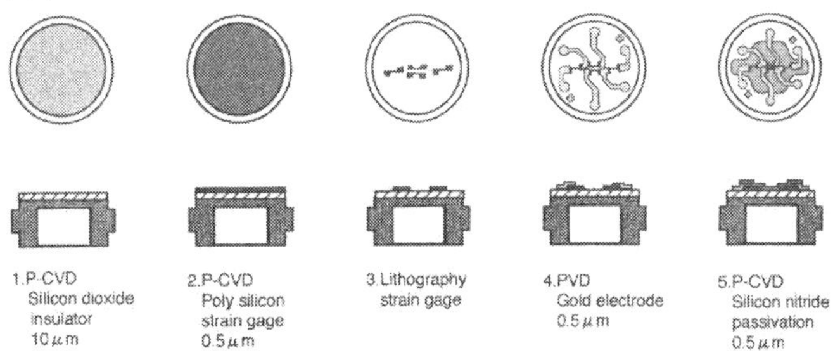

P-CVD : plasma-enhanced chemical vapor deposition
PVD : physical vapor deposition

Pressure Sensor Package Steel Chip Welded to Package for industrial & automotive applications

Biocompatible titanium can be used for medical biosensor applications

email:dsparks@m2ntechnologies.org

Post Dicing Packaging Microfluidic Interfaces 3D Printed or Laser Welded Tubing

3D Printing enables the combining of the MEMS sensor element with the fluidic packaging interface

After wafer dicing the microfluidic chip can have bottom or side metal tubing connections.

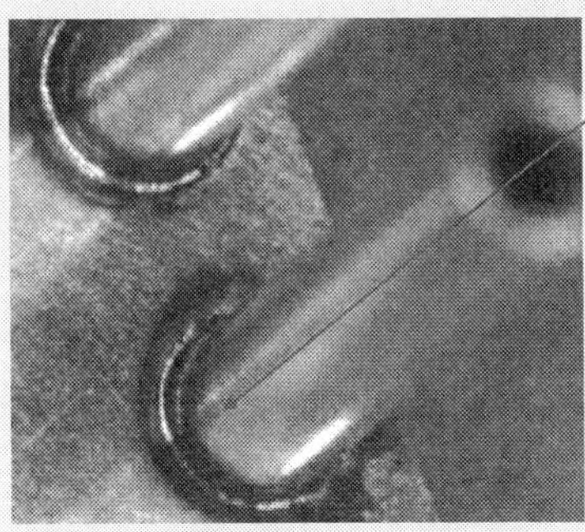

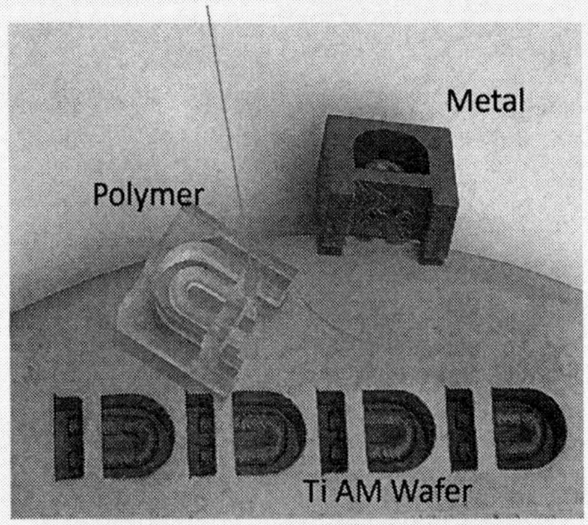

- Dual stainless tubing laser welded to the bottom of the chip
- 3D Printed female tubing inset ports

3D printed metal and plastic side tubing inlets and outlets on each chip

website: https://m2ntechnologies.org/ email:dsparks@m2ntechnologies.org

Convergence-Will MEMS Fabs have 3D Printers?

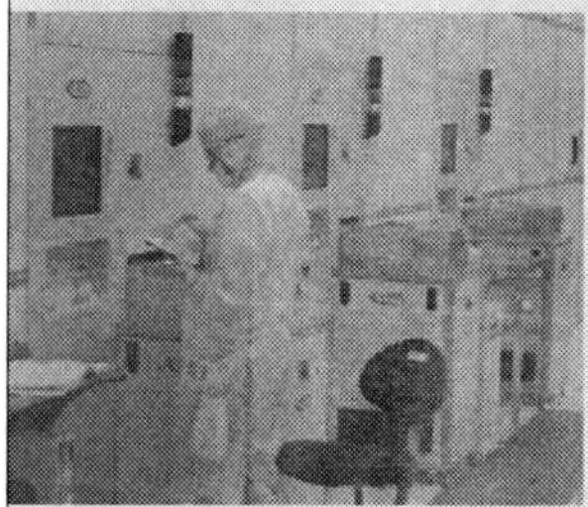

Wafer fabs have photo, thermal, plasma etch bays

Will they have an AM bay in the future?

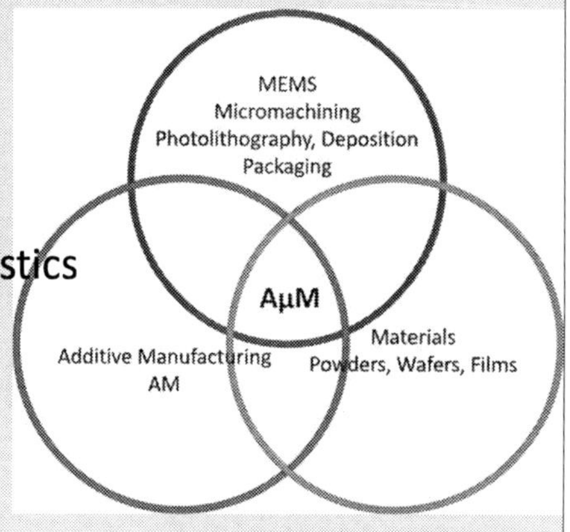

- Can use them for maintenance- fast replacement parts for fab equipment- virtual warehouse
- Quick MEMS prototype packages
- Print MEMS wafers from metals, alloys like stainless steel and plastics

3D Printer Farms

website: https://m2ntechnologies.org/ email:dsparks@m2ntechnologies.org

Conclusions

Sensors Converge

3D Printed MEMS wafers can be a new platform for fabricating sensors and can broaden the material and structural micromachining capability over conventional silicon and Pyrex wafer processing, while reducing processing & development time

These 3D printed MEMS substrate materials include materials like stainless steel, super alloys and titanium for industrial, aerospace, automotive and medical implant applications

The convergence of conventional sub-micron photolithography and AM+MEMS wafers offers significant advantages over traditional silicon MEMS devices by adding micron and even submicron circuit and feature dimensions for high-volume, low-cost manufacturing, ideal for harsh environments.

Contact Info: Doug Sparks, 1-734-732-7825 & dsparks@m2ntechnologies.org

© M2N Technologies LLC
website: https://m2ntechnologies.org/ email:dsparks@m2ntechnologies.org

NEXTFLEX

ADDITIVE ELECTRONICS FOR NOVEL WEARABLE DEVICES

DR. PATRICIA BECK, DR. ROBERT MALAKHOV, JEFF BERGMAN

Outline

NEXTFLEX

I. NextFlex Overview
II. Flexible Hybrid Electronics
III. Rigid to Flex Conversion
  a. Phase I: Thin Die Attach
  b. Phase II: Design and Manufacturing an FHE Prototype
  c. Phase III: Transition to Volume Manufacturing
IV. Process Improvements and Wearable Applications
V. Summary

Where Nextflex (a Public/Private Partnership) Fits

NEXTFLEX

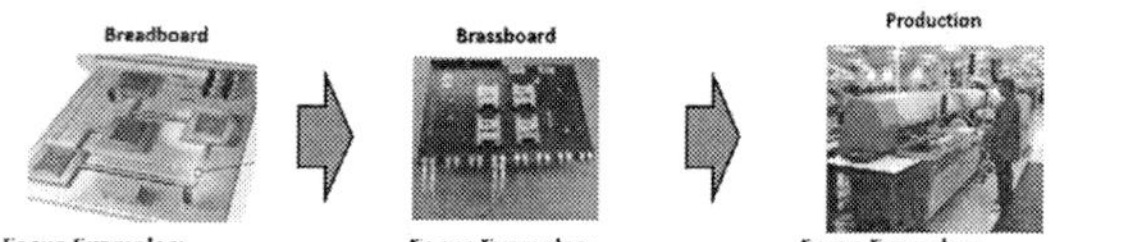

Focus Examples:
- Technology and Industrial Base
- Materials
- Cost and Funding

Focus Examples:
- Design
- Process Capability and Control
- Quality Management

Focus Examples:
- Manufacturing Workforce
- Facilities
- Manufacturing Management

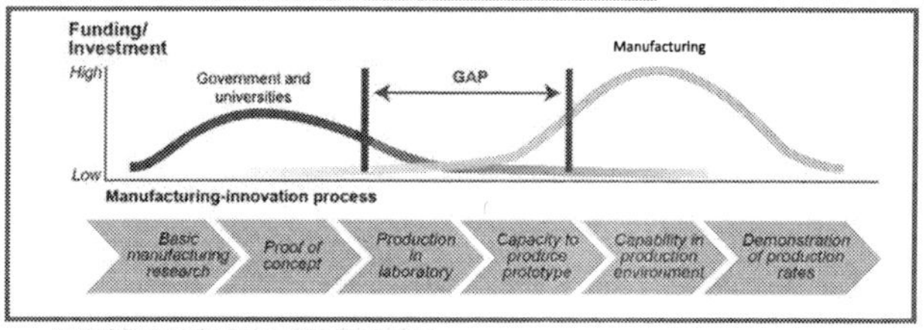

Source: GAO adapted from Executive Office of the President.

Pre Material Solution Analysis			Materiel Solution Analysis	Technology Maturation and Risk Reduction		Engineering & Manufacturing Development		Production & Deployment	
MRL 1 Basic Mfg Implications Identified	**MRL 2** Mfg Concepts Identified	**MRL 3** Mfg Proof of Concept Developed	**MRL 4** Manufacturing Processes In Lab Env't	**MRL 5** Components In Production Relevant Env't	**MRL 6** System or Subsystem In Production Relevant Env't	**MRL 7** System or Subsystem In Production Representative Environment	**MRL 8** Pilot Line Demonstrated Ready for LRIP	**MRL 9** LRIP Demonstrated Ready for FRP	**MRL 10** FRP Demo'd Lean Production Practices in Place
TRL 1 Basic Principles Observed	**TRL 2** Concept Formulation	**TRL 3** Proof of Concept	**TRL 4** Breadboard in Lab	**TRL 5** Breadboard in Representative Environment	**TRL 6** Prototype in Representative Environment	**TRL 7** Prototype in Operational Environment		**TRL 8** System Qual	**TRL 9** Mission Proven

Printing and Processing, Thin Die Integration & Testing Services for Commercial and Agency Projects

NEXTFLEX

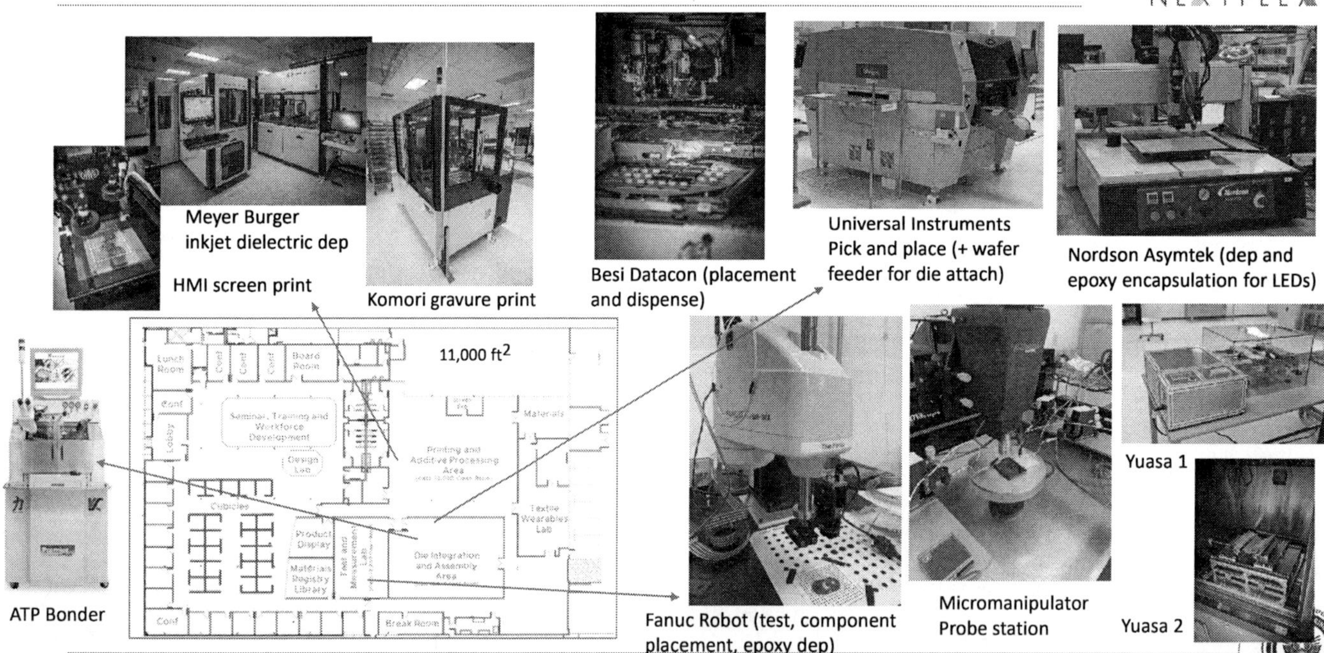

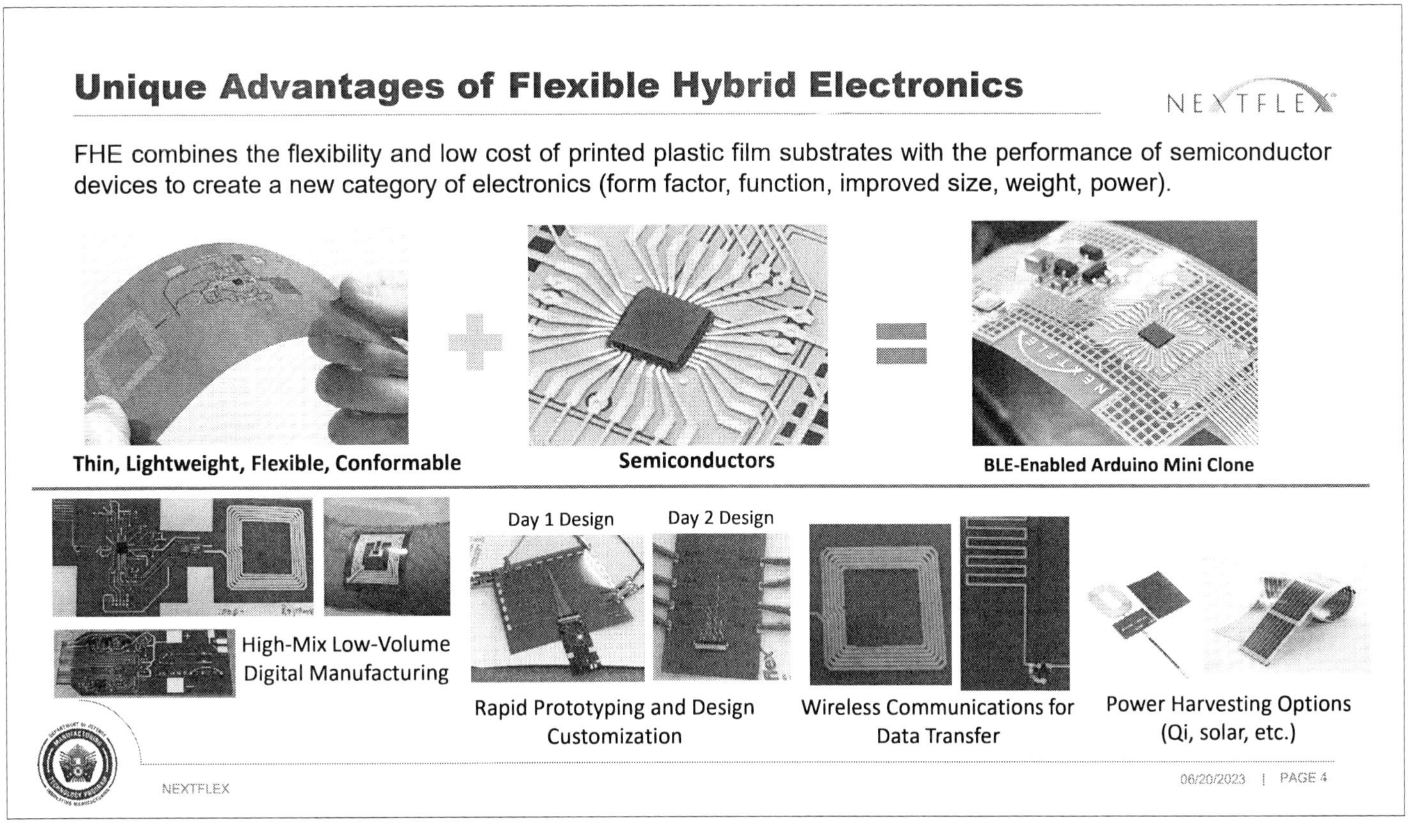
Unique Advantages of Flexible Hybrid Electronics
NEXTFLEX
FHE combines the flexibility and low cost of printed plastic film substrates with the performance of semiconductor devices to create a new category of electronics (form factor, function, improved size, weight, power).
Thin, Lightweight, Flexible, Conformable
Semiconductors
BLE-Enabled Arduino Mini Clone
High-Mix Low-Volume Digital Manufacturing
Day 1 Design
Day 2 Design
Rapid Prototyping and Design Customization
Wireless Communications for Data Transfer
Power Harvesting Options (Qi, solar, etc.)
NEXTFLEX
06/20/2023 | PAGE 4

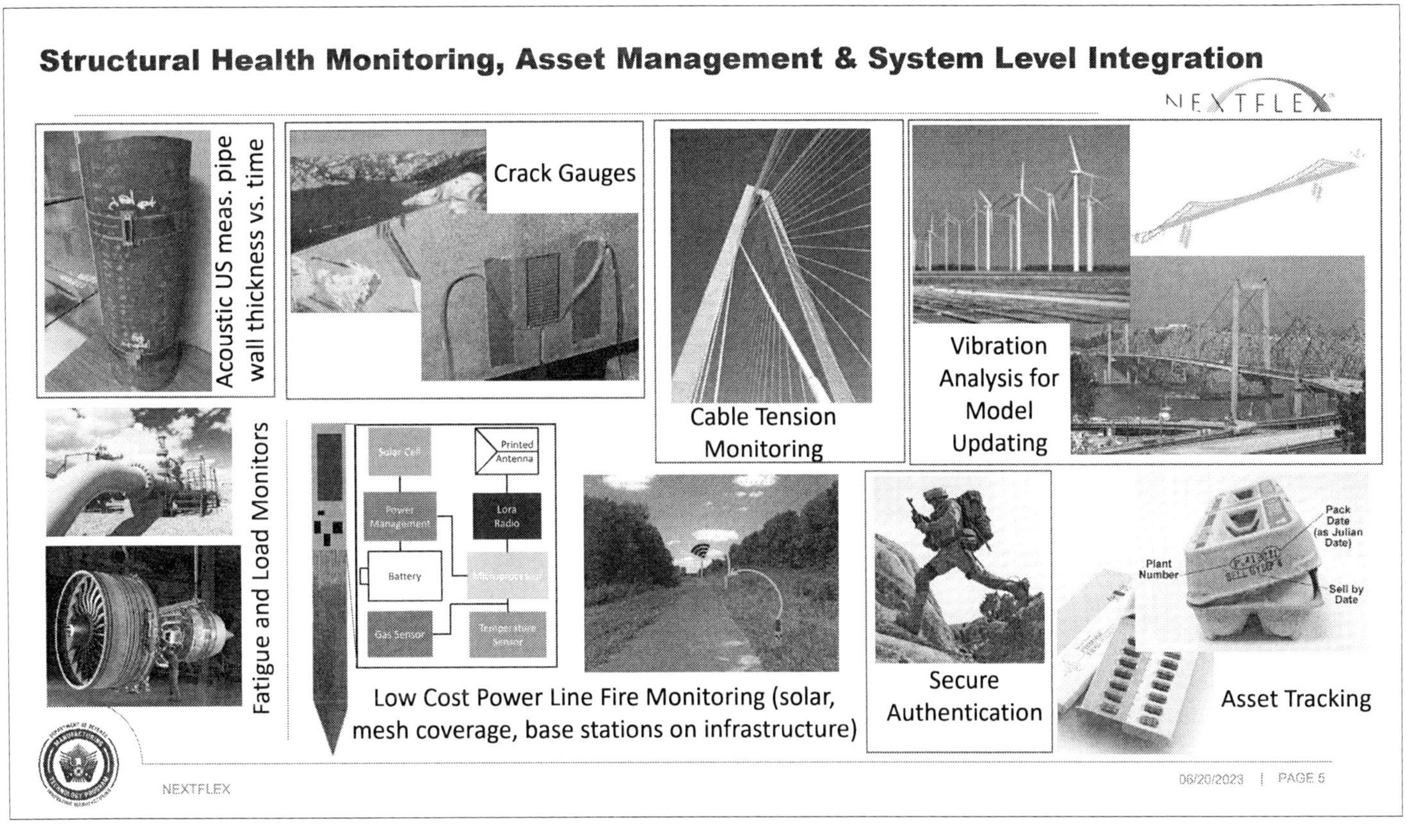
Structural Health Monitoring, Asset Management & System Level Integration
NEXTFLEX
Acoustic US meas. pipe wall thickness vs. time
Crack Gauges
Cable Tension Monitoring
Vibration Analysis for Model Updating
Fatigue and Load Monitors
Solar Cell
Printed Antenna
Power Management
Lora Radio
Battery
Microprocessor
Gas Sensor
Temperature Sensor
Low Cost Power Line Fire Monitoring (solar, mesh coverage, base stations on infrastructure)
Secure Authentication
Pack Date (as Julian Date)
Plant Number
Sell by Date
Asset Tracking
NEXTFLEX
06/20/2023 | PAGE 5

Rigid to Flex Conversion of an Arduino® Microcontroller

NEXTFLEX®

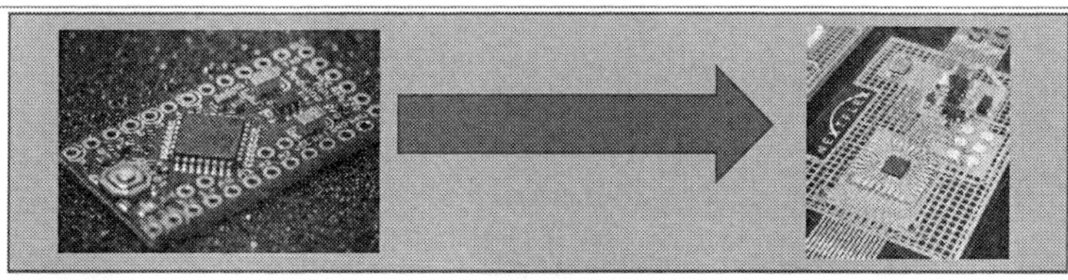

System Design → Layout → Print → Die Bond → SMT Assembly → Encapsulation → Test & Characterization

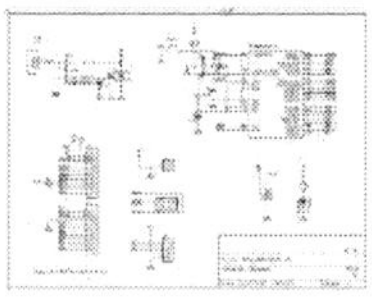

Single layer interconnect

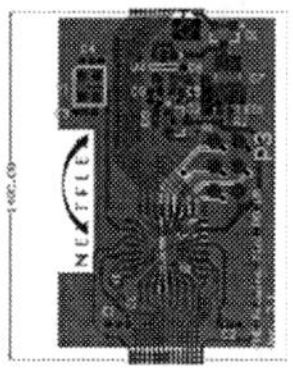

System Layout

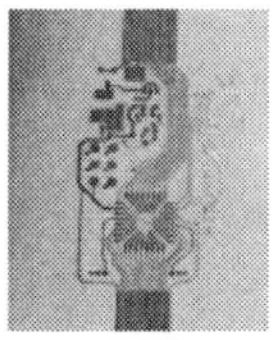

Ink Jet
Aerosol Jet
Screen Print

Flip Chip Attach

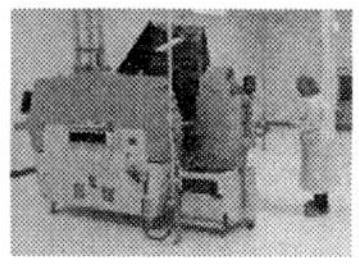

Pick & Place

Apply Bead of UV Epoxy then Insert-Molding or Adhesive Glob Top

Electrical
Physical
Environmental

Greater than 50% reduction in the number of process steps (7 FHE) vs. rigid PCB manufacturing (19)

Commercial Off-The-Shelf IC's Are Not Made for FHE

NEXTFLEX®

Packaged IC's are large and do not bend or flex.

Advanced packaging wafer-level based technologies like Wafer Large Scale Chip Package (WLCSP) have large Ball Grid Arrays (BGA) which prevent thinning to our target of 50 microns or less. Solder balls of 350-micron diameter on a 50-micron die will not help reliability.

Our goal is to use wafers – thinned and diced – for direct integration into FHE devices.

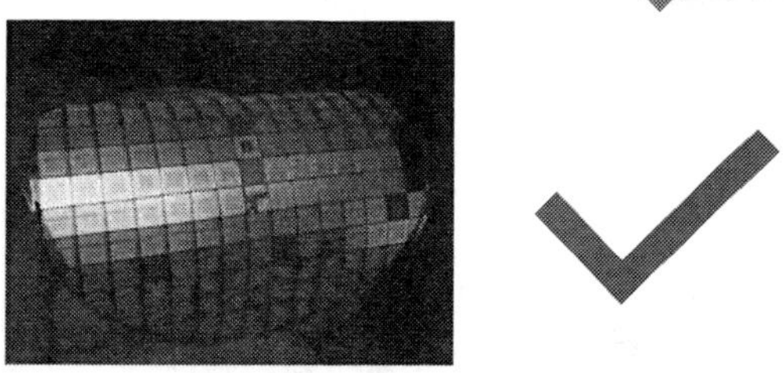

Challenge: Thinning and Dicing To <50 Microns

NEXTFLEX

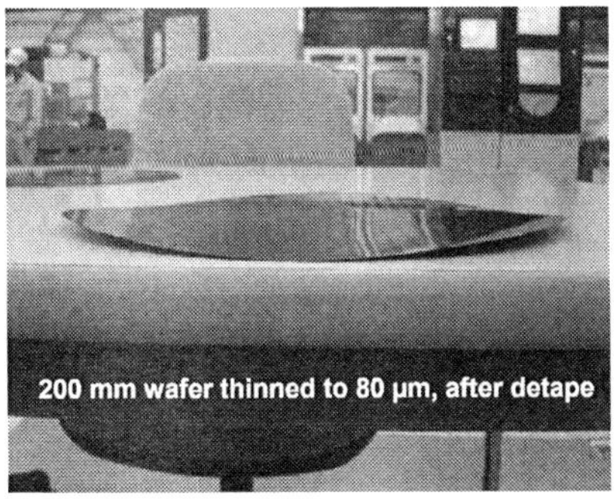

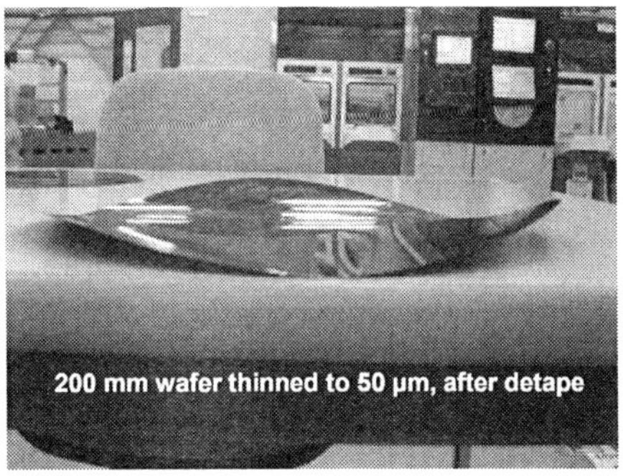

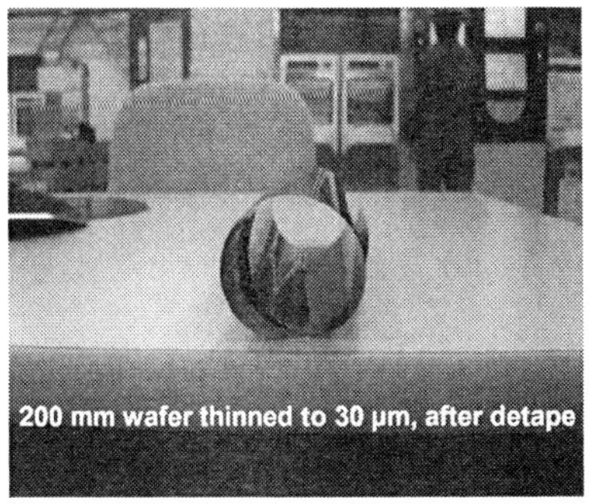

After thinning, there is the further challenge of pick and place of these ultra thin die
Requires ejection tool using multiple ejection pins per die and small distances between tape and pickup tool

Creating a Process Platform for Integration

NEXTFLEX

Instead of attempting to narrow down the selection of devices to integrate into an FHE system, we created a process flow where any type of device available in wafer form can be integrated:

Thinning
Dicing/Singulation
Attach

Bare die from Wafer Level Chip Scale Package (WLCSP) – bumped or unbumped

Die preparation for integration on FHE board
ENIG (Electroless Nickel Immersion Gold) bumping of contact pads
Au stud bumping of contact pads

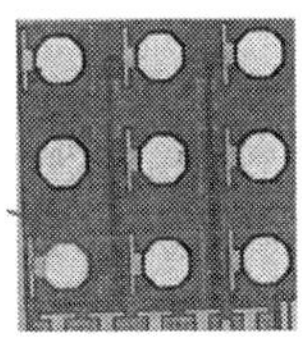

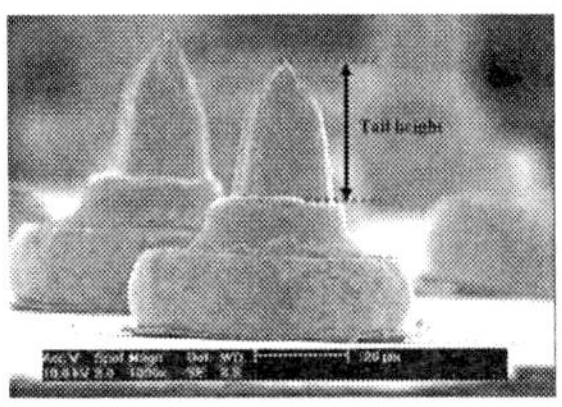

(Quad Flat No Lead)

Phase II - FHE Design and Prototype

NEXTFLEX

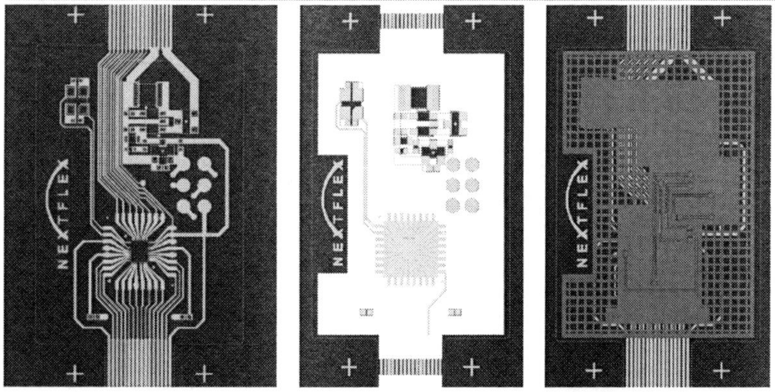

Front Side Metal | Dielectric Front | Backside Metal

Print Files

- Design of the boards for two layers per side, one metal and one dielectric
- Laser cutting of vias in substrate prior to printing
- Laser ablation after printing for tuning of fine features and details
- Design was created to be manufactured on an 8-inch x 12-inch sheet

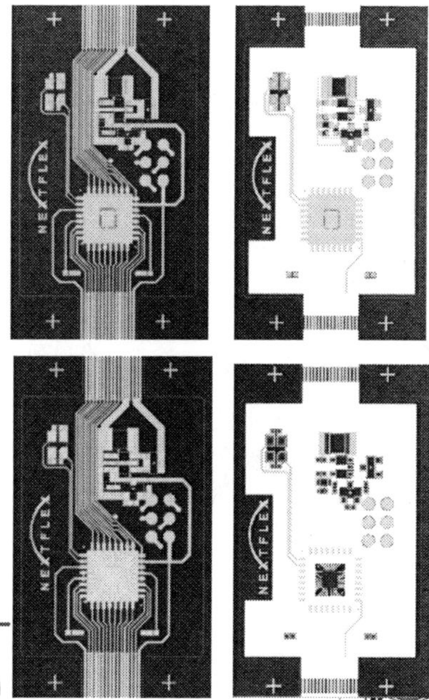

Laser Ablation

Down Selection of Printing Process

NEXTFLEX

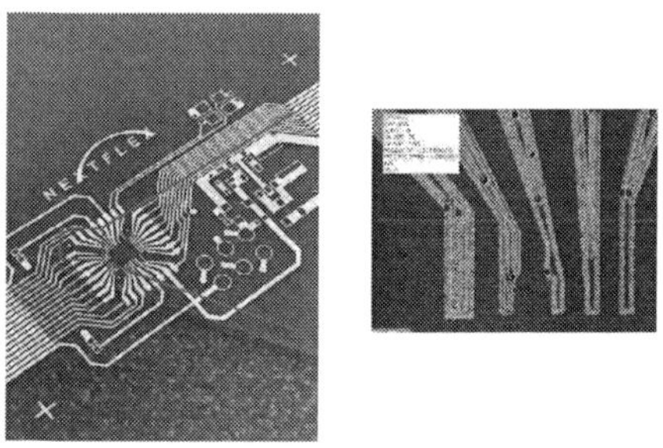

Aerosol Jet

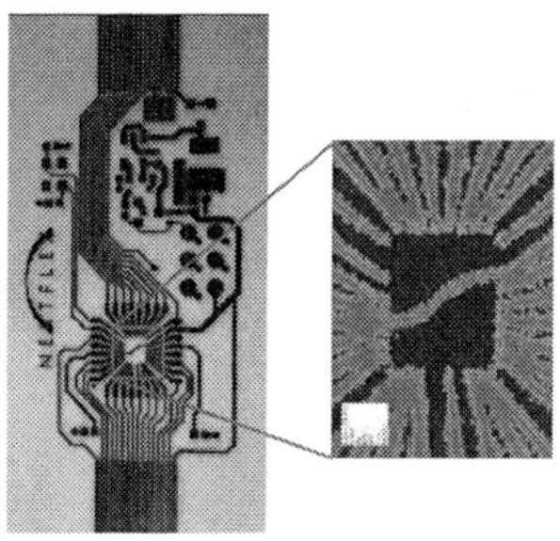

Inkjet

- Multiple printing processes were evaluated for the print
  - primary candidates: Aerosol Jet, Ink Jet and Screen Printing
- Screen printing was chosen as preferred fabrication method
  - Fast print time
  - Good ink thickness
  - Acceptable resolution

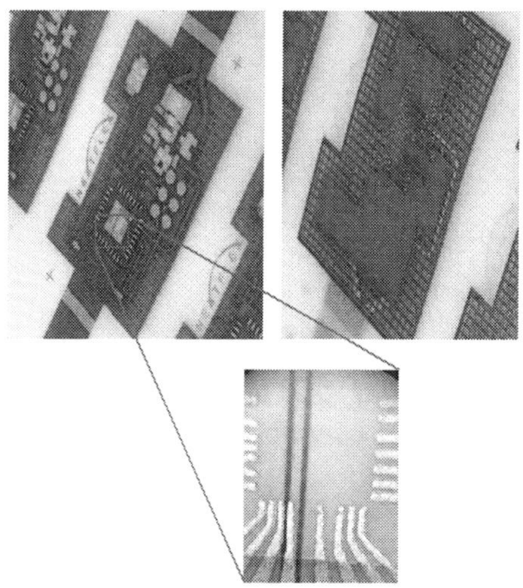

Screen Print front and back of FHE Arduino-compatible microcontroller

Flexible Arduino®-Compatible Microcontroller Before Encapsulation

NEXTFLEX

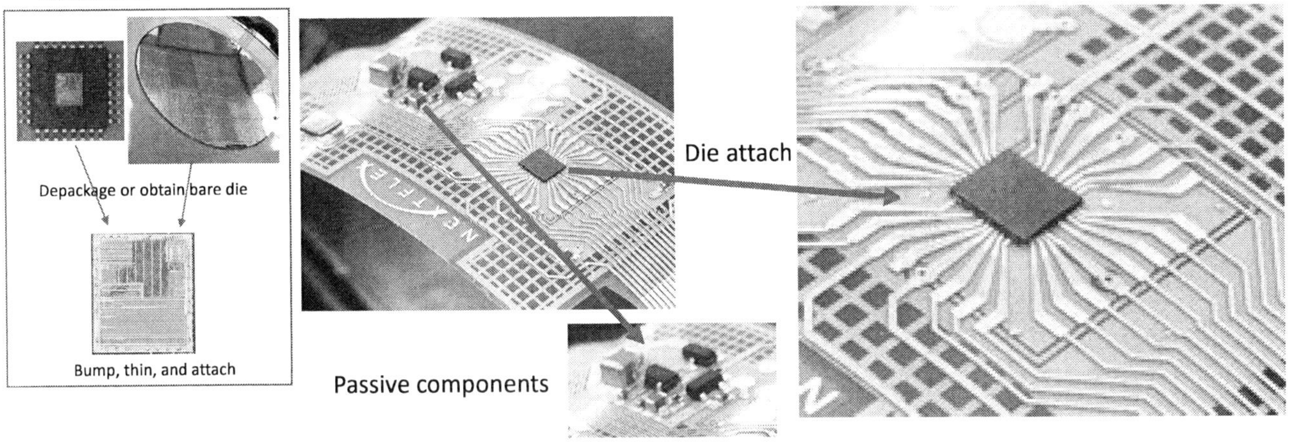

- To develop the flexible-design bare Microchip ATmega328 (microcontroller used in all Arduino minis) die were obtained through package removal of commercially sourced IC's before being able to obtain bare die
- Both passive components and bare die were attached to the printed traces on the substrate to assemble the full device
- Once the assembly was complete the device build was finalized via encapsulation of the IC

NEXTFLEX 06/20/2023 | PAGE 12

Encapsulation

NEXTFLEX

- IC's on the device were encapsulated using a syringe-deposited silicone
- Each IC was separately encapsulated to maximize the flex of the IC
- Once the silicone was deposited it was cured at room temperature
- A dielectric was screen-printed
- Later encapsulation would be by pouring and insert-molding

NEXTFLEX 06/20/2023 | PAGE 13

Transition to Manufacturing: Concept

Goal: Develop a mass-produced flexible copy of the Arduino®-compatible Mini Microcontroller board to:

- Validate ability to mass produce printed hybrid electronics
- Minimize the cost of the device
- Create and validate an 8-bit microcontroller platform for potential future applications

Rigid Arduino Mini Board

Flexible Prototype

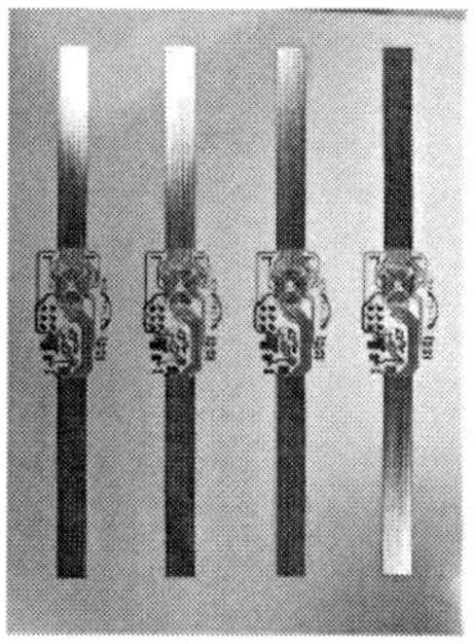

Mass Produced

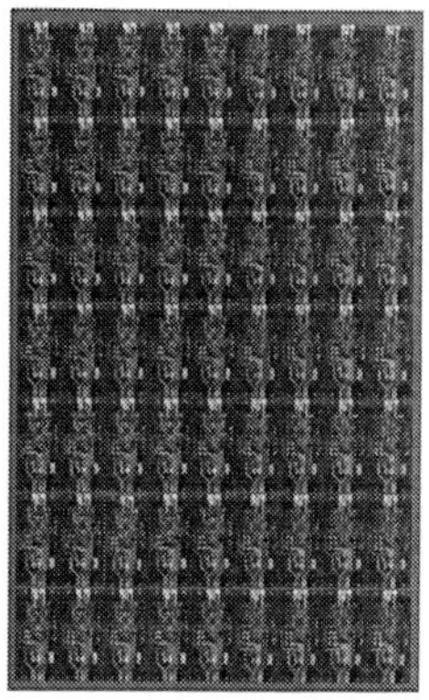

Case Study: Design Process & Application of Design Rules

Schematic and layout were performed in Mentor Graphics design software

Desired bend locations were determined and components placed accordingly

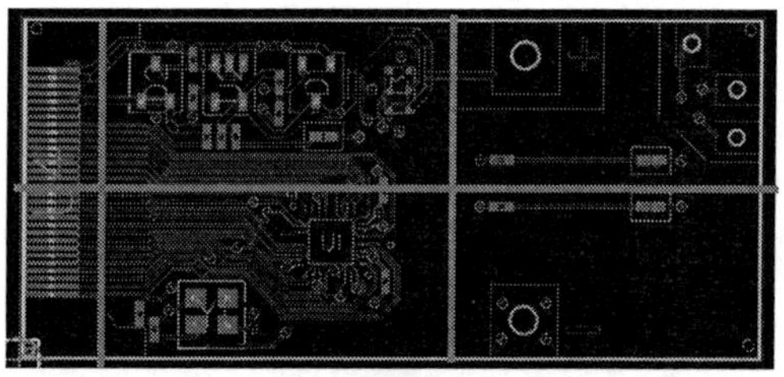

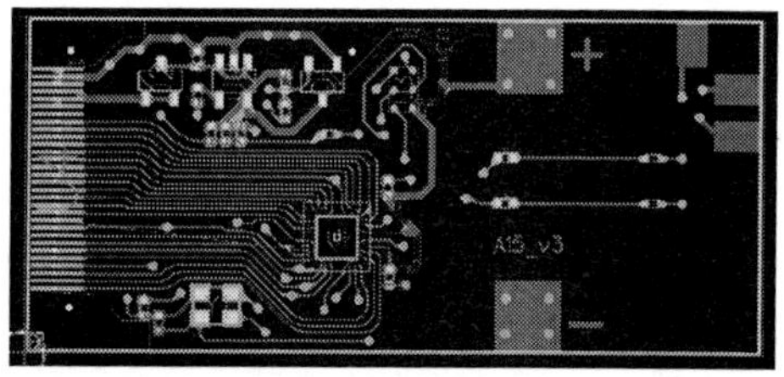

Graphical files for printer were generated in Fab3000

3D Models were generated

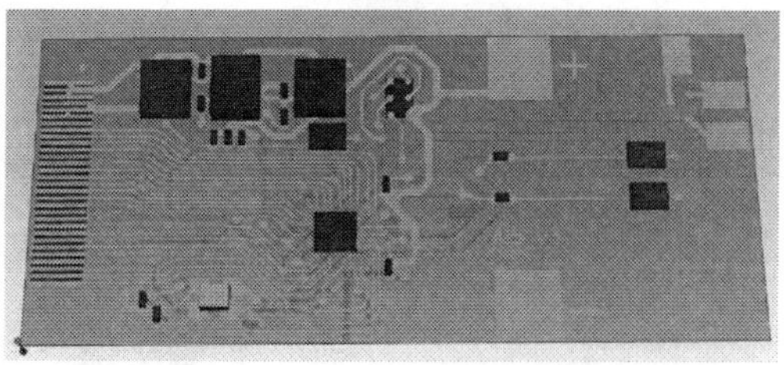

Applied design rules include:

- Minimum trace l/s of 150 um/150 um
- Minimum via (80 um)
- Minimum pad size (250 um)
- Mechanical layout based on desired bend locations

Case Study: Redesign for Volume Fabrication

NEXTFLEX

Removal of extraneous ears of "wristband" circuitry

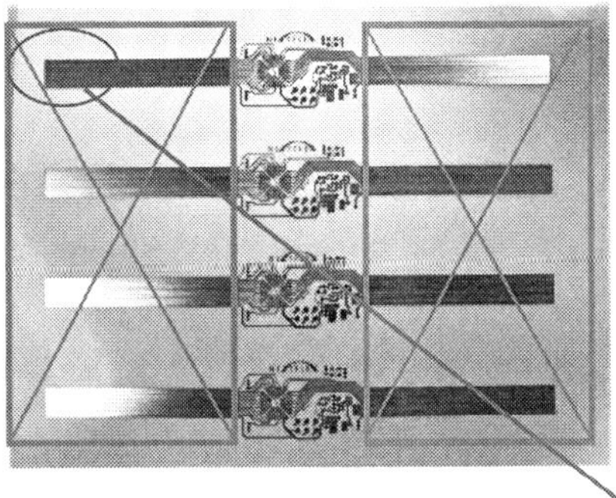

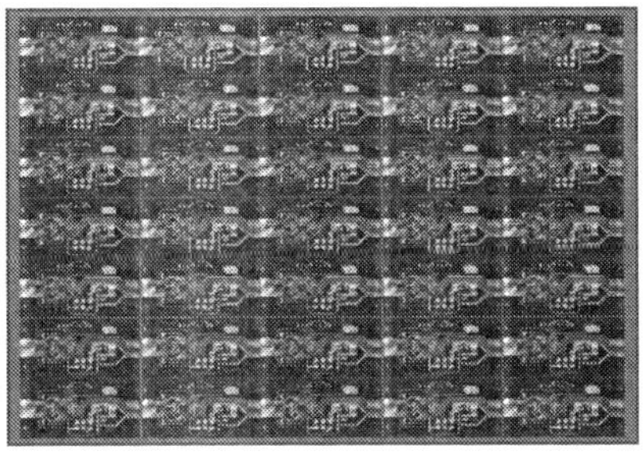

High device density per sheet to minimize waste

Move all ZIF pins to one side to simplify connections

Addition of LEDs and interface pads [power and SPI (serial peripheral interface) for testing and prototyping]

Removal of backup QFN pads to shrink die attach area

Standardization of passives to 0402 (4 mil x 2 mil US standard) size to maximize bend

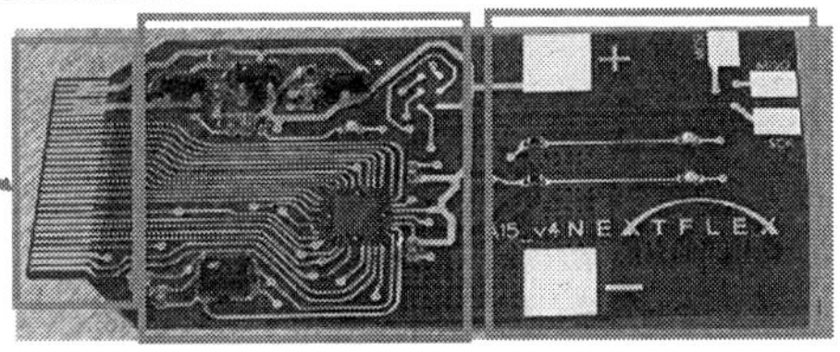

Packing of components into smaller area

Automated Programming

NEXTFLEX

- Programming was automated using a FANUC® robot
- Robot would automatically detect, properly place pogo pin connector on pads, program and test each device on the sheet using computer vision

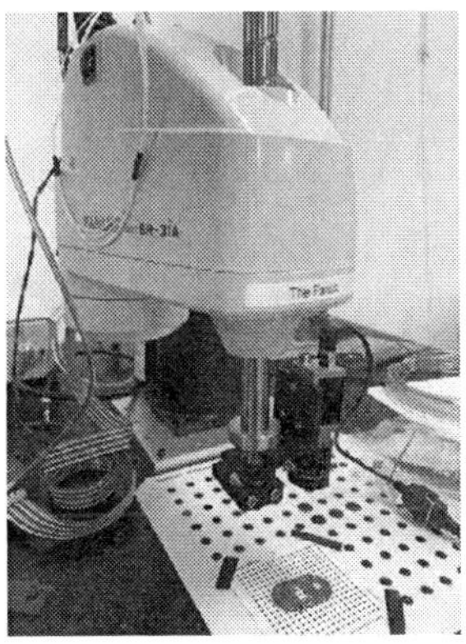

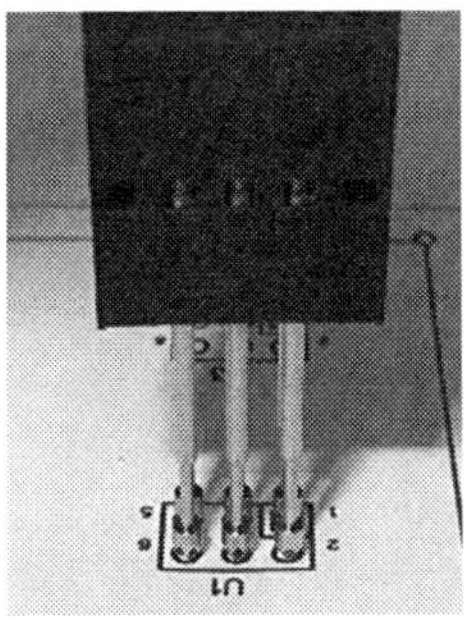

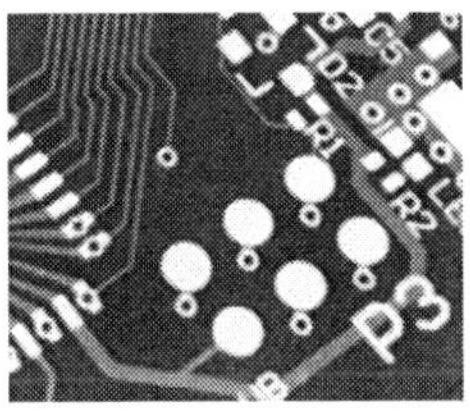

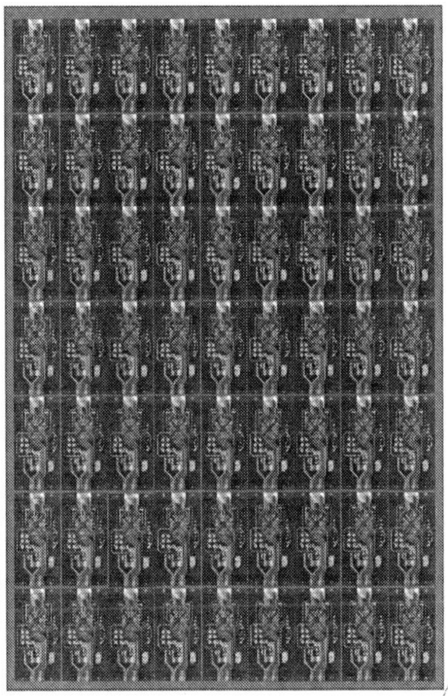

Singulation

- Up to 35 devices are produced on a single 8"x12" sheet
- Once fabrication of an entire sheet had been completed and the devices are tested, the devices are singulated and prepared for distribution

NEXTFLEX 06/20/2023 | PAGE 18

IMPROVEMENTS AND APPLICATIONS

NEXTFLEX

Stud Bumping for Fine Pitch Integration

NEXTFLEX

- Starting with unpackaged die
- Pads are inset below the passivation layer requiring bumps to allow for flip-chip attach
- Gold pads also remove issues with oxide layers on aluminum pads

Two Options

- ENIG (Electroless Nickle Immersion Gold)
  - Low Cost
  - Scalable
  - Limited pitch due to mushrooming
  - Limited control over where plating occur
- Stud Bumping
  - Higher Cost
  - Scalable
  - Ability to do fine pitch bumping (8 um gaps)
  - No plating in undesired areas
  - Spikes easily into silver traces

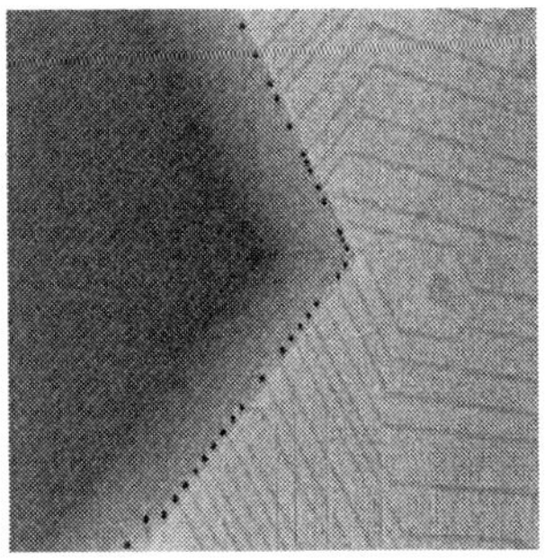

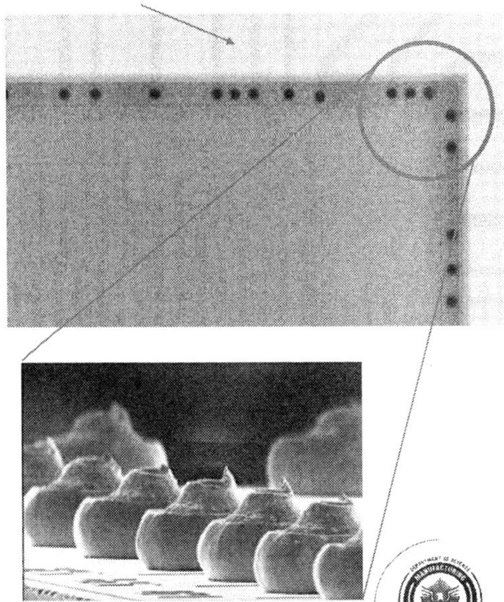

Die Interconnect Methods

NEXTFLEX

Laser ablation

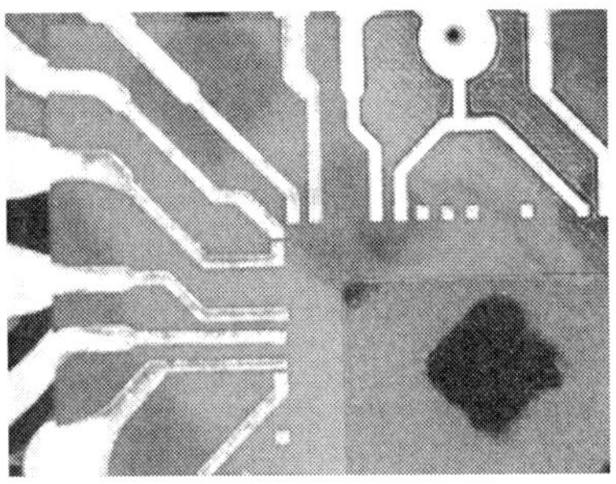

- **ESI 5200 femtosec green laser**
- Widest material set
- Thickest trace height
- Spot size ~10um

Aerosol jet

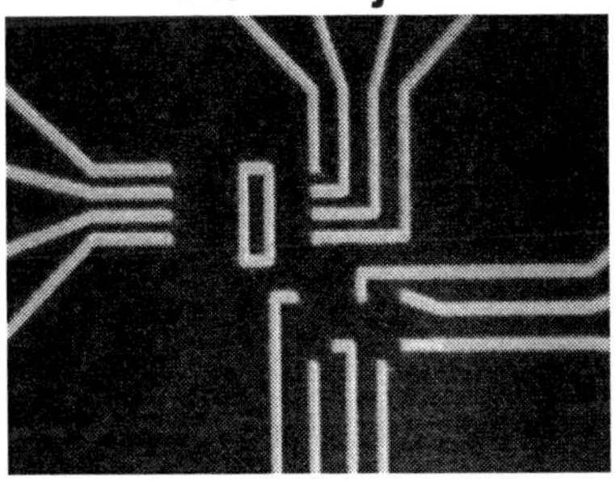

- **Optomec AJ5X**
- Great for prototyping
- Multi-axis printing
- Wide material set

Gravure offset

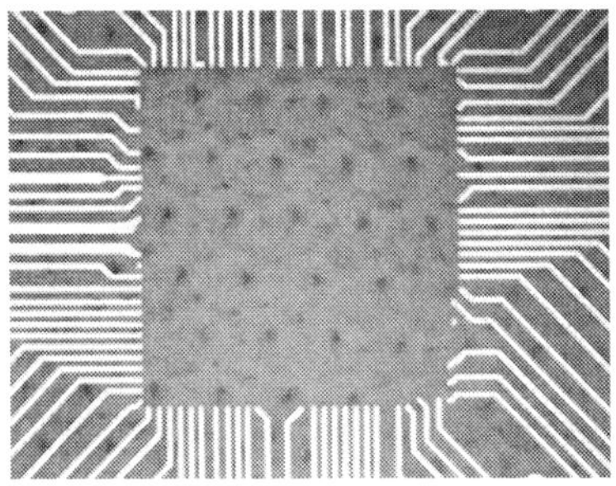

- **Komori sheet-fed**
- Fastest process by sheet
- Excellent edge definition
- Thin trace height ~2um

Pads-Up Die Attach

NEXTFLEX

- Die attach alternate methods
  - Pads up & Print to pads
    - Print ramp for interconnect (aerosol jet or extrusion)

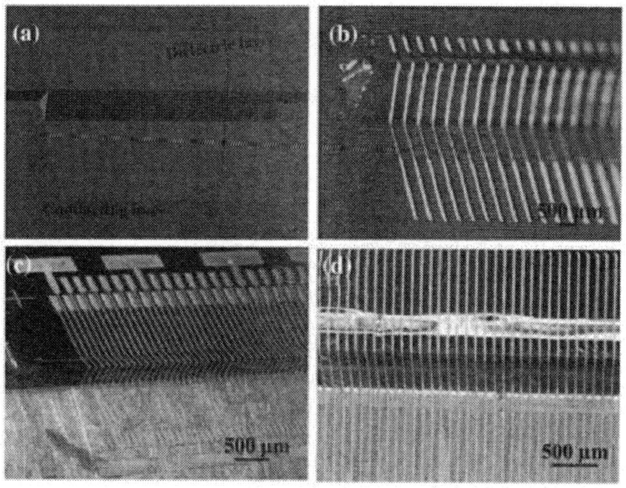

- Others
  - Flip chip w/ **magnetic field-oriented particles**
  - Stencil print bumps on substrate / attach with non-conductive underfill

Wearable Chemical and Environmental Sensor

NEXTFLEX

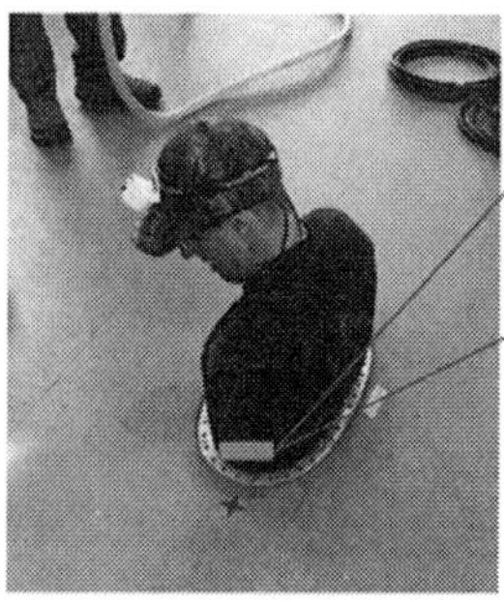

Confined Space Monitoring

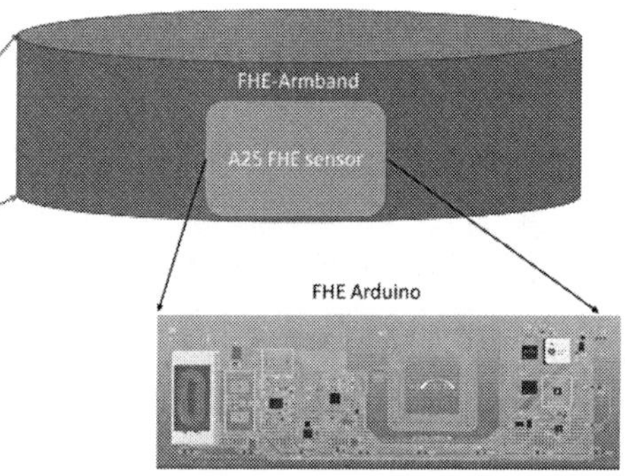

Low cost repeaters can be placed at intervals to rebroadcast message to personnel outside the immediate area

Microcontrollers are capable of mesh networking

C: charging chip
A: nRF52840
BLE: BT antenna
T&H: Temp and Humidity sensor
CS: chemical sensor (NS)
L: LED/sound indicator

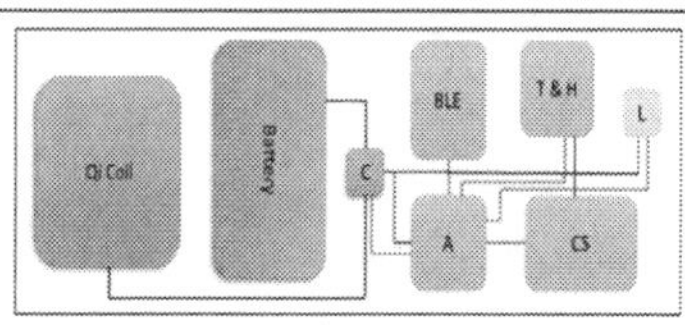

Block Diagram

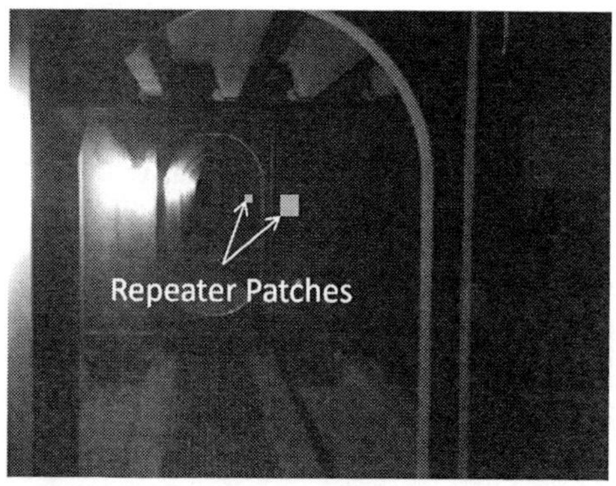

Sensing built into clothing can monitor for health and safety issues and send warnings when safety issues are detected

Multi-Domain Operations Wearable Sensor System

NEXTFLEX

- Wearable Sensor System
- Unobtrusive monitoring of soldiers
- Provides real-time data
  - Vital signs
  - Stress
  - Heat/cold injuries
  - Local environmental data
  - Signs of fatigue
- Flexible electronics laminated onto a regular shirt
- RF communications interface with wearable/embedded sensors

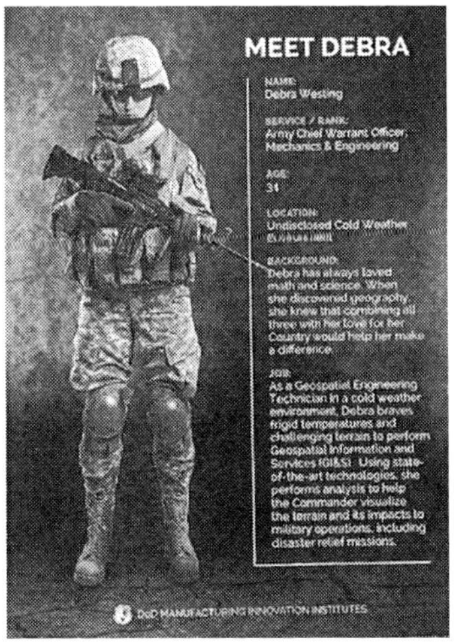

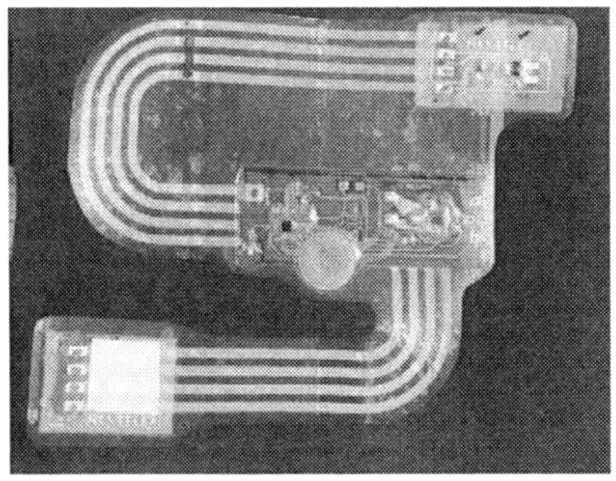

Microcontroller with Textile Integration

NEXTFLEX

Capacitive Touch System (CTS) enables touch localization along a conductive fabric surface.

A microcontroller FHE board can be integrated into the CTS to develop a fully flexible solution.

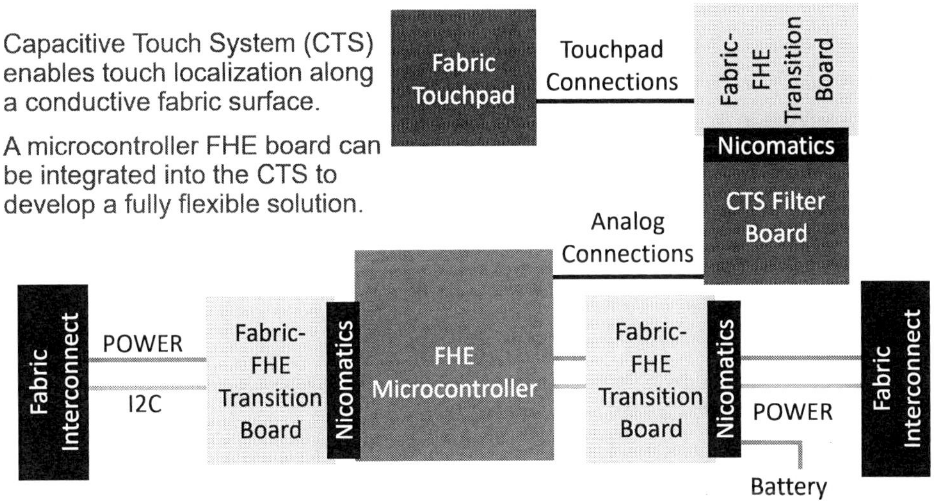

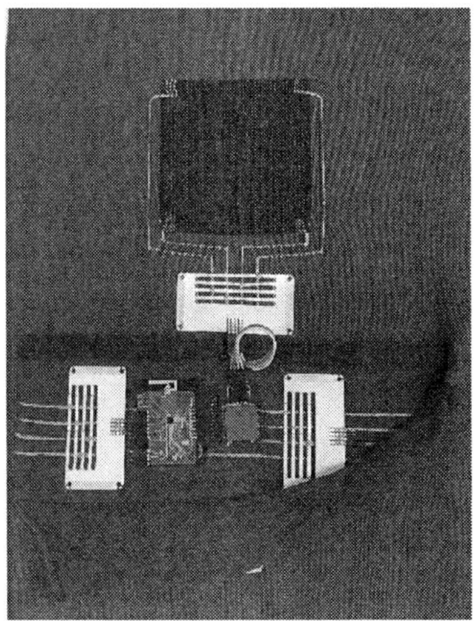

Sensing built into clothing requires leads in fabric – conductive threads, switches, touch sensors – but processing will be in additive components. Interfaces are important. Are they rigid or flexible? Electrical? Electro-optic?

Summary – A US Electronics Manufacturing Opportunity

NEXTFLEX

Sensor Integration
- MEMS pressure & inertial
- CMOS chemical & optical
- Printed sensors
- Microfluidics

Microcontroller and Communications
- Low power microcontrollers
- BLE, NFC, LoRa, Zigbee, etc.
- Printed antennas

Power
- Primary / secondary battery
- Wireless charging
- Energy harvesting

<u>Fully customizable</u>
- Shape & size
- Materials & environmental capability
- Expected lifetime & life cycle (reusable/disposable)
- Cost target

Flexible Hybrid Electronics enables unique products
- Wearables, medical devices, machinery monitoring, secure authentication, IOT sensor nodes
- Structurally integrated sensors
- Conformal antenna arrays on aircraft

Printing and additive processes allow for new form factors, high mix, digital manufacturing

The FHE toolkit enables tighter integration of circuits and novel packaging
- Bare die integration, eliminating discretes, new design freedom
- Structural & system level integration

It takes a multidisciplinary effort to build FHE:
- Electronics, printing, robotics, material science, plastics processing, software

This material is based on research sponsored, in part, by Air Force Research Laboratory under agreement numbers FA8650-15-2-5401 and FA8650-20-2-5506 and Other Transaction number HQ00342190017 as conducted through the flexible hybrid electronics manufacturing innovation institute, NextFlex. The U.S. Government is authorized to reproduce and distribute reprints for Governmental purposes notwithstanding any copyright notation thereon. The views and conclusions contained herein are those of the authors and should not be interpreted as necessarily representing the official policies or endorsements, either expressed or implied, of Air Force Research Laboratory or the U.S. Government

Sensors Converge

E-Textile Based Systems Using Different Modalities for Damage Detection and Status Monitoring for Military and Other Applications

June 20–22, 2022 | Santa Clara, CA

#SensorsConverge

About…

DCS Corporation

DCS is a premier professional services firm providing advanced research and development, engineering, prototyping, technical, and programmatic support services to the DoD and other national security-focused customers.

dcs corp

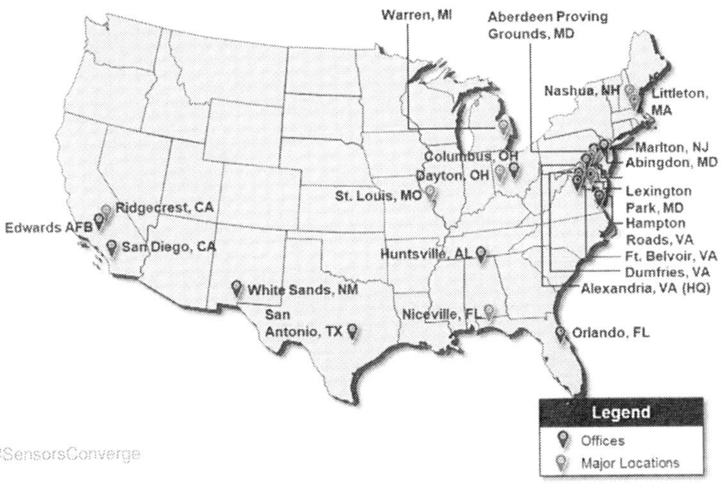

Headquarters DCS Corporation
6909 Metro Park Drive
Alexandria, VA 22310

#SensorsConverge

Sensors Converge

What Was the Problem?

- The Defense Health Agency (DHA) was seeking a medical simulation to model the impacts to E-textiles that coincide with bodily injury. Once established, the expectation is to use the e-textile impact to infer bodily damage.
- The objective of this program was to develop a set of E-textile materials and measurement systems to meet the needs for a damage detection testbed system.

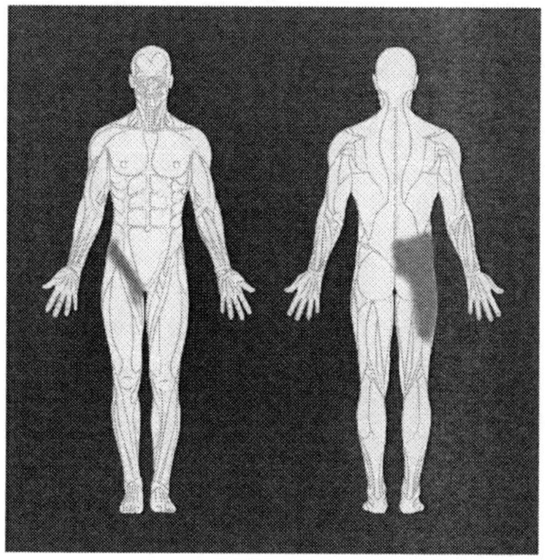

#SensorsConverge

Sensors Converge

Why Were We the Right Partner?

DCS has the capability to design, fabricate, and evaluate textile articles, including those that feature embedded electrical functionality.

- Fiber/Yarn characterization
  - Mechanical
  - Electrical
  - Melt Properties
- Fabric Characterization
  - Electrical
  - EMI Shielding
  - Environmental
- Network Formation
  - Ultrasonic welding station
  - Portable ultrasonic welding system
  - Soldering stations
- Network Characterization
  - Impedance (LCR) Meter
  - Time-domain reflectometer
  - Oscilloscopes

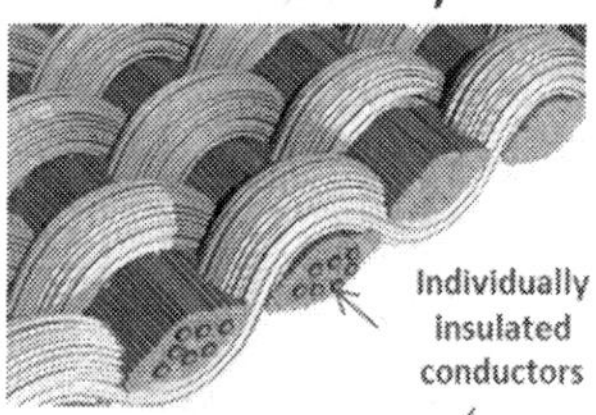

- Prototype Fabrication
  - Cut and sew stations
  - Sewing machines
  - Sergers
  - Rivet and fastener presses
- System testing and qualification
  - Current capacity
  - Environmental
  - Launderability
  - Signal Integrity

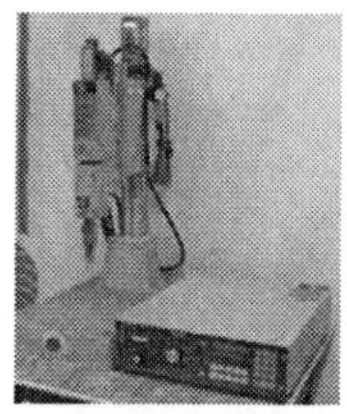

#SensorsConverge

Sensors Converge

Phases of Textile Development

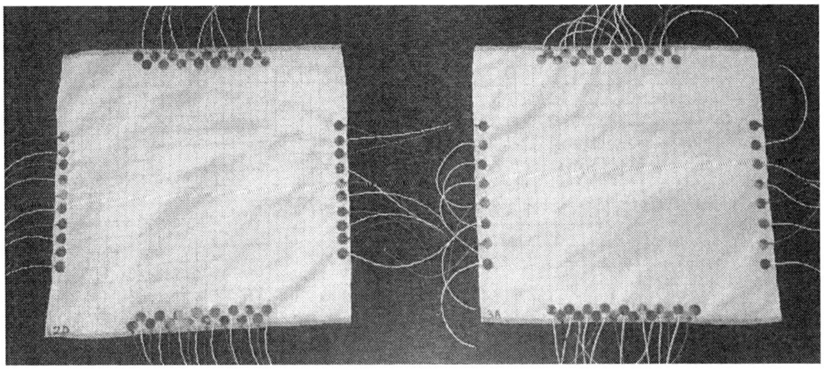

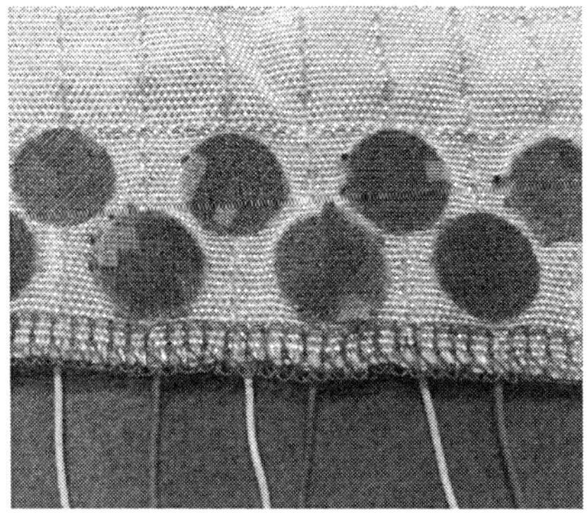

- Functionalized E-textile samples using DCS optimized ultrasonic welding techniques
- This staggered approach caused undesired variability in the trace capacitance, so a new technique was explored

#SensorsConverge

Sensors Converge

Phases of Textile Development

- Replacing the rounded horn with an oblong horn allowed more trace connections, facilitating a denser grid pattern.

- 13.5" x 13.5" swatch allowed for a 20 x 20 sensor grid

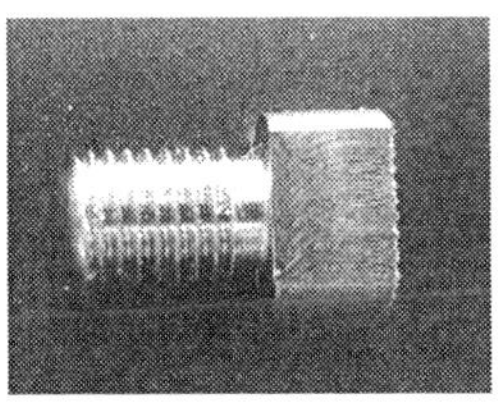

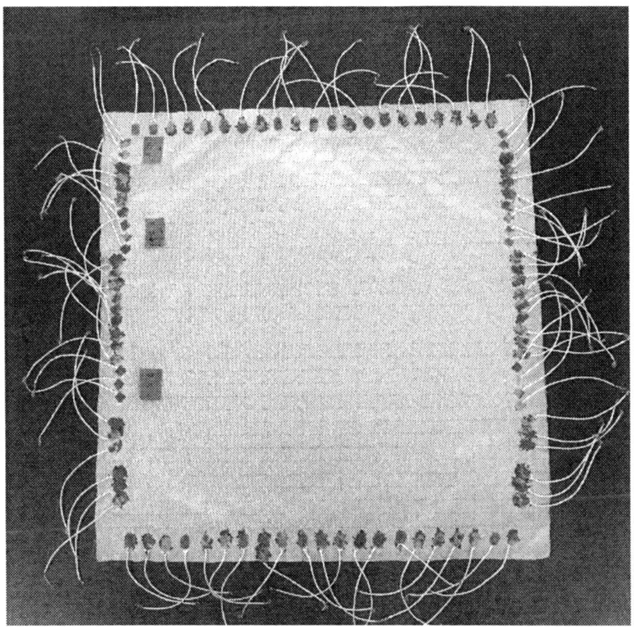

#SensorsConverge

Sensors Converge

Thermal Sensor Integration

- Using conductive fibers made from dissimilar metals to produce an embedded thermocouple
- The most consistent performer was Chromel and Stainless-Steel pairing
- The performance was still several times less sensitive than a standard T-type thermocouple, but as both metals are typically used for negative terminals that is expected.

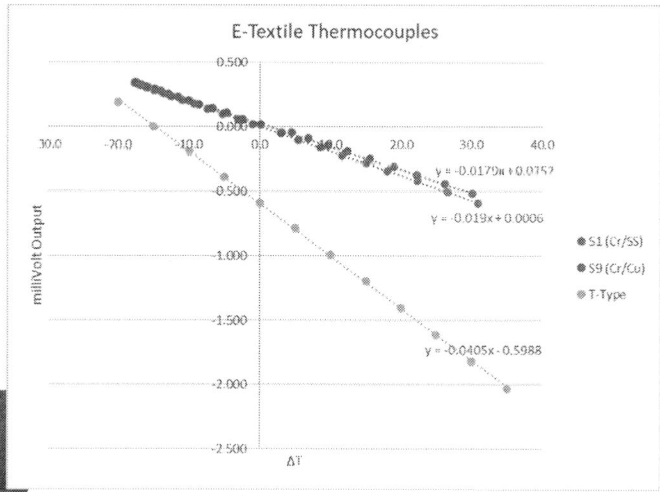

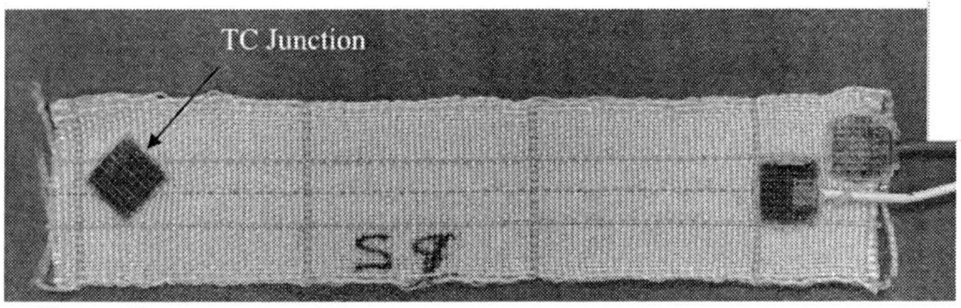

#SensorsConverge

Sensors Converge

Thermal Sensor Integration

- An improvement can be made by replacing the chromel with constantan wire, but due to project limitations that was outside scope
- A linear fit of the data shows an 18.6 µV/°C sensitivity at Tcold = 0°C.

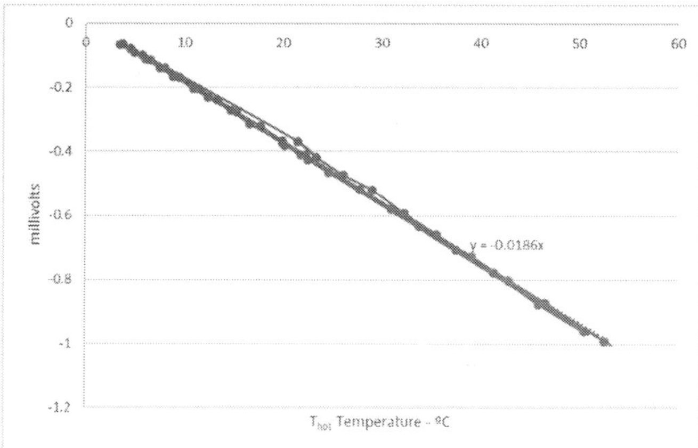

Thermocouple Type	Sensitivity (µV/°C)
S1 E-Textile (Chromel/Stainless Steel & Copper)	18.6
K (Chromel/Alumel)	41.276
E (Constantan/Chromel)	76.373
S (Platinum/Pt+Rhodium)	9.587

#SensorsConverge

Sensors Converge

Moisture Detection

- Created samples of varying spacing
- .5" (Top), 0.25" (Middle), and 0.125" (Bottom)
- Relationship between the spacing and the capacitive coupling was found to be linear

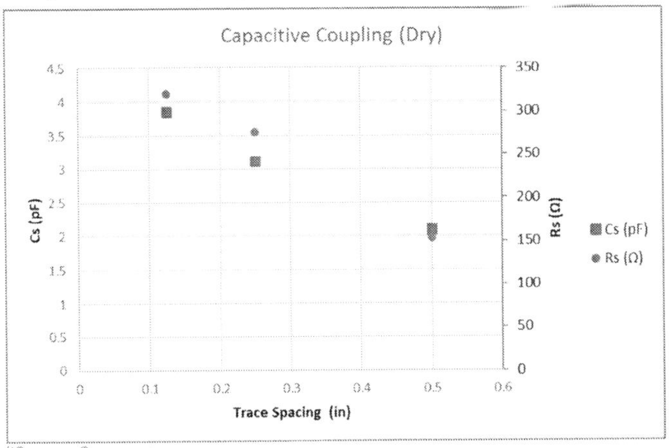

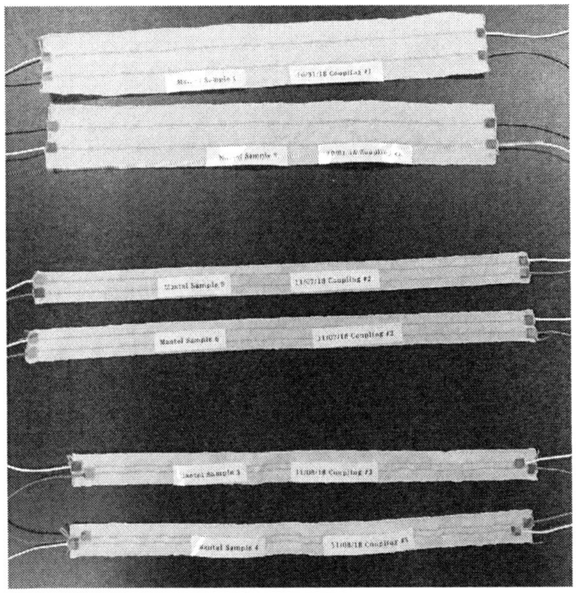

#SensorsConverge

Sensors Converge

Moisture Detection

- Introducing water greatly increased capacitive coupling
- Using the known dielectric constants materials, the type of saturation could be deciphered.

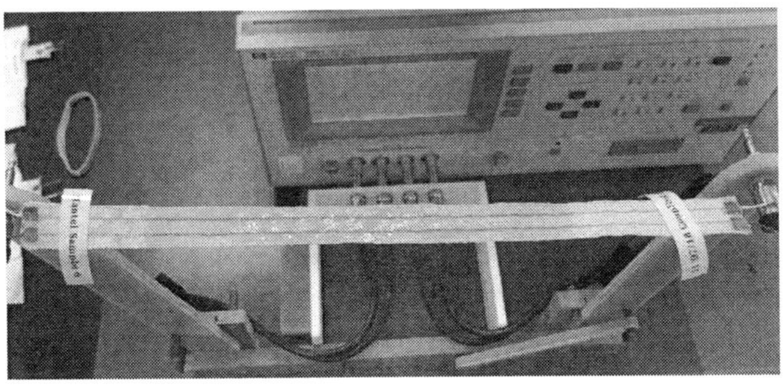

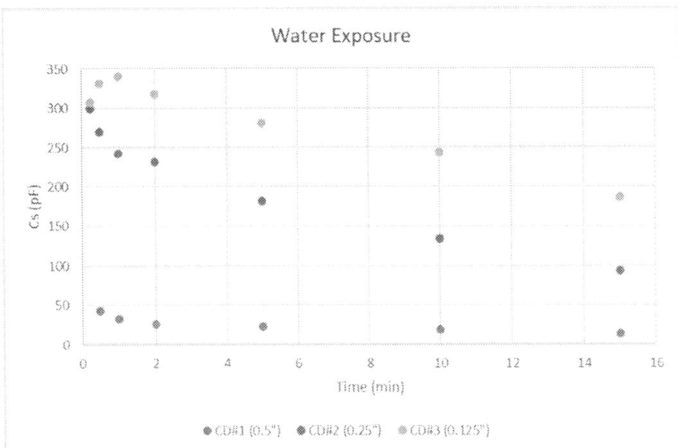

#SensorsConverge

Sensors Converge

Moisture Detection

- The blood simulant selected was ¼ strength Ringer's solution (R1)
- Clean tap water (Tav) was used as comparison
- The presence of salts in the R1 solution increased coupling, allowing for a clear difference in the results
- The 4x-6x increase in capacitance readings is easily noted and can be used to status monitoring and fluid differentiation.

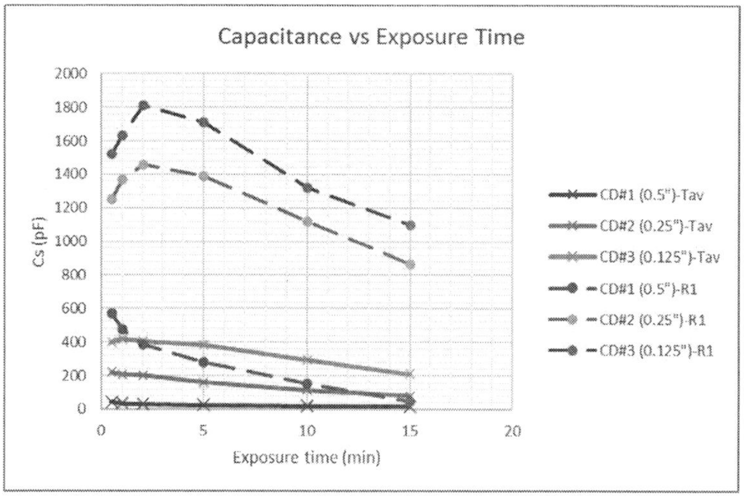

#SensorsConverge

Sensors Converge

Frequency Sweep Evaluation

- Using low, medium, and high frequency sweep patterns to evaluate rectangular sample response
- Even though the low frequency band produced relatively lower capacitance values its consistency and reliability made it the preferred operating band.

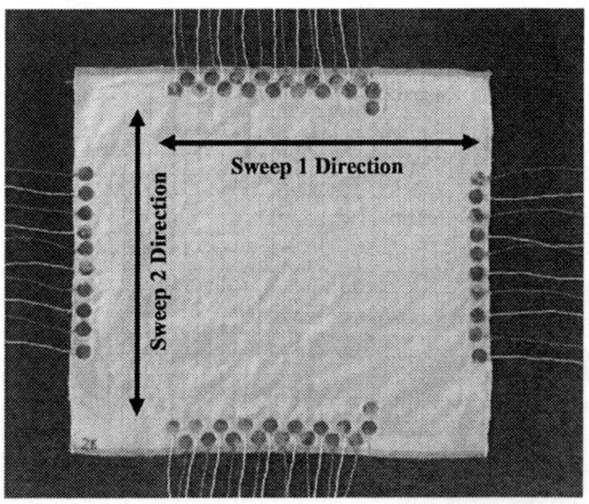

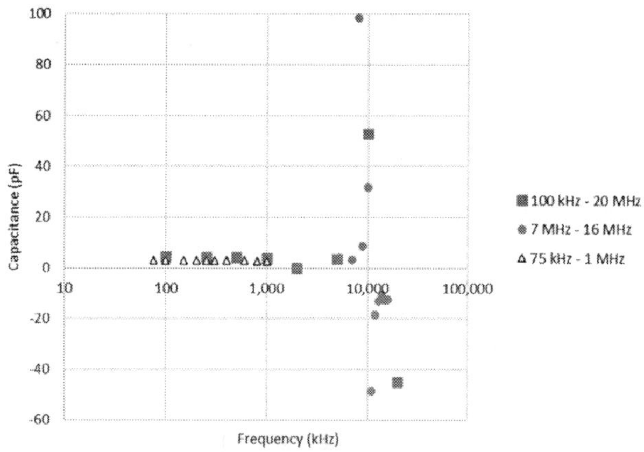

#SensorsConverge

Sensors Converge

2D – Perturbation

- A Teflon block was placed on the intersection points
- By subtracting out the base measurements from the Teflon measurements, a model could be made.
- Comparing this model to other bare measurements changes can be observed

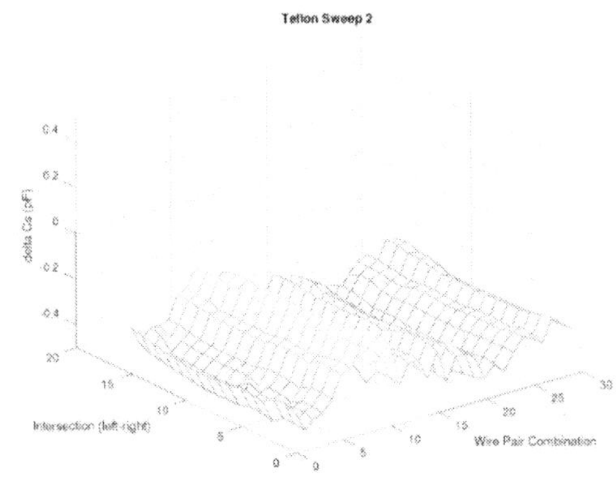

Cut Detection

- Adding puncture wounds to the material
- The cut traces show up in the 3D plot of the material with much lower capacitance
- a 'shadowing' effect can be seen emanating from the area of damage over the runs of the pairs broken.

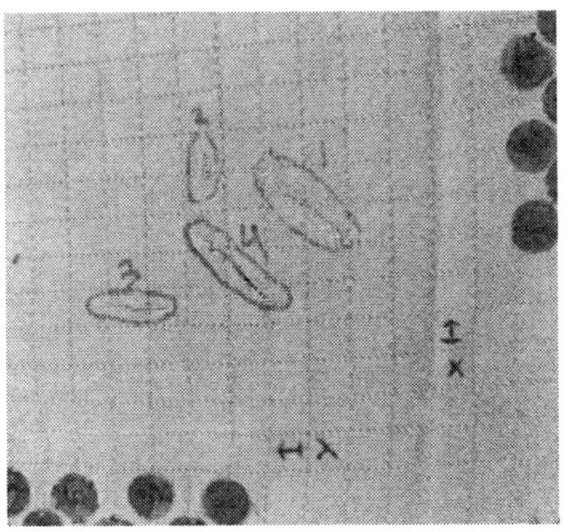

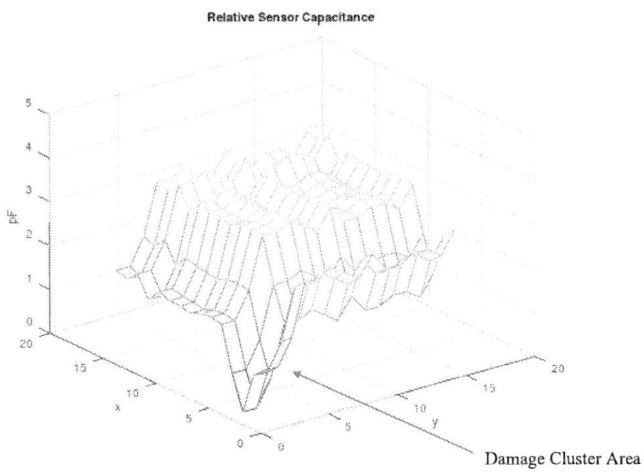

Measurement Complications. Solution: Auto-shielding

- Measurement of a small capacitance in a physically large structure is difficult without a fixture and method for control for external influences.
- Without a way to mask or shield the sensor, error compensation and filtering would need to be applied in software
- Auto shielding is a means of implementing a grounded shield to protect a measurement from external influences
- All of the sense lines not used for a pairwise measurement are grounded to the shield connection

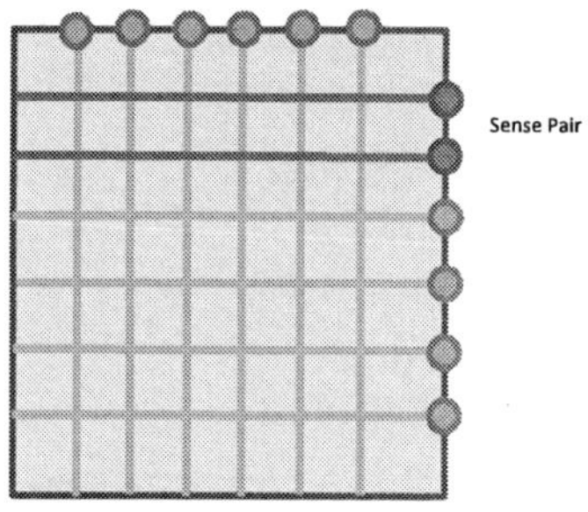

Grid E-Textile Sensor – MEASUREMENT 1

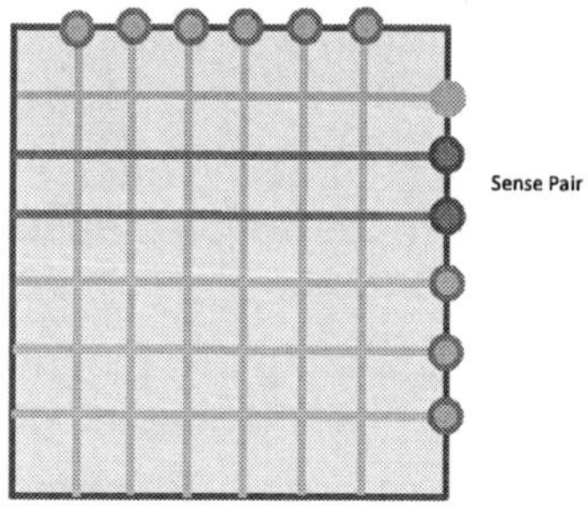

Grid E-Textile Sensor – MEASUREMENT 2

#SensorsConverge

Sensors Converge

Measurement Complications. Solution: Auto-shielding

- By selectively connecting to a grounded shield circuit, several sources of error are eliminated, including:
  - Distributed proximity effect
    - Local changes are picked up by non-sampled pairs, which couple back into the sense pair during measurement
  - EMI influence
    - Large areas of ungrounded conductor act as antenna for local EMI, coupling back into the sense pair measurement
  - Position variance
- Measurement stability was noticeably improved

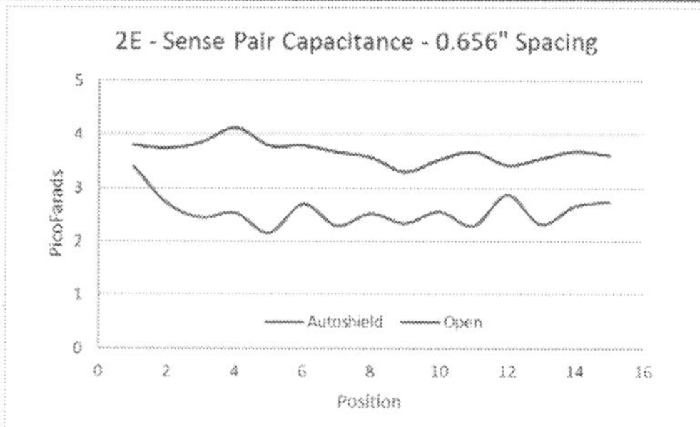

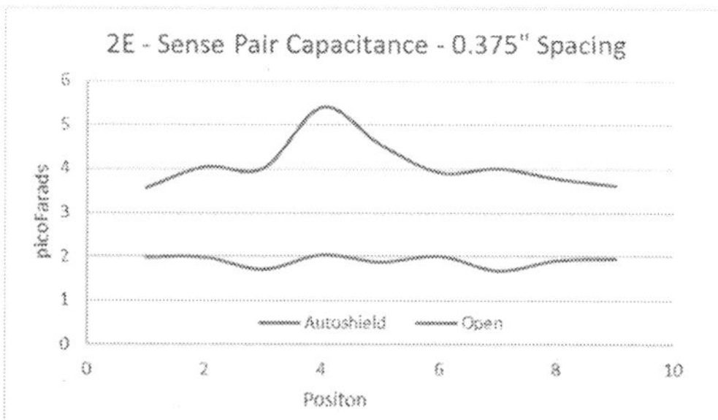

#SensorsConverge

Sensors Converge

Functionalizing Samples

- All of this work has been through manual sampling and modeling from a static test bench
- To allow for closer to real time testing a jig assembly with software monitoring was designed
- Coupled with automated auto-shielding, the sense pairs can be polled rapidly allowing for continual model updates.

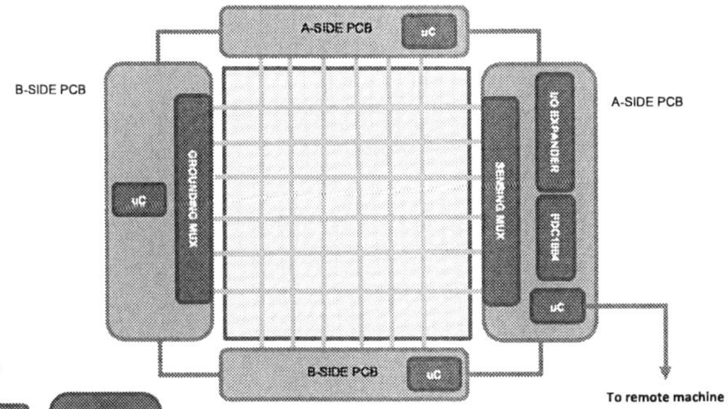

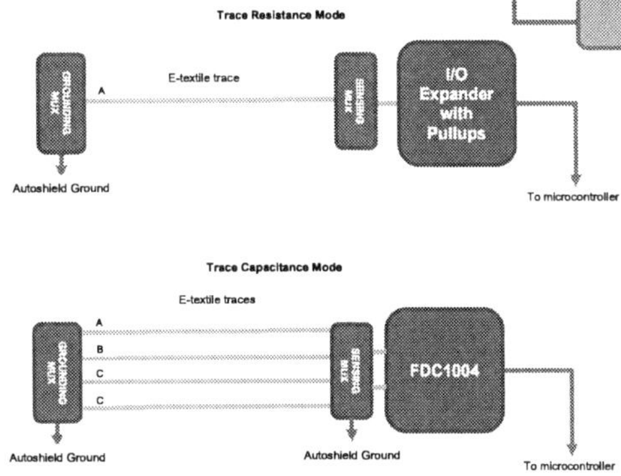

#SensorsConverge

Sensors Converge

Functionalizing Samples

- Rigid printed circuit boards were used to tension the structure and route out the sensing pairs
- Sequencing of the MUXes through this scheme to meet the needs of the resistance and capacitance measurements was controlled by a microcontroller module offboard

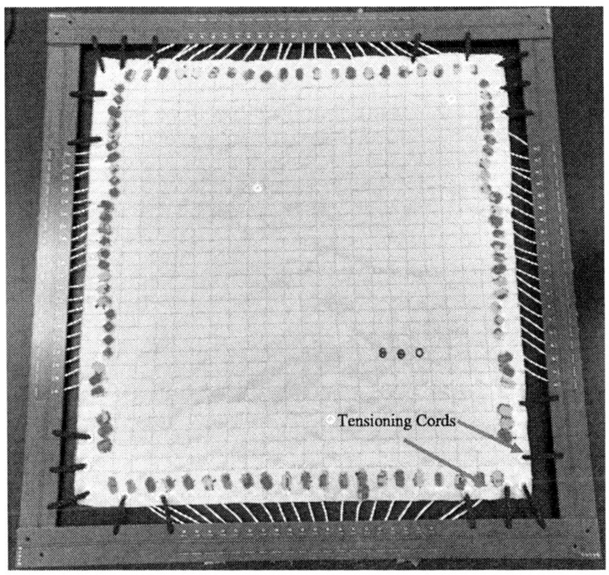

#SensorsConverge

Sensors Converge

Future Development of Sense Network

- Rigid PCBs do not facilitate use in garments or blankets
- Flex PCBs can be used along edges, sonically welded to replace wires
- Data processing and control can be offloaded to a larger unit integrated into a handled or unit mounted device
- For garments, seems can be used as panel connection points
- Patchwork blankets can be produces by combining smaller sections of sensing E-textile
- Adding stretch using new conductive fibers will bring additional sensing modalities to expand the sensing capability

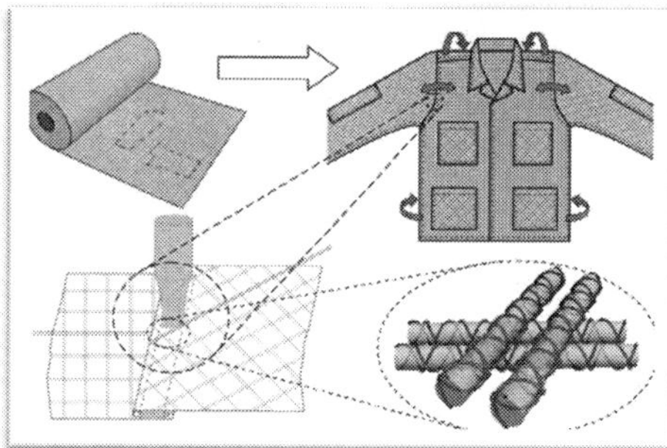

#SensorsConverge

Sensors Converge

DCS Ongoing/Future Development

- Creating E-textiles capable of USB 3.0 gen 2 data speeds and reliability
- Integrating electrical networks for communication and power delivery into stretch fabrics, allowing for deformation.
- Development of new E-textile connectors to facilitate more natural connections and less hard points
    - Using additive manufacturing to have contacts embedded into a non-conductive housings
    - Utilize rigidized flex-circuits to have direct interface between E-textile and connector
- Electrifying nylon webbing by embroidering E-yarns into belts, straps, and slings

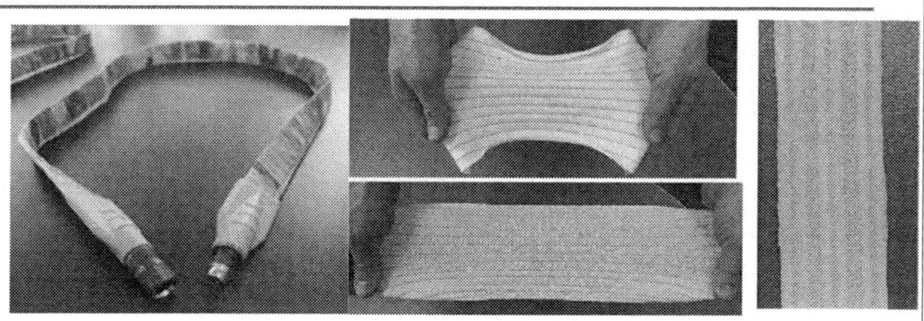

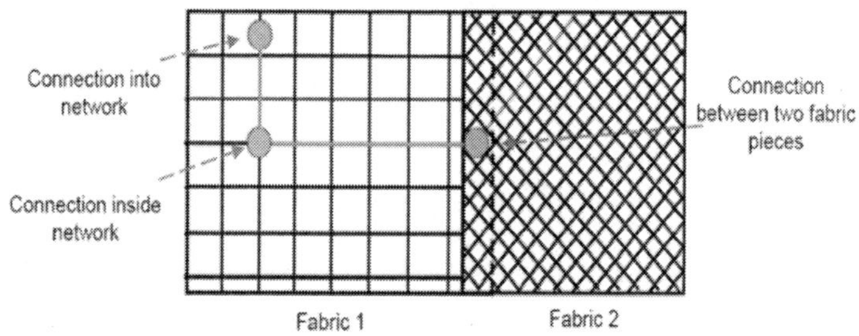

#SensorsConverge

Sensors Converge

Thank You for Your Attention

- Please contact me with any questions or with interest in what DCS can provide for you

PRINTED / FLEXIBLE /STRETCHABLE AND FUNCTIONAL FABRIC/ E-TEXTILE SENSORS AND SENSOR-BASED SYSTEMS: TECHNOLOGY LAUNCHPADS TO ENABLE EMERGING APPLICATIONS

PART 1: INTRODUCTION AND OVERVIEW

Sensors Converge Precon
Santa Clara California Convention Center
June 20, 2023

Roger H. Grace
President, Roger Grace Associates
rgrace@rgrace.com
www.rgrace.com

ROGER GRACE ASSOCIATES
MARKETING COUNSEL

SESSION OVERVIEW

- 10 Speakers (including me…providing introduction and summary))
- 20-minute presentations, two-25 minute keynotes
- Q and A to occur at the conclusion of the a.m. and p.m. sessions…using 3" x 5" notecards for questions from audience
- 15 minute mid-session breaks, one hour lunch break
- Kindly complete the questionnaire and it will be collected before the conclusion of the afternoon session…$50 Amazon gift card to the lucky winner
- The most highly concentrated presentation of speakers on the topic of printed/flexible/stretchable and e-textile/smart fabric sensors to date
- For the first time we will address 3D printing…thanks to Doug Sparks
- Virtually all-new program from previous with small number of "return" speakers
- Copies of the presentations will be made available by Questex

ROGER GRACE ASSOCIATES
MARKETING COUNSEL

A.M. SESSION

- 9:00-9:05 Welcome... Roger Grace, Roger Grace Associates, Workshop Organizer and Chairman
- 9:05-9:25 Roger Grace, Roger Grace Associates, Introduction and Overview of Printed, Flexible, Stretchable and Functional/E-Fabric Sensors and Sensor-Based Systems
- 9:25-9:50 Ravinder Dahiya Ph.D., Northeastern University, High-Performance Printed Electronics on Flexible Substrates (KEYNOTE)
- 9:50-10:10 Rob Podoloff, Tekscan, Design Considerations when Embedding Tactile Force Sensors-What OEMs Need to Know
- 10:10-10:30 Radislav Potyrailo Ph.D., GE Research, Conventional versus New Generation Gas Sensing: Meeting the Demanding Needs of Flexible Electronics and Emerging Markets
- 10:30-10:45 Morning Break
- 10:45-11:05 Doug Sparks Ph.D., Micro2Nano Technologies, 3D Printing Enables Complex Manufacturing Processes for Sensors
- 11:05:11:25 Robert Malakhov Ph.D., NextFlex, Additive Hybrid Electronics for Novel Wearable Devices
- 11:25-11:45 Maurizio "Mac" Macagno, Sensoria Health, A Gait Lab in a Textile Sensor-Infused Sock
- 11:45-12:00 Q and A
- 12:00-1:00 Lunch (Hosted)

ROGER GRACE ASSOCIATES
MARKETING COUNSEL

P.M.SESSION

- 1:00-1:10 Welcome... Roger Grace, Roger Grace Associates, Workshop Organizer and Chairman
- 1:10-1:35 Helena Alves Ph.D., INESC (Portugal), Self-Sustainable Textile Sensor Power Sources Based on Low-Cost Printing (KEYNOTE)
- 1:35 -1:55 Stephanie A.T. Brown, U.S. Army Combat Capabilities Development Command, Sensored Soldier at the Tactical Edge
- 1:55 -2:15 Sean Garbarino, DCS, E-Textile Based Systems for Damage Detection and Status Monitoring for Military and Other Applications
- 2:15-2:35 Roger Grace, Roger Grace Associates, Summary and Conclusions of Printed, Flexible, Stretchable and Functional/E-Fabric Sensors and Sensor-Based Systems
- 2:35-3:00 Q and A

ROGER GRACE ASSOCIATES
MARKETING COUNSEL

Copyright © 2023 Roger Grace Associates

MEA CULPA

- My colleagues have oft-times accused me of making "text-rich" presentations…and while I agree…the rationale for this is that I wish to provide the attendee with information that they can "take home" and use…rather that trying to remember my rambling comments or taking copious notes to collect the data points.
- I trust that you can appreciate my position on this…and thank you for your kind understanding.

ROGER GRACE ASSOCIATES
MARKETING COUNSEL

PRESENTATION OUTLINE

- Definitions
- Why printable/flexible/stretchable and E-Textile/smart fabric sensors?
- Situational analysis
- Market analysis
- Technology status of printed/flexible system functionalities
- Manufacturing process
- Industry activities
  - Commercial
  - Research/Academic
- Critical Success Factors
- Monetizing
- Summary/Conclusions/Recommendations

ROGER GRACE ASSOCIATES
MARKETING COUNSEL

ROGER GRACE BACKGROUND

- Education: BSEE, MSEE (Raytheon Graduate Fellow) Northeastern University, Boston, MA; MBA Program, California Berkeley
- Design Engineer with specialty in microwave and RF, 13 years...Raytheon, Avco
- Applications Engineer, RF semiconductors, 3 years, Avantek/HP
- Marketing Manager, MEMS, 3 years, Foxboro ICT
- Marketing Consultant, MEMS, Sensors and Semiconductors, 40 years
- Guest Lecturer, University of California Berkeley, 1990-2003
- Alumni Engineer of the Year, 2004, Northeastern University
- Co-Founder ,Past President and Board member of Micro ,Nano and Emerging Technology Commercialization Education Foundation (MANCEF)
- Published over 70 papers and articles on MEMS/Sensors/Commercialization
- Organized and Chaired over 30 technical sessions worldwide on MEMS/Sensors
- Board membership...Florida MEP, University of Michigan WIMSS, Northeastern University High Rate Nanomanufacturing Center
- Organizing committee includes IEEE Transducers 2009,COMS, Smart Systems Integration (EU), Advanced Microsystems for Automotive Applications (EU), Bestowed Inaugural "Sensor Industry Impact Award" by Sensors Expo/Sensors Magazine 2016

ROGER GRACE ASSOCIATES
MARKETING COUNSEL

ROGER GRACE ASSOCIATES OVERVIEW

- Founded in 1982,a pioneer in the MEMS/Sensors strategic marketing and analysis sector www.rgrace.com
- Clients include the "who's who" of industrial and government organizations worldwide
- Headquartered in Bonita Springs, Florida / San Francisco, California
- Focus on MEMS/Sensors and Capital Equipment markets
- Capabilities include...refer to next PPT.
  - Custom market research...product definition, application opportunity assessment,
  - New product introductions
  - Market strategy development
  - Merger and Acquisition (M&A) due diligence
  - Sales and distribution channel development
  - Integrated marketing communications
    - Promotion
    - Public Relations
    - Positioning and Branding

ROGER GRACE ASSOCIATES
MARKETING COUNSEL

TECHNOLOGY COMMERCIALIZATION* PROCESS MODEL

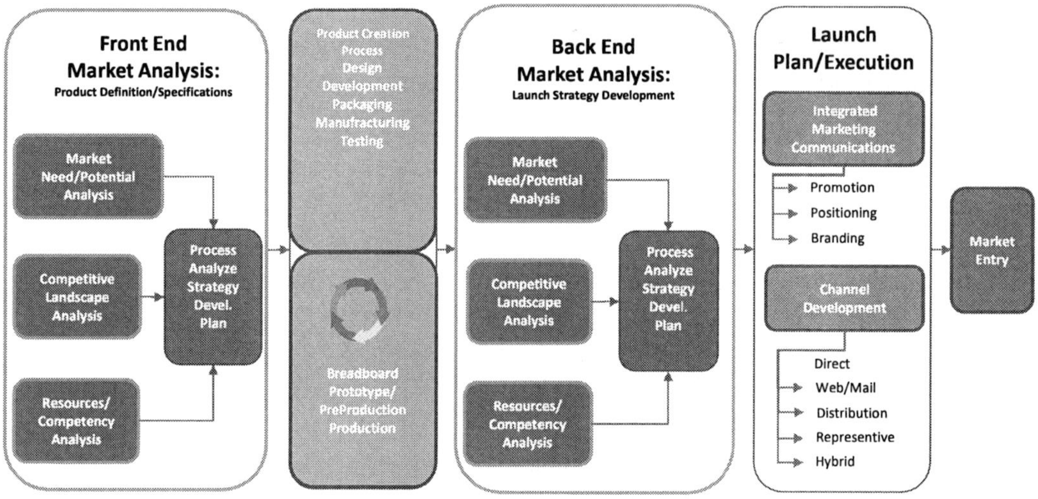

*Def: Process or cycle of introducing a new product or production method to the market

Roger Grace Associates supports its clients in front and back-end market analysis as well as in the product launch plan and execution

ROGER GRACE ASSOCIATES
MARKETING COUNSEL

MARKET RESEARCH METHODOLOGY

- PRIMARY: OVER 120 in-person, in-lab and telephone in-depth interviews with technology participants beginning in early 2015…and continuing
- SECONDARY: Data mining vis-à-vis the web …addressing the entire ecosystem of participants
- Attendance at several technical conferences and trade shows
- Participation in webinars

ROGER GRACE ASSOCIATES
MARKETING COUNSEL

WHY PRINTED / FLEXIBLE / STRETCHABLE & E-TEXTILE / SMART FABRIC

Attribute	Benefit	
	Cost	Functionality
Printed	• Low Infrastructure • Low Unit (R-2-R)	• Large device size • Arraying capability • Low profile • Ease of hybrid integration • Reduced time to market
Flexible		• Application driven (especially human interface)
Stretchable		• Application driven (especially human interface)
E-Textile/ Smart Fabric	• Low Infrastructure • Low unit	• Application driven (especially human interface) • Large device size • Arraying capability • Low profile

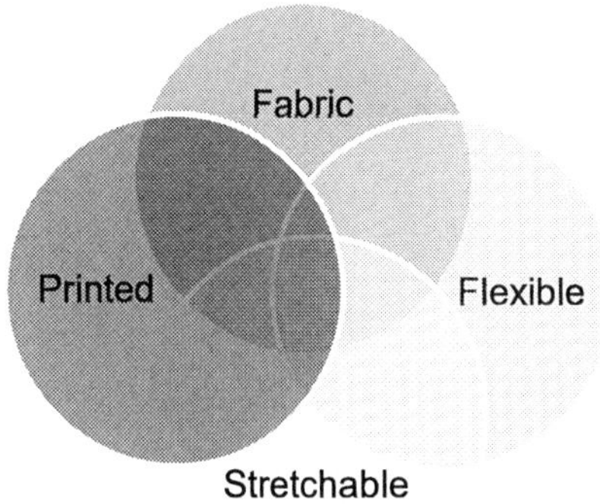

ROGER GRACE ASSOCIATES
MARKETING COUNSEL

COMMERCIALIZATION DRIVING FUNCTIONS

- Small size / low profile / low weight
- Ability to conform to attaching surfaces…especially in bio applications
- Robust and highly reliable vis-à-vis judicious material selection
- Low manufacturing cost based on existing batch mode processing with the ability to be scaled to a uber- high volume / uber low cost roll-to-roll (R2R) or weaving manufacturing approach
- Enhanced performance over discrete 3-D solutions because of their size and geometry
- Device-to-device uniformity
- Low CAPEX requirements for manufacturing
- Ease for integration (including discrete) of other functionalities onto same or layered carriers…hybrid approaches
- Ability for arraying
- Large area coverage capability
- Expected to benefit from momentum of popularity of Flexible Hybrid Electronics (FHE) and associated manufacturing capabilities

ROGER GRACE ASSOCIATES
MARKETING COUNSEL

Copyright © 2023 Roger Grace Associates

SENSOR-BASED SYSTEM SOLUTIONS

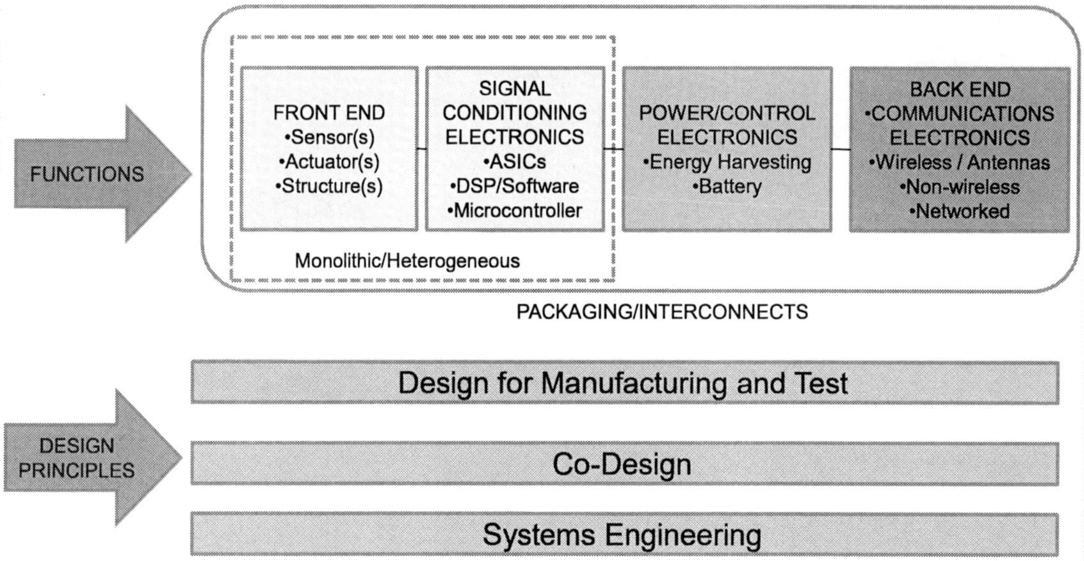

ROGER GRACE ASSOCIATES
MARKETING COUNSEL

SITUATIONAL ANALYSIS

- Printed/flexible sensors are a logical extension of printed displays (OLED) and Flexible Hybrid Electronics (FHE) electronics…and are chemistry and materials (not electronically) driven and are truly a convergence of technologies
- First commercially success in 1985 by Interlink Electronics and followed by Tekscan …Force Sensing Resistors (FSR)
- To be considered as a compliment / not replacement to Silicon functionalities
- Use much the same infrastructure as printed electronics
- Sensors typically have simple structures and thus easy to manufacture
- Flexible / extensible manufacturing processes:
  - Batch mode for low-to-medium volume applications
  - Roll-to-Roll (R2R) for large volume applications
- Only a small number of companies currently in volume production
- Significant activity in agencies, research labs and universities worldwide
- Many possible application opportunities with a focus on major opportunities for wearables e.g. sports monitoring and home healthcare monitoring
- High volume application opportunities expected to fuel dramatic growth
- Adequate market research coverage to date…i.e. IDTechEx, Modor, Research and Markets
- Limited design and analysis tools currently available

ROGER GRACE ASSOCIATES
MARKETING COUNSEL

SENSOR PRODUCT LIFE CYCLES

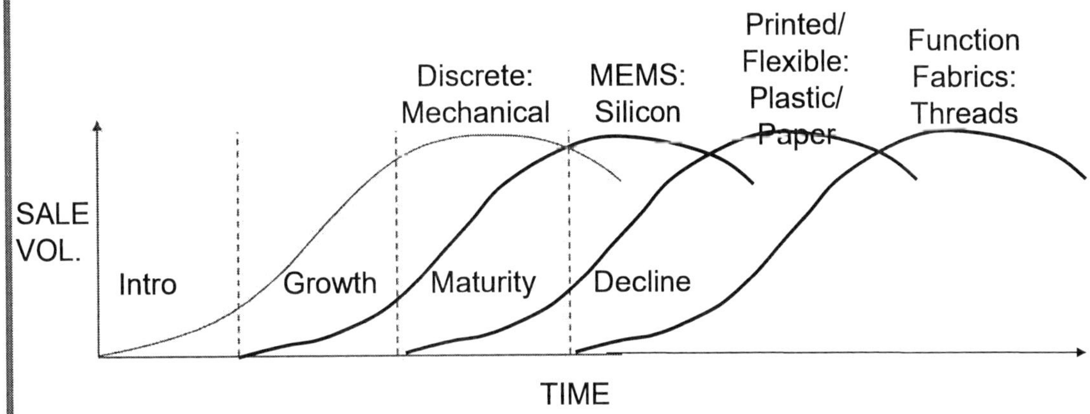

ROGER GRACE ASSOCIATES
MARKETING COUNSEL

WHERE IT ALL BEGAN

Johannes Gutenberg; Mainz, Germany 1440

ROGER GRACE ASSOCIATES
MARKETING COUNSEL

ECOSYSTEM

- Broad and in-depth (many suppliers for each) ecosystem in place in the value chain
- Suppliers include:
  - Materials, chemicals
  - Equipment
  - Sensors
  - Interconnects
  - Integration
  - Packaging
  - End product design
  - Manufacturing
  - Design, layout and analysis tools
  - Sales and distribution of final product
- Collaboration up and down the value chain will be critical for participants success…one cannot successfully go it alone

ROGER GRACE ASSOCIATES
MARKETING COUNSEL

EMERGING HIGH VOLUME APPLICATION OPPORTUNITIES

- It is common knowledge that many high volume applications exists…however the big question is which are the most lucrative ones and when?
- Need to take into account the "Grace / Walsh 30 year development process for MEMS"
- Current acknowledged current application opportunities include:
  - Package tracking
  - International monitoring of the environment by chemical / gas sensors connected by mobile networks
  - Disposables….e.g. diapers
  - Wearables …Personal health / fitness monitoring e.g. "e-medical"/ military battlefield
  - Food, beverage and drug status monitoring…e.g. UCBerkeley
  - Patient activity monitoring

ROGER GRACE ASSOCIATES
MARKETING COUNSEL

DEVICE MATERIAL COST COMPARISON

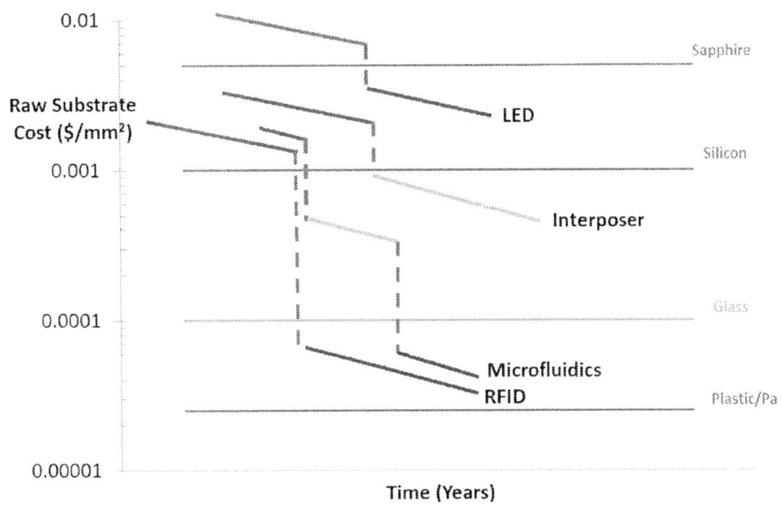

Source: AM Fitzgerald /adapted from P. Werbaneth

ROGER GRACE ASSOCIATES
MARKETING COUNSEL

DESIGN & MANUFACTURING PROCESS

- Complex process flow…lots of "landmines" to avoid
- Critical to have design & manufacturing "kickoff" meeting to bring all aspects of the design & manufacturing involved and addressed from day 1
- Decision on printing process driven by several factors…Sheet fed or Roll-to-Roll
  - Volume
  - Specifications
- Scalability…start with sheet-fed for prototypes and low volumes…migrate to Roll-to-Roll for large volumes
- Selection of base materials and inks is critical to performance and manufacturability
- "Converters" or…packagers…integrate the sheets into the final products
  - Cutting
  - Lamination
  - Connection to the outside world

ROGER GRACE ASSOCIATES
MARKETING COUNSEL

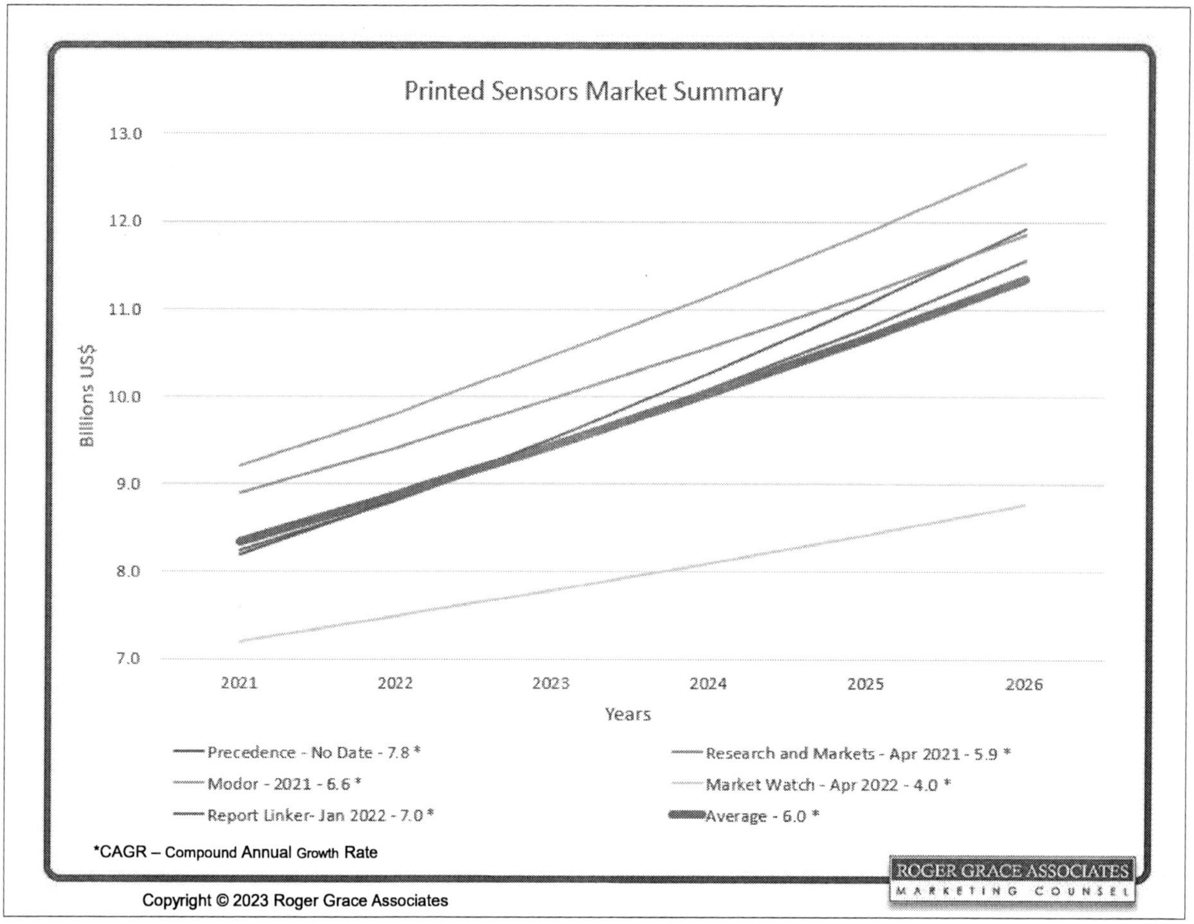
Printed Sensors Market Summary
13.0
12.0
11.0
10.0
9.0
8.0
7.0
Billions US$
2021
2022
2023
2024
2025
2026
Years
Precedence - No Date - 7.8 *
Research and Markets - Apr 2021 - 5.9 *
Modor - 2021 - 6.6 *
Market Watch - Apr 2022 - 4.0 *
Report Linker- Jan 2022 - 7.0 *
Average - 6.0 *
*CAGR – Compound Annual Growth Rate
ROGER GRACE ASSOCIATES
MARKETING COUNSEL
Copyright © 2023 Roger Grace Associates

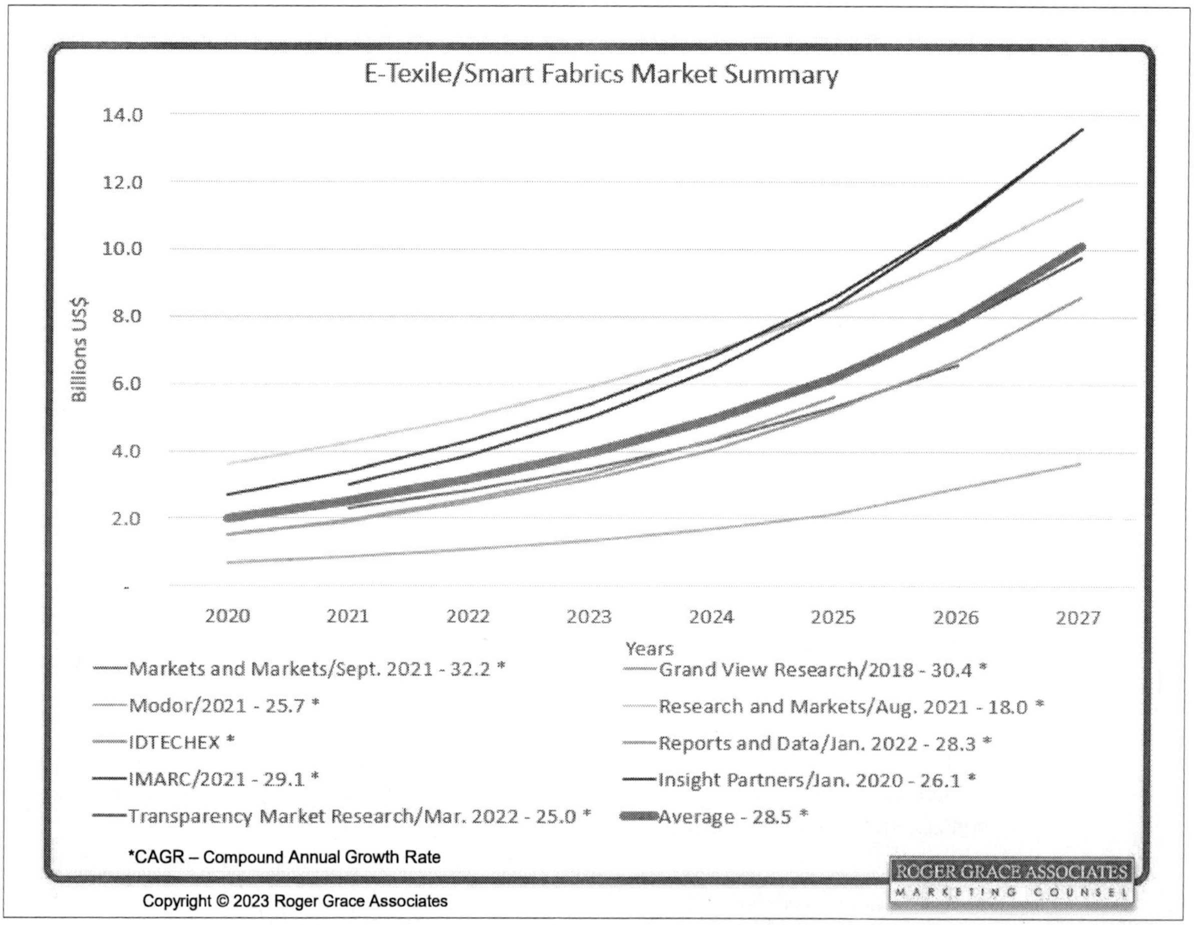
E-Textile/Smart Fabrics Market Summary
14.0
12.0
10.0
8.0
6.0
4.0
2.0
-
Billions US$
2020
2021
2022
2023
2024
2025
2026
2027
Years
Markets and Markets/Sept. 2021 - 32.2 *
Grand View Research/2018 - 30.4 *
Modor/2021 - 25.7 *
Research and Markets/Aug. 2021 - 18.0 *
IDTECHEX *
Reports and Data/Jan. 2022 - 28.3 *
IMARC/2021 - 29.1 *
Insight Partners/Jan. 2020 - 26.1 *
Transparency Market Research/Mar. 2022 - 25.0 *
Average - 28.5 *
*CAGR – Compound Annual Growth Rate
ROGER GRACE ASSOCIATES
MARKETING COUNSEL
Copyright © 2023 Roger Grace Associates

PRINTED / FLEXIBLE /STRETCHABLE AND FUNCTIONAL FABRIC/ E-TEXTILE SENSORS AND SENSOR-BASED SYSTEMS: TECHNOLOGY LAUNCHPADS TO ENABLE EMERGING APPLICATIONS

PART 2: APPLICATIONS / SUMMARY/CONCLUSIONS

Sensors Converge Precon
Santa Clara California Convention Center
June 20, 2023

Roger H. Grace
President, Roger Grace Associates
rgrace@rgrace.com
www.rgrace.com

ROGER GRACE ASSOCIATES
MARKETING COUNSEL

▪

COMMERCIAL ACTIVITIES

ROGER GRACE ASSOCIATES
MARKETING COUNSEL

CURRENT COMMERCIALIZATION PLAYERS

- Limited "reported" activity in sensors production
- No apparent large volume producers
- No apparent "big dogs" involved (yet)…e.g. Bosch, ST, ADI, Freescale …however we believe that "big dogs" are funding efforts in P/F and FF vis-à-vis subcontracts with research institutes and universities
- Over 100 smaller players worldwide addressing individual parameters
- Virtually all current participants not "traditional" sensor companies but rather materials / chemical companies e.g. Brewer Science
- Sensor parameters currently being addressed include:
  - Chemical/gas
  - Touch/force/pressure
  - Temperature
  - Humidity
  - Bio
  - Air flow
  - Imaging
  - Conducting electrodes

ROGER GRACE ASSOCIATES
MARKETING COUNSEL

SUPPLIER LANDSCAPE

Company	Force/Touch	Temperature	Humidity	Gas	Electrodes	Bio-Chem	Imaging	Shock	Time of Flight	Flow	Other
BodiTrack/Vista Medical (Canada)	•										
Brewer Science		•	•								
Drop Sense (Spain)					•						
Electrozyme						•					
Flexpoint	•		•							•	
GSI Technologies					•						
Interlink Electronics	•										
ISORG (France)							•				
MC10						•					
Nikkoia (France)							•				
Peratech (UK)	•										
Piezotech (France)					•			•	•		
Plastic Electronics GmbH (Austria)	•										
PolyIC (Germany)	•										
PST (So. Africa)		•									
Sensitronics	•										
Spec Sensors				•							
Synkera				•							
Tactonic	•										
Tekscan	•										
Temptime		•									
T-Inc	•										

Not exhaustive
Alphabetical order

ROGER GRACE ASSOCIATES
MARKETING COUNSEL

TEKSCAN

- Location: Norwood MA
- Introduced: Early 1990's
- Brand name: Flexiforce
- Parameter sensed: Force, rate of change of force, relative change in force, touch, contact
- Construction: Two layers of polyester substrates with printing of layer of conductive silver (connections) and layer of pressure sensitive ink attached by an adhesive bond
- Applications include sports/fitness consumer, medical devices, robotics, control and diagnostic

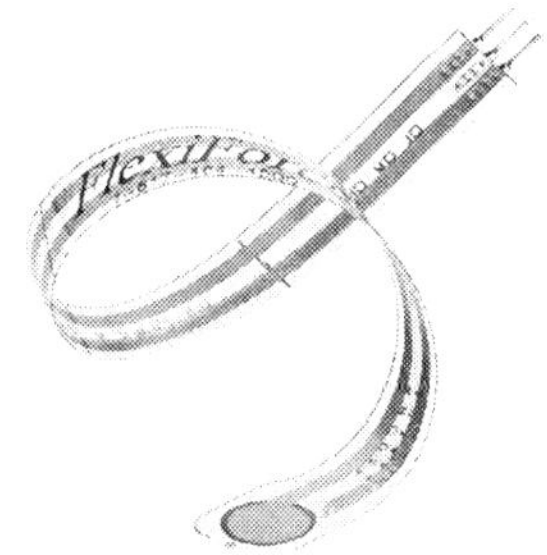

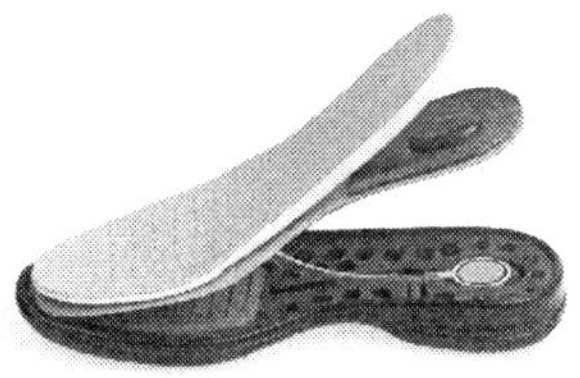

ROGER GRACE ASSOCIATES
MARKETING COUNSEL

ISORG

- Location: Grenoble, France
- Parameter sensed: imaging sensor
- Visible/NIR up to 900 nm.
- Low dark current
- Large dynamic range
- PET plastic foil: 32 x 32 cm. moving to 60 x 60 cm.; 5 x 5 cm. device
- PET backplane
- Applications: whole -hand fingerprint analysis/biometrics, medical x-ray imaging ,IoT inventory analysis
- CEA-Leti spinoff in 2009
- Received 28M Euro infusion

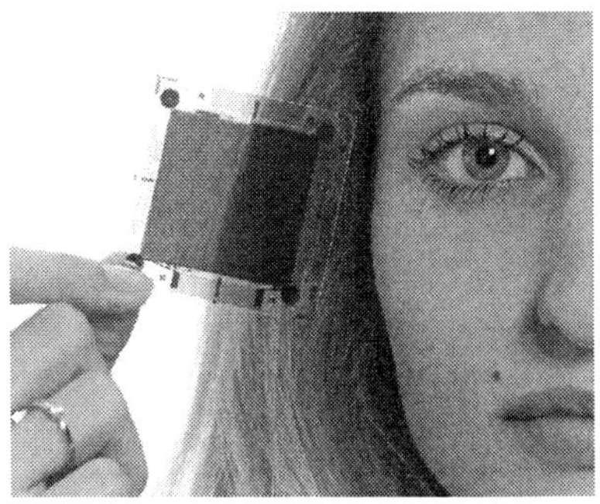

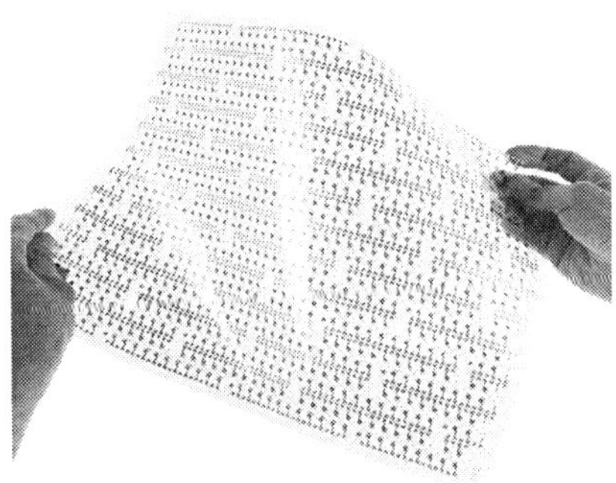

ROGER GRACE ASSOCIATES
MARKETING COUNSEL

HOLOGENIX / CELLIANT

- Founded: 2017 in LA
- Works on principle of certain minerals plus 88 trace elements react to heat and emit full spectrum IR energy
- Proprietary minerals added to liquid phase of the polymeric thread extrusion process
- Currently EU Class 1 medical device
- FDA classified as medical device with no class determination
- Applications include apparel, medical/wound care, diabetes
- Products include T-shirts (UnderArmor), socks, sheets (Pure Care) Mattresses (Bear)

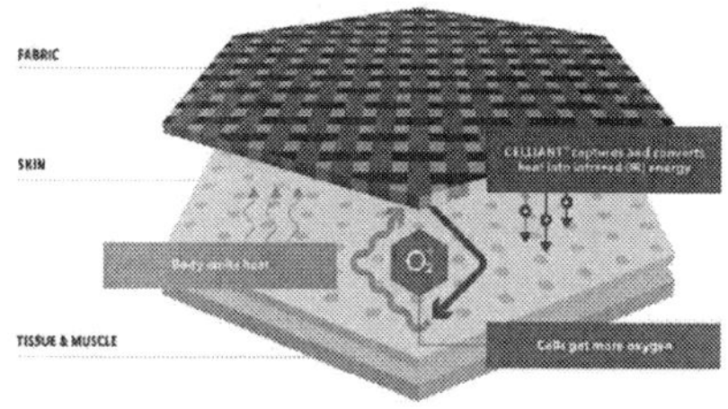

ROGER GRACE ASSOCIATES
MARKETING COUNSEL

Applications

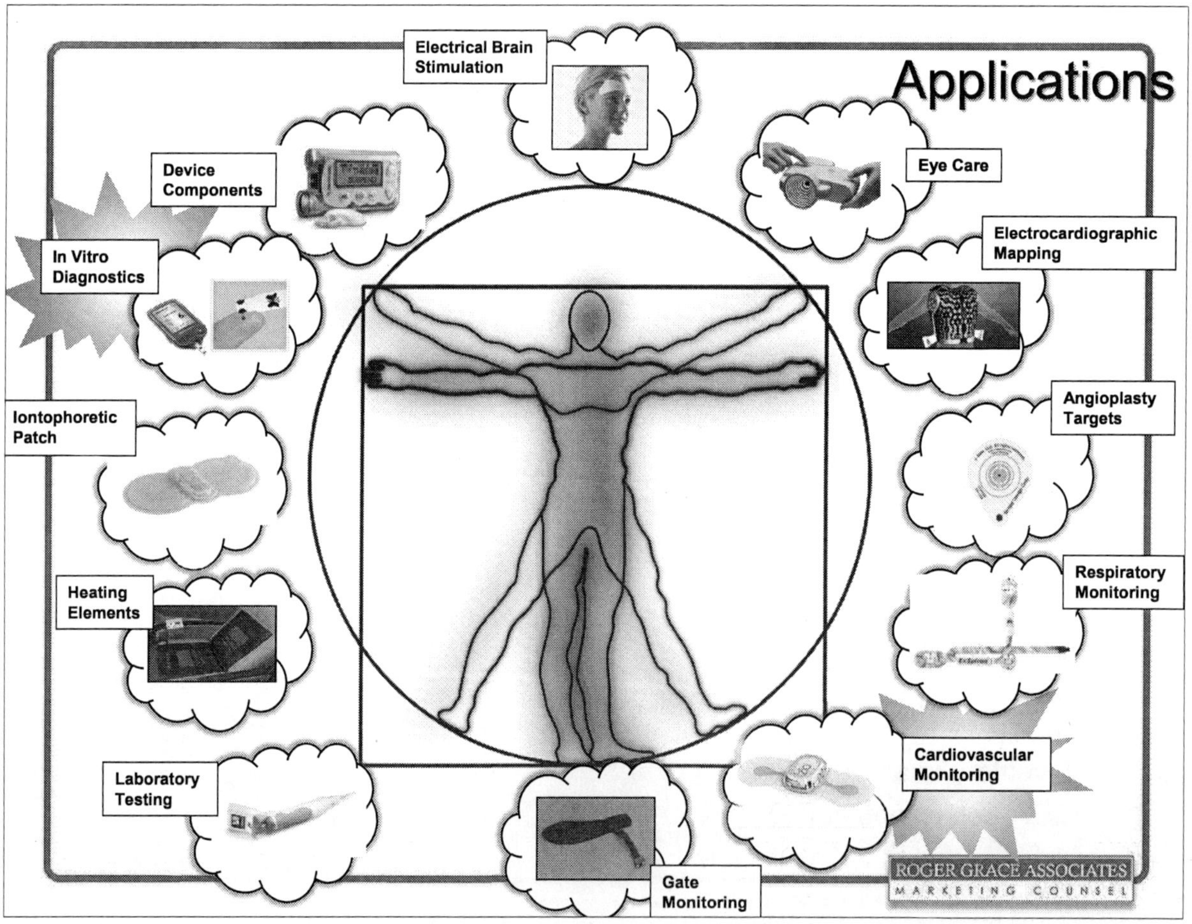

ROGER GRACE ASSOCIATES
MARKETING COUNSEL

WEARABLES:THE FUTURE OF MEDTECH*

- Definition:
  - On-body vs. off-body
  - Apple watch vs. Sensoria T-Shirt
- Objective: provide "transparent computing"...Davide Vigano/CEO Sensoria
- Forcing Factors
  - "the pandemic transformed healthcare"...Alfred Poor, Editor, Heath Tech Insider
  - Rate of adoption acerated by
    - Aging-in-place
    - Adoption of telemedicine/telehealth
    - Recent developments in AI
- Applications...remote and on-person monitoring
  - Post-procedure
  - Physical therapy
  - Chronic illness
- Technical Issues...Hardware
  - Hybrid/"pod" approach for sensing, computation, communication, power
  - Packaging/interfacing sensor platforms to systems

*key take-aways from the WEAR Conference...June 7-9, 2022 Scottsdale, AZ

ROGER GRACE ASSOCIATES MARKETING COUNSEL

WEARABLES:THE FUTURE OFMEDTECH*(CONT.)

- Market Growth (Research and Markets Report: "Global Smart Wearables" Feb. 2023)
  - $20.64 B(2022)
  - $34.39B(2027)
  - CAGR=10.2%
- Technical Issues...Software/Data
  - What needs to be measured to impact decisions
  - How is it displayed to optimize efficacy
- Barriers to Commercialization
  - Data security
  - Regulation
  - CDC billing code approval
  - Broadband and smart phone access
- Companies to Watch
  - Butler Technologies...Smart T-Shirt
  - Hologenix...Smart power T-shirt (Under Armor)
  - Liquid Wire...sensors and connectivity solutions
  - Nextiles...smart fabric sensors
  - Sensoria...Smart socks, T-Shirts and bras

ROGER GRACE ASSOCIATES MARKETING COUNSEL

UNIVERSITIES / RESEARCH INSTITUTES ACTIVITIES

ROGER GRACE ASSOCIATES
MARKETING COUNSEL

R&D LANDSCAPE OVERVIEW

- Considerable R&D activity in sensor development (and their integration) into systems a.k.a. products in many research institutes and universities: Asia
  - ITRI-Taiwan
  - Sungkyonk wan University-Korea
- Europe
  - CEA-Leti France
  - CSEM Switzerland
  - Fraunhofer Europe (67 with approx. 10 involved in P/F Electronics including Chemnitz/ENAS, Munich/EMFT, Dresden/IPMS and Berlin/IZM)))
  - IMEC/ Holst Netherlands
  - VTT Finland
  - INESC Portugal
- US

– Arizona State University	GE Research	Western Michigan University
– Northeastern University	parc	Ohio State
– Stanford	UMASS Amherst	N.C. State
– UC Berkeley	UMASS Lowell	
– UC San Diego	UC Irvine	

ROGER GRACE ASSOCIATES
MARKETING COUNSEL

PRINTOCENT CLUSTER

- Location: Oulu, Finland
- Started: 2008 www.Printocent.fi
- Facilities (shared):
  - VTT
  - OUAS
  - University of Oulu
- Funding: 40M Euros (EU and Regional)
- Turnover of companies (2019): 25M Euros
- Total number of companies in cluster: 40
- Number of companies catalyzed: 30
- Number of jobs created: 300
- Purpose: Provide open access to companies for scale-up of manufacturing capabilities for the creation and manufacturing of "printed intelligence"
- Created a six-part series of webinars in mid-2020 on "Printed Intelligence"
- Offers free…"Handbook of Printed Intelligence" as pdf download

ROGER GRACE ASSOCIATES
MARKETING COUNSEL

US PUBLIC / PRIVATE CONSORTIA

- AFFOA (Advanced Functional Fabrics of America) www.affoa.org.
  - Location: Cambridge, MA (MIT)
  - Founded in 2016
  - Funding:$75M (US DOD) with grants from governments, industry and academia totaling approximately $325M
  - Focus: Enabling manufacturing
- NEXT FLEX / SEMI www.nextflex.org.
  - Location: San Jose, CA
  - Founded in 2015
  - Funding:$75M (US DOD) with grants from governments, industry and academia totaling approximately $325M
  - Focus: Enabling manufacturing (flexible hybrid approach)

ROGER GRACE ASSOCIATES
MARKETING COUNSEL

INTEGRATION CHALLENGES

- The future success will reside in the ability of suppliers to judiciously select the required functionalities of the individual circuit functions and determine the optimum format/platform for their realization in specific applications
- Monolithic vs. heterogeneous vs. hybrid integration strategies…TBD
- Connectivity of individual devices
- Packaging/encapsulation of total solution
- Reliability issues…especially with wearables continuous washing/drying
- Modelling challenges
- Determination of the manufacturing method to minimize cost, maximize functionality and maximize reliability e.g. Flextronics, Jabil
- Major efforts underway in EU to address this issue…also with NextFlex in the US

ROGER GRACE ASSOCIATES
MARKETING COUNSEL

SYSTEM INTEGRATION

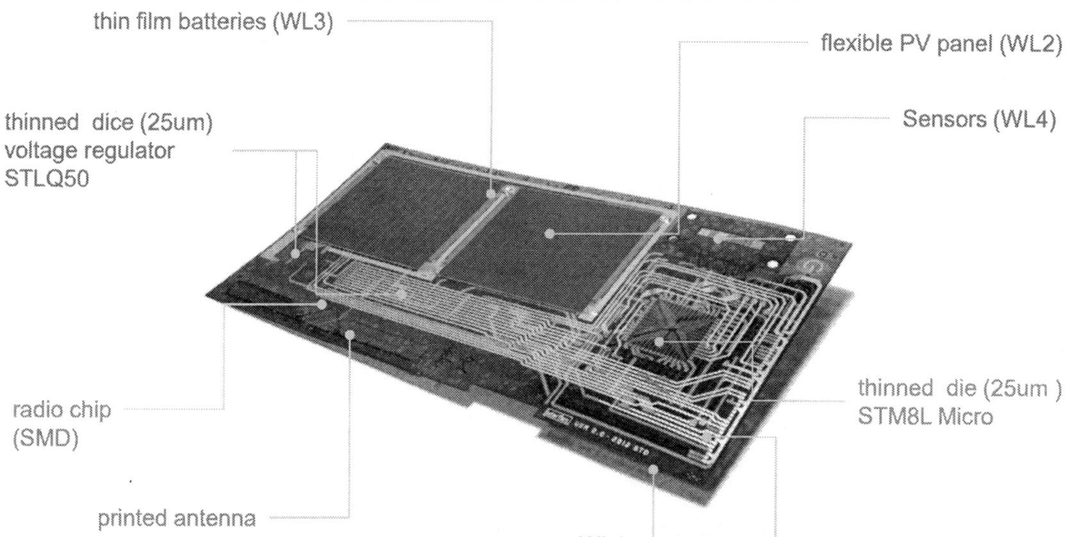

- multi foil based
- energy autonomous
- thin and flexible

INFOTECH automation
cea
BOSCH Invented for life
Henkel
Fraunhofer EMFT

ROGER GRACE ASSOCIATES
MARKETING COUNSEL

CRITICAL SUCCESS FACTORS

- Ability to demonstrate value- add to critical applications
- Ability of to demonstrate equal- to -better performance vs. competitive approaches…and my market research say "yes"
- Growth of the wearables market uncertainty
- Ability of non-flexible/non-organic functional solutions to accommodate application requirements
- Entry of additional players (with big R&D Budgets) to help commercialize the technology
- Adoption of standard processes based on the broad availability of materials
- Continuation of robust funding of research activities by governments …e.g. Next Flex (US), AFFOA (US), PrintoCent (Finland)
- Ability of existing sensor companies to adopt a paradigm shift from a electromechanical technology mindset to that of a materials one
- Continuation of over-hyping of flexible electronics opportunities
- BOTTOM LINE….I believe there is lots of uncertainty at this time…"as goes flexible hybrid electronics so goes its sensors"…R. Grace

ROGER GRACE ASSOCIATES
MARKETING COUNSEL

MONITIZING

- FACT…Its hard to make money just providing sensors (J. Bryzek)
- Need to add value…look for system solutions
- Actively seek partnerships/collaborations … e.g. PST / ThinFilm (licensing)
- Possible acquisition strategy
- Ride the wave of the printed electronics (PE) growth
- Find and get designed into applications that can exploit the unique benefits of these sensor technologies and address unmet market needs especially in wearables

ROGER GRACE ASSOCIATES
MARKETING COUNSEL

SUMMARY / CONCLUSIONS

- Limited:
  - number of success stories to date
  - number of commercial companies in volume production
  - number of parameters currently being measured:
    - Pressure / force / touch
    - Gas analyses
    - Temperature
    - Humidity
- Solid growth foreseen by several market research groups
  - Printed: CAGR (average) =6% (2021-2026)?
  - Functional Fabric: CAGR (average)= 28% (2020-2027)
- Growth forcing functions
  - Replacement of existing solutions…lower cost, enhanced functionality
  - Creation of new solutions based on enabling nature of P/F/S and FF
- Will require a significant marketing/applications pull vs. technology push
- A "systems solution" approach will be required…not just a sensor!
- Wearables for military, sport fitness, disposables, package tracking, e-healthcare and environmental monitoring expected to propel market
- Ability to scale to R-2-R for large volume/low cost application opportunities

ROGER GRACE ASSOCIATES
MARKETING COUNSEL

SUMMARY / CONCLUSIONS (cont.)

- Low cost CAPEX makes commercialization by many organizations possible
- I believe that the success of Printed/Flexible/Stretchable and Functional Fabric/E-Textile sensors will weigh heavily on the success of flexible hybrid electronics (FHE) …the future will be interesting

ROGER GRACE ASSOCIATES
MARKETING COUNSEL

UPCOMING EVENTS OF NOTE

- IEEE Sensors Council-FLEPS (www.ieee-fleps.org)... Boston/Northeastern University...July 9-12, 2023...connect with Prof. Ravinder Dahiya for details
- Semicon West/NextFlex (www. nextflex.org)...San Francisco, CA...July 11-13, 2023
- WEAR (www.wear.com) San Diego...December 4-6, 2023

ROGER GRACE ASSOCIATES
MARKETING COUNSEL

FURTHER READING

- Articles by Roger Grace on P/F/S and E-Textile/Smart Fabric sensors have appeared in:
  - Electronic Products-June, 2015 Electronic Products; July 2015
  - Sensors Magazine Newsletter-September 25, 2015
  - Sensor Magazin (Germany)-November 2015
  - Commercial Micromanufacturing Magazine (UK)-December 2015
  - Commercial Micromanufacturing Magazine (UK)-May/June 2018

...and all available on the Roger Grace Associates website www.rgrace.com in the drop down tab..."Articles"

ROGER GRACE ASSOCIATES
MARKETING COUNSEL

Since this was a shortened presentation due to time constraints…

the entire presentation will be available to attendees by kindly requesting it via email to me at …rgrace@rgrace.com

Please come by the Roger Grace Associates booth #324 and enter to win a smart T-shirt and Smart socks courtesy of Hologenix

ROGER GRACE ASSOCIATES
MARKETING COUNSEL

Sensors Converge

Self-sustainable textile sensors power sources based on a low-cost printing solution

June 20–22, 2023 | Santa Clara, CA

#SensorsConverge

Textile Electronics

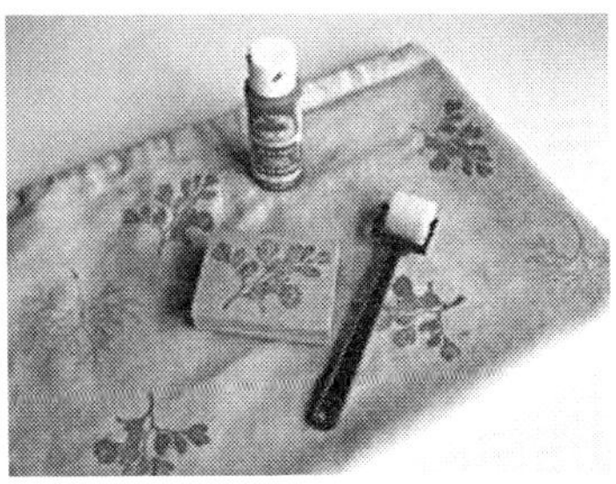

#SensorsConverge

Sensors Converge

Power Challenge

Sensor and communication devices

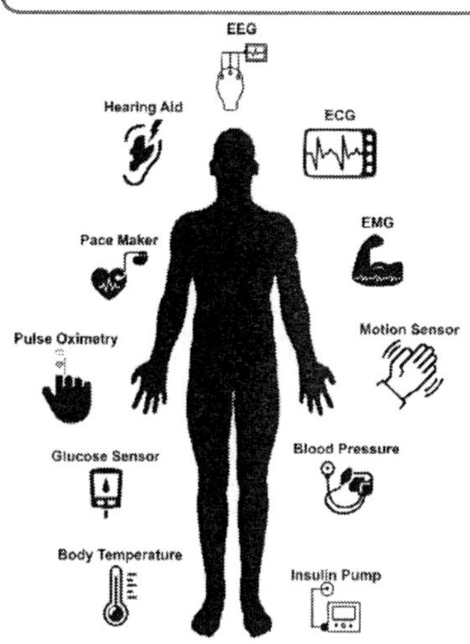

Rely on batteries

- Frequent recharging
- Limited lifetime
- Environmental hazard

Additional Problems

#SensorsConverge

Sensors Converge

Self-sustainable Textile Power Supply Devices

- From sources in the body
  - Triboelectric, Piezolectric, Thermoelectric

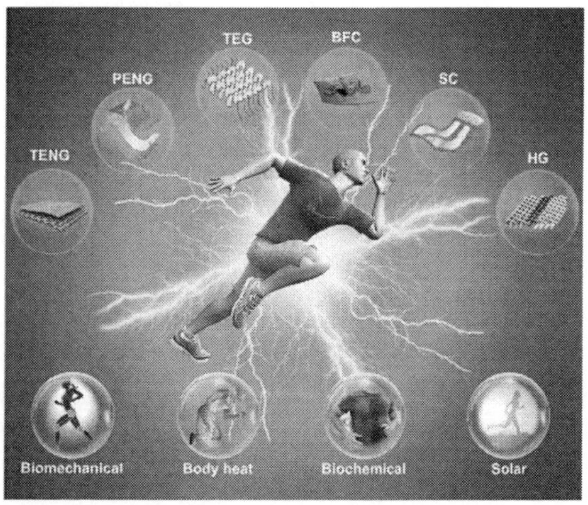

- From the surrounding environment
  - Radio Frequency, Photovoltaic, Ultrasonic

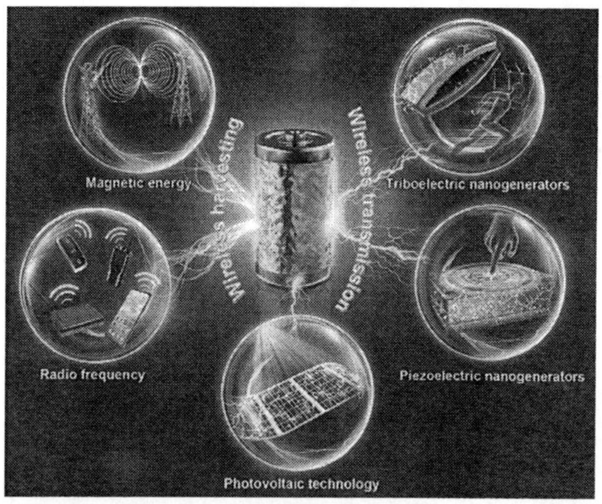

#SensorsConverge

Sensors Converge

Triboelectric devices

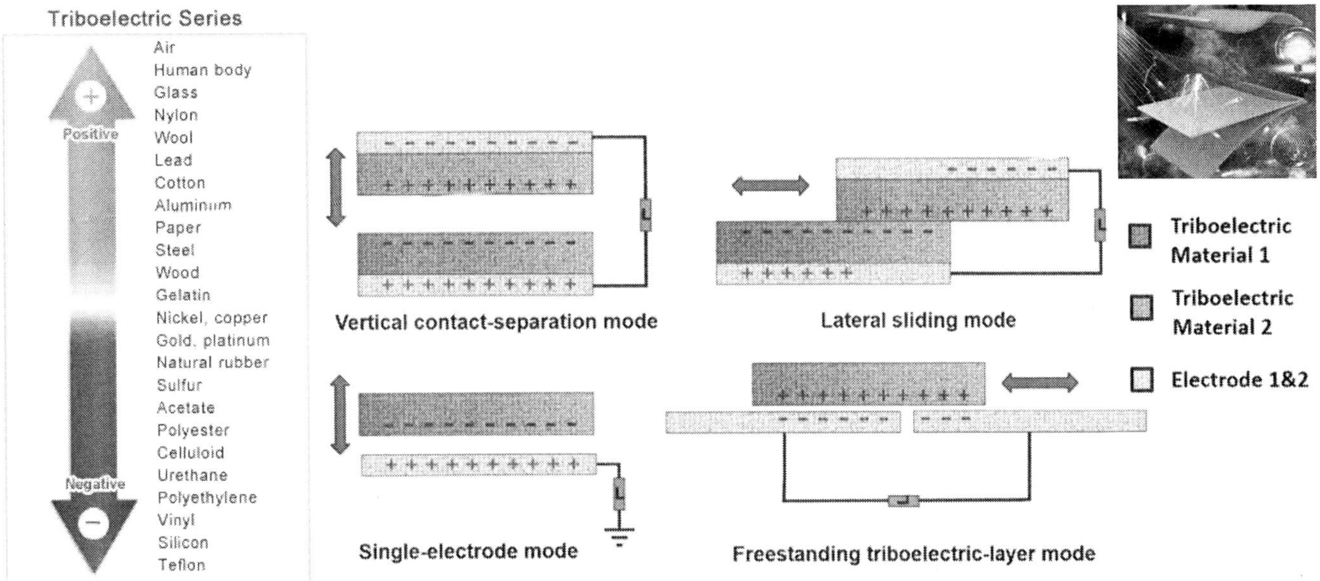

Triboelectric devices

- Main Challenges:
  - Power densities low due to low effective contact area relating to their structure
    - fiber-TENG up to 953 mW/m^2
    - fabric-TENG up to 8920 mW/m^2
  - Complex fabrication process (particularly fiber-based TENGs)
  - Processes compatible with standard large-scale textile manufacturing
  - Metal electrode reduces flexibility

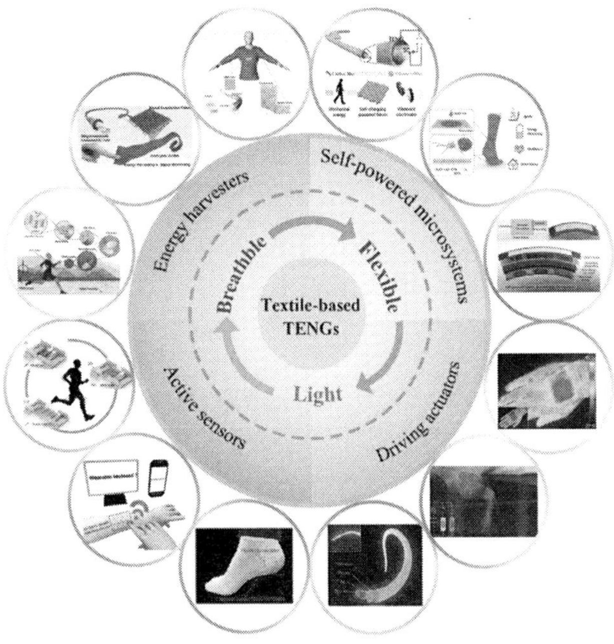

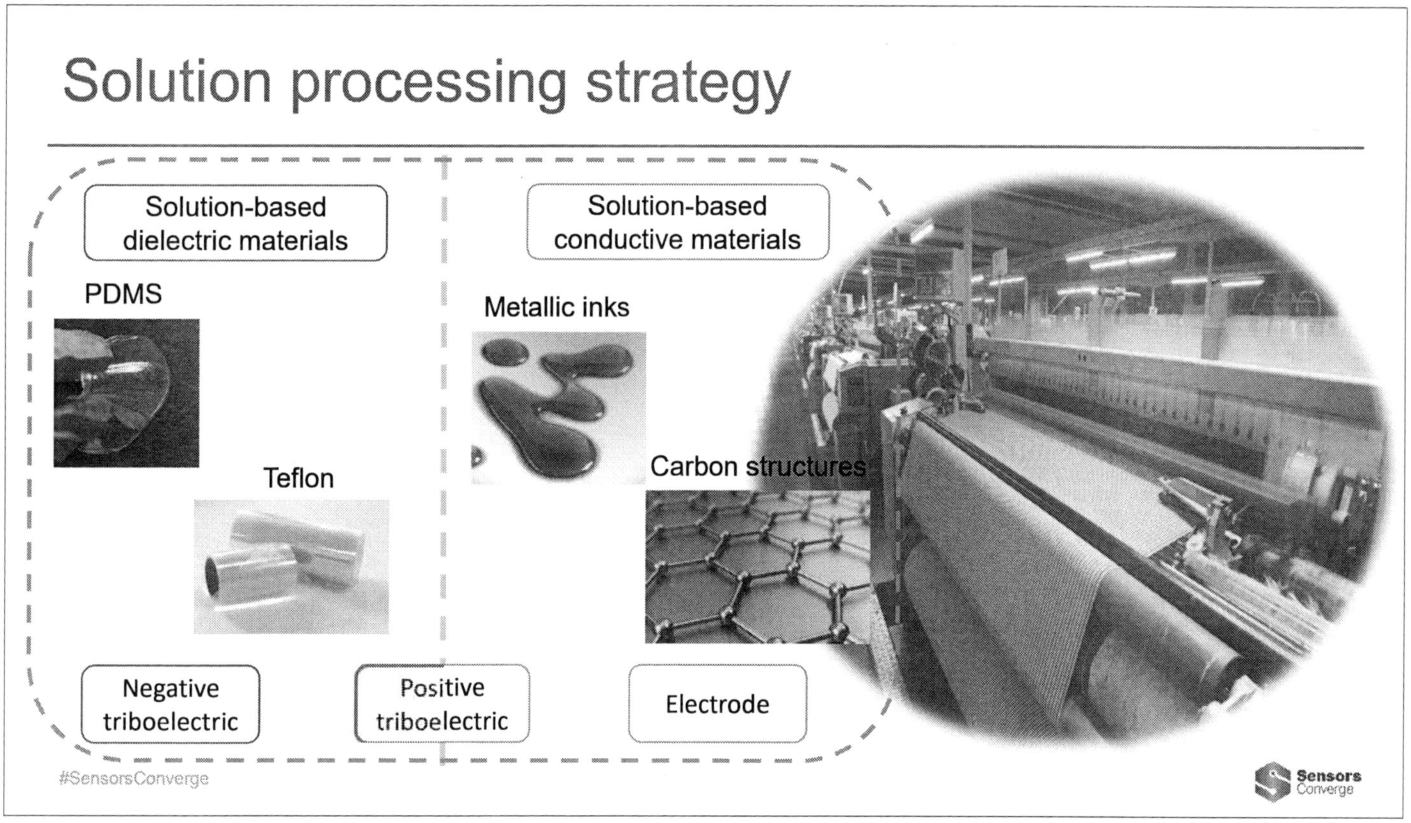
Solution processing strategy
Solution-based dielectric materials
PDMS
Teflon
Solution-based conductive materials
Metallic inks
Carbon structures
Negative triboelectric
Positive triboelectric
Electrode
#SensorsConverge
Sensors Converge

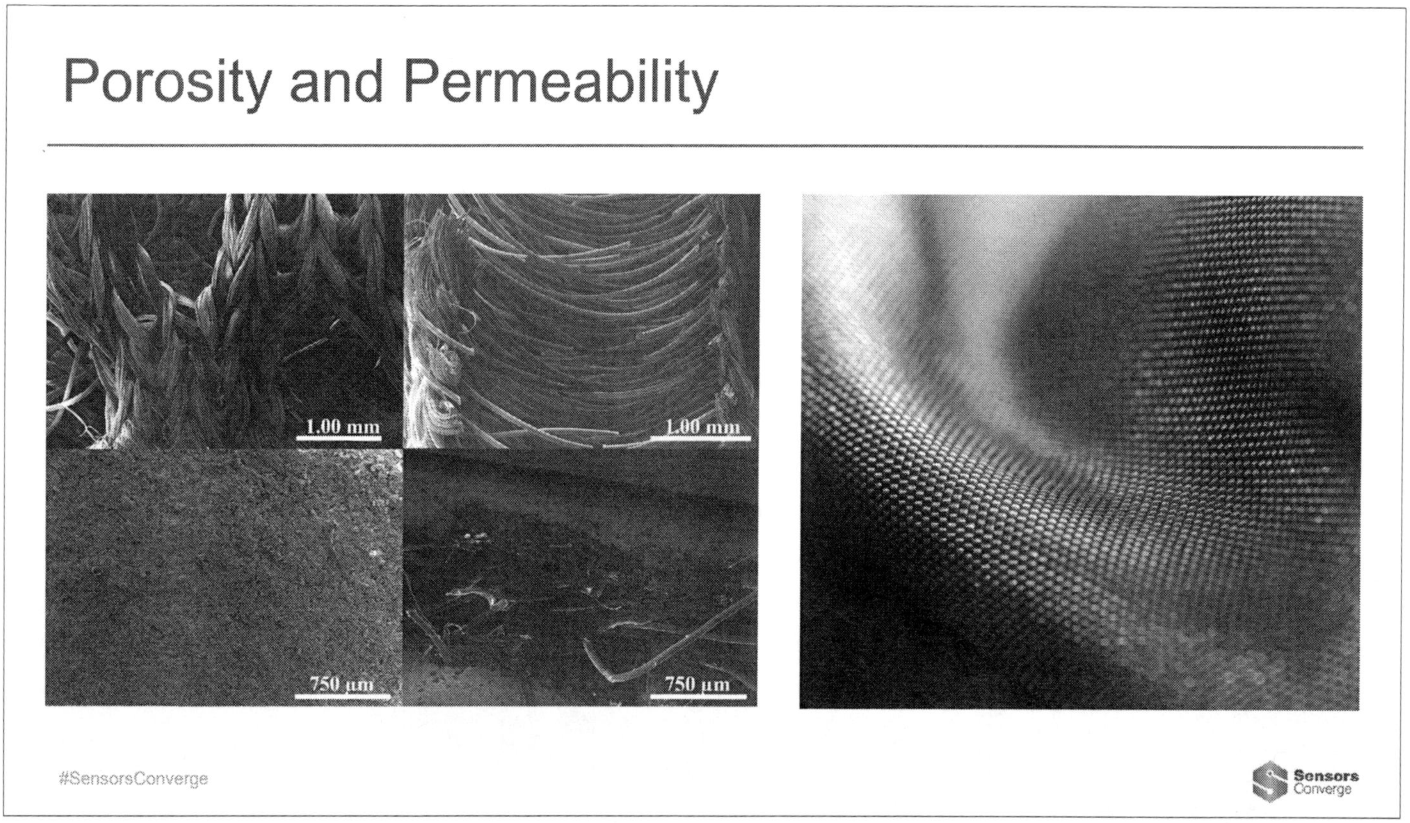
Porosity and Permeability
1.00 mm
1.00 mm
750 μm
750 μm
#SensorsConverge
Sensors Converge

Porosity and Permeability

Adhesive layer

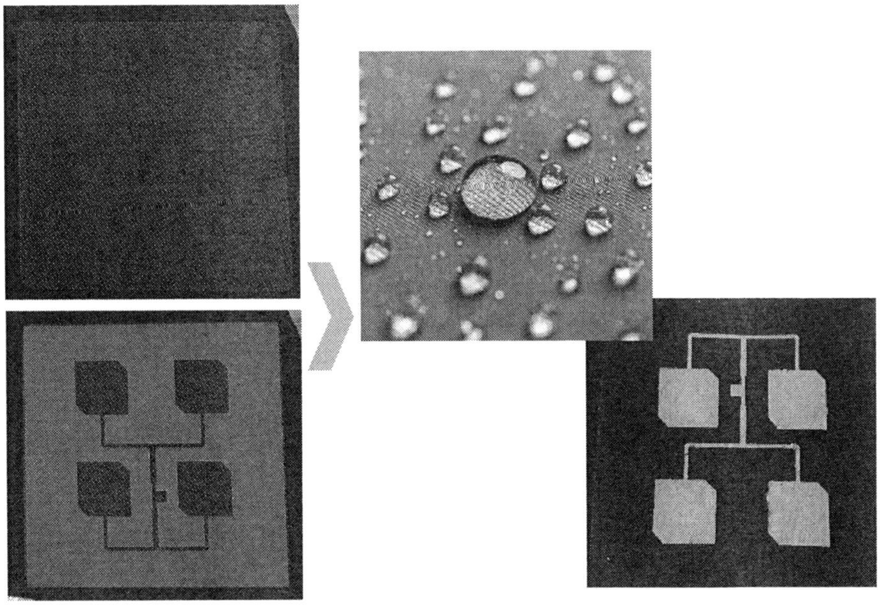

#SensorsConverge

Sensors Converge

Planarization

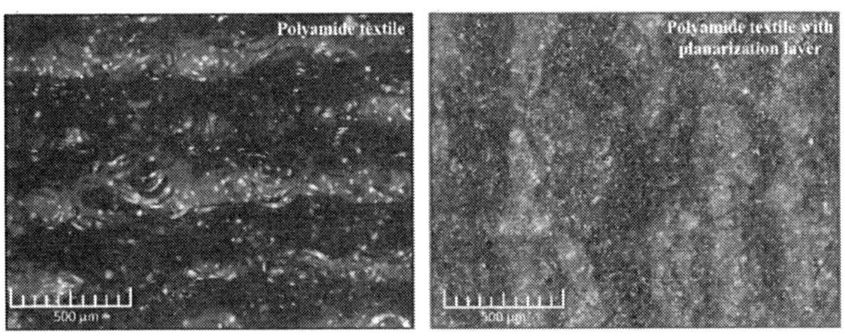

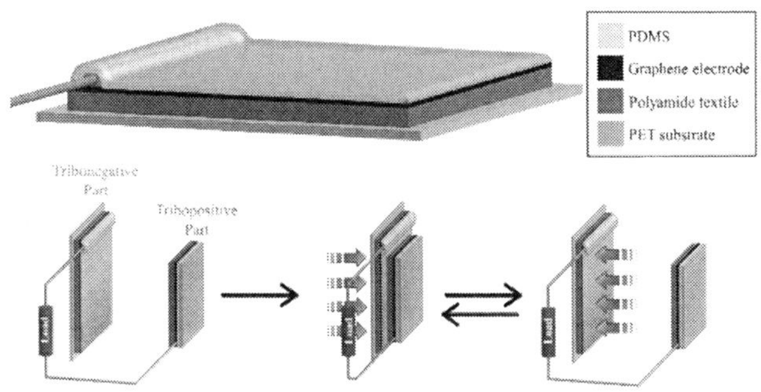

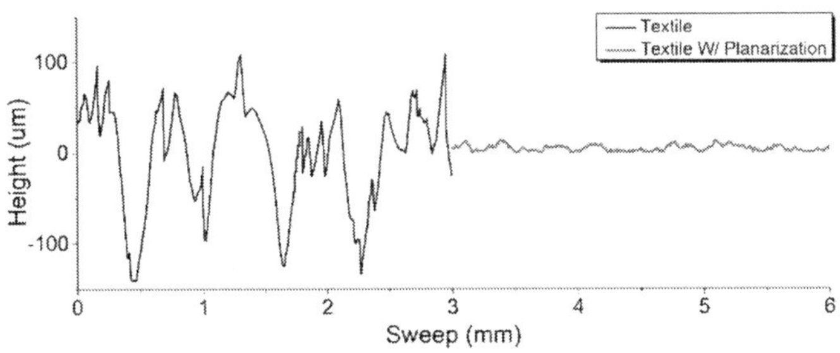

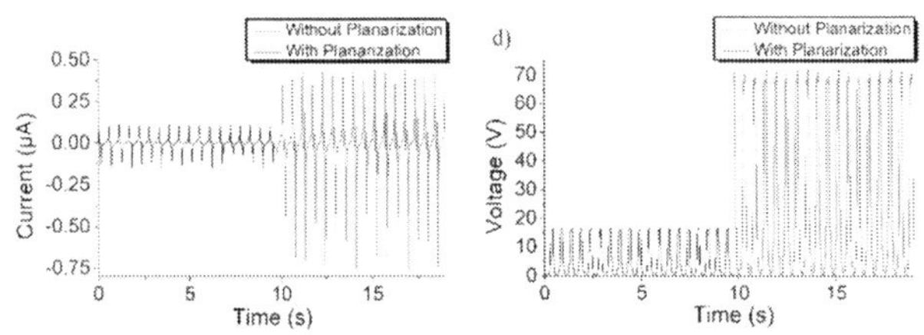

#SensorsConverge

Sensors Converge

Deposition

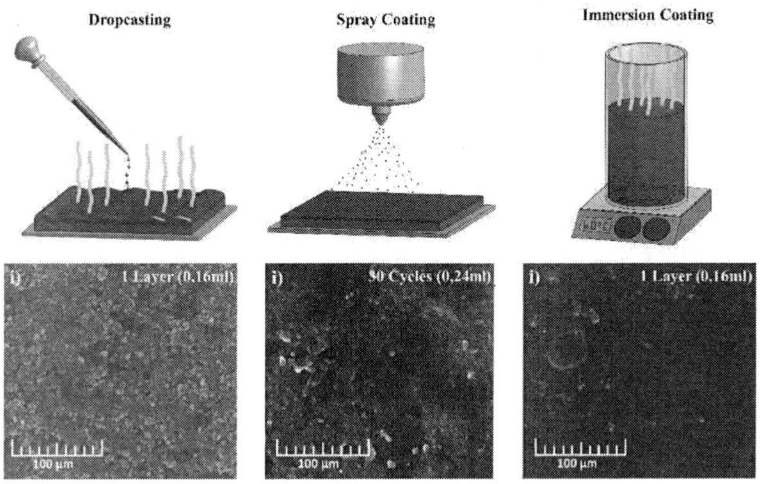

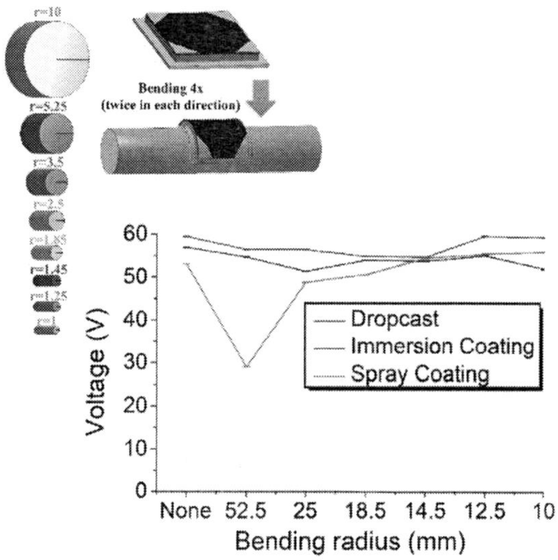

#SensorsConverge

Sensors Converge

Frequency and Area Dependency

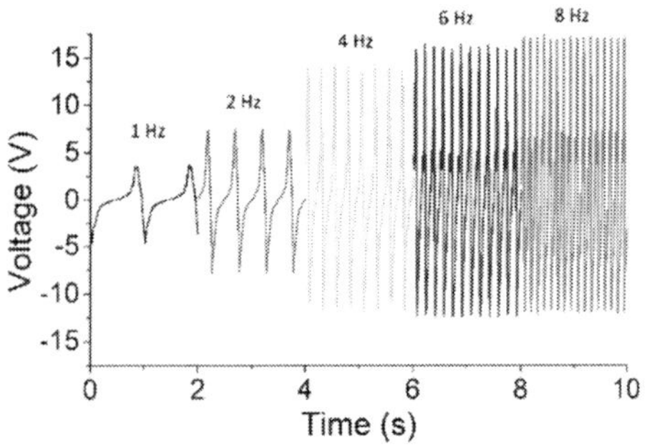

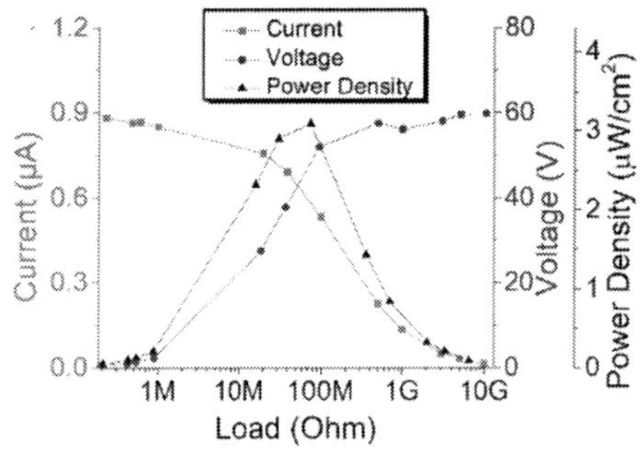

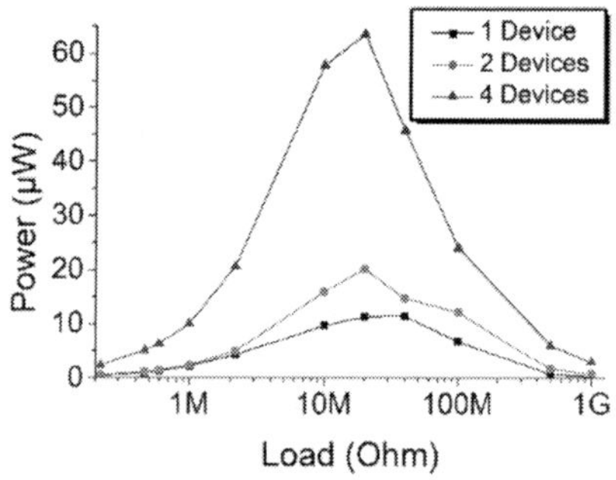

#SensorsConverge

Sensors Converge

Biomechanical Sensor

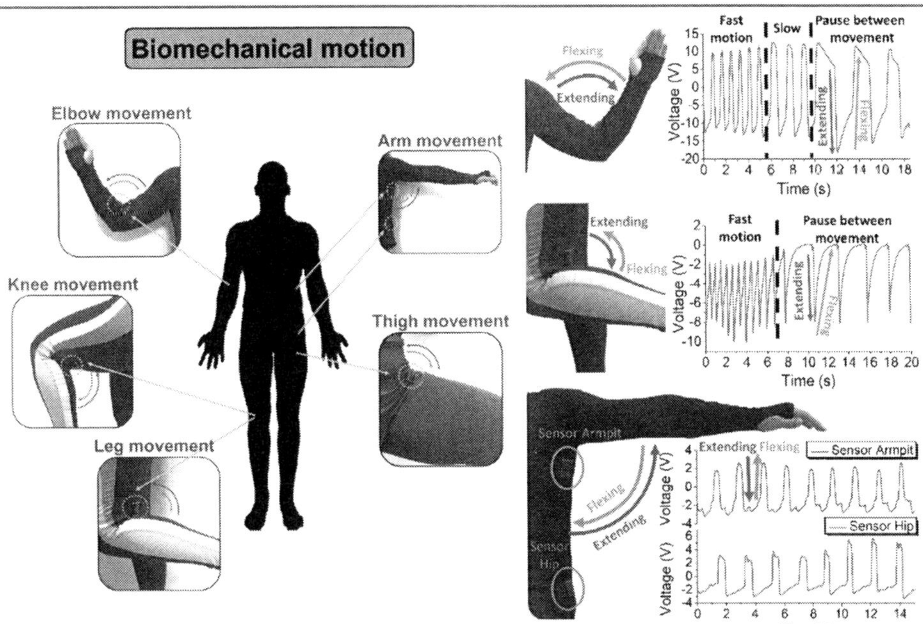

#SensorsConverge

Sensors Converge

Radio Frequency Energy Harvesters

- Ambient RF Energy Sources

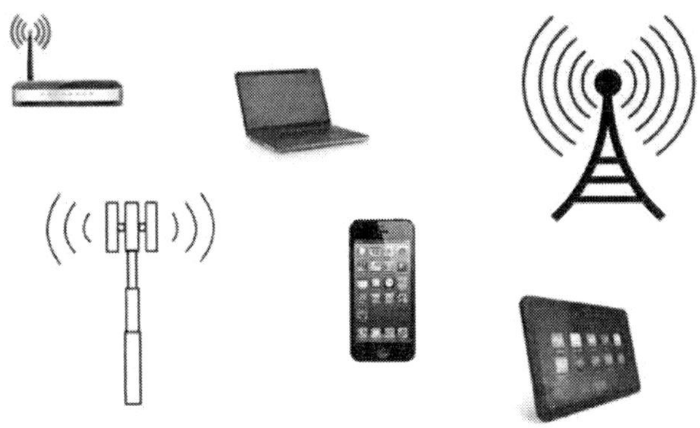

- Operation

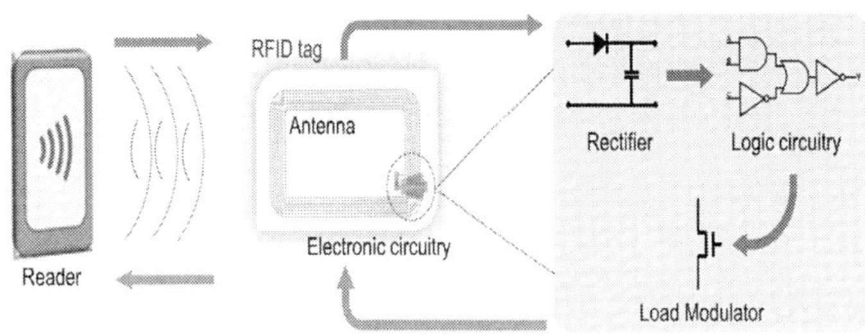

#SensorsConverge

Sensors Converge

Flexible Textile Antennas - Dielectric

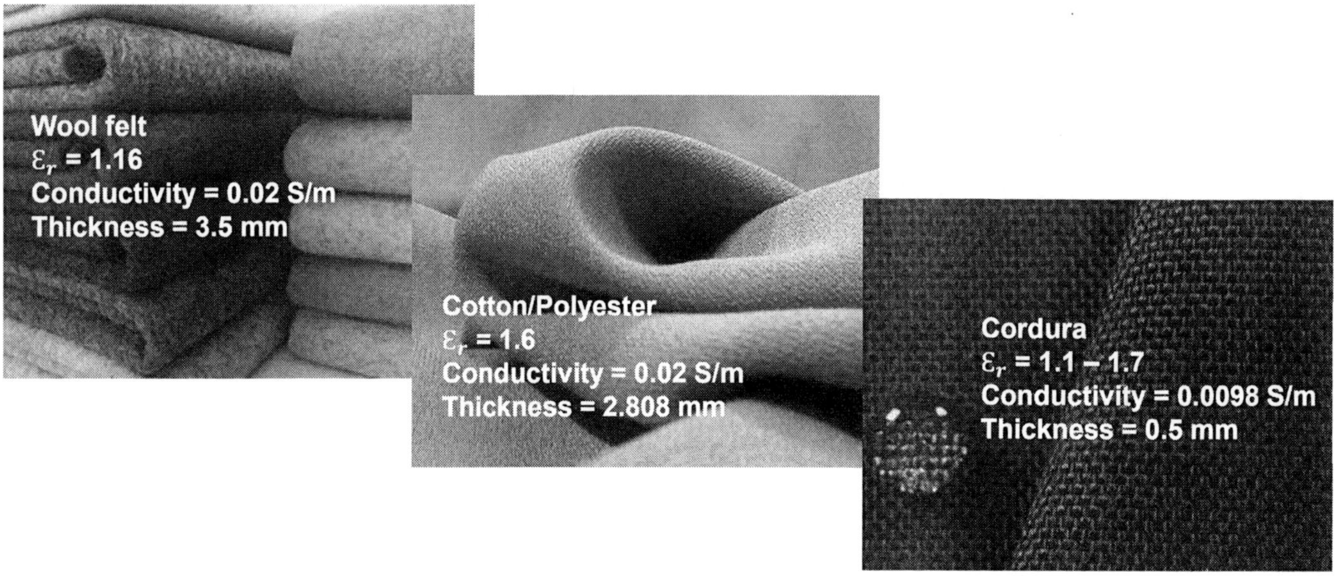

#SensorsConverge

Sensors Converge

Sustainable Fabrics

#SensorsConverge

Sensors Converge

Flexible Textile Antennas - Conductor

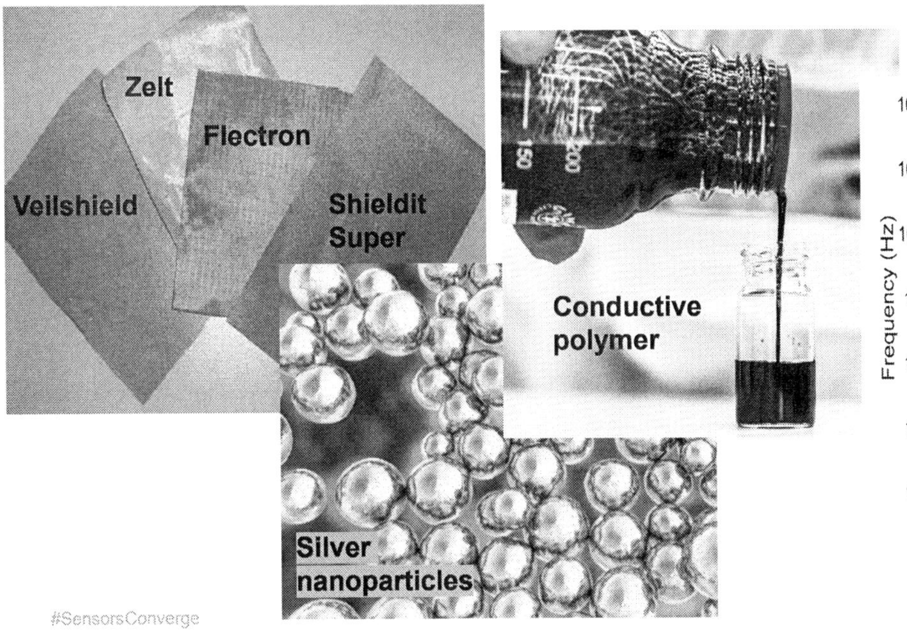

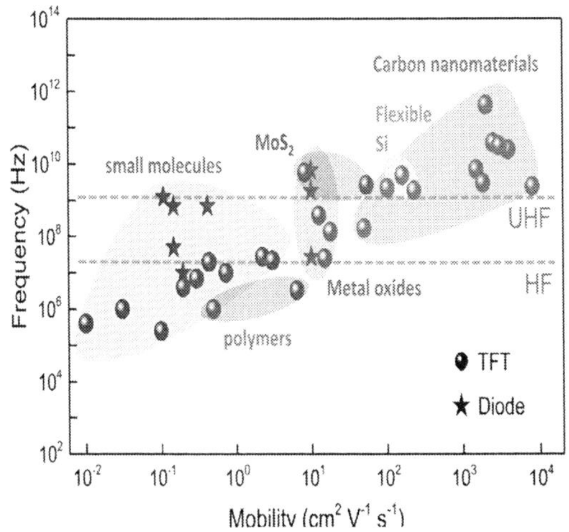

#SensorsConverge

Sensors Converge

Printed Antenna

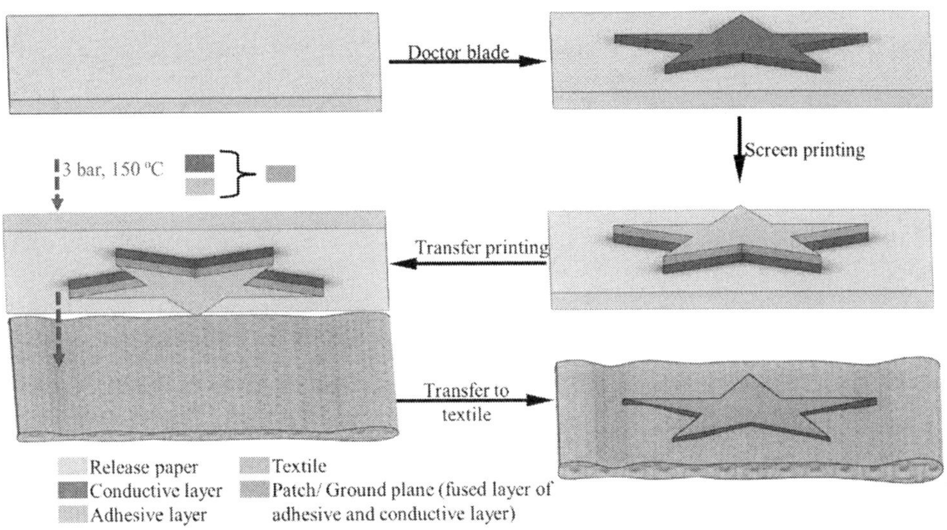

#SensorsConverge

Sensors Converge

Output

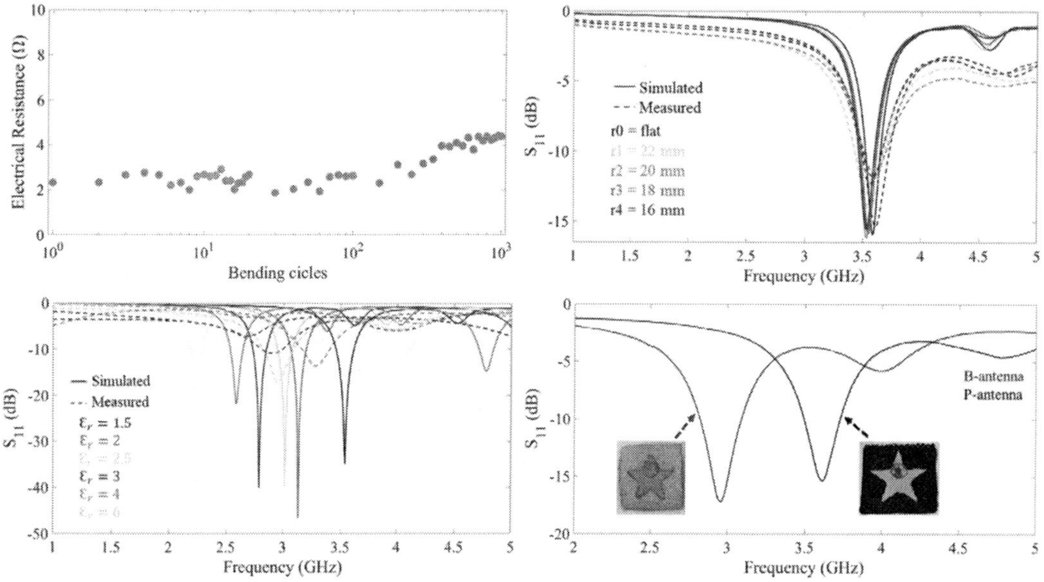

#SensorsConverge

Sensors Converge

Wearable Antenna

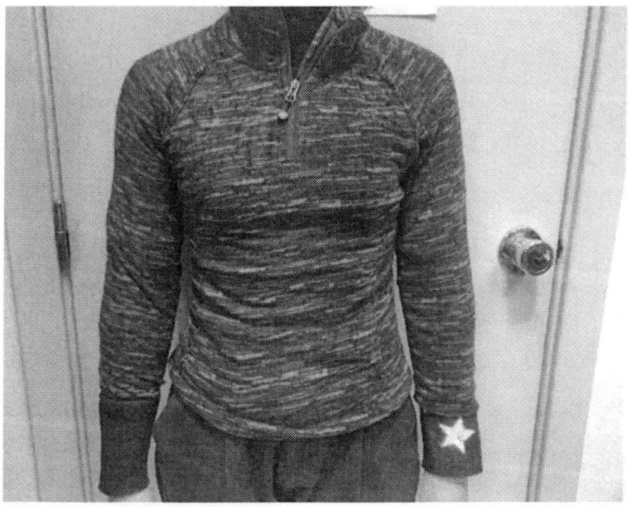

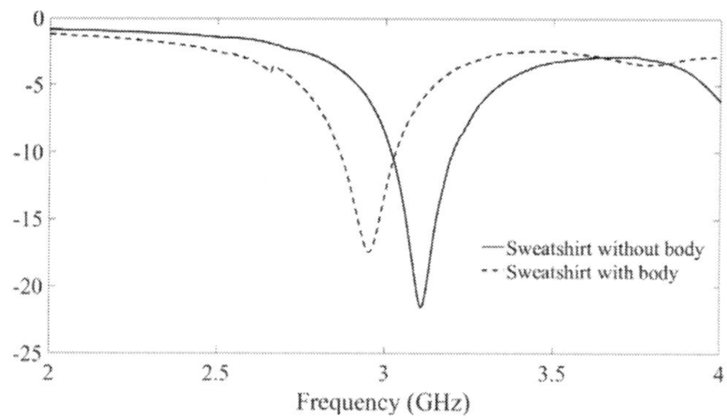

#SensorsConverge

Sensors Converge

Acknowledgments

- PhD students
  - Ismael Domingos
  - Joana Tavares

- Collaborators
  - Monica Craciun (U. Exeter)
  - Pedro Pinho (Telecommunications Institute)

- Funders

PRR Plano de Recuperação e Resiliência · REPÚBLICA PORTUGUESA · Financiado pela União Europeia NextGenerationEU · FCT Fundação para a Ciência e a Tecnologia

#SensorsConverge

Sensors Converge

Sensors Converge

A Gait Lab in a Textile Sensor-Infused sock

Maurizio Macagno, CTO & Co-Founder, Sensoria Health Inc.

June 20–22, 2023 | Santa Clara, CA

#SensorsConverge

The Garment is the Computer

sensoria HEALTH

Passion & Background

- Experience in **Healthcare** and **Direct-to-Consumer Tech**
- Founders Former **Microsoft Executives**
- Based in Redmond (WA) **USA** with R&D unit already active and operating in **Italy**
- Multiple **utility and design patents obtained**
- **Sensoria Italia Srl** R&D controlled company established in Naples at UNINA Campus.

Microsoft

XBOX LIVE

Core Capabilities

*Full stack integrated **sensor-infused smart garments**, AI/ML Algos, mobile patient apps and clinician cloud dashboards.*

- Delivered **new textile sensors** and **microelectronics**, generating novel datasets for patients and clinicians
- Developed **signal processing** capabilities, **ML/AI algorithms** coupled to footwear, apparel and other accessories. From analog to digital patient experiences
- Built a full **mobile + cloud-based remote patient monitoring platform (RPM)** including a mobile set of interfaces improving quality of life and patient outcomes.

www.sensoriahealth.com

Multidisciplinary Team

- **Healthcare** experts
  Software engineers
  Materials engineers
  Signal processing engineers
  Data scientists
  Electrical engineers
  Mechanical engineers
  Hardware and software designers and UX **Designers**
- Prestigious research academic

THE MICHAEL J. FOX FOUNDATION FOR PARKINSON'S RESEARCH

Shepherd Center

Baylor College of Medicine

Keck Medicine of USC

What is Gait?

- Gait is the pattern of movement when a person walks, runs or engage in any other form of locomotion
- It encompasses the coordinated actions of various body parts, as well as the rhythm and timing of those movements

- Each individual has a unique gait pattern, influenced by:
  - Body structure
  - Muscle strength
  - Neurological control

#SensorsConverge

Sensors Converge

Gait Analysis

- WHAT: studying and evaluating the characteristics of an individual's gait
- WHY: assess and diagnose movement abnormalities, detect musculoskeletal or neurological problems, design appropriate interventions or treatments in the rehab process
- WHERE: clinical, research and sports science (biomechanics, rehabilitation, orthopedics, etc.)

- HOW:
  - Quantitative analysis
  - Qualitative analysis

#SensorsConverge

Sensors Converge

Qualitative Gait Analysis

- Visual observation
- Subjective assessment
- Expert clinician / trained professional to observe:
  - Posture
  - Symmetry
  - Range of motion
  - Foot strike pattern
  - Observable abnormalities from normal gait
- Subjective, relies on the expertise and experience of the observer

#SensorsConverge

Sensors Converge

Quantitative Gait Analysis

- Use of objective measurements and technology to analyze and quantify different gait parameters

- Technology used:
  - Motion Capture systems
  - Force plates
  - Electromyography (EMG)
  - Wearable sensors
- **Usually expensive tech, confined in the lab**

#SensorsConverge

Sensors Converge

(Some) Gait Parameters

Temporal Parameters	Spatial Parameters	Derived Metrics
Step Count	Step Length	Gait Velocity
Cadence	Stride Length	Symmetry Index
Step time	Distance	Balance (Center of Pressure / Mass)
Stride Time (Gait Cycle)	...	...
Single Support / Double Support		
Stance Time / Swing Time		
...		

Gait Assessments: Many Conditions

- Frailty (Aging, fall detection, risk of fall analysis)
- Neuropathy
- Neurological Disorders (Parkinson's, MS, ALS, Cerebral Palsy, Stroke, Ataxia, etc.)
- Circulatory Disorders (ie: PAD, etc.)
- Diabetic Foot Ulcers (DFU)
- Pre and post-surgery: TKA/TKR and TKH
- All lower body rehabilitation scenarios (post traumatic events, etc.)
- Amputees, using a prosthetic device
- …

Taking the lab outside of the lab with wearables

- Counting steps is not enough to properly monitor, diagnose and treat any of the previous conditions
- A wrist worn device may never be able to provide accurate gait data from gait impaired subjects
- Traditional gait labs systems:
  - are expensive, bulky, hard to set up
  - cannot be used outside the clinic
  - are only a snapshot in time of each patient
  - require patients to travel
- A wearable device able to perform gait assessments:
  - is not a replacement for a gait lab
  - should be its natural extension, complementing its data in small clinics, at home and in the community
  - ENABLING RPM: Remote Patient Monitoring (or asynchronous telemonitoring) is the device driven, automatic collection of health data from a subject, often from outside conventional care settings, which is then electronically and securely transmitted to a provider for use in care and related support services

#SensorsConverge

Sensors Converge

How about a smart sock?

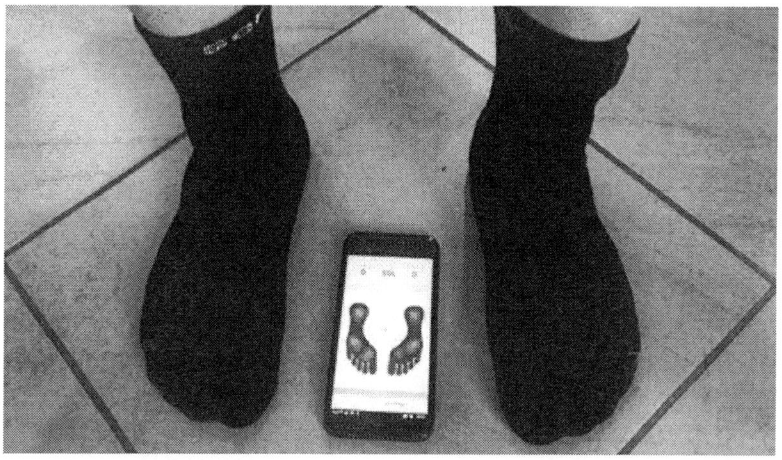

Monitoring All Core Patient Gait Metrics & Balance

#SensorsConverge

Sensors Converge

Sensoria Smart Sock(s) specs

- Sensoria Smart Sock:
    - Traditional sock
    - 3 textile pressure sensors
    - Dock for electronic device
- Sensoria Core device:
    - Bluetooth Smart
    - Onboard 9-axis IMU
- Data collection apps for research and analysis
- End user (Consumer + Healthcare apps)
- Several utility patents assigned and pending

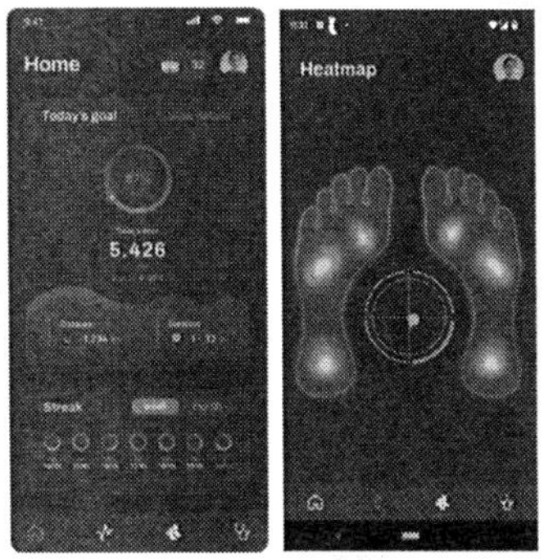

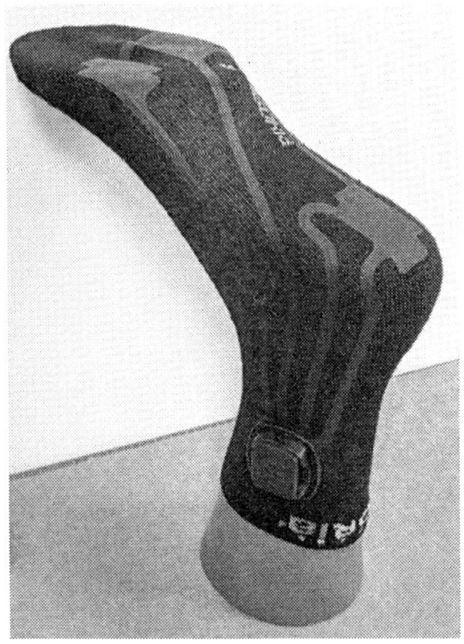

Sensoria® Sock for Gait Analysis

Clinically proven to be on par or better than gold standard gait labs

Gathers gait data for post-stroke or neuro condition monitoring and rehab

Sensoria Walk app provides actionable feedback to patient

Haptic motor provides feedback to users

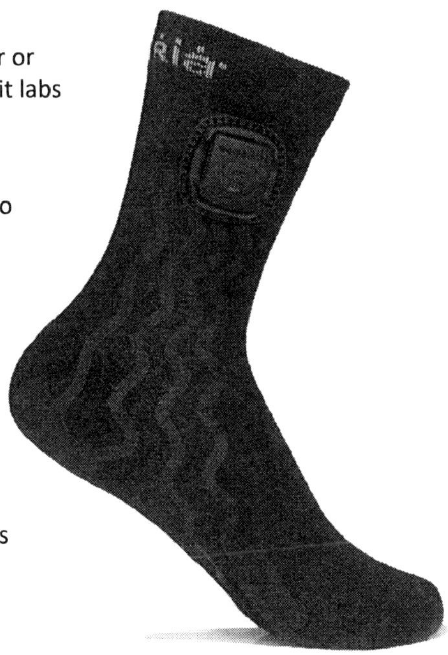

Balance and fall detection

Real time data shared with user and clinicians

Enables GDPR and HIPAA Compliant RPM Dashboards

Easy to wear and use at home and in the community

Textile Sensor's characteristics

- Characteristic curve similar to traditional FSRs
- 10-12 mils (0.25-0.30mm) thick
- Wearable, washable
- Suited for integration in a garment
- Pressure estimation curve fit:

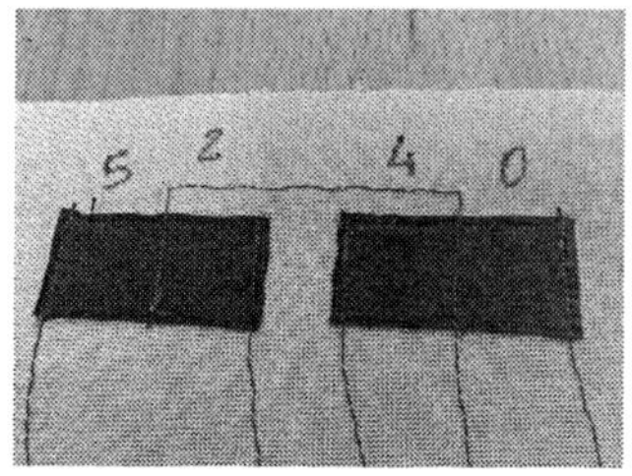

$$P_{est} = \frac{a \times ADC^{-b} + c}{Surface}$$

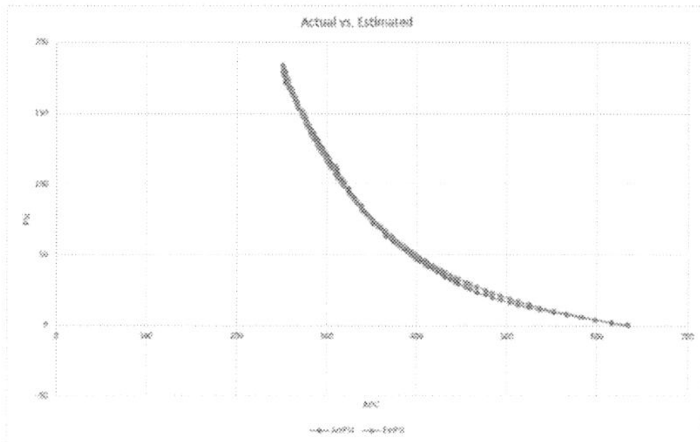

Sensoria Sock vs. Gait Lab

- Sensoria sock has been independently studied by several researchers
- Noteworthy study:
  - https://www.ncbi.nlm.nih.gov/pmc/articles/PMC8472002/
  - University of Sherbrooke
  - Comparing Sensoria Smart Socks to traditional gait lab systems

"We proposed a system to determine the spatio-temporal parameters of gait based on an easy-to-use non-cumbersome sock system that could be worn with all shoe types. These characteristics are very important for a wearable system to be used in a free-living environment and for a long period of time. ***The proposed system has been proven to be accurate for the estimation of temporal gait parameters and had better accuracy than a system commonly used in clinical applications (Mobility Lab) in estimating spatial parameters.*** *The IMU-instrumented sock systems could potentially be used for the estimation of the spatio-temporal parameters of gait in clinical settings and in free-living conditions, but the data should be interpreted with spatial precautions in patients with severely reduced gait speed. Further studies are needed to validate the system in different conditions and populations." Prof. Patrick Boissy*

Study Description

- Objective: Assess the accuracy of Sensoria Smart Socks
- Using a validated algorithm (TEARDRIP) for the estimation of spatial-temporal gait parameters
- 25 healthy participants (HP) + 21 patients with foot impairment (psoriatic arthritis) PsA
- Estimations of:
  - Cadence (CAD)
  - Gait Cycle Duration (GCD)
  - Gait Speed (GS)
  - Stride Length (SL)
- Slow, Normal, Fast walking speeds
- Comparison vs. MoCap system (*) on treadmill walking
- Comparison vs. established multi-IMU (**) based overground and treadmill walking

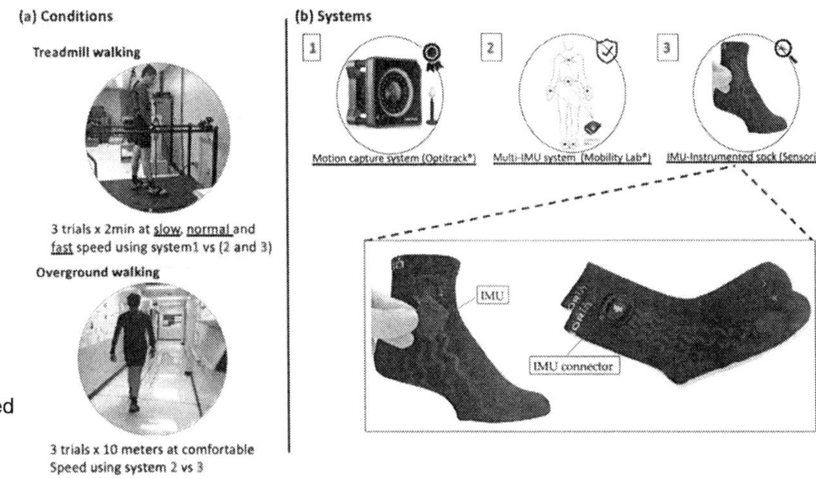

(*) 8 x Optitrack Prime 13W cameras

(**) Mobility Lab (ML) system (APDM Wearable Technologies)

#SensorsConverge

Sensors Converge

Overall results

- Good agreement between the Mo-Cap system and Sensoria Socks in estimating the spatio-temporal parameters at normal and fast speeds for both HP and PsA
- Better accuracy of GS and SL than ML (both HP and PsA)
- Precision (inter-session reliability):
  - Overground walking: excellent (all speeds)
  - Treadmill (fast speed): excellent
  - Treadmill (slow and normal speed): moderate-to-good

Table 1

Descriptions of the spatio-temporal parameters and the comparison between healthy and PsA patients.

Variables	Systems	Healthy Participants	PsA Patients	p
		Mean ± SD	Mean ± SD	
CAD (steps/min)	IMU-instrumented sock	116.45 ± 7.25	109.05 ± 7.79	0.002
	Mobility Lab	117.18 ± 7.23	107.14 ± 10.94	0.001
GCD (s)	IMU-instrumented sock	1.04 ± 0.06	1.11 ± 0.08	0.002
	Mobility Lab	1.03 ± 0.07	1.14 ± 0.14	0.003
GS (m/s)	IMU-instrumented sock	1.46 ± 0.16	1.18 ± 0.22	<0.001
	Mobility Lab	1.34 ± 0.14	1.04 ± 0.23	<0.001
SL (m)	IMU-instrumented sock	1.46 ± 0.13	1.13 ± 0.24	<0.001
	Mobility Lab	1.37 ± 0.12	1.14 ± 0.18	<0.001

Overground walking

#SensorsConverge

Sensors Converge

Overall Results (cont.)

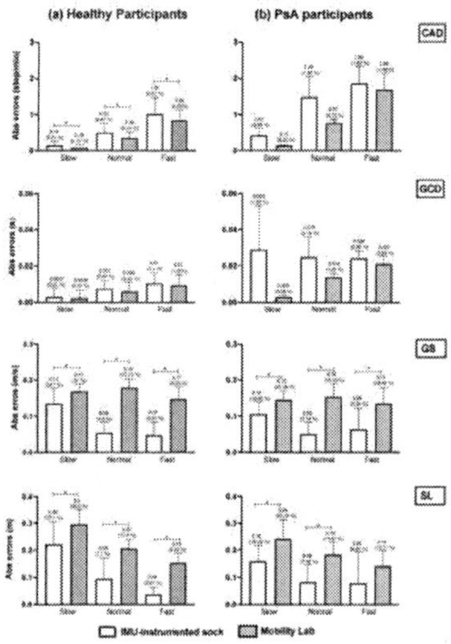

Table 2

Intersession reliability of the spatio-temporal parameters estimated by the TEADRIP algorithm applied to the IMU-instrumented sock recordings and those estimated by the Mobility Lab system for treadmill walking in HP. Intra Class Correlation Coefficient (ICCs) and their 95% CI for the treadmill 2MWT at slow, normal, and fast walking speeds.

Parameter	System	Speed		
		Slow (0.45 m/s)	**Normal (1.12 m/s)**	**Fast (1.6 m/s)**
CAD	IMU-instrumented sock	0.712 (0.34 to 0.88)	0.88 (0.72 to 0.95)	0.934 (0.85 to 0.97)
	Mobility Lab	0.734 (0.40 to 0.88)	0.88 (0.7 to 0.95)	0.938 (0.86 to 0.97)
GCD	IMU-instrumented sock	0.755 (0.44 to 0.9)	0.902 (0.76 to 0.96)	0.936 (0.85 to 0.0.73)
	Mobility Lab	0.778 (0.5 to 0.9)	0.891 (0.725 to 0.95)	0.935 (0.85 to 0.972)
GS	IMU-instrumented sock	0.625 (0.14 to 0.84)	0.657 (0.2 to 0.85)	0.719 (0.4 to 0.88)
	Mobility Lab	0.746 (0.41 to 0.089)	0.835 (0.62 to 0.93)	0.757 (0.44 to 0.89)
SL	IMU-instrumented sock	0.633 (0.2 to 0.84)	0.681 (0.5 to 0.92)	0.914 (0.757 to 0.97)
	Mobility Lab	0.798 (0.54 to 0.91)	0.874 (0.7 to 0.95)	0.916 (0.8 to 0.97)

Sock vs. ML, 2 min treadmill walk

#SensorsConverge

Enabling Telerehab and Remote Patient Monitoring

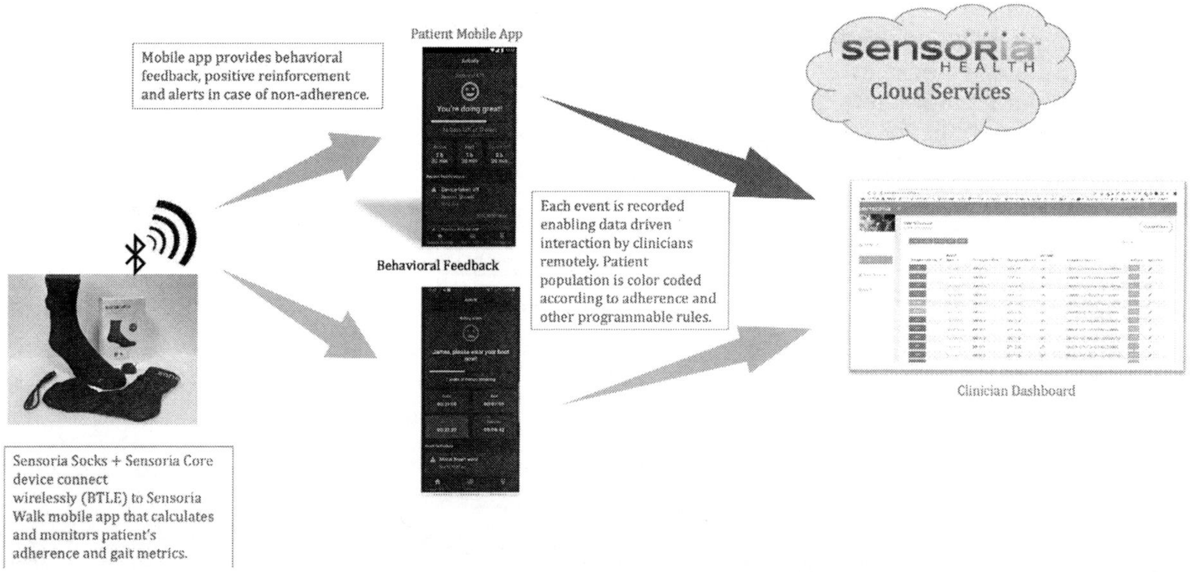

#SensorsConverge

Sensors Converge

THANK YOU!

Maurizio Macagno, CTO & Co-Founder, Sensoria Health Inc.

June 20–22, 2023 | Santa Clara, CA

#SensorsConverge

Baylor College of Medicine

Defender powered by Sensoria Boot vs Garmin: Actigraphy and Adherence

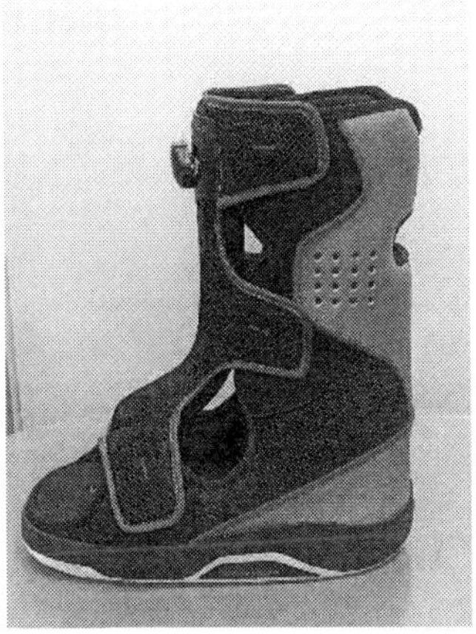

Moin U. Atique

Postdoctoral Fellow

Department of Surgery

Baylor College of Medicine

NIH National Institute of Diabetes and Digestive and Kidney Diseases

Sensoria Core

sensoria HEALTH

- Nine Axis IMU
- Auto ON/OFF
- BTLE
- Rechargeable Battery
- Connects to dedicated smartwatch app.

#SensorsConverge

NIH National Institute of Diabetes and Digestive and Kidney Diseases

Sensoria Android 4G/LTE Watch Patient App

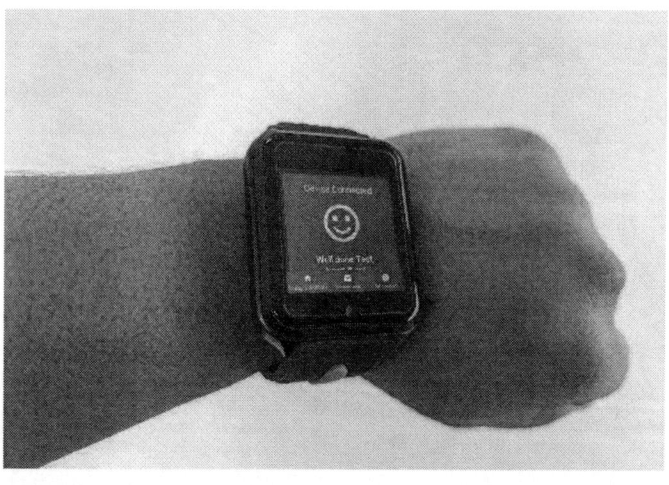

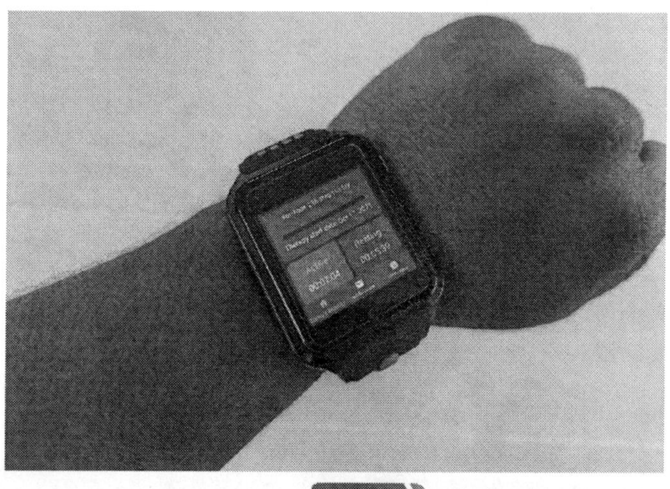

#SensorsConverge

NIH National Institute of Diabetes and Digestive and Kidney Diseases

expertreviews | Technology | Home & Garden | Baby & Kids | Health & Beauty | Sports & Leisure | Travel | Best Buys

Garmin Vivosmart 4

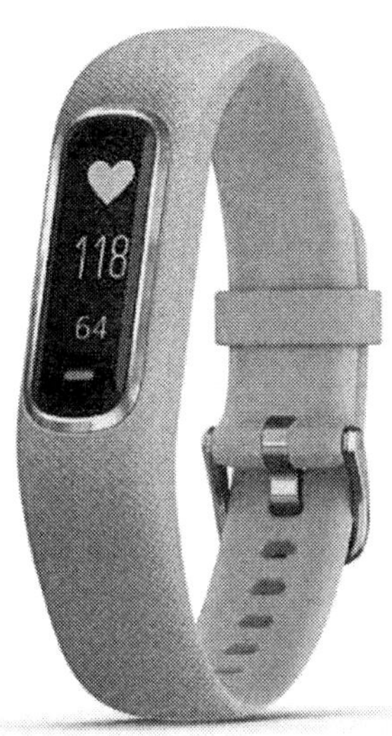

can choose which app's notifications are sent to the fitness tracker so not to be bombarded constantly and I found they always arrived promptly.

As for battery life, Garmin promises up to seven days between charges, although that figure will drop by a few days if you choose to enable Pulse OX at night. If anything, however the Vivosmart 4 seemed to exceed those estimates. After three days of use with Pulse OX activated, the battery indicator icon still had three of its five bars filled, so I'd expect it to reach six days with the SPO2 sensor enabled and yet more still without it.

Garmin Vivosmart 4 review: Verdict

There are a few things that prevent the Vivosmart 4 from gaining a five-star review and Best Buy award, namely its lack of GPS and cycling mode. Plus, you can easily make the case that its rivals such as the Fitbit Charge 3 are better looking.

However, if you're not looking for a device that lets you track outdoor activities to the nearest ten metres, Garmin's Vivosmart 4 does everything you could ask a fitness tracker to do.

With automatic activity, sleep and stress tracking, it builds a detailed picture of your overall fitness and health that its rivals simply can't match. Crucially, this wealth of data is summarised in bite-sized form in the excellent Body Battery score, which can inform your exercise schedule, so you get fitter without over-training.

Consider that the Vivosmart 4's smart features are more reliable than those of its main rival, the Fitbit Charge 3, and there's no question which device I'd recommend. The Garmin beats the Fitbit on pretty much all counts.

Converge

Baylor College of Medicine

Mean Step Counts (Sensoria vs Garmin)

Defender Boot – Sensoria Core

- Three speed levels (Slow, Habitual, Fast)
- 3 trials per speed
- 50 steps on each walk.

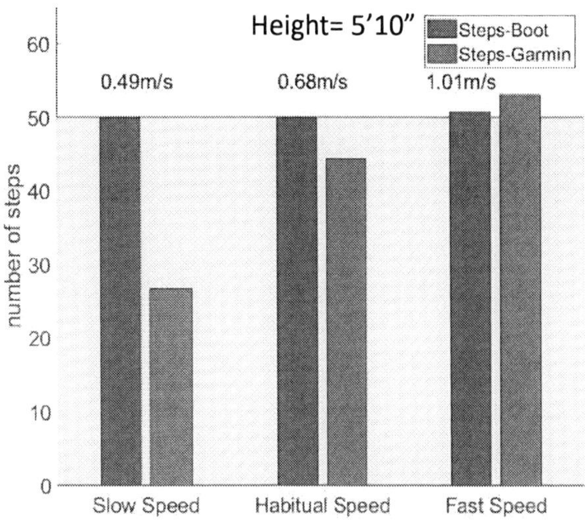

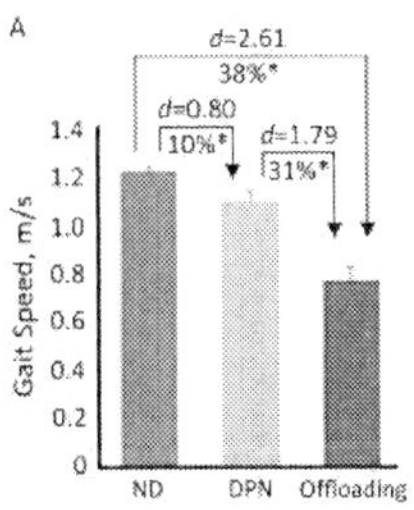

Comparison between ND, DPN, and Offloading groups for, gait speed[1].

(1) Ling, E., Lepow, B., Zhou, H., Enriquez, A., Mullen, A. and Najafi, B., 2020. The impact of diabetic foot ulcers and unilateral offloading footwear on gait in people with diabetes. *Clinical Biomechanics*, *73*, pp.157-161

NIH National Institute of Diabetes and Digestive and Kidney Diseases

Baylor College of Medicine

Mean Error (Defender Boot vs Garmin watch)

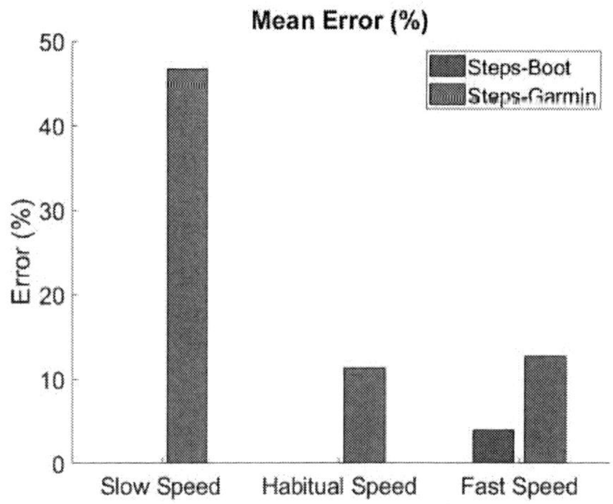

National Institute of Diabetes and Digestive and Kidney Diseases

U.S. ARMY

DEVCOM SOLDIER CENTER

U.S. ARMY COMBAT CAPABILITIES DEVELOPMENT COMMAND SOLDIER CENTER

Sensored Soldier at the Tactical Edge

20 JUNE 2023

Controlled by:	DEVCOM Soldier Center
Controlled by:	FCDD-SCD-RTC
PAO Approval No.	
Distribution Control:	Approved for Public Release
POC:	Stephanie Brown, stephanie.a.brown88.civ@army.mil

SOLDIERS OUR CREDENTIALS

INTRODUCTION

DEVCOM SOLDIER CENTER

Photos courtesy of dvidshub.net and army.mil

APPROVED FOR PUBLIC RELEASE

COMBAT OF THE FUTURE

What does the future look like…

- **Large-scale, Multi-domain operations**
- **Distributed operations**
- **Transparent battlefield**

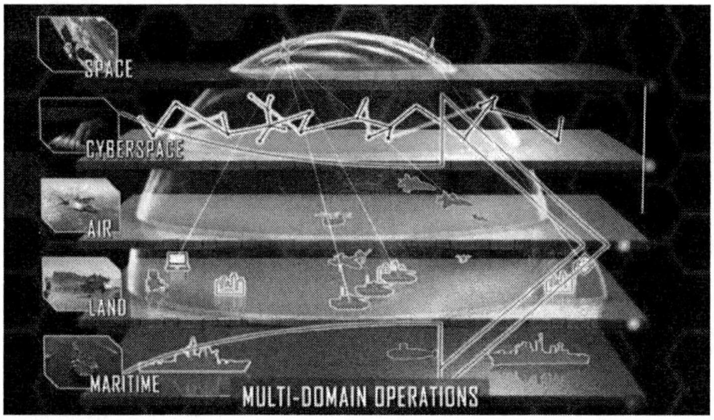

Photos courtesy of dvidshub.net and army.mil

APPROVED FOR PUBLIC RELEASE

3

APPROVED FOR PUBLIC RELEASE

COMBAT OF THE FUTURE

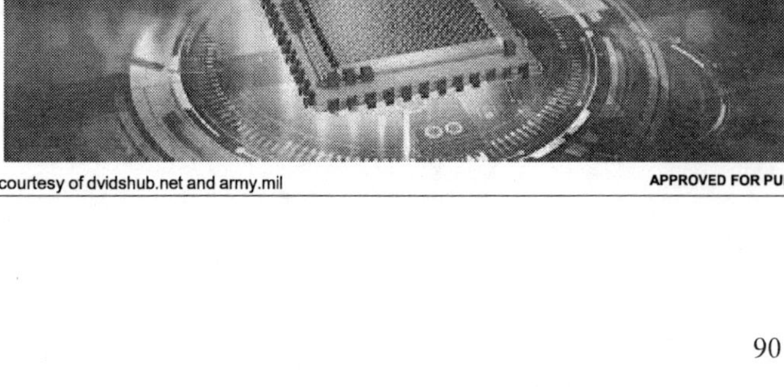

What are the persistent problems…

- **Overwhelming amount of data**
- **Processing speed to understand the battlefield**
- **Need to look farther, think faster & act smarter**

Photos courtesy of dvidshub.net and army.mil

APPROVED FOR PUBLIC RELEASE

4

CURRENT ARMY INVESTMENTS

DEVCOM SOLDIER CENTER

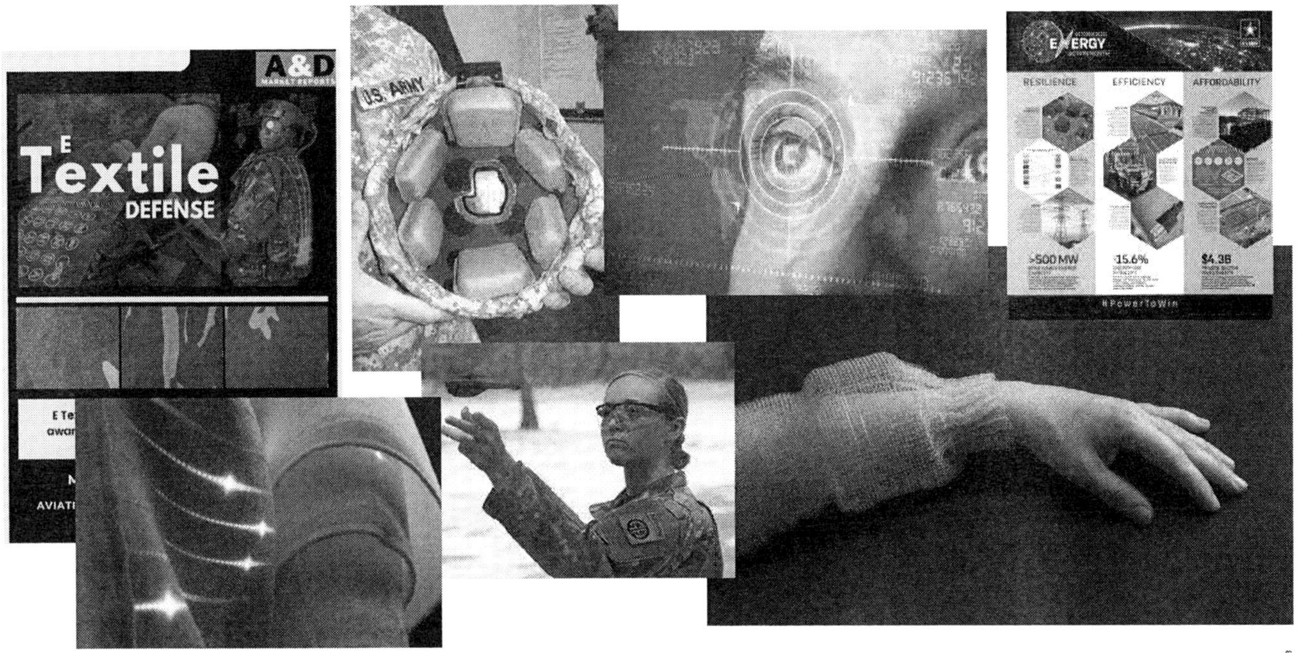

Photos courtesy of dvidshub.net and army.mil

DEVCOM SOLDIER CENTER: OVERVIEW

DEVCOM SOLDIER CENTER

MISSION: To provide the Army with innovative science and technology solutions to optimize the performance of our Soldiers.

VISION: Ensuring dominance through superior scientific and engineering expertise.

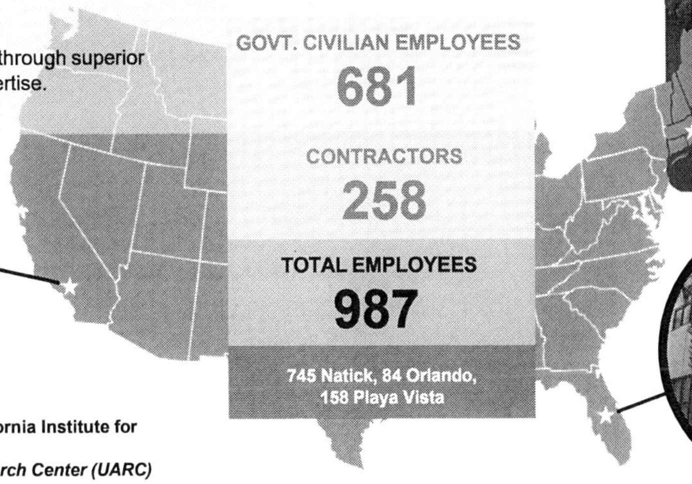

MILITARY EMPLOYEES
48

GOVT. CIVILIAN EMPLOYEES
681

CONTRACTORS
258

TOTAL EMPLOYEES
987

745 Natick, 84 Orlando, 158 Playa Vista

★ **Natick Soldier Systems Center**
Natick, MA

University of Southern California Institute for Creative Technologies
A University Affiliated Research Center (UARC)
Playa Vista, CA

Central Florida Research Park
Orlando, FL

APPROVED FOR PUBLIC RELEASE

DEVCOM SOLDIER CENTER: SOLDIER PROTECTION

SOLDIER CENTRIC DESIGN

Materials:

- Multifunctional Materials
  FR, EMI Shielding, Vector Protection, Thermal Mgt
- Protective Materials & Systems
  Ballistic, Chem-Bio, Signature Mgt
- Composite Materials
- Helmet Prototyping & Testing
- Ballistic Material Development, Testing & Integration

Equipment:

- Combat Clothing & Individual Equipment
- Dress Clothing
- Chemical/Biological Protective Materials & Ensembles
- Load Carriage Systems
- Textile Prototyping & Testing
- Individual Hydration
- Cold Weather Clothing & Individual Equipment

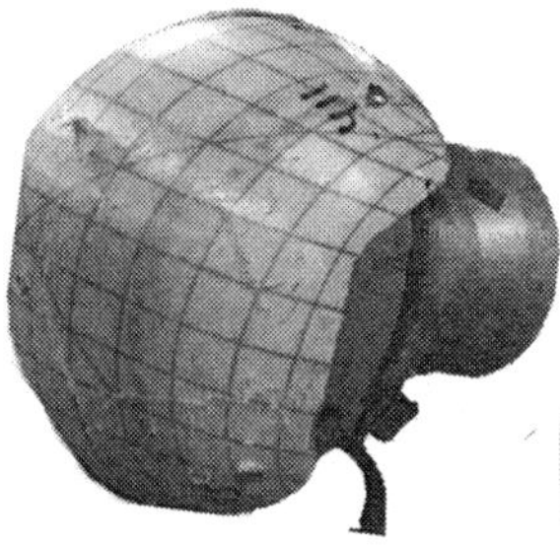

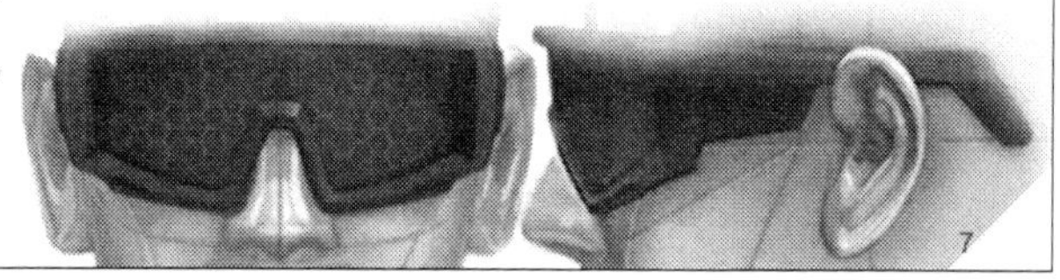

APPROVED FOR PUBLIC RELEASE

7

APPROVED FOR PUBLIC RELEASE

DEVCOM SOLDIER CENTER: SOLDIER SUSTAINMENT

SOLDIER CENTRIC DESIGN

Combat Feeding

Food Engineering and Nutrition:
- Food preservation & stabilization
- Novel food processing technology
- Functional food prototyping

Food Protection and Packaging:
- Food contamination mitigation
- CBRN packaging solutions
- Microbiological testing of foods

Food Service Logistics:
- Innovative Military Ration Engineering & Food Processing Technologies
- Mechanical & Chemical Engineering for Refrigeration, Combustion and Sanitation

Cargo and Personnel Delivery:

- GN&C technology for GPS denied/degraded environment
- Novel multi-use aerial dispersion systems
- Sensor development for safety devices
- Powered payload delivery system design

Material Development

Material Development and Optimization:
- Support and guidance for Electromagnetic Interference (EMI) and X-ray Shielding
- Designs and build systems for unique customer applications
- Design for energy efficiency

Additive Manufacturing:
- Additive Manufacturing Design and Fabrication
- Complete Machining and Welding Facility
- Heavy Textile Design and Fabrication Facility

APPROVED FOR PUBLIC RELEASE

APPROVED FOR PUBLIC RELEASE

DEVCOM SOLDIER CENTER: SOLDIER EFFECTIVENESS

SOLDIER CENTRIC DESIGN

Training, Simulation and Learning Technologies

- Mixed and Augmented Reality Technologies for Training
- Synthetic Natural Environments
- Live Training Technologies
- Medical Training Technologies
- Artificial Intelligence and Machine Learning
- Adaptive Training
- Distributed Simulation
- Training Effectiveness
- Cyber Training Simulations
- Data at the Point of Impact
- Quantitative and Qualitative Analysis

Physical/Cognitive/ Biological

- State Assessment
- Quantification of Close Combat Task Performance
- Predictive Performance Models
- Neuromodulation
- Exoskeleton
- Gut Microbiome
- Anthropometric Modeling
- Human Factors Product Test and Evaluation
- Soldier-Centeric Design
- Muscle & Immune Cell Model & Nutritional Intervention

Soldier & Technology Integration:

- Sensors and situational awareness
- Leader Planning & Decision Tools
- Network and the "right" information

Performance Enablers:

- Efficient Power & Energy Solutions
- Climate Conditioning For Extremes
- Robotics for Soldier and Squad

APPROVED FOR PUBLIC RELEASE

9

APPROVED FOR PUBLIC RELEASE

DEVCOM SOLDIER CENTER: WICKED PROGRAM SCHEMA

Multidomain Concealment - *Invisible Soldier*
How does the Army enable the Soldier and small unit to delay and degrade detection by the enemy (human and non-human) across the electromagnetic (EM) spectrum, in order to disrupt the kill chain and maintain freedom of maneuver

Unburden and Enable the Soldier/Squad - *Enabled Soldier*
How does the Army optimally equip and protect Soldiers as an integrated weapon system and the squad as an integrated combat platform

Decision Dominance - *Enhanced Soldier*
How can the Army enhance the Soldier and small unit's situational understanding and optimize the decision-making process to achieve decision dominance

Small Unit Logistics at the Edge - *Sustained Soldier*
How does the Army keep small units resupplied in a distributed and contested environment

APPROVED FOR PUBLIC RELEASE

10

APPROVED FOR PUBLIC RELEASE

ARMY S&T INVESTMENTS

DEVCOM SOLDIER CENTER

INSTITUTE FOR SOLDIER NANOTECHNOLOGIES
MASSACHUSETTS INSTITUTE OF TECHNOLOGY
ISN

affoa

U.S. ARMY

DEVCOM SOLDIER CENTER

U.S. Army H2F Holistic Health and Fitness

ARTIFICIAL INTELLIGENCE INTEGRATION CENTER
ARMY FUTURES COMMAND

DEVCOM ARMY RESEARCH LABORATORY

JPE CBRND

DARPA

DEVCOM C5ISR CENTER

HEROES
UMass Lowell / US Army

DEVCOM ARMAMENTS CENTER

CABCS
CENTER FOR APPLIED BRAIN & COGNITIVE SCIENCES
Tufts University & US Army CCDC Soldier Center

APPROVED FOR PUBLIC RELEASE

11

APPROVED FOR PUBLIC RELEASE

E-TEXTILES FOR THE SOLDIER

DEVCOM SOLDIER CENTER

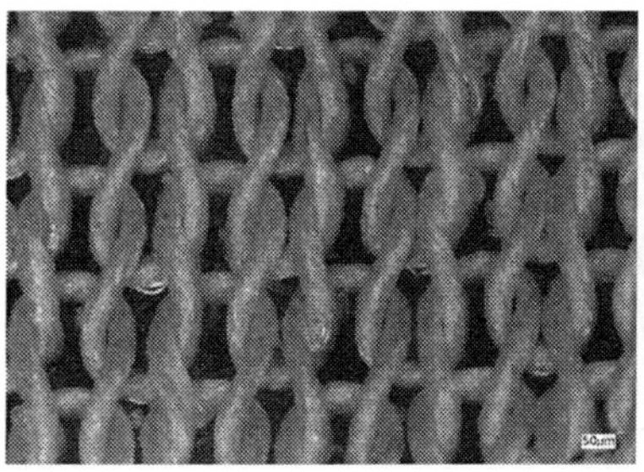

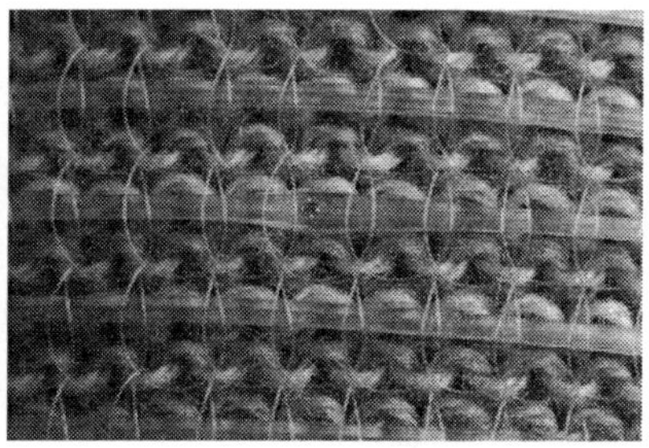

- Army's integration of knitted conductive yarn as breadboard to transmit power and data from sensors to power source, making the textile an integration platform and reducing snag hazards for Soldiers

- Army partnered with MIT creating acoustic fabric that can "hear" converting audible sounds into electrical signals using piezoelectric materials

- MIT Army-funded research in programmable fiber that uses nano technology embedded into fibers to power sensors, store and analyze the data, and transmit to outside sources

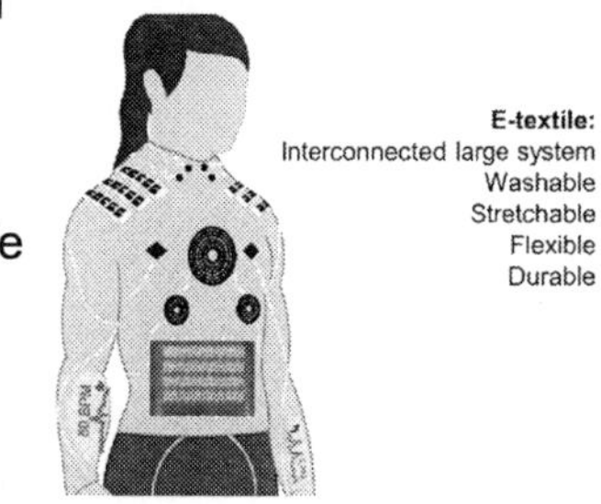

Photos courtesy of dvidshub.net and army.mil

APPROVED FOR PUBLIC RELEASE

12

SOLDIER ROBOTICS & AUTONOMOUS SYSTEMS

- Develop, integrate, assess and demonstrate advanced levels of autonomy for squad level small UAS (SBS / SRR) to increase SA, Soldier Lethality and reduce cognitive burden during Close Combat operations
- Leverage and mature SUAS algorithms from ARL and others for Autonomous Navigation, Search, Perch and Stare, Human-Agent teaming, Targeting, and Collaborative Behaviors
- Demonstrate capabilities in operational representative environments during frequent Soldier touchpoints
- Demonstrate capability on a government defined open architecture to support transition to PoRs and reduce program risk and cost
- Inform future Robotics and Autonomous Systems Requirements

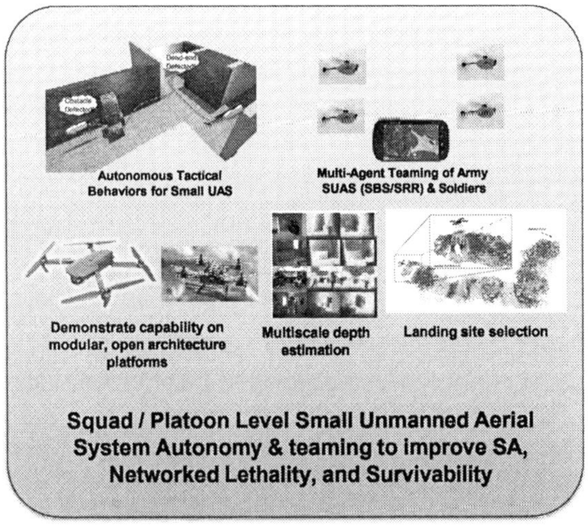

Enabling focus on the **fight** NOT flight

SENSORED SOLDIER: MULTI-DOMAIN REMOTE SENSING

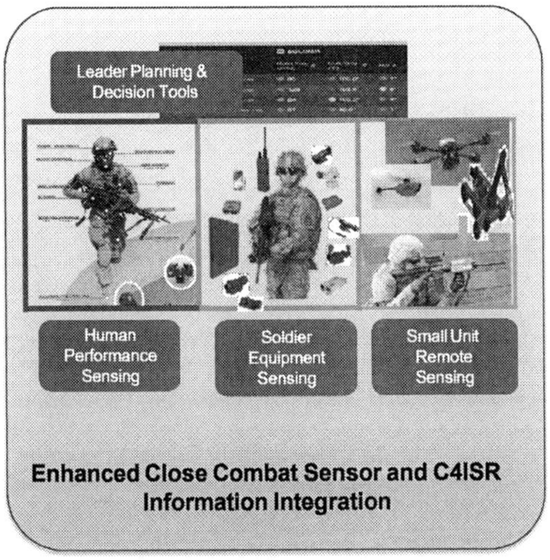

Provide Soldier platform sensing across the formation and throughout the continuum of operations: planning, rehearsal, actions on the objective and After Action Review (AAR).

- **Leader Planning & Decision Tool** components transitioned to Programs of Record (PoR) that guide operational usage of physiological, equipment, and remote sensing hardware and information.
- **Human Performance Sensing and Integration** software components transitioned to PoRs that guide operational usage; Integration of MASTR-E and third party physiological and cognitive sensing across the Squad workflow.
- **Soldier Equipment Sensing and Integration** components transitioned to PM Close Combat Squad and other PoRs that guide operational usage and user experience of equipment status sensing across the Squad workflow.
- **Remote Sensing and Integration** software components transitioned to PoR that guides operational usage and user experience of remote squad sensing status across the Squad workflow.

UX/UI: MULTIMODAL INPUT TECHNIQUES

DEVCOM SOLDIER CENTER

- Multimodal human-machine interaction (HMI) techniques (e.g., gesture, gaze, voice, head movements) can enable fast, accurate, and user-friendly control of augmented reality (AR) head-worn displays (HWDs).
- Best implementation and combination of multimodal inputs to optimize human performance when interacting with AR during operations is currently unknown.
- Multimodal inputs can improve performance but have the potential to cognitively overburden the user if not optimally combined and/or paired with complementary tasks.

Project Objectives:

- Identify performance-optimized pairings of multimodal inputs to common AR tasks and input handoff best practices for enhanced tactical AR use.
- Incorporate augmented/virtual reality HWDs, physiology-based input technologies and algorithms (e.g., gesture-sensing wearables, eye and gaze depth tracking, voice recognition, IMU), and quantitative and qualitative human performance metrics to address these needs.

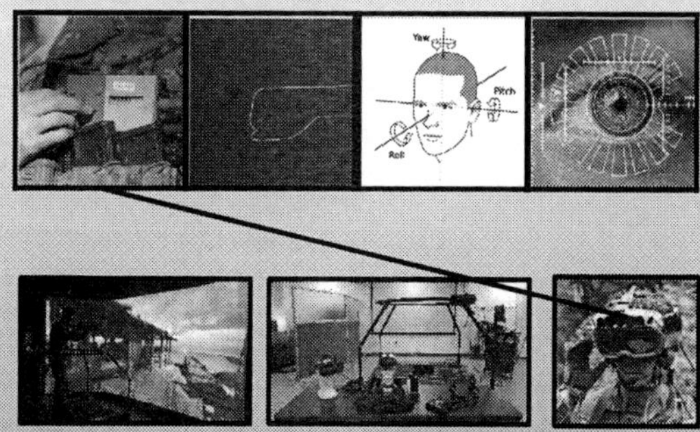

Enable fast, accurate, and user-friendly multimodal control of augmented reality.

INTEGRATED SOLDIER SYSTEMS

DEVCOM SOLDIER CENTER

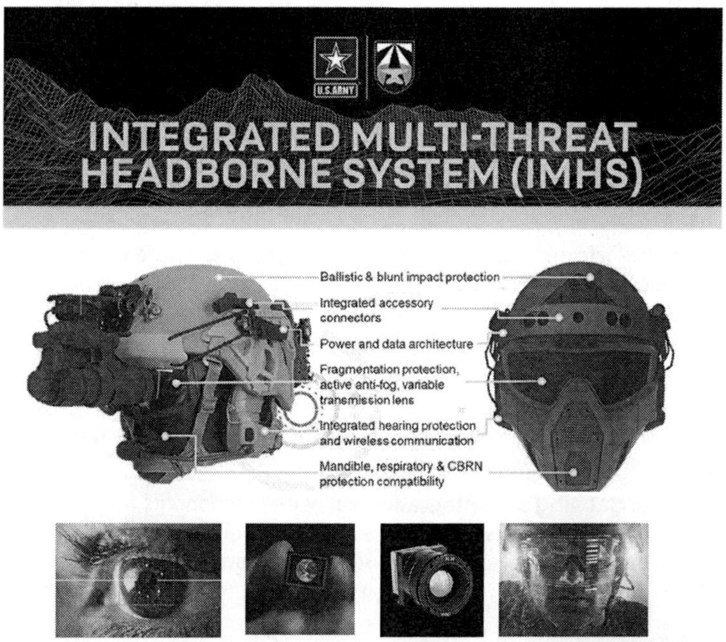

- Integration of Soldier-worn sensor technologies and accessories
- Interface control document to standardize parts and attachment types
- Common on body interfaces, power distribution, and and data architecture for interoperabili

APPROVED FOR PUBLIC RELEASE

HP MEASUREMENT & PREDICTION

Increase Soldier & Squad Capability (Smarter (decide), Faster (move), more Lethal (threat elimination) & Precise (reduction of ambiguity)) through advanced training tools, optimization & enhancement strategies, and Soldier-system characterization & integration in order to increase lethality and resilience under close combat stress.

HP Analytics for Decision Dominance
Development of advanced human performance analytics and platforms to quantify Soldier and Small Unit performance and readiness for targeted interventions and decision dominance

Trade Space Parameters for Soldier & Squad Lethality
Inform acquisition decisions thru development of methods, metrics, and M&S to quantify the impacts of Soldier equipment and technology on the lethality trade space for both the Soldier and Small Unit.

Enhancement for Soldier & Squad Overmatch
Optimize and enhance Soldier/Squad cognitive/physical capacity and resiliency to adverse conditions. Aim to achieve decreased lost duty time, increased readiness, increased recovery and optimize/enhance tactical performance.

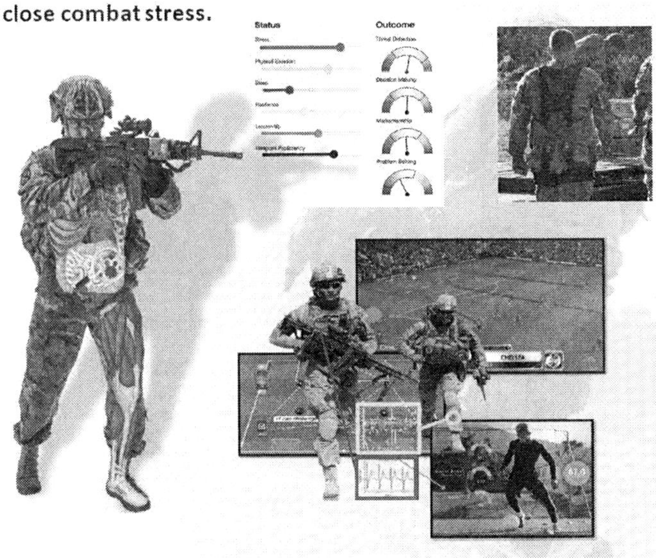

APPROVED FOR PUBLIC RELEASE 17

APPROVED FOR PUBLIC RELEASE

LEVERAGING COTS WEARABLES

<u>Framing Question</u>: can wearables provide commanders with warfighter readiness and performance information to enhance multi-domain operational decision making?

Inform Decision Making
Learn what decisions could be made at each echelon & domain

Minimize Warfighter Burden
Identify tools to automate and supplements warfighter/leadership readiness status and reporting tasks

Move Data Regionally
Demonstrate data movement across vast distances (1,000's mi)

Integrate DoD Stakeholders
Integrate wearables capabilities from across the DoD

JPEO CBRND Wearables Program- Lorenz Hankla, PM

APPROVED FOR PUBLIC RELEASE 18

APPROVED FOR PUBLIC RELEASE

LEVERAGING COTS WEARABLES

DEVCOM SOLDIER CENTER

Framing ... ess and performa ... ?

Inform

Learn wh... made at ea...

...hter Burden

...mate and ...ter/leadership ... reporting tasks

Move...

Demon... across vast...

...takeholders

...capabilities

APPROVED FOR PUBLIC RELEASE

19

APPROVED FOR PUBLIC RELEASE

LEVERAGING COTS WEARABLES

DEVCOM SOLDIER CENTER

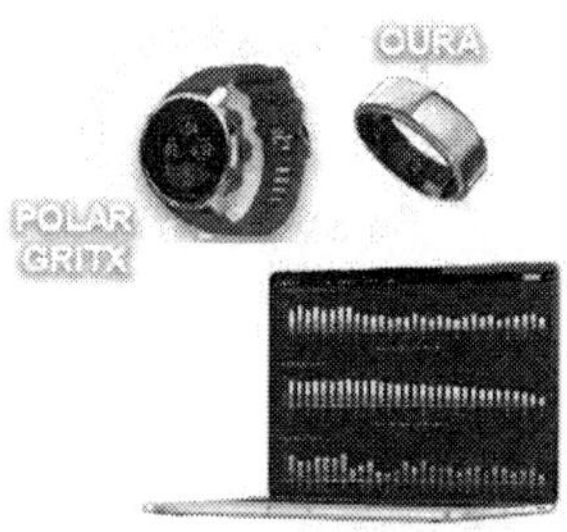

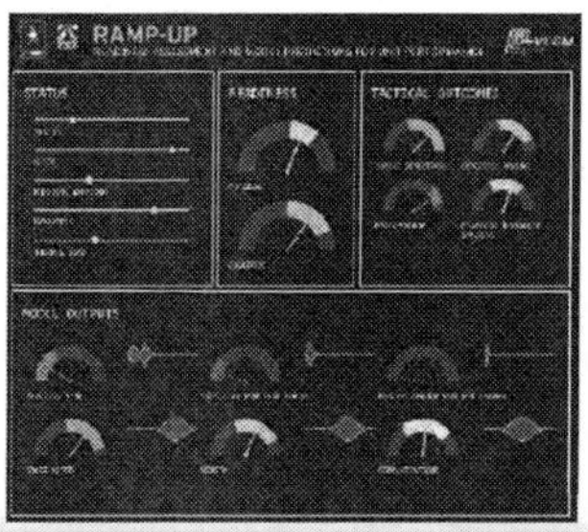

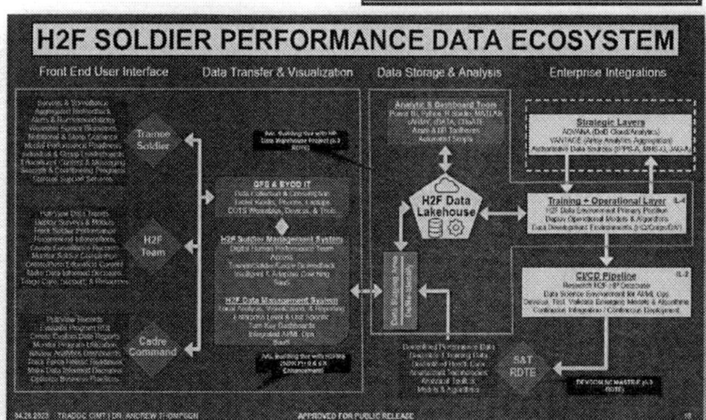

APPROVED FOR PUBLIC RELEASE

20

APPROVED FOR PUBLIC RELEASE

FUTURE APPLICATIONS & OPPORTUNITIES

DEVCOM SOLDIER CENTER

- Human Performance sensing to determine real-time states
- Eye tracking for HUD interfacing and targeting
- Health status monitoring for intervention
- Injury prevention
- Medical applications (triage/casualty care and prolonged care)
- Environment sensing (acoustic, optical, thermal, CBRNE, etc.)
- Adversary sensing (detection and monitoring)

Photos courtesy of dvidshub.net and army.mil

APPROVED FOR PUBLIC RELEASE

21

APPROVED FOR PUBLIC RELEASE

CHALLENGES

DEVCOM SOLDIER CENTER

Photos courtesy of dvidshub.net and army.mil

APPROVED FOR PUBLIC RELEASE

22

DEVCOM SOLDIER CENTER
THANK YOU.
SOLDIERS: OUR CREDENTIALS
PROTECTED • OPTIMIZED • LETHAL

U.S. ARMY

Sensors Converge

A Hands-On Introduction to The Zephyr Project RTOS

June 20–22, 2023 | Santa Clara, CA

#SensorsConverge

The Speaker

Mohammed Billoo
(www.mab-labs.com)

www.linkedin.com/in/mab-embedded

@mabembedded

BIOS Food Newsletter

#SensorsConverge

Sensors Converge

Agenda

- Why?
- Getting Started
- Unique Features
- What's Next?
- Q&A

#SensorsConverge

Sensors Converge

Why?

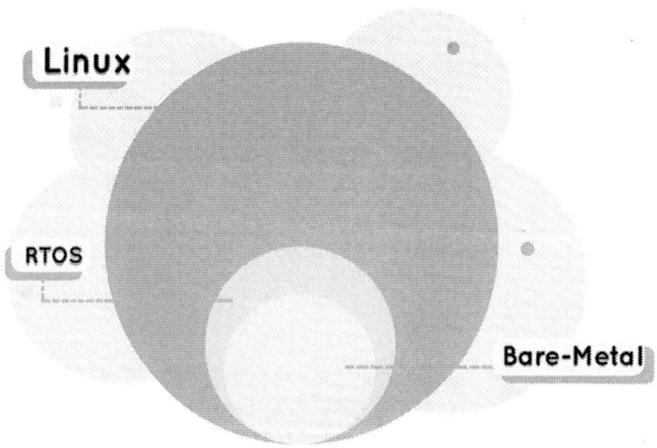

#SensorsConverge

Sensors Converge

RTOS vs Bare Metal

- An RTOS Saves Development Time
- Minimal additional code size
- Serves as a HAL to MCU synchronization features
- Avoids requiring us to implement these features
  - Reinvent the wheel
  - Time-consuming
- Tested thoroughly

#SensorsConverge

Sensors Converge

RTOS Benefits

- Don't reinvent the wheel
- API that implements standard features
  - Task/thread
  - Queue
  - Semaphore
  - Mutex
- Leverage MCU hardware
  - ARM
  - Assembly to enable/disable interrupts
- Leverage compiler for increased optimization

www.eringillespiecartoons.wordpress.com

#SensorsConverge

Sensors Converge

Why The Zephyr Project RTOS?

- Self-contained
  - Drivers included
  - Subsystems included
  - No need to manually retrieve other repositories
- Vendor agnostic
  - Support for CPUs from many vendors
  - Support for extensive list of development boards
- Examples for all subsystems/peripherals
- VS Code Plugins

NORDIC SEMICONDUCTOR

life.augmented ARDUINO RISC-V

#SensorsConverge

Sensors Converge

The Zephyr Project RTOS

- It's not Linux!
- "Zephyr"
- It's an RTOS
  - Direct access to hardware
  - No rings/privileged mode*
- Organization is different from other RTOSes
  - Collection of repositories
  - Uses a "meta-tool" called West

Zephyr™

#SensorsConverge

Sensors Converge

Getting Started

- nRF Connect for Desktop
- An application that sets up a complete Zephyr development environment
- VS Code Plugins!
  - Create a new project
    - Based on an example
  - Open existing project
  - Configure Zephyr
  - Build and debug a project

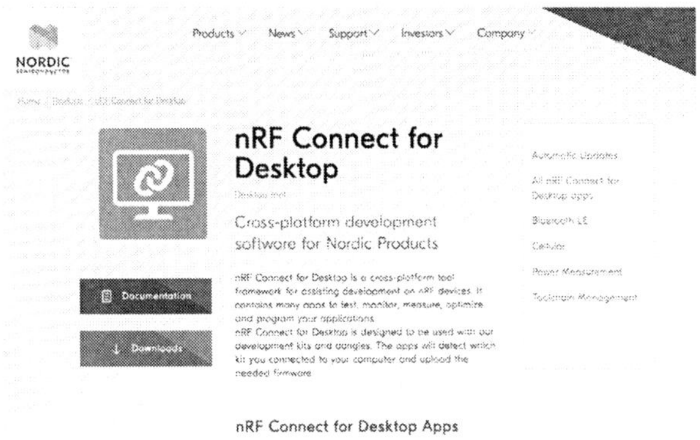

#SensorsConverge

Sensors Converge

nRF Connect For Desktop

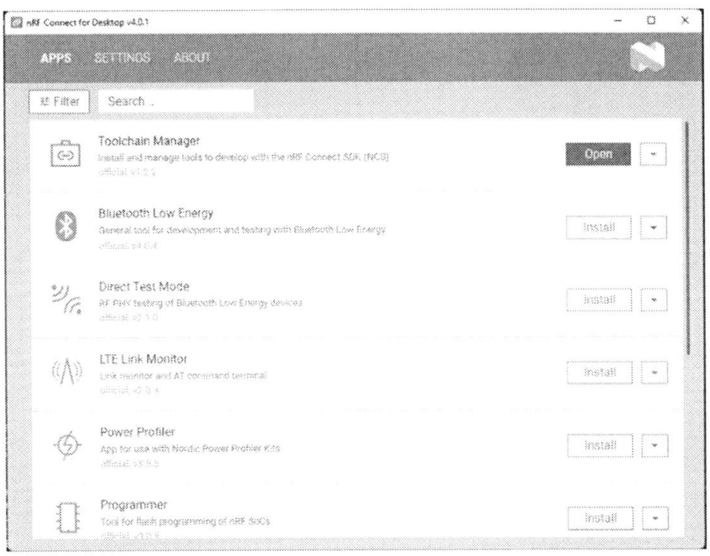

#SensorsConverge

Sensors Converge

nRF Connect For Desktop

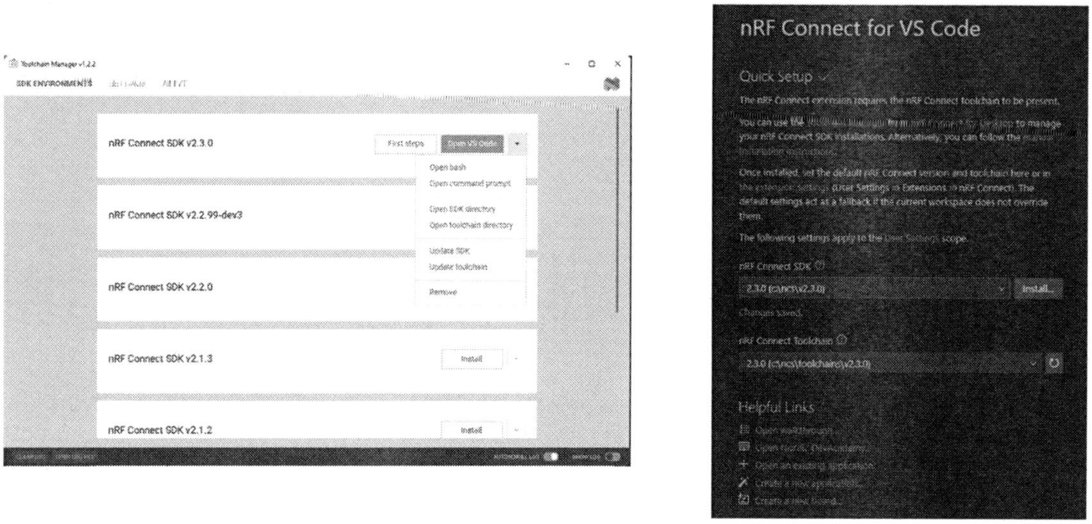

Hello World!

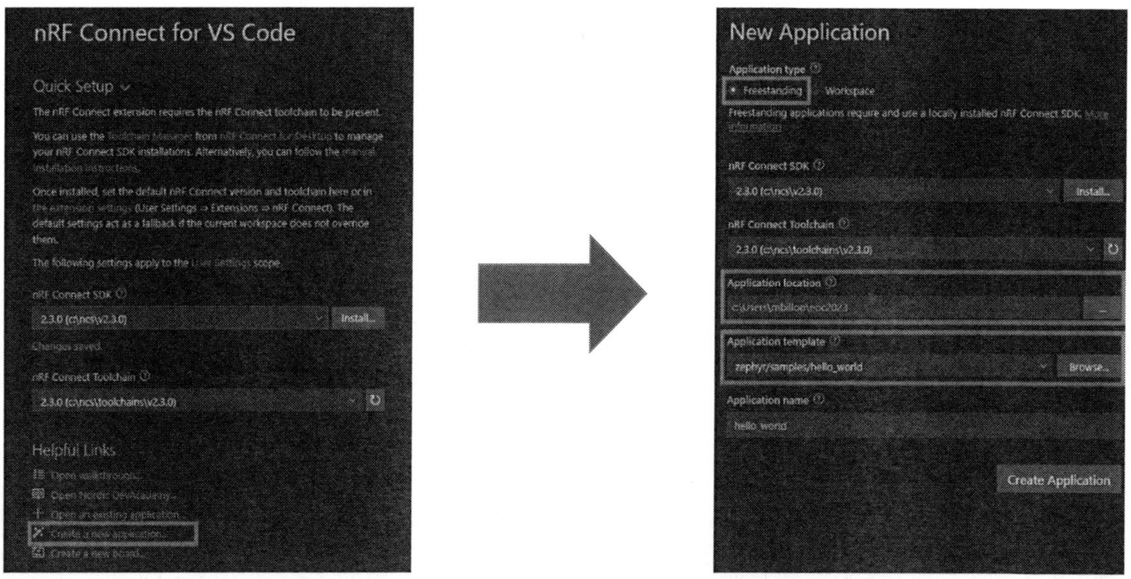

Hello World (nRF Connect Plugin)

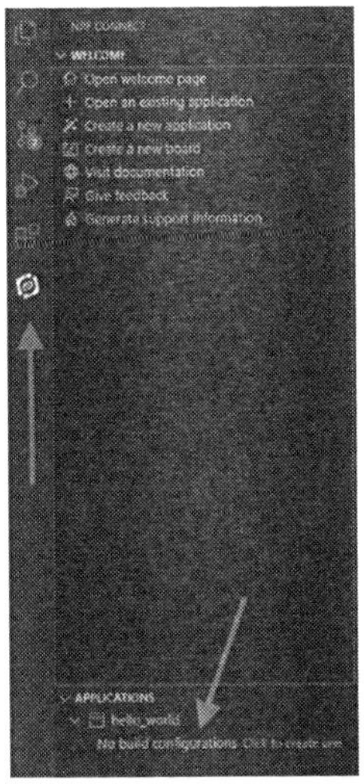

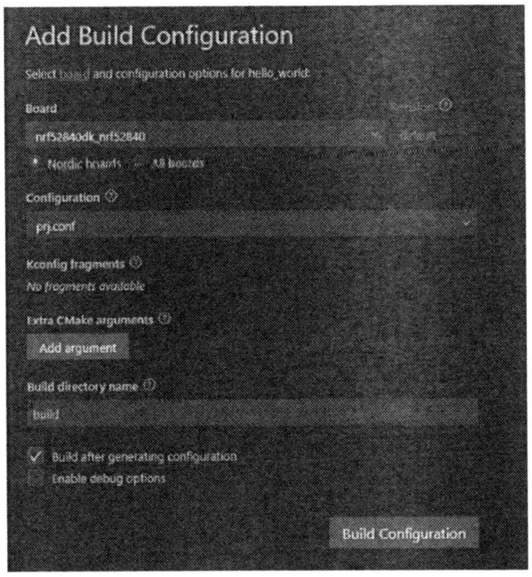

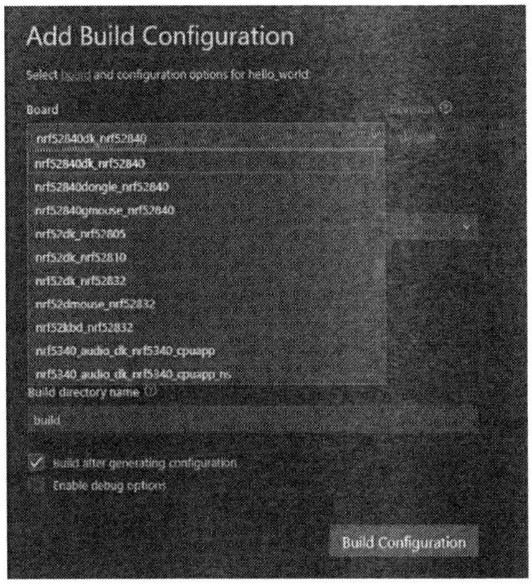

Hello World!

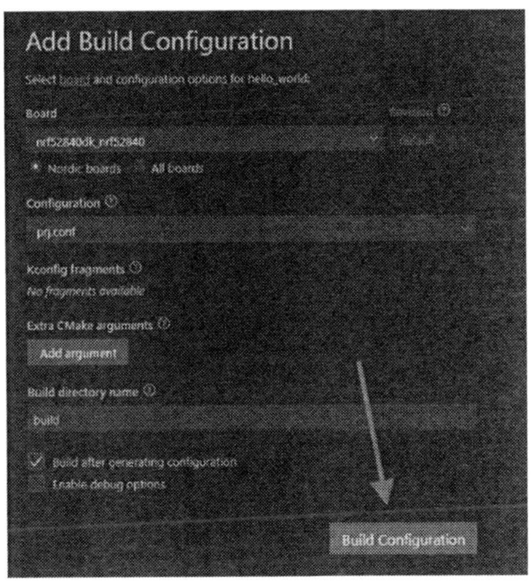

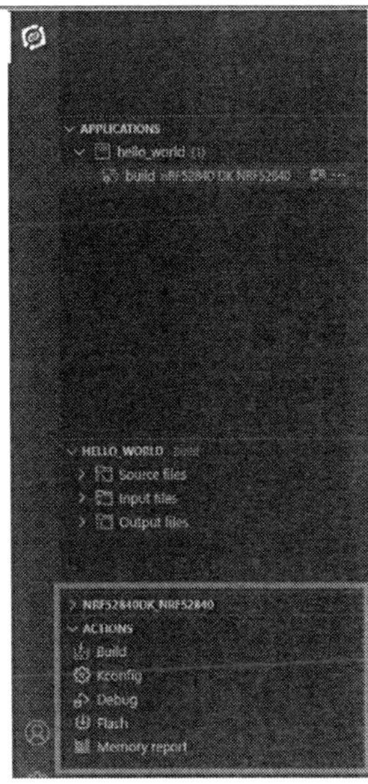

Hello World!

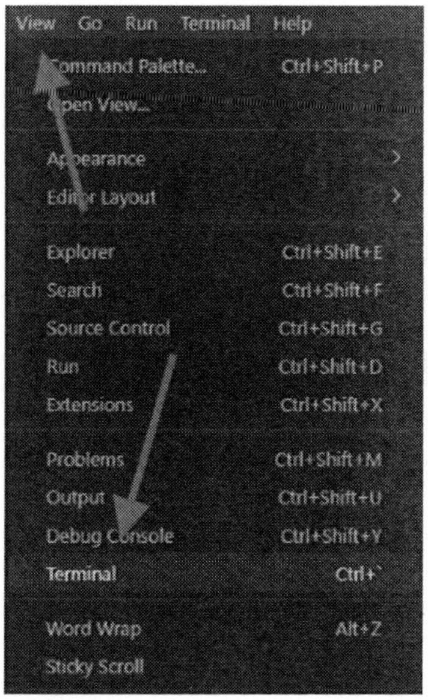

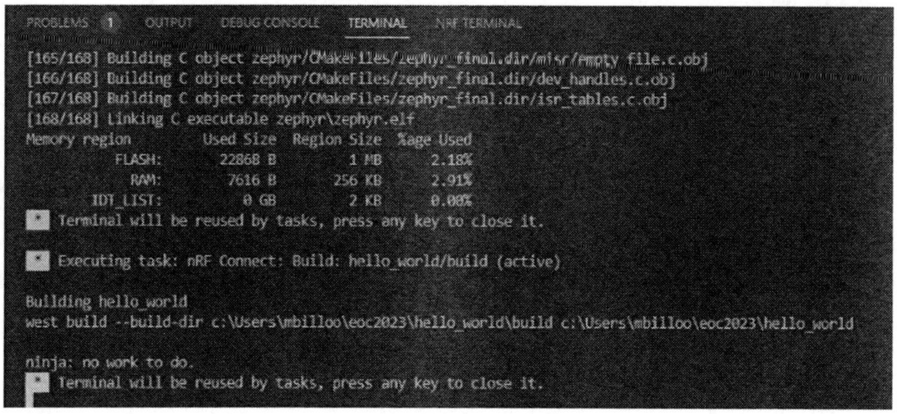

#SensorsConverge

Sensors Converge

Hello World!

#SensorsConverge

Sensors Converge

Hello World!

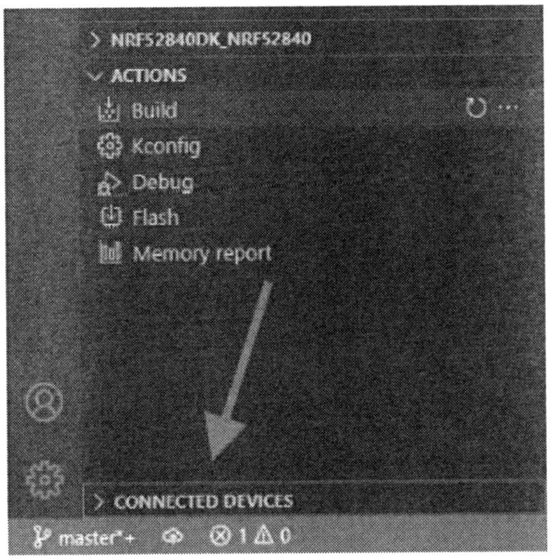

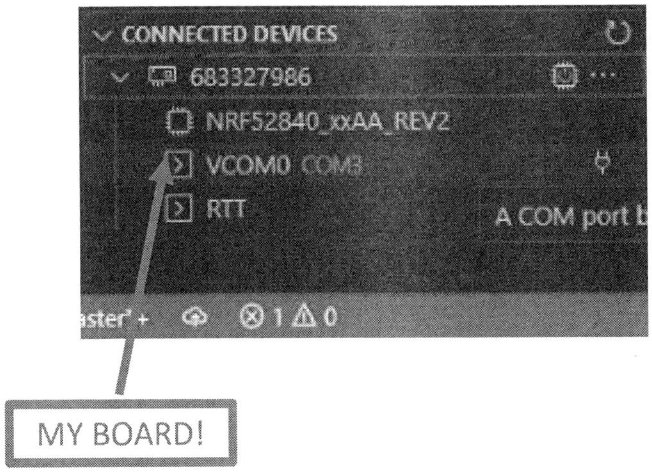

#SensorsConverge

Hello World!

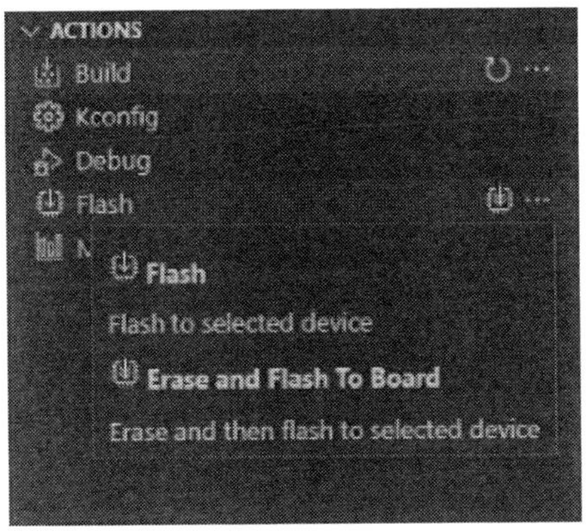

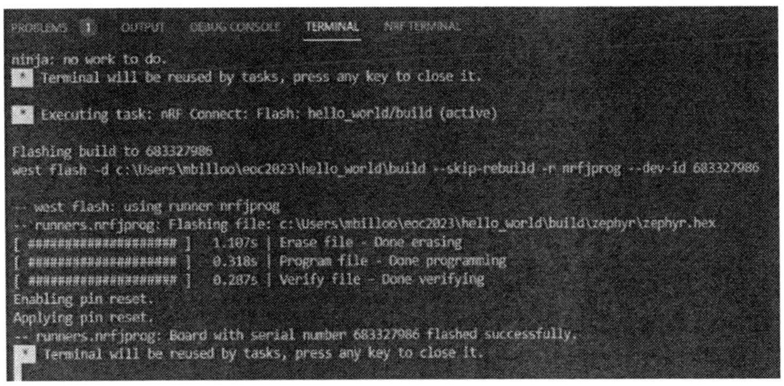

#SensorsConverge

Hello World!

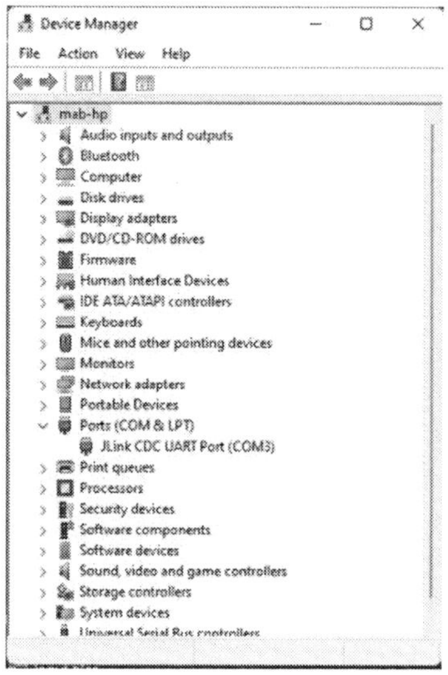

Hello World!

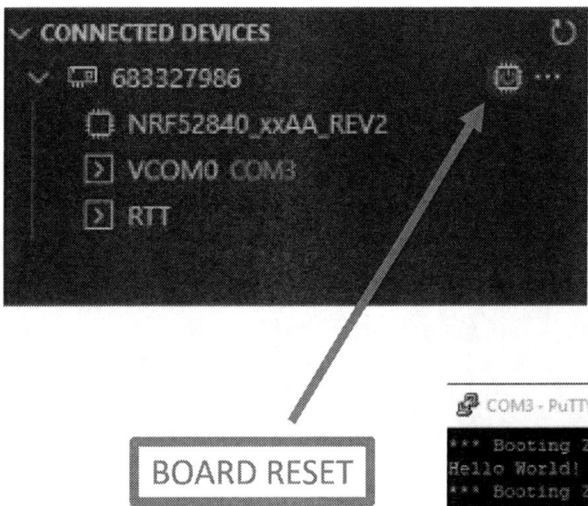

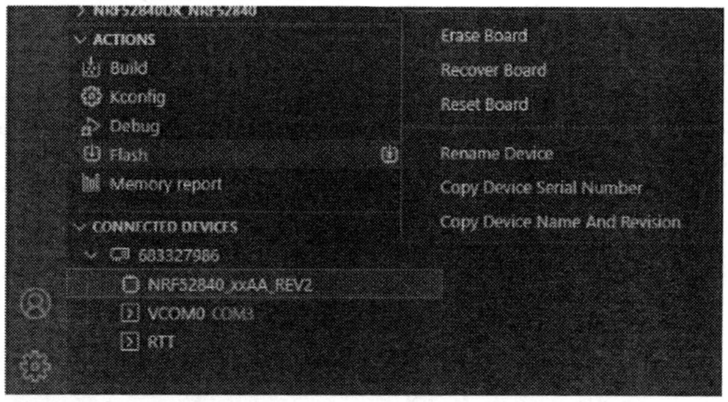

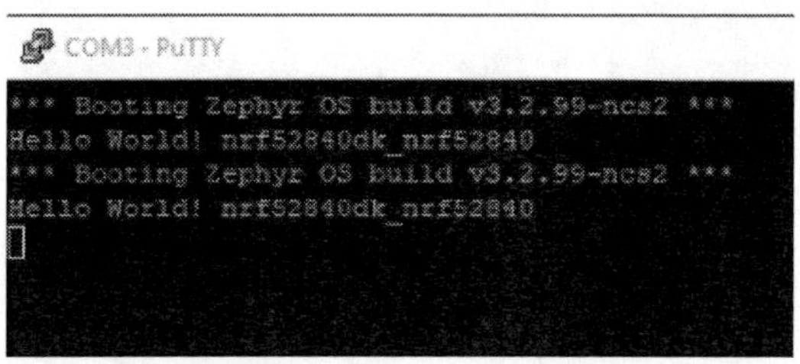

KConfig

- Borrowed from Linux
- Used to configure Zephyr features
  - Subsystems
- Similar to specifying macros in other RTOSes
  - All features (not just kernel options)!
- Configuration
  - Can be filed based
    - "prj.conf"
  - Or use GUI

Zephyr™

#SensorsConverge

Sensors Converge

KConfig

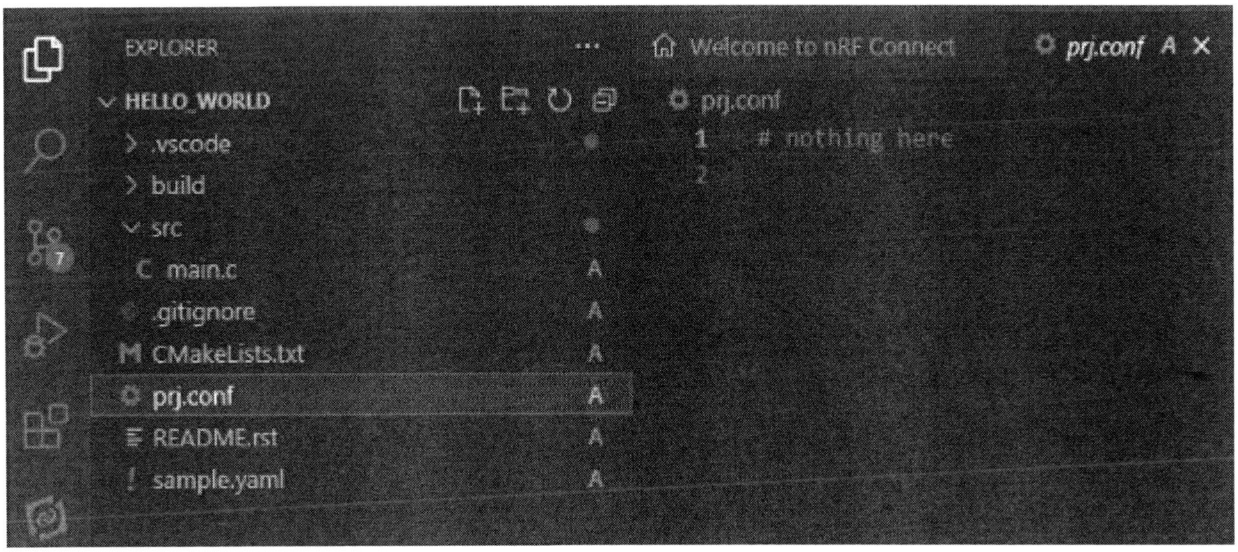

#SensorsConverge

Sensors Converge

KConfig

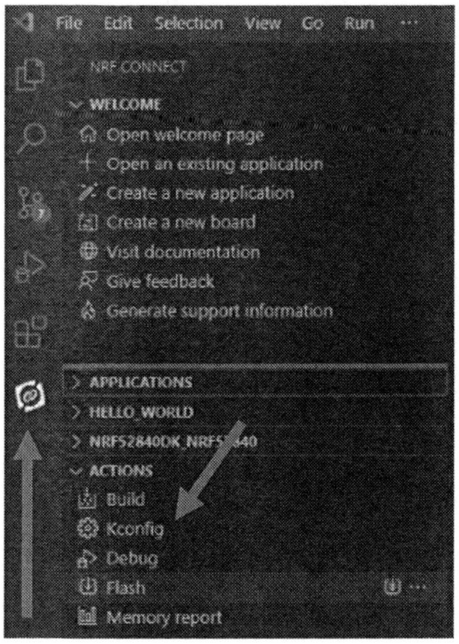

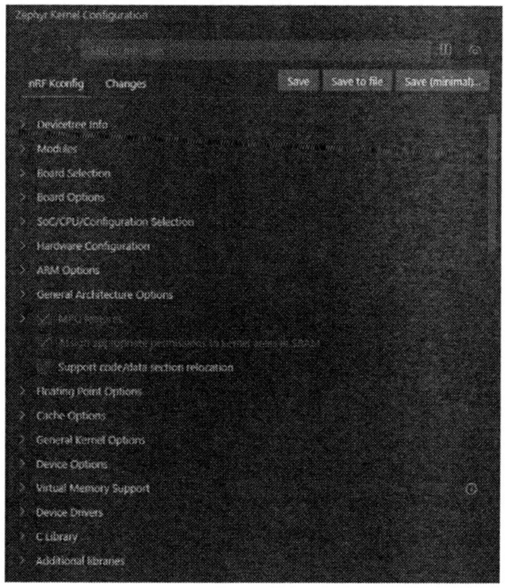

#SensorsConverge

Sensors Converge

KConfig

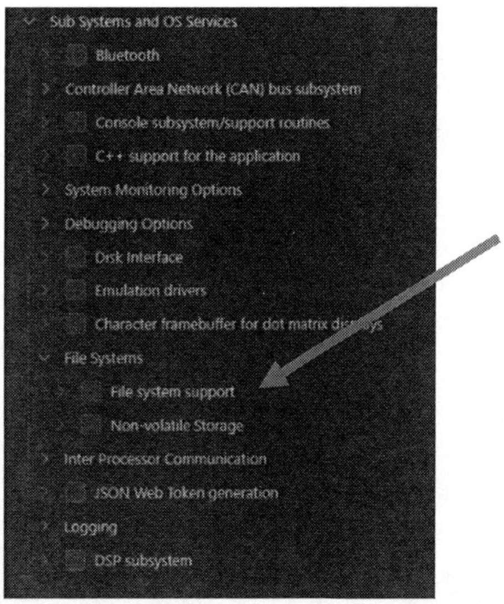

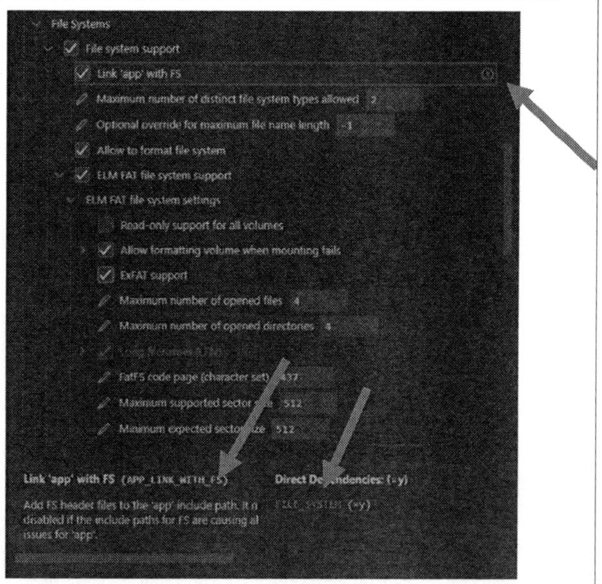

#SensorsConverge

Sensors Converge

KConfig

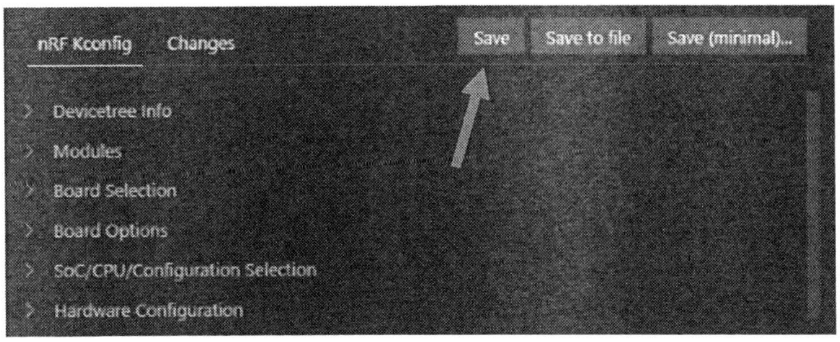

CHANGES WILL NOT BE SAVED TO prj.conf!

BAD FOR VERSION CONTROL!

#SensorsConverge

KConfig

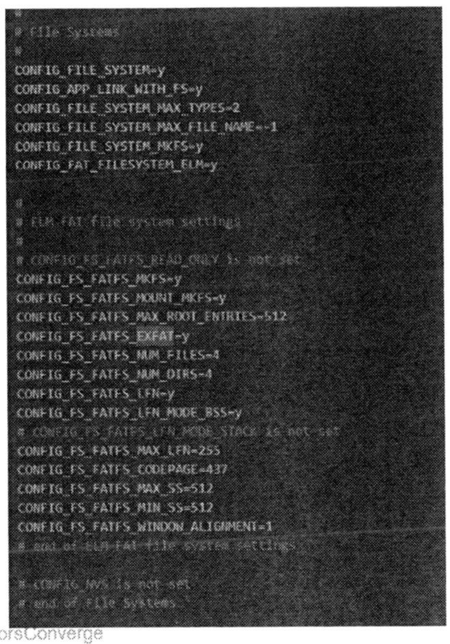

```
#
# File Systems
#
CONFIG_FILE_SYSTEM=y
CONFIG_APP_LINK_WITH_FS=y
CONFIG_FILE_SYSTEM_MAX_TYPES=2
CONFIG_FILE_SYSTEM_MAX_FILE_NAME=-1
CONFIG_FILE_SYSTEM_MKFS=y
CONFIG_FAT_FILESYSTEM_ELM=y

#
# ELM FAT file system settings
#
# CONFIG_FS_FATFS_READ_ONLY is not set
CONFIG_FS_FATFS_MKFS=y
CONFIG_FS_FATFS_MOUNT_MKFS=y
CONFIG_FS_FATFS_MAX_ROOT_ENTRIES=512
CONFIG_FS_FATFS_EXFAT=y
CONFIG_FS_FATFS_NUM_FILES=4
CONFIG_FS_FATFS_NUM_DIRS=4
CONFIG_FS_FATFS_LFN=y
CONFIG_FS_FATFS_LFN_MODE_BSS=y
# CONFIG_FS_FATFS_LFN_MODE_STACK is not set
CONFIG_FS_FATFS_MAX_LFN=255
CONFIG_FS_FATFS_CODEPAGE=437
CONFIG_FS_FATFS_MAX_SS=512
CONFIG_FS_FATFS_MIN_SS=512
CONFIG_FS_FATFS_WINDOW_ALIGNMENT=1
# end of ELM FAT file system settings

# CONFIG_NVS is not set
# end of File Systems
```

CAN COMMIT CHANGES TO prj.conf

ADD build DIRECTORY TO .gitignore

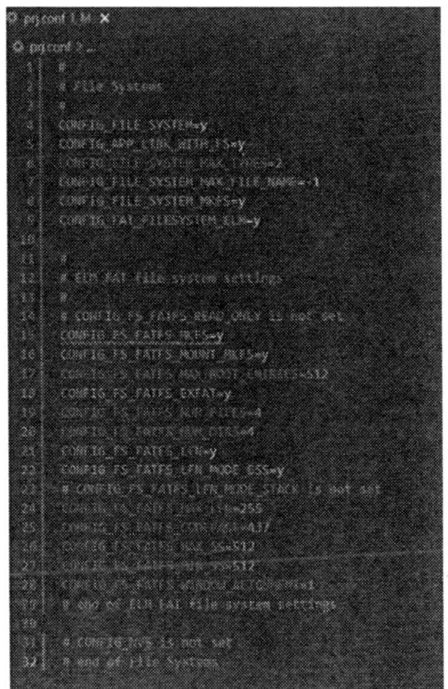

#SensorsConverge

Devicetree

- Borrowed from Linux
- Used to configure hardware
  - Pinmux
  - Pinout
  - Board peripherals
- Part of the build process
  - Start with "top-level" device tree file (provided by vendor)
    - Contains references to other device tree files
      - Pinout configuration
  - Can customize devicetree using "overlays"
    - Custom hardware

Devicetree Overlay

- For custom hardware
- Change peripheral pinout
- Enable subsystem
  - Sometimes enablement is done via devicetree (instead of KConfig)

Devicetree Overlay

- Example: Enabling ADC and SPI-SD card support

```
/ {
    aliases {
        adcctrl = &adc;
    };
};

&adc {
    status = "okay";
};
```

```
sdhc0: sdhc@0 {
    compatible = "zephyr,sdhc-spi-slot";
    reg = <0>;
    status = "okay";
    label = "SDHC_0";
    mmc {
        compatible = "zephyr,sdmmc-disk";
        status = "okay";
    };
    spi-max-frequency = <24000000>;
};
```

#SensorsConverge

Sensors Converge

Devicetree Overlay

- Example: Changing default pins

```
&spi1 {
    status = "okay";
    pinctrl-0 = <&mab_spi>;
    pinctrl-1 = <&mab_spi>;
    pinctrl-names = "default", "sleep";
    cs-gpios = <&gpio0 2 GPIO_ACTIVE_LOW>;
```

```
&arduino_i2c {
    pinctrl-0 = <&mab_i2c>;
    pinctrl-1 = <&mab_i2c>;
    pinctrl-names = "default", "sleep";
};
```

```
&pinctrl {
    mab_spi: mab_spi {
        group1 {
            psels = <NRF_PSEL(SPIM_SCK, 0, 26)>,
                <NRF_PSEL(SPIM_MOSI, 0, 27)>,
                <NRF_PSEL(SPIM_MISO, 1, 8)>;
        };
    };

    mab_i2c: mab_i2c {
        group1 {
            psels = <NRF_PSEL(TWIM_SDA, 1, 15)>,
                <NRF_PSEL(TWIM_SCL, 1, 14)>;
        };
    };
};
```

#SensorsConverge

Sensors Converge

What's Next?

- Typical RTOS data structures and paradigms
- Threads/tasks
- Thread/task synchronization
  - Mutex
  - Semaphore
- Thread/task communication
  - Workqueue
  - FIFO

#SensorsConverge

Sensors Converge

Intermediate Topics

- Connectivity
- BLE
  - Custom advertised name
  - Standard services/characteristics
    - Battery
  - Custom services/characteristics
- WiFi
  - AP mode
  - Station mode

#SensorsConverge

Sensors Converge

Advanced Topics

- West Manfiest
- nRF Connect for Desktop uses Nordic's own West manifest under the hood
- Maybe beneficial to bring West manifest in-house
  - Ensure that all source code is from a particular version
    - Unknown updates may break functionality
  - Helpful for client projects
- Blog post
  - Getting Started With Zephyr: West Manifest Customization
  - https://www.embeddedrelated.com/showarticle/1505.php

#SensorsConverge

Sensors Converge

Thank You!

June 20–22, 2023 | San Clara, CA

#SensorsConverge

Sensors Converge

MODERNIZING EMBEDDED SOFTWARE

June 20–22, 2023 | Santa Clara, CA

#SensorsConverge

BENINGO EMBEDDED GROUP

Simplifying Concepts, Delivering Success℠ | 2

THE SPEAKER

Jacob Beningo

Beningo Embedded Group
President

Focus: Embedded Software Consulting

An independent consultant who specializes in the design of real-time, microcontroller based embedded software.

He has published three books;

- Reusable Firmware Development
- MicroPython Projects
- Embedded Software Design

Writes a weekly blog for DesignNews.com focused on embedded system design techniques and challenges.

Visit www.beningo.com to learn more ...

BENINGO
EMBEDDED GROUP

EMBEDDED ONLINE CONFERENCE

www.embeddedonlineconference.com

Preconference
Organized By:

Embedded
Online
Conference

1 Embedded Systems Preconference Track Overview

BENINGO EMBEDDED GROUP

SESSION OVERVIEW

Agenda

9:00 – 9:30	Modern Embedded Software Development Strategies and Processes
9:30 – 10:15	Designing Secure Embedded Devices for an Interconnected World
10:25 – 11:10	Sensing on a Mars Analogue Astronaut Mission
11:15 – 12:00	The Best Defense is Offensive Programming
12:00 – 12:50	Lunch
1:00 – 1:50	Where's the killer app for TinyML?
2:00 – 2:50	A Hands-on Introduction to The Zephyr Project RTOS

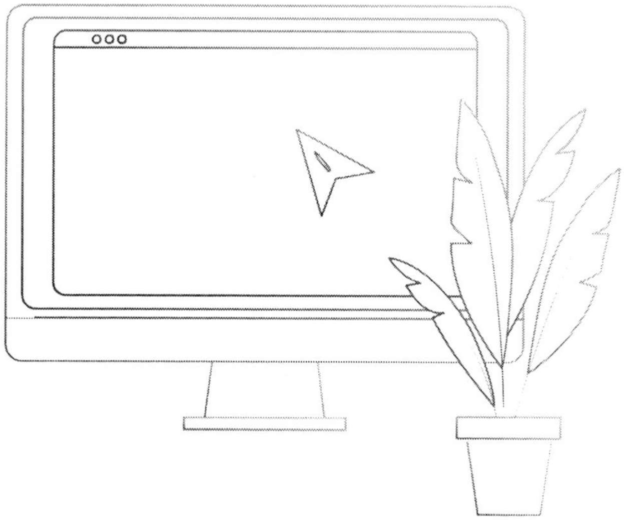

BENINGO EMBEDDED GROUP

Simplifying Concepts, Delivering Success℠

MODERNIZING EMBEDDED SOFTWARE

Session 0000 – Modern Embedded Software Development Strategies and Processes

2 Embedded Software Challenges

BENINGO
EMBEDDED GROUP

EMBEDDED SOFTWARE CHALLENGES

What challenges are you facing?

MODERN CHALLENGES

Challenges Facing Embedded Developers

Quality

- Buggy software
- Constant bug fixes
- Customer complaints

Development Costs

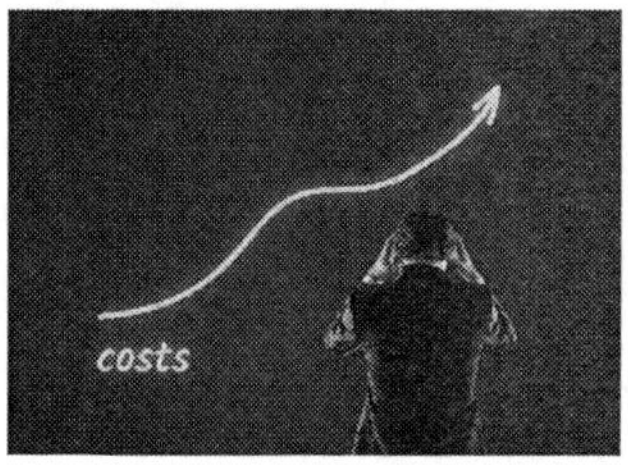

- Smaller budgets
- More features
- Increased complexity

Time to Market

- More debugging
- Missed deadlines
- Integration woes

Scalable Solutions

- Tightly coupled code
- Vendor dependency
- Inflexible architecture

2 Software Design Philosophy

SOFTWARE DESIGN PHILOSOPHY

Fight the biggest fire

SOFTWARE DESIGN PHILOSOPHY

Traditional Thinking

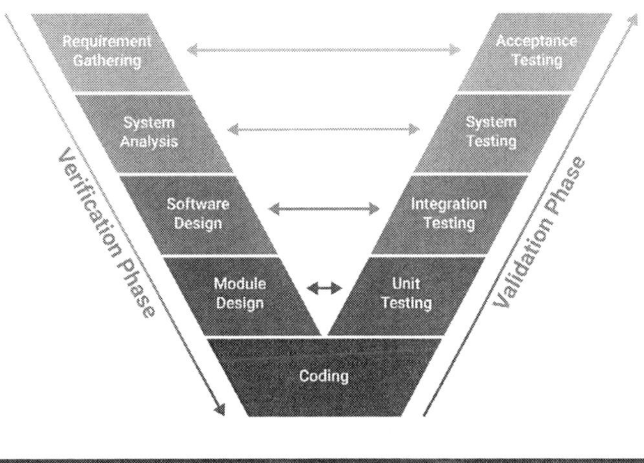

SOFTWARE DESIGN PHILOSOPHY

Agile Methodologies

At its core, Agile is about[1]:

1) **Individuals and interactions** over processes and tools
2) **Working software** over comprehensive documentation
3) **Customer collaboration** over contract negotiation
4) **Responding to change** over following a plan

"Some folks think that Agile is about going fast. It's not. It's never been about going fast. Agile is about knowing, as early as possible, just how screwed we are."
-- Bob Martin

[1]Clean Agile, Bob Martin

SOFTWARE DESIGN PHILOSOPHY

Successful Embedded Software

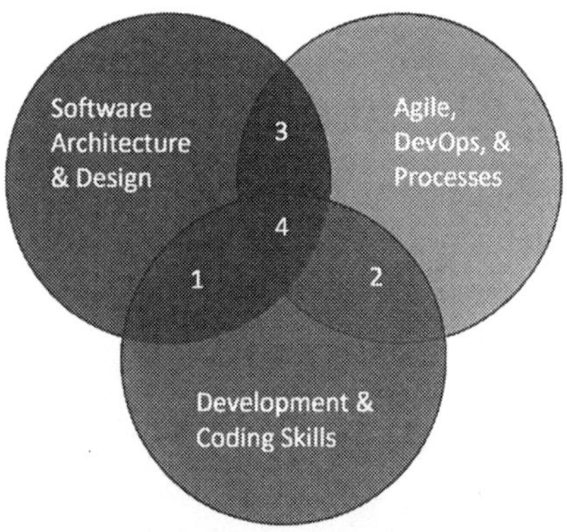

1 - Late, Inconsistent, Quality Issues
2 - Late, Rework, Lost / Meandering
3 - Never completed
4 - Successful Delivery

BENINGO
EMBEDDED GROUP

SOFTWARE DESIGN PHILOSOPHY

Define the principles that are most important to you.

- Principle #1 – Data Dictates Design
- Principle #2 – There is No Hardware (only data)
- Principle #3 – KISS the Software
- Principle #4 – Practical, Not Perfect
- Principle #5 – Scalable and Configurable
- Principle #6 – Test, Test, and Test
- Principle #7 – Security is King

Action Item:

Identify and write down your top 7 principles.

Put them in a place you can readily see them!

BENINGO
EMBEDDED GROUP

SOFTWARE DESIGN PHILOSOPHY

Successful Embedded Software

- Process dictates design
- Design dictates Process
- What is being accomplished?
  - Proof-of-concept
  - Production system?
  - Simulation?

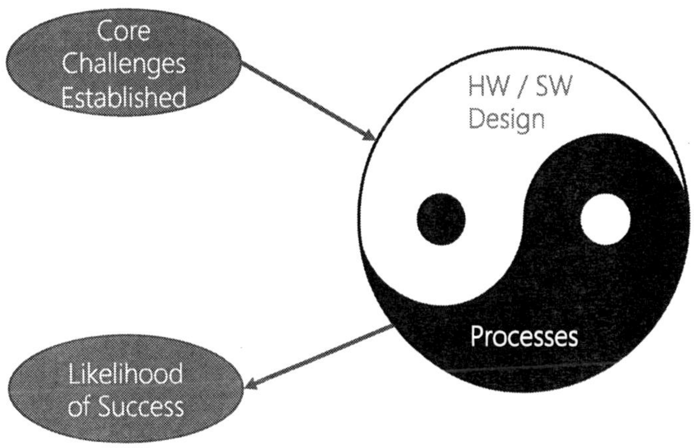

3 Modern Build Processes

BENINGO
EMBEDDED GROUP

Simplifying Concepts, Delivering Success℠ | 18

MODERN BUILD PROCESSES

What is your vision of the ultimate build process?

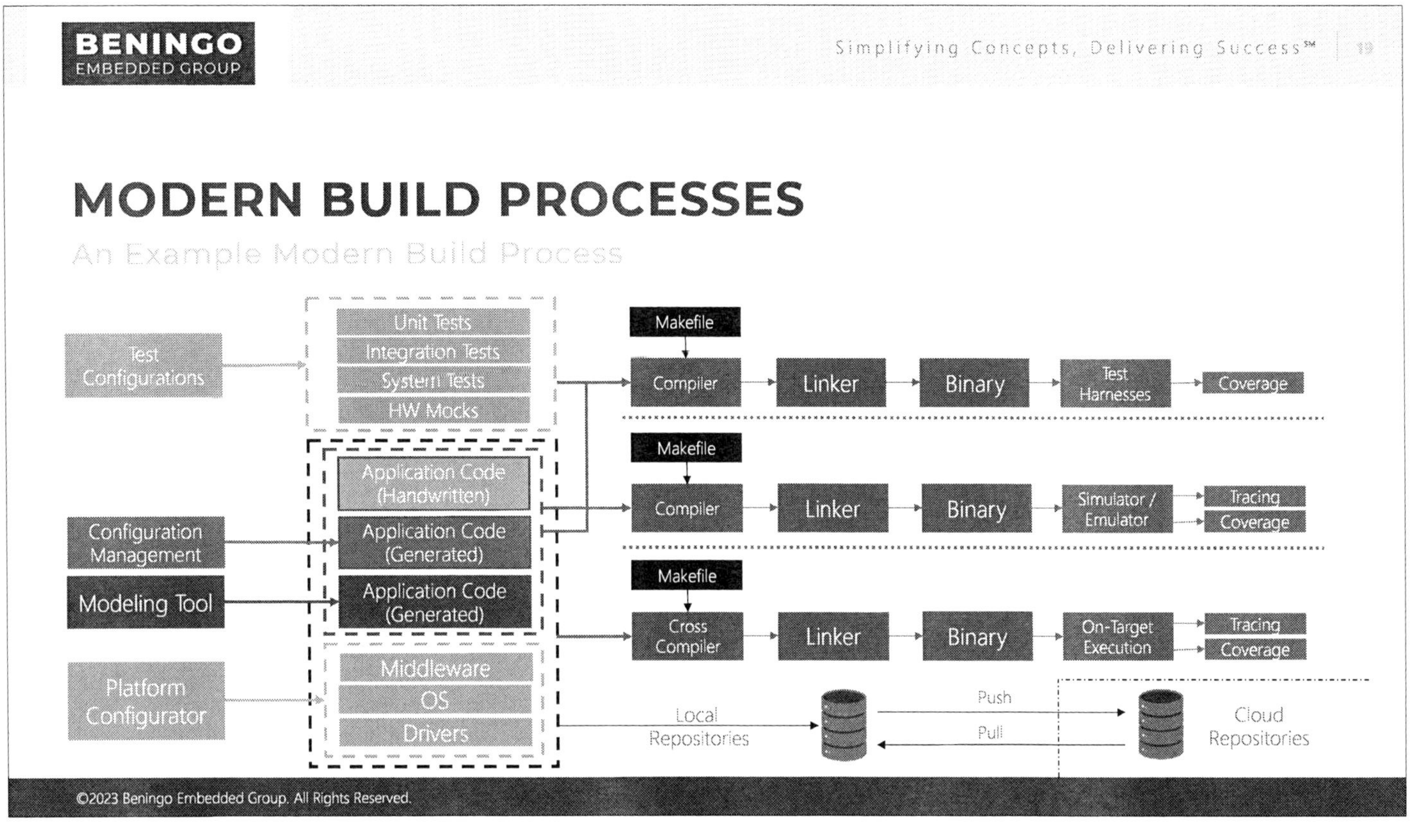
BENINGO
EMBEDDED GROUP
Simplifying Concepts, Delivering Success℠
19
MODERN BUILD PROCESSES
An Example Modern Build Process
Test Configurations
Unit Tests
Integration Tests
System Tests
HW Mocks
Configuration Management
Modeling Tool
Application Code (Handwritten)
Application Code (Generated)
Application Code (Generated)
Platform Configurator
Middleware
OS
Drivers
Makefile
Compiler
Linker
Binary
Test Harnesses
Coverage
Makefile
Compiler
Linker
Binary
Simulator / Emulator
Tracing
Coverage
Makefile
Cross Compiler
Linker
Binary
On-Target Execution
Tracing
Coverage
Local Repositories
Push
Pull
Cloud Repositories
©2023 Beningo Embedded Group. All Rights Reserved.

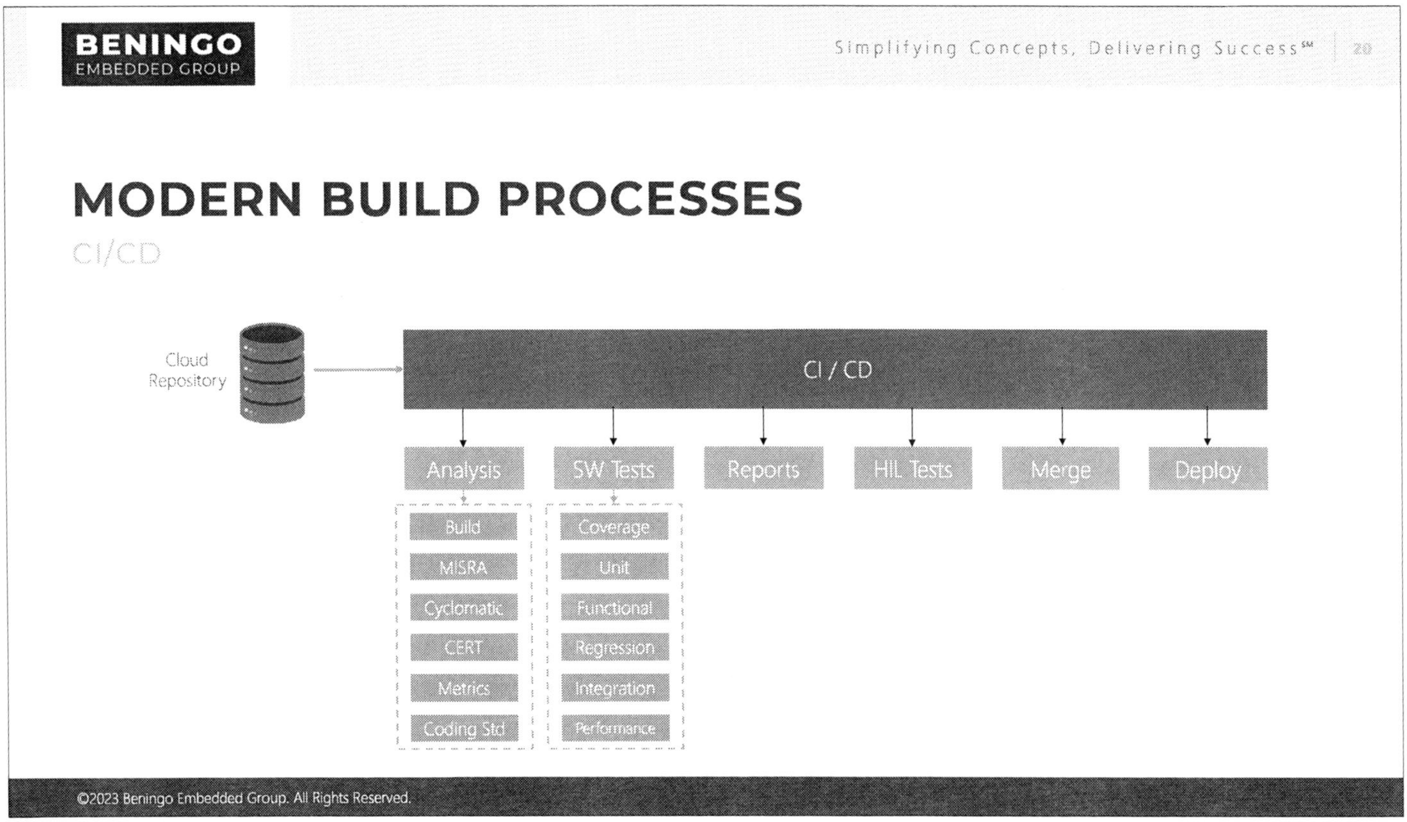
BENINGO
EMBEDDED GROUP
Simplifying Concepts, Delivering Success℠
20
MODERN BUILD PROCESSES
CI/CD
Cloud Repository
CI / CD
Analysis
SW Tests
Reports
HIL Tests
Merge
Deploy
Build
MISRA
Cyclomatic
CERT
Metrics
Coding Std
Coverage
Unit
Functional
Regression
Integration
Performance
©2023 Beningo Embedded Group. All Rights Reserved.

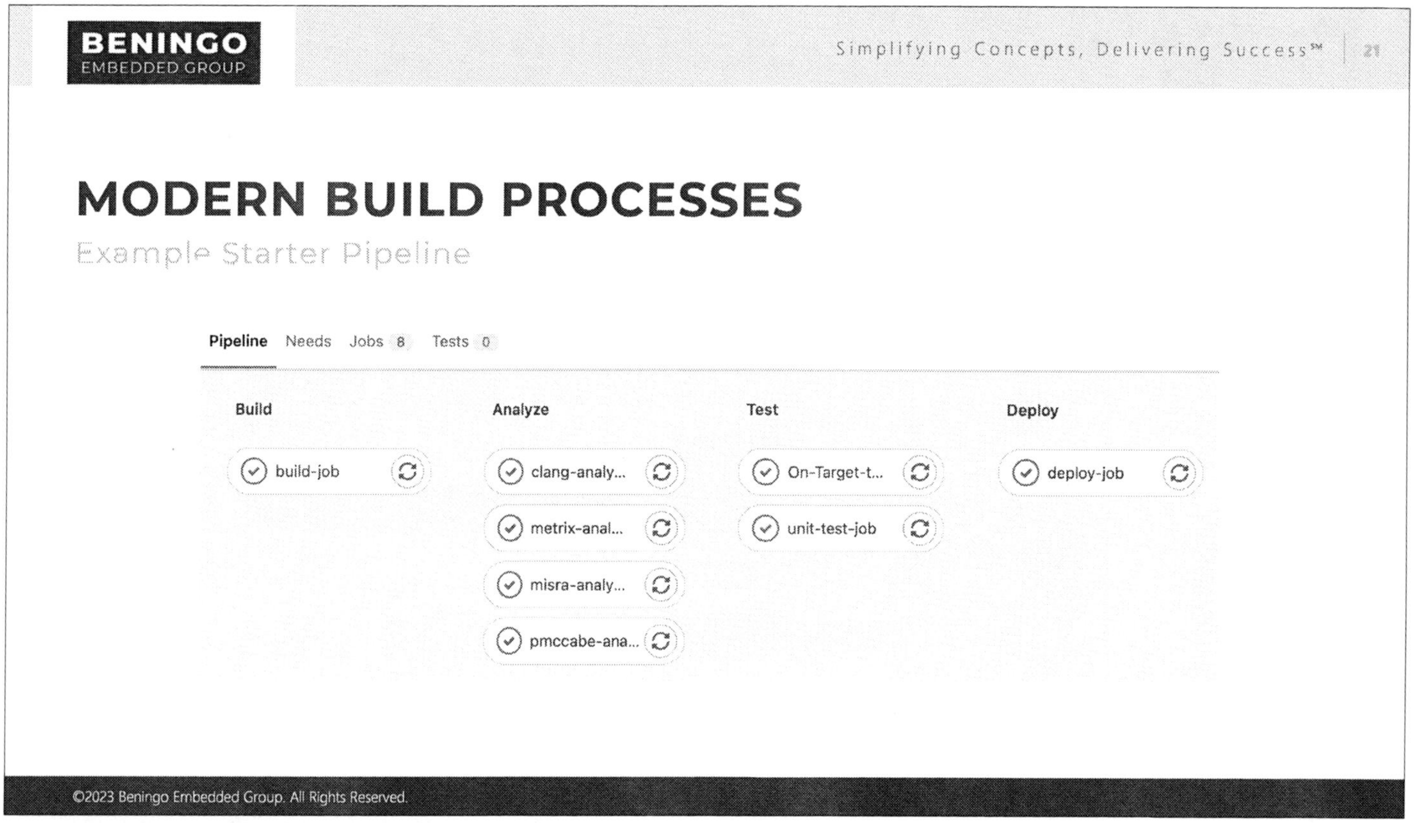
BENINGO
EMBEDDED GROUP
Simplifying Concepts, Delivering Success℠
21
MODERN BUILD PROCESSES
Example Starter Pipeline
Pipeline
Needs
Jobs 8
Tests 0
Build
Analyze
Test
Deploy
build-job
clang-analy...
On-Target-t...
deploy-job
metrix-anal...
unit-test-job
misra-analy...
pmccabe-ana...
©2023 Beningo Embedded Group. All Rights Reserved.

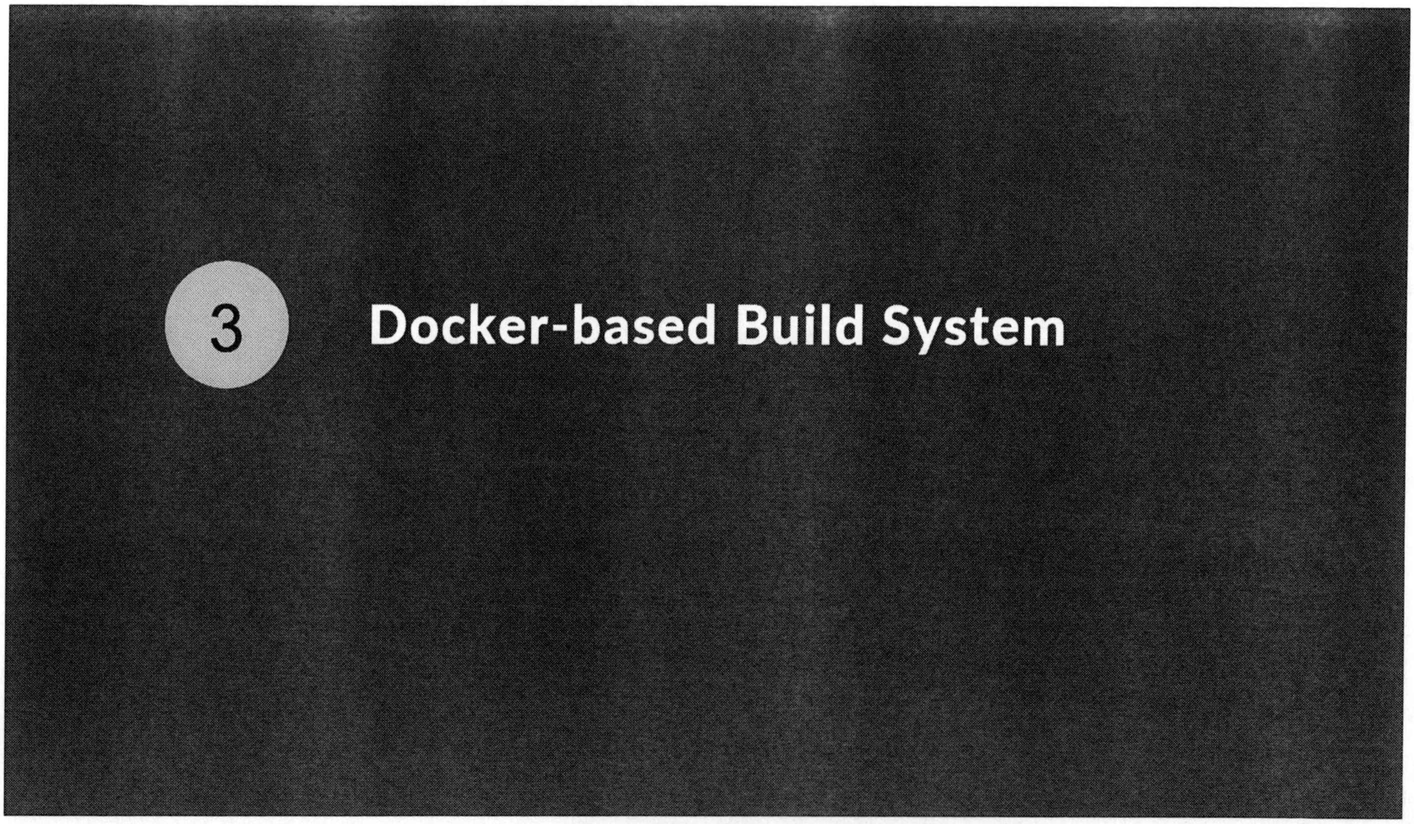
3
Docker-based Build System

BENINGO EMBEDDED GROUP

DOCKER-BASED BUILD SYSTEM

With CI/CD

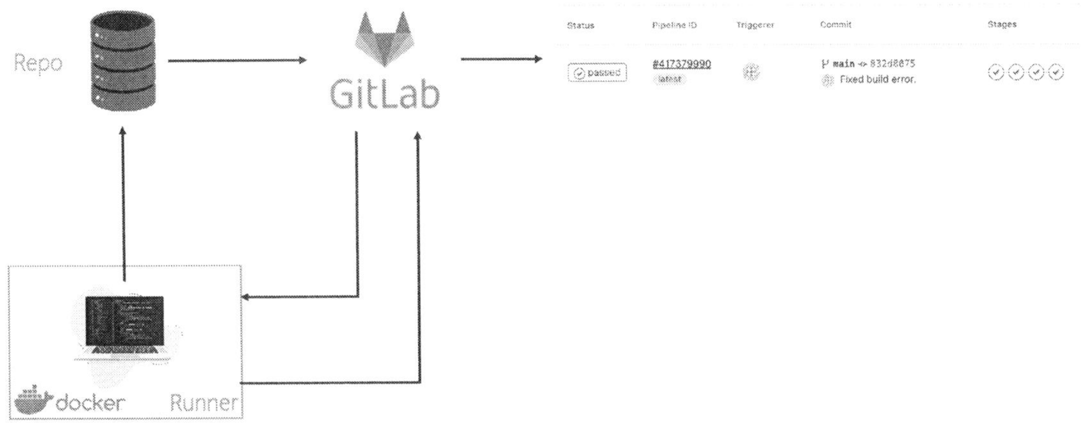

BENINGO EMBEDDED GROUP

DOCKER-BASED BUILD SYSTEM

Example Dockerfile

```
FROM ubuntu:latest
ENV REFRESHED_AT 2023-03-24

# Download Linux support tools
RUN apt-get update && \
    apt-get clean &&  \
    apt-get install -y autoconf && \
    apt-get install -y libtool && \
    apt-get install -y \
        build-essential \
        wget \
        curl \
        git  \
    python3 python-setuptools python3 python3-pip python3-setuptools

# Set up a development tools directory
WORKDIR /home/dev
ADD . /home/dev

# Install the arm toolchain and C++ support
RUN apt-get install -y --no-install-recommends gcc-arm-none-eabi
ENV PATH $PATH:/home/dev/gcc-arm-none/bin
RUN apt-get install -y --no-install-recommends libstdc++-arm-none-eabi-newlib
```

```
# Download Static analyzer and formatting tools
RUN apt-get install -y clang clang-tools clang-format clang-tidy cppcheck
RUN pip install cpplint

# Metric analyzers and code coverage tools
RUN apt-get install -y pmccabe
RUN pip install metrixpp
RUN pip install gcovr

# Install the debugging tools
RUN apt-get install -y --no-install-recommends stlink-tools

# Install doxygen and graphviz for documentation
RUN apt-get install -y doxygen graphviz

# Clean up
RUN apt-get clean all
```

DOCKER-BASED BUILD SYSTEM

Dockerfile with Test Harness

```
# Install and configure CppUTest
WORKDIR /home/cpputest

RUN git clone --depth 1 --branch v4.0 https://github.com/cpputest/cpputest.git .
RUN autoreconf . -i
RUN ./configure
RUN make install

ENV CPPUTEST_HOME=/home/cpputest

# Set our working directory back to app
WORKDIR /home/app
```


3 Tuning Up Your Design Cycle

TUNING UP YOUR DESIGN CYCLE

Development is Dynamic not Static

A simple process:

1. Identify your ideal build, CI/CD, and processes
2. Audit where you are today
3. Define a roadmap to your ideal design cycle

Important Notes:

- Will require a lot of thought
- May require outside assistance
- Will be evolutionary
- Won't be accomplished in the short term

QUESTIONS

THANK YOU

BENINGO
EMBEDDED GROUP

Sensors Converge

The Best Defense is Offensive Programming

June 20–22, 2023 | Santa Clara, CA

#SensorsConverge

Tyler Hoffman
Co-Founder & VP Developer Experience, MemFault

Tyler Hoffman

Co-Founder and VP of Developer Experience, Memfault

- I love developer tools, primarily for embedded engineers
- Previously: Firmware Engineer @ Pebble, FitBit
- I write on Memfault's Interrupt blog and give talks
- https://interrupt.memfault.com

fitbit pebble Memfault

#SensorsConverge

Sensors Converge

Does this look **Familiar?**

```
void process_something(sData *data) {
    uint8_t *buf = malloc(256);
    if (buf == NULL) {
        LOG("Malloc failed");
        return;
    }
}
```

#SensorsConverge

It's defensive, **but poorly done**

```
void process_something(sData *data) {
    uint8_t *buf = malloc(256);
    if (buf == NULL) {
        LOG("Malloc failed");
        return;
    }
}
```

- Pretends like it's recoverable
- Requires implementation knowledge
- Often leads to silent failures and confusion
- *Someone* has to eventually deal with the error. Maybe your future self.

#SensorsConverge

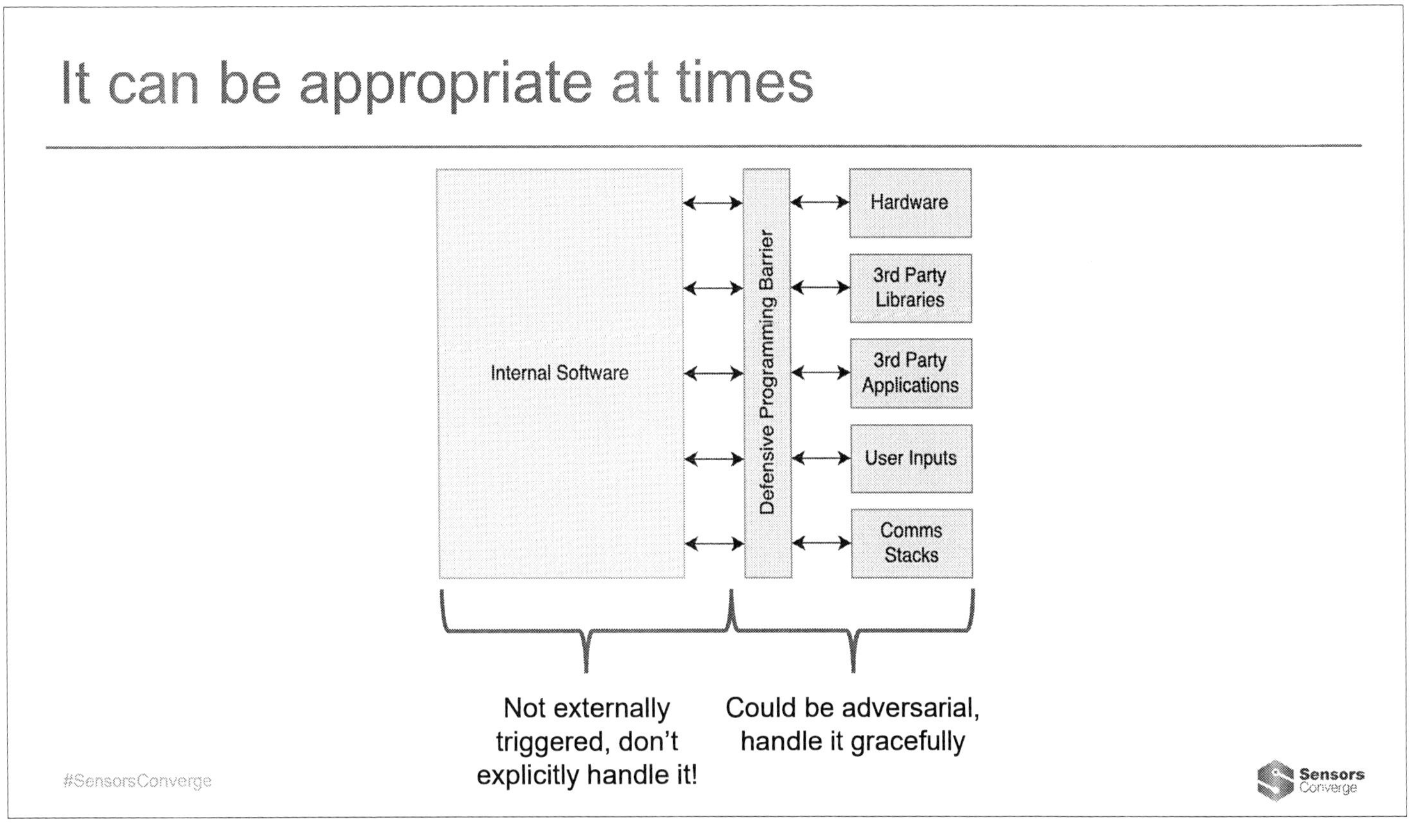
It can be appropriate at times
Internal Software
Defensive Programming Barrier
Hardware
3rd Party Libraries
3rd Party Applications
User Inputs
Comms Stacks
Not externally triggered, don't explicitly handle it!
Could be adversarial, handle it gracefully
#SensorsConverge
Sensors Converge

#1 takeaway from this talk
int do_something(void) {
uint8_t *buf = malloc(128);
if (buf == NULL) {
return -1;
}
}
void do_something(void) {
uint8_t *buf = malloc(128);
ASSERT(buf != NULL);
}

Agenda

1. What is Offensive Programming?
2. Production Usage
3. Examples
4. Best Practices

#SensorsConverge

Sensors Converge

What is Offensive Programming?

Offensive Programming

```
void do_something(void) {
    uint8_t *buf = malloc(128);
    ASSERT(buf != NULL);
}
```

Raise errors immediately – and loudly

https://interrupt.memfault.com/blog/asserts-in-embedded-systems

Internal Software Modules

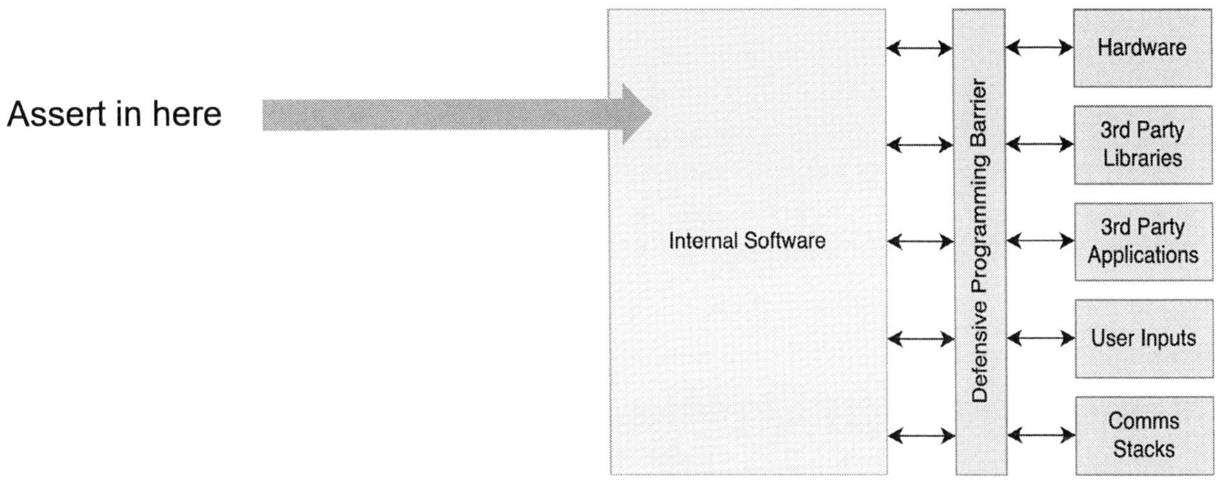

Internal Software Modules

Drivers	RTOS	Algorithms
BLE Application	GUI	Protocols
Services	Resource Management	State Machines

Majority of the software stack is in our control

#SensorsConverge

Sensors Converge

Reasons to use Assert

- Infinitely better than documentation
- Asserts provide breadcrumbs (file & line number)
- Raise alarms close to the root issue
- Safest thing to do in undefined state is to reset
- You control the assert handler
- Capture extra data, logs, a coredump. Anything!

```
void do_something(void) {
    uint8_t *buf = malloc(128);
    ASSERT(buf != NULL);
}
```

Fail fast! – especially during development and testing

#SensorsConverge

Sensors Converge

What you should assert on

Program Error

- Invalid arguments
- Out-of-order API calls

Undefined Behavior

- Memory corruption
- Security issues

Resource Exhaustion

- Malloc failures
- Stack overflow

Performance

- Queues full
- Watchdog timers

Many of these are very difficult to reproduce

#SensorsConverge

Sensors Converge

Wait a minute... ASSERT? Liberally?!

Yes. Even in production (most of the time)

The problem is that our devices are now resetting with no debugger attached.

That's where Memfault comes in...

Production Usage

Production Environments

Every bug will surface in production

- 1 in 10,000 bugs are real
- Production has the greatest matrix of test cases
- Log if assertions aren't possible in some cases
- **Diagnostics need to be collected**

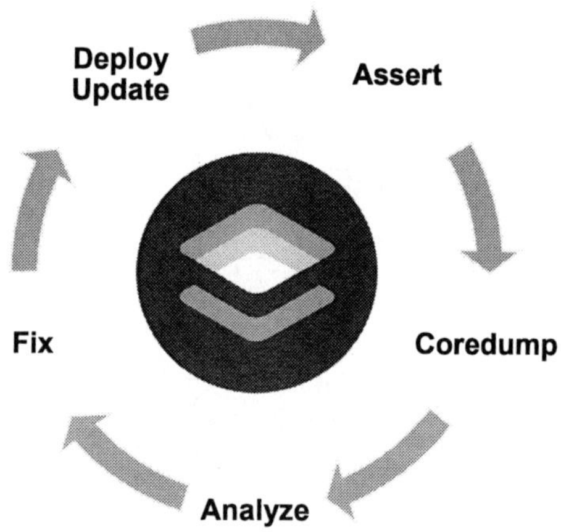

Offensive Programming + Diagnostics = Quicker Fixes

#SensorsConverge

Sensors Converge

Prerequisites for Production

Diagnostics & monitoring is a requirement

- [x] Basic telemetry & logging
- [x] Proper fault handling
- [x] Assert implementation
- [x] Some path to receive error data
- [x] Devices can firmware update

Memfault

Logs, Metrics, Crashes

Memfault SDK

#SensorsConverge

Sensors Converge

What to capture on an assert

- File and line number of the assert
- Expression value (if configured to do so)

- Backtrace of the asserted task
- Arguments and variables within the call stack
- Global and static variable values
- State of all data structures (heap, queues, etc.)

Debugger attached
or
Memfault

#SensorsConverge

Sensors Converge

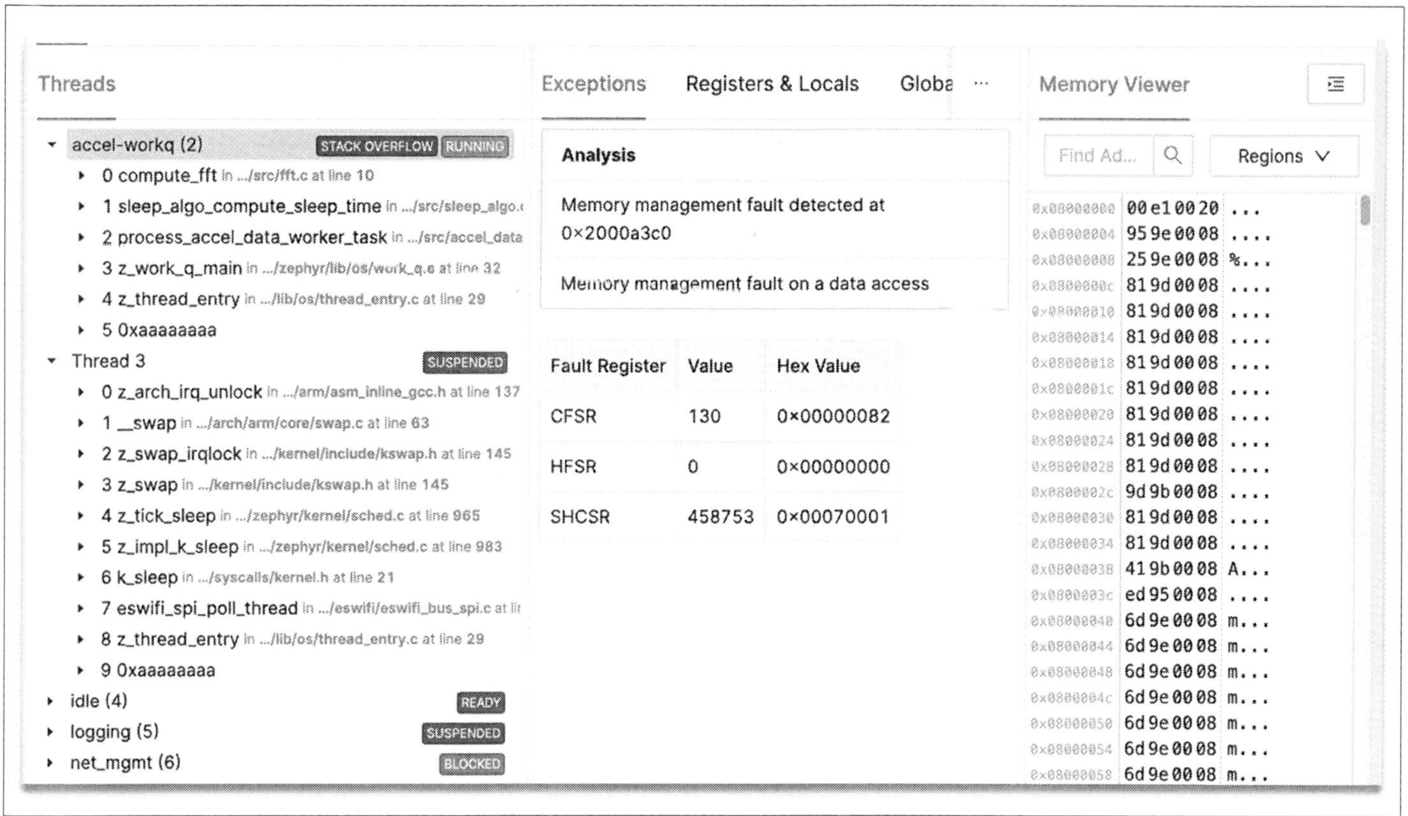
Threads
accel-workq (2) STACK OVERFLOW RUNNING
0 compute_fft in .../src/fft.c at line 10
1 sleep_algo_compute_sleep_time in .../src/sleep_algo.c
2 process_accel_data_worker_task in .../src/accel_data
3 z_work_q_main in .../zephyr/lib/os/work_q.c at line 32
4 z_thread_entry in .../lib/os/thread_entry.c at line 29
5 0xaaaaaaaa
Thread 3 SUSPENDED
0 z_arch_irq_unlock in .../arm/asm_inline_gcc.h at line 137
1 __swap in .../arch/arm/core/swap.c at line 63
2 z_swap_irqlock in .../kernel/include/kswap.h at line 145
3 z_swap in .../kernel/include/kswap.h at line 145
4 z_tick_sleep in .../zephyr/kernel/sched.c at line 965
5 z_impl_k_sleep in .../zephyr/kernel/sched.c at line 983
6 k_sleep in .../syscalls/kernel.h at line 21
7 eswifi_spi_poll_thread in .../eswifi/eswifi_bus_spi.c at li
8 z_thread_entry in .../lib/os/thread_entry.c at line 29
9 0xaaaaaaaa
idle (4) READY
logging (5) SUSPENDED
net_mgmt (6) BLOCKED
Exceptions
Registers & Locals
Globa
Analysis
Memory management fault detected at 0x2000a3c0
Memory management fault on a data access
Fault Register
Value
Hex Value
CFSR 130 0x00000082
HFSR 0 0x00000000
SHCSR 458753 0x00070001
Memory Viewer
Find Ad...
Regions
00e10020 ...
959e0008 ....
259e0008 %...
819d0008 ....
819d0008 ....
819d0008 ....
819d0008 ....
819d0008 ....
819d0008 ....
819d0008 ....
819d0008 ....
9d9b0008 ....
819d0008 ....
819d0008 ....
419b0008 A...
ed950008 ....
6d9e0008 m...
6d9e0008 m...
6d9e0008 m...
6d9e0008 m...
6d9e0008 m...
6d9e0008 m...
6d9e0008 m...

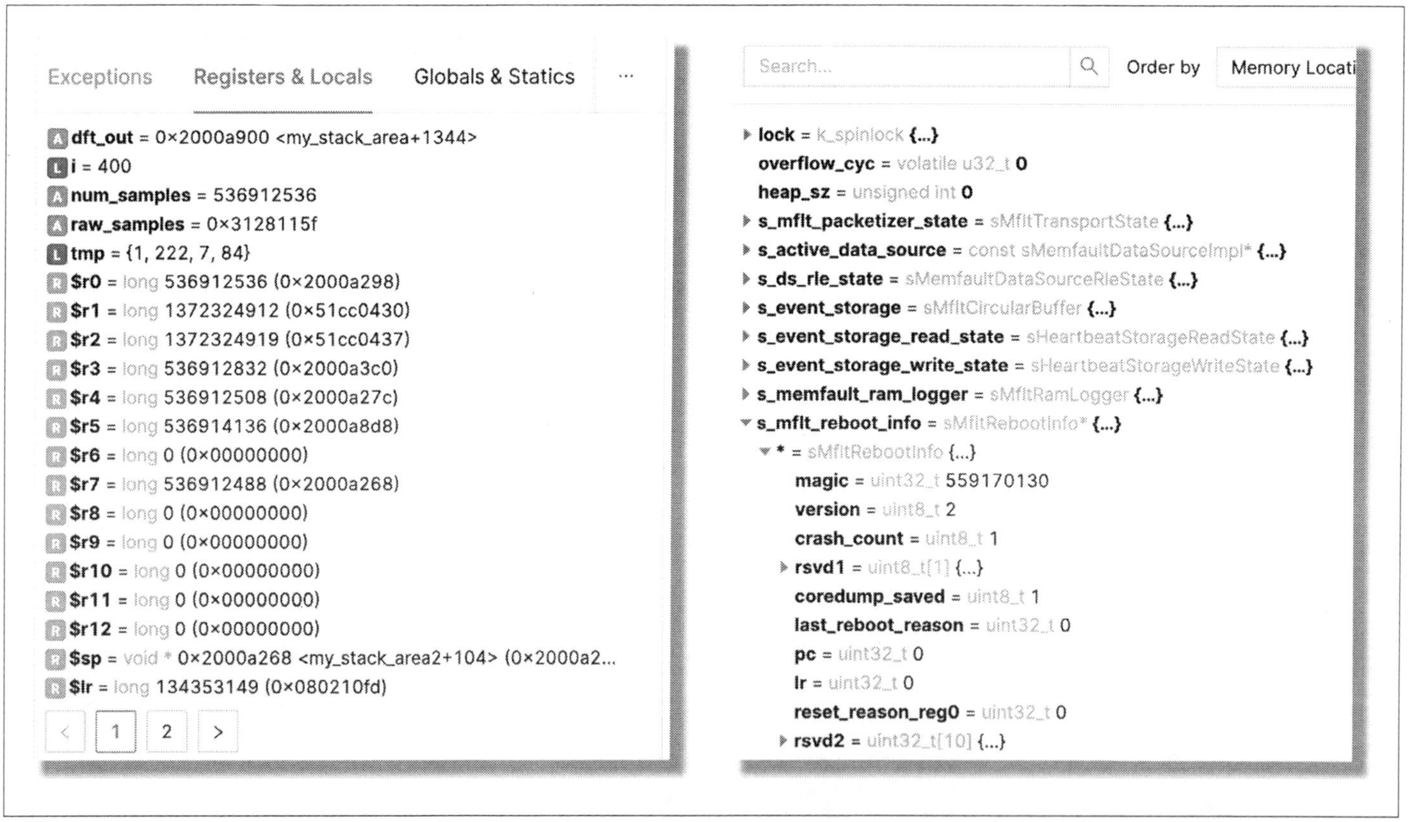
Exceptions
Registers & Locals
Globals & Statics
dft_out = 0x2000a900 <my_stack_area+1344>
i = 400
num_samples = 536912536
raw_samples = 0x3128115f
tmp = {1, 222, 7, 84}
$r0 = long 536912536 (0x2000a298)
$r1 = long 1372324912 (0x51cc0430)
$r2 = long 1372324919 (0x51cc0437)
$r3 = long 536912832 (0x2000a3c0)
$r4 = long 536912508 (0x2000a27c)
$r5 = long 536914136 (0x2000a8d8)
$r6 = long 0 (0x00000000)
$r7 = long 536912488 (0x2000a268)
$r8 = long 0 (0x00000000)
$r9 = long 0 (0x00000000)
$r10 = long 0 (0x00000000)
$r11 = long 0 (0x00000000)
$r12 = long 0 (0x00000000)
$sp = void * 0x2000a268 <my_stack_area2+104> (0x2000a2...
$lr = long 134353149 (0x080210fd)
1 2
Search...
Order by
Memory Locati
lock = k_spinlock {...}
overflow_cyc = volatile u32_t 0
heap_sz = unsigned int 0
s_mflt_packetizer_state = sMfltTransportState {...}
s_active_data_source = const sMemfaultDataSourceImpl* {...}
s_ds_rle_state = sMemfaultDataSourceRleState {...}
s_event_storage = sMfltCircularBuffer {...}
s_event_storage_read_state = sHeartbeatStorageReadState {...}
s_event_storage_write_state = sHeartbeatStorageWriteState {...}
s_memfault_ram_logger = sMfltRamLogger {...}
s_mflt_reboot_info = sMfltRebootInfo* {...}
* = sMfltRebootInfo {...}
magic = uint32_t 559170130
version = uint8_t 2
crash_count = uint8_t 1
rsvd1 = uint8_t[1] {...}
coredump_saved = uint8_t 1
last_reboot_reason = uint32_t 0
pc = uint32_t 0
lr = uint32_t 0
reset_reason_reg0 = uint32_t 0
rsvd2 = uint32_t[10] {...}

Offensive Programming Examples

With Memfault as your "debugger"

Argument Validation

```
void device_set_name(char *name,
                     size_t name_len) {
  ASSERT(name && name_len <= 32);
  ...
}

bool device_get_name(char **buf,
                     size_t buf_len) {
  ASSERT(buf && buf_len >= 32);
  ...
}
```

Developer errors → Raise the alarm immediately

Argument Validation

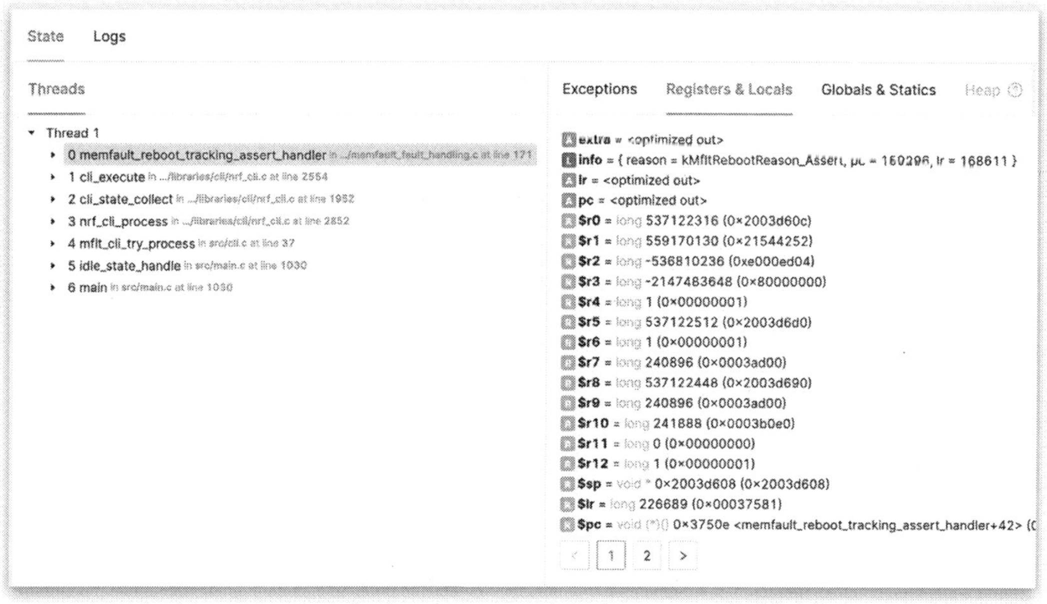

State machine transition errors

```
void on_commit(eState prev_state) {
  ASSERT(prev_state == kState_Flushing
      || prev_state == kState_Idle);
}
```

Ensure that states happen in order and as expected

Malloc returns NULL

```
void *malloc_assert(size_t n) {
  void *p = malloc(n)
  ASSERT(p);
  return p;
  ...
}
```

For allocations that should never fail

Likely means a memory leak

#SensorsConverge

Sensors Converge

Memfault Memory View

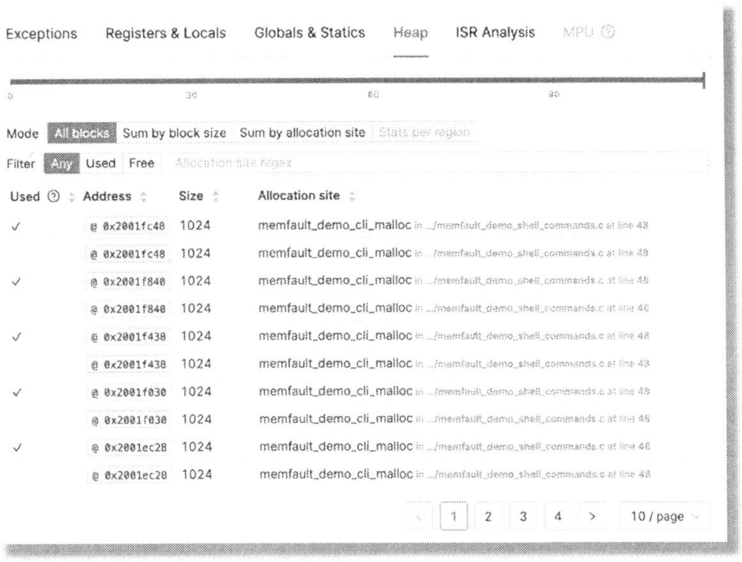

#SensorsConverge

Sensors Converge

Full Queue

```
void critical_event(void) {
  ...
  const bool success =
      xQueueSend(q, &item, 1000 /* wait 1s */)
  ASSERT(success);
  ...
}
```

Track down performance issues using a timeout

#SensorsConverge

Sensors Converge

Resource Depletion – full queue

```
(gdb) queue_print s_event_queue
-----
Queue Status: 10/10 events in queue (FULL!)
0: Addr: 0x200070c0, event: BLE_PACKET
1: Addr: 0x200070a8, event: TICK_EVENT
2: Addr: 0x20007088, event: BLE_PACKET
3: Addr: 0x20007070, event: BLE_PACKET
4: Addr: 0x20007050, event: BLE_PACKET
5: Addr: 0x20007038, event: BLE_PACKET
6: Addr: 0x20007018, event: BLE_PACKET
7: Addr: 0x20007000, event: BLE_PACKET
8: Addr: 0x20006fe0, event: BLE_PACKET
9: Addr: 0x20006fc8, event: BLE_PACKET
```

Weren't processing BLE packets fast enough

#SensorsConverge

Sensors Converge

Detecting software stalls

```
void timing_sensitive_task(void) {
  const bool success =
      mutex_lock(&s_mutex, 1000 /* 1 second */);
  ASSERT(success);
  {
    ...
  }
}
```

Fail if mutex not grabbed in reasonable time

#SensorsConverge

Sensors Converge

Detecting software stalls

```
void timing_sensitive_task(void) {
  // Task watchdog will assert a stall
  mutex_lock(&s_mutex, INFINITY);
  {
    ...
  }
}
```

Let the software watchdog detect the stall

#SensorsConverge

Sensors Converge

Detecting software stalls

#SensorsConverge

Sensors Converge

Stack Overflow Detection

Many RTOS's have this built-in now. Double check yours!

https://embeddedartistry.com/blog/2020/05/18/implementing-stack-smashing-protection-for-microcontrollers-and-embedded-artistrys-libc/

https://www.freertos.org/Stacks-and-stack-overflow-checking.html

https://docs.zephyrproject.org/latest/reference/usermode/memory_domain.html#hardware-stack-overflow

#SensorsConverge

Sensors Converge

Failing even faster: Compile-time errors

```
typedef struct PACKED {
  uint32_t count;
  uint8_t buf[12];
  uint8_t new_value; // ADDED
} MyStruct;

_Static_assert(sizeof(MyStruct) <= 16, "Oops, too large!");
```

```
$ gcc test.c
test.c:14:1: error: static_assert failed due to requirement
    'sizeof(MyStruct) <= 16' "Oops, too large!"

_Static_assert(sizeof(MyStruct) <= 16, "Oops, too large!");
^              ~~~~~~~~~~~~~~~~~~~~~~~
1 error generated.
```

#SensorsConverge

Sensors Converge

Best Practices

Watch out for boot loops

Boot loop detection is a must

- You control the assert handler
- Capture extra data, logs, a coredump. Anything!
- Don't assert on boot
- Count # reboots within time interval
- Boot into safe mode
- Only FWUP, diagnostics pull, and factory reset

https://interrupt.memfault.com/blog/device-firmware-update-cookbook

#SensorsConverge

Sensors Converge

Build asserts into wrappers

```
void *malloc_assert(size_t size) {
    uint8_t *buf = malloc(128);
    ASSERT(buf != NULL);

    /* Collect breadcrumbs */

    return buf;
}
```

Clean and simple

#SensorsConverge

Sensors Converge

Debug builds are your friend

Internal testing is the best kind of testing

On internal builds:

- Enable more aggressive asserting
- Tighten timeout durations
- Send builds to small groups externally
- Test. Experiment. Try things. Be creative.

- Every Pebble internal firmware build

#SensorsConverge

Sensors Converge

Takeaways

- Don't play defense against bugs
- Fail fast and capture data
- Test internally as much as possible
- Keep asserts in production
- We at Memfault would love to help

#SensorsConverge

Sensors Converge

Thank You!

- memfault.com
- twitter.com/memfault
- linkedin.com/company/Memfault
- interrupt.memfault.com
- **We're hiring!**

Memfault

#SensorsConverge

Sensors Converge

Questions?

802.11ah - HaLow

June 2023

NEWRACOM

802.11ah HaLow

STANDARD & SPECIFICATION

IEEE 802.11 IEEE 802.11ah

CERTIFICATION & PROMOTION

HaLow Wi-Fi Alliance

Characteristics of IEEE 802.11ah HaLow

Frequency Band	License-exempt bands below 1 GHz, excluding the TV white spaces – Example: 863-868.6 MHz (Europe), 915.9 -928.1 MHz (Japan), 755-787 MHz (China), 917- 923.5 MHz (Korea), 866-869 MHz, 920-925 MHz (Singapore), and 902-928 MHz (U.S.)
Channel Width	1/2/4/8/16 MHz
Range	1Km + (outdoor)
End Node Transmit Power	Dependent on regional regulations (from 1 mW to 1 W)
Data Rate	150 Kbps ~ 346.666 Mbps
Devices per Access Point	8,191
Standard Body	IEEE 802.11 working group
Topology	Star, Tree

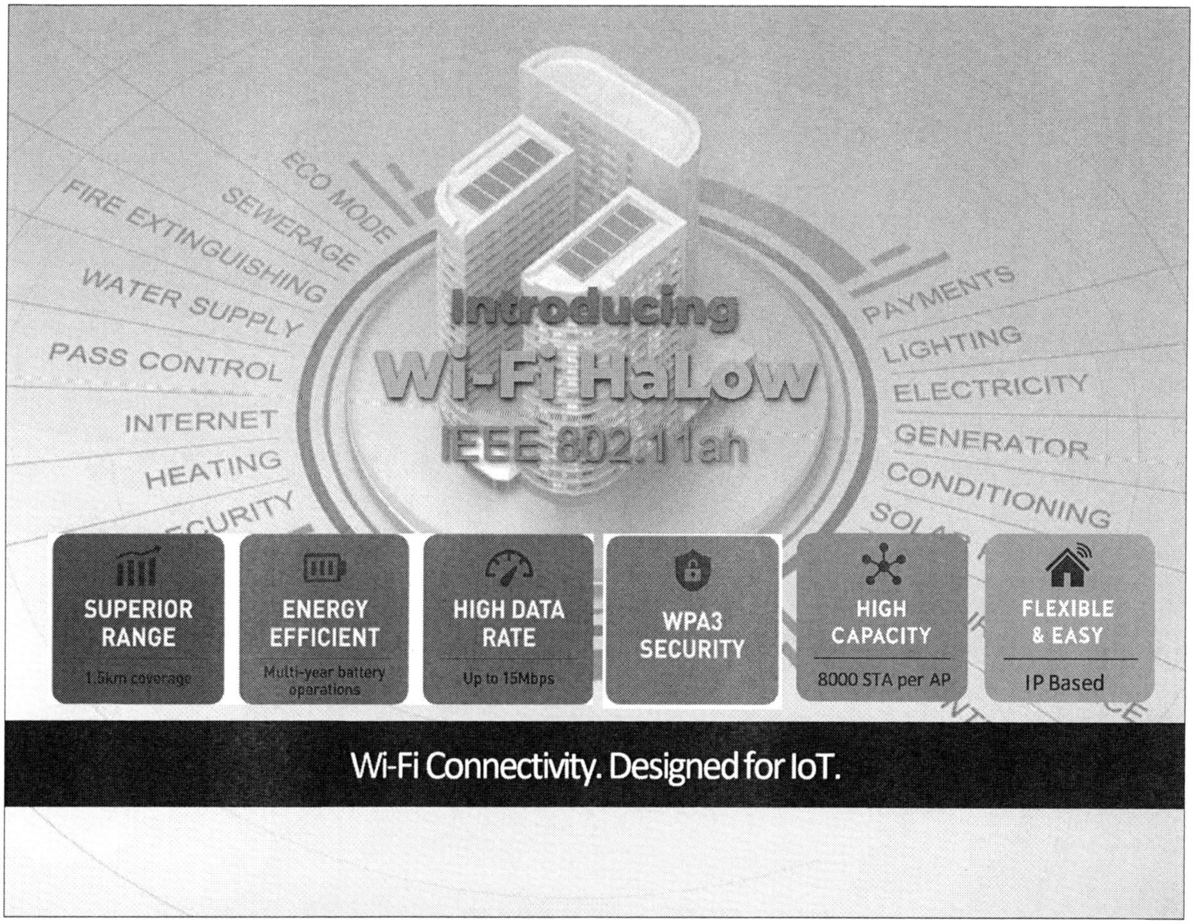
ECO MODE
SEWERAGE
FIRE EXTINGUISHING
WATER SUPPLY
PASS CONTROL
INTERNET
HEATING
SECURITY
PAYMENTS
LIGHTING
ELECTRICITY
GENERATOR
CONDITIONING
Introducing
Wi-Fi HaLow
IEEE 802.11ah
SUPERIOR RANGE
1.5km coverage
ENERGY EFFICIENT
Multi-year battery operations
HIGH DATA RATE
Up to 15Mbps
WPA3 SECURITY
HIGH CAPACITY
8000 STA per AP
FLEXIBLE & EASY
IP Based
Wi-Fi Connectivity. Designed for IoT.

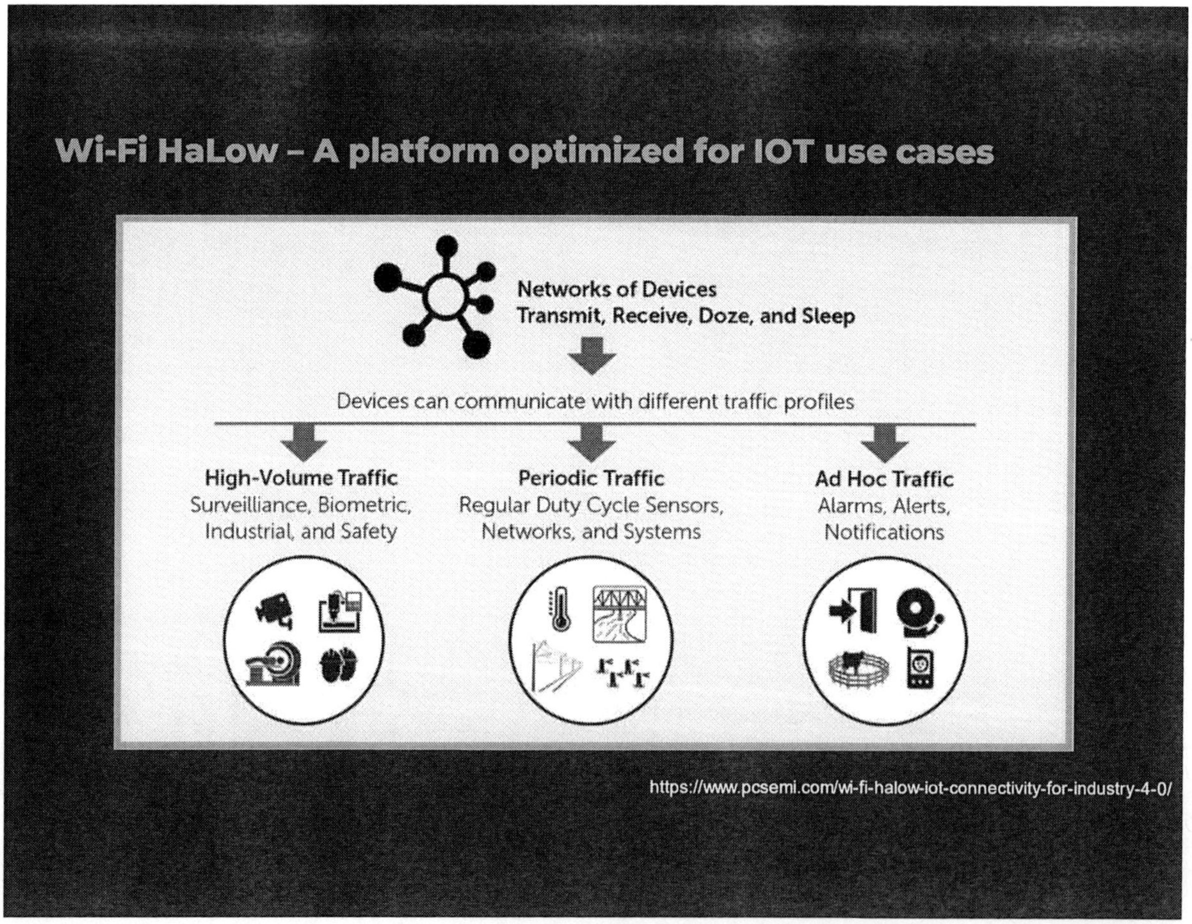
Wi-Fi HaLow – A platform optimized for IOT use cases
Networks of Devices
Transmit, Receive, Doze, and Sleep
Devices can communicate with different traffic profiles
High-Volume Traffic
Surveilliance, Biometric, Industrial, and Safety
Periodic Traffic
Regular Duty Cycle Sensors, Networks, and Systems
Ad Hoc Traffic
Alarms, Alerts, Notifications
https://www.pcsemi.com/wi-fi-halow-iot-connectivity-for-industry-4-0/

Long Range / High Thruput

NEWRACOM

IoT Comparison – Range & Data Rate

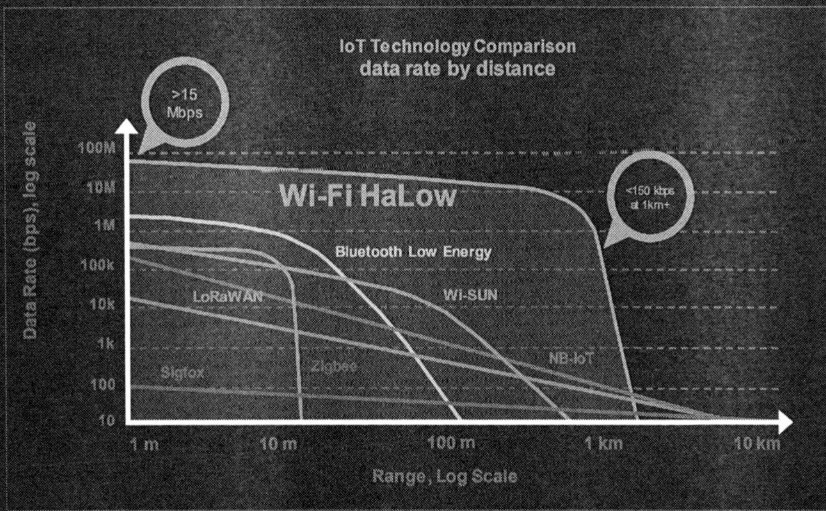

Source: 'Wi-Fi HaLow: Wi-Fi for IoT Applications' by Wi-Fi Alliance, May 2020.

5

Wi-Fi Technology Portfolio - HaLow

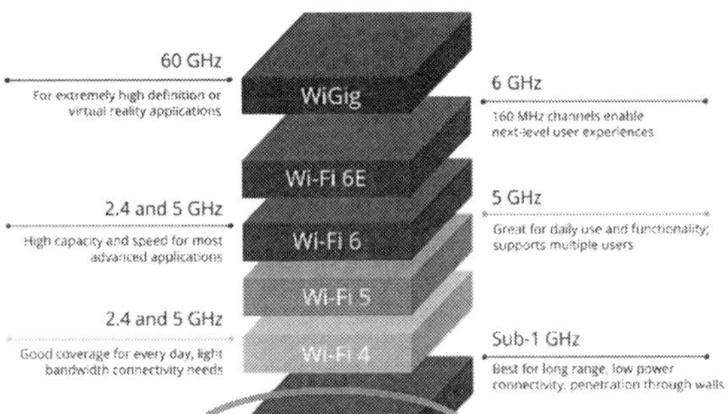

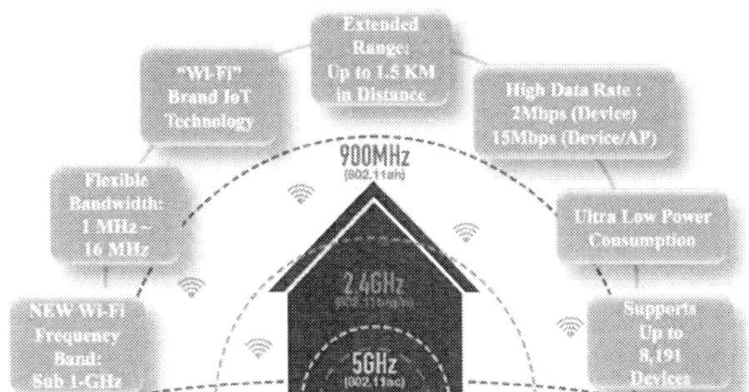

NRC7292 – Long Range

NEWRACOM

- Field Test at Business District
  - 1.79 Mbps avg. throughput @ 500m
  - 2MHz channel bandwidth
  - 922.5MHz center frequency
  - 17dBm transmit power
  - Noisy channel environment
  - Dipole antenna

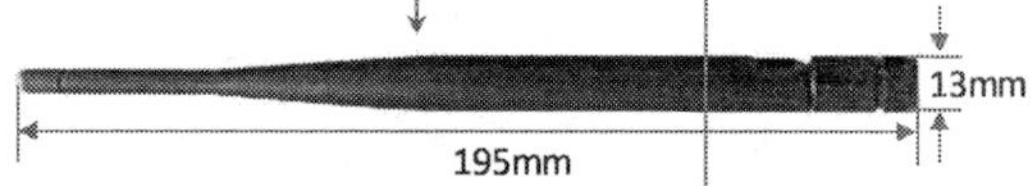

-55dBm peak RFID interference

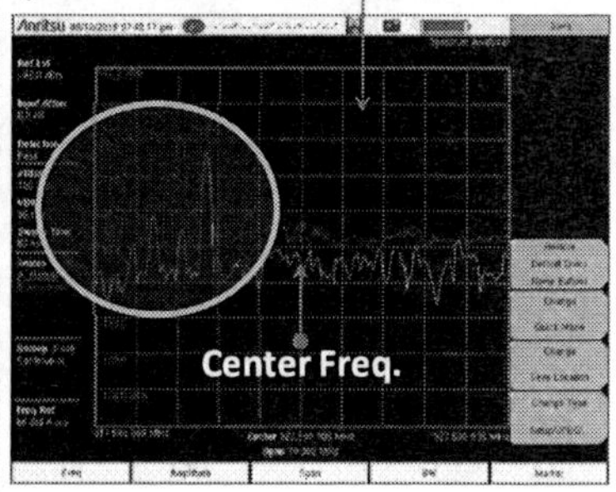

Confidential & Proprietary 7

NRC7292 – Long Range

NEWRACOM

- Field Test at Seawall
  - 2.58 Mbps avg. throughput @ 3km
  - 2MHz channel bandwidth
  - 924.5MHz center frequency
  - 17dBm transmit power
  - Low interference environment
  - PCB pattern antenna

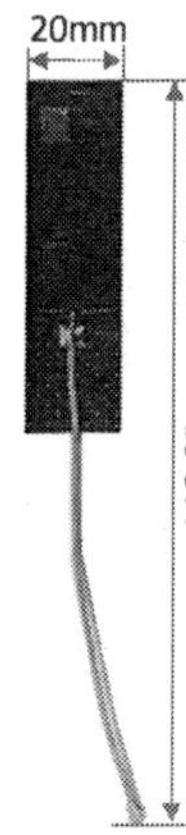

Confidential & Proprietary 8

802.11ah HaLow

NEWRACOM

- IEEE 802.11ah uses a sub-1GHz bandwidth, which allows a greater coverage of a distance up to 1.5 km while transmitting data at reasonable rates. Therefore, it is suitable for almost all IoT applications such as smart home, smart city, smart energy, smart building, smart factory and smart farm.

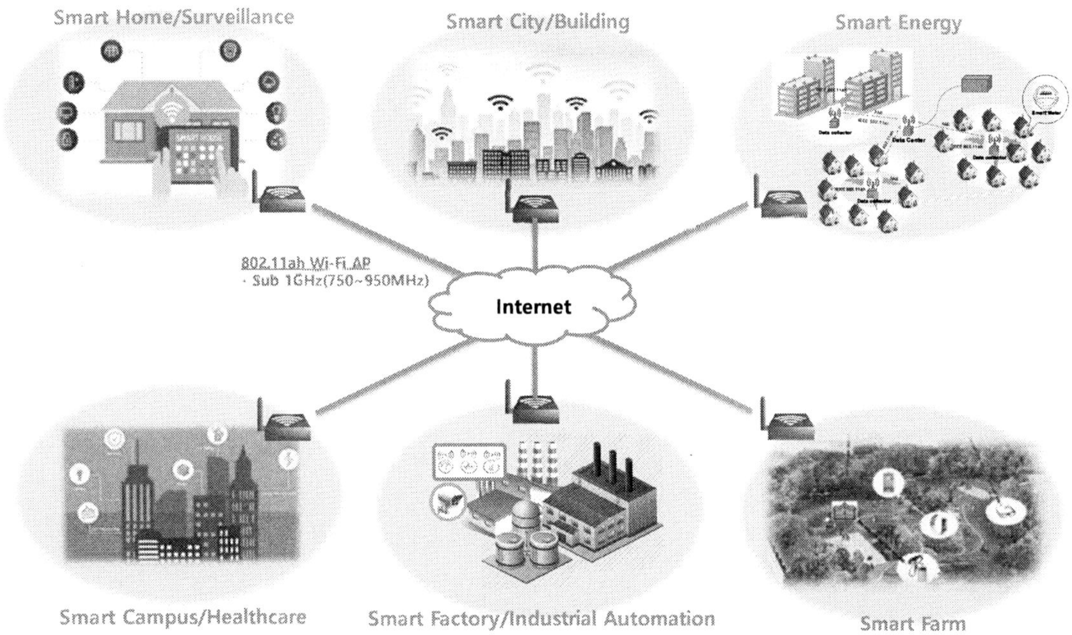

Confidential & Proprietary 9

Applications: Smart Building

NEWRACOM

- **Advantages**
  - One AP can cover about 300m distance and multiple floors
  - Simple configuration (star or tree topology)
  - Mbps throughput enable large amount of data gathering for big data analysis
  - Saving Installation cost for wired network and regular fee
- **Use Cases**
  - Building energy management system (Meters & gauges)
  - HVAC & air-conditioner
  - Various sensor devices
  - Lighting system
  - Security & surveillance system
  - Facility & equipment maintenance
  - Communication between indoor and outdoor unit
  - Backhaul network for other short-range devices (Wi-Fi, BT, Zigbee, z-wave etc.)

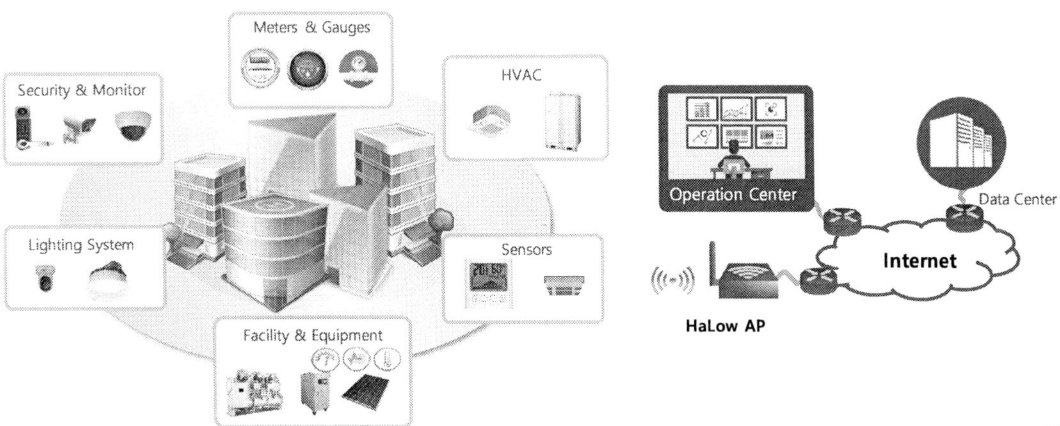

Confidential & Proprietary 10

Applications: Smart Factory

NEWRACOM

Advantages

- Coverage : 300~500m with max 1024 STA per AP
- Mbps throughput enables sensor signal data collection for big data analysis or pattern recognition
- Low latency suitable for emergency warning or failure detection

Use Cases

- Equipment and process monitoring and diagnosis
- Realtime sensor data collection (vibration, temp/humidity, strain gauge or leakage)
- Safety or security
- CCTV/Thermal camera
- Factory Energy Management System (FEMS)
- Wearable (Helmet camera, Watch, Walky-talky, etc.)

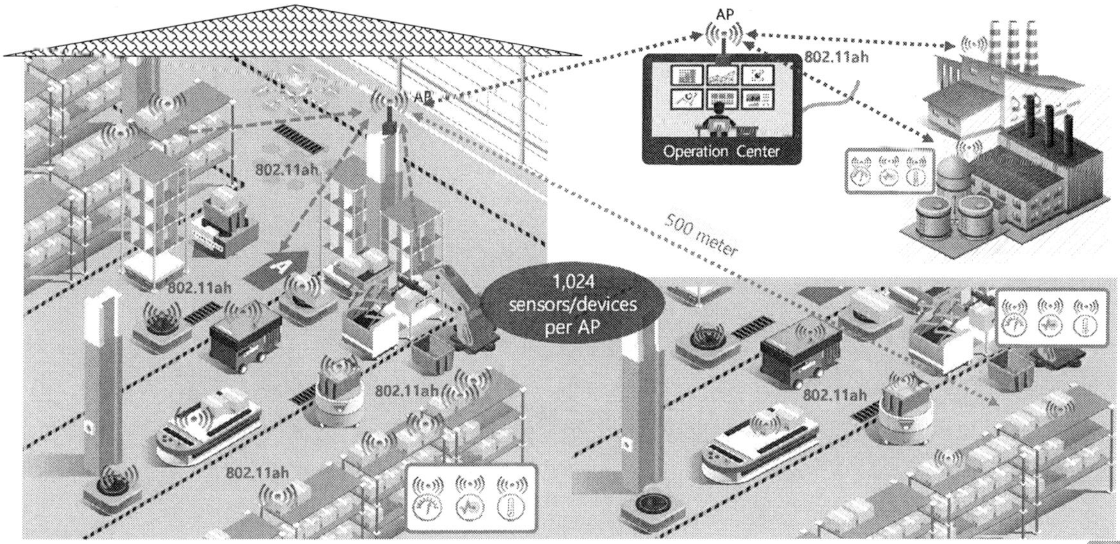

Confidential & Proprietary

11

Applications: Smart Cattle Care

NEWRACOM

Cattle Tracking & Monitoring

- IoT sensors (temperature, humidity, etc.) are implanted in the animal's skin/ear (cow, pig, lamb, etc.) for tracking and monitoring activity levels and disease with Wi-Fi HaLow-enabled tags which support extended coverage with secured data
- Keep tracking cattle's activity levels and healthy condition during the transportation process

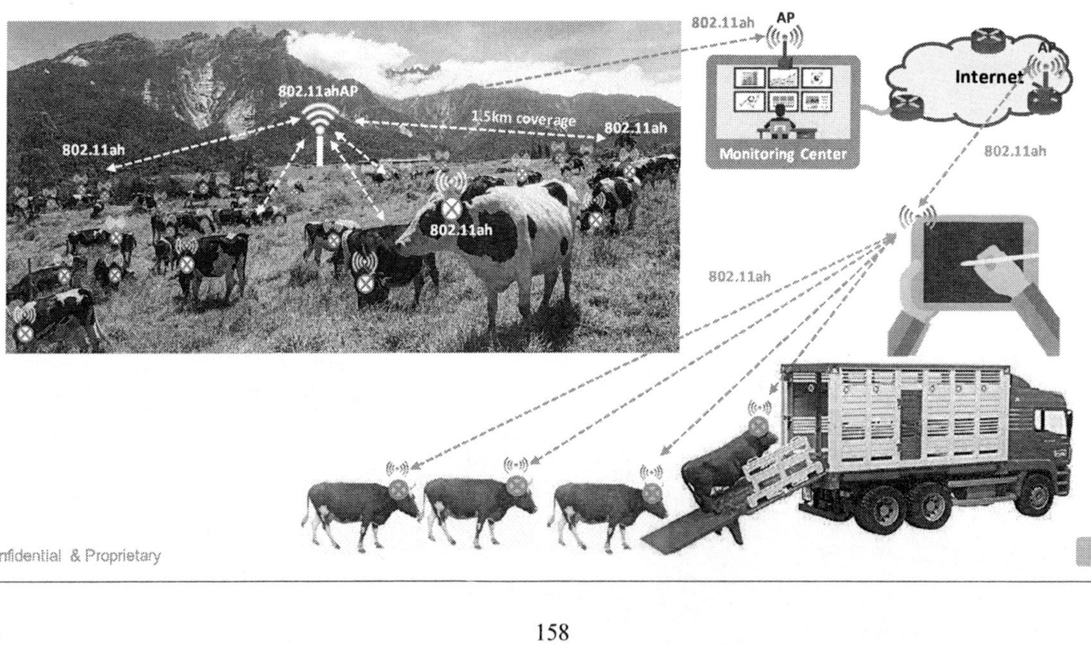

Confidential & Proprietary

12

Thank you
NEWRACOM

Sensors Converge

Matter over Wi-Fi Training Session

June 20–22, 2023 | Santa Clara, CA

#SensorsConverge

Table of contents

#SensorsConverge

Sensors Converge

Table of contents

#SensorsConverge

Sensors Converge

What is Matter?

- Matter is a unifying, IP-based connectivity protocol built on proven technologies, helping connect to and build reliable, secure IoT ecosystems.
- Simplicity, Interoperability, Reliability and Security

https://csa-iot.org/members/

csa connectivity standards alliance

#SensorsConverge

Sensors Converge

Matter Smart Home Fabric example

IKEA Dirigera

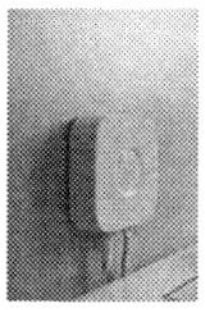

Philips Hue

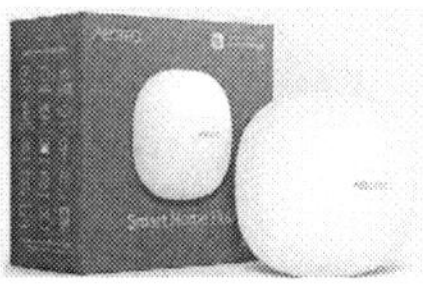

Samsung SmartThings Hub

Apple TV 4K

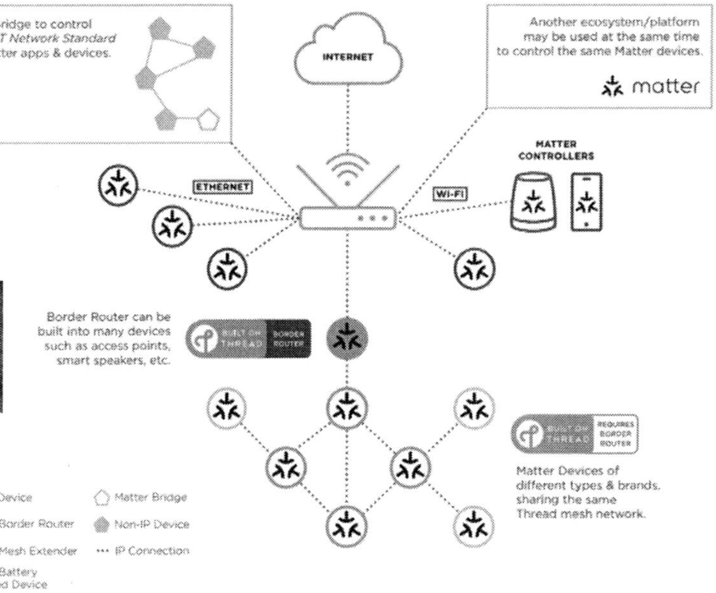

Today 90+% of Smart Speakers are Wi-Fi only

Echo Dot (Wi-Fi)

#SensorsConverge

Sensors Converge

Matter Concepts and Terminology

- **Node:** An addressable entity which supports the Matter protocol stack and has its own Operational Node ID and Node Operational credentials.
- **Fabric:** A logical collection of communicating Nodes, sharing a common root of trust, and a common distributed configuration state.
- **Commissioning:** Sequence of operations to bring a Node into a Fabric by assigning an Operational Node ID and Node Operational credentials.
- **Cluster:** A specification defining one or more attributes, commands and dependencies, that supports an independent utility or application function. The term may also be used for an implementation or instance of such a specification on an endpoint.

#SensorsConverge

Sensors Converge

Matter Concepts and Terminology (Contd.)

- Matter Onboarding Payload: It allows onboarding a device into a Matter network
  - Payload Contents:
    - Version, Vendor & Product ID, Discriminator ID, Custom Flow, Discovery Capabilities Bitmask, Discriminator Value and Passcode.
  - Payload Representation:
    - QR Code
    - Manual Entry
    - NFC Tag (v1.x)

Payload: MT:8IXS142C00KA0648G00

This QR code is unique for your device. You may print a copy of this for subsequent use.

Print QR Code

#SensorsConverge

Sensors Converge

Matter Concepts and Terminology

- Matter Ecosystem

Fabric 1

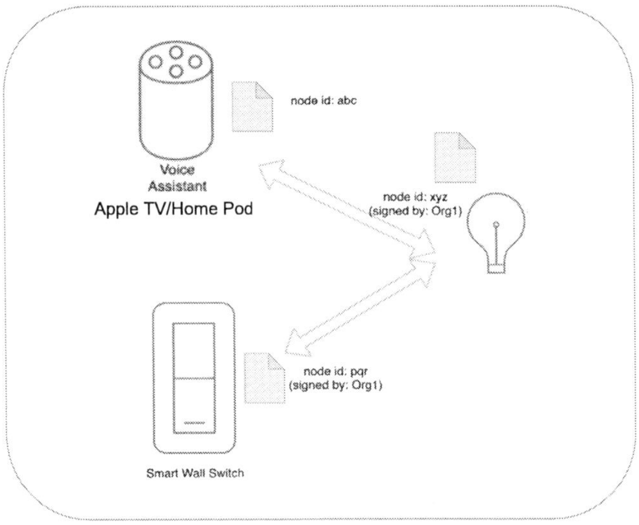

#SensorsConverge

Sensors Converge

Matter Concepts and Terminology

- Multi-Admin Control:

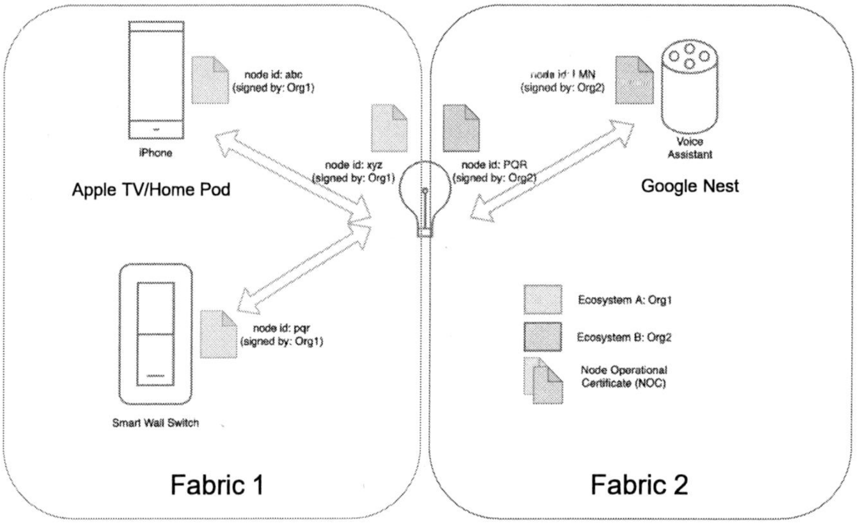

#SensorsConverge

Sensors Converge

Table of contents

#SensorsConverge

Sensors Converge

Architecture Overview of Matter

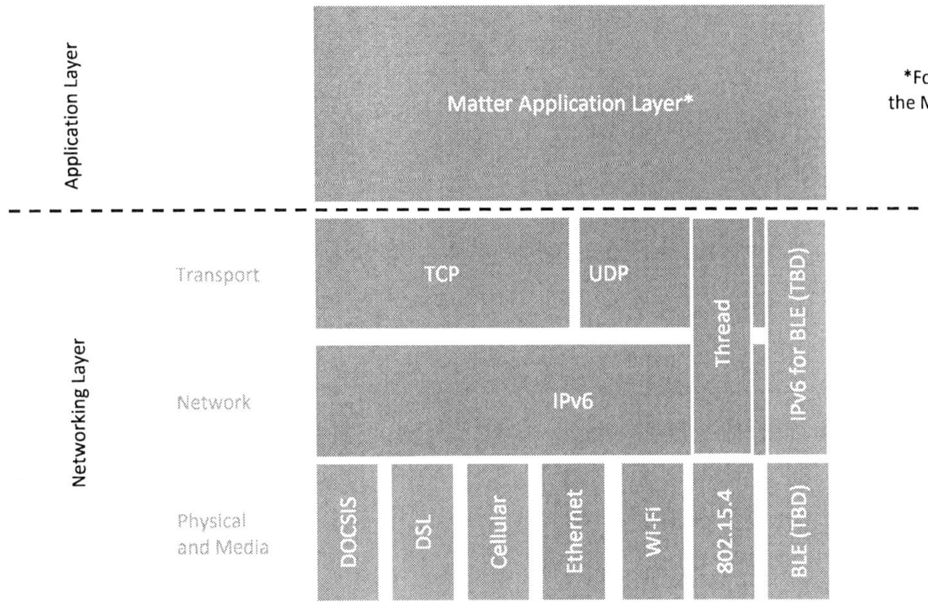

*For "Matter over Wi-Fi" solutions the Matter app layer runs on the HOST

#SensorsConverge

Sensors Converge

Table of contents

1.
2.
3. Matter Commissioning and Certification
4.
5.
6.
7.
8.

#SensorsConverge

Sensors Converge

Matter – the expected user experience

User brings a new device into Smart Home

User scans QR device with Commissioner

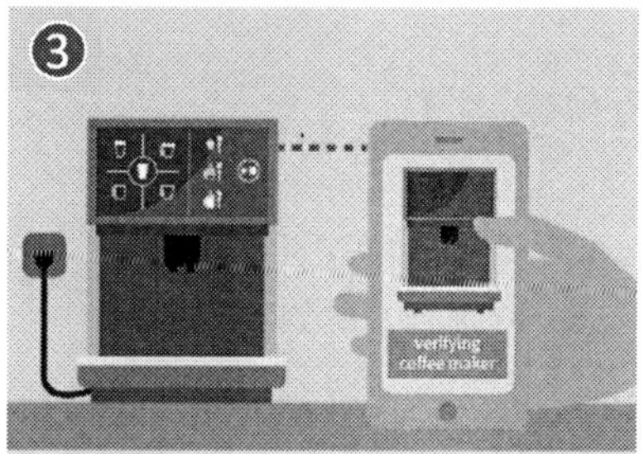

Device is verified and provisioned

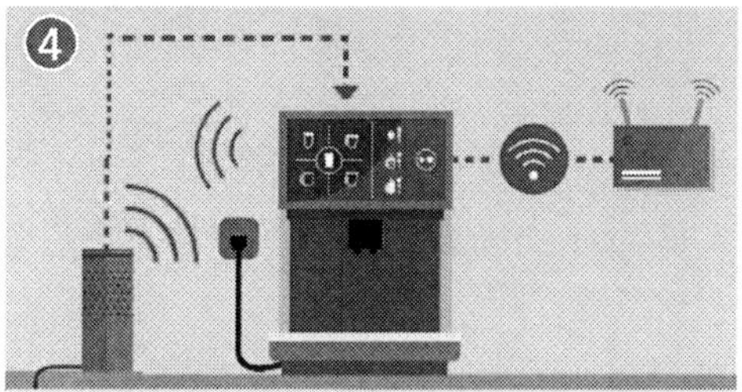

Device connects to secure home network

Device operates smoothly in Smart Home

#SensorsConverge

Sensors Converge

Matter commissioning – user view

Factory

Store

1. Device is manufactured and shipped
2. User brings device to smart home
3. User intros device to commissioner (Tablet, phone, smart speaker, etc.)
4. User initiates commissioning
5. Device is commissioned
6. Device operates smoothly in smart home

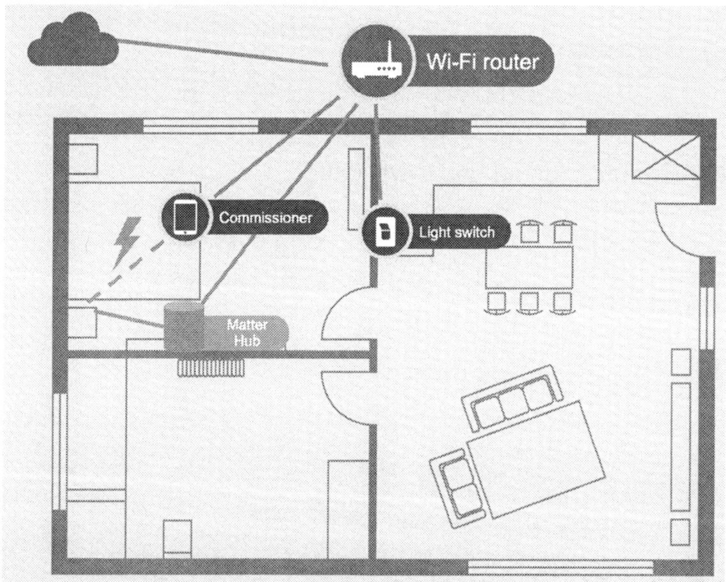

#SensorsConverge

Sensors Converge

Matter Raises the Bar for IoT security, privacy & ease-of-use

1. Easy, secured, and flexible device commissioning
2. Validation that each device is authentic and certified
3. Up-to-date info via Distributed Compliance Ledger
4. Strong device identity so only your devices can join your smart home
5. Secured unicast communications
6. Secured group communications
7. Multiple administrators and controllers, maximizing choice
8. Verified access controls to prevent unauthorized actions
9. Secured, standard software updates
10. Verification of software integrity

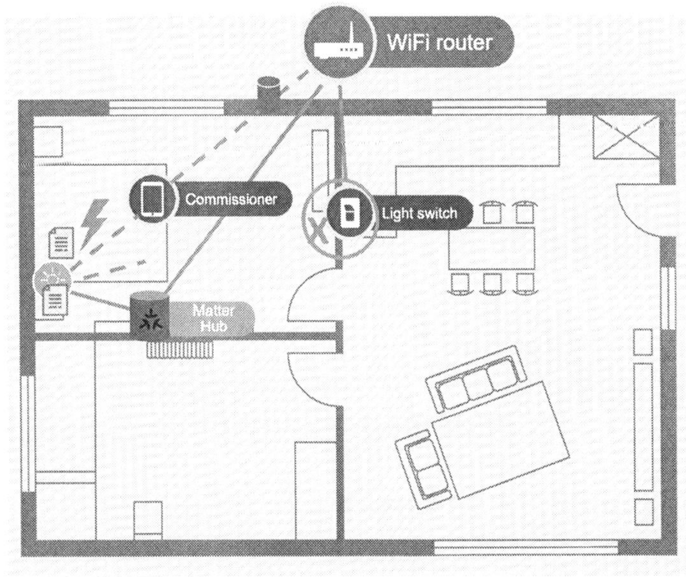

#SensorsConverge

Sensors Converge

Matter Device Pairing Flow

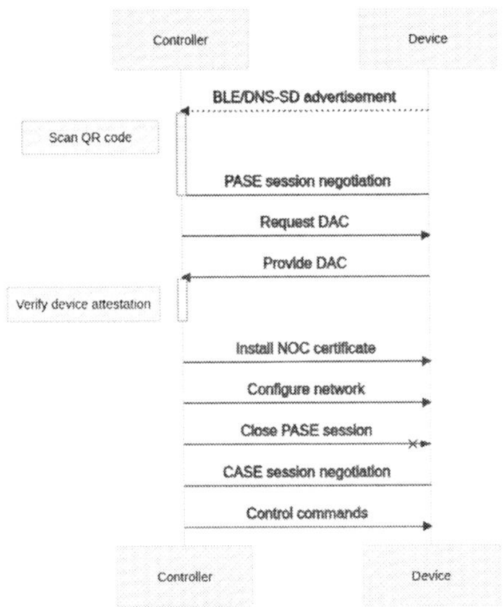

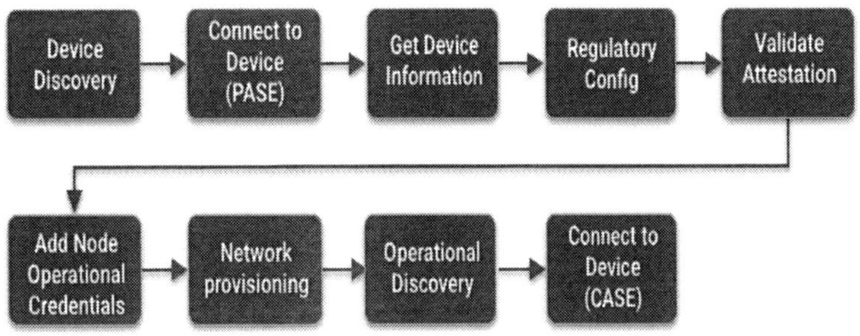

- DNS-SD- Domain Name System- Service Discovery
- PASE- Passcode Authenticated Session Establishment
- DAC- Device Attestation Certificate
- NOC- Node Operational Certificate
- CASE- Certificate Authenticated Session Establishment

#SensorsConverge

Sensors Converge

Matter PKI – Customer Pain Points lead to Integrated Solution Opportunity

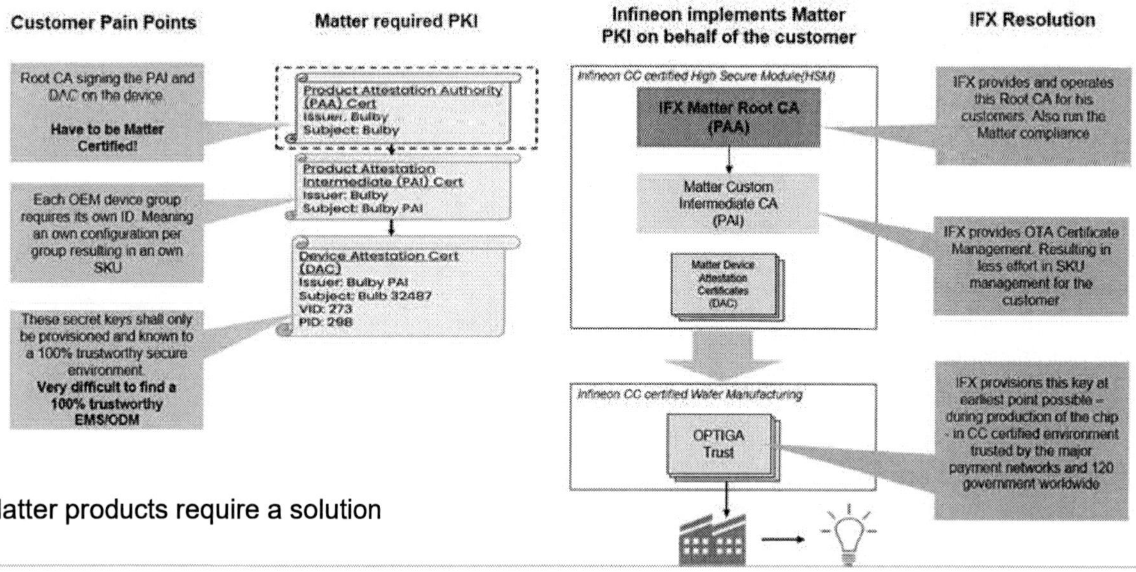

All Matter products require a solution

#SensorsConverge

Sensors Converge

Matter Commissioning – Part of Edge SE 'Cradle to Grave' Flow

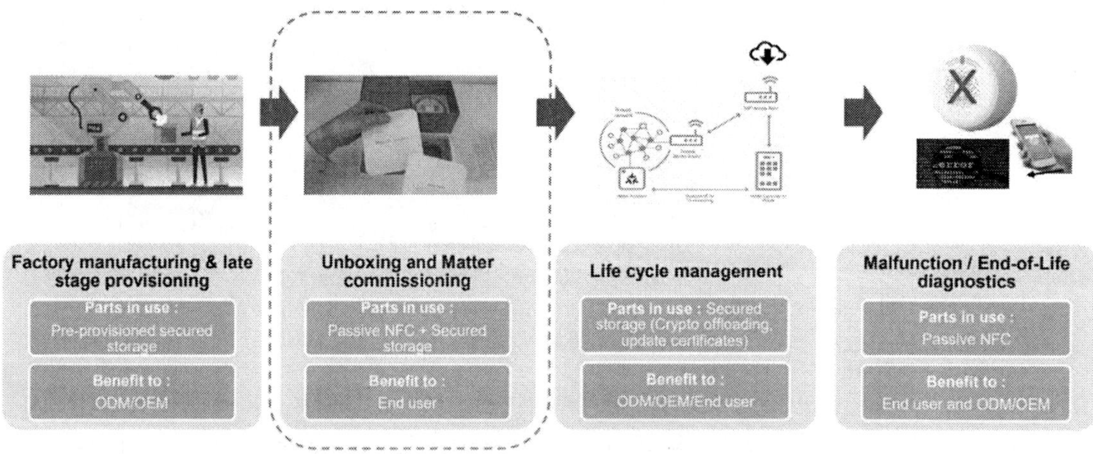

All SEs will come with its own **Cloud Provisioning Service** offered by IFX, thereby making it a full package for OEMs (Chip + Services).

#SensorsConverge

Sensors Converge

Matter Certification Process – 1/2

Become a Member

01

Read Connectivity Standards Alliance Policies and Governing Documents and become a member.

Request a Manufacturer ID / Vendor ID

02

Contact the Alliance Certification Team to reserve your Manufacturer ID or Vendor ID.

Select a Compliant Platform or Network Transport

03

For Zigbee and Smart Energy end products, we have established access to Compliant Platforms from multiple silicon vendors. Select one from the list of certified Compliant Platforms.

For Matter end products, you have the choice of various network transport options, including Wi-Fi, Thread, and Ethernet. Note that you will need to obtain certification for your network transport form the relevant standards organization before you certify your Matter device with the Alliance.

Choose a Testing Provider

04

Select from Connectivity Standards Alliance authorized Test Providers at locations all around the world.

https://csa-iot.org/certification/testing-providers/

#SensorsConverge

Sensors Converge

Matter Certification Process – 2/2

Send Product to be Tested

05

After scheduling testing with an Authorized Test Provider, the facility will make arrangements for testing samples and Protocol Implementation Conformance Statement (PICS) documents to be submitted. Test Provider will issue a final report to the Connectivity Standards Alliance when testing is successfully completed.

PICS proforma templates are available in the Members Area

Submit Certification Application

06

Complete and submit an application for certification in the Connectivity Standards Alliance Certification Tool. Instructions for requesting a Certification Tool account and creating/submitting applications can be found in the Connectivity Standards Alliance Members Area.

Application Pending

07

Connectivity Standards Alliance Certification Team will review your application and, if necessary, request action on specific identified items or information required to make a determination of approval or rejection. At any time during this process, you may reach out to the Connectivity Standards Alliance Certification Team with any questions.

Upon Approval

08

After your product certification is approved, you will receive a formal certificate from the Alliance and may immediately begin using the Certified Product logo. Certified Product logos have usage guidelines that govern how they are used. Please review the applicable sections before affixing. Logos are provided to the applicant's contact for the certification. For more information about Alliance logos and their usage, please contact us.

Matter products will also receive a Certification Declaration (CD) blob file and a certified product record entered in the Distributed Compliance Ledger (DCL).

Infineon has taken P6+43012 through the Matter pre-certification test process

#SensorsConverge

Sensors Converge

Table of contents

#SensorsConverge

Sensors Converge

Matter Spec: What applications are covered today? What's planned next?

Application	V1.0 (R)	V1.1 (P)		V1.x (P)
Lighting Devices (bulbs, switches, etc.)	☑			
Smart Speaker	☑			
Smart Lock	☑			
Smart Thermostat	☑			
Security Sensors (motion, occupancy, etc.)	☑			
TV	☑			
Smart Appliance (Washing, Fridge, AC)		☑	→	☑
Smart Appliance (HVAC, Dish, Dryer,....)		☑	→	☑
Robot Vacuums		☑	→	☑
IP Cameras/Video Doorbells		☑	→	☑
Easy Wi-Fi onboarding, Sleepy Devices		☑		
Bug fixes		☑		
Air Quality Detectors, Garage Door				☑

#SensorsConverge

Sensors Converge

Broad Secure Connected Portfolio Delivers Matter Compliance for Your Application

Matter over Thread

- CYW30739 Module
- 1MB External flash
- +20dBm PA for improved RF performance
- OPTIGA™ Trust M for hardware security
- User Experience - Best interoperability with installed base of Access Points and phones sharing IP heritage
- Memory efficient program execution

Matter over Wi-Fi

- Flexible scalable secure platform - PSoC6 + CYW43xxx Wi-Fi/BT Combo family
- Ultra low power by design – very low sleep, transmit, and receive current
- Low power system architecture – host offloads for keep-alive functions allowing host processor to sleep for longer periods
- High-performance RF ensures the most robust connection which substantially reduces power consumption

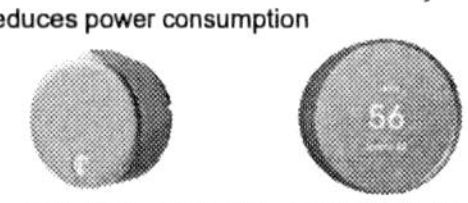

Enhanced Security

- Any Matter certified device needs to be provisioned with the set of credentials, OPTIGA™ Trust M will act as (productive) Trust Anchor for customer specific Matter credentials
- Certificates / keys need to be personalized and securely stored in a trust anchor, Infineon will provide a Matter certified Root CA* and PKI* infrastructure for customers
- Trust anchor for higher cryptographic operations required, OPTIGA™ Trust M hardware cryptographic accelerators will support Host MCU with Matter onboarding

PKI – Private Key injection CA – Certificate Authority

#SensorsConverge

Sensors Converge

Table of contents

1.
2.
3.
4.
5. Infineon Matter Roadmap
6.
7.
8.

#SensorsConverge

Sensors Converge

Matter Roadmap Summary

Wi-Fi MCU		802.15.4/BLE SoC
MCU	Wi-Fi Combo	

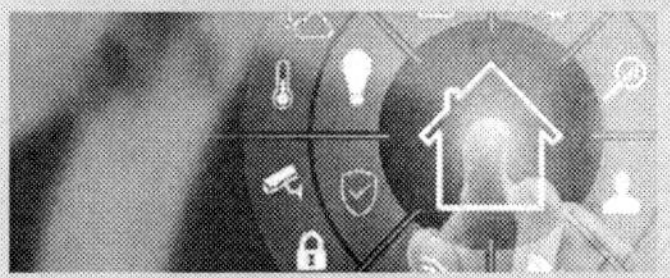

PSoC™ 64
150 MHz Cortex-M4 /100 MHz M0+, Security
2MB Flash/1MB RAM
* H1/23

PSoC™ 62
150 MHz Cortex-M4 /100 MHz M0+
2MB Flash/1MB RAM
Now

PSoC™ 6
MCUs for the broad base of IoT and consumer applications, bringing best in class low power, connectivity, and security

Wi-Fi Combo (11n and 11ac)
Complete portfolio with low power keep alive across 11n and 11ac, offer ac friendly ultra low power series optimized for battery powered connected home solution

For Wi-Fi the SW API hooks into Matter stack in MCU

CYW43439
SB 1x1 11n HT40
SDIO, BT5.0, UART/SDIO
Now

CYW43012
ULP DB 1x1 11n HT20
11ac Friendly
SDIO/SPI, BT5.0
Now

CYW4373
DB 1x1 11ac HT80
SDIO/PCIe
BT5.2, UART/USB
Now

CYW54590
DB 2x2 11ac HT80
SDIO/PCIe
BT5.1, UART
* H2/23

Bluetooth LE and Thread
High-Performance, Low Power Multi-Protocol MCU with integrated Security for Embedded and Hosted applications
BLE 5.x and Thread stack supporting Matter

30739 Module
BLE5.1/Thread/ Matter
CM4 SoC
1M Flash/512K, 5dBm Tx
* H2/23

Matter stack | MCU | Wi-Fi combo | Thread/Matter BLE combo | Availability

#SensorsConverge

Sensors Converge

Table of contents

#SensorsConverge

Sensors Converge

Building Matter

1. Matter over Wi-Fi

Platforms:

- Raspberry Pi (core developmental)
- Smart Home Hubs:
    - Apple TV, HomePod mini
    - Smart Things Hub
    - Google Nest Hubs
    - Amazon Eco

- CHIP GitHub Repo (V1.0-branch https://github.com/project-chip/connectedhomeip)
- ModusToolBox™

#SensorsConverge

Sensors Converge

Prerequisites (Hardware & Software Tools)

- 2x CY8CKIT-062S2-43012 Wi-Fi BT Pioneer Kit
- 1x iPhone/iPad with iOS 16.2 or +
- 1x Apple TV 4K/Apple HomePod mini
- 1x WLAN Access Point with Network connection
- ModusToolBox™ ver. 3.0+

#SensorsConverge

Sensors Converge

Matter Demo Hardware Setup

- Lock App on PSoC™ 6 CY8CKIT 43012 Wi-Fi BT Pioneer Kit #1
- Light App on PSoC™ 6 CY8CKIT 43012 Wi-Fi BT Pioneer Kit #2
- Homepod Mini
- iPad

#SensorsConverge

Sensors Converge

Kits Functionalities

Kit	Baud Rate	Factory Reset Mechanism	Action Button	Indication
CY8CKIT 062S2 43012	115200	Button Press (User Button 2)	User Button 1	LED 9
CYSBSYSKIT-DEV-01	115200	NA	NA	LED 4 Blue Power
XENSIV™ BGT60TR13C	NA	NA	NA	LED D1 Red/Green

#SensorsConverge

Sensors Converge

Getting Started with Matter on MTB

- Install & Open MTB 3.0
- Make sure you are familiar with workspace creation and related operations
- Create a folder in workspace
- Click New Application in the Start group of the Quick Panel

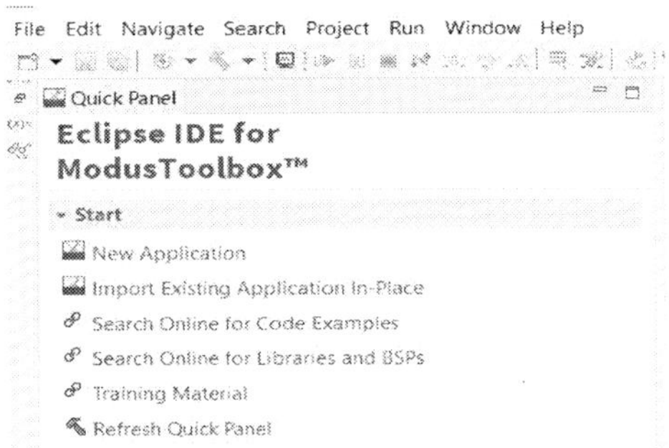

#SensorsConverge

Getting Started with Matter on MTB

- Select the BSP as CY8CKIT-062S2-43012 which will be used in this sample Lock application and click Next

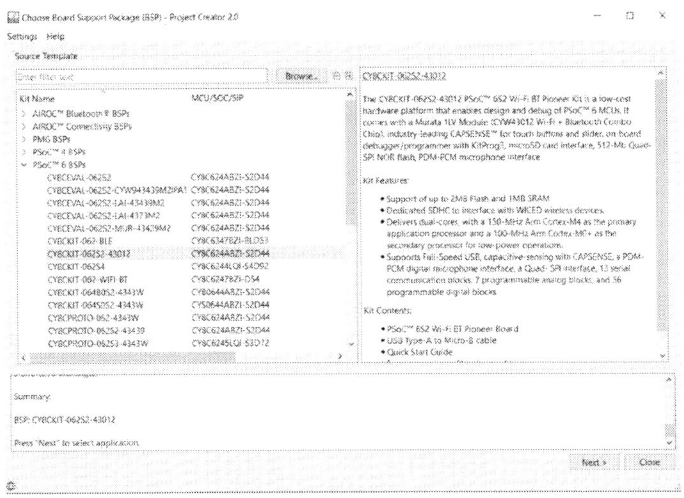

#SensorsConverge

Getting Started with Matter on MTB

- Under Connectivity, select Matter Wi-Fi Door Lock as the sample application and click Create

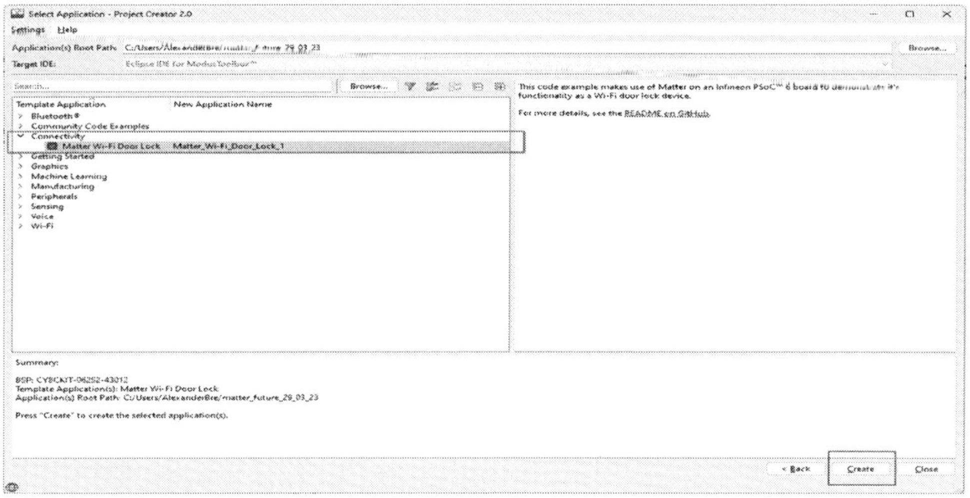

#SensorsConverge

Getting Started with Matter on MTB

- Build and flash the example application onto the Kit

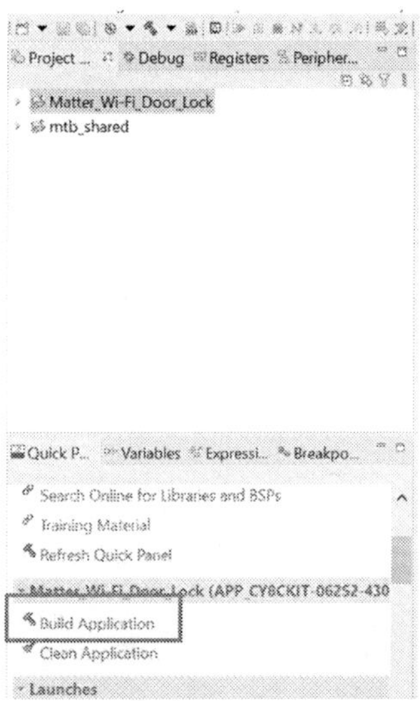

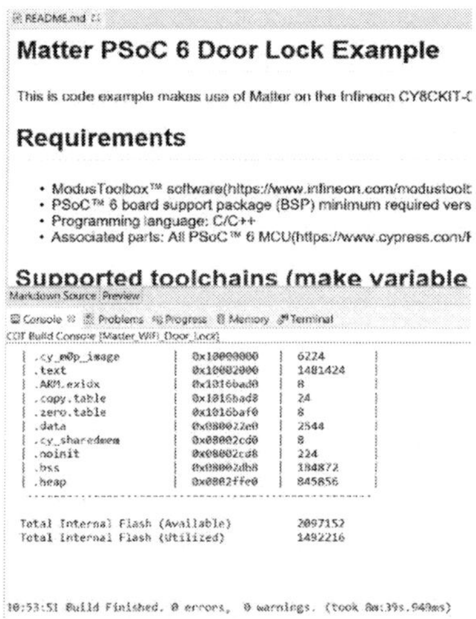

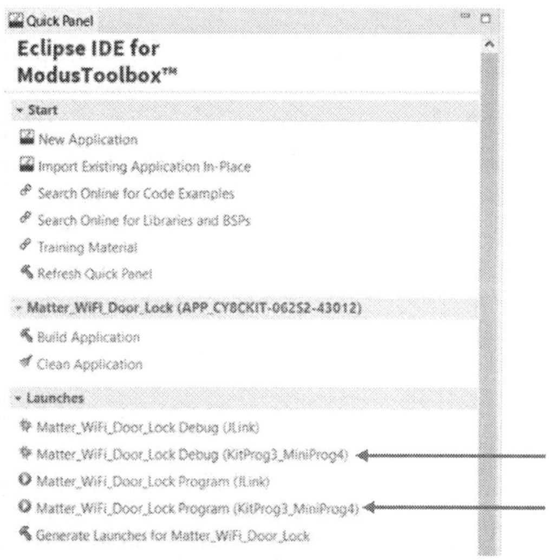

#SensorsConverge

Matter over Wi-Fi Smart Lock Cluster Resource Usage – A breakdown

Description	Flash Usage (KB)
Matter SDK	400
MTB shared	1,004
Total Flash	1,404

Description	Flash Usage (KB)
WHD (43012)	485
LWIP	168
BT Stack	90
mBed TLS	96
MTB HAL	26
WCM	8
WPA3	12
PDL	36
FreeRTOS	11
Miscellaneous	72
MTB Shared	1004

Matter over Wi-Fi can only be supported on PSoC6 2M Flash variant

#SensorsConverge

Sensors Converge

Table of contents

#SensorsConverge

Sensors Converge

Adding a Matter Accessory to Apple Homepod Mini Matter Controller

- Adding accessories using QR scan

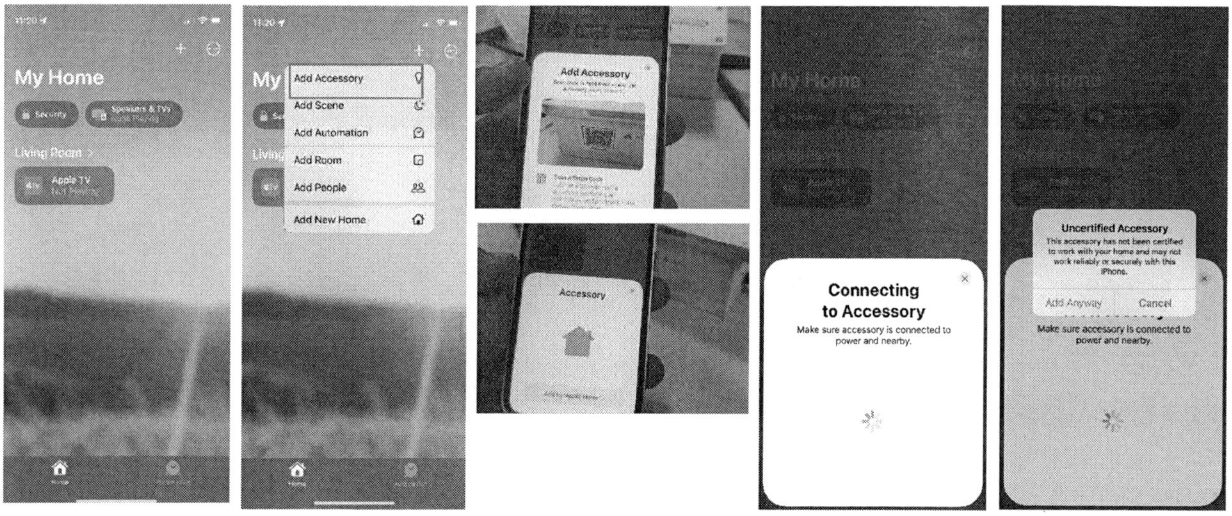

#SensorsConverge

Sensors Converge

Adding a Matter Accessory to Apple Homepod MiniMatter Controller

- Selecting location & naming for accessories

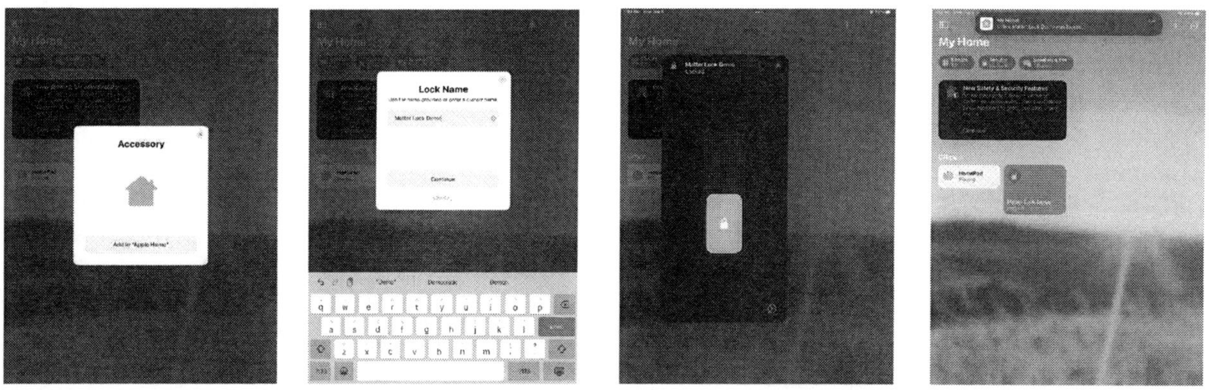

#SensorsConverge

Sensors Converge

Table of contents

#SensorsConverge

Sensors Converge

Resources

Matter lock Example Code GitHub Repo:
https://gitlab.intra.infineon.com/wpp/ce/mtb/mtb-example-psoc6-matter-door-lock

Chip Repo:
https://github.com/project-chip/connectedhomeip/

Boards:
https://www.infineon.com/cms/en/product/evaluation-boards/cy8ckit-062s2-43012/
https://www.infineon.com/cms/media/pss-3dmodels/xensiv-connected-sensor-kit/

Download Matter 1.0 Spec : here
Additional details :
https://www.infineon.com/cms/en/product/promopages/matter-over-thread-30739-802.15.4/

#SensorsConverge

Sensors Converge

Call to Action

1

Learn More
Webinars on Matter

2

Demo Environment

Order development kits:
PSoC™ 6 Pioneer Kit
Sensor Kit

XENSIV™ connected sensor kit

3

Download Matter Lock Ex.

4

Drive discovery into customers looking to use Matter

For more information go to www.Infineon.com/matter

#SensorsConverge

Sensors Converge

Sensors Converge

nichicon america

Optimization of Energy Storage in IoT Devices

June 20, 2023 | Santa Clara, CA

Mark Gebbia, Sales Application Engineering Manager

#SensorsConverge

Company Data

Company Name	NICHICON CORPORATION
Established	August 1, 1950
Employees	5,209
Revenue	184.725 million Yen March 31, 2023
Stock Listings	Tokyo Section 1
Product Lines	Aluminum, Polymer Aluminum, Hybrid Polymer Aluminum, Small Lithium-Titanate Rechargeable Batteries, Film Capacitors, EDLC Capacitors, Functional Modules, Positive Thermistors, Switching Power Supplies, ICEL by Nichicon Films, Capacitors for Applied Systems and Equipment

#SensorsConverge

Sensors Converge

Nichicon Products at a Glance

Aluminum Electrolytic Capacitors

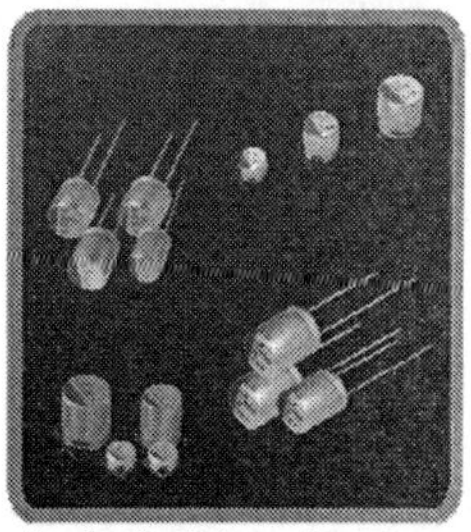

Conductive Polymer Capacitors

Hybrid Aluminum Polymers

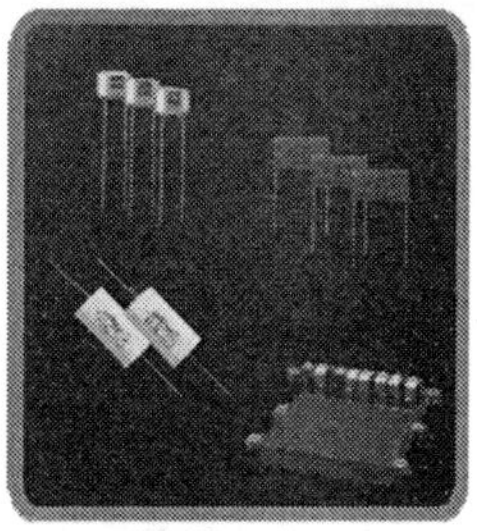

Film Capacitors

Electric Double Layer Capacitors

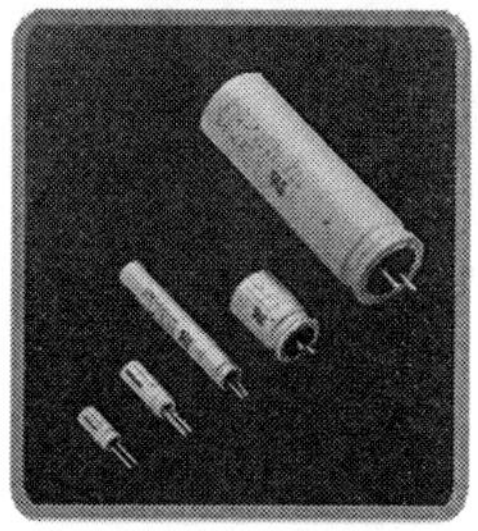

Small LTO Rechargeable Battery

#SensorsConverge

Sensors Converge

Sensors Converge

EDLC/Supercapacitors

#SensorsConverge

Electric Double Layer Capacitor's

- Activated Carbon electrodes
  - Extremely large surface area
- No dielectric - unlike standard capacitors
  - Energy stored on surface
- Energy stored in carbon/ electrolyte interface area on both plates. (Electric Double layer)
- Environmentally safe electrolyte (Nichicon EDLC's)

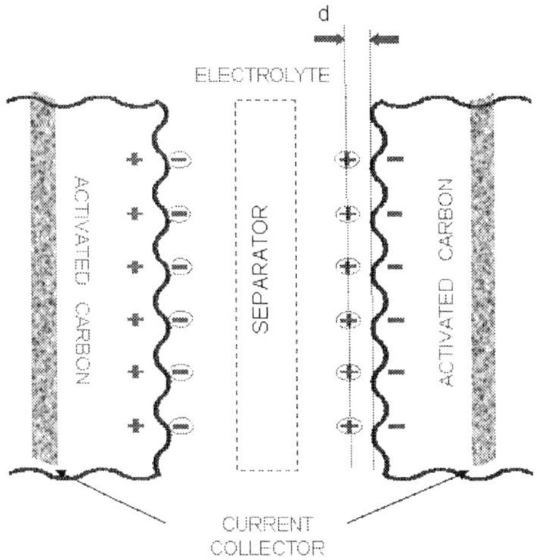

#SensorsConverge

Sensors Converge

Electric Double Layer Capacitor's

✓Capacitance values up to several thousands of Farads in a single package.

✓Voltage limited to 2.7VDC per capacitor cell.

✓Maximum temperature 70°C, 85°C with voltage derating.

✓Discharge times can be very short (<1second).

✓Up to 1,000,000 charge/discharge cycles.

✓Applications: Battery backup, Battery alternative, Pulse power, DC-DC converters, Actuators, LED displays, Scanners, Wind power, Audio systems

#SensorsConverge

Sensors Converge

Sensors Converge

Lithium-Ion Rechargeable Batteries

#SensorsConverge

Why Lithium?

- ✓Lightest metal in the periodic table
- ✓Greatest electrochemical potential
- ✓Largest specific energy/kg
- ✓Wider temperature range
- ✓High reliability
- ✓Long cycle life (Compared to other battery types)
- ✓Higher charging/ discharging rate

#SensorsConverge

Sensors Converge

How a Li-ion Battery Works

Charging

Charging current causes Li-ions to be released. Flow from cathode to Anode.

Discharge

Li-ion flow from Anode to cathode. Electrons (Current) flows into circuits.

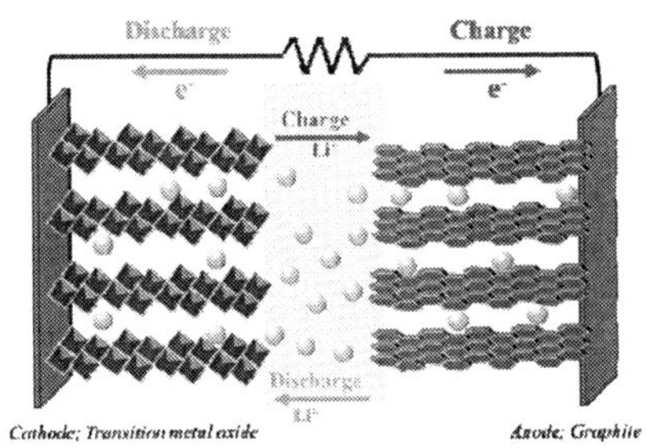

Anode

$LiM^*O_2 \underset{\text{Discharge}}{\overset{\text{Charge}}{\rightleftharpoons}} Li_{1-x}MO_2 + xLi^+ + xe^-$ M=Metal oxide (Ni, Co, Mn etc)

Cathode

$6xC + xLi^+ + xe^- \underset{\text{Discharge}}{\overset{\text{Charge}}{\rightleftharpoons}} xC_6Li$

Combined reaction

$LiM^*O_{2+}6xC \underset{\text{Discharge}}{\overset{\text{Charge}}{\rightleftharpoons}} Li_{1-x}MO_2 + xC_6Li$

Special "Negative Electrode" of LTO

What's the difference between the LTO and conventional Lithium-Ion Rechargeable Batteries?

Negative Electrode

Conventional Lithium-Ion Rechargeable Battery		Lithium Titanate Rechargeable Battery
LiC_6 (Graphite)	→	**LTO** ($Li_4Ti_5O_{12}$)

Li-ion reaction is 0.1V
Thick SEI (solid electrolyte interphase)
Higher electrolyte decomposition
Higher resistance

LTO reaction 1.55V
Thin SEI(solid electrolyte interphase)
Low electrolyte decomposition
Low resistance

Li-ion Batteries vs EDLC

EDLC

- Can be charged/ discharged repeatedly thousands of time
- More stable with temp.
- Higher power density
- Wider temperature range
- Non flammable
- Board mountable

Li-ion Batteries

- Higher energy density
- Discharge over a longer period of time
- Smaller in size
- Low cost
- Higher voltage

#SensorsConverge

Sensors Converge

Discharge (EDLC vs Battery)

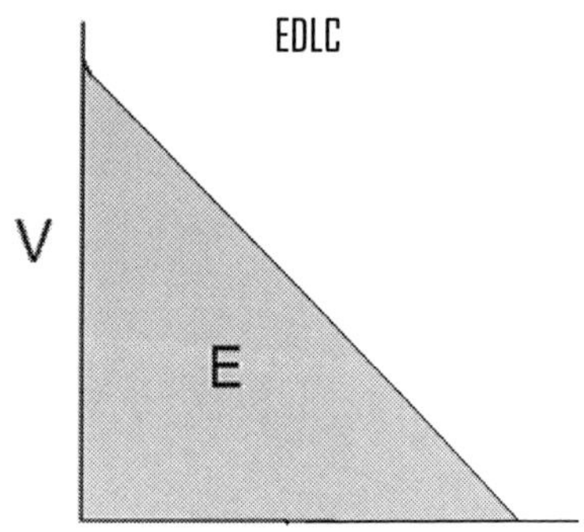

Q=CV

EDLC's – voltage drops as parts discharge

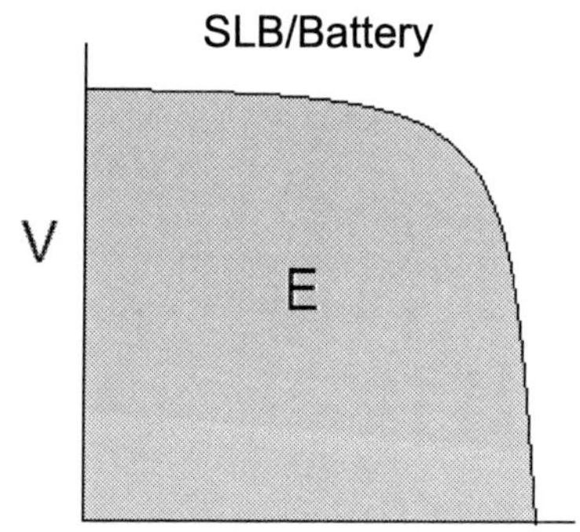

Q=It

Battery – Voltage constant until discharge complete

#SensorsConverge

Sensors Converge

Circuit Board Energy Storage Devices

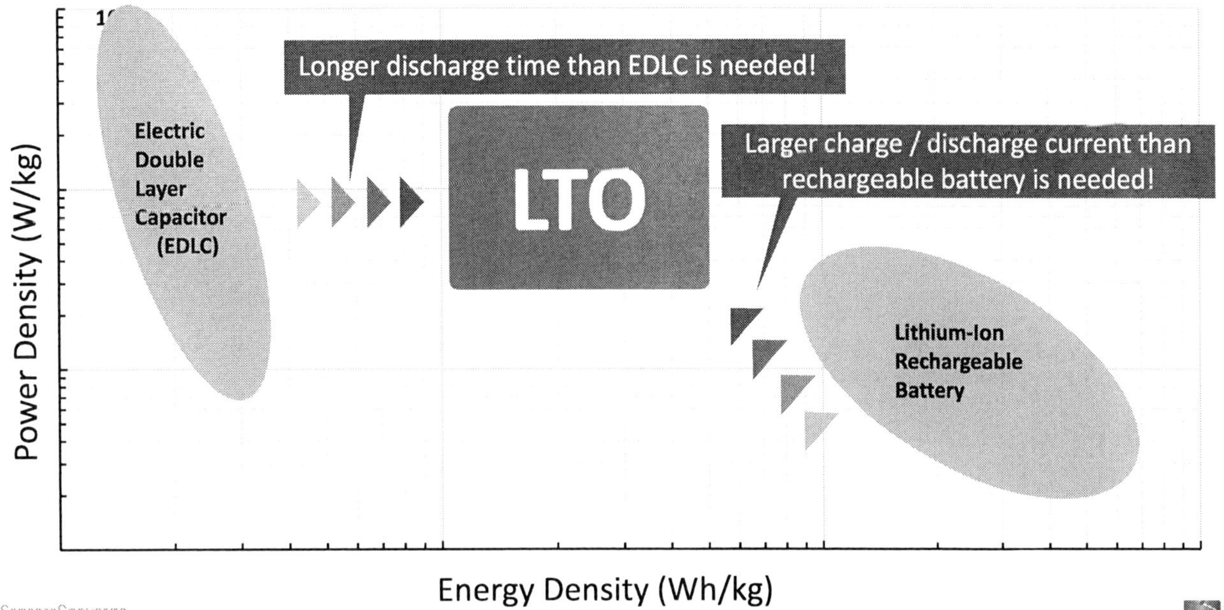

#SensorsConverge

Sensors Converge

Long Life (LTO vs. Li-ion)

Long Life: Over 80% capacity after 20,000 charge/discharge cycles.

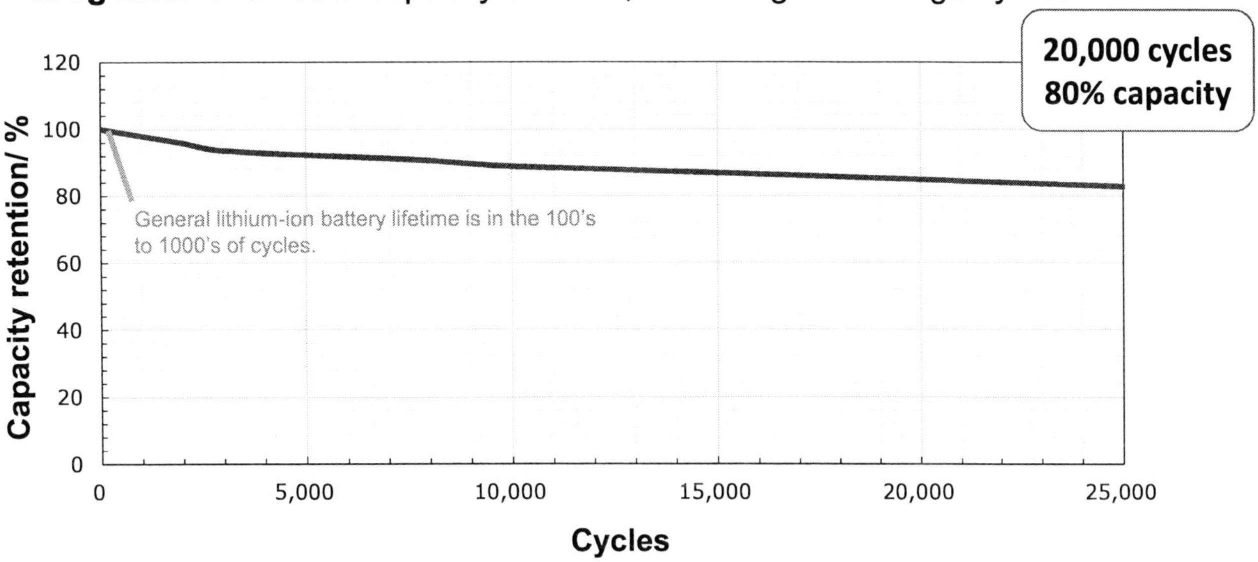

#SensorsConverge

EDLCs can do 1,000,000 charge/ discharge cycles

Sensors Converge

Charge/Discharge Characteristics

Rapid charge/discharge is possible : Power density similar to EDLC.

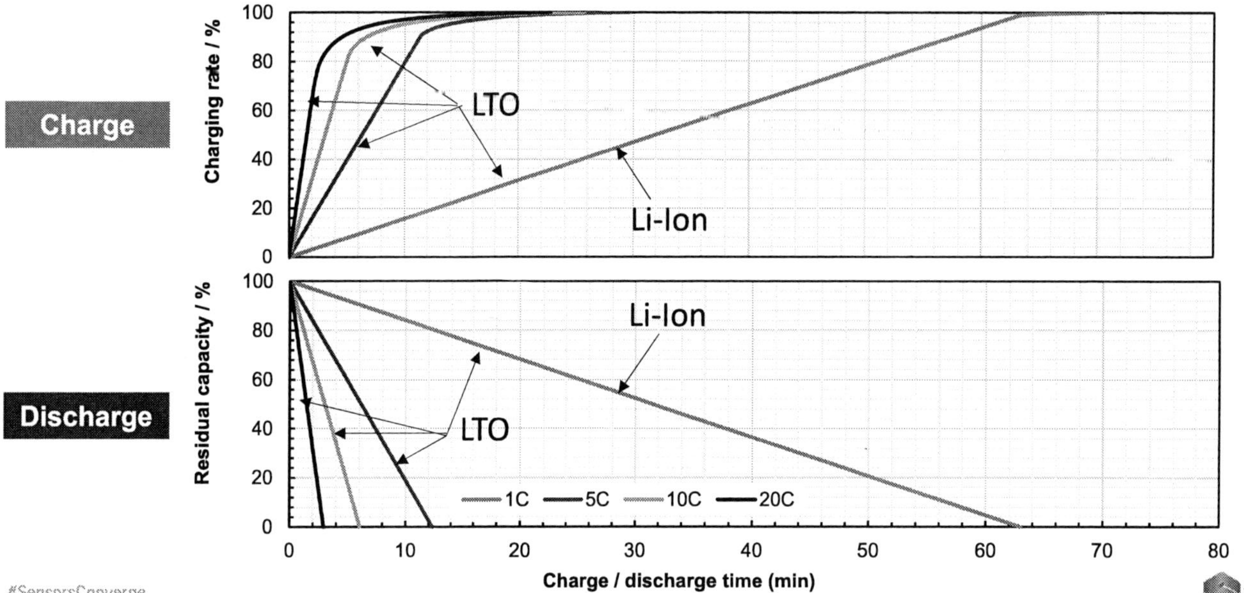

#SensorsConverge

Low-current Charging

Test conditions
Charging current; 5μA (=0.014C)

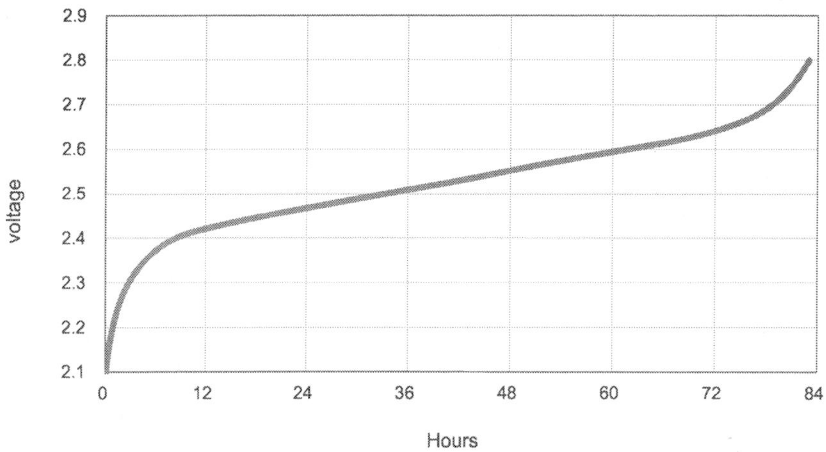

EDLCs & Li-ion cannot be charged at this low of a charging current

#SensorsConverge

Discharge to 0V (Depth of Discharge)

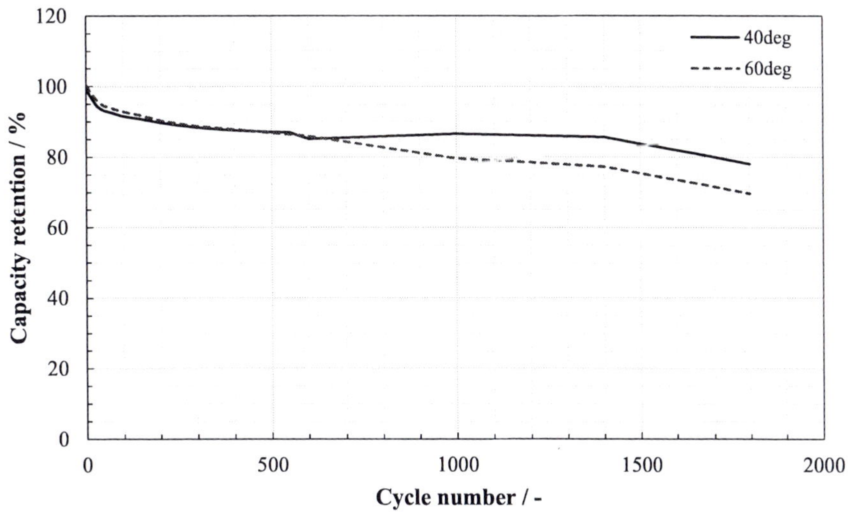

EDLC not damaged if discharged to 0V
Li-ion can become damaged

#SensorsConverge

Sensors Converge

Overcharge

<u>LTO battery</u>

Can withstand up to 20% over rated voltage

<u>EDLC</u>

Can withstand up to SVDC (~8%)

<u>Li-ion</u>

Can become damaged

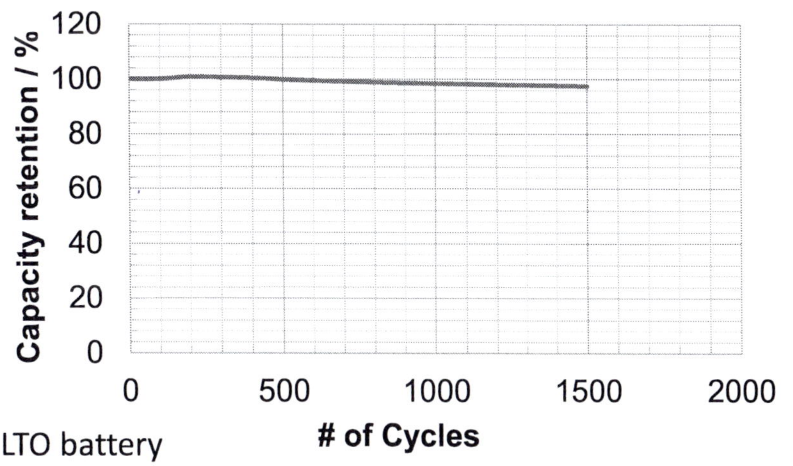

LTO battery

#SensorsConverge

Sensors Converge

Self Discharge (EDLC vs LTO)

LTO self discharge superior to EDLC

	EDLC	LTO
Temp(°C)	25	25
Charge Voltage (VDC)	2.7	2.8
Time (days)	30	40
Final voltage (VDC)	1.97	2.66
ΔVDC	-27.04	-5

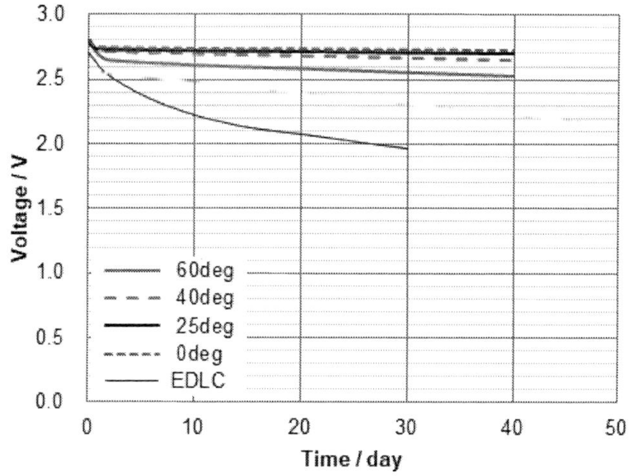

#SensorsConverge

Sensors Converge

Temperature Characteristics

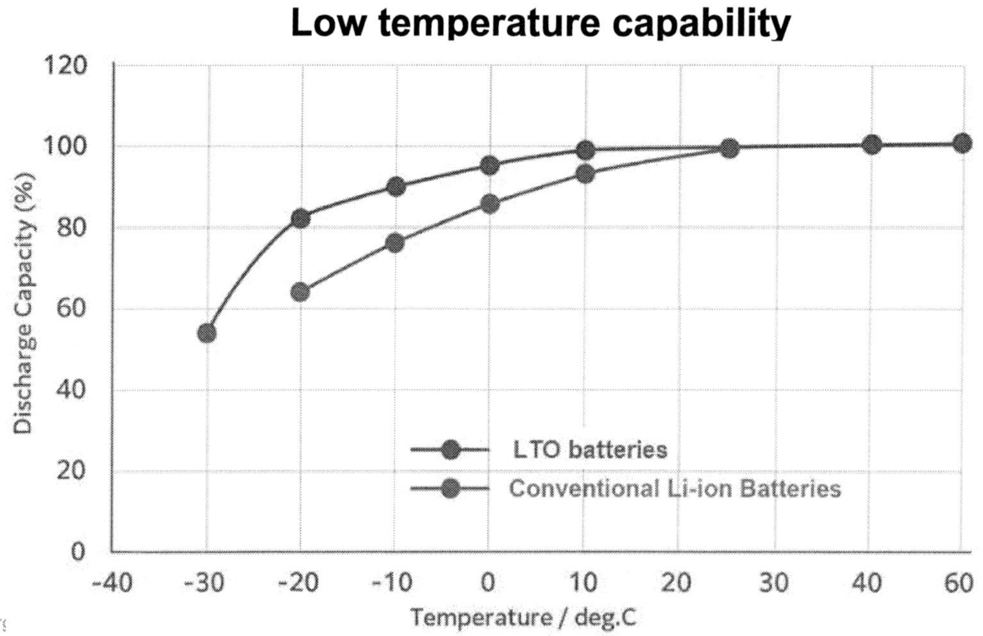

#SensorsConver

Sensors Converge

LTO No Lithium Deposition

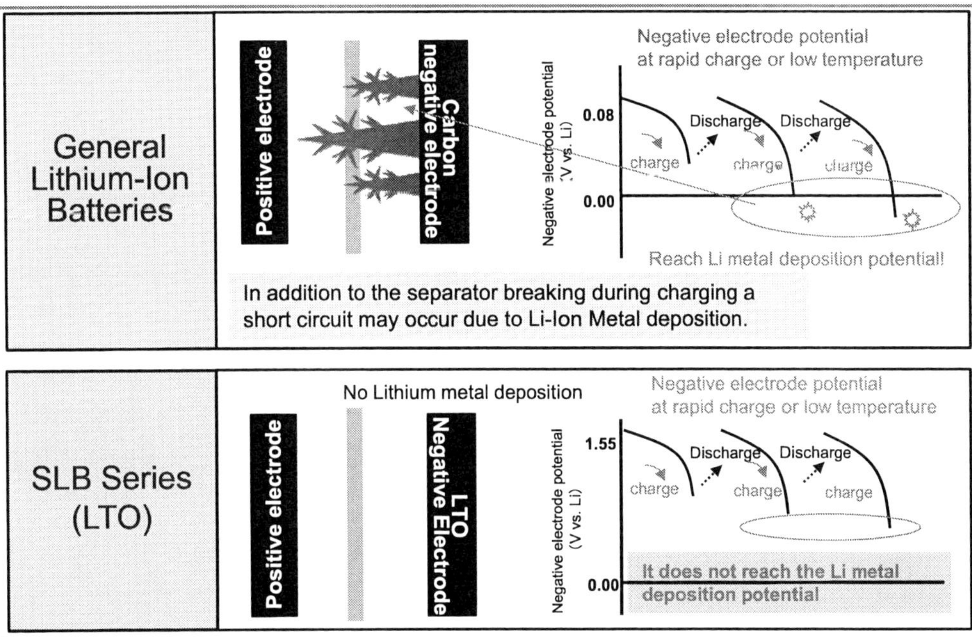

#SensorsConverge

Sensors Converge

Safety

Extremely low risk of **rupture or ignition** from internal short circuit (LTO).

No.	Test Item	Result (Li-ion)	Result (LTO)
1	Crushing	ignition	Extremely low risk of rupture or ignition
2	Nail penetration test	ignition	Extremely low risk of rupture or ignition
3	Blunt nail test	ignition	Extremely low risk of rupture or ignition
4	External short circuit	ignition	Extremely low risk of rupture or ignition
5	Over charge	ignition	Extremely low risk of rupture or ignition
6	Forced discharge	ignition	Extremely low risk of rupture or ignition

JIS C 8712 test criteria

LTO Rechargeable Battery

Safe

Crush Test

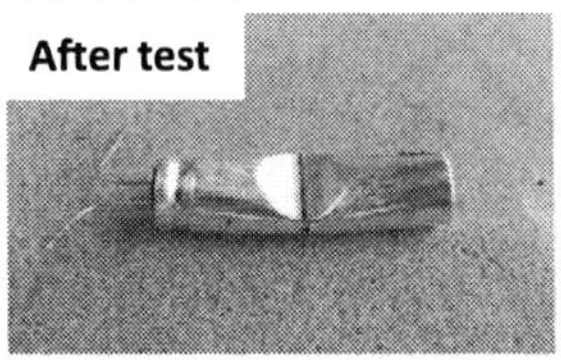

Nail penetration test

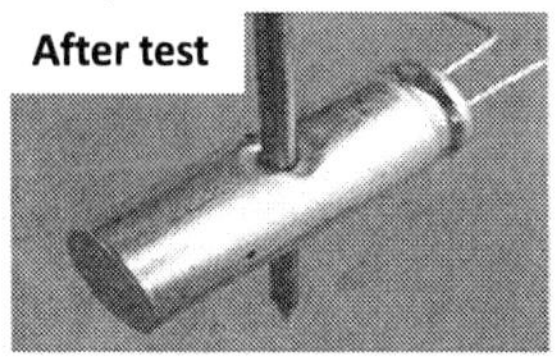

#SensorsConverge

Sensors Converge

Comparison (EDLC vs Li-ion vs LTO)

	EDLC	Li-ion	LTO
# of cycles	>500k	<5k	20k+
Widest Temp Range (without de-rating)	-40/70°C	-20/60C	-30/80°C
Max Voltage	3.8V	3.7V	2.8V
Board-mountable (solderable)	Yes	no	Yes
Energy Density	Lowest	Highest	Middle
Safe to use	No fire	Fire	No fire
Abuse (over voltage/ Discharge)	SVDC	none	Yes
Low charging current (<1C)	None	None	0.01C
Discharge rate	1C	5C	20C (100C)

#SensorsConverge

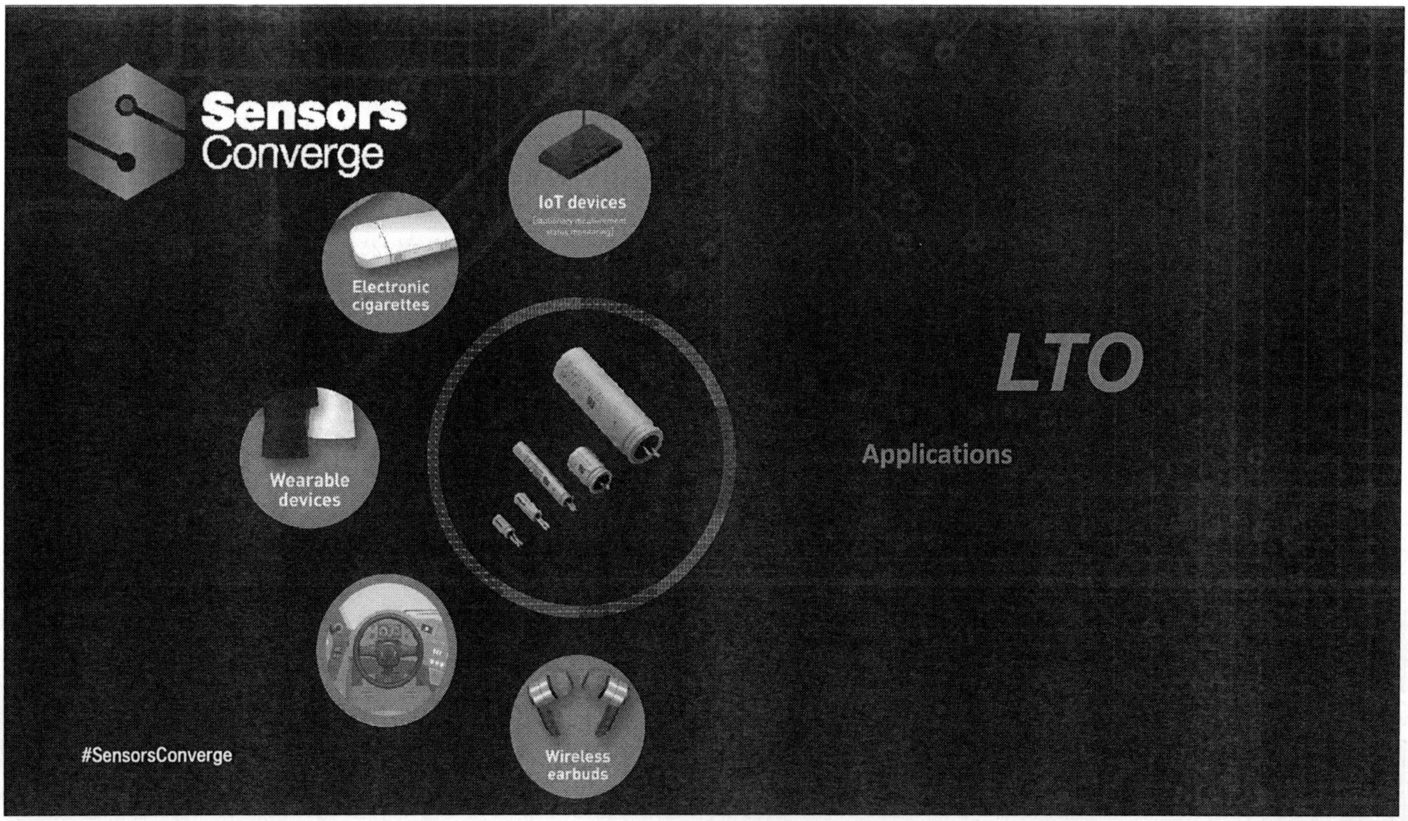

IoT Applications

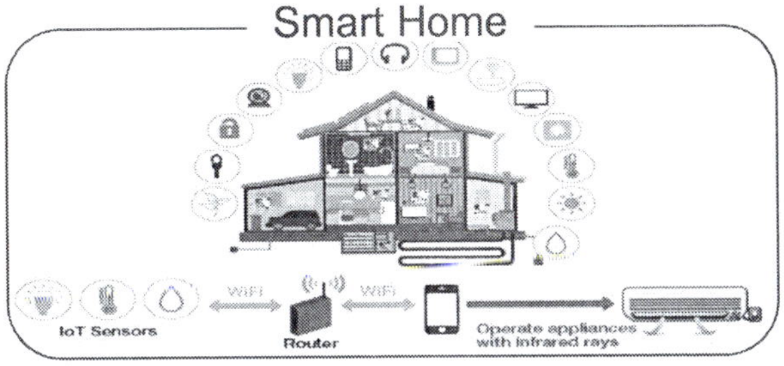

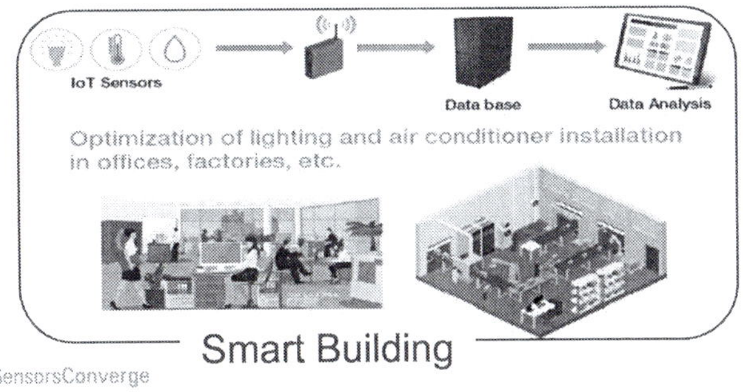

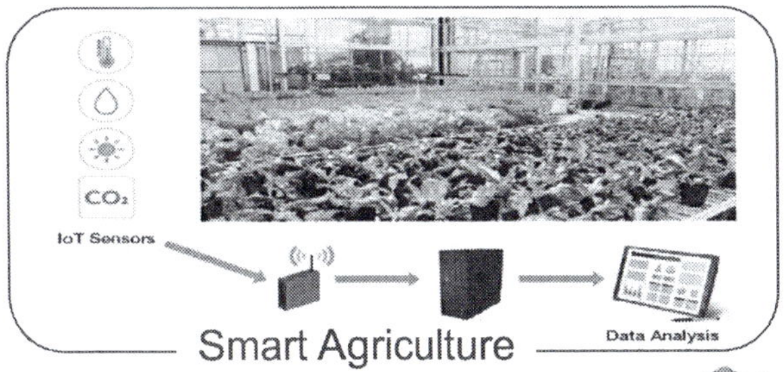

#SensorsConverge

Sensors Converge

Stylus Pen – Samsung

Galaxy

Samsung Electronics Co., Ltd.

Galaxy Series S Pen
Galaxy Note 10 / Note 10+
Galaxy Note 20 / Note 20 Ultra
Galaxy S22 Ultra
Galaxy S23 Ultra

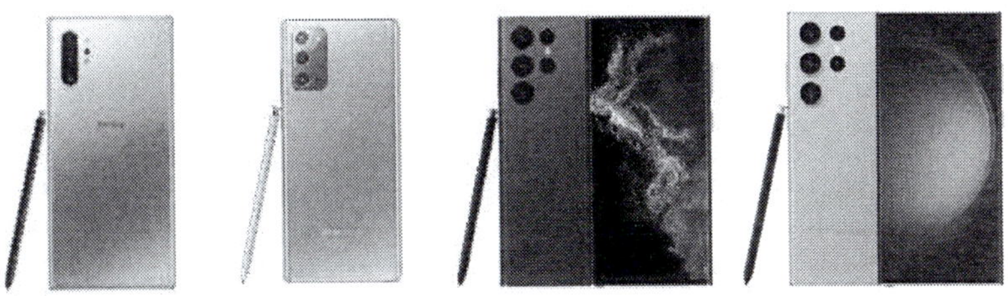

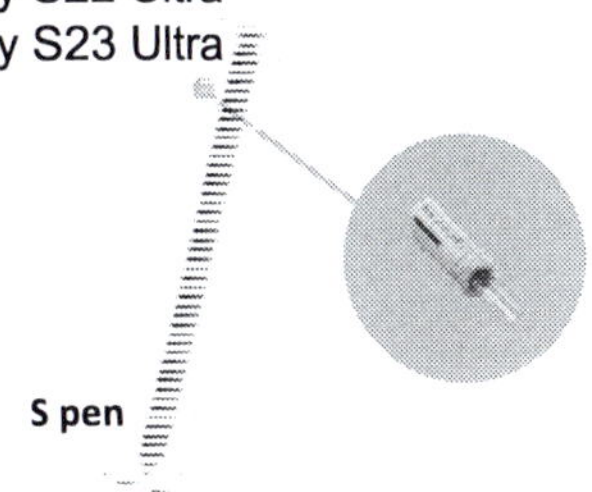

* Previous smartphone models used EDLC capacitors. The EDLC has been replaced with the Nichicon LTO battery in a φ3x7Lmm case size.

The key for Samsung adoption was the LTO ability to handle the increased power consumption that is required due to new S Pen functions.

#SensorsConverge

Sensors Converge

Source: https://www.ifixit.com/Teardown/Samsung+Galaxy+Note10++5G+Teardown/125590

Maintenance Free Sensor Network

Ricoh
By
Nisshinbo

LTO battery is used by Ricoh for their environmental sensing device – EH Environmental Sensor D201/D202. Monitoring of refrigerated, high temperature and high humidity environments with wireless and maintenance-free.

Advantages of adopting LTO

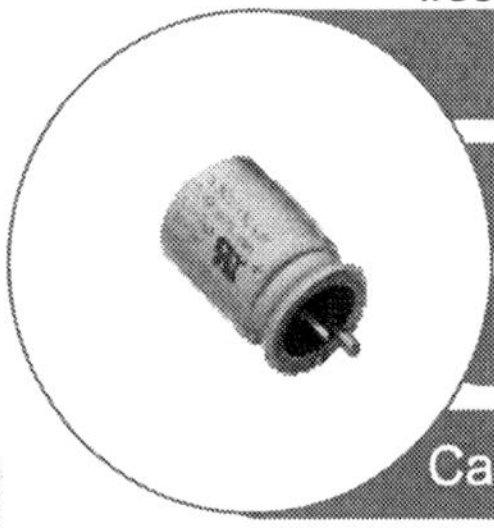

- Long-life cycle batteries for maintenance-free operation!
- Rapid discharge (20C) for wireless (e.g. BLE) is possible!
- Low current charging (0.01C) with environmental power generation!
- Can be charged and discharged at low temperatures (-30°C)

Advantages of installing environmental sensors:

- Visualization of the work environment comfort level.
- Significant reduction in record and management
- Cost reduction in product management

#SensorsConverge

Sensors Converge

Electric Shelf Label - Prototype

Maintenance-free ESL

Electronic Shelf Tag, which is maintenance-free and can be updated frequently. Powered by in-store lighting and can be updated by using a PC or mobile device

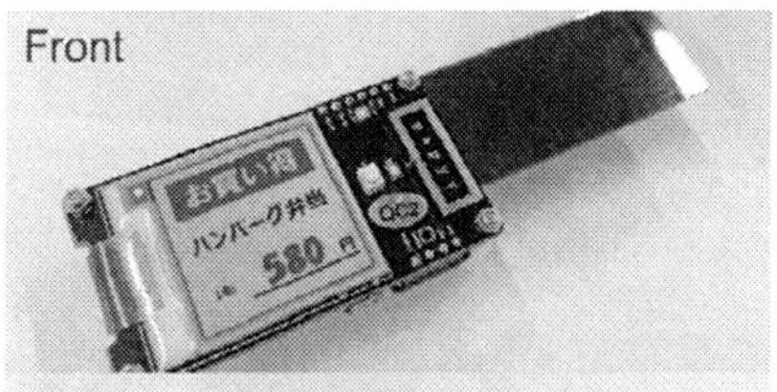

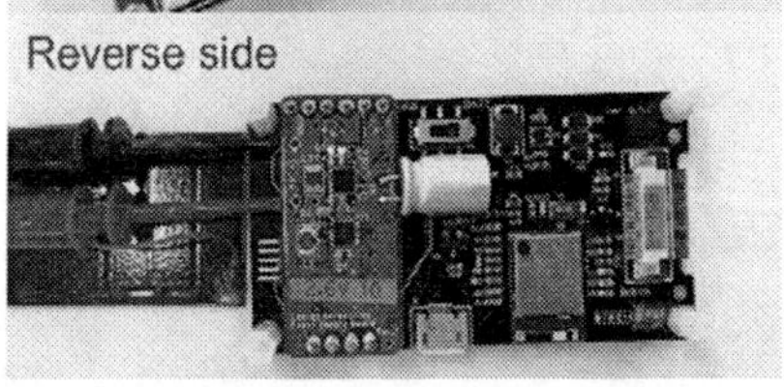

NISSHINBO

Three advantages of maintenance-free electronic shelf tag.

Can be frequently rewritten because it is powered by solar cells
Electricity is generated by the light energy obtained from the store lighting, allowing you to eliminate the limitation on the number of rewrites available.

Power saving circuit and rechargeable battery for maintenance-free operation.
Driven by energy harvesting, no battery replacement is required!

BLE / NFC communication allow for management and promotional updates on the fly.
Rewriting the shelf tag data in the application and guiding the user to the link via NFC communication.

#SensorsConverge

Sensors Converge

Sensors Converge

Small Lithium-Titanate Rechargeable Battery

#SensorsConverge

Wound vs Coin Cell Battery

Specification	Coin cell	Through hole
Image		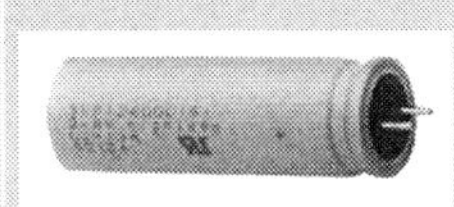
Chemistry	Lithium nickel manganese cobalt dioxide	LTO
Capacity (mAh)	150	150
Voltage (VDC)	3.7	2.8
Dimensions (DxL)	24.5x4.3 mm	12.5x40 mm
Temp Range	-20°C to 80°C	-30°C to 60°C (80°C)
Charge rate	0.5C (~3 hours)	20C (3 minutes)
Discharge rate	0.2C	20C (100C)
Weight (grams)	5.4	9

#SensorsConverge

Sensors Converge

Sensors
Converge
nichicon
america
Booth 729
#SensorsConverge

Sensors Converge

Major Research Collaborations Driving Energy Harvesting TRL progression and Power IoT Ecosystem

Cristina Rusu – RISE, Research Institutes of Sweden

Mike Hayes – Tyndall National Institute

#SensorsConverge

June 20–22, 2023 | Santa Clara, CA

Presentation Outline

Introduction to RISE & Tyndall

EH leverage opportunities

- Sweet spot
- Power IoT Ecosystem

Initiatives 1, EnABLES, Energy ECS, Stargate, Smart Memphis

Initiatives 2 – Technology platform concepts

- PMIC, eSiP
- Simulation model, metrology of real-life applications

Conclusions

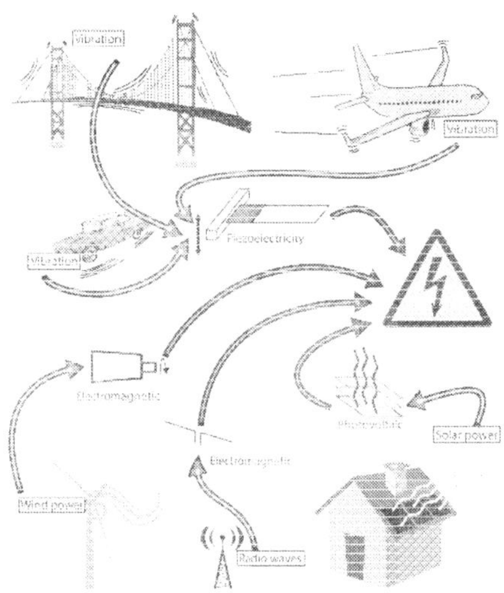

#SensorsConverge

Sensors Converge

Sweden's research institute

RISE

Business and innovation areas

Founded in 2016

3,000 **employees**

130+

Testbeds and **demonstration environments**

Smart hardware dept.

- **Expertise** -

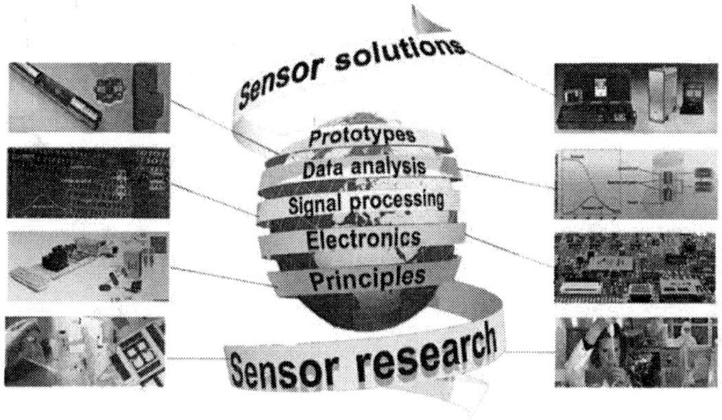

#SensorsConverge

Sensors Converge

Tyndall National Institute (Ireland)

Tyndall National Institute

Leading European R&D centre - integrated ICT hardware & systems.

Specializing in:

- Electronics & IC Design
- Photonics
- Materials
- Devices
- Circuits and Systems

- o Lead institute for Irish Photonics Integration Centre and European Space Agency Space Solutions Centre Ireland.
- o We host industry aligned research centres; Microelectronic Circuits Centre Ireland & International Energy Research Centre
- o 600 staff, >200 industry partners
- o €45M operating costs, >85% through competitive funding
- o >200 publications & 300 publications per annum

#SensorsConverge

Sensors Converge

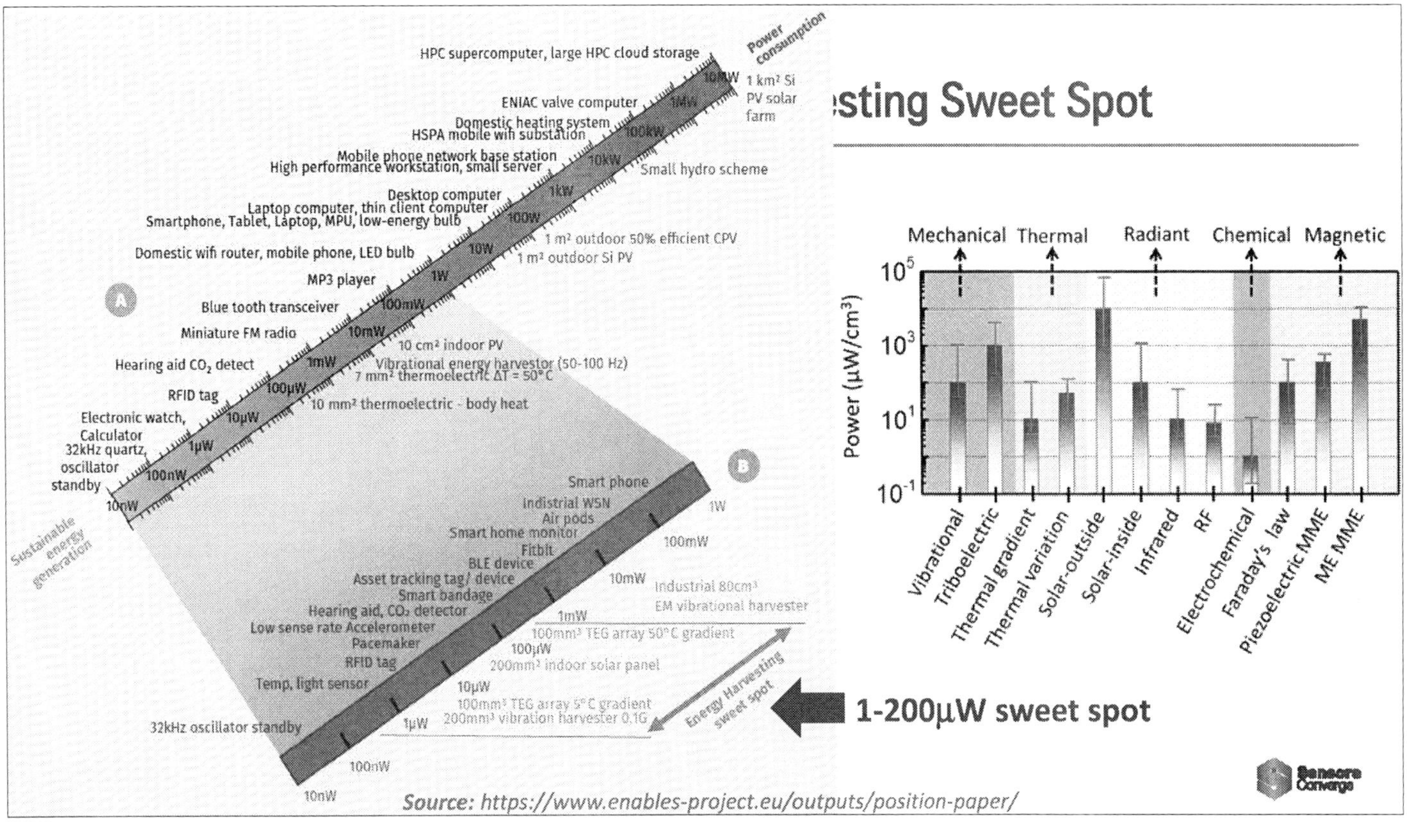

…sting Sweet Spot
Power consumption
HPC supercomputer, large HPC cloud storage
1 km² Si PV solar farm
ENIAC valve computer
Domestic heating system
HSPA mobile wifi substation
Mobile phone network base station
High performance workstation, small server
Small hydro scheme
Desktop computer
Laptop computer, thin client computer
Smartphone, Tablet, Laptop, MPU, low-energy bulb
1 m² outdoor 50% efficient CPV
1 m² outdoor Si PV
Domestic wifi router, mobile phone, LED bulb
MP3 player
Blue tooth transceiver
Miniature FM radio
10 cm² indoor PV
Hearing aid CO2 detect
Vibrational energy harvestor (50-100 Hz)
7 mm² thermoelectric ΔT = 50°C
RFID tag
10 mm² thermoelectric - body heat
Electronic watch, Calculator
32kHz quartz, oscillator standby
Sustainable energy generation
Smart phone
Indistrial WSN
Air pods
Smart home monitor
Fitbit
BLE device
Asset tracking tag/ device
Smart bandage
Hearing aid, CO2 detector
Low sense rate Accelerometer
Pacemaker
RFID tag
Temp, light sensor
32kHz oscillator standby
Industrial 80cm³ EM vibrational harvester
100mm³ TEG array 50°C gradient
200mm² indoor solar panel
100mm³ TEG array 5°C gradient
200mm³ vibration harvester 0.1G
Energy Harvesting sweet spot
Mechanical Thermal Radiant Chemical Magnetic
Power (μW/cm³)
Vibrational
Triboelectric
Thermal gradient
Thermal variation
Solar-outside
Solar-inside
Infrared
RF
Electrochemical
Faraday's law
Piezoelectric MME
ME MME
1-200μW sweet spot
Source: https://www.enables-project.eu/outputs/position-paper/
Sensors Converge

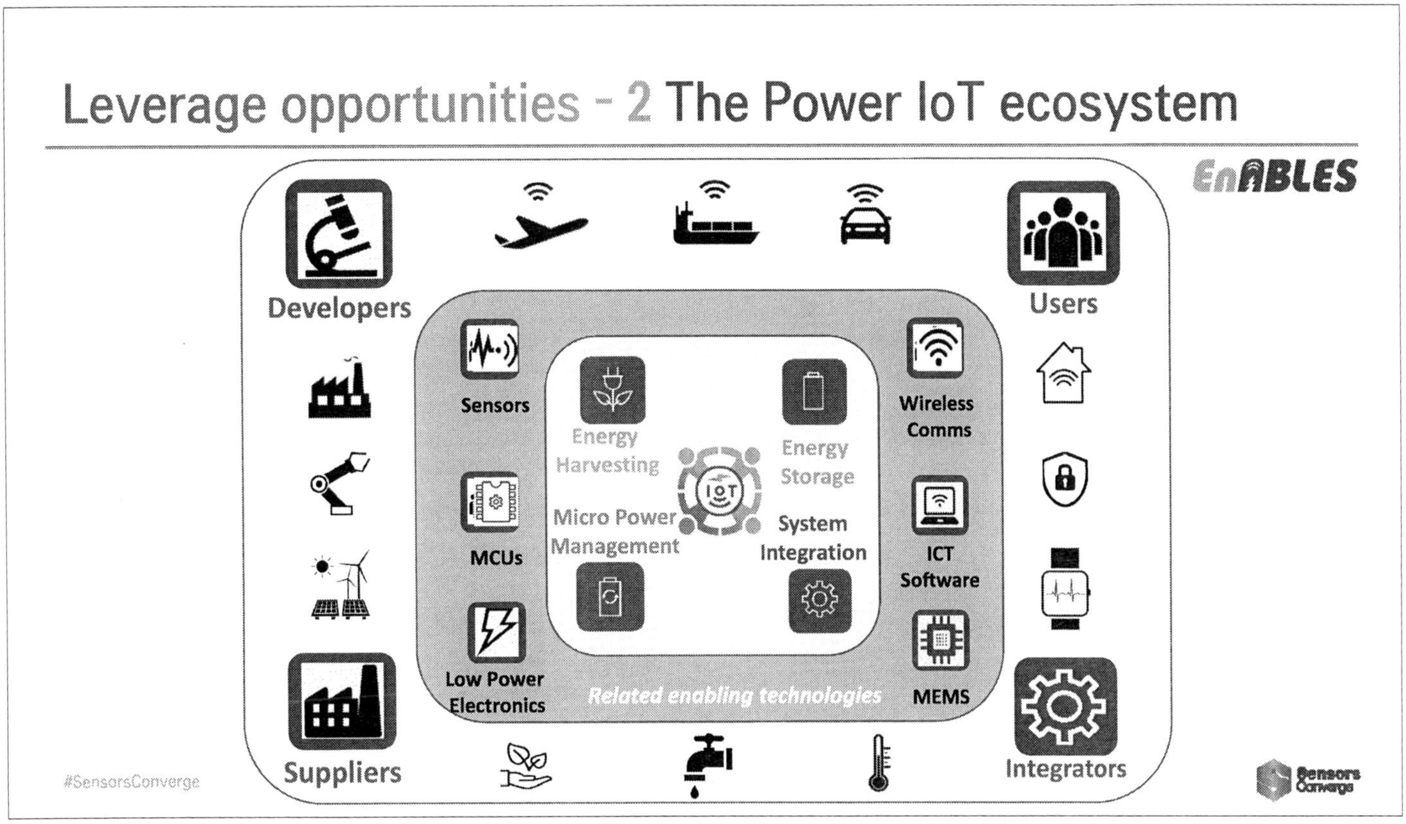

Leverage opportunities - 2 The Power IoT ecosystem
EnABLES
Developers
Users
Sensors
Wireless Comms
Energy Harvesting
Energy Storage
Micro Power Management
System Integration
MCUs
ICT Software
Low Power Electronics
Related enabling technologies
MEMS
Suppliers
Integrators
#SensorsConverge
Sensors Converge

INITIATIVES – 1 Application driven projects & 2 Tech platforms

CONNECT Networks of the Future

RoWBUST

MISCHIEF

ENERGY ECS

EnABLES

STARGATE

Gripen of Sweden

SMART MEMPHIS

#SensorsConverge

Sensors Converge 7

Piezo harvester powering wireless sensor on Gas Turbine

STARGATE SEVENTH FRAMEWORK PROGRAMME

! *Different resonances* in *various directions*

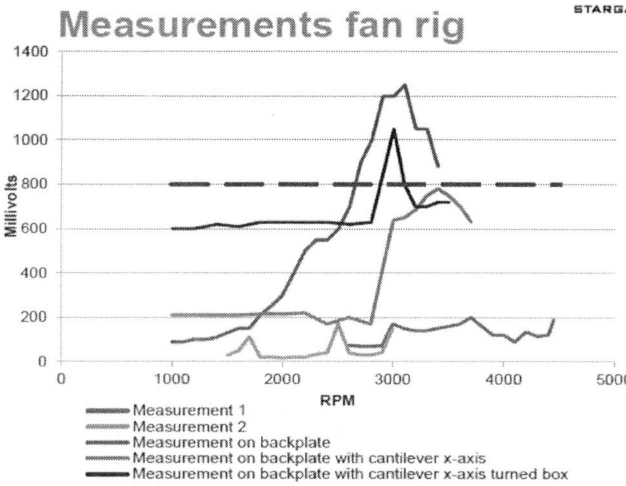

MIDE EH (80 - 175 Hz)

#SensorsConverge

CHALMERS

Sensors Converge

Gas Turbine 2(3) - Developments

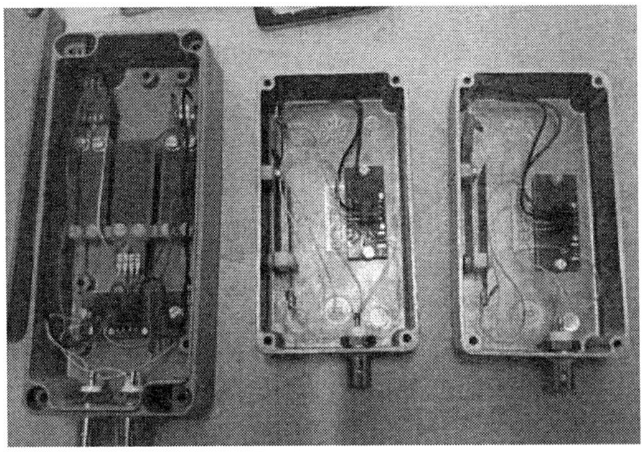

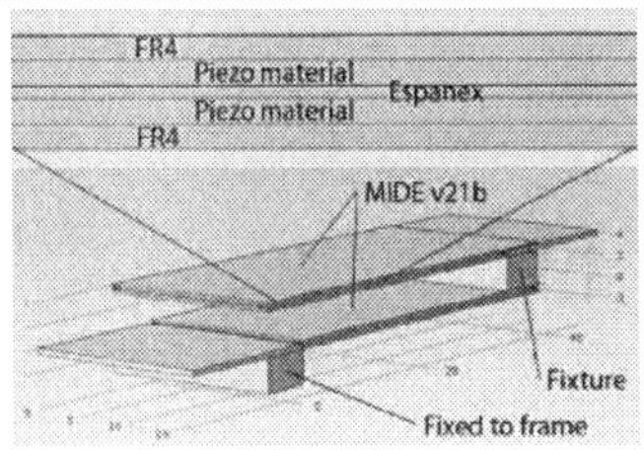

Backfolded harvester

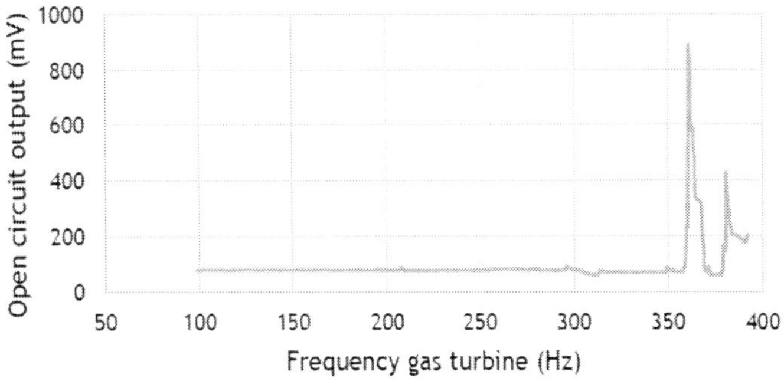

- ✓ Harvester tested up to 100°C
- ! Cables → ✓ Multi core (damps vibrations)
- ! Mounting support - eigenfrequency

#SensorsConverge

CHALMERS

Gas Turbine 3(3) - Results

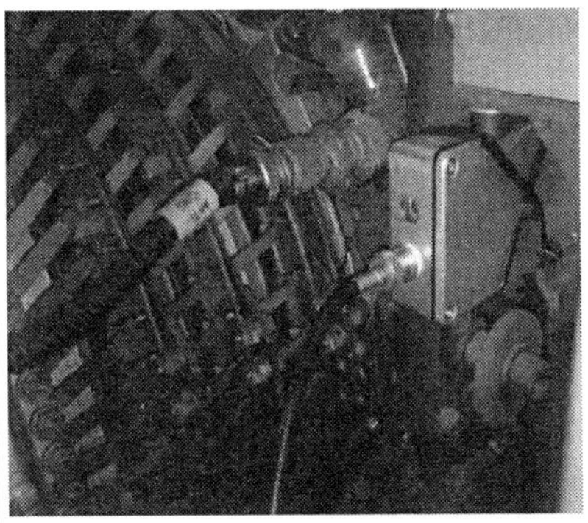

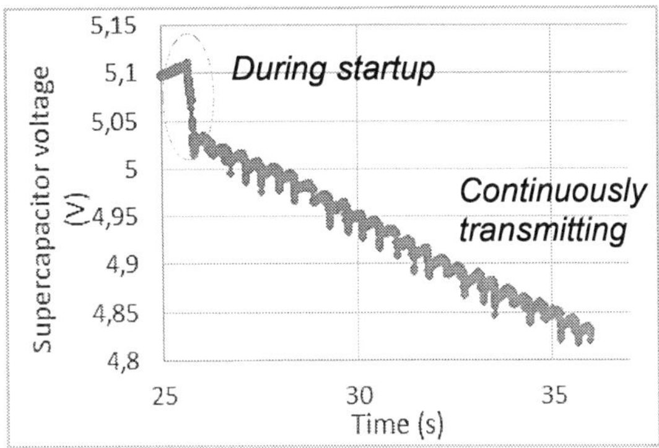

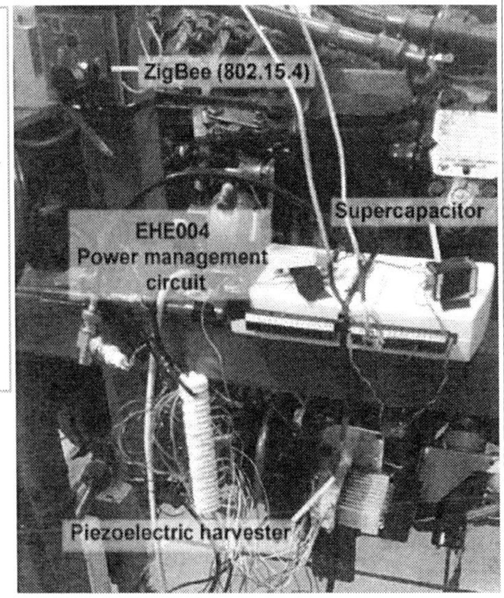

- ! 4 supercapacitors connected in series
- ! Discharge while powering Wi-Fi ↔ Rechargeable battery

#SensorsConverge

CHALMERS

Pacemaker 1(3) - Requirements

EU H2020 **Smart-Memphis**

Smart MEMs Piezo based energy Harvesting with Integrated Supercapacitor and packaging

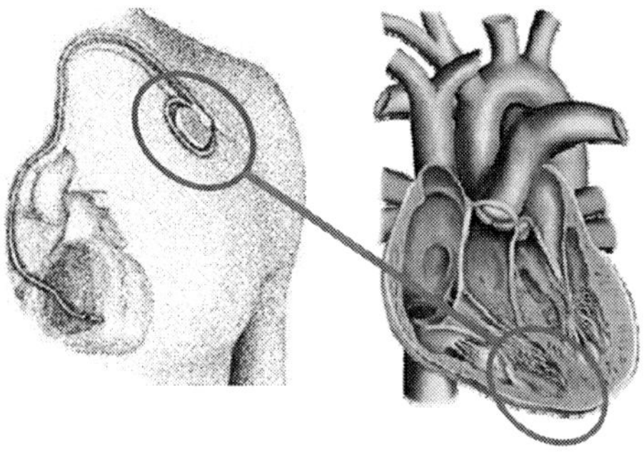

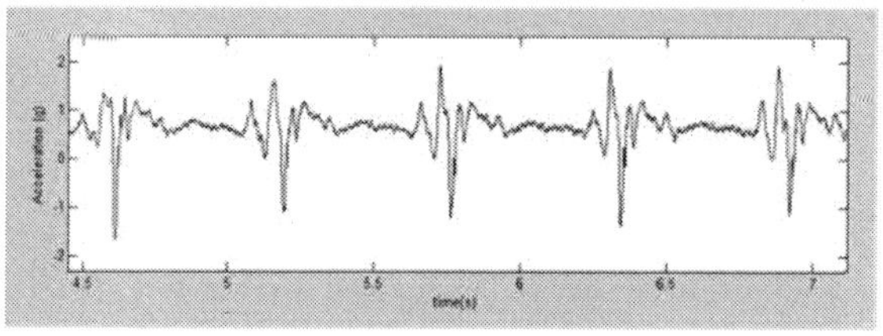

Resonance frequency: 10- 30 Hz

Acceleration: ⟨ 1 g

Size: 0.3 - 1 cm^3

Needed power: 10 – 20 μW

#SensorsConverge

Pacemaker 2(3) - Challenges

- MEMS design ↔ bulk PZT ↔ low frequency
- Resonating structure ↔ damping, pressure encapsulation
- Heart measurements ↔ EH position
- Excitation data ↔ shaker pre-compensation

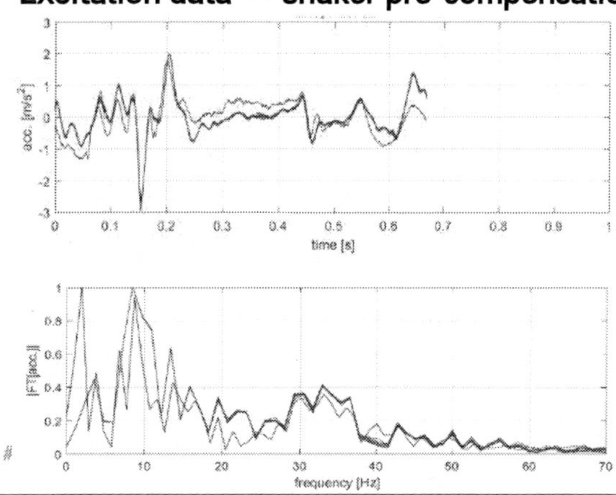

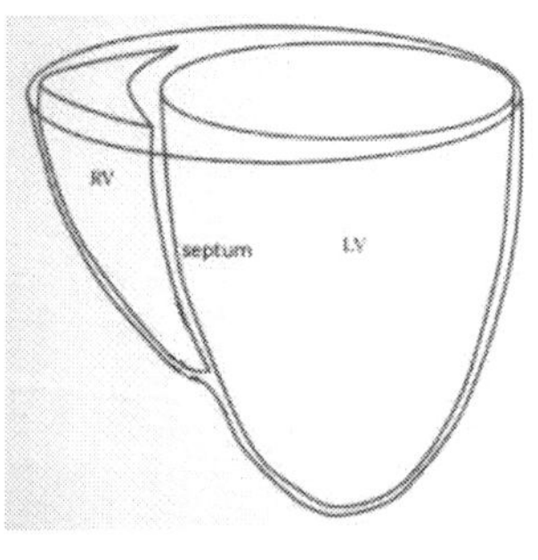

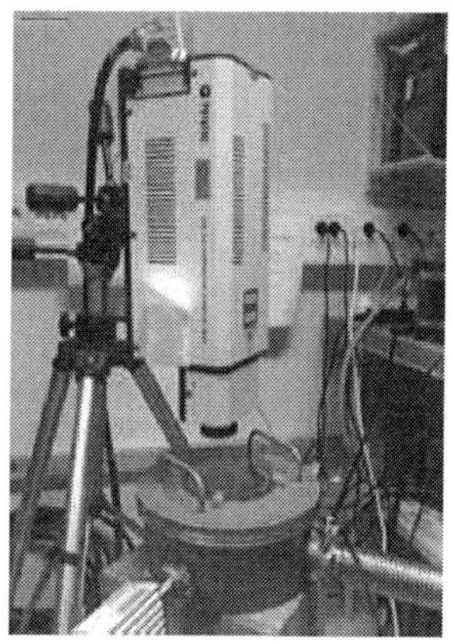

Pacemaker 3(3) - Commercialisation

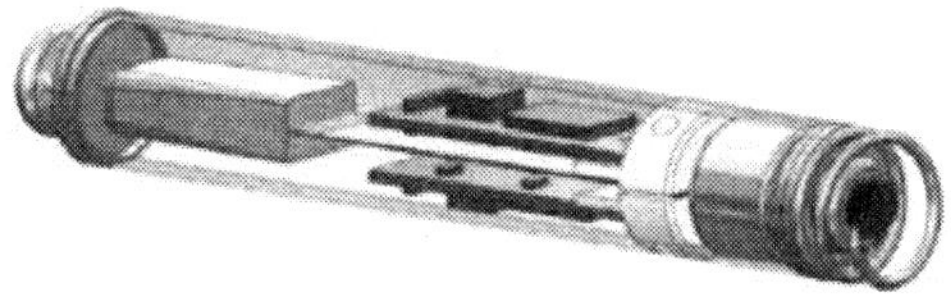

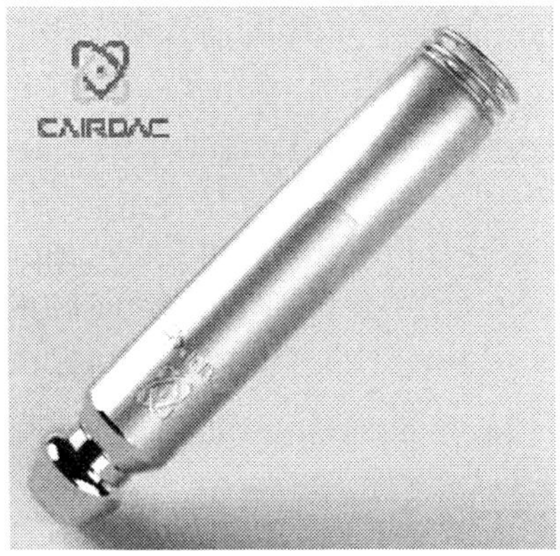

! Investment: prototype → commercialization (many M€)

- Reproducibility
- Reliability

#SensorsConverge

Energy ECS - Smart and secure energy solutions for future mobility

ECSEL Joint Undertaking

2021 – 2024

https://energyecs.eu

ENERGY ECS

UC2 - Smart transportation demo – port of Cork

ENERGY ECS

Collaboration with Irish SME NetFeasa

Self powered: >10 year battery life

Tyndall EH PMIC & simulation model

- Minimize device power consumption
- Size the EH & storage components

RISE Discrete power management solution

- Associated project with CONNECT - also look at
  - Optimising network energy efficiency & NODE efficiency
  - Optimizing based on Energy available, Criticality, Interference, etc.

CONNECT Networks of the Future

netfeasa

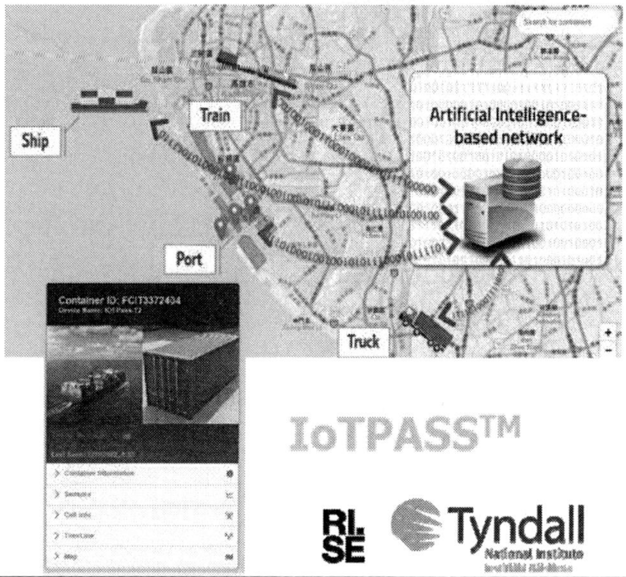

RISE Tyndall National Institute

#SensorsConverge

UC5 – Smart tire 1(2)

RISE nokian TYRES ENERGY ECS

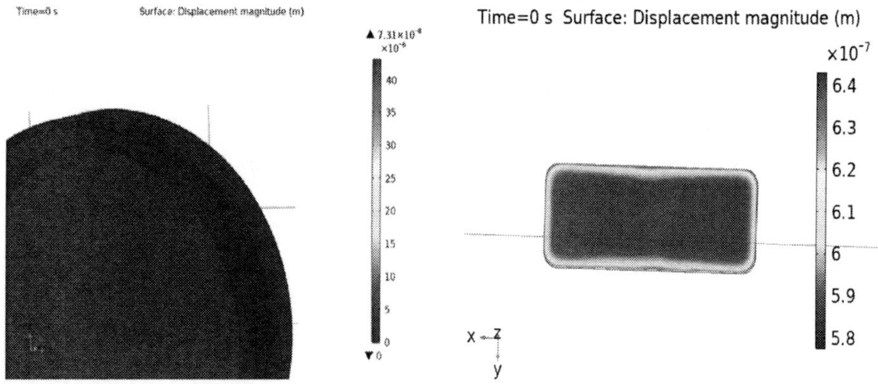

! Simultaneous simulation tire & piezo deformation

! Tire material data

#SensorsConverge

Sensors Converge

UC5 – Smart tire 2(2)

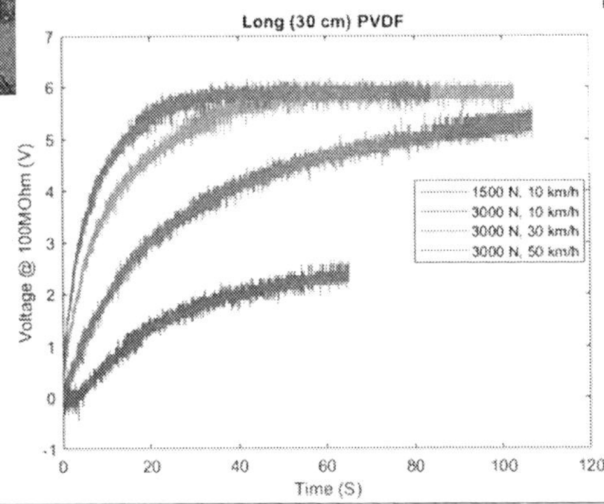

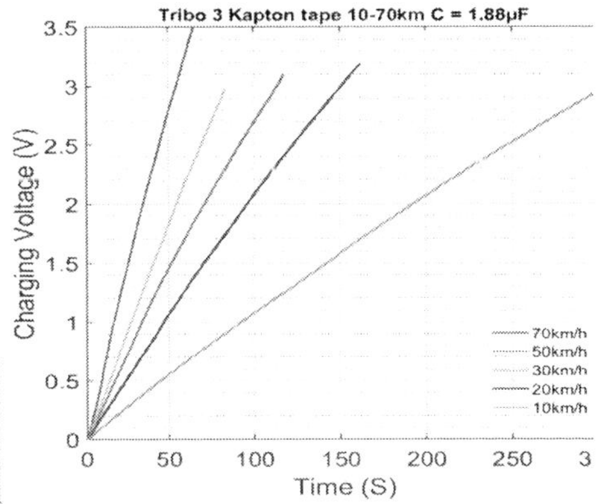

! Robust integration on tire

! Long-term reliability

> 20 mJ **available energy** (after electronics)

#SensorsConverge

INITIATIVES – 2 Technology platform concepts

- **PMIC** (Power Management IC)
- **eSiP** (energy Source in Package)
- **Simulation model**
- **Metrology of Real life Applications** (ambient energy & power consumed)

#SensorsConverge

"MISCHIEF" Multi-source energy harvesting **PMIC**

- ***Highest efficiency*** switch-mode, energy harvesting PMIC at 10s of μW point
  - Cold-start and operation over ≈1 μW to 200mW
  - Can convert low level ambient energies that are currently unusable (50mV, 10uW)
- ***Lowest quiescent current*** (I_Q) in low power regulation mode, <200nA
- Highest **end-to-end system** efficiency
- Innovate high frequency ZVS switching ***Buck Boost can handle*** both battery voltage (≈ 3V) and LV (≈ 1V8)
- Potentially can dramatically reduce size of external inductor
- Modular Flexible Mixed Signal blocks - technology Platform proofed for

FAST TRACK LOW RISK development of Next Gen control & features

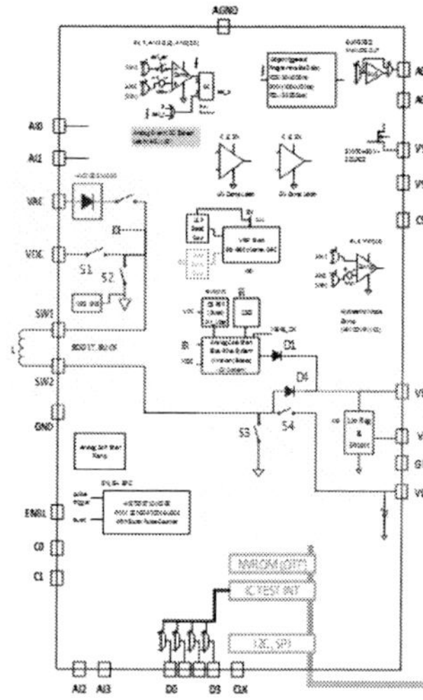

#SensorsConverge

eSiP - energy Source in Package

Integration: Ener Harv, Ener Storage, Micro PM

- Progress from COTS to research platforms

Integration Technologies:

- PCB, PCB-embedding, Flexible
- Micro-Transfer Printing (MTP)

Integrate into a SELF POWERED smart patch demo (next slide)

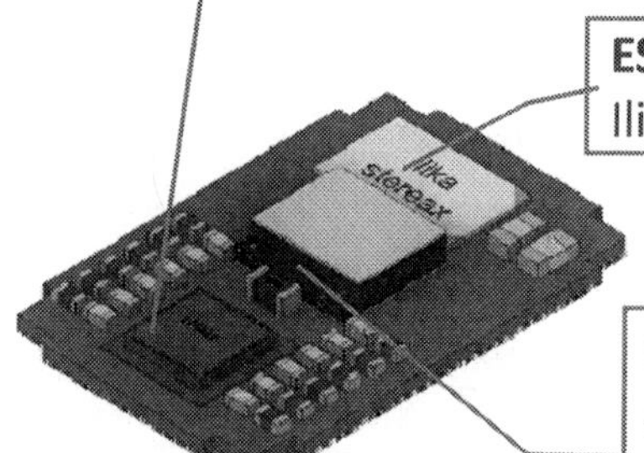

MPM: Power Management IC (PMIC):
COTS then Tyndall

ES: MicroBattery: 200-500 μAh
Ilika, Cymbet, iTEN then Tyndall

EH: Si-based Thermoelectric Generator:
TEG – (COTS then Tyndall TEG)
Wire bond to PCB

#SensorsConverge

Integration eSIP & PMIC into TEG powered patch

CONNECT
Networks of the Future

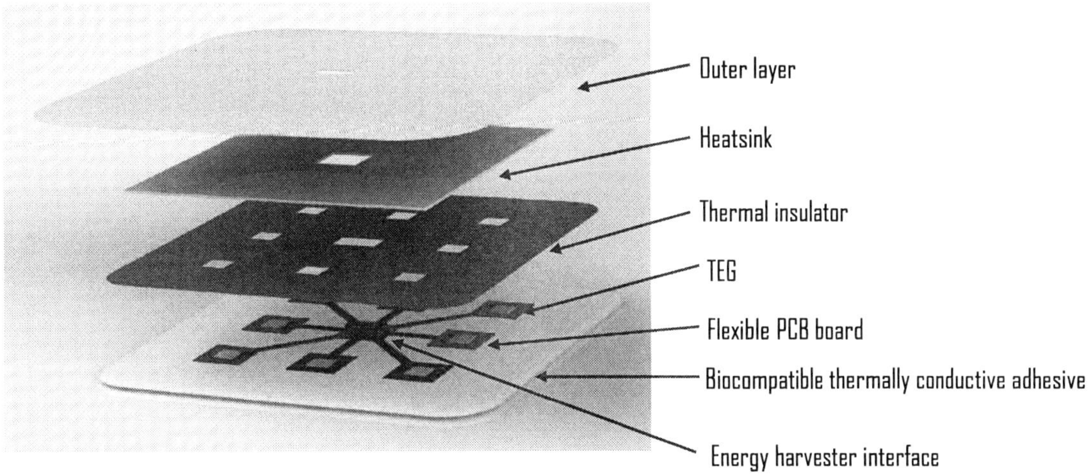

Developing a simulation model to optimise power transfer and component sizing

#SensorsConverge

Initial concept created for Irish DTIF project HOLISTICS

Sensors Converge

Smart patch - Miniaturised, wearable, self-powered

CONNECT
Networks of the Future

- Leveraging work done on HOLISTICS (Irish Gov. funded)
- **Self powered (30μW)** with 35°C temp source
- BLE temp reading every 78 sec to mobile app
- **Reconfigurable** (can miniaturize)
- **Simulation models** will optimise for lower airflow and/or increased functionality (e.g. pulse, motion, SPO_2)

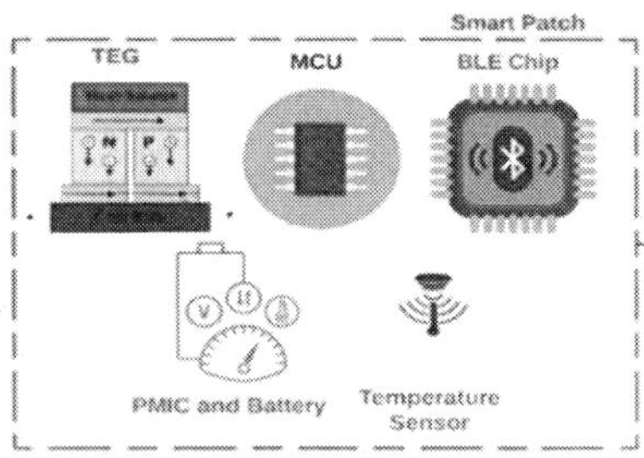

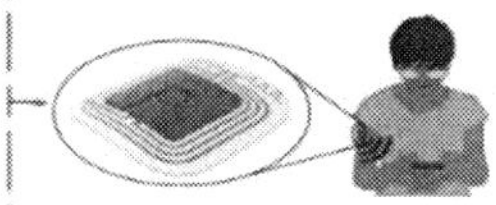

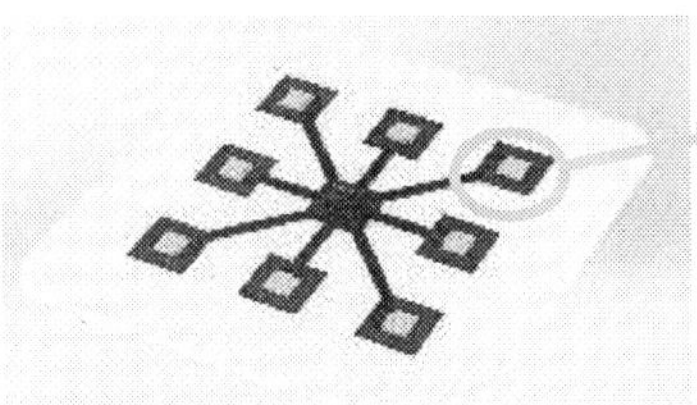

~70x70x3mm

Novel array of TEGs

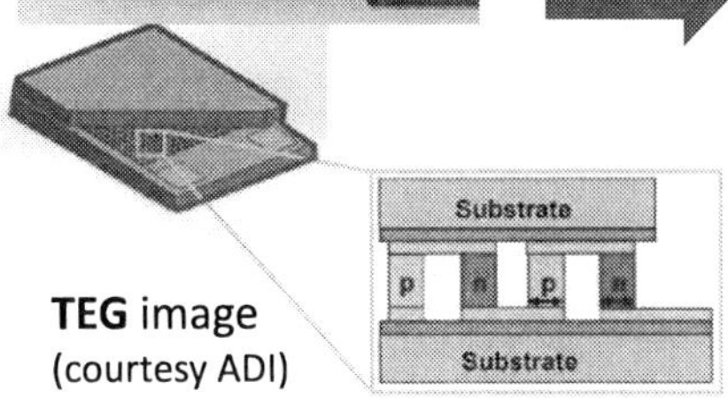

TEG image
(courtesy ADI)

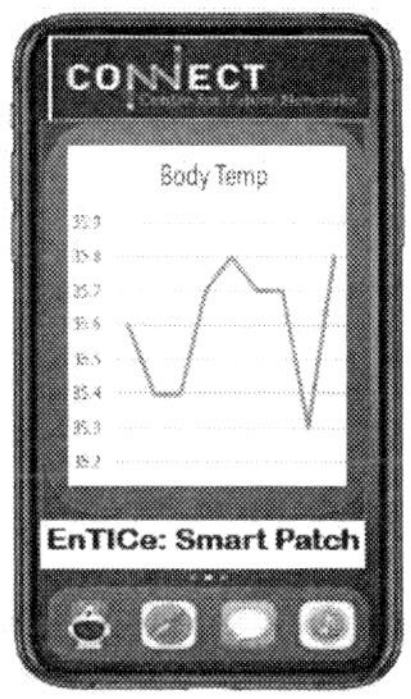

#SensorsConverge

Sensors Converge

Simulation model - EH Powered WSN battery life

- Help installers select hardware components for a potential energy harvesting deployment
- No Energy Harvesting or WSN expertise needed
- Can also be used to optimise component sizes

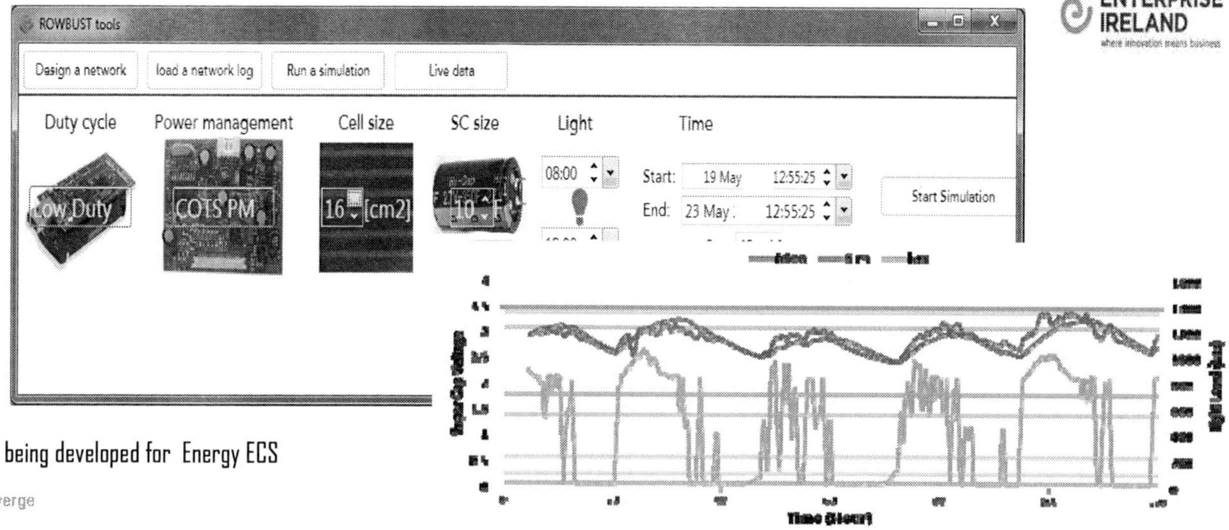

Variant of this being developed for Energy ECS

#SensorsConverge

Metrology - EH demo 1(3)

- ➢ Max/ min opened/ closed claws
- ➢ Gripping logs
- ➢ Lifting logs

- Vibrations from shock
- Mechanical vibration
- Heat from hydraulics

#SensorsConverge

Metrology - EH demo 2(3)

Metrology - EH demo 3(3)

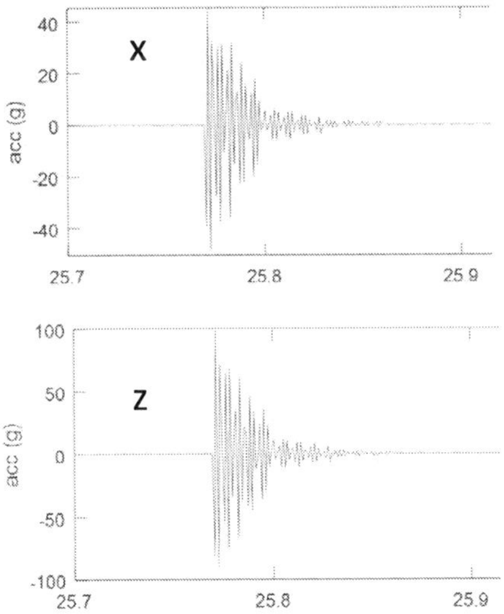

- Accelerations 80 – 200 g but extremely short period
- Temperature gradient ~ 10 – 15°C

! Correct mounting of measurement device

Metrology - Proof of Concept: Pump maintenance

Pump characteristics for harvester design and tuning

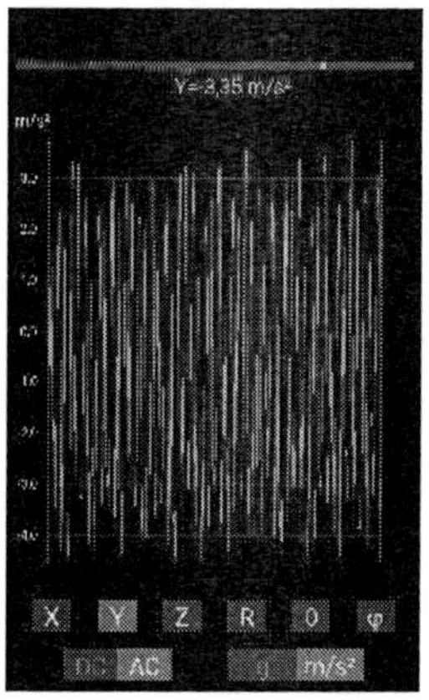

Raw acceleration Y-led on pump

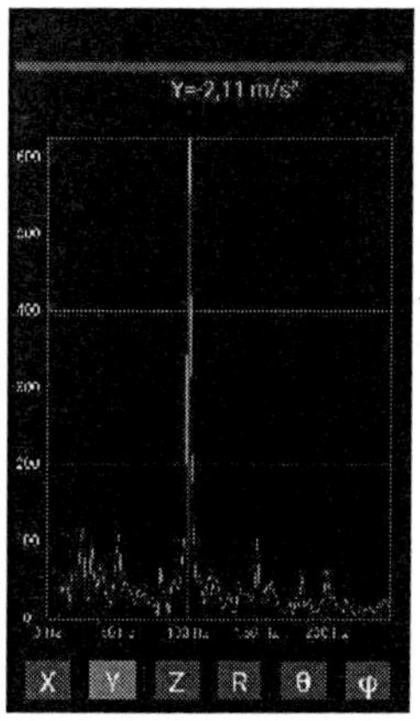

Amplitude spectrum over frequency

Tuned harvester setup attached to pump

! Correct mounting of measurement device for vibration spectra

#SensorsConverge

Sensors Converge

Conclusions

- In many applications: energy harvesting will not replace batteries but··· there is interest/need to increase battery lifetime and/or reduce cables.
  - There is a sweet spot where significant extension and in some cases autonomy can be achieved
  - The stakeholders need to collaborate to achieve this
- Market acceptance is very much application dependant:
  - Chosen harvester solution ↔ Energy source
  - Component is not a system
  - Implementation is complex
- Energy Harvesting application is still new & requires significant progress & robustness
- Collaboration with industry is essential
- Use project and tech platforms to drive best practice and learn from real life deployments

#SensorsConverge

Sensors Converge

Acknowledgements

SMART MEMPHIS

EnABLES

EU Project 730957

CONNECT Networks of the Future

Gripen of Sweden

HOLISTICS

Irish government DTIF

STARGATE

ENERGY ECS

EU JU # 101007247

MISCHIEF

VINNOVA

Sweden's innovation agency

Science Foundation Ireland sfi For what's next

ENTERPRISE IRELAND where innovation means business

#SensorsConverge

Sensors Converge

Contacts

Cristina Rusu
Energy Harvesting system
Sensors & Systems
cristina.rusu@rise.se

Mike Hayes
Energy Harvesting Power
Management & Systems
michael.hayes@tyndall.ie

#SensorsConverge

Sensors Converge

Sensors Converge

PowerFilm. MADE IN THE USA SOLAR

Pre-Conference Symposium 1: Charge controllers, who needs them? Optimizing MPPT for Energy Harvesting Applications

June 20, 2023 | Santa Clara, CA

Brad Scandrett, VP of Engineering, PowerFilm, Inc

#SensorsConverge

Components of an EH System

Storage Element

Charge Controller or EH PMIC

Transducer (TEG, Piezo, RF, Solar)

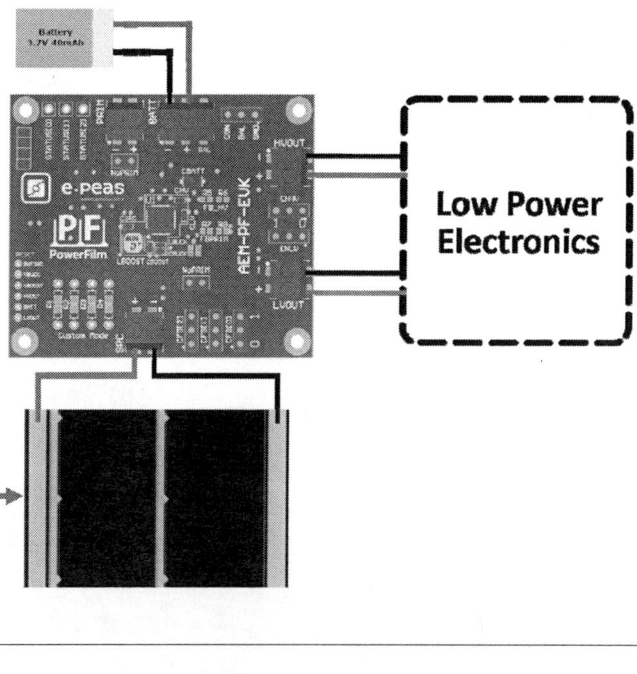

#SensorsConverge

Sensors Converge

Energy Harvesting Power Sources

Thermoelectric (TEG): Heat energy is converted into electric power. Charges in thermoelectric materials diffuse from the hot to the cold, producing a current. Up to 0.6uW/cm^2/Deg K.

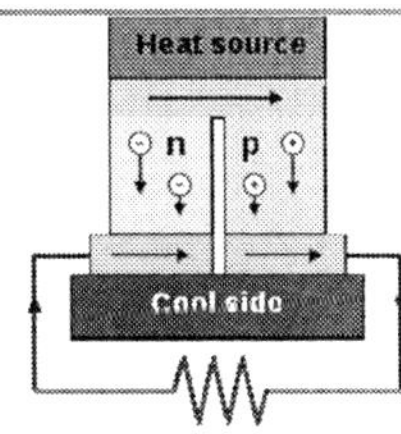

Piezo and Electrodynamic: Motion (kinetic energy) is converted into electric power using the piezoelectric effect or magnetic induction.

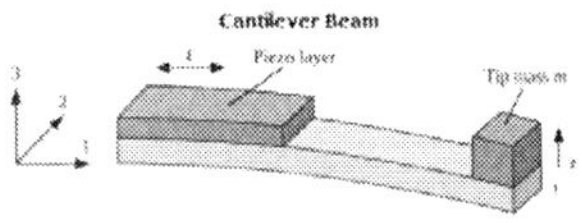

Radio Frequency (RF): Radio waves contain energy which can by converted to electric power using a rectifying antenna (far field) or magnetic coupling (near field). Up to 1.6uW/cm^2

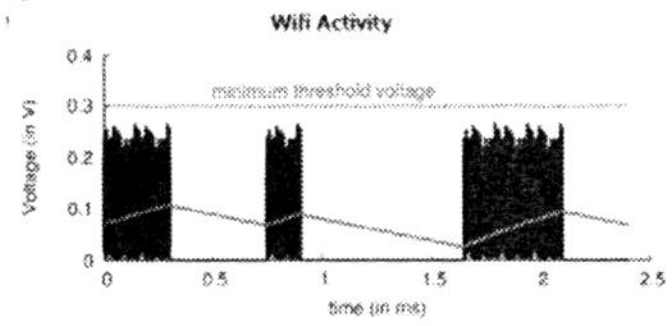

Photovoltaic (Solar): Solar cells absorb light and convert the energy to electric power. An electric field inside the material forces charges apart producing a current. 3.2uW/cm^2/100lux

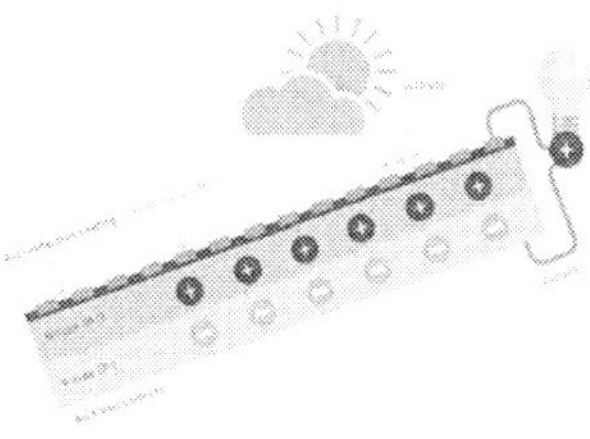

#SensorsConverge

Solar Cell IV Curve

- Power output of module based on operating point on IV curve which is determine by the impedance of the connected load
- Current changes proportionally with light intensity
- Voltage only slightly decreases until <10% light intensity
- Below 10% light voltages changes are no longer insignificant

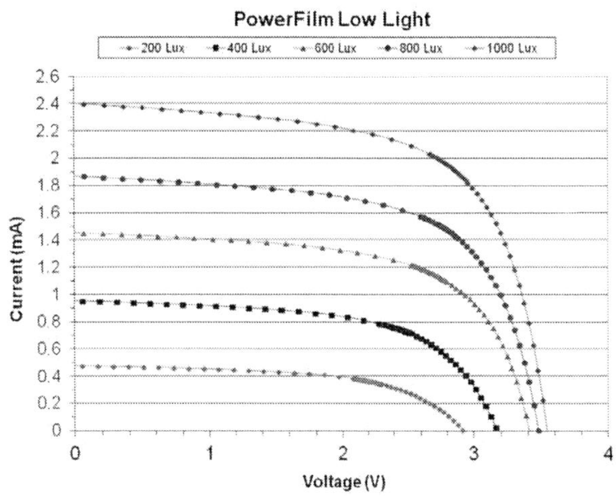

#SensorsConverge

Why do I need a charge controller? - IV Curve

- To maximize power collection from a generator the load and source impedance must match. The charge controller serves this function.
- Impedance of the source will change depending on configuration

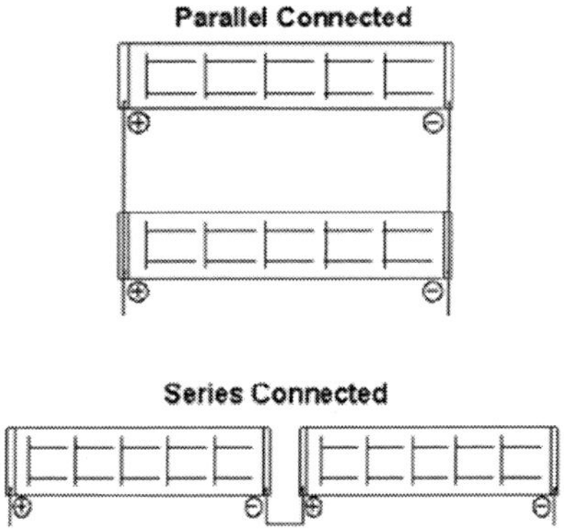

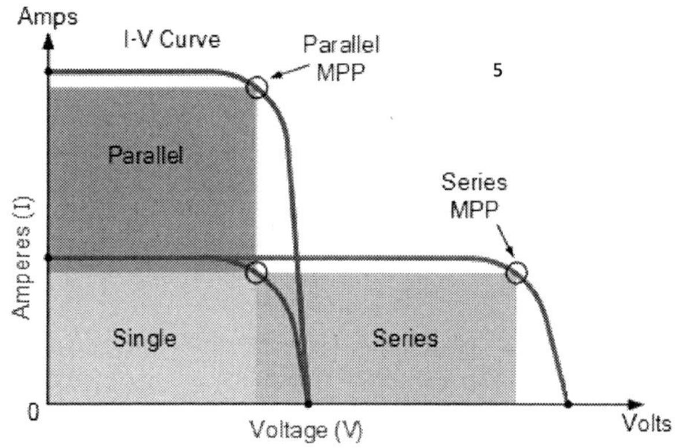

Why do I need a charge controller? - IV Curve

- MPPT vs PWM Power difference depending on state of charge for a battery.
- MPPT will provide a increase of 20% in power delivered to a battery at the end of the charge vs PWM. While providing over 55% more power when a battery is fully depleted.

MPPT VS PWM 12V

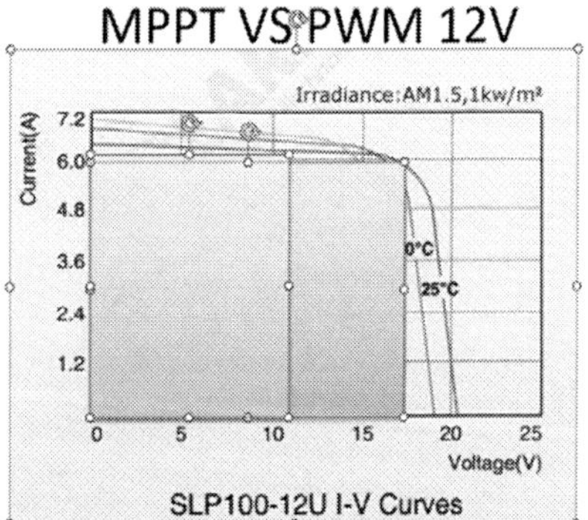

Battery Low (10.5V)

MPPT VS PWM 12V

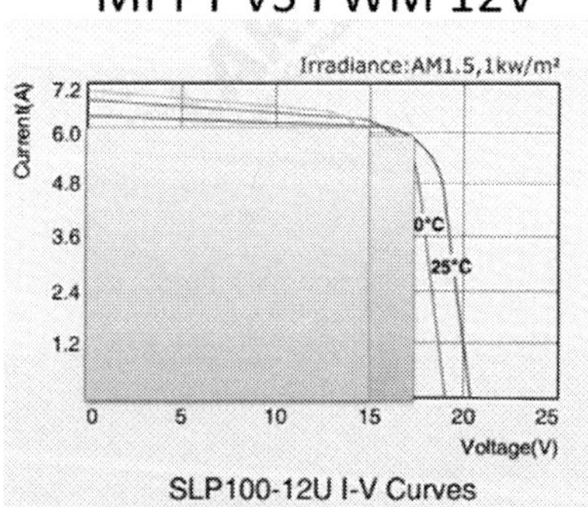

Battery Full 13.5V

What Does MPPT Mean on a Data Sheet?

- Types of MPPT
  - Fixed voltage set point
  - Ratio power point (Vpp/Voc)
  - True Maximum power point (MPPT)

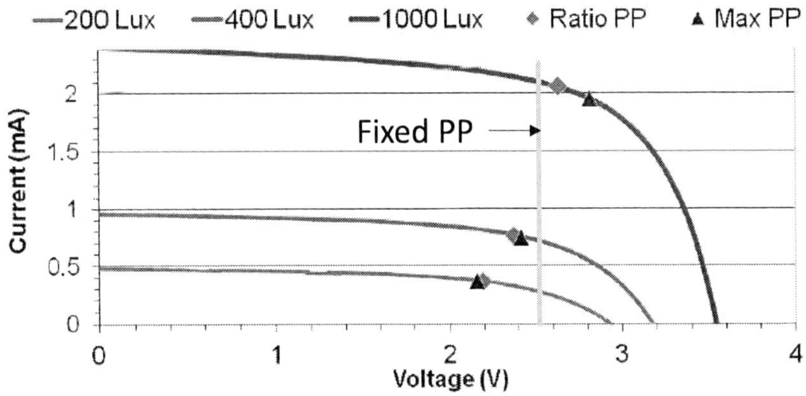

#SensorsConverge

Sensors Converge

Charge Controllers

- DC-DC Converters with Maximum Power Point Tracking (MPPT)
  - Boost – Track input voltage and increase voltage to battery voltage on output
  - Buck – Track input voltage and decrease voltage to battery voltage on output
  - Power Management IC (PMIC) – Boost or buck designed specifically for low power operation
  - Works well with all battery types and chemistries.

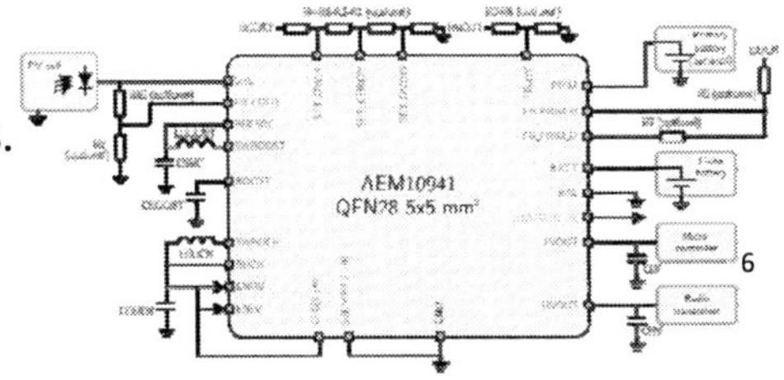

6

#SensorsConverge

Sensors Converge

Charge Controllers

- Pulse Wave Modulation (PWM) – Uses pulses to connect solar panel to battery to control charging rate and maximum charge voltage
- Typically microprocessor or dedicated PWM charging IC
- Low Cost, fewer parts than MPPT charging circuits
- Very reliable for non-Microprocessor based designs
- Works with all battery types and chemistries

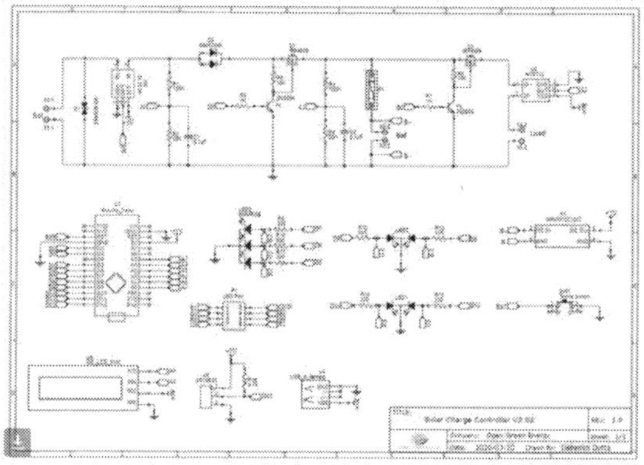

#SensorsConverge

Sensors Converge

Charge Controllers

- Direct Charging
  - Directly connects panel to battery
  - Panel voltage must be designed to match battery
  - Can include over voltage protection
  - Unprotected systems must have solar current output less than 1% of battery amp-hour capacity
  - Not recommended to pair with lithium batteries technologies
  - Works well with capacitors and lead acid batteries

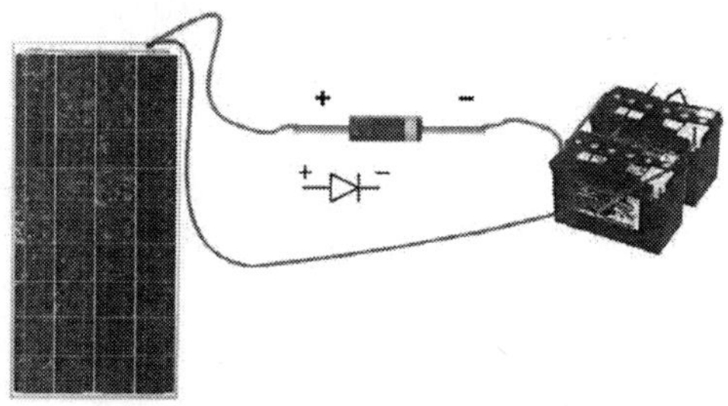

#SensorsConverge

Sensors Converge

Features Offered by PMICs

- Very low power collection (≥80mV, ≥1μA)
- Very low current consumption (<0.5μA)
- Integrated battery charging
- Switcher shutdown for reduced EMI during wireless transmission
- UV/OV protection
- Power Good Output Signals
- Integrated comparator
- Primary battery backup
- 2s super cap balancer
- Dual EH inputs
- Regulated outputs
- High efficiency (>90%)

#SensorsConverge

Sensors Converge

Selection Criteria

	PWM	Fixed PPT	Ratio PPT	Maximum PPT	Direct
Power	uW to W	uW to W	uW to W	uW to W	uW to W
Efficiency	60-90%	85-95%	90-95%	90-95%	80-95%
Topology	Buck	Buck, Boost	Buck, Boost	Buck, Boost	Direct
Low or Varying Power Transducer Optimized	No	No	Yes	Yes	No
Cost	$$	$$	$$$	$$$$	$

#SensorsConverge

Sensors Converge

Getting Started

Development kits are a great way to start and available with many different harvesters and radios

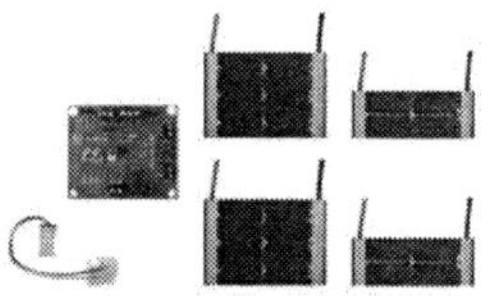

AEM10941 – EPeas[7]

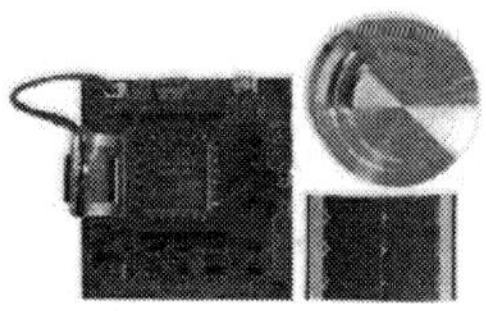

EMH-UNIV-1 – Xidas[8]

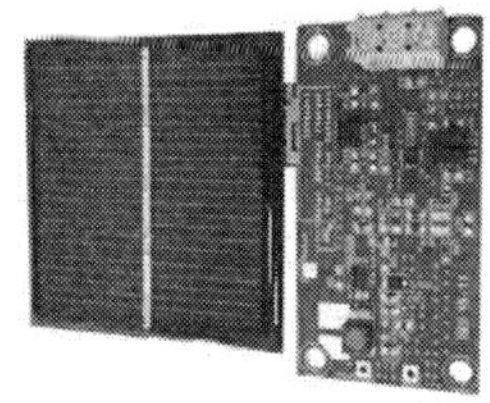

SPV1040 – STMicro[9]

MAX20361 – Maxim[14]

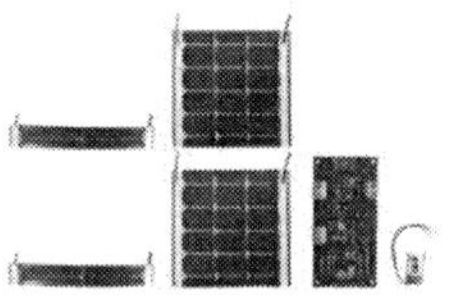

BQ25570 – TI and nRF52832 – Nordic[11]

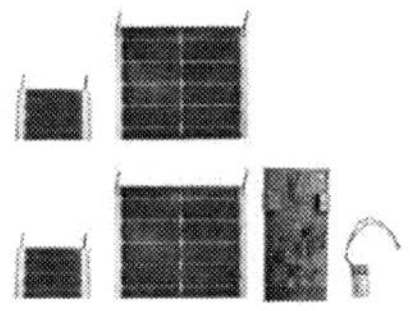

BQ25570 & CC2650 – TI[12]

ADP5091 – Analog Devices[13]

EH IC Comparison Chart

IC Part Number	MFG	startup voltage	Sampling Time	Min Current Power	Max Current Power	MPPT programmable	Input voltage range	AC Input	Quiescent Current	LDO Reg	LDO Reg	Protection	Primary Battery	Super Cap	size(mm)	Price 100pcs
AEM10941	EPeas	380mV	5 sec	3uW	110mA	Ratio 70,75,85,90%	50mv-5V	No	400nA	1.2/1.8V	20mA	OC/ODC	yes	Yes	5 x 5	3.87
EHM-UNIV-1	Xidas	380mV		6uW	150mA	MPPT	3.6V	Yes (EM)	390nA	1.5-3.6V	150mA	OC/ODC	No	Yes	25 x 25	45.5
SPV1040	STMicro	300mV			1.8A	MPPT	0.3-5.5V	No	60uA	2-5.2V	NA	OV/OC/OT	No	No	3 x 4.4	3.28
BQ25570RGRR	Ti	600mV	16 Sec	5uW	230mA	MPPT programmable	0.1-5.1	No	488nA	2-5.5V	110mA	OV/ODC	No	Yes	3.5 x 3.5	5.42
ADP5091/2	Analog Devices	380mV	16 Sec	6mW	600mW	MPPT	0.08-3.3V	No	510nA	1.5-3.6V	150mA	OV/ODC	Yes	No	4 x 4	5.81
MAX20361	Analog Devices	400mV	64 Sec	15uW	300mW	Ratio Programmable	0.225-2.5V	No	1.43uA	NA	NA	OV	No	Yes	1.63 x 1.23	3.30(Qty1k)
CC2650	TI	Bluetooth Low Energy Transceiver														
nRF52832	Nordic Semi	Bluetooth Low Energy Transceiver, Bluetooth Mesh														

Questions??

#SensorsConverge

Sensors Converge

References

1. HEHN, THORSTEN. Cmos Circuits for Piezoelectric Energy Harvesters. SPRINGER, 2016.
2. Paul, Douglas. "Thermoelectric Energy Harvesting." School of Engineering University of Glasgow, U.K, School of Engineering University of Glasgow, U.K.
3. http://www.stion.com/technology/photovoltaic-effect/
4. Pinuela, Manuel, et al. "Ambient RF Energy Harvesting in Urban and Semi-Urban Environments." IEEE Transactions on Microwave Theory and Techniques, vol. 61, no. 7, 2013, pp. 2715–2726., doi:10.1109/tmtt.2013.2262687.
5. "Solar Cell I-V Characteristic and the Solar Cell I-V Curve." Alternative Energy Tutorials, www.alternative-energy-tutorials.com/energy-articles/solar-cell-i-v-characteristic.html.
6. AEM10941 Solar Harvesting | Photovoltaic Energy Harvesting | e-peas, https://e-peas.com/product/aem10941/
7. https://www.digikey.com/en/products/detail/powerfilm-inc/DEV-EPEAS/14008990 or https://www.powerfilmsolar.com/products/development-kits/aem-pf-evk-solar-development-kit-with-e-peas-pmic
8. https://xidasiot.com/power/eh-edu-1
9. https://www.digikey.com/en/products/detail/stmicroelectronics/STEVAL-ISV012V1/3083468
10. https://www.digikey.com/en/products/detail/nowi/NH2D0245-EVAL-BOARD/13694744
11. https://www.digikey.com/en/products/detail/powerfilm-inc/DEV-BLE-NS/12088517 or https://www.powerfilmsolar.com/products/development-kits/solar-development-kit-with-nordic-ble
12. https://www.digikey.com/en/products/detail/powerfilm-inc/DEV-BLE-TI/9559450 or https://www.powerfilmsolar.com/products/development-kits/solar-development-kit-with-ti-ble
13. https://www.digikey.com/en/products/detail/analog-devices-inc/ADP5091-2-EVALZ/6189737
14. https://www.digikey.com/en/products/detail/maxim-integrated/MAX20361EVKIT/13279720
15. https://www.instructables.com/ARDUINO-PWM-SOLAR-CHARGE-CONTROLLER-V-202/
16. https://www.pcdvd.com.tw/showthread.php?t=1200800&page=2

#SensorsConverge

Sensors Converge

Sensors Converge

Fraunhofer ISIT

Pre-Conference Symposium 1: Leveraging mechanical MEMS energy harvesting for IoT applications

June 20, 2023 | Santa Clara, CA

Dr. Björn Gojdka, Fraunhofer Institute for Silicon Technology ISIT, Germany

#SensorsConverge

Agenda

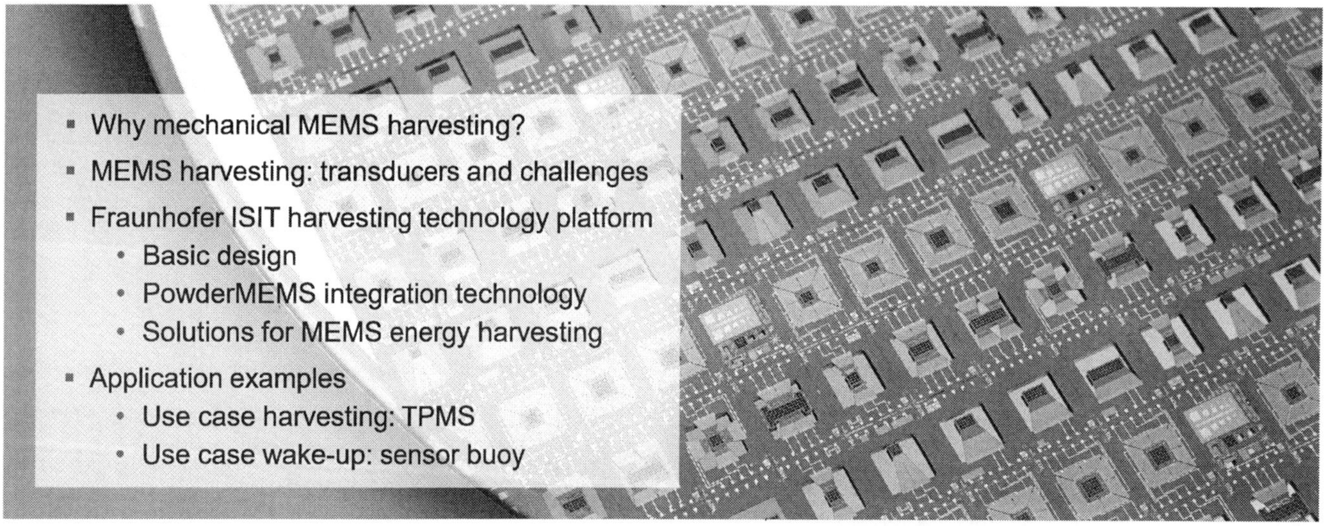

- Why mechanical MEMS harvesting?
- MEMS harvesting: transducers and challenges
- Fraunhofer ISIT harvesting technology platform
  - Basic design
  - PowderMEMS integration technology
  - Solutions for MEMS energy harvesting
- Application examples
  - Use case harvesting: TPMS
  - Use case wake-up: sensor buoy

Why MEMS energy harvesting?

"A huge challenge ahead of us for the 20 next years, is to **reduce the energy footprint** of the IoT by designing objects that … **use any source of energy** one could think about such as **vibration, heat and light**." - *Prof. Reinhold Dauskardt, Stanford University [1]*

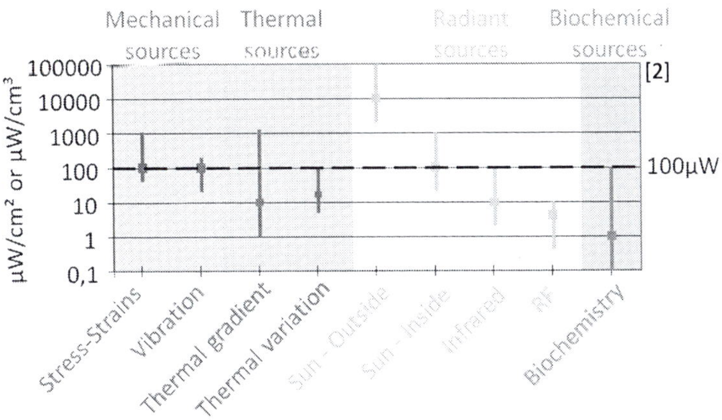

- Light great energy source
- No light, no thermal gradients?
  → mechanical sources required
- Miniaturized, autonomous wireless sensor nodes
  → micro energy harvesting

[1] World Materials Forum, France (2018), Big Data/AI for Materials Efficiency
[2] S. Boisseau et al. (2012), https://doi.org/10.5772/51360

#SensorsConverge 06/20/2023 Dr. Björn Gojdka, Fraunhofer Institute for Silicon Technology ISIT, Germany Sensors Converge

Extension of battery life – what's realistic?

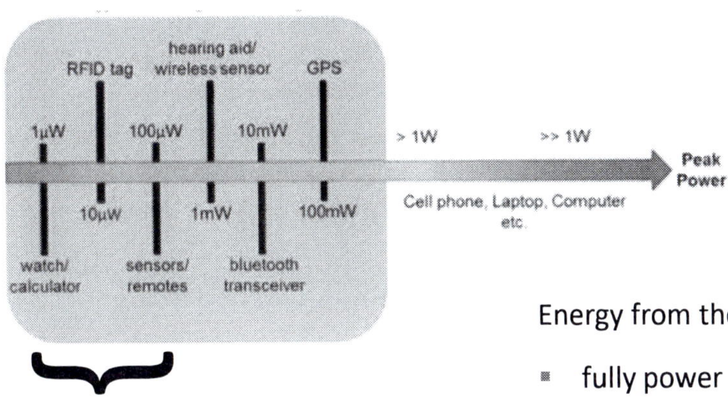

MEMS energy harvesting

Energy from the environment can be harvested to…

- fully power an electronic device
- complement a battery
- lossless stand-by, i.e. zero-power wake up

[1] ConFlow Power Group, "Market Research on Energy Harvesting for IoT Devices" (2020)

#SensorsConverge 06/20/2023 Dr. Björn Gojdka, Fraunhofer Institute for Silicon Technology ISIT, Germany Sensors Converge

Transducers for mechanical MEMS harvesters

Electromagnetic

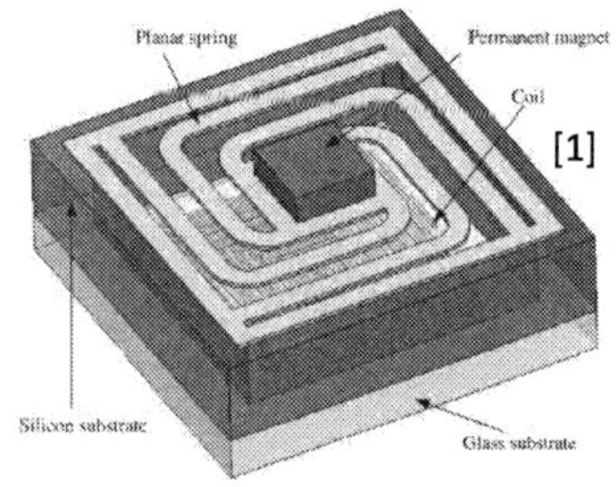

- Typical configurations yield <100 mV order of magnitude
- Monolithic manufacturing of magnets and coils challenging

Electrostatic

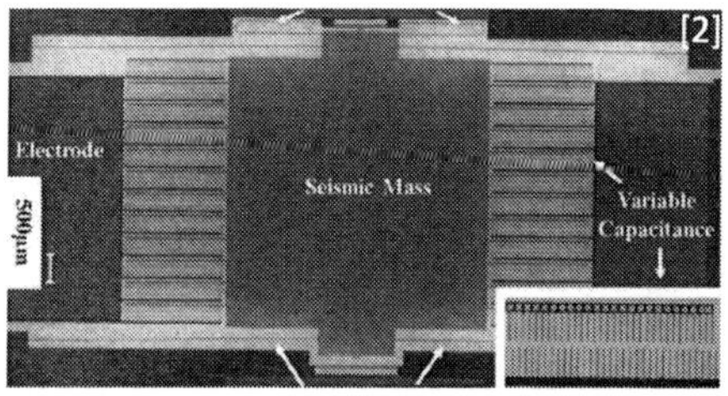

- Power scales with mass vs. fragile comb structures
- Voltage/charge source required

Piezoelectric

- High power density
- Useful voltage level
- Established for mass manufacturing

[1] Wang et al. (2007), https://doi.org/10.1016/j.mejo.2007.10.002
[2] B. Vysotskyi (2019), https://theses.hal.science/tel-01968067

Piezoelectric energy harvester

Table 1. Summary of maximum energy densities of three kinds of transducers.[1]

Type	Energy density (mJ cm^{-3})	Equation	Assumptions
Piezoelectric	35.4	$(1/2)\sigma_y^2 k^2/2c$	PZT 5 H*
Electromagnetic	24.8	$(1/2)B^2/\mu_0$	0.25 T
Electrostatic	4	$(1/2)\varepsilon_0 E^2$	3×10^7 V m^{-1}

* replacing PZT with AlN / AlScN piezoelectric power density becomes even more superior

Advantages of piezoelectric energy harvesters

- Well-suited for mass microfabrication
- Typical output voltages 1-20 V
- Highest power output density
- Current development of AlScN potentially increases power output 2-4-fold

[1] S. Roundy et al. (2003), https://doi.org/10.1088/0964-1726/13/5/018

Challenges of MEMS energy harvesting

- Generation of sufficient power output
- High q-factors of MEMS oscillators -> narrow excitation frequency band; typ. f_{res} = 1-3 kHz
- Application-specific excitation geometries: linear, rotational, shock, contact, non-contact

Solution?

- A dedicated MEMS design for each application scenario?
  - MEMS need volume (or high cost per device)

→ Versatile MEMS harvesting technology platform required

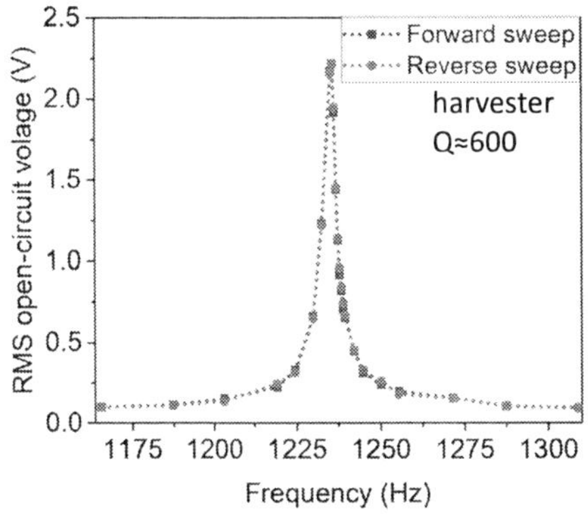

M.T. Bodduluri (2022), https://doi.org/10.3390/mi13060863

Fraunhofer ISIT MEMS Energy Harvester

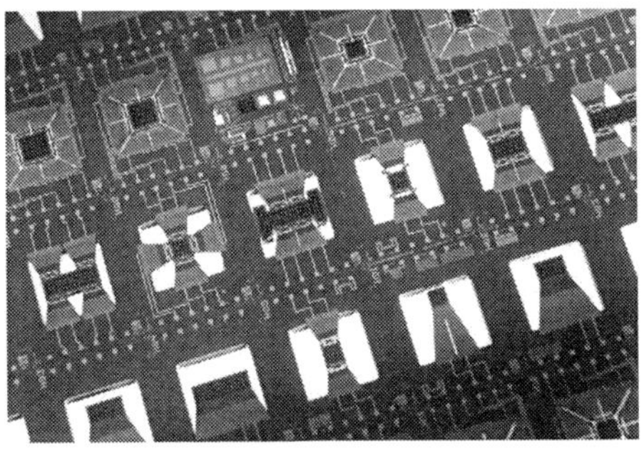

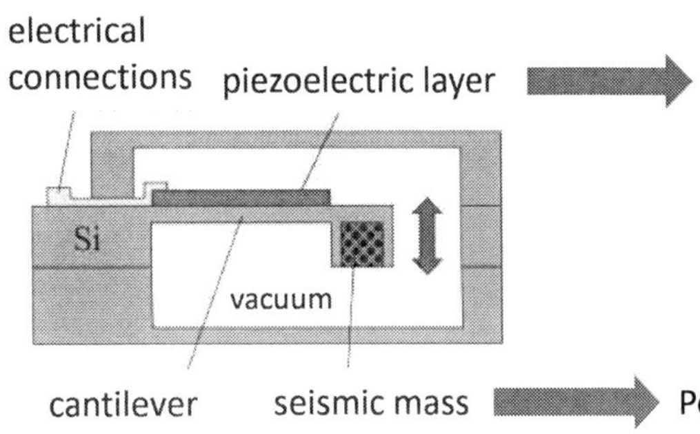

3. Aluminum (Scandium) Nitride AlN / AlScN

PowderMEMS

1. Variable mass density
2. Integrated Micromagnets

PowderMEMS micromanufacturing

1. Dry filling of microcavities	2. Solidification by atomic layer deposition	3. Substrate conditioning for post-processing

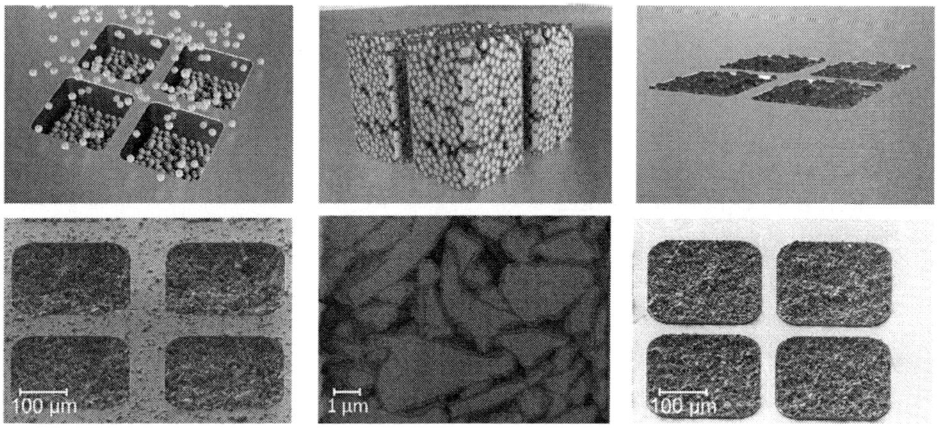

Unique set of micromanufacturing properties:

- free choice of materials
- tuning of local mass density
- precise wafer-level integration of 3D micromagnets

T. Lisec et al. (2022), https://doi.org/10.3390/mi13030398

1. PowderMEMS: variable mass density

Same design, variable resonance frequency

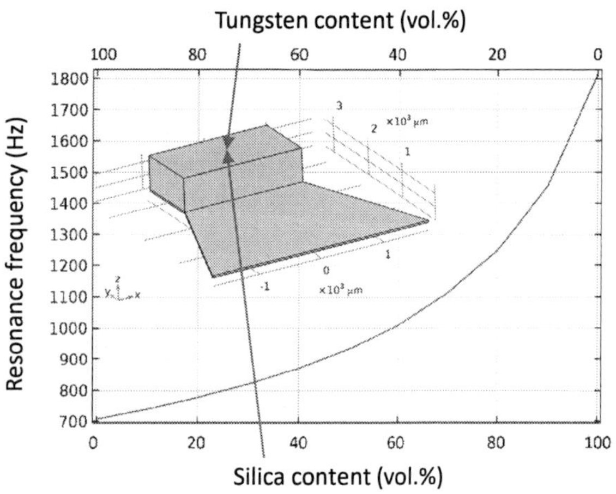

Proof mass made of powder mixtures

- variation of mass density in the same MEMS design
- tuning of resonance frequency without changing the design
- adaption to different excitation spectra with same design and same manufacturing flow

2. PowderMEMS: integration of micromagnets

Same design, various excitation modes

- contactless harvesting
- linear, rotational, shock excitations
- magnetic field sensing

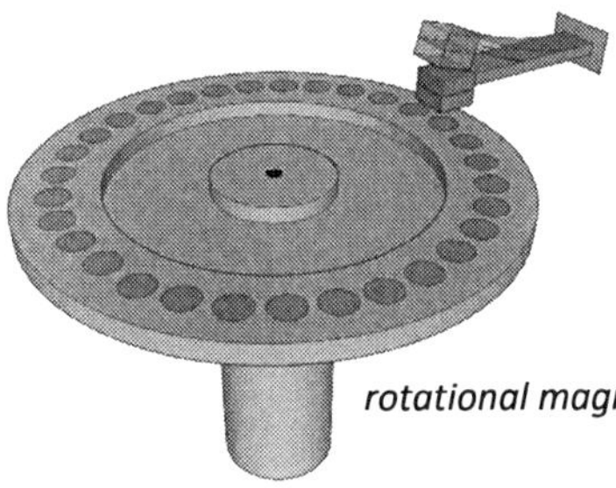

rotational magnetic excitation

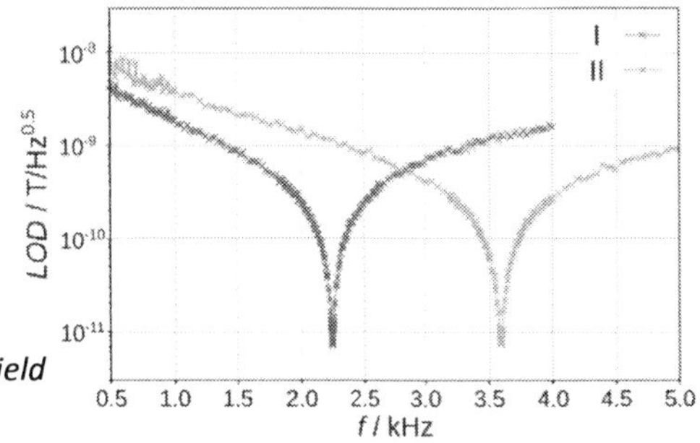

excitation by ac magnetic field

F. Niekiel (2019), https://doi.org/10.1016/j.sna.2019.111560

Rotational contactless harvesting

Magnetic plucking setup

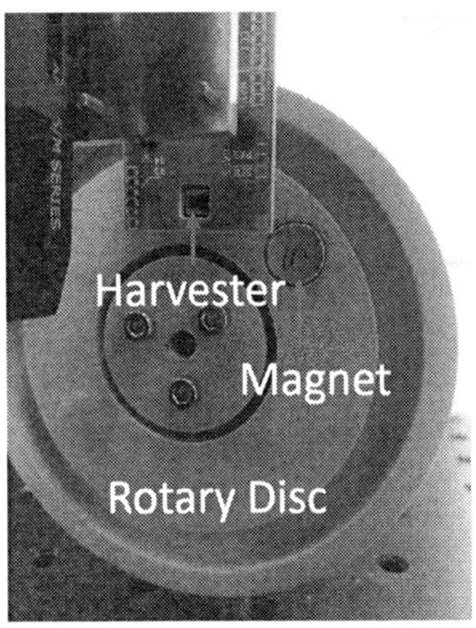

Harvester response

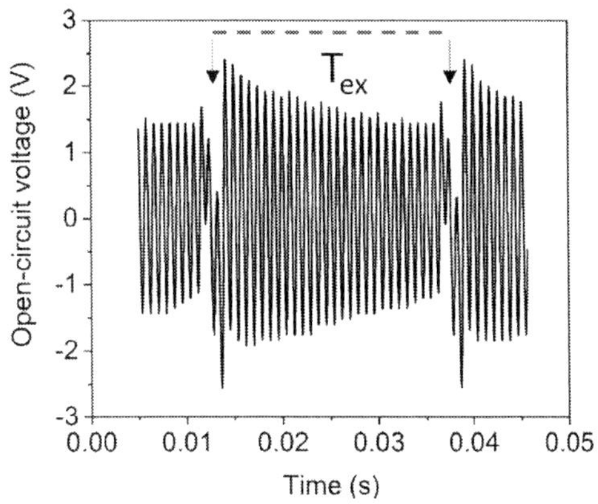

Frequency up-conversion:

- Harvester f_{res}≈1kHz
- f_{exc}=42 Hz
- „shock"-like excitation

M.T. Bodduluri (2022), https://doi.org/10.3390/mi13060863

3. Power boost: AlScN vs. AlN

Magnetic plucking

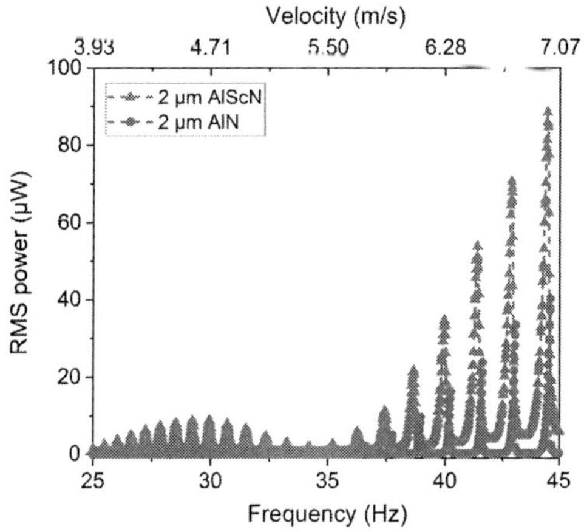

Excitation in resonance

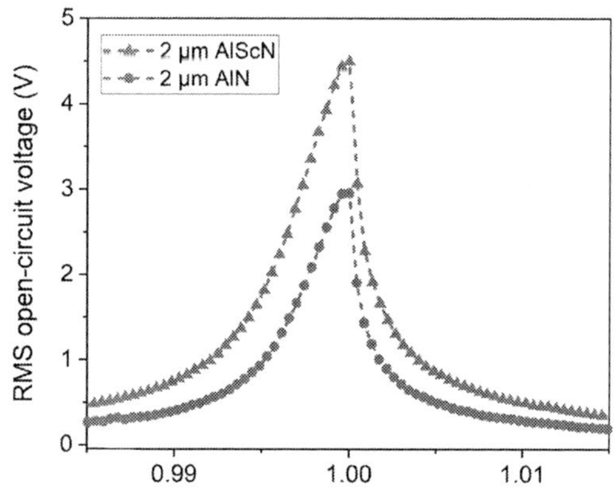

→ AlScN power output 2-4 times higher than AlN, under development

Application: tire pressure monitoring system (TPMS)

[1]

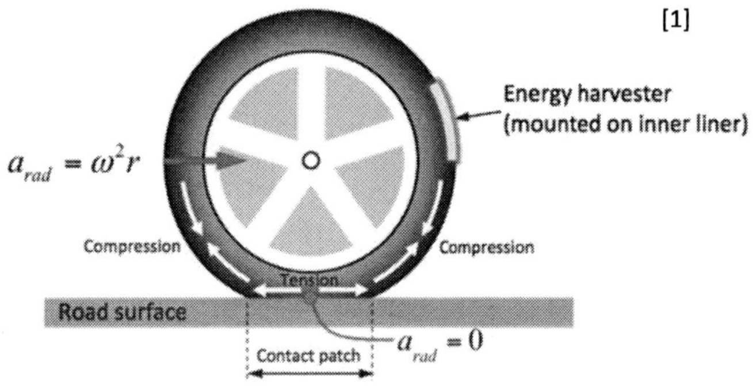

[2]

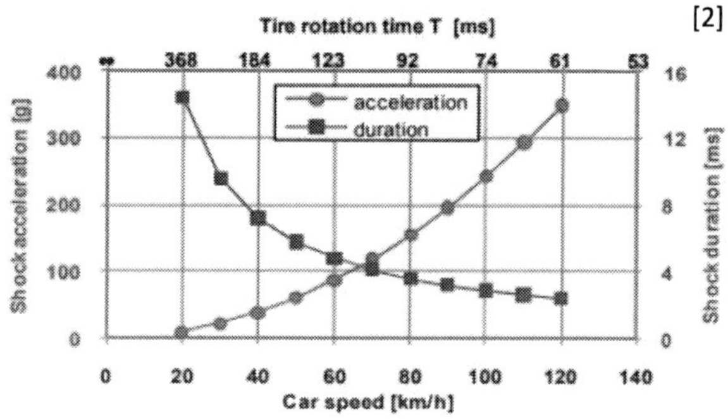

[3]

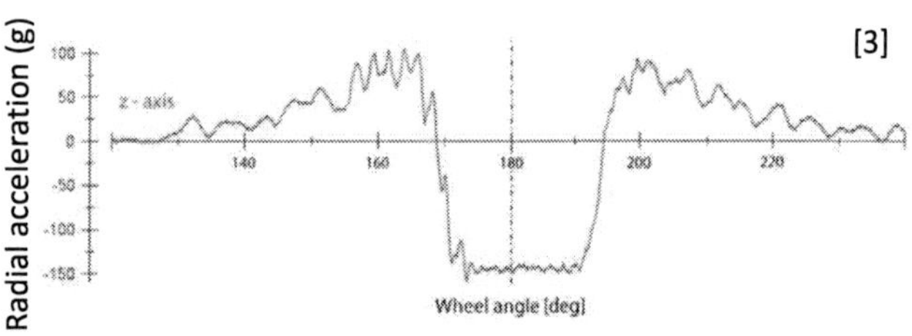

- no light; abundant mechanical energy
- power consumption 20-100 µW [4]

[1] C. R. Bowen et al. (2015), https://doi.org/10.1002/aenm.201401787
[2] R. Elfrink (2011), https://doi.org/10.1109/IEDM.2011.6131639
[3] Niskanen et al. (2014), https://doi.org/10.1080/00423114.2014.898777
[4] M. Germer (2022), https://doi.org/10.1109/JIOT.2022.3152547

Piezoelectric MEMS for TPMS

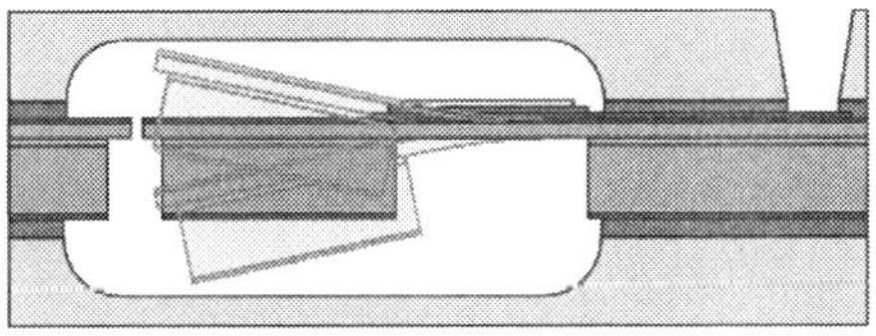

[1]

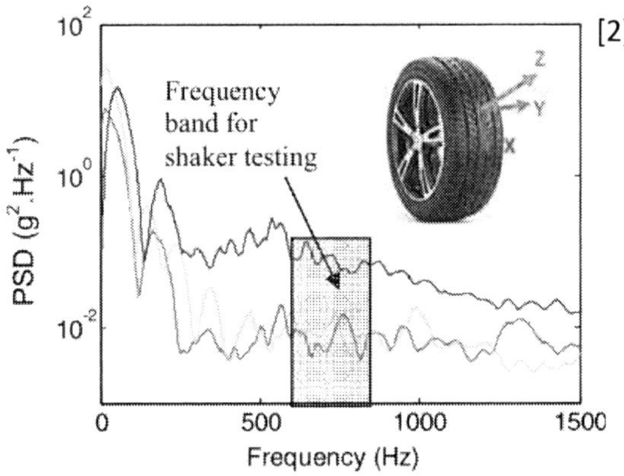

[2]

- Power output [1]: 42µW @ 70 km/h
- ISIT technology platform estimated to reach 100µW @ 50 km/h
  - integration of PowderMEMS tungsten mass
  - AlScN instead of AlN
  - challenge: output vs. stability

[1] Elfrink et al. (2011), https://doi.org/10.1109/IEDM.2011.6131639
[2] Renaud et al. (2013), https://doi.org/10.1109/Transducers.2013.6626861

Application: zero power wake-up

General idea:

- battery-powered system
- few relevant events; completely off
- harvester generates wake-up voltage
- virtually no power consumption during off time, P_{leak}<0.1 nW

Right: comparison of periodically listening sensor module vs. event-based passive wakeup (eZ430-RF2480 board, MSP430F2274 microcontroller, CC2480 radio module and LSM6DSOX gyro)

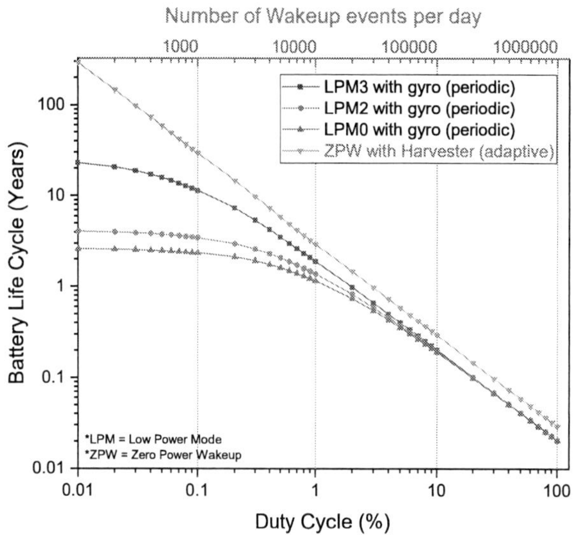

M. Ahmed et al. (2022), https://doi.org/10.3390/mi13030407

Example: Autonomous sensor buoy

Scenario:

- Few relevant sensor events, e.g. freak wave
- very long lifetime without battery replacement
- „dirty“ conditions

Illustration of scenario

Project OTC-BASE, funded by the German Federal Ministry for Education and Research

Example: Autonomous sensor buoy

Wake-up demonstrator

- single event/impact suffices
- no sophisticated electronics required

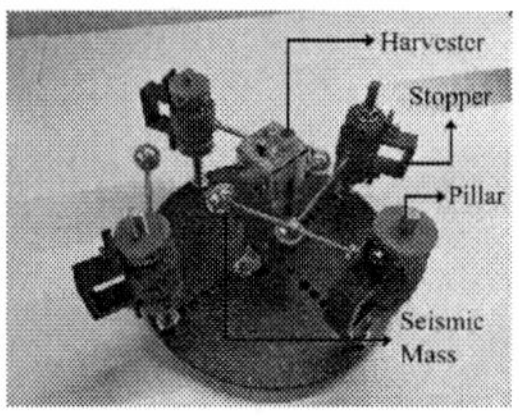

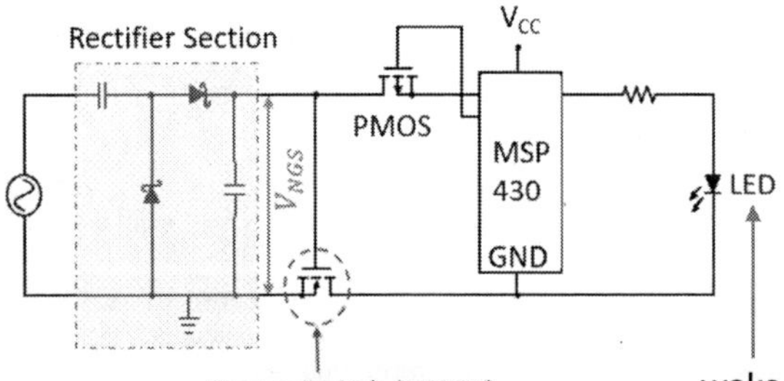

wake-up indicator (finally sensor, GPS etc.)

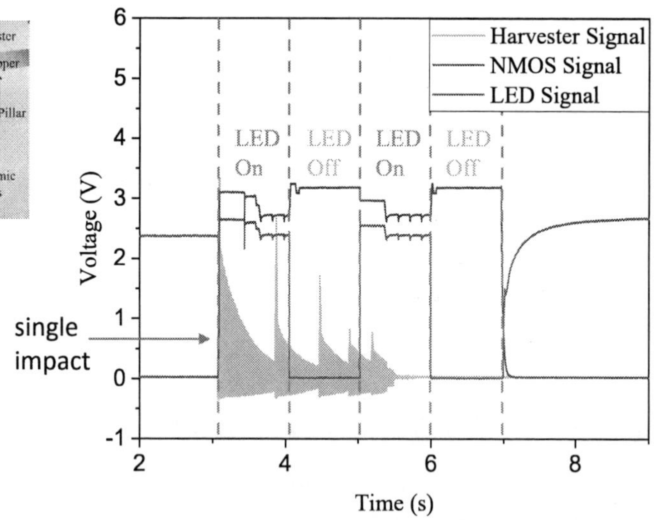

Project OTC-BASE, funded by the German Federal Ministry for Education and Research

Summary

Energy harvesting can enhance device life in IoT applications by
- providing an infinite power source, replacing the battery
- complementing a battery
- extending battery life with zero-power standby

Depending on the application, challenges are
- narrow bandwidth
- sufficient power output
- costs for application-specific designs

Fraunhofer ISIT's technology platform
- adaption of resonance frequency in a MEMS design
- high performance AlScN transducer
- flexible excitation

Fraunhofer

Fraunhofer-Gesellschaft

Contact

Dr.-Ing. Björn Gojdka
Fraunhofer ISIT
Business Unit MEMS Applications
Bjoern.Gojdka@isit.fraunhofer.de
Tel. +49 4821 171412

Confidential

VUERON

LiDAR Solution Provider for Automotive

Sensors Converge

June 20–22, 2023 | Santa Clara, CA

Overview

Since 2019, Vueron has achieved milestones and built various business references, attracting over $10 million in investments

Overview

Name	Vueron Technology Co., Ltd.
Foundation	October 10th 2019
CEO	Joseph Kim
Office	HQ Seoul, South Korea San Jose office Munich office
Team	45 (32 engineers)
Key milestones	• Obtain one LiDAR only self-driving permit in Korea / California / Nevada • Revealed smart Infra LiDAR solution • Revealed eco-friendly, self-driving truck

History

2023. 01	Release VueTruck – eco-friendly, self-driving truck
2022. 06	Obtained AV permit in US (CA / NV)
2021. 12	Pre-A Funding U$10m (KDB, Bon Angels and more)
2021. 02	Obtained AV permit in Korea
2020. 11	Release VueTwo – Smart infra solution
2020. 07	Release VueOne – Automotive solution
2020. 05	Seed Funding(Naver, BonAngels)
2019. 10	Vueron Technology Foundation

Sensors Converge

Strictly Private and Confidential

History

Driven by our mission to make people safer,
Vueron is dedicated to addressing the challenges of the autonomous driving industry and smart cities with Vueron LiDAR solution

Value

Mission "To make people safer by providing the best LiDAR solution"

Business LiDAR H/W, LiDAR S/W → Integration / Module

Product

VueOne	• Autonomous Driving / ADAS
VueTwo	• Smart infrastructure
VueTruck	• Eco-friendly, self-driving truck

Global Networks

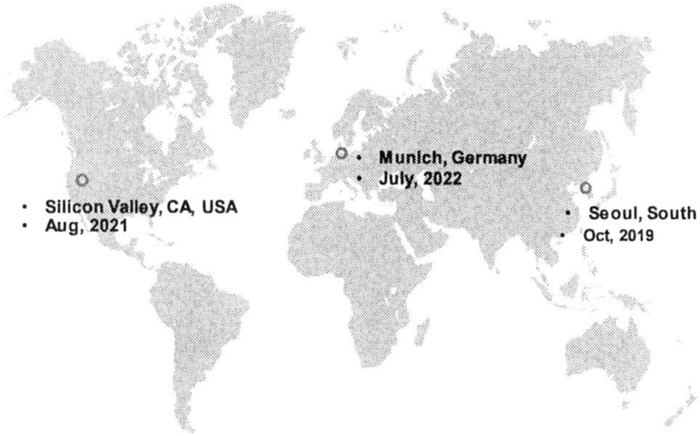

Sensors Converge

Vueron Product Description : Software

LiDAR software provides essential information for autonomous driving system by pre-processing millions of data points per second from LiDAR hardware

LiDAR Hardware

• **Hardware only provides point information**
– Point X, Point Y, Point Z, and Point Intensity

LiDAR Software

• **Software provides object information**
– Position, Size, Direction, Velocity, and more

Sensors Converge

Vueron Product Description : VueOne

VUERON

VueOne is a LiDAR perception software for autonomous driving and ADAS system

Basic output

- Car
- Commercial Vehicle
- Pedestrian
- Cyclist
- Unknown object
- Velocity
- Object contour

Functions

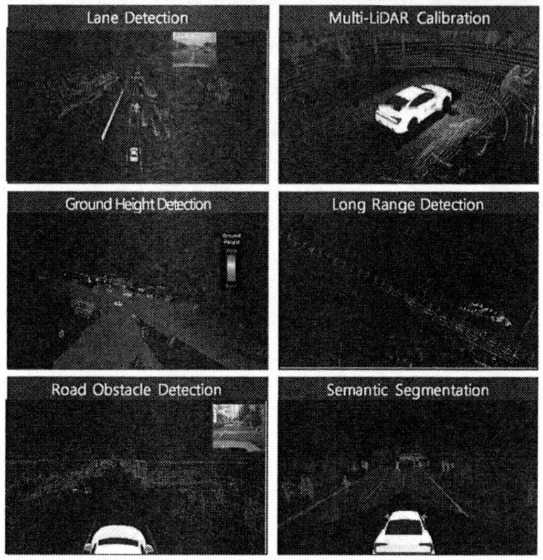

Platforms

intel. NVIDIA. RENESAS TEXAS INSTRUMENTS

Vueron Product Description : VueTwo

VUERON

VueTwo is the best LiDAR perception software for smart infrastructure

Basic output

- Object Class (People, Car, and more*)
- Distance
- Height
- Velocity
- Direction
- Trajectory

* More classes are available upon request.

Functions

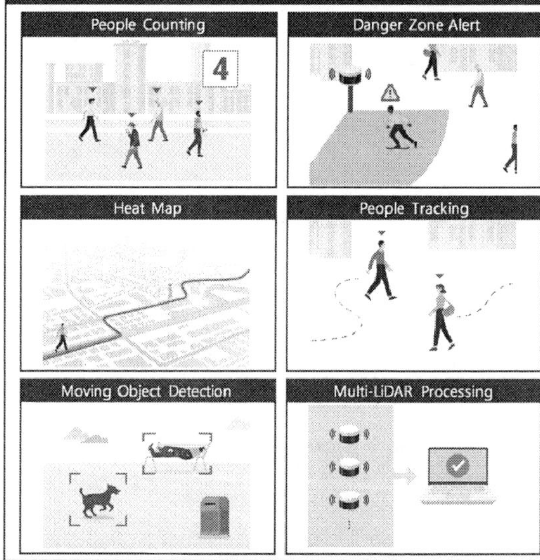

Platforms

intel. 4G NVIDIA. HARDKERNEL

Vueron Product Description : VueTruck

VueTruck is a specially designed Lv 4 autonomous trucking system for the delivery of fresh and frozen foods from hubs to customers

VueTruck - 001

System configurations

Operations

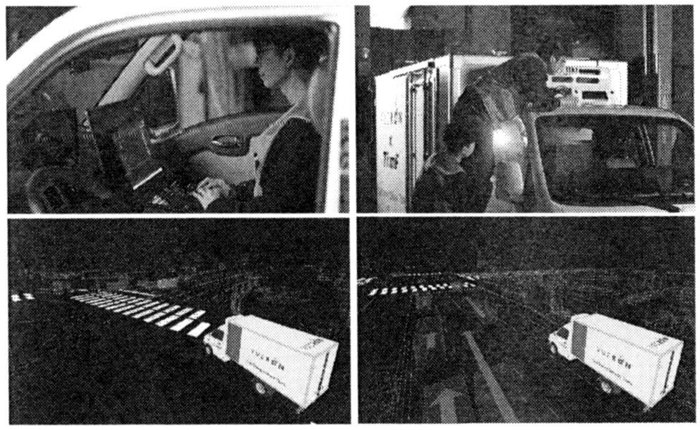

Key summary

1. Lv.4 autonomous trucks powered by our cutting-edge LiDAR solution, VueOne.
2. Sustainable delivery solution by utilizing electric trucks and refrigeration boxes
3. Providing highly reliable services through our partnership with 'TeamFresh', Korea's #1 cold-chain logistics company

VueOne's Competitiveness : Summary

VueOne enables the clients to deploy the best LiDAR solution with top level of safety and performance for autonomous driving to their current mass-produced vehicles

Core Competencies		VueOne's competitiveness
1 High Safety & Performance	• Due to insufficient S/W development ability, LiDAR H/W manufacturers try to build up ecosystem by securing S/W partnering companies	• World's first to obtain an autonomous driving license in Korea and US with only one LiDAR • Continue to upgrade S/W performance with 8 test vehicles equipped with LiDAR
2 Applicability to Mass-Produced Vehicles	• Competitors' LiDAR solutions require a large capacity database and processing ability; cannot with low performance/power MCU → Inevitable to equip high-performance GPU with high power consumption	• 100% Compatible with every LiDAR in the world • Available solution not only in GPU but also in low performance & power MCU
3 Co-Work References in Automotive Sector	• For AV Solution commercialization, accumulative collaboration with OEM / Tier 1 and related partnering companies is the main point	• Numerous POC projects and government tasks carried out for several years with automotive OEM and Tier 1 • Co-development experiences with global partners such as LiDAR H/W, Chipmaker, etc.

VueOne's Competitiveness : ① High Safety & Performance

Using test vehicles with autonomous driving license in Korea and US,
Vueron is constantly reviewing and upgrading its safety & performance level suitable for autonomous vehicles

Autonomous Driving License

World's 1st company obtaining
AV permit with 1 LiDAR in Korea and USA(CA / NV)

[redacted]

- Feb '21, Obtained AV permit in Korea
- Jun '22, Obtained AV permit in CA, USA
- Jul '22, Obtained AV permit in NV, USA
- Dec '22, Prepare for obtaining AV permit in Germany

Autonomous Driving Test Vehicle

Continuous review and upgrade of S/W performance with
8 test vehicles equipped with LiDAR Solution(H/W + S/W)

- Perform driving test with 4 cars(Sedan, Truck, SUV) having AV permit in Korea and 2 cars in USA
- 2 LiDAR Solution Demo Vehicles (both in and outside of Korea)

Sensors Converge

Strictly Private and Confidential

VueOne's Competitiveness : ① High Safety & Performance

[Appendix] VueOne's Performance Benchmark

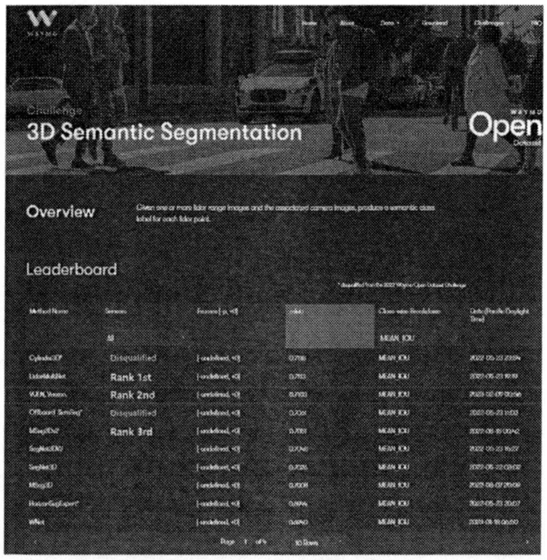

World 2nd in Waymo Benchmark
(3D Semantic Segmentation)

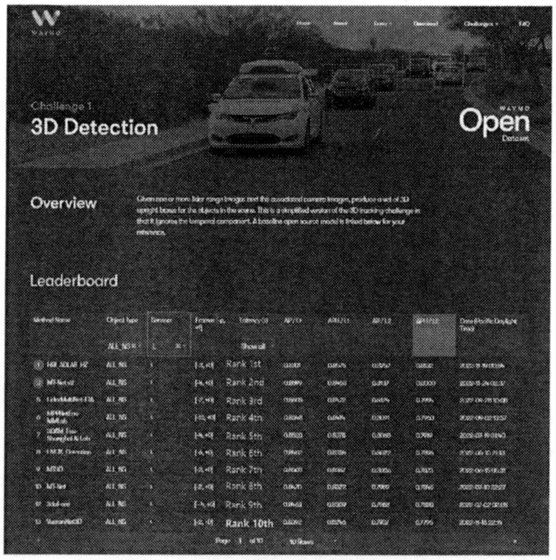

World 10th in Waymo Benchmark
(3D Object Detection)

Sensors Converge

Strictly Private and Confidential

Vueron's Competitiveness : ② Applicability to mass-produced vehicles

VUERON

VueOne is also a LiDAR software that can be 100% compatible with all types of LiDAR hardware and run with not only high-performance GPUs but also low-end MCUs

Applicability to LiDAR Hardware

InnoVusion LUMINAR AEVA OUSTER Cepton Velodyne HESAI AEYE INNOVIZ TECHNOLOGIES

- Regardless of manufacturer and product type, 100% compatible LiDAR S/W

Applicability to Processor

RENESAS TEXAS INSTRUMENTS NVIDIA intel

- LiDAR S/W available in not only with high-performance GPU, but also with MCU in mass-produced vehicles now using with low-power & low-performance

VueOne is the only one LiDAR software in the world that can immediately adapted to any LiDAR hardware and domain environment desired OEMs and Tier 1

VueOne's Competitiveness : ③ Co-Work References in Automotive Sector

VUERON

Vueron has deep understanding of the automotive vehicles sector through numerous accumulated projects with Automotive OEMs and Tier 1

Global OEM

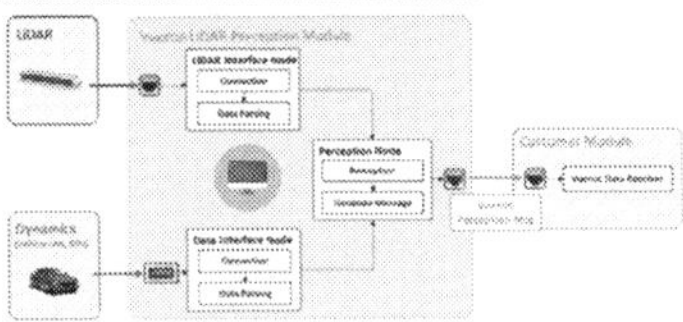

- PoC project to provide the perception s/w for LiDAR sensor that is considered mass production

Global OEM

- PoC project to provide the sensor fusion software development(incl. LiDAR perception) for truck platooning system

Global Tier-1

- PoC project to provide the LiDAR perception s/w for autonomous shuttle

Global Tier-1

- PoC project to provide the LiDAR perception s/w for ADAS lamp system

VUERON

Thank you

Contact : Noah Jang/ noah.jang@vueron.org

Sensors Converge

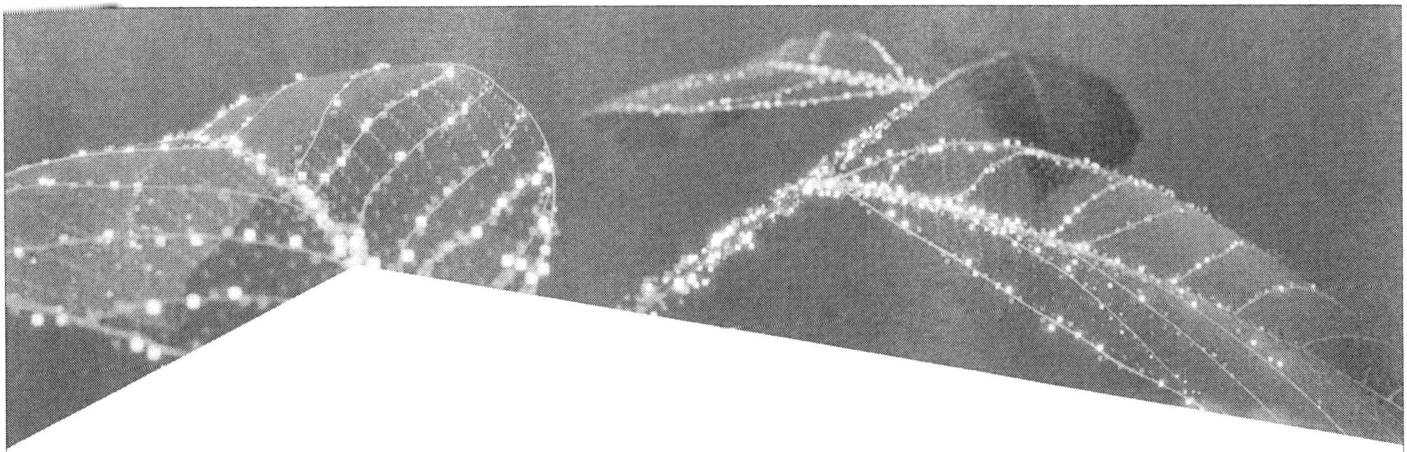

Infineon XENSIV™ sensors At the forefront of the sensorization of things

Raj Khattoi
Senior Director, Power & Sensor Systems

#SensorsConverge

Sensors Converge

The future is here

Infineon

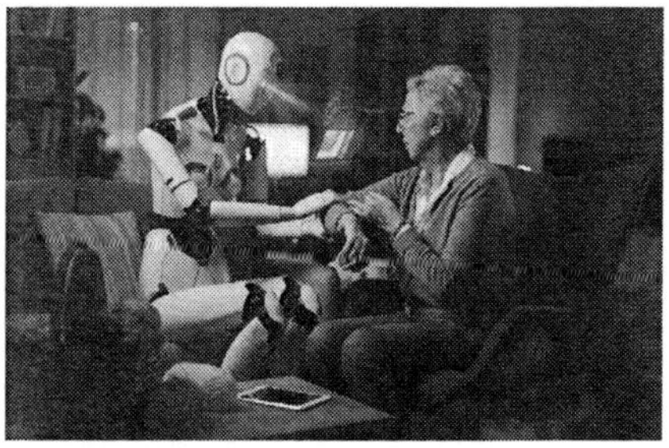
Human Machine Co-existence

Smart homes

Generative AI and AR/VR

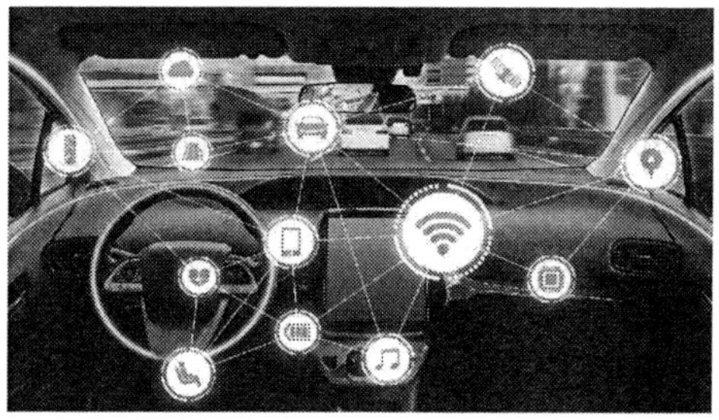
Intelligent and autonomous cars

#SensorsConverge

Sensors Converge

Infineon sensors have applications in every industry

Infineon

Smart home and building

- Activity recognition
- Attention monitoring

Retail, PoS, digital signage

- Traffic monitoring
- Attention monitoring
- Voice interface

Surveillance and safety

- Intrusion detection, alarm systems
- Safety systems, social distancing
- People counting, traffic monitoring

Smartphone

- Voice pick up, voice detection
- 3D authentication, AR

Notebooks, tablets, conferencing

- Audio communications
- Human presence, anti-peeking
- Augmented reality

Hearables and wearables

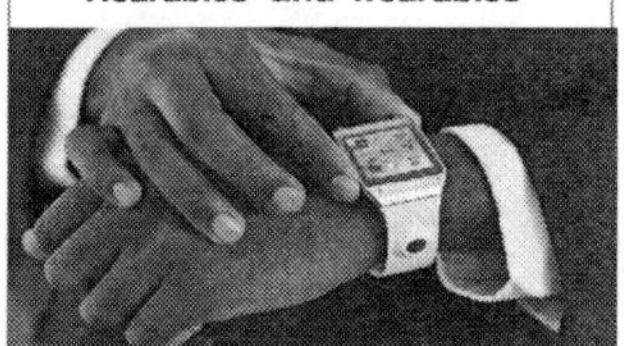

- Bio sensing
- Contextual awareness, AR/MR
- Voice UI, ANC, touch/gesture UI

Service robots

- Navigation
- Contextual awareness
- User interface

Car and mobility

- Occupancy monitoring
- Safety
- User interface

#SensorsConverge

Sensors Converge

XENSIV™ consumer and industrial sensors

infineon

Touch sensors

Pressure and CAPSENSE™

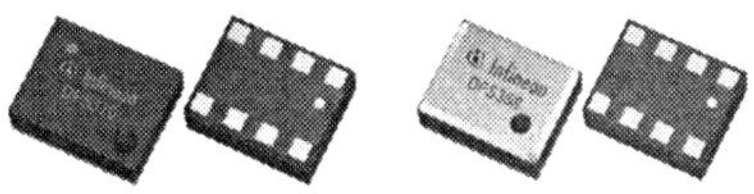

Microphones

3D time-of-flight (ToF) camera

High resolution depth

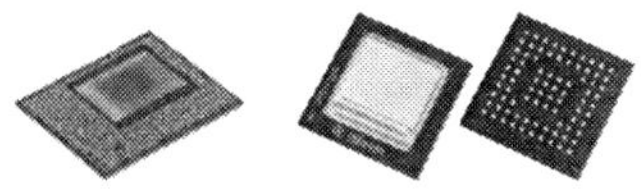

CO_2-based gas sensor

3D RADAR technology

#SensorsConverge

Sensors Converge

---

infineon

XENSIV™ microphones

Sensors Converge

High performance XENSIV™ microphones enable new audio use cases

Advanced audio functionality

Feature	Category	Category	Feature
Low self-noise to capture the faintest and far-field sounds	High SNR	Robustness	**Ingress protection (IP57)** and **filters** for **RF** suppression reduce integration cost and manufacturability
Enables **best-in-class** transparent hearing and **active noise cancelling** functionality	High SNR	Low power consumption	**Ultra-low power** digital microphones and selectable power modes for long-lasting battery life
Low signal **distortions** even at high sound pressure levels	High AOP	Low part variability	**Tight** sensitivity, phase and LFRO **matching** for beamforming applications and ANC control loop design
Handling of high **signal peaks** for reliable ANC performance	High AOP		

Automated speech recognition

Connecting the real to the digital world
(for digital assistants, talk-to-text)

Active noise cancellation

Suppression of unwanted sounds
(for advanced earbuds, headsets)

Beamforming and audio zoom

Changing audio recording directivity
(for cameras, smart glasses, conference devices)

Transparent / Advanced hearing

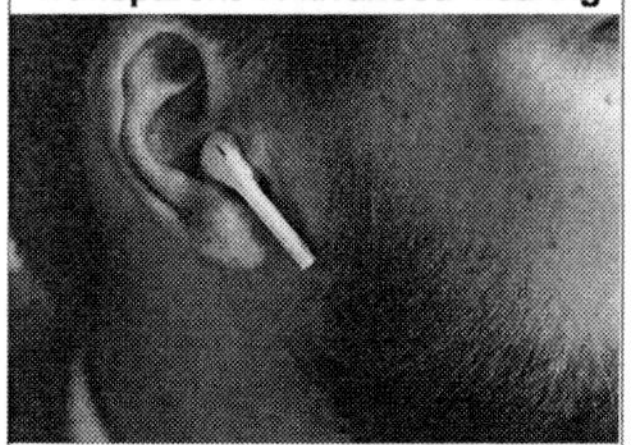

Adaptive audio experience
(for hearables and headphones)

MEMS, ASIC and package: Building blocks of a MEMS microphone

Infineon Microphone System – Head Quarter in Munich, Germany

MEMS	ASIC	Package
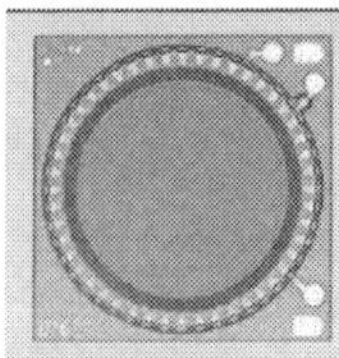	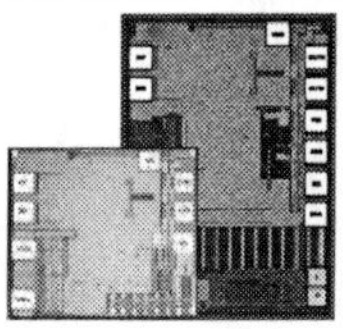	
Micro electro-mechanical system	ASIC contains circuitry for MEMS	Package protects the device and enables pick-and-place
Membrane and backplate forming a capacitor	Charge pump for membrane	Shielding (EMI)
Capacitor is modulated by acoustic waves	Amplifier stages	Package volume is forming an acoustical back volume
	LDO for clean supply	
	Calibration logic	

Infineon owns all building blocks of MEMS microphones – allowing to identify and develop MEMS, ASIC and package combinations optimized to each application

Infineon's sealed dual membrane technology is a revolutionary step forward for capacitive MEMS microphones

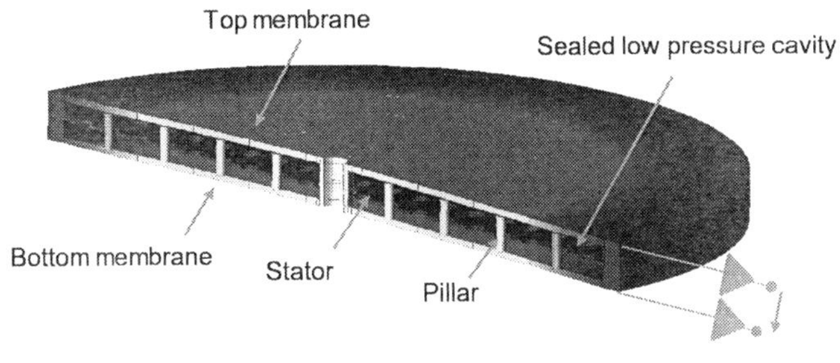

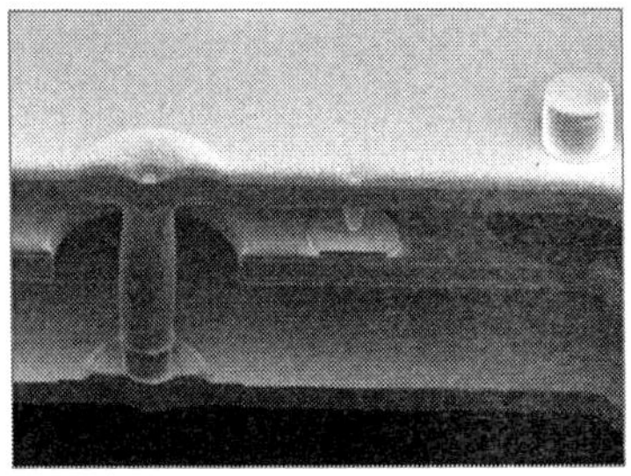

- True-differential topology
  - Enables ultra-high SNR of up to 75 dB SNR (80 dB for dual MEMS)
  - Distortion improvement by cancellation of even order distortion
- IP57 environmental robustness leads to less field returns and better manufacturability

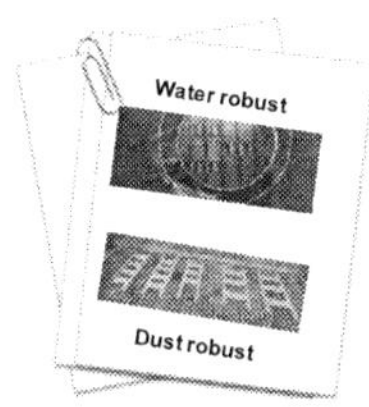

#SensorsConverge

XENSIV^{TM} radar

#SensorsConverge

Smart presence detection with Infineon radar sensors

Reducing energy consumption while improving user experience

Smart thermostats & displays

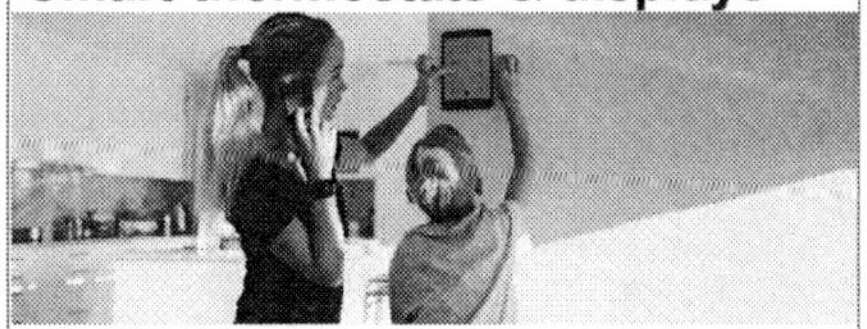

- Activation by proximity sensing
- Enhance booting time & user experience
- Support gesture control

Smart lighting systems

- Activate only where people are located
- Indoor & outdoor
- Higher sensitivity than PIR sensors

Room air conditioners

- Turn on & off devices based on presence & vacancy detection
- Steer airflow away from people's position

Security systems

- Start camera & recording only by movements inside the covered area
- Reduce number of false alarms

Laptops & monitors

- Turn off / reduce brightness by absence detection
- Increased battery lifetime
- Lock the screen to protect data

TV

- Turn off screen by absence detection
- Pause & resume streaming content based on presence & absence

#SensorsConverge

Sensors Converge

Radar solutions – Helping companies reduce carbon footprint

- Number of smart homes worldwide will exceed 500 million by 2026.
- Smart activation & deactivation based on radar presence & absence detection saves energy.
- Radar sensors can add additional functionalities to increase comfort & safety in a smart environment.

Article: bit.ly/3CoMYUt

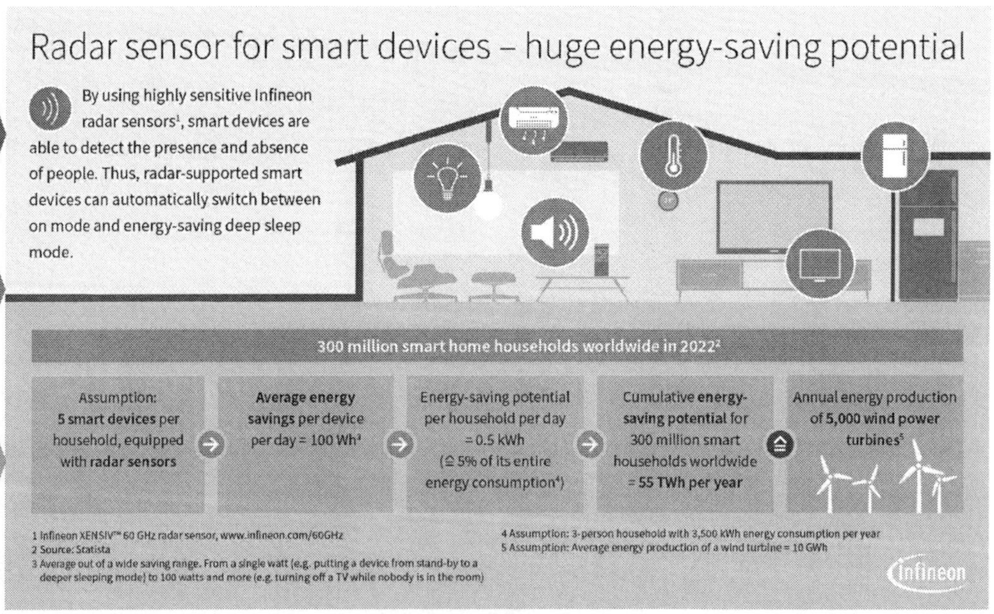

#SensorsConverge

Sensors Converge

Portfolio that caters to all use cases

Increasing functionality

	BGT60LTR11AIP	BGT60UTR11AIP	BGT60TR13C
	 6.7 x 3.3 mm	 4.05 x 4.05 mm	 6.5 x 5.0 mm
Positioning	Smart & cost-effective **PIR replacement**	**Compact and cost-efficient** radar chip for FMCW operations	Enable **advanced radar sensing** including presence, tracking and gesture control
Operating mode	**Doppler Radar** with integrated detectors	**FMCW** (5.5 GHz BW)	**FMCW** (5.5 GHz BW)
Value proposition	**Completely autonomous mode:** Most convenient way to implement radar in your system	**Smallest 60 GHz chip** with integrated antennas on the market	**Maximum functionality and flexibility:** Develop the most demanding radar use cases
Target use cases	**Motion detection,** Presence detection (short range)	Presence detection, gesture control, vital sensing, 1D ranging, material classification	Presence detection, gesture control, vital sensing, segmentation, tracking, distance
Target applications	Lighting, monitors, TV, cameras, IoT/smart-home applications, door openers, toilets, …	Smart Home, Smart appliances, health care devices, TVs, laptops, Service robots, …	Smartphones, laptops, smart home applications, health- & babycare devices, …

#SensorsConverge

XENSIV™ CO2 sensors

#SensorsConverge

Thanks to our leadership in MEMS technologies, we have realized a new generation of miniaturized CO_2 sensors

Infineon

From photoacoustic spectroscopy principle...

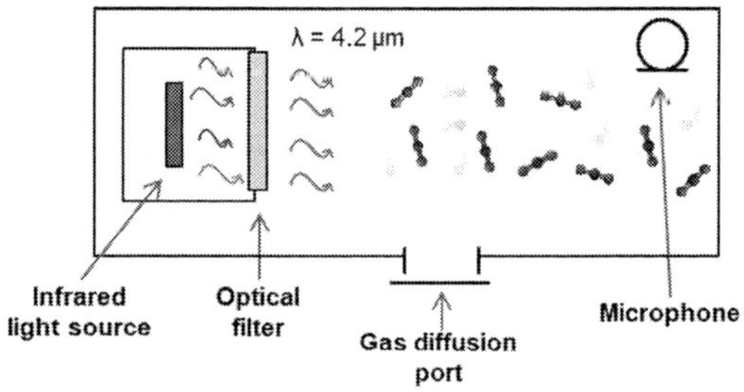

The PAS principle allows for a direct, accurate and selective measurement of CO2

- A MEMS-based IR emitter generates a light pulse at a specific wavelength selective to CO2
- CO2 molecules absorb the light and vibrate, creating a sound wave with an amplitude directly related to the concentration
- The sound wave is detected by a MEMS microphone

...to mass produced XENSIV™ PAS CO2 sensor

All key components are developed by Infineon

- The PAS CO2 sensor achieves **the accuracy & stability of high-end** NDIR CO2 sensors in a 4x smaller size
- **Compliant with major standards and regulations** for indoor air quality (e.g.: WELL, LEED, ASHRAE)
- Suitable for **high volume standard assembly processes** with surface mount assembly

#SensorsConverge

Sensors Converge

XENSIV™ PAS CO2 is targeting many applications for indoor air quality monitoring and energy saving

Infineon

HVAC

Air quality devices

Consumer devices

Smart home & building

Air quality awareness

Higher comfort levels

Healthier life

Lower energy consumption

Increased productivity

Energy cost savings

#SensorsConverge

Sensors Converge

CAPSENSE™ sensors

CAPSENSE™ and applications

- Capacitive sensing has changed the face of the modern products and the way users interact with them
- CAPSENSE™ is Infineon's proprietary capacitive sensing technology used in touch user interfaces
- Replaced over 6+ Billion conventional buttons

Capacitive sense buttons

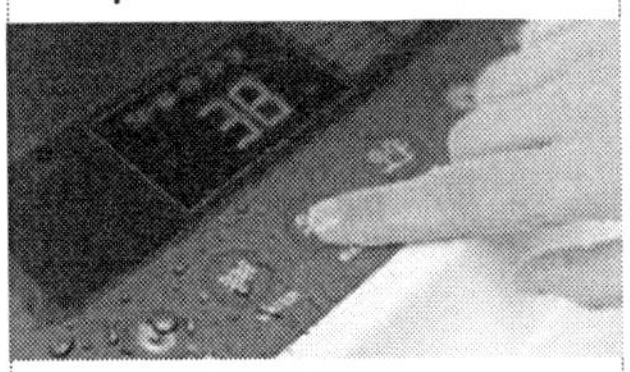

Capacitive sense sliders

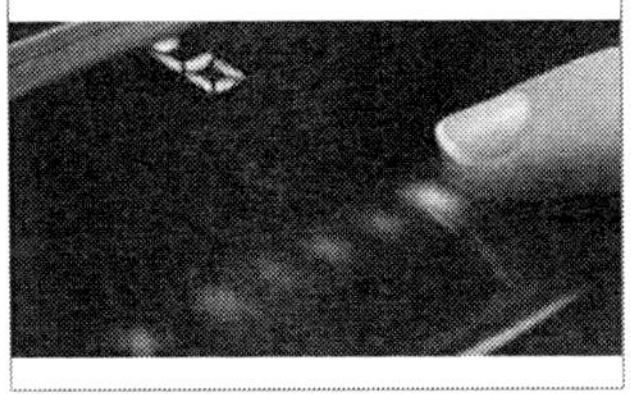

Metal proximity

Proximity detection

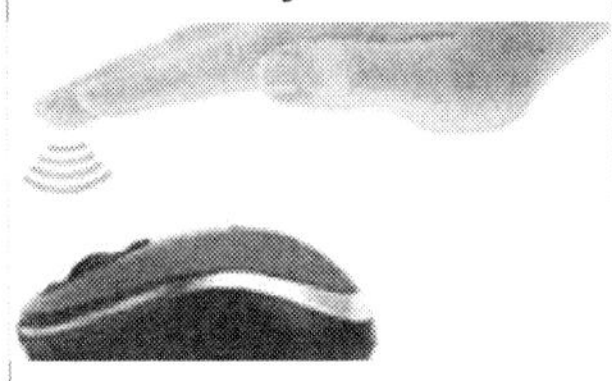

Specific absorption rate

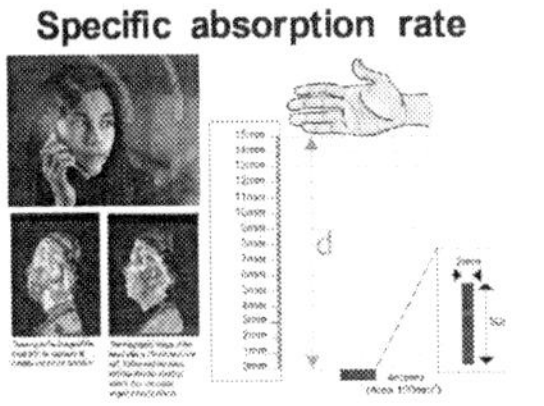

Capacitive liquid level sensing

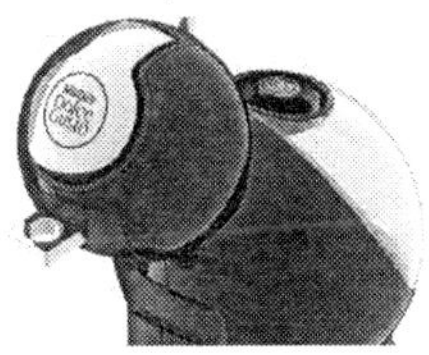

Capacitive force sensing

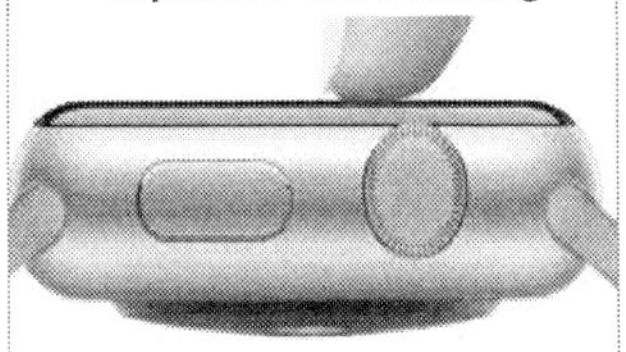

Absolute capacitance sensing

#SensorsConverge

CAPSENSE™ touch-sensing technology

infineon

Infineon CAPSENSE™

1 Signal-to-noise ratio
- A high SNR is indicative of highly reliable touch interface

2 Low power
- Ultra-low power standby current
- Sensing in Deepsleep domain

3 HMI response
- Fast reaction to user interaction
- 120 Hz for smooth user experience

4 Noise immunity
- Best-In-Class noise immunity
- Reliably works in harsh conditions

5 Multi-sensing
- Enable large and complex touch sensing interfaces

6 Reliable sensing
- Immunity to liquid, snow etc
- Operate with thick gloves temp

#SensorsConverge

Sensors Converge

5th generation sensing technology – Multi sense converter

infineon

Feature	Higher SNR	Lower power	Higher refresh rate	Improved linearity	Supply rejection
Differential (rail-rail) sensing	✓				
Ratio metric sensing	✓				
Autonomous scanning		✓	✓		
Multi-channel	✓		✓		
Dithering				✓	
Full wave conversion (2x CMOD)					✓

#SensorsConverge

Sensors Converge

XENSIV™ automotive sensors

#SensorsConverge

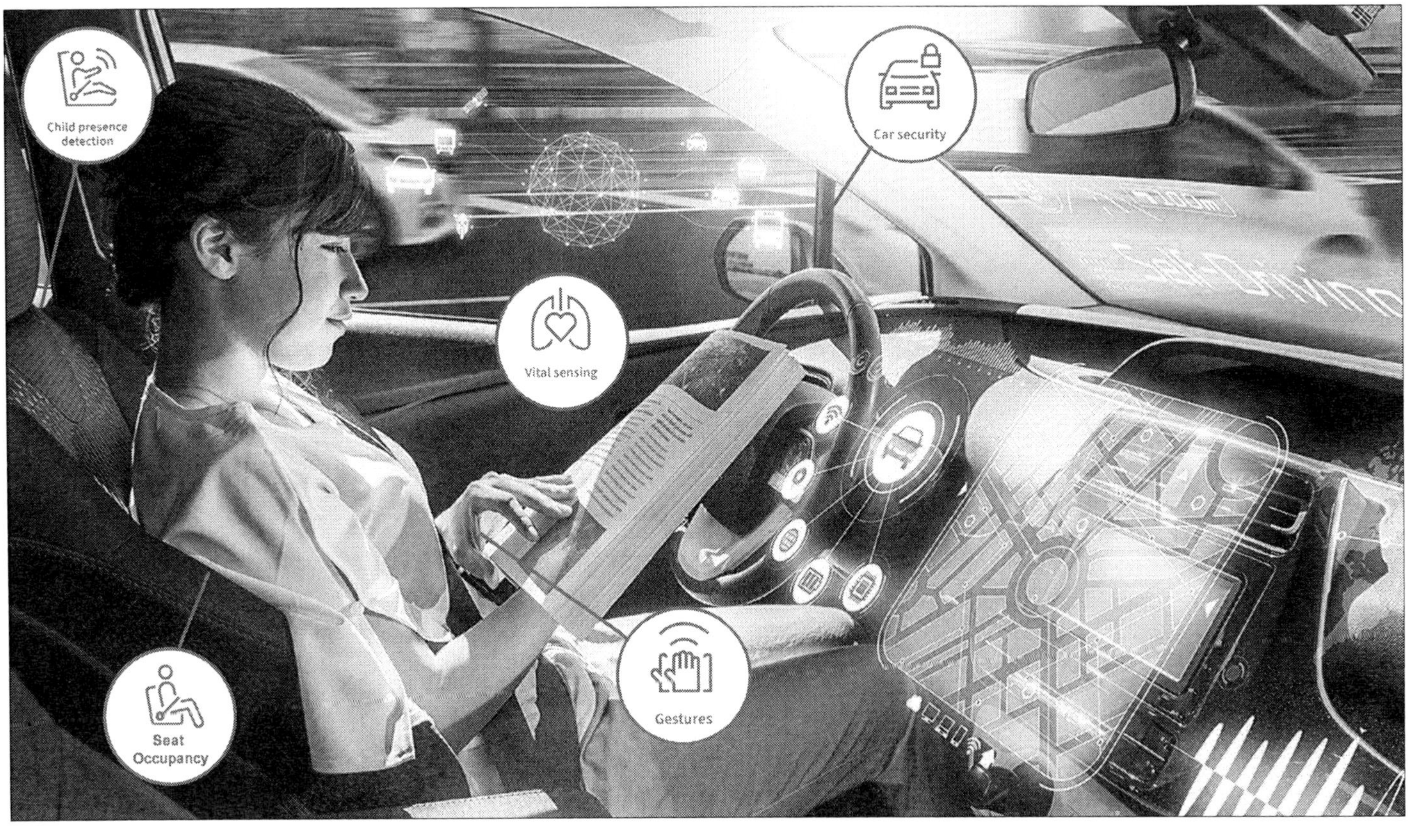

A broad sensor portfolio for automotive
Leading market positions in key applications

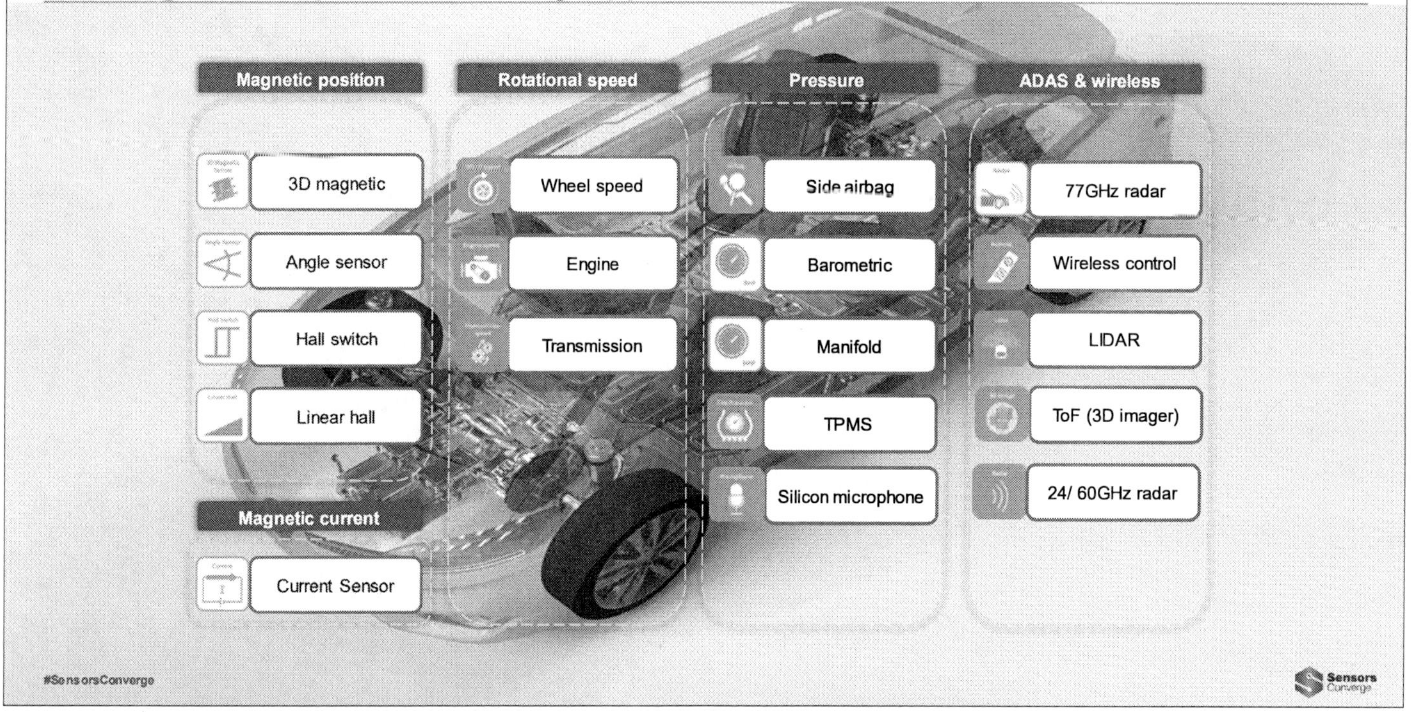

From 'sensor' to 'sensor system solutions'

An holistic sensor systems approach is required to successfully create new use cases

infineon

Sensor and IC technology
- Sensor technology, heterogeneous packaging, power management

Edge AI
- Tools, DNN, edge NPU

Layers of analytics from sensor to cloud
- Runtimes, containerization, load balancing, OTA

Connectivity and security
- Interoperability, ease of use, reliability, energy efficiency

#SensorsConverge

Sensors Converge

Edge analytics and AI

infineon

Radar gesture recognition example
(Cortex M4, DNN 30KB)

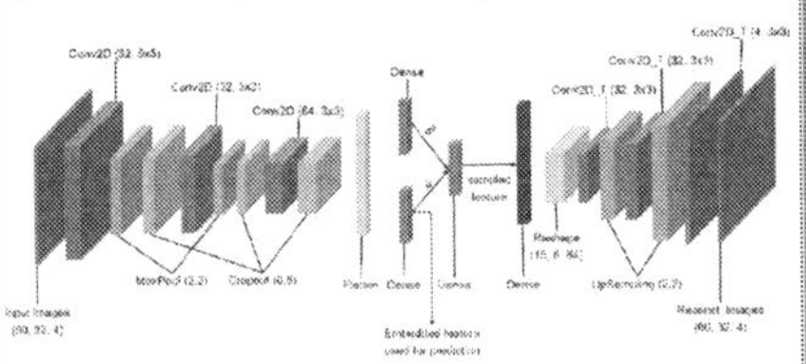

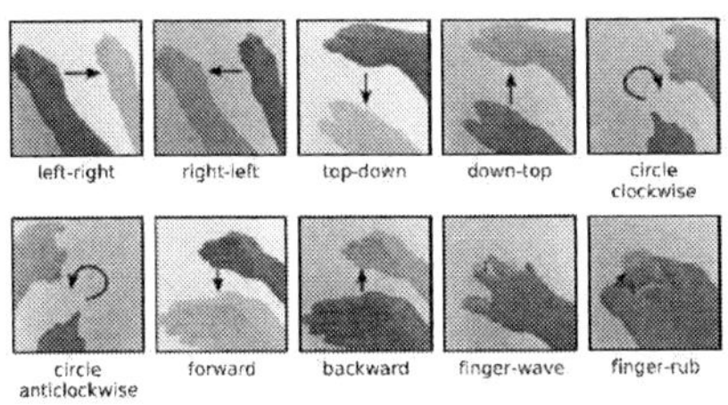

Large deep neural networks can be adapted to small embedded systems

Embedded NN development framework

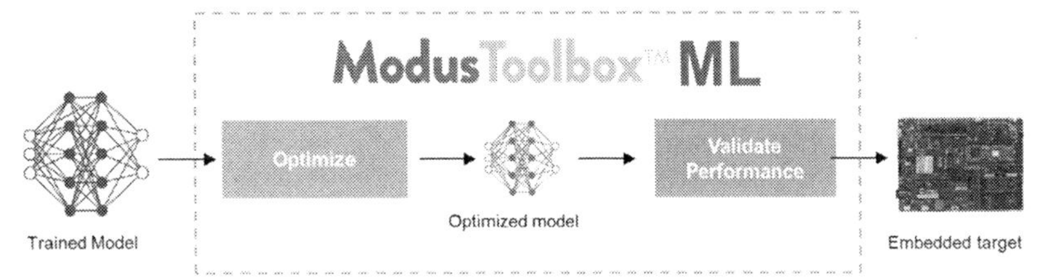

Datasets creation and management

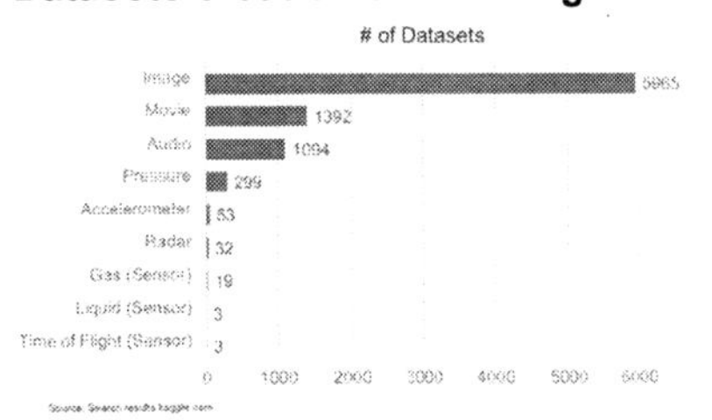

Embedded NPU and signal processing

ARM/RiscV core	AI & DSP acceleration engine
Memories	App SW AI models

#SensorsConverge

Sensors Converge

Layers of analytics from edge to cloud

Load balancing sensor-edge-hub-cloud

A critical business choice: cost of ownership, upgradability, energy consumption, user experience depend on it

- Energy efficiency
- Privacy
- Latency

A mix of analytics layer which can be moved dynamically

- Complexity
- Flexibility
- Upgradability
- Data fusion

OTA upgrades,
Edge containerization
runtime (incl. MCU)

Interoperable
connectivity & security
frameworks (eg. Matter)

#SensorsConverge

Sensor system in action

XENSIV™ connected sensor kit (CSK)

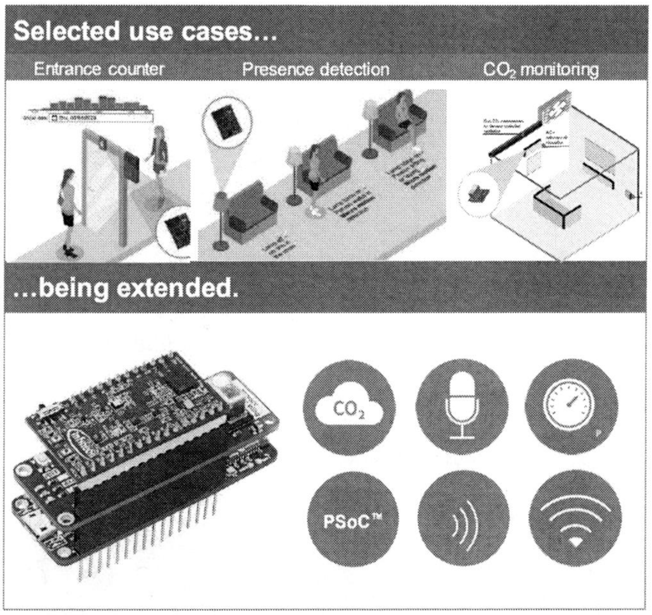

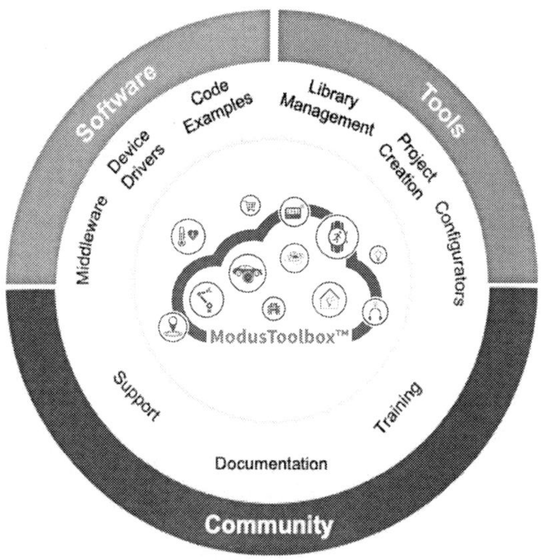

#SensorsConverge

Infineon

#SensorsConverge

Sensors Converge

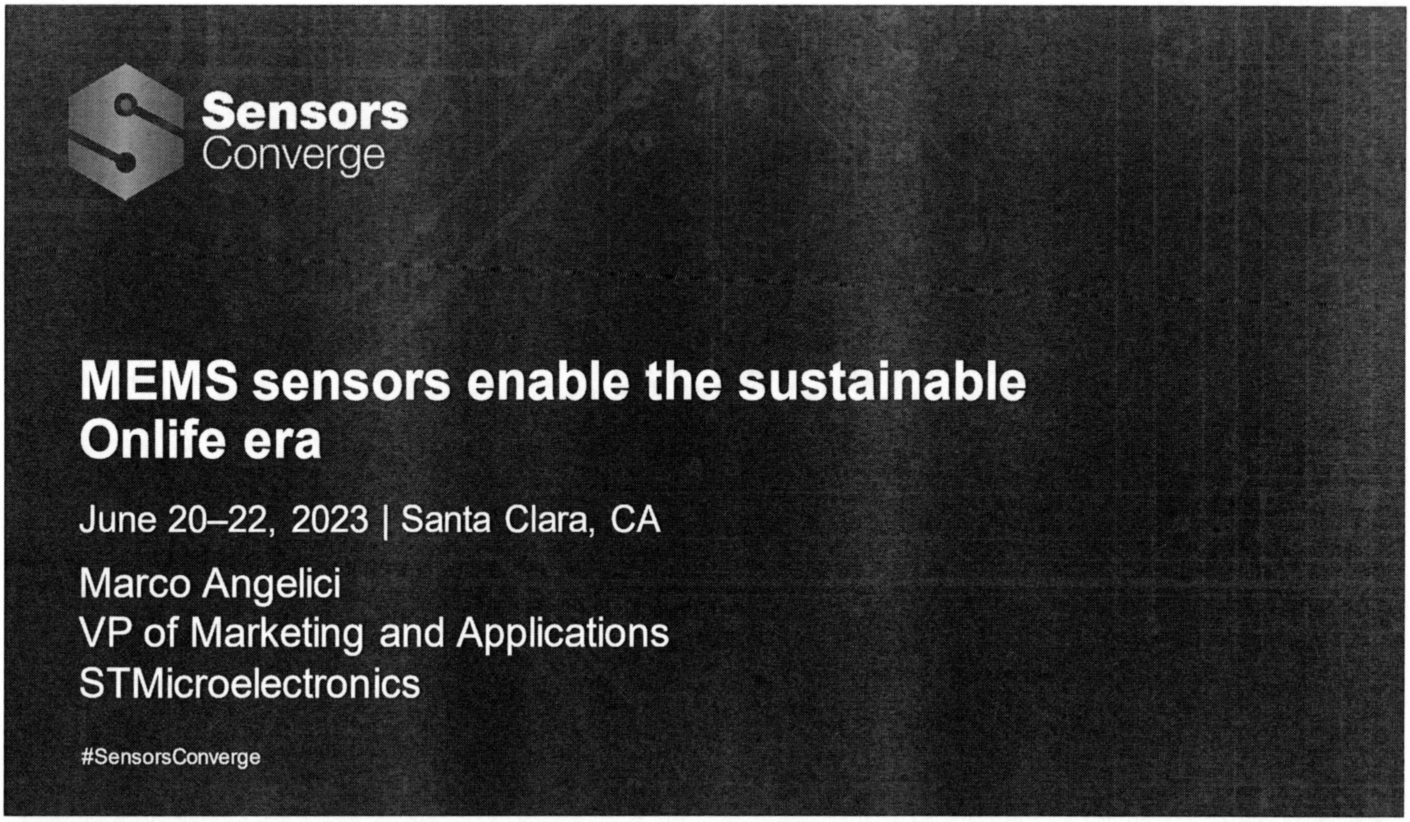
Sensors
Converge
MEMS sensors enable the sustainable Onlife era
June 20–22, 2023 | Santa Clara, CA
Marco Angelici
VP of Marketing and Applications
STMicroelectronics
#SensorsConverge

The right path is by no means obvious

Main focus on CO_2 emissions

Carbon dioxide emissions reached ~**34 Gtons** in 2020, where power sector represents the major contributor with 40% of the total

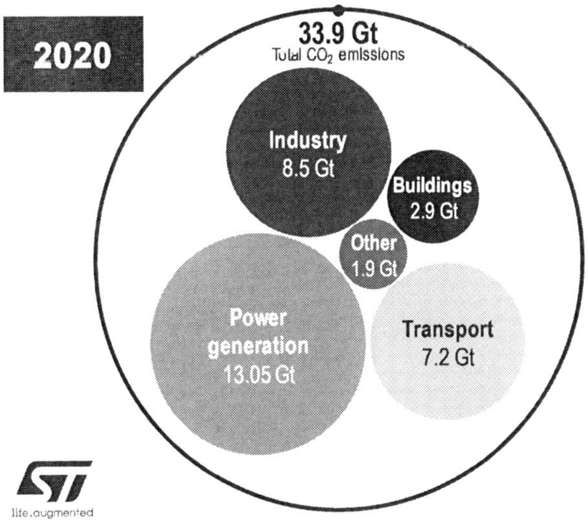

Additional energy will be required to achieve this transformation

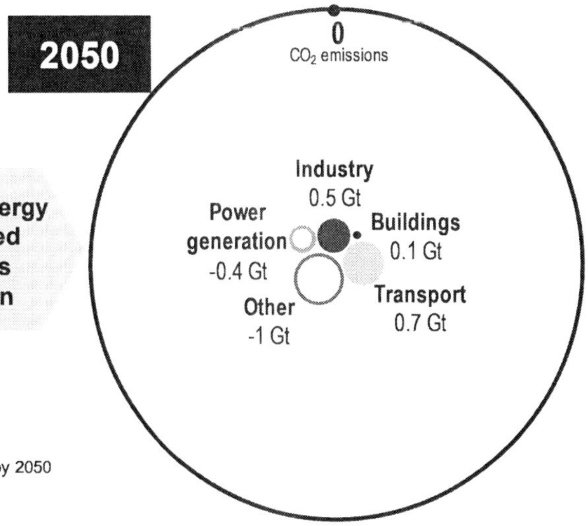

Source: IEA, Net Zero by 2050

life.augmented

3

The path to carbon neutrality

Energy generation

From fossil to renewable energy sources

Industry

Use of highly efficient equipment

Transportation

Migration to electric vehicle

Building

Low emission energy source and efficient systems

life.augmented

4

Electricity generation worldwide trend

Electricity generation worldwide is forecast to triple in the next three decades, reaching **83,000 terawatt-hours by 2050**

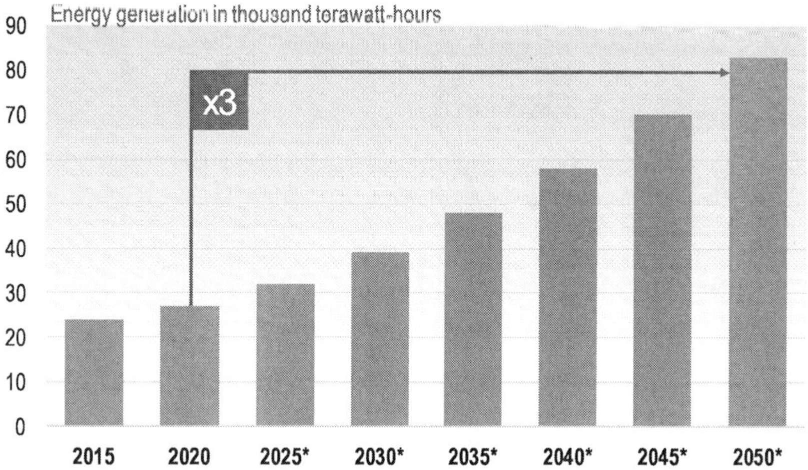

3x power generation largely **driven by decarbonization efforts** and **electrification** of the transportation and building sectors

Source: Statista, Worldwide; McKinsey & Company

life.augmented

5

A complex equation

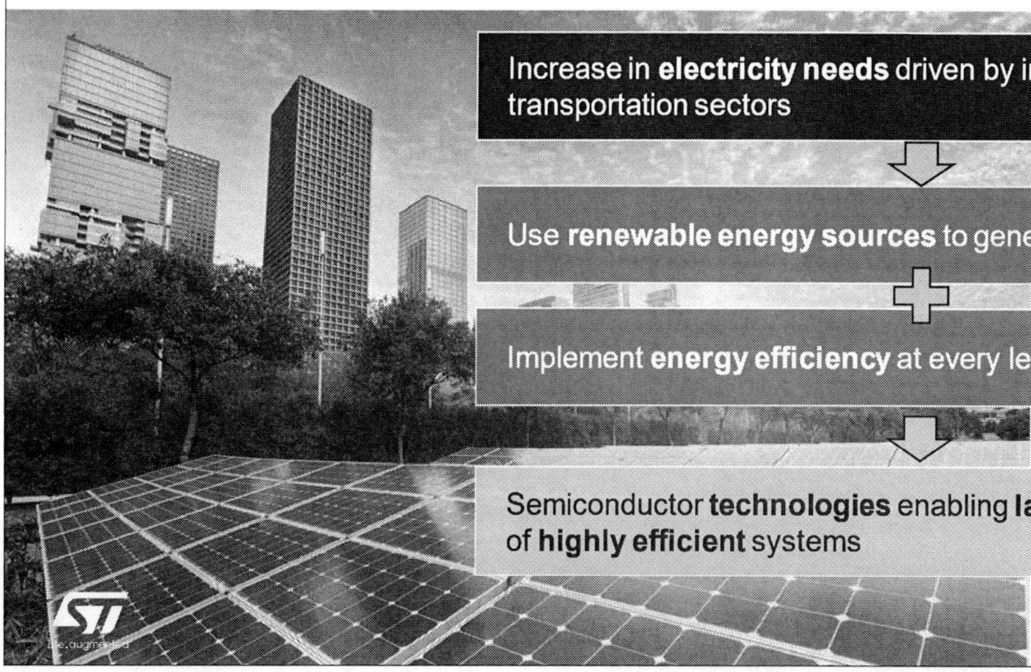

Increase in **electricity needs** driven by industry, buildings and transportation sectors

Use **renewable energy sources** to generate electricity

Implement **energy efficiency** at every level

Semiconductor **technologies** enabling **large-scale** deployment of **highly efficient** systems

6

What do human expect from technology today?

Sustainable

Technologies that **protect** and **help humans protect** the planet

Human centered

Technologies that improve the **interaction** with the world around us, remain **non-invasive** and **secure** while developing our **creativity**

life.augmented

Sensors at the heart of our interactions with the digital world

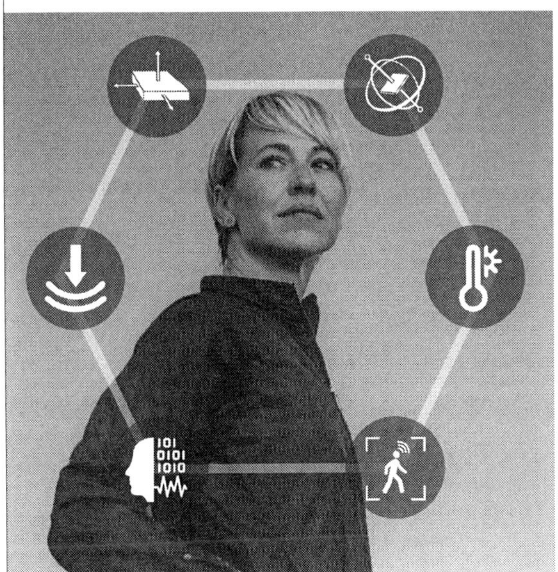

Human centered + **Sustainable**

Sensors are the key components to **bridge** the **physical** and the **digital worlds**

Sensors becoming **smart** answer **human expectations** while ensuring a **sustainable future**

life.augmented

Smart sensors making our world a better place

Offline Era

2000

A paradigm change in the man-machine interface

MEMS technology: from a concept to a product.

Online Era

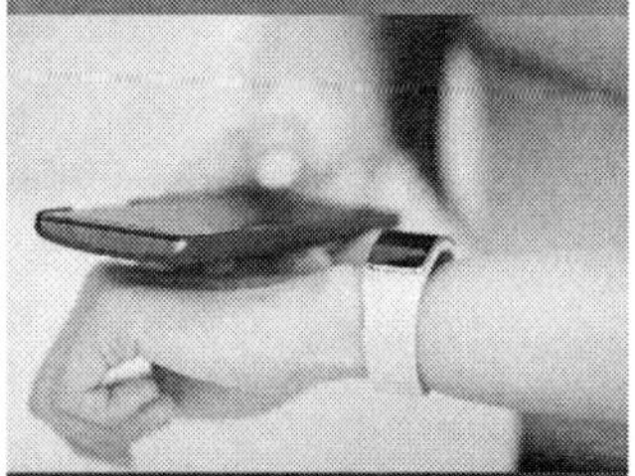

2010

Sensor proliferation and connections to the Cloud

Performance improvement and technology fusion.

Onlife Era

2020

The fusion of technology and life

MEMS sensors able to sense, process, and act.

Sustainable Onlife

Sustainable sensorization of the world

MEMS sensors sending only the **meaningful data** to the cloud

life.augmented

9

Key attributes of MEMS sensors

Smart

Sensors able to **process data**

Open

Sensors configured to **your needs**

Accurate

Sensors providing a **correct set of data**

Meaningful data provided in an optimal way

Human centered

Sustainable

life.augmented

10

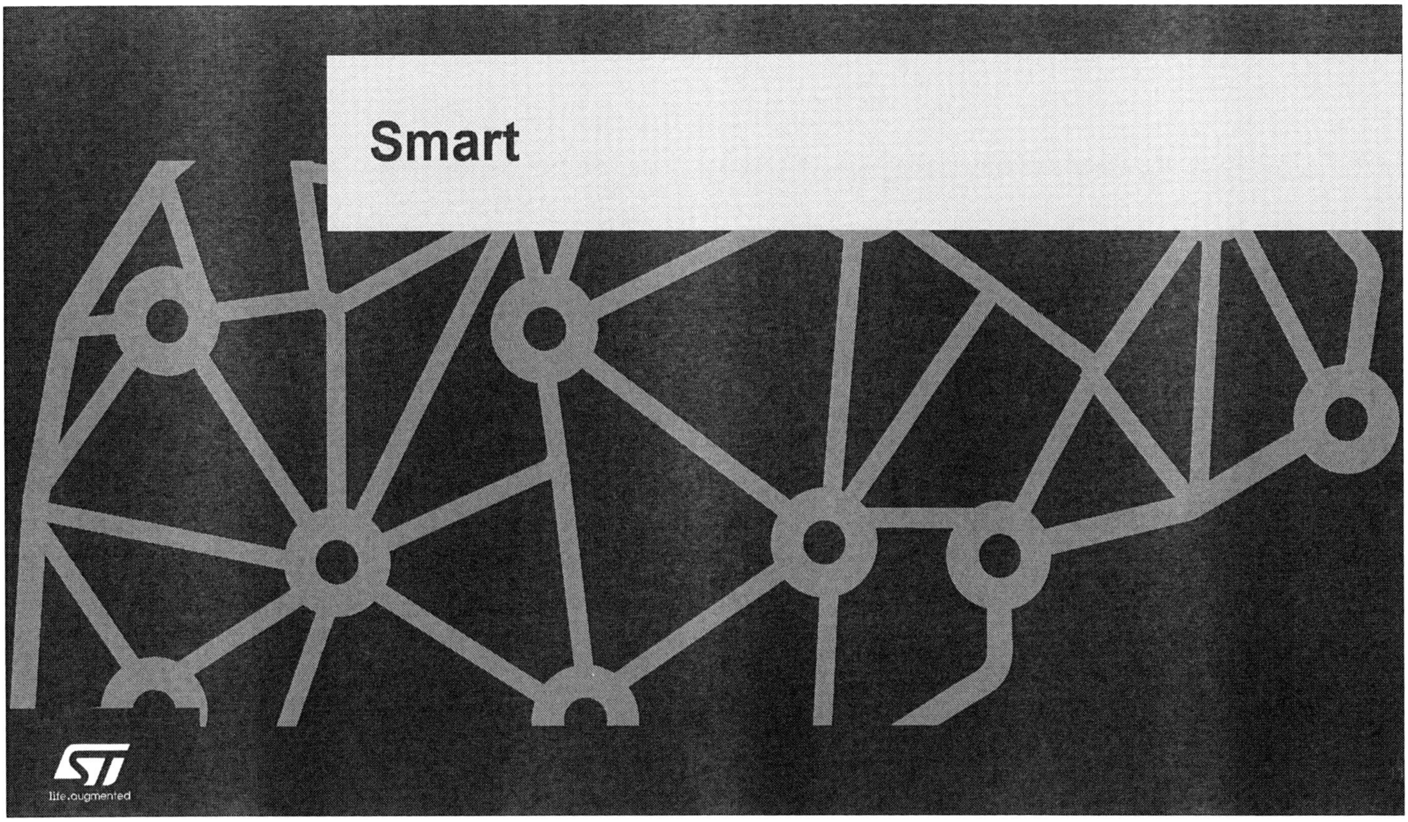
Smart
life.augmented

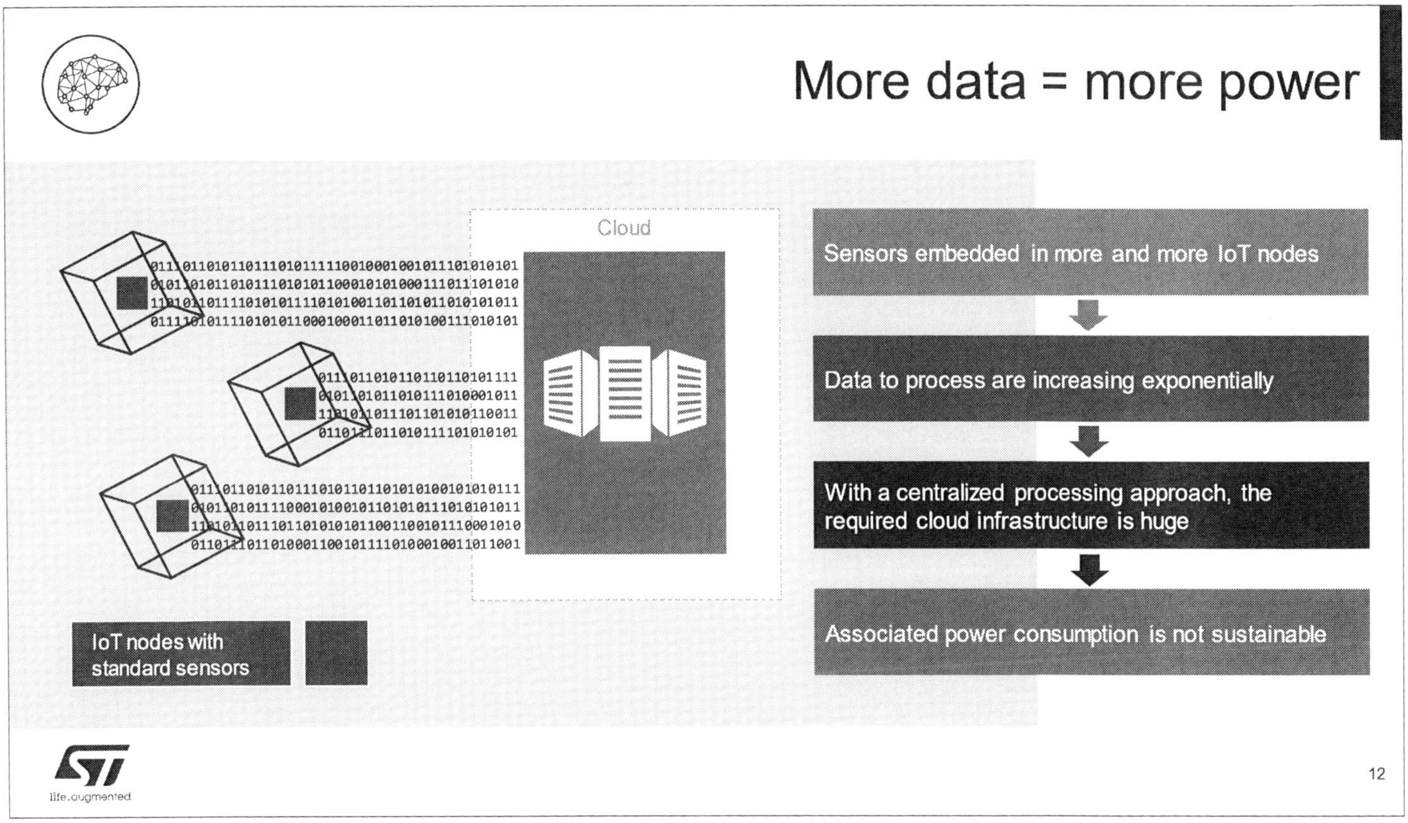
More data = more power
Cloud
IoT nodes with standard sensors
Sensors embedded in more and more IoT nodes
Data to process are increasing exponentially
With a centralized processing approach, the required cloud infrastructure is huge
Associated power consumption is not sustainable
life.augmented
12

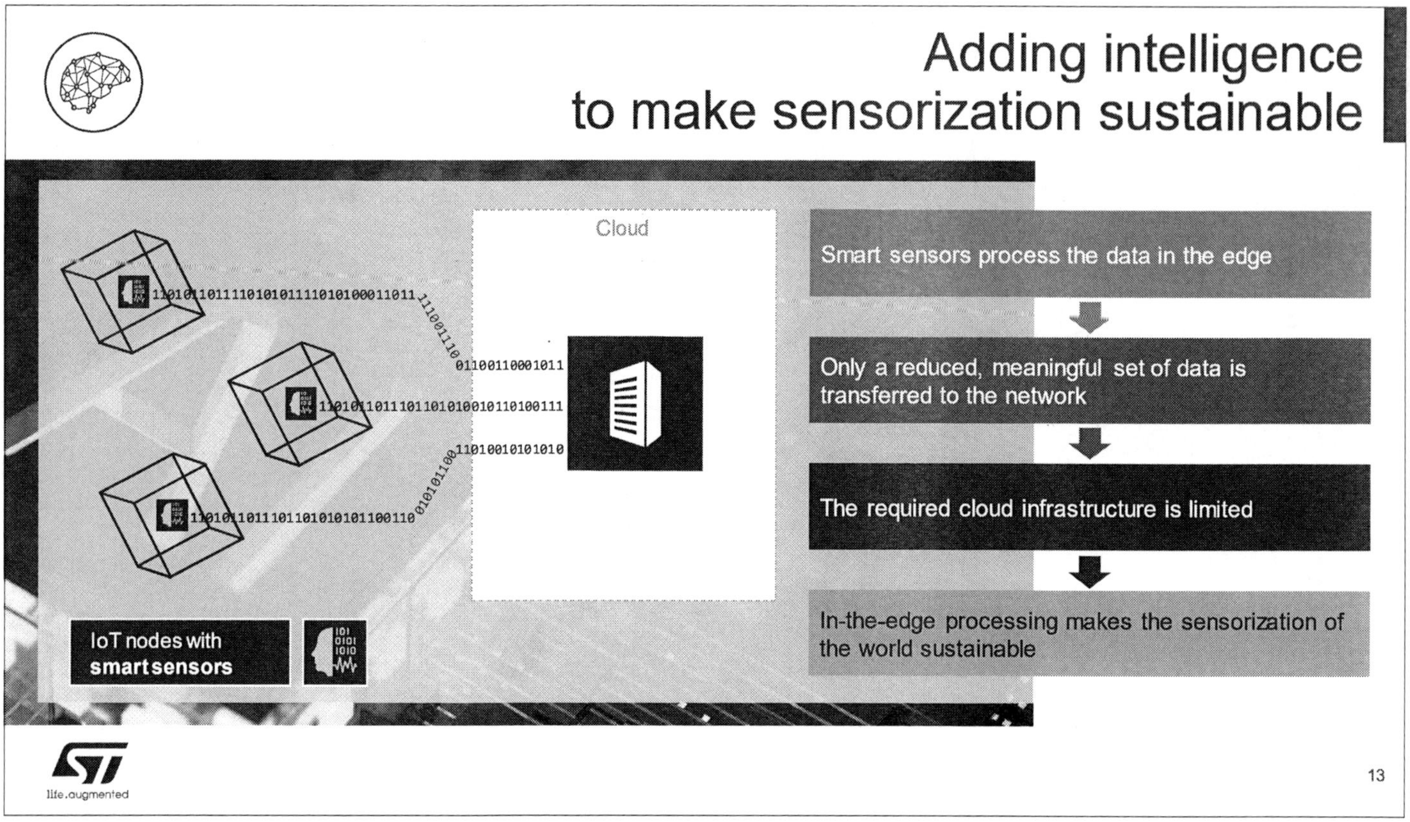
Adding intelligence
to make sensorization sustainable
Cloud
Smart sensors process the data in the edge
Only a reduced, meaningful set of data is transferred to the network
The required cloud infrastructure is limited
In-the-edge processing makes the sensorization of the world sustainable
IoT nodes with
smart sensors
life.augmented
13

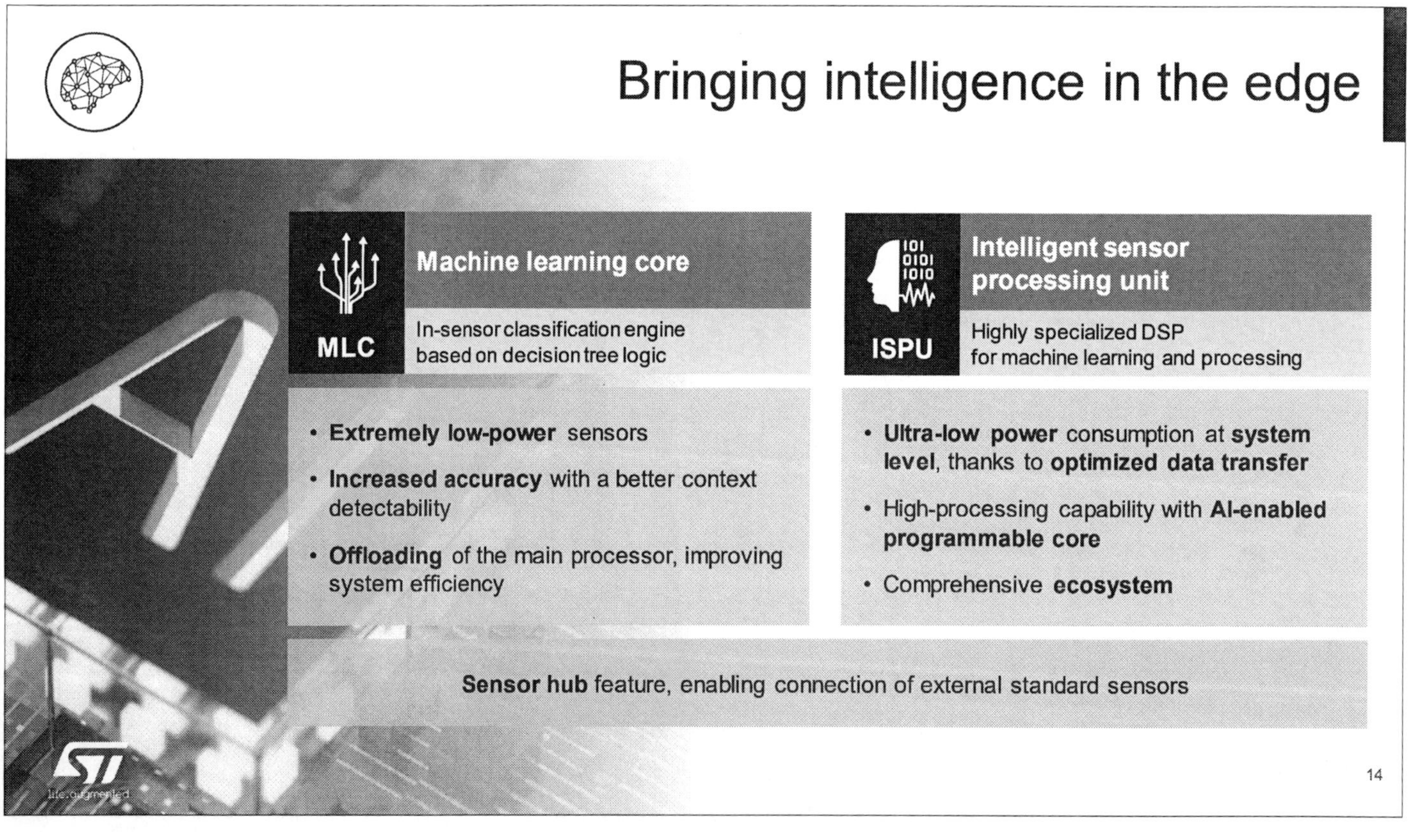
Bringing intelligence in the edge
Machine learning core
MLC
In-sensor classification engine based on decision tree logic
Intelligent sensor processing unit
ISPU
Highly specialized DSP for machine learning and processing
• Extremely low-power sensors
• Increased accuracy with a better context detectability
• Offloading of the main processor, improving system efficiency
• Ultra-low power consumption at system level, thanks to optimized data transfer
• High-processing capability with AI-enabled programmable core
• Comprehensive ecosystem
Sensor hub feature, enabling connection of external standard sensors
life.augmented
14

Open
life.augmented

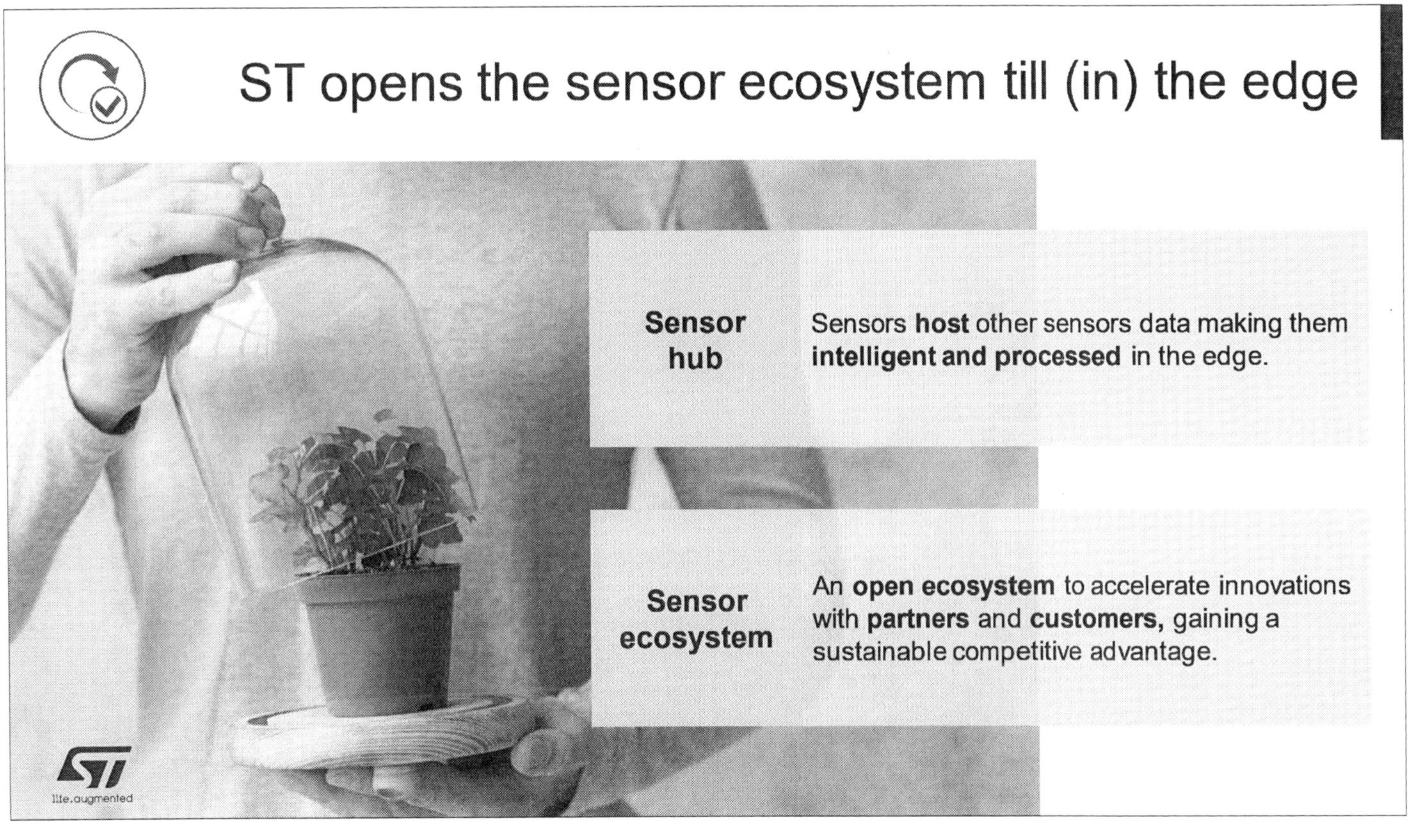
ST opens the sensor ecosystem till (in) the edge
Sensor hub
Sensors **host** other sensors data making them **intelligent and processed** in the edge.
Sensor ecosystem
An **open ecosystem** to accelerate innovations with **partners** and **customers,** gaining a sustainable competitive advantage.
life.augmented

ST MEMS sensor hub

Enabling connection of external standard sensors

Helps to **integrate data from other sensors** (up to 4) by connecting them directly to our sensors

Data from all sensors are **processed in ST MEMS sensor**

Allows keeping the **intelligent in-the-edge**, further improving energy efficiency

life.augmented

17

ST MEMS sensor ecosystem

OPEN

Jointly create value for customers

- Leveraging **on partners**
- **Sharing** state-of-the-art, high-quality components
- Shortening customer's **time-to-market**
- New strategic set-up: **flexibility and sustainability**

18

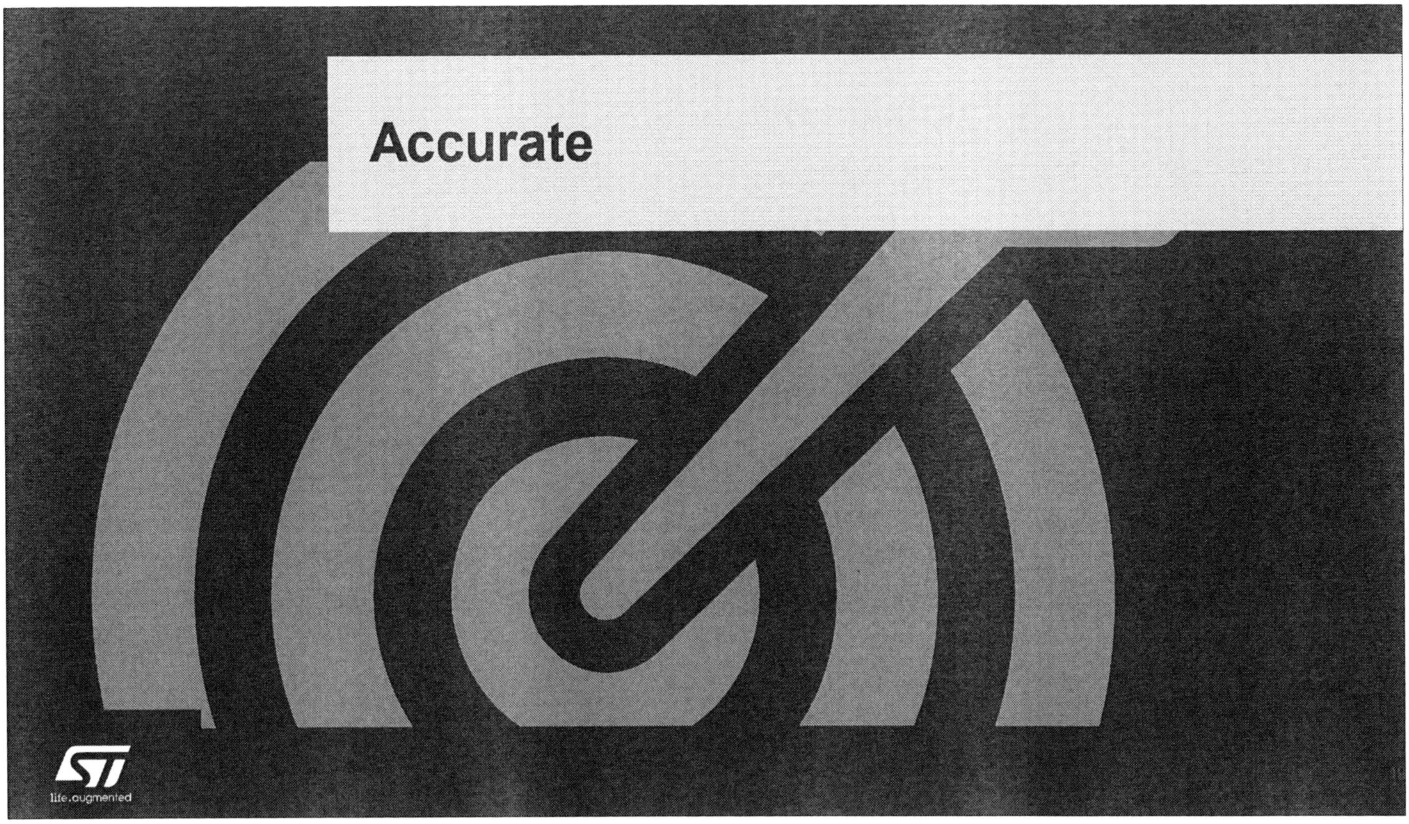
Accurate
life.augmented

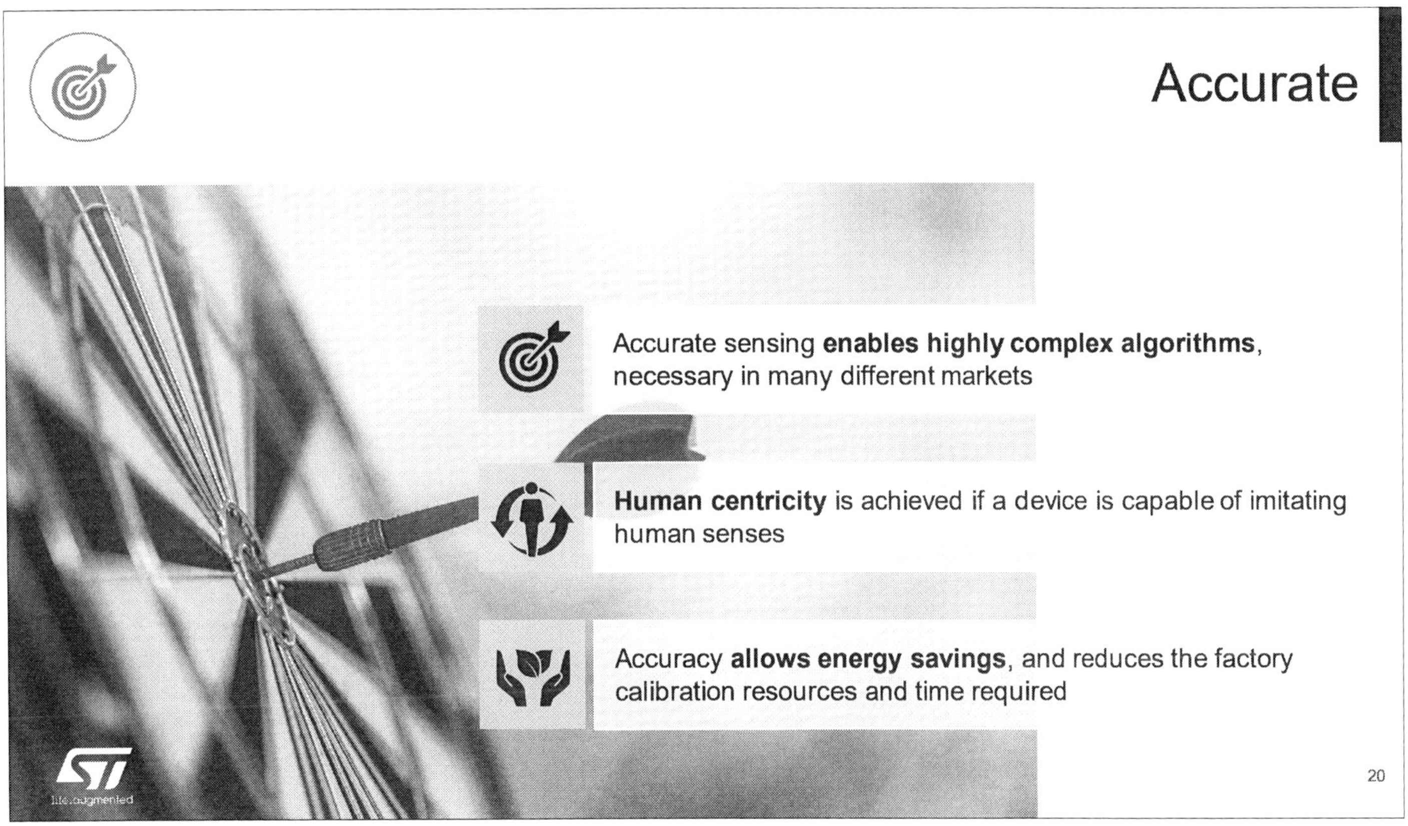
Accurate
Accurate sensing **enables highly complex algorithms**, necessary in many different markets
Human centricity is achieved if a device is capable of imitating human senses
Accuracy **allows energy savings**, and reduces the factory calibration resources and time required
life.augmented
20

ST smart sensors
contributing to carbon neutrality
life.augmented

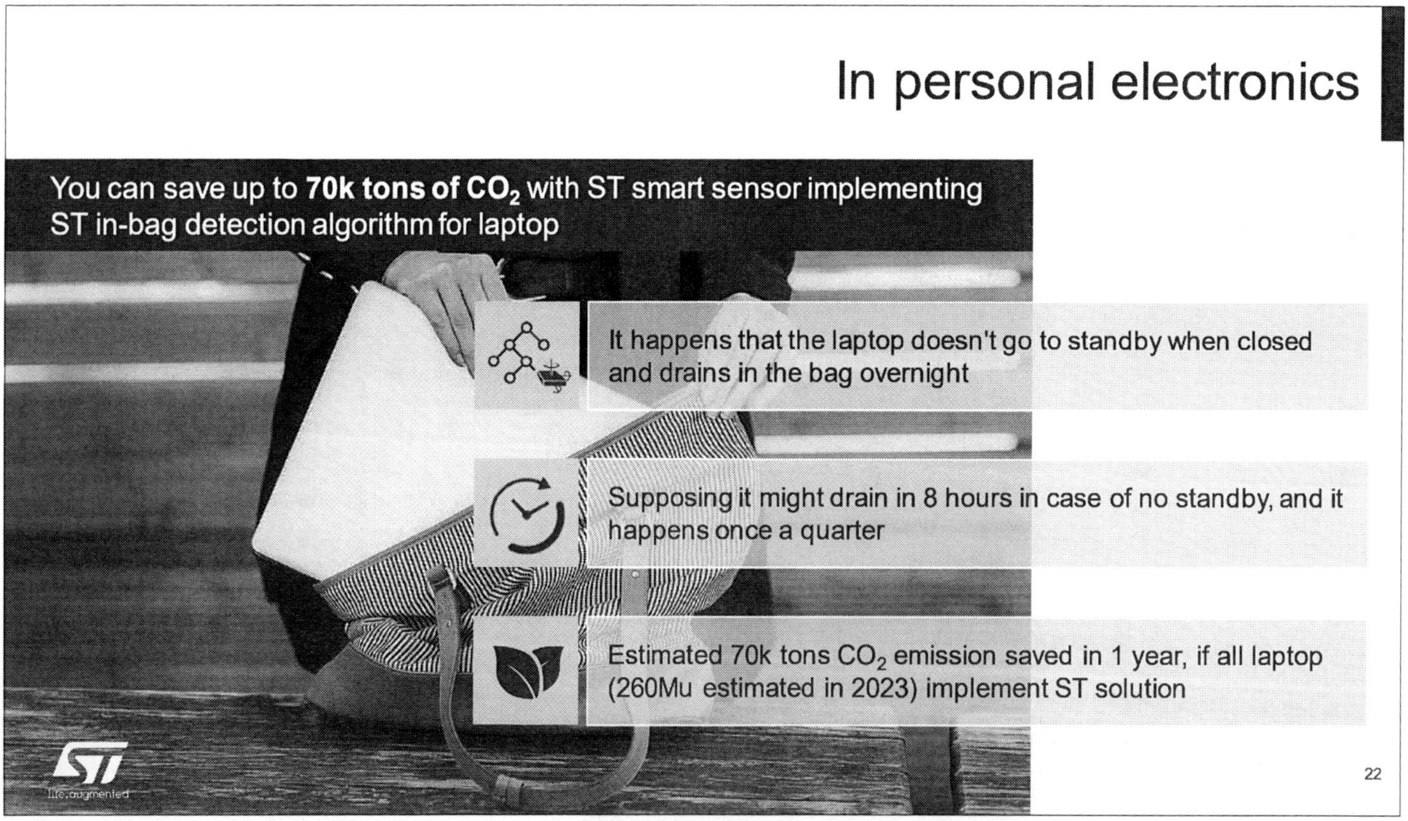
In personal electronics
You can save up to **70k tons of CO_2** with ST smart sensor implementing ST in-bag detection algorithm for laptop
It happens that the laptop doesn't go to standby when closed and drains in the bag overnight
Supposing it might drain in 8 hours in case of no standby, and it happens once a quarter
Estimated 70k tons CO_2 emission saved in 1 year, if all laptop (260Mu estimated in 2023) implement ST solution
life.augmented
22

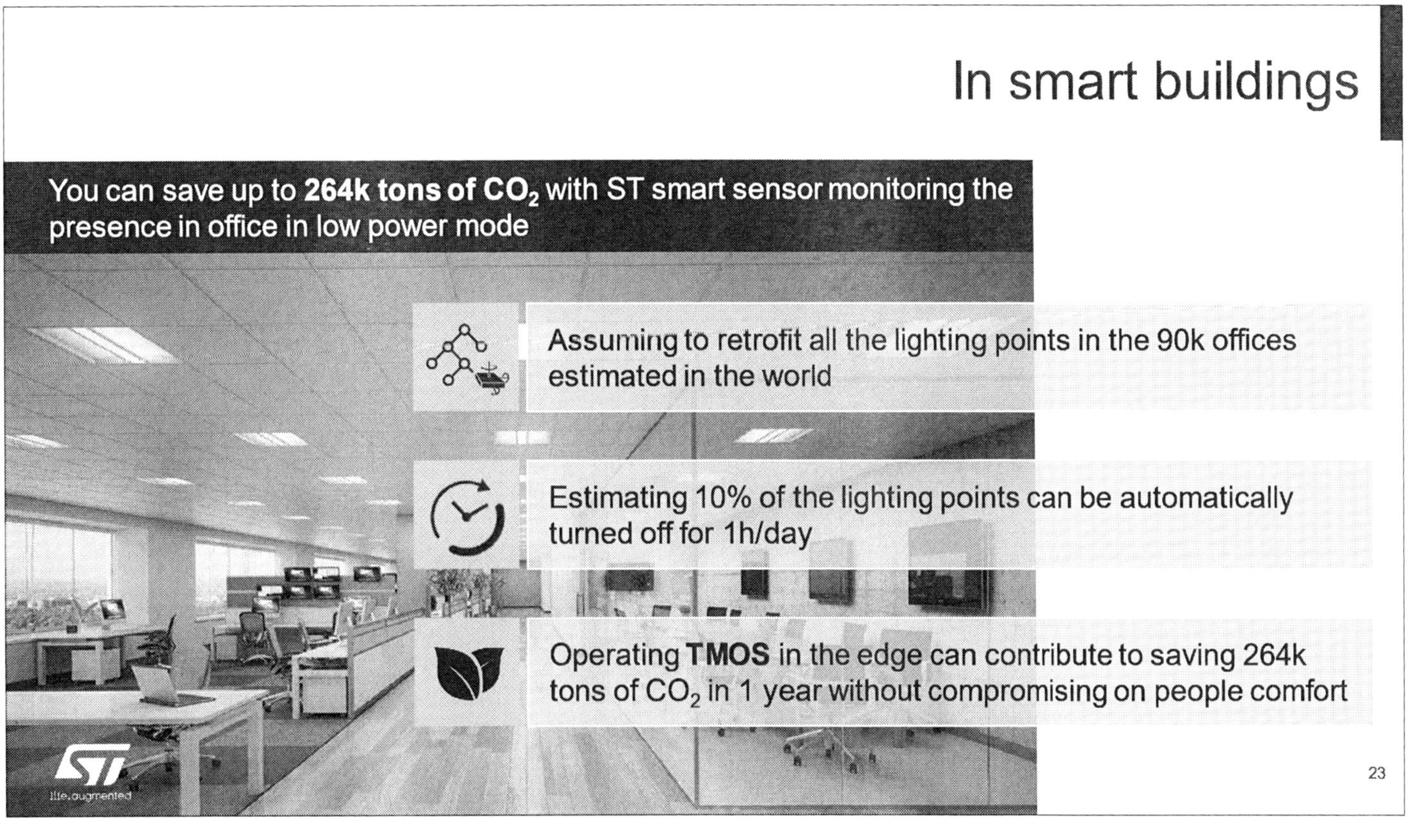
In smart buildings
You can save up to **264k tons of CO_2** with ST smart sensor monitoring the presence in office in low power mode
Assuming to retrofit all the lighting points in the 90k offices estimated in the world
Estimating 10% of the lighting points can be automatically turned off for 1h/day
Operating **TMOS** in the edge can contribute to saving 264k tons of CO_2 in 1 year without compromising on people comfort
life.augmented
23

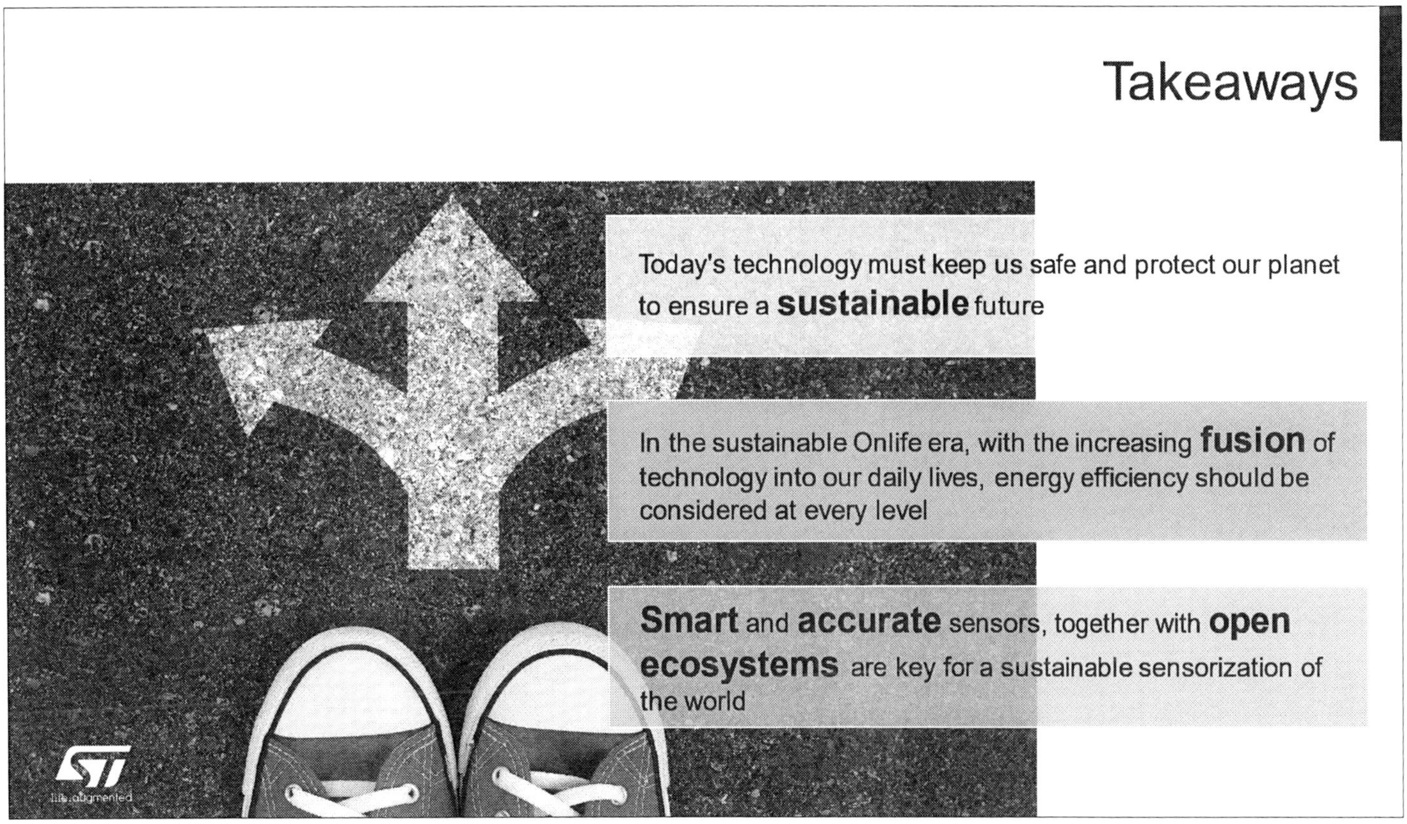
Takeaways
Today's technology must keep us safe and protect our planet to ensure a **sustainable** future
In the sustainable Onlife era, with the increasing **fusion** of technology into our daily lives, energy efficiency should be considered at every level
Smart and **accurate** sensors, together with **open ecosystems** are key for a sustainable sensorization of the world
life.augmented

Our technology
starts with You

Find out more at www.st.com/MEMS

life.augmented 25

Sensors Converge

Sensors: Saving Lives, Enabling Sustainability

June 20–22, 2023 | Santa Clara, CA

Dr. Christian Peters
Director Smart Sensors & Hardware Systems
Research and Technology Center and Bosch Center of Artificial Intelligence
Robert Bosch LLC

#SensorsConverge

Sensors: Saving Lives, Enabling Sustainability

Sensors are everywhere

Sensors are omnipresent and increase our comfort significantly.

But sensors can do more... way more!

2 Dr. Christian Peters | 2023-06-21

BOSCH

Sensors: Saving Lives, Enabling Sustainability

50,457

Lives are saved by accelerometers in airbags*)

3 Dr. Christian Peters | 2023-06-21

*) as of 2017

BOSCH

Sensors: Saving Lives, Enabling Sustainability

4,100

Lives are saved by gyroscopes in ESC in 2010-2014

75%

Risk reduction of fatal single vehicle rollover

4 Dr. Christian Peters | 2023-06-21

ESC: Electronic Stability Control

BOSCH

Sensors: Saving Lives, Enabling Sustainability

660

lives saved by pressure sensors in TMPS per year!

5 Dr. Christian Peters | 2023-06-21

TMPS: Tire Pressure Monitoring System

BOSCH

Sensors: Saving Lives, Enabling Sustainability

10,120

lives saved by pressure sensors in smartphones per year!

6 Dr. Christian Peters | 2023-06-21

BOSCH

Sensors: Saving Lives, Enabling Sustainability

Fall detection

devices enabled by IMUs and pressure sensors

7 Dr. Christian Peters | 2023-06-21

IMU: Inertial Measurement Unit

BOSCH

Sensors: Saving Lives, Enabling Sustainability

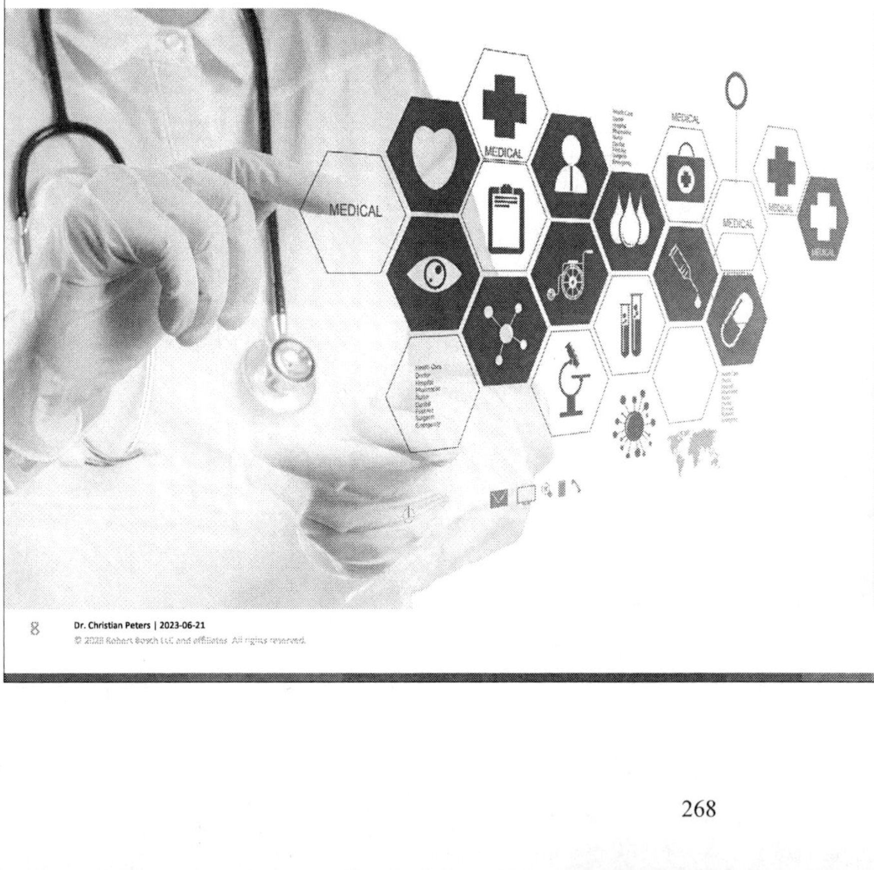

Future

Early detection of rare and common disease

Enabling personalized treatments

8 Dr. Christian Peters | 2023-06-21

BOSCH

Sensors: Saving Lives, Enabling Sustainability

Sensors

will enable sustainability

9 Dr. Christian Peters | 2023-06-21

BOSCH

Sensors: Saving Lives, Enabling Sustainability

$511M

gas saved by pressure sensors in TMPS per year!

10 Dr. Christian Peters | 2023-06-21

BOSCH

Sensors: Saving Lives, Enabling Sustainability

20%

of global carbon emissions are caused by wildfires

11 Dr. Christian Peters | 2023-06-21

BOSCH

Sensors: Saving Lives, Enabling Sustainability

1/3

of the world's food is wasted

12 Dr. Christian Peters | 2023-06-21

BOSCH

Sensors: Saving Lives, Enabling Sustainability

13 Dr. Christian Peters | 2023-06-21

BOSCH

Sensors Converge

PowerFilm SOLAR
MADE IN THE USA

Solar Power for Indoor Systems

June 20, 2023 | Santa Clara, CA

Brad Scandrett, VP of Engineering, PowerFilm, Inc

#SensorsConverge

Components of an EH System

Storage Element

Charge Controller or EH PMIC

Transducer (TEG, Piezo, RF, Solar)

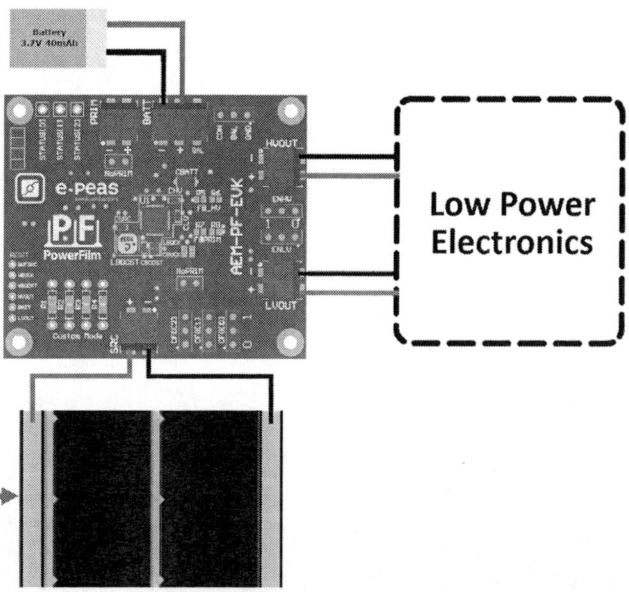

#SensorsConverge

Sensors Converge

Choosing the Right Solar for an EH System

What's commercially available?

How does it work?

SOLAR

Light Energy Spectrum

Solar efficiencies quoted under light spectrum of AM1.5 at 1000W/m^2 and 25˚C

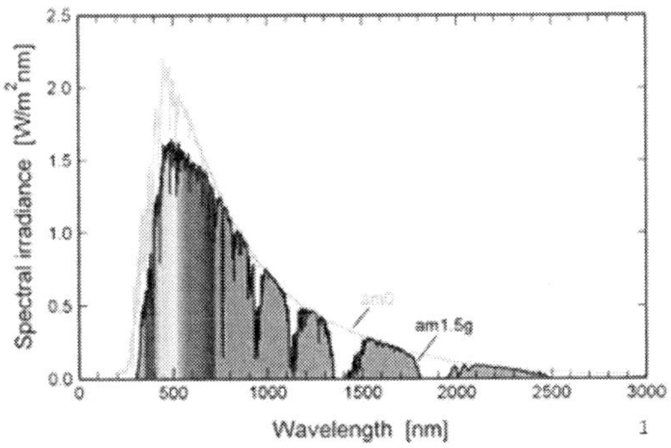

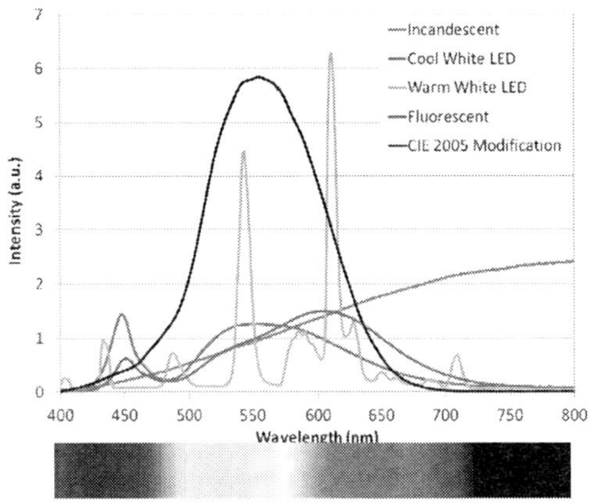

Spectrum of energy efficient light sources limited to visual range

Quantum Efficiency

Parameter that describes a solar cell's absorption efficiency at each wavelength

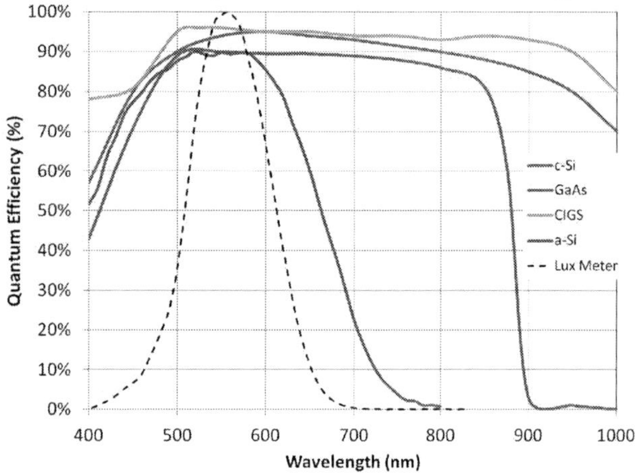

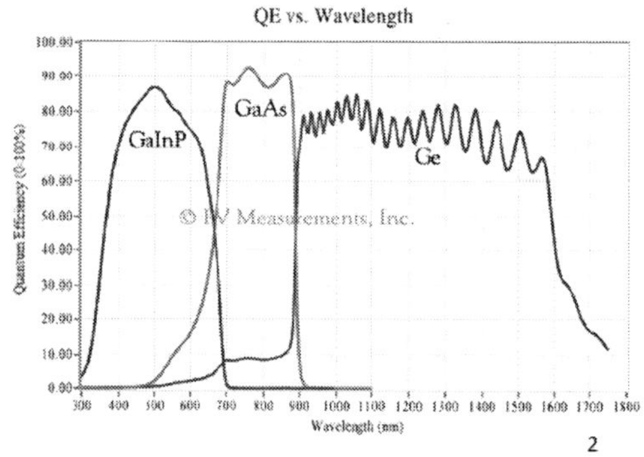

2

Cell matching will limit indoor performance of multi-junction cells

#SensorsConverge

Solar Cell - IV Curve

- Solar cells are diodes
- Collected power depends on resistance across cell
- Current changes proportional to light intensity
- Voltage depends on a cell's shunt resistance

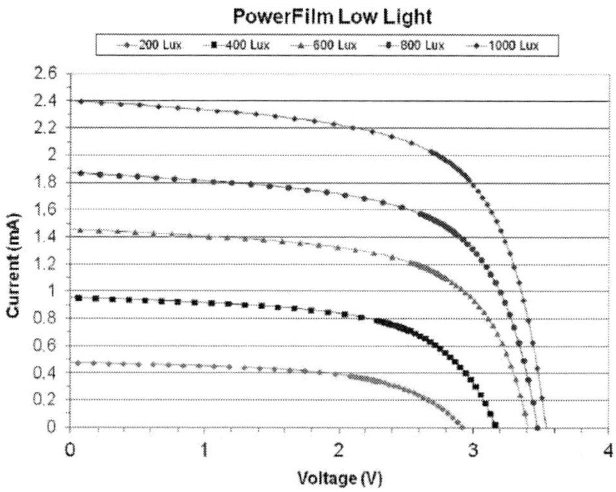

#SensorsConverge

Solar Voc vs Light Intensity

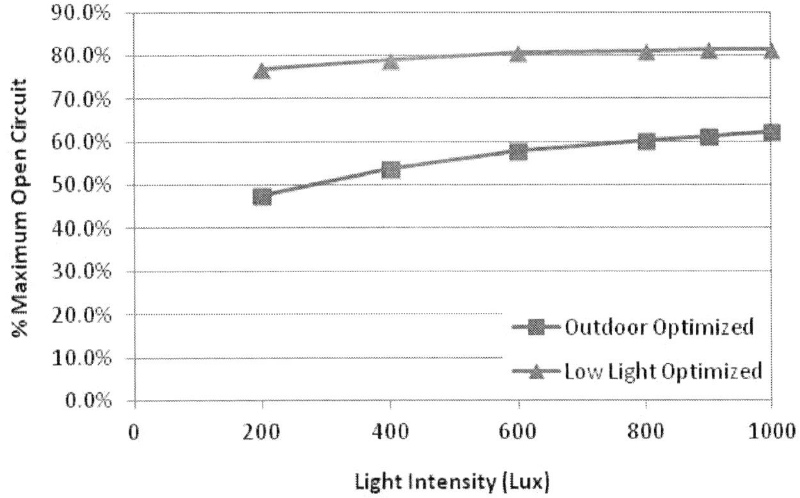

#SensorsConverge

Sensors Converge

Energy Harvesting Solar Power Sources

	a-Si	c-Si	GaAs	CIGS
Weight	Light	Moderate	Light to Moderate	Light to Moderate
Area	Moderate	Low	Very Low	Moderate
Indoor Performance	High	Low to Moderate	Low to High	Very Low
Durability	Excellent	Poor	Good	Moderate
Flexibility/Conformability	Excellent	Poor	Poor to Good	Good
Thickness	Thin	Thick	Thin to Thick	Thin to Thick
Cost	Moderate	Low	High	Moderate
Shade Tolerance	Excellent	Poor	Poor	Poor to Moderate
Manufacturing	Moderate	Moderate to Complex	Complex	Moderate

#SensorsConverge

Sensors Converge 2

Light Source 3000K LED

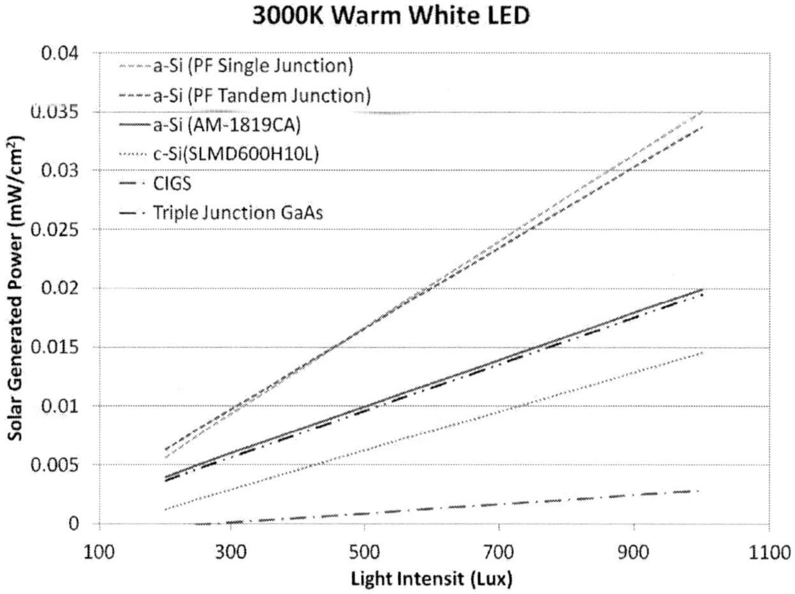

6

#SensorsConverge

Sensors Converge

Light Source 5000K LED

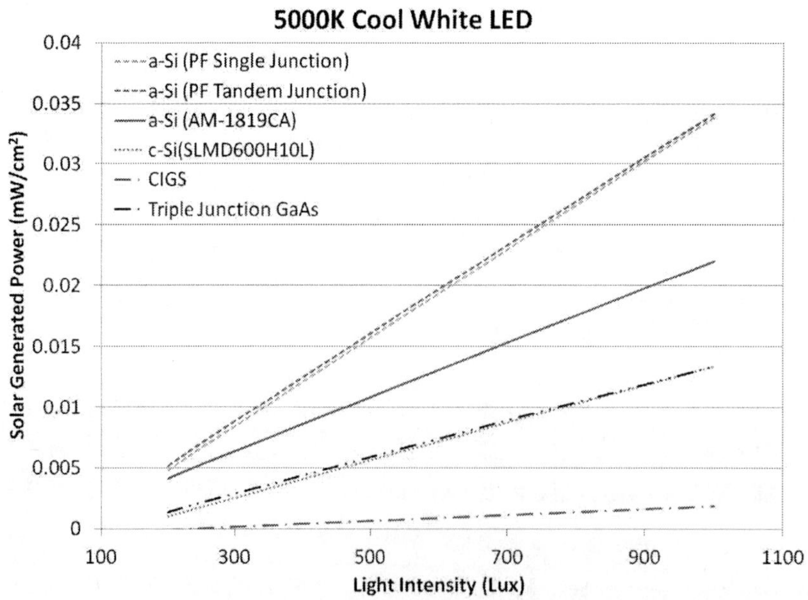

6

#SensorsConverge

Sensors Converge

Light Source Fluorescent

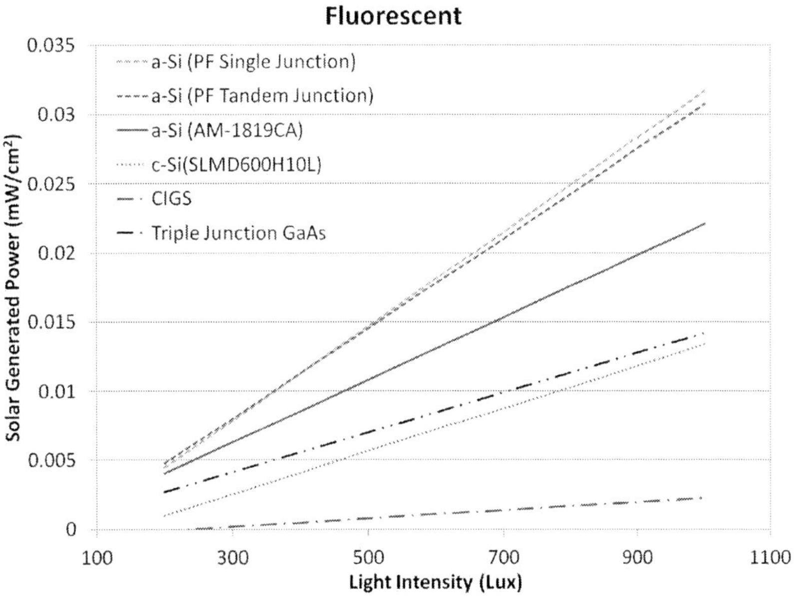

6

#SensorsConverge

Sensors Converge

Light Source Incandescent

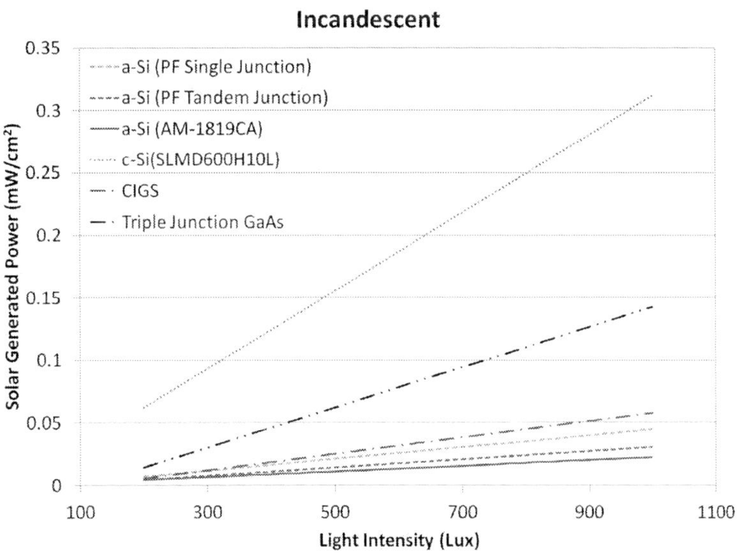

#SensorsConverge

Sensors Converge

Selection Criteria

- Rated efficiency has no correlation with indoor performance – Quantum efficiency and leakage do
- Light source spectrum has a major impact
- a-Si collects the most power in energy efficient indoor lighting

Technology	Rated Efficiency %	Current Density (mA/cm^2) at 1000Lux Fluorescent	LED	Incandescent
CIGS	8.5%	0.002	0.003	0.058
Si	18.0%	0.013	0.015	0.310
a-Si	6.0%	0.032	0.035	0.045
Triple Junction GaAs	30.0%	0.014	0.020	0.142

#SensorsConverge

Sensors Converge

Estimating Solar Requirements

- Energy harvester efficiency (90%, high solar voltage improves EH IC efficiency)
- Desired days to recharge from worst case given by safety factor (5 days)
- Illumination (12 hours/day)

$$\text{Solar Generation Capability} = \left[\frac{\frac{\text{Capacity Required}}{\text{Days to Recharge}} + \text{Daily Power Consumption}}{\text{Illumination Time}}\right]$$

- Illumination Intensity – PowerFilm a-Si Solar Module LL2.4-75-200, 0.29mW @ 200Lux, 1.91mW @ 1000Lux

Daily Power Consumption (mWh)	Capacity Required (mWh)	Days to Fully Recharge	Illumination Time (hours/day)	Solar Generation Capability (mW)
1.57	15.7	5	12	0.44
			12	0.15
6.9	69	5	12	1.92
			12	0.64

Charger efficiency is 90%

#SensorsConverge

Sensors Converge

OPV Considerations

- Organic Solar Modules or Organic Photovoltaics (OPV) Considerations
- High temperature degradation.
  - High temperatures ($T \gg 300$ K), mechanical stress, or contact with water can, in principle be overcome by engineering solutions like encapsulation or active cooling(13)
- UV Degradation;
  - UV light Is well known to cause degradation in OSCs, photodegradation is typically studied with UV cutoff filters, which have a typical cutoff wavelength of around 380 nm. Using a cutoff filter leads to lower light-harvesting potential of the OSCs and hence a loss in maximum current and performance of the devices.
- Moisture/Humidity Degradation;
  - There are no significant changes in the *J–V* characteristics of unencapsulated P3HT:PCBM cells using PMA as HTL during the course of 4 h in damp heat (85 °C/85% RH), while PEDOT:PSS-based devices are completely nonfunctional after such treatment.(14)
  - With regard to the thermal stability, the state-of-the-art device based on a PBDBT:ITIC blend with an initial 11.2% PCE achieved a T_{80} lifetime of >250 h after heating at 100 °C in a nitrogen-filled glove box (26).
- Light induced Degradation;
  - Samples that were illuminated with green light degraded linearly with *SE*h*, reducing their PCE by ≈15% within 100 *SE*h*, the samples degraded with blue light were suffering from a burn-in-like degradation behavior, in the beginning, reducing PCE by ≈50% within 100 *SE*h* (13)
- Encapsulation Solutions;
  - Glass-encapsulated annealed OPVs show good environmental stability with 4.8% loss in efficiency after 4,736 h and an estimated T_{80} lifetime (80% of the initial power conversion efficiency) of over 20,750 h in the dark under ambient condition and T_{80} lifetime of 1,050 h at 85 °C and 30% relative humidity.

#SensorsConverge

Sensors Converge

Conclusions

- Solar enables self sustaining sensors indoors and outside
- Rated solar efficiency has no correlation with indoor or low light intensity performance
- a-Si excels at producing power indoors
- a-Si has proven history of endurance in the field
- CIGS low performance/lack of availability
- GaAs can perform indoors, look for Single Junction devices
- OPV's are still in development
- The devil is in the details!

#SensorsConverge

Sensors Converge

Getting Started

Development kits are a great way to start and available with many different harvesters and radios

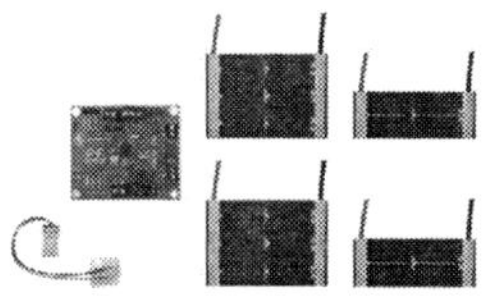

AEM10941 – EPeas[7]

EMH-UNIV-1 – Xidas[8]

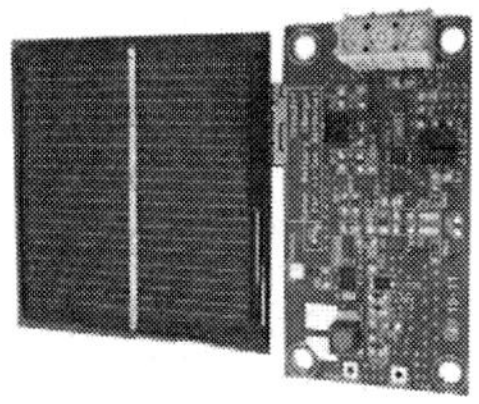

SPV1040 – STMicro[9]

MAX20361 – Maxim[14]

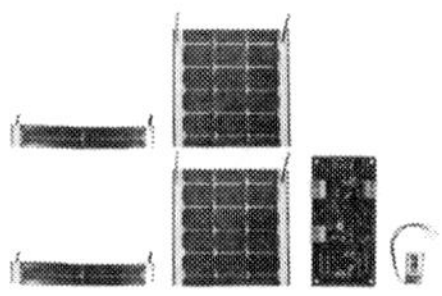

BQ25570 – TI and nRF52832 – Nordic[11]

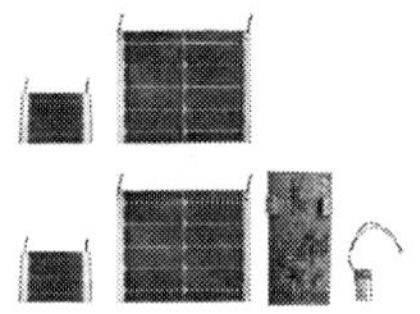

BQ25570 & CC2650 – TI[12]

ADP5091 – Analog Devices[13]

#SensorsConverge

Questions??

Do you have systems that you'd like to optimize and power via energy harvesting? PowerFilm can help! We would love to hear about your application and help make your vision a reality. Visit us at **Booth 962** or contact us www.powerfilmsolar.com

#SensorsConverge

References

1. "IoT: Number of Connected Devices Worldwide 2012-2025." Statista, www.statista.com/statistics/471264/iot-number-of-connected-devices-worldwide/.
2. "LEDs and Photosynthesis." Berry Gardener, 9 Feb. 2016, www.berrygardener.com/tags/light/.
3. https://www.noao.edu/education/QLTkit/ACTIVITY_Documents/Safety/LightLevels_outdoor+indoor.pdf
4. https://www2.pvlighthouse.com.au/resources/courses/altermatt/The%20Solar%20Spectrum/The%20global%20standard%20spectrum%20(AM1-5g).aspx
5. http://www.pvmeasurements.com/Products/Discontinued-Products/qex7-solar-cell-spectral-response-quantum-efficiency-ipce-measurement-system.html
6. Arthur, Battery Types Used in Solar Lighting. LEDWatcher.com. 1/15/16. http://www.ledwatcher.com/battery-types-used-in-portable-and-solar-lighting/ 10/20/2016.
7. Zhang, Yin, "Performance Characteristics of Lithium Coin Cells for Use in Wireless Sensing Systems" (2012). All Theses and Dissertations. Paper 3588.
8. http://batteryuniversity.com/learn/article/how_to_prolong_lithium_based_batteries
9. M. Jensen. "Coin cells and peak current draw". White Paper SWRA349.
10. https://www.labdevice.ch/products-1/100ma-range-current-probe/
11. Particle. Whitepaper, "Power Management for IoT Devices". (2017). https://www.particle.io/white-papers/power-management-for-iot-devices?sent=true&submissionGuid=5f28f939-95a3-439b-ab68-c1677f6d80da
12. Non-fullerene acceptor organic photovoltaics with intrinsic operational lifetimes over 30 years https://www.pnas.org/doi/10.1073/pnas.1919769117
13. Revealing Photodegradation Pathways of Organic Solar Cells by Spectrally Resolved Accelerated Lifetime Analysis https://onlinelibrary.wiley.com/doi/10.1002/aenm.202202564
14. Overcoming Moisture-Induced Degradation in Organic Solar Cells https://onlinelibrary.wiley.com/doi/10.1002/adem.202300595

HaiLa

Ultra Low Power RF Communications

Ambient Power Enabled IoT Sensing

Presenter: Vytas Kezys, Chief Scientist, HaiLa Technologies, Inc.
Sensors Converge 2023, Santa Clara

Enabling sustainable IoT sensing with
ultra-low power wireless connectivity

Massive IoT deployments: The Battery Problem

Critical need for actionable data & automation

Drives potential for **massive IoT adoption** in wireless sensor networks

End-user and operator needs

Minimize power, maintenance costs, and waste

Maximize sensor lifecycle

Barriers to sustainable IoT sensor network growth

Power hungry wireless connectivity

CapEx and OpEx for millions of battery replacements

E-waste generation

Solution: Ambient Power Enabled IoT

IoT sensing application example

Building automation

Mounted → Accessible for battery changes

HVAC Efficiency
• Temperature/humidity • Current monitoring (fan/pump) • Pressure/airflow

Security & Emergency
• Access control • Smoke/fire/CO2 detection

Comfort
• Lighting/air quality/occupancy

Requires ultra-long battery life for lower CapEx/OpEx

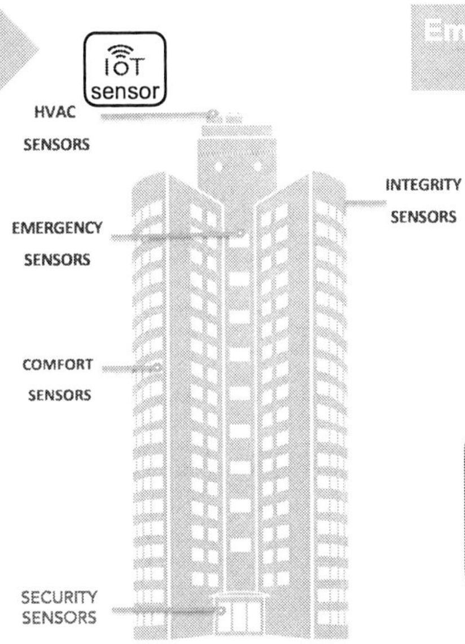

Embedded → Non-accessible for battery changes

Building Materials
• Mold/moisture detection • Water leaks • Electrical hotspots • Strain gauges

Requires ambient power (battery-free) IoT sensors based on extreme low power wireless communications

Wireless power efficiency challenges

New, power-efficient sensor technologies (e.g., silicon, MEMS)	Battery life is often dominated by the radio sub-system
Radio sub-system power consumers	Transmitter: ○ Generation of a stable RF carrier + RF amplifiers ○ Can be dominant power consumers especially at high transmission duty cycles Receiver: ○ Needed for channel sensing, synchronization via beacons, etc. ○ Will be dominant power consumer at low transmission duty cycles

Ambient Power IoT: How do we get there?

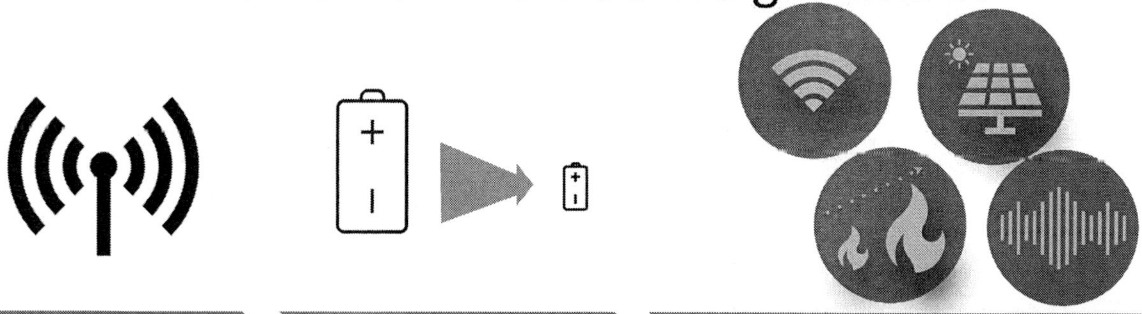

Reduce radio power consumption → **Interim: Enable use of small, lifetime battery** → **Ultimate goal: Enable energy harvesting from ambient power sources**

Today: High power radio solutions → Near future: Ultra-low power RF technology → RX: Envelope detector or channelized receiver with long sleep cycles

TX: Backscatter

Backscatter on Wi-Fi explained

Bistatic Backscatter (TX and RX in different AP)

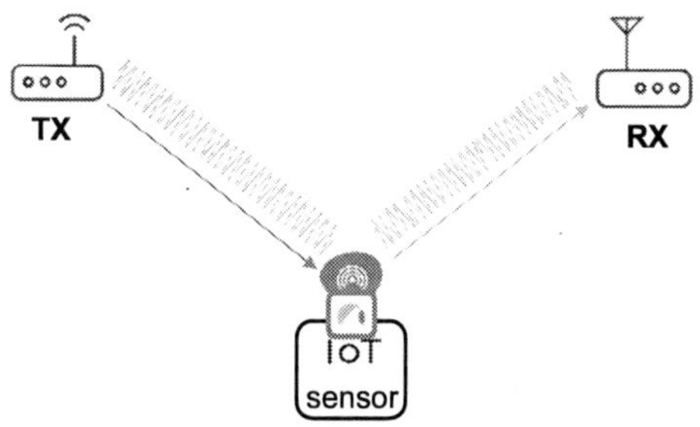

Monostatic Backscatter (TX and RX are colocated in AP)

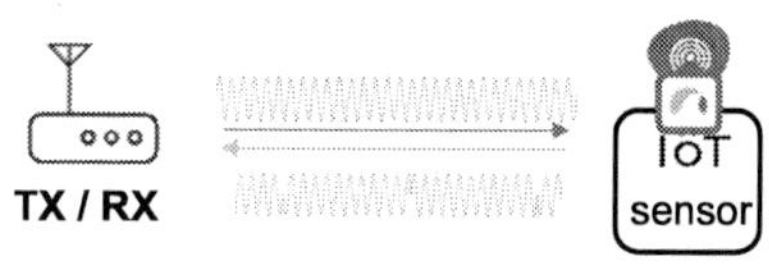

Backscatter is a modulated reflection of an ambient RF signal, in this case a Wi-Fi signal

- A conventional transmitter (TX) sends standard Wi-Fi signal
- IoT sensor tag backscatters (reflects) the Wi-Fi signal on a different Wi-Fi channel with the sensor data embedded
- The reflected signal is received by a Wi-Fi device (RX) as a standard Wi-Fi signal
- IoT sensor tag data can be extracted at the receiver, the network edge or in the Cloud
- Can be configured as bi-static or monostatic

Ubiquitous Wi-Fi, IoT sensing, and ultra-low power RF

Optimized use of existing infrastructure: Wi-Fi

- Avoid yet another radio protocol
- Wi-Fi is ubiquitous
- It can be tailored to meet battery life longevity requirements for wireless IoT
- IEEE 802.11 AMP is an active group defining the path to ambient powered IoT over Wi-Fi

Infrastructure enhancements for backscatter on Wi-Fi

- Enhancing coverage
  - Macro diversity (more infrastructure)
  - Joint transmission (Wi-Fi 8)
  - Multi-antenna sensor tags
- Self-jamming cancellation

Expectations for backscatter on Wi-Fi

- Projected battery life of 20 years with 2-minute sensor updates

Demonstrating Wi-Fi backscatter for IoT sensing

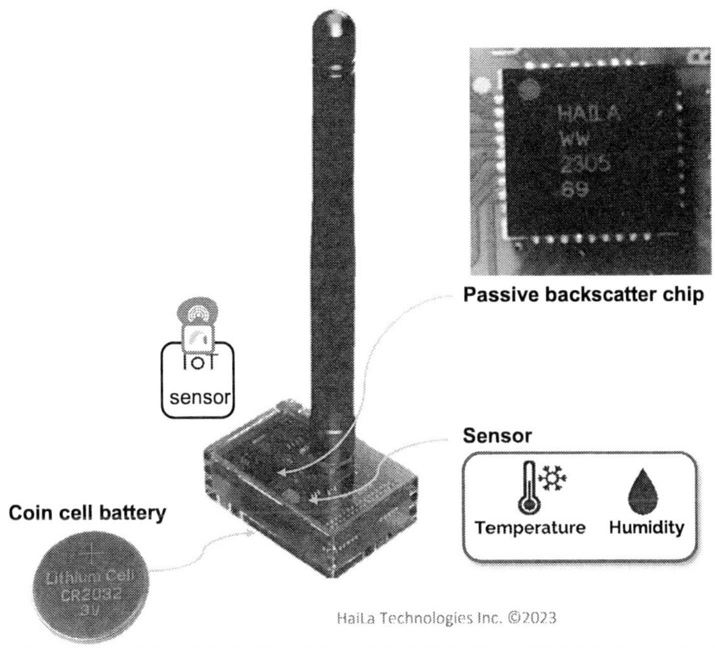

Key Takeaways

Battery problem	Massive deployment of IoT sensors needs a solution to mitigate battery waste and eliminate altogether
Sensor radio power	Industry working towards lower power radios
Ambient IoT	Need a step-function improvement in radio designs to eliminate IoT sensor batteries
Ease of adoption	Leverage ubiquitous, existing, global wireless networks
New enabling technology	Passive backscatter over Wi-Fi

Thank You

Sensors Converge

Archimedes Controls A150 and ARCOS IIOT platform

Wenli Yu, CEO
Archimedes Controls Corp.

- June 20–22, 2023 | Santa Clara, CA

#SensorsConverge

Company's Vision, Mission and Value

- Our Vision – **IoT Everywhere**. The rising popularity of IoT devices and edge computing are becoming the main driving force for ever increased needs for application specific sensors and gateways powered by cloud-based IoT services.

- Our Long Term Mission and Commitment - **Innovation**. Archimedes Controls is committed to develop, build and offer our customers the most reliable and cost-effective IoT services and products through continuous innovation and operational excellence.

- Our Value – **Simplicity.** Our cloud-based IoT platform ARCOS™ is a universal control platform supporting organically developed as well as 3rd party devices through a secured https link for analog and digital sensors, cameras, gateways and alarm devices with a few minutes of setup time.

#SensorsConverge

Sensors Converge

Vertical Applications

Data Center and Edge Security

- Per-user, per-rack and security protected environmental, assets and access monitoring.
- Reduces the number of on-site visits.
- Secures and provides detailed health information about the edge data center's environment and physical security.
- Protects remote IT equipment operating conditions under 24 x 7 x 365 surveillance.
- 10-year battery operated wireless sensors.
- Integrated IP security cameras.
- Warnings and alarms notification and records.

Industrial Controls & Automation

- Temperature and humidity monitoring.
- Water leak detection monitoring.
- Real time power consumption monitoring.
- Metal detection or separation for structural monitoring.
- Vibration, tamper, shake, move, tilt detection for physical security.
- IP security cameras.
- Pre-set warning triggers and notification.
- Analytics and AI tools for data analysis and prediction.
- 3rd party devices support.
- Historic data recording for audit and compliances.

Agriculture & Food Safety

- Mission critical temperature and humidity monitoring.
- Airborne particle counts and air quality PM1.0, PM2.5 and PM10 for nearby wildfire monitoring
- Smoke detection
- Liquid level monitoring for fuel and any liquid tanks and storages
- Water leak detection.
- Tamper and break-in detection
- 2G, 3G, 4G/5G cloud-based
- Data access from anywhere in the world.
- 24x7 automatic monitoring, recording and warning messaging.
- Analytics and AI tools for analysis and prediction.

Environmental & Transportation

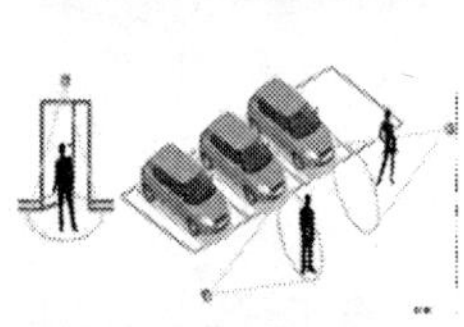

- Temperature and humidity monitoring.
- Airborne particle counts and air quality PM1.0, PM2.5 and PM10.
- Smoke detection.
- Explosive gas detection.
- Water leak detection.
- HVAC performance monitoring.
- Metal detection or separation for structural monitoring.
- Vibration, tamper, shake, move, tilt detection for physical security.
- Traffic flow analysis.
- Parking garage/lot safety and security
- Automated parking assistance.

#SensorsConverge

Sensors Converge

A150 System Platform

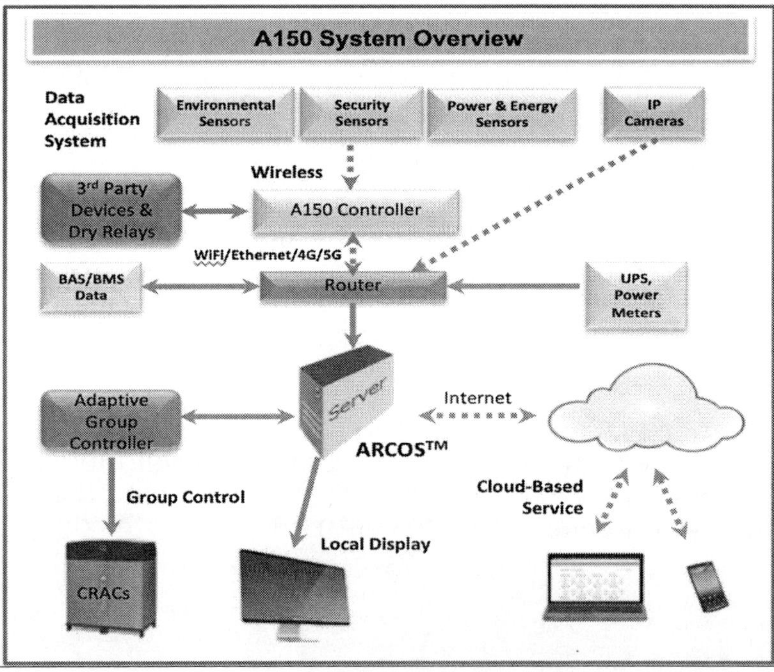

#SensorsConverge

Sensors Converge

Vertical Applications

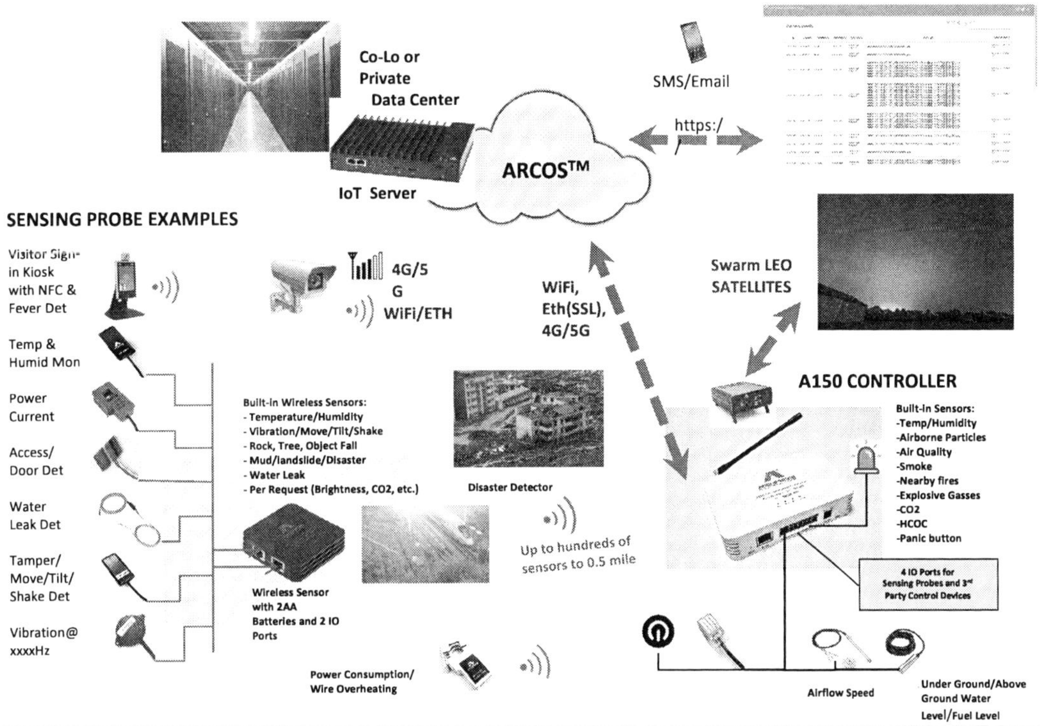

Introducing A300 Satellite IoT CPE

NEW

Applications:

- **Connecting IoT Gateways to Swarm LEO Satellites**
- **National Strategic Fuel Reserve and Assets Monitoring**
- **Security Tracking in Desert, Mountains and Ocean**
- **Granary Monitoring and Food Safety**
- **Global Emergency Alert and Notification**

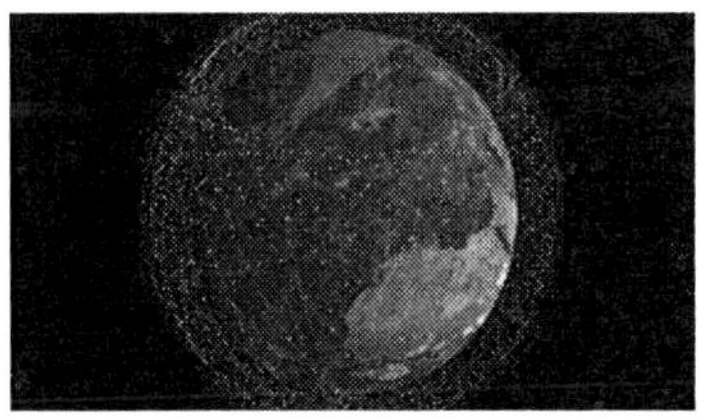

LEO Satellites

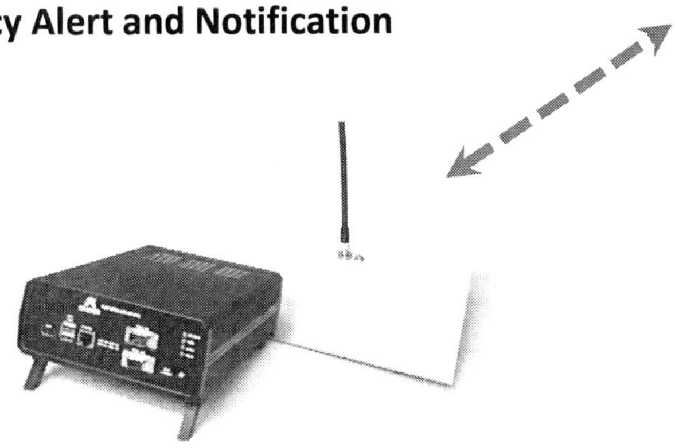

A300 Satellite IOT CPE

A300 Satellite IoT CPE

NEW

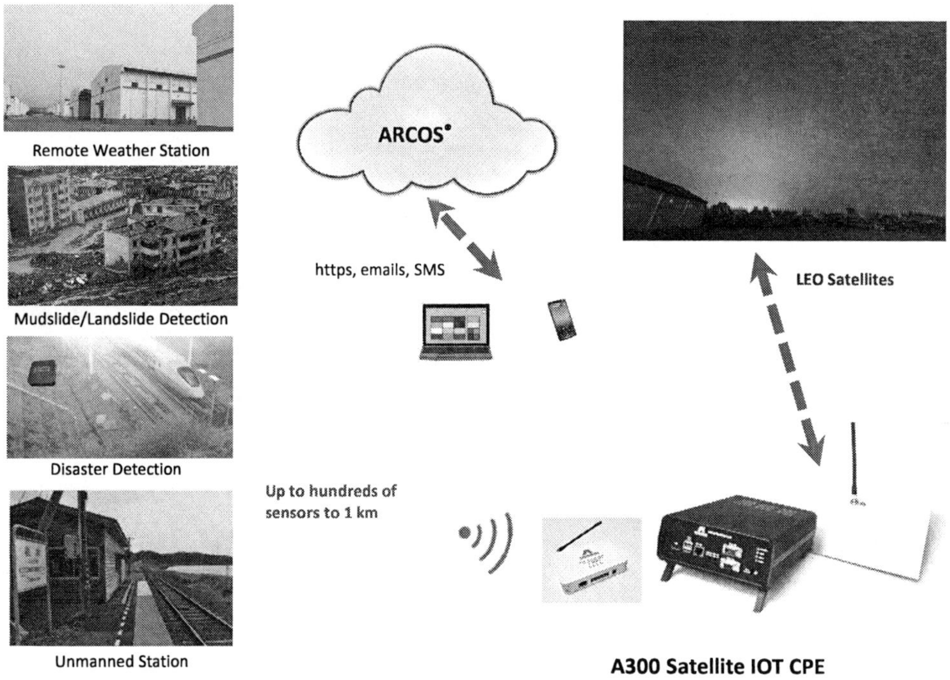

Fully Integrated Analytics - OpenSearch

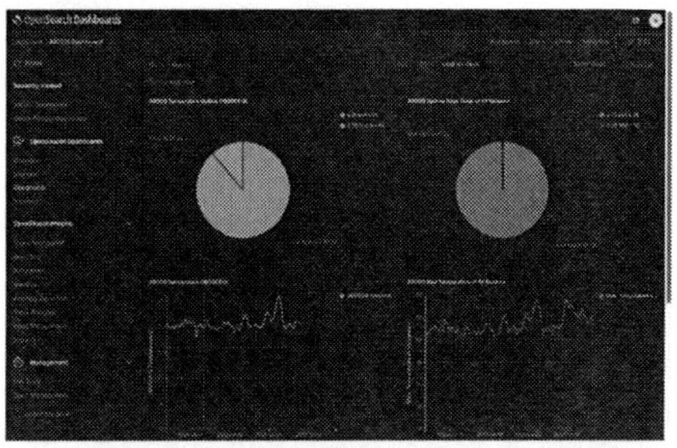

- OpenSearch provides custom reports, charts, dashboards, histograms, data graphs, heatmaps, and measure analysis, warnings, etc.

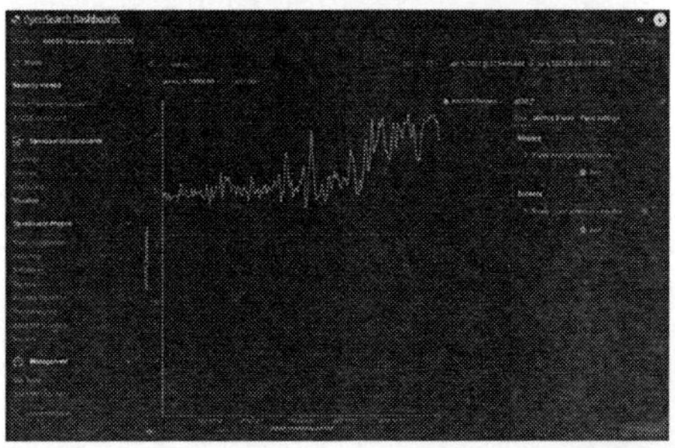

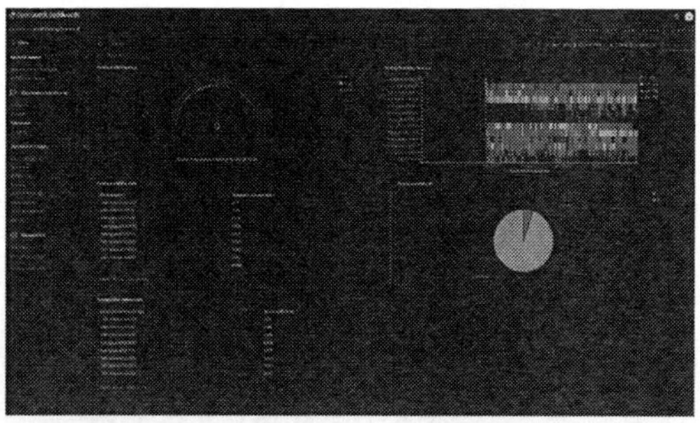

#SensorsConverge

Sensors Converge

Machine Learning (ML) Based Anomaly Detection

- Integrated powerful machine learning (ML) based Anomaly detection with anomaly grade and confidence level and warnings

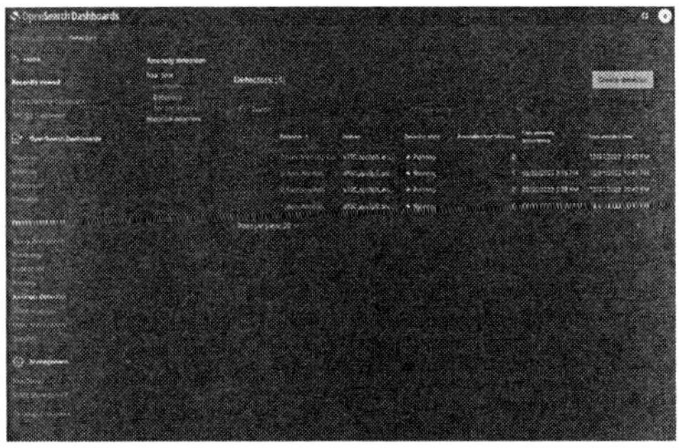

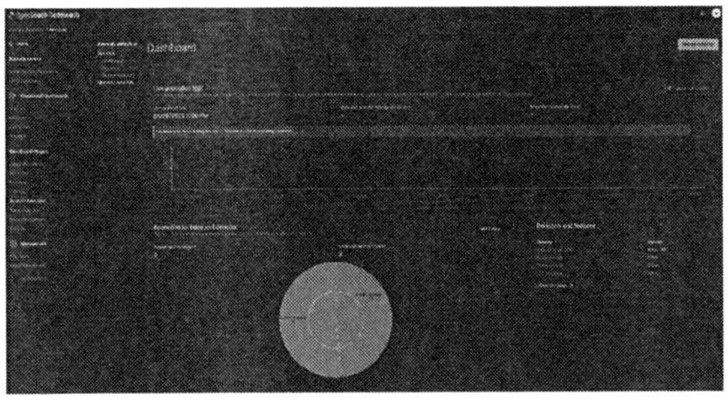

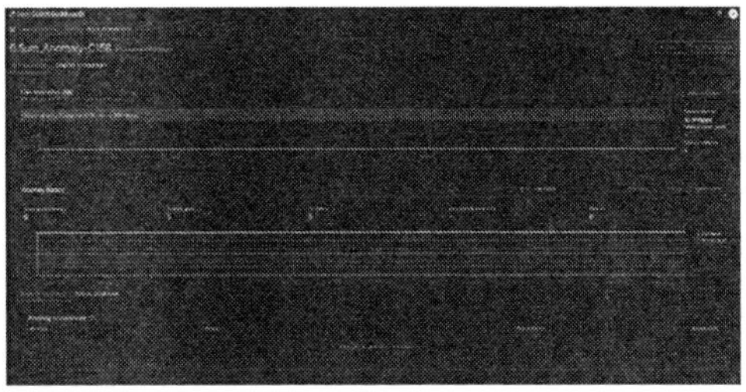

#SensorsConverge

Sensors Converge

ARCOS® Cloud Service

- Offers both SaaS and Purchase options for hardware sensors, gateways and cloud software
- Silicon Valley, US based data center for extra security
- Supports all Archimedes platform and sensor data globally
- Global 24x7 remote physical security monitoring
- Dedicated server for each customer
- Customer access at any time from anywhere in the world

Use Case – Security Monitoring

#SensorsC

Sensors Converge

Use Case – Fuel Supply & Demand Management

- Smart gas station fuel usage management for major fuel suppliers and government monitoring
- Smart fuel delivery tracking via mobile network
- Virtual geofencing, line crossing detection, vehicle recognition

Smart Fuel Tracking and Monitoring System

Use Case – Disaster Monitoring and Alert

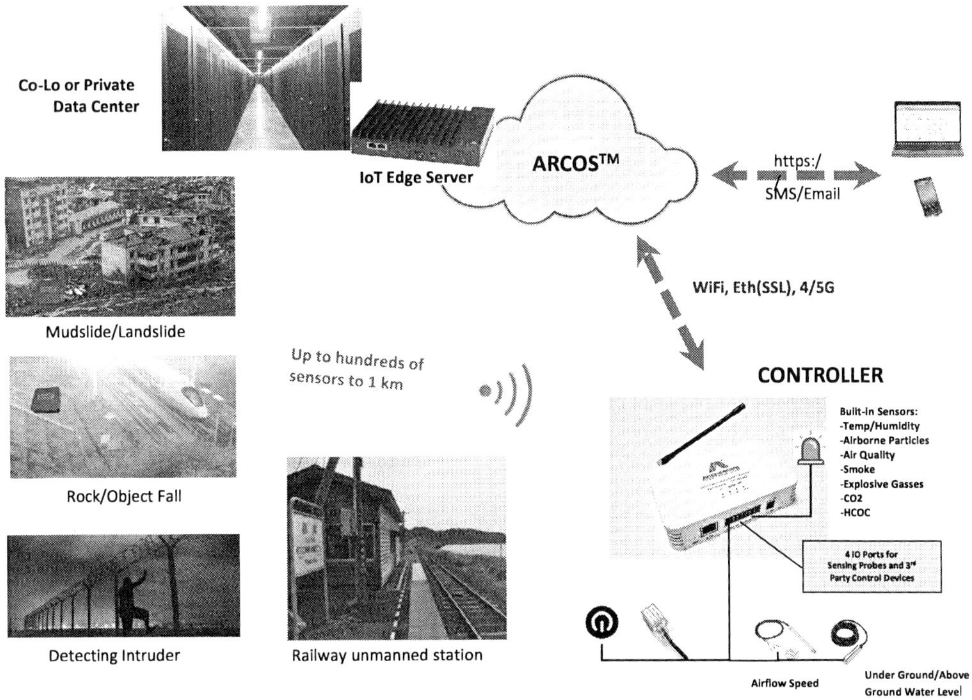

Use Case – Agriculture, Granary

- Grains such as wheat, corns and soy beans considered national strategic economic resources, along with its storage environment such as granary's temperature, humidity and surrounding air composition are a few very important environmental parameters in modern agriculture.

- In a typical granary, grains are safely stored and kept for 2 to 5 years for many reasons. Due to specific security requirements, reliability, ultra low power, automatic 24x7 monitoring and wireless all the way are critical and desirable at all levels.

Use Case - Private Cloud Control Center

- ❑ Private cloud-based software management
- ❑ Site view, dashboards, 3D heat map, warnings, historic charts, property assets management, etc.
- ❑ Accessible from anywhere via secured link for alarms, videos, data
- ❑ Alerts to emails and mobile phones via SMS
- ❑ User privileged accounts
- ❑ AI and ML based video detection
- ❑ Supports integration to existing warning system

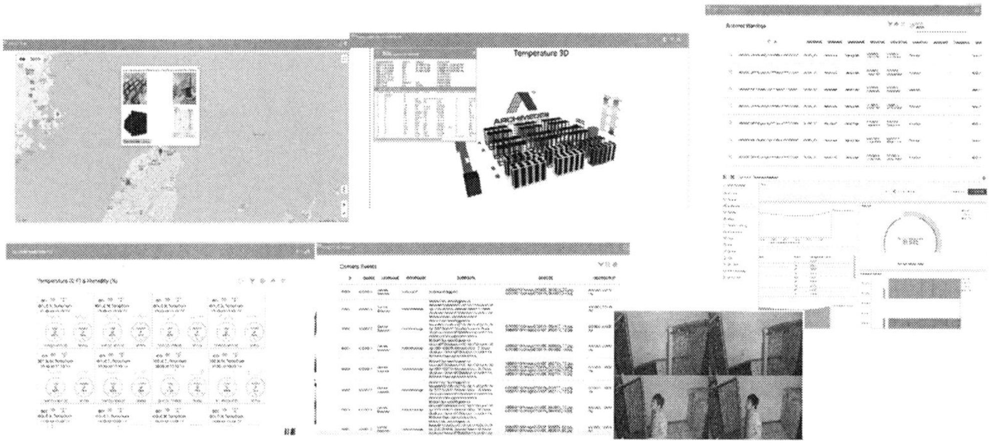

Archimedes Controls

A150 Wireless Sensors/Gateway System
and
ARCOS® IoT Cloud Service

Wenli Yu, CEO
wenli.yu@archimeescontrols.com
Mobile: 301-370-0496

www.ArchimedesControls.com

June 2023

Sensors Converge

Sensors Converge

Innovative MEMS-Based Thermal Conductivity Sensors for Hydrogen Detection

Federico Pasquini, Director, Sales and Marketing, N.E.T. s.r.l,

June 21, 2023 | Santa Clara, CA

#SensorsConverge

Agenda

1. THE HYDROGEN ECONOMY IS UPON US
2. APPLICATIONS AND DETECTION SCENARIOS
3. HYDROGEN SAFETY CONCERNS
4. COMMON HYDROGEN DETECTION TECHNOLOGIES
5. THERMAL CONDUCTIVITY SENSORS
6. NET KATHAROMETER GAS TECHNOLOGY
7. NET MAK (MEMS ANALOGUE KATHAROMETER)
8. CONCLUSIONS

n.e.t. innovative gas sensing

Federico Pasquini | Director, Sales&Marketing
email | federico.pasquini@nenvitech.com
www.nenvitech.com

twenty years of advanced solutions for gas detection 20 YEARS

#SensorsConverge

Sensors Converge

THE HYDROGEN ECONOMY IS UPON US

- A global sustainability effort is undergoing to significantly increase use of hydrogen between here and 2050.
- More and more, in the upcoming future, hydrogen will be used to decarbonize entire economic sectors.
- Hydrogen is highly energetic and extremely environment friendly: it can be created from water using renewable sources such as wind and solar power.
- Hydrogen combustion only releases water vapor into the atmosphere.

APPLICATIONS AND DETECTION SCENARIOS

HEAVY INDUSTRY

LITHIUM BATTERY LEAKS

NATURAL GAS SUBSTITUTE IN GRIDS

FUEL CELLS

#SensorsConverge

Sensors Converge

HYDROGEN SAFETY CONCERNS

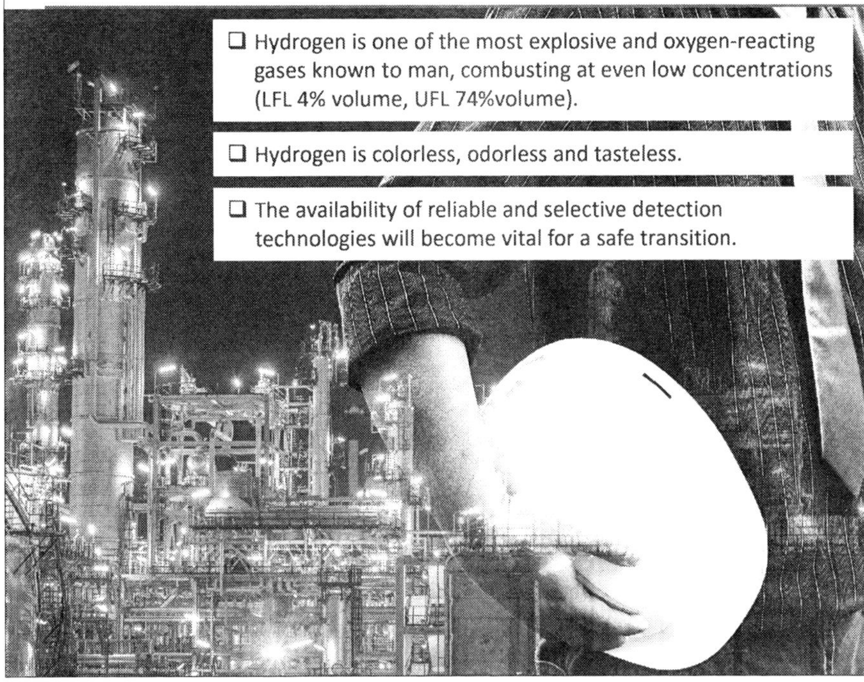

- ❑ Hydrogen is one of the most explosive and oxygen-reacting gases known to man, combusting at even low concentrations (LFL 4% volume, UFL 74%volume).
- ❑ Hydrogen is colorless, odorless and tasteless.
- ❑ The availability of reliable and selective detection technologies will become vital for a safe transition.

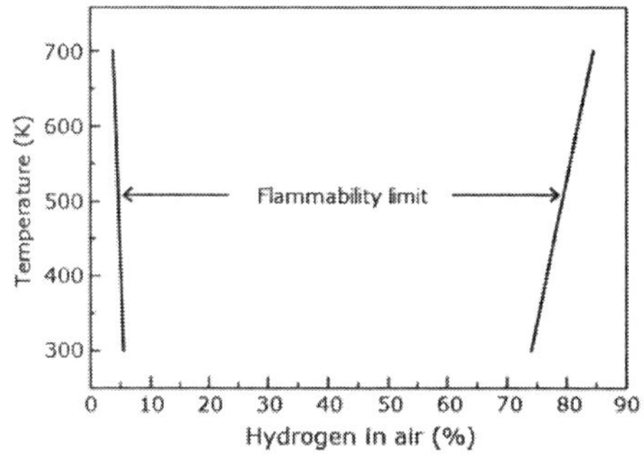

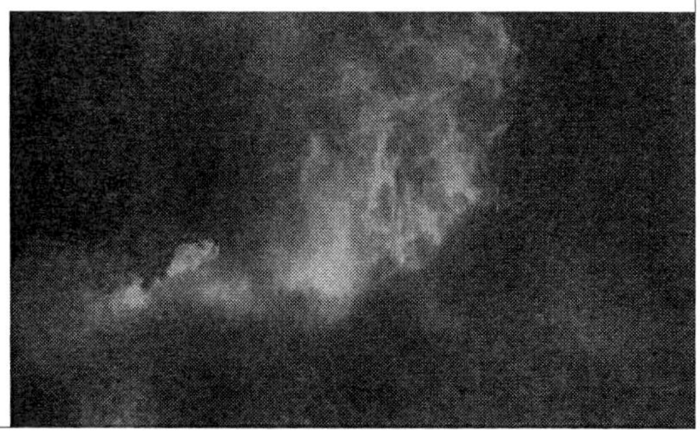

COMMON HYDROGEN DETECTION TECHNOLOGIES

ELECTROCHEMICAL CELLS
- ❑ Detection range: up to 5.000ppm (0.5%vol)
- ❑ Typical long-term drift: 2%/month
- ❑ Typical operating life: 24 months in air
- ❑ Cross sensitivity to other gases
- ❑ Potential replacement required after high exposures
- ❑ Can only operate in presence of Oxygen

CATALYTIC BEAD SENSORS
- ❑ Detection range: up to 100% LFL (4%vol)
- ❑ Effectively Linear to 60% LEL
- ❑ Typical long-term drift: 5% LEL/3 Months
- ❑ Reacts to any flammable gas
- ❑ Potential replacement required after high exposures
- ❑ Susceptible to contamination and poisoning
- ❑ Can only operate in presence of Oxygen

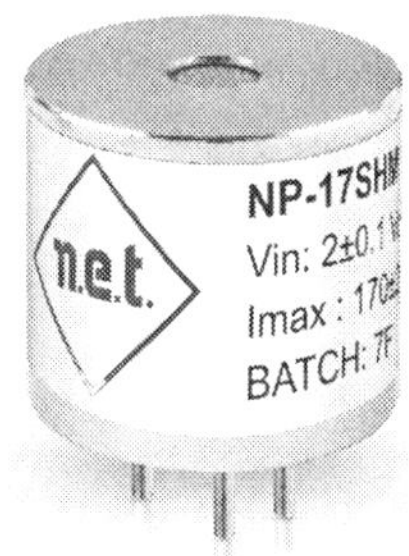

#SensorsConverge

Sensors Converge

THERMAL CONDUCTIVITY SENSORS

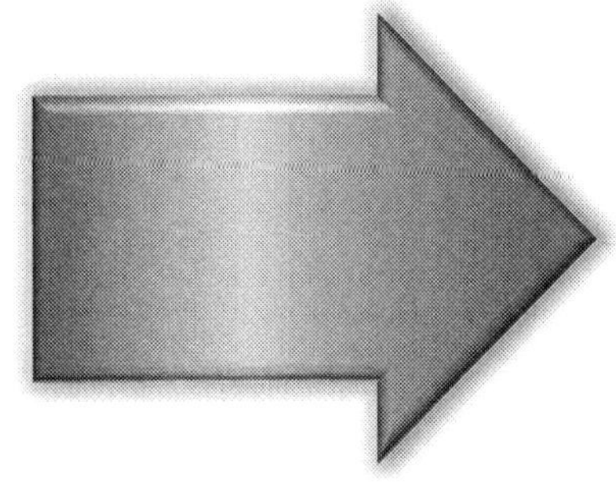

- A thermal conductivity sensor, also known as a katharometer, is a common technology allowing measurement of the concentration of flammable gases, also above the Lower Flammability Level (LFL).
- Traditional thermal conductivity sensors suffer from high power requirements and demand high level of precision and craftsmanship in manufacturing.
- Employing very repeatable, high-volume Single-wafer CMOS (Complementary metal-oxide-semiconductor) MEMS technology, is significantly lowering production costs and power consumption.

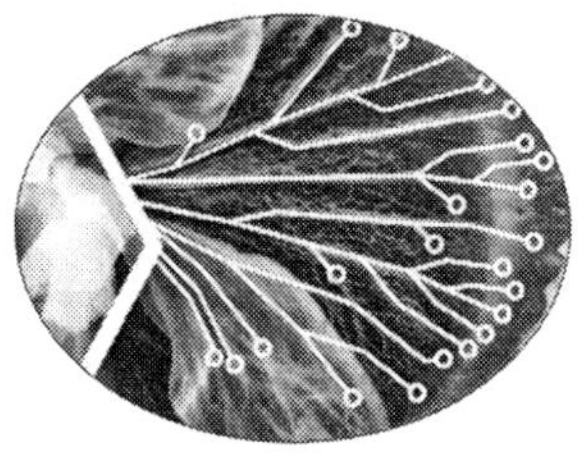

#SensorsConverge

Sensors Converge

NET KATHAROMETER GAS TECHNOLOGY

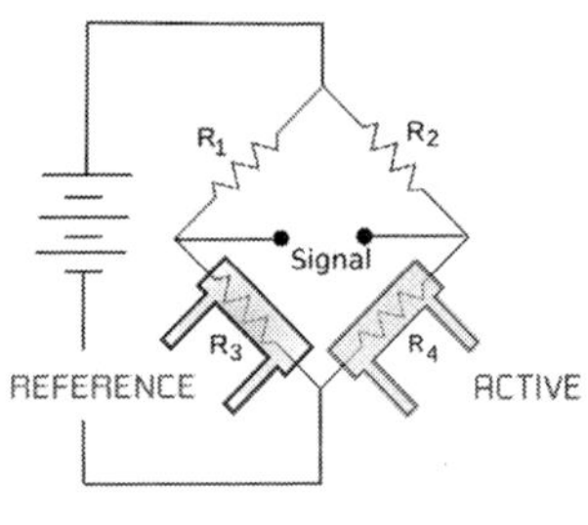

Both dies are heated using constant current and run in a classic Wheatstone bridge circuit.

- Thermal conductivity sensors measure the concentration of gases having thermal conductivity significantly different to a reference gas (normally, air), between 0 and 100% volume.
- Thermal conductivity sensors measure the change in heat loss of the active die in the presence of the target gas.
- Thermal conductivity sensors perform best in applications where interfering gases are absent, or their cross sensitivity is within the acceptable margin of error required by the application.
- Thermal conductivity sensors are most effective when detecting gases with low molecular weight, which correspond to greater thermal conductivity – such as **Hydrogen**, possessing possesses the highest thermal conductivity of all known gases, and Helium.

#SensorsConverge

Sensors Converge

NET MAK (MEMS ANALOGUE KATHAROMETER)

KATHAROMETER
gas technology

- ❑ Detection range: ppm to 100% volume
- ❑ Long-term reliability (0.5 % F.S./year), no chemical reaction/contamination
- ❑ Reliable in harsh environments
- ❑ Fast response time (< 1.4 s)
- ❑ High resolution (2 ppm of H_2)
- ❑ Long expected lifetime
- ❑ Internal heat cavity, minimizing conduction and natural convection
- ❑ Can operate without the presence of Oxygen
- ❑ Industry proven technology (used for flow and vacuum pressure sensors)
- ❑ Low working temperature (~2ºC above ambient)
- ❑ intrinsically safe, while avoiding condensation
- ❑ MEMS membrane-based sensor: great resistance to mechanical shocks
- ❑ Environmental compensation
- ❑ Standard industrial size and footprint
- ❑ Standard industrial output (voltage, bridge, Modbus)

#SensorsConverge

Sensors Converge

CONCLUSIONS

- ❑ Thermal conductivity is a promising technology for the detection of Hydrogen
- ❑ Effective in different application conditions, included harsh environments
- ❑ CMOS MEMS technology ensure reliable and cost-effective production
- ❑ Safe and stable technology: no chemicals, no optics/lamps, no resonating/moving parts
- ❑ Low power consumption
- ❑ A need for a strong environmental compensation and effective calibration

THANK YOU FOR YOUR ATTENTION

n.e.t.
innovative gas sensing

Federico Pasquini | Director, Sales&Marketing
email | federico.pasquini@nenvitech.com
www.nenvitech.com

twenty years of advanced solutions for gas detection 20 YEARS

BOOTH #745

#SensorsConverge

Sensors Converge

Sensors Converge

Intelligent sensing: past, present, and future

Mahesh CHOWDHARY, Fellow, Sr. Director, MEMS Software Solutions
MEMS subgroup, STMicroelectronics

June 20–22, 2023 | Santa Clara, CA

Visit us in Booth #936

#SensorsConverge

MEMS sensors' three key elements

Transducer	ASIC	Package
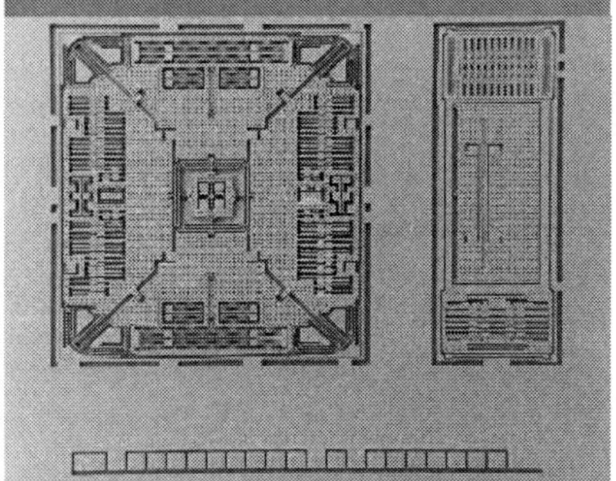		
Micron-sized **transducer** realized through a specific process called Micro-Machining	A dedicated **ASIC** with embedded smart functionalities	Dedicated **package** and **calibration** features

life.augmented

2

Sensors: past

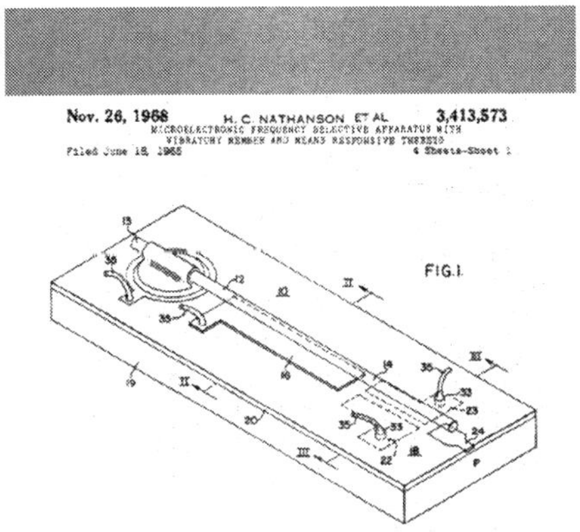

Early 1960s: Invention of MEMS: Resonant Gate Transistor used as frequency filter for ICs.

2006: game controllers using accelerometers for swinging, shaking, tilting. **2008** generation introduced the use of gyro-scopes for complex movements

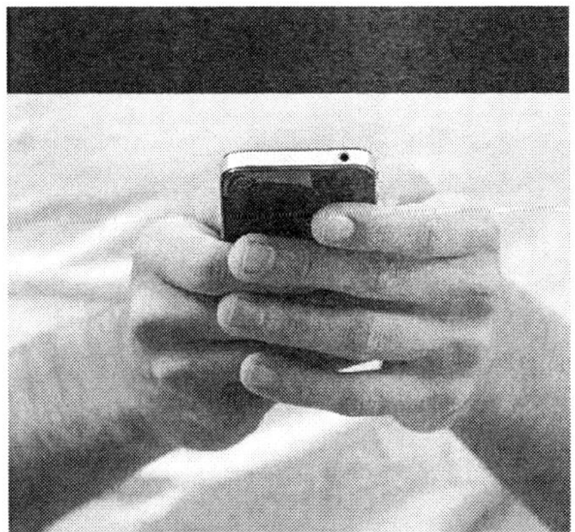

2007: first full touchscreen smartphone with an accelerometer to adjust portrait / landscape mode

life.augmented

3

Sensors: past

- Early sensors: MEMS sensing element + ASIC for signal conditioning and data acquisition
- Most intelligence resided on uControllers or application processors
- There was gradual addition of intelligence in sensors through embedded features on sensor ASIC

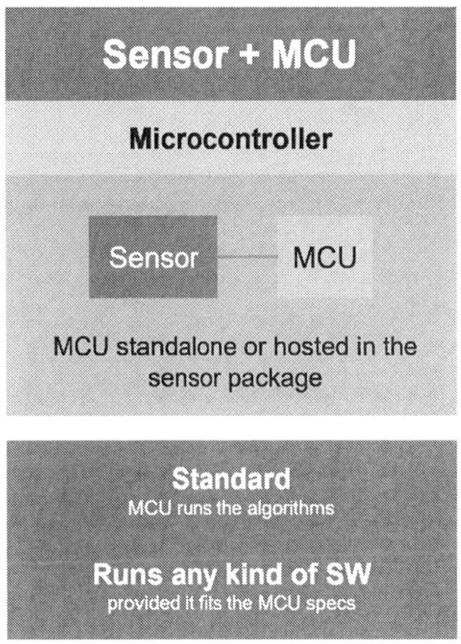

life.augmented

4

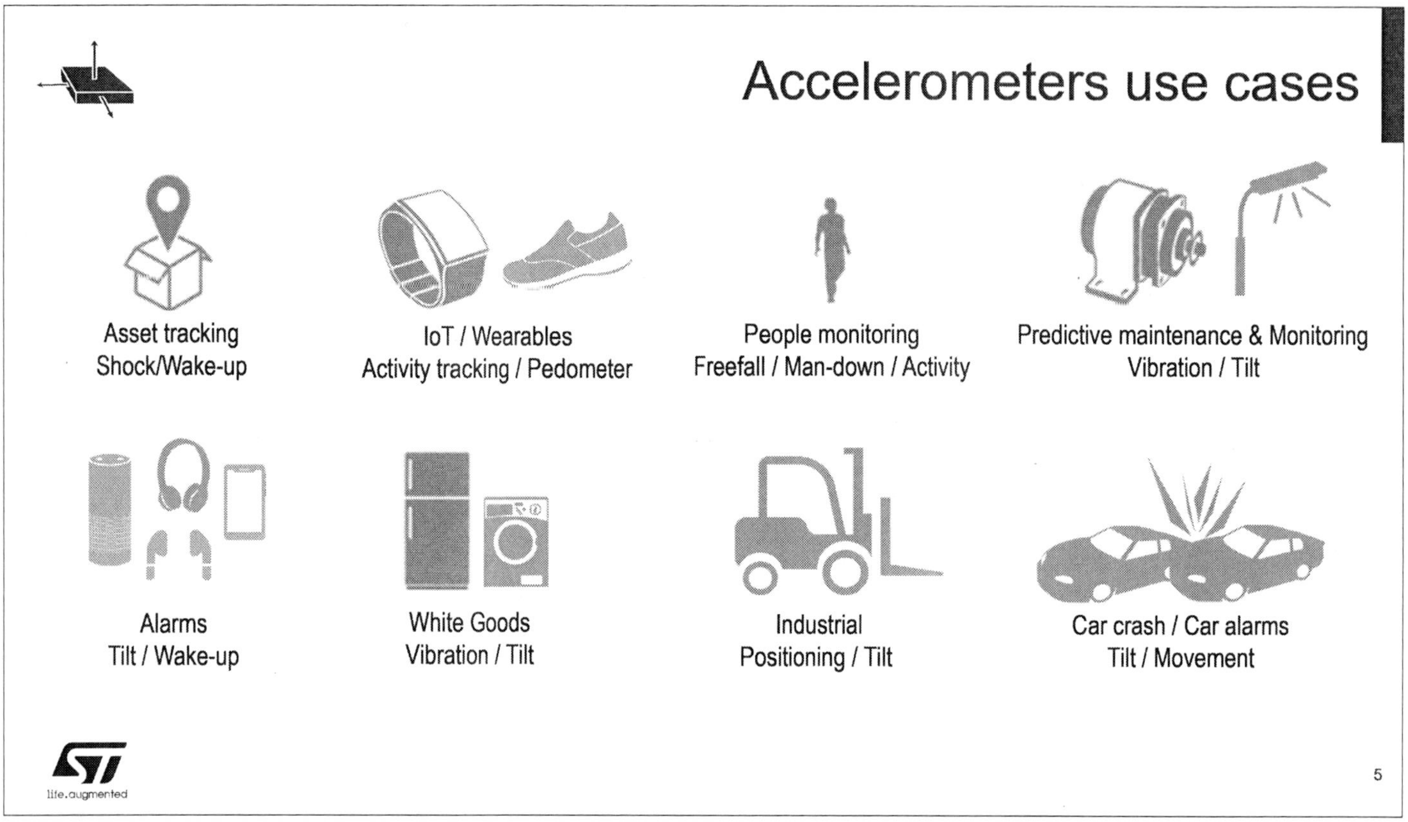
Accelerometers use cases
Asset tracking
Shock/Wake-up
IoT / Wearables
Activity tracking / Pedometer
People monitoring
Freefall / Man-down / Activity
Predictive maintenance & Monitoring
Vibration / Tilt
Alarms
Tilt / Wake-up
White Goods
Vibration / Tilt
Industrial
Positioning / Tilt
Car crash / Car alarms
Tilt / Movement
life.augmented
5

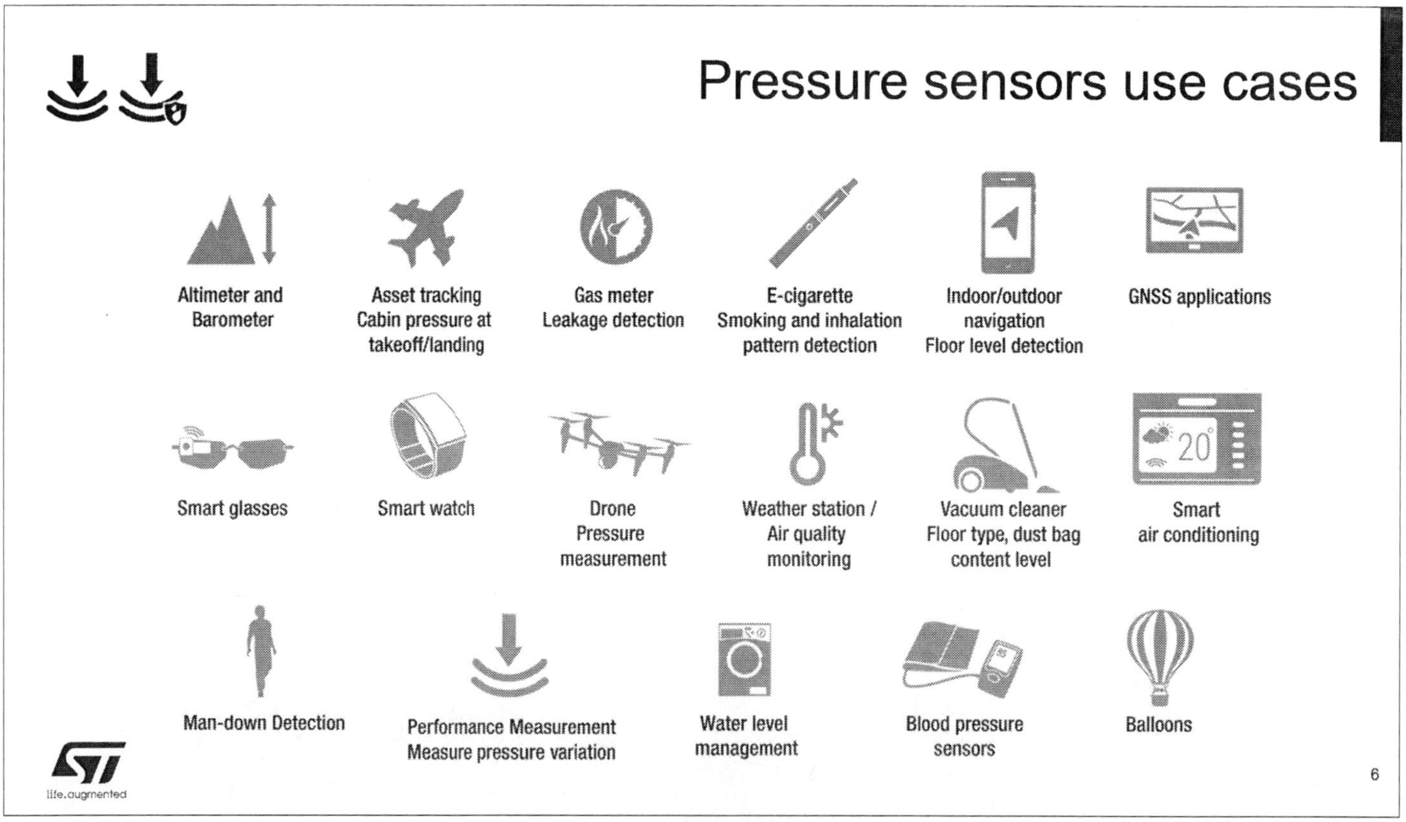
Pressure sensors use cases
Altimeter and
Barometer
Asset tracking
Cabin pressure at
takeoff/landing
Gas meter
Leakage detection
E-cigarette
Smoking and inhalation
pattern detection
Indoor/outdoor
navigation
Floor level detection
GNSS applications
Smart glasses
Smart watch
Drone
Pressure
measurement
Weather station /
Air quality
monitoring
Vacuum cleaner
Floor type, dust bag
content level
Smart
air conditioning
Man-down Detection
Performance Measurement
Measure pressure variation
Water level
management
Blood pressure
sensors
Balloons
life.augmented
6

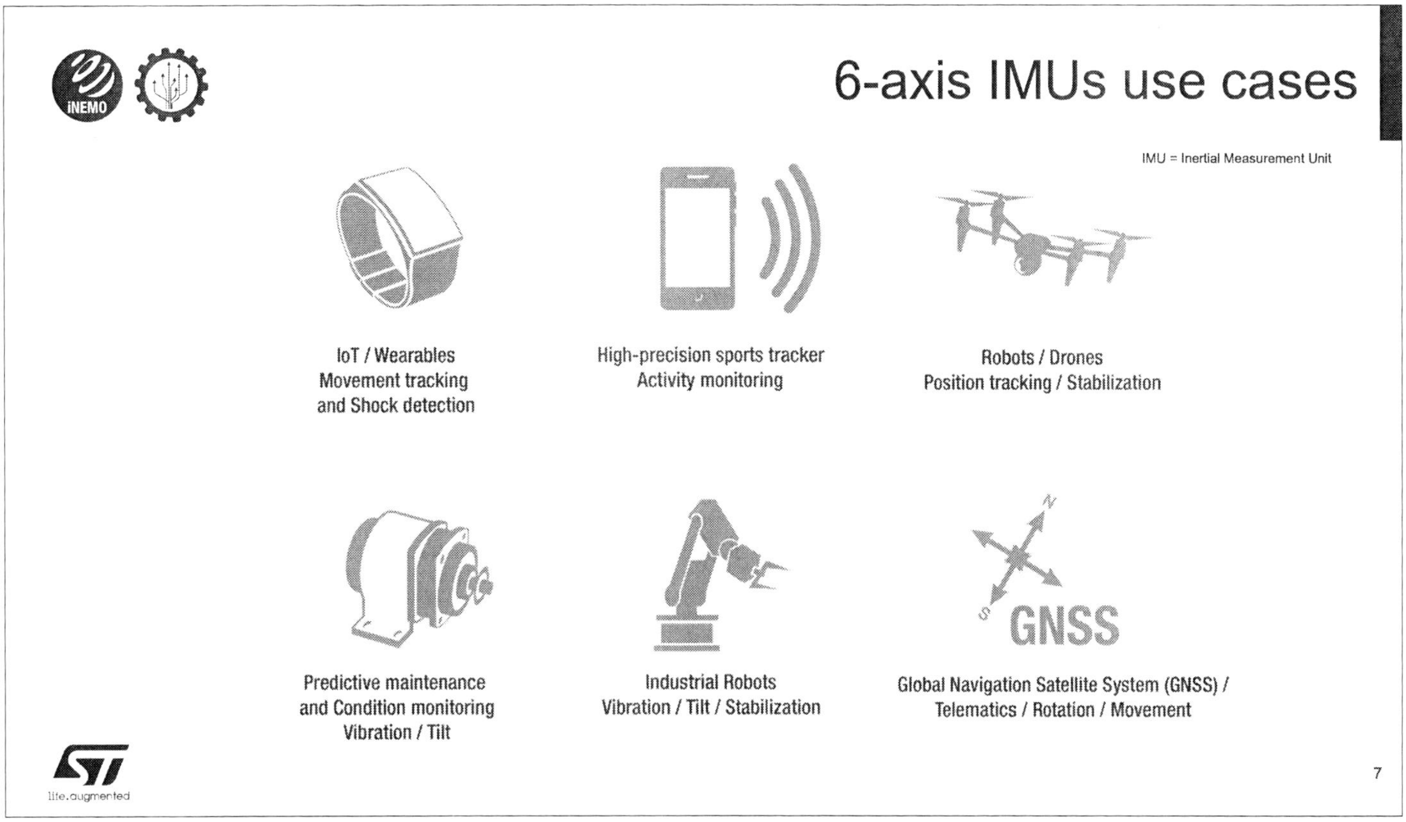
6-axis IMUs use cases
iNEMO
IMU = Inertial Measurement Unit
IoT / Wearables
Movement tracking
and Shock detection
High-precision sports tracker
Activity monitoring
Robots / Drones
Position tracking / Stabilization
Predictive maintenance
and Condition monitoring
Vibration / Tilt
Industrial Robots
Vibration / Tilt / Stabilization
N
S
GNSS
Global Navigation Satellite System (GNSS) /
Telematics / Rotation / Movement
life.augmented
7

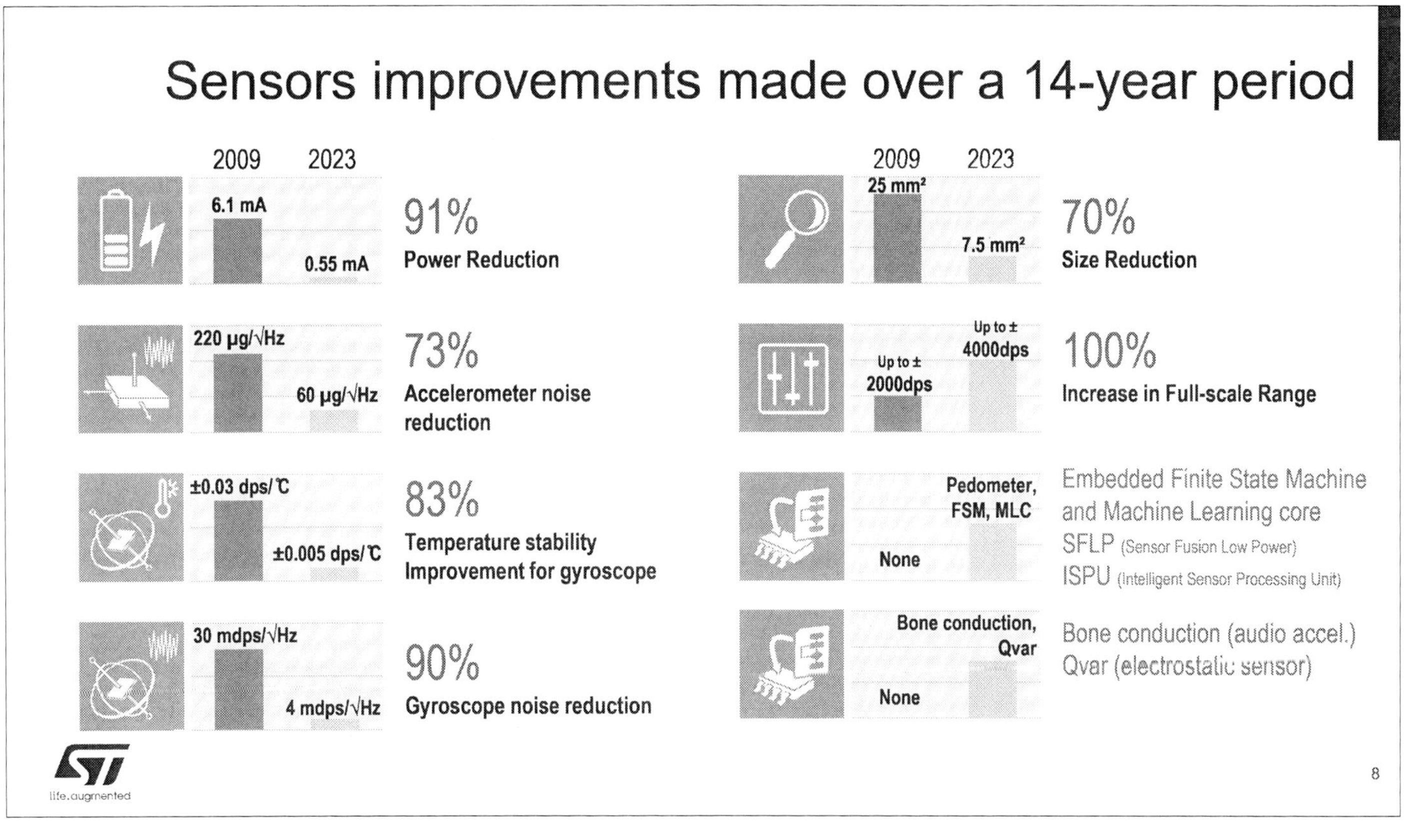
Sensors improvements made over a 14-year period
2009
2023
6.1 mA
0.55 mA
91%
Power Reduction
220 µg/√Hz
60 µg/√Hz
73%
Accelerometer noise reduction
±0.03 dps/℃
±0.005 dps/℃
83%
Temperature stability Improvement for gyroscope
30 mdps/√Hz
4 mdps/√Hz
90%
Gyroscope noise reduction
2009
2023
25 mm²
7.5 mm²
70%
Size Reduction
Up to ± 2000dps
Up to ± 4000dps
100%
Increase in Full-scale Range
None
Pedometer, FSM, MLC
Embedded Finite State Machine
and Machine Learning core
SFLP (Sensor Fusion Low Power)
ISPU (Intelligent Sensor Processing Unit)
None
Bone conduction, Qvar
Bone conduction (audio accel.)
Qvar (electrostatic sensor)
life.augmented
8

Intelligent sensor: present

Intelligent sensors offer a variety of embedded features	Sensors with embedded sensor fusion to generate orientation	Intelligent sensors have Finite State Machine (FSM)	Intelligent sensors have Machine Learning Core (MLC)
Pedometer Significant motion detect, Wake-up, Free fall detection, 6D orientation, ..	They compute the orientation of device in 3D space outputting Euler Angles or Quaternion	They use a computational model represented by the FSM, a set of predefined states and transition rules	They offer a unique combination of high-quality measurements and capabilities to process data using ML algorithms on the sensor

life.augmented

9

Sensors with Finite State Machine

FSM is an in-sensor behavioral model composed of a finite number of states and transitions between states

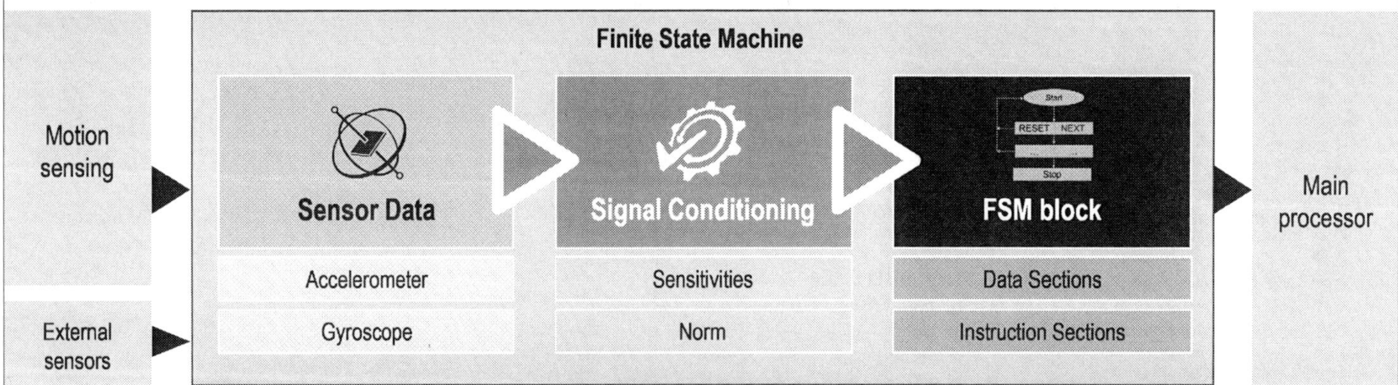

FSM is able to generate interrupt signals activated by user-defined motion patterns

life.augmented

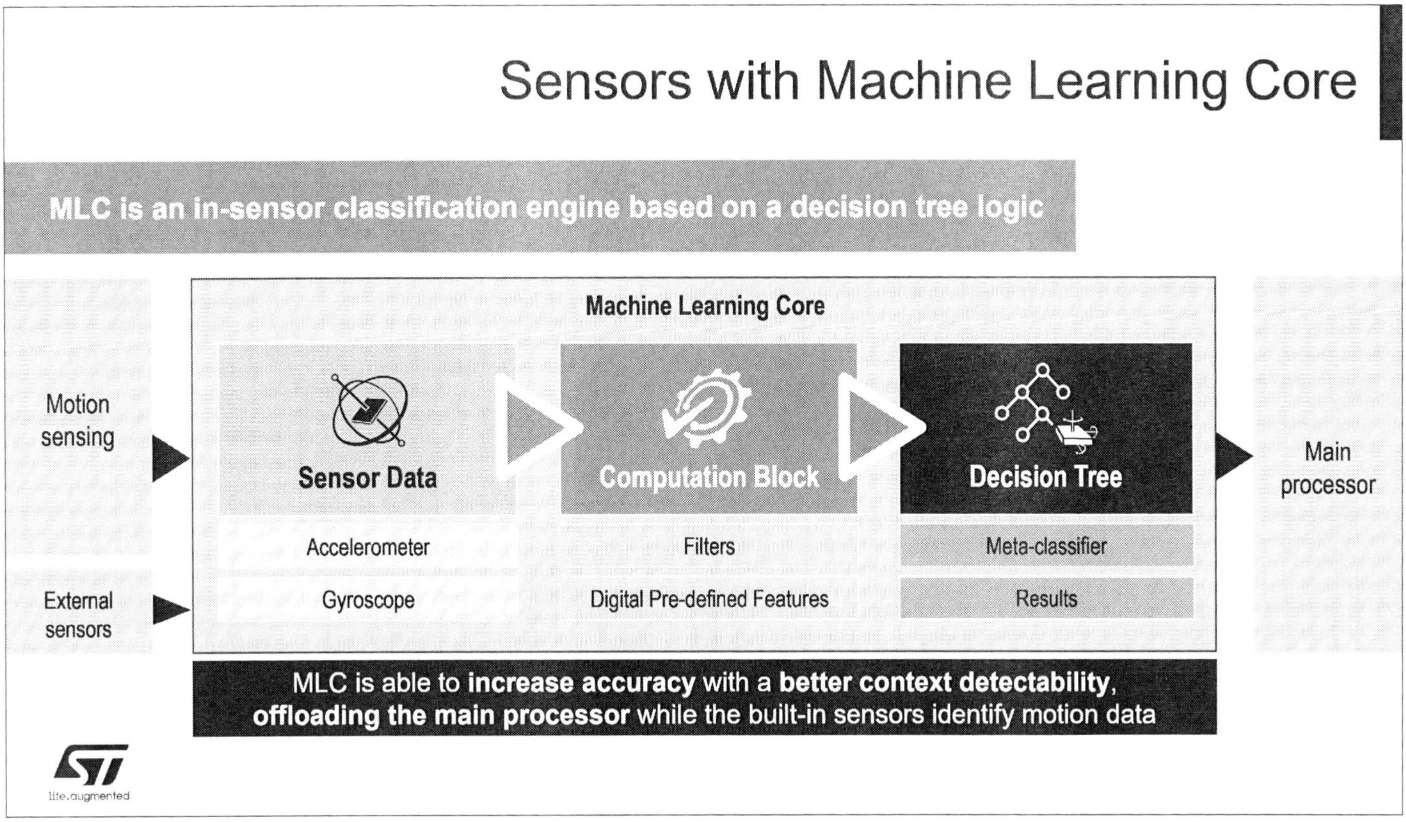
Sensors with Machine Learning Core
MLC is an in-sensor classification engine based on a decision tree logic
Machine Learning Core
Motion sensing
External sensors
Sensor Data
Accelerometer
Gyroscope
Computation Block
Filters
Digital Pre-defined Features
Decision Tree
Meta-classifier
Results
Main processor
MLC is able to increase accuracy with a better context detectability, offloading the main processor while the built-in sensors identify motion data
life.augmented

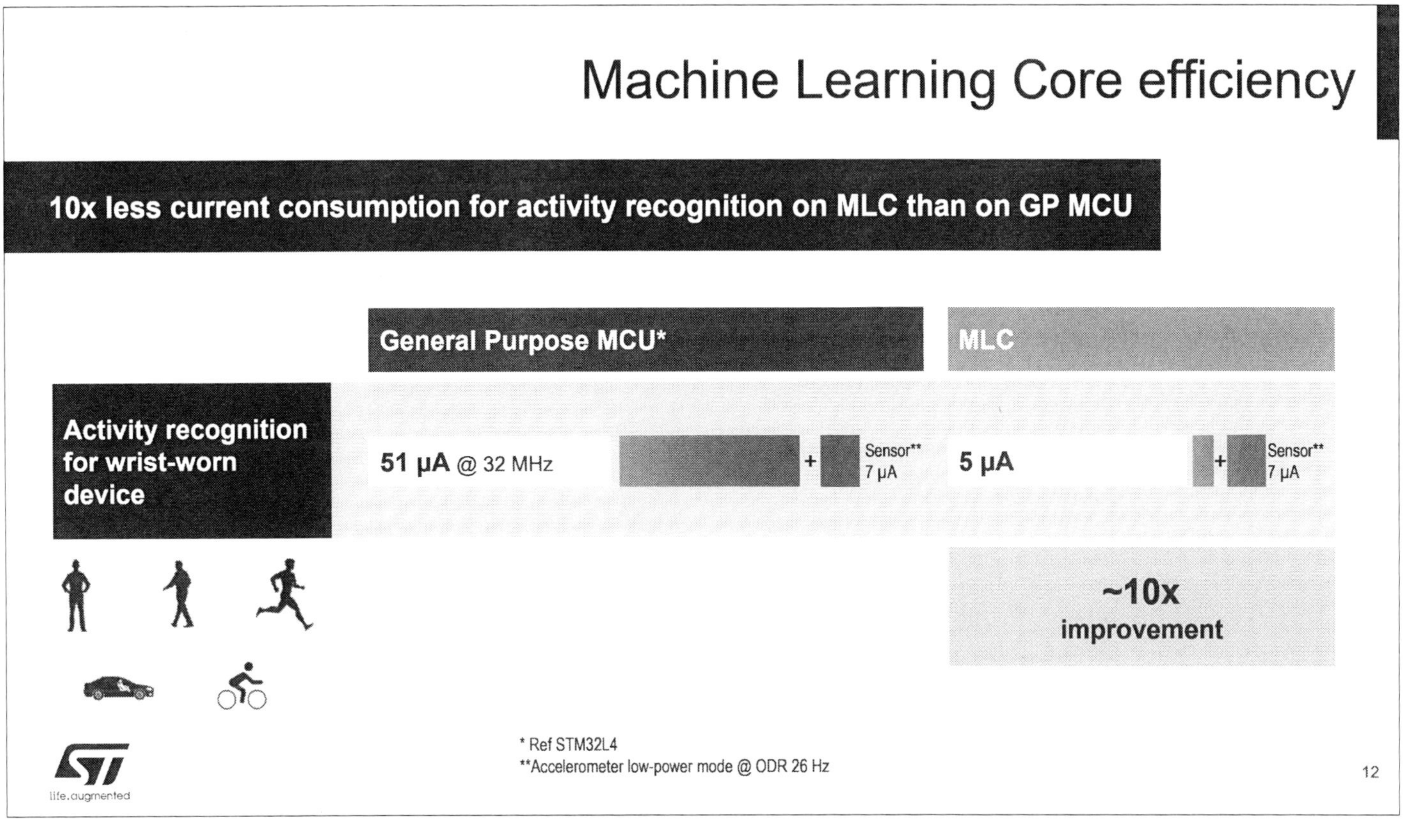
Machine Learning Core efficiency
10x less current consumption for activity recognition on MLC than on GP MCU
General Purpose MCU*
MLC
Activity recognition for wrist-worn device
51 µA @ 32 MHz
+
Sensor** 7 µA
5 µA
+
Sensor** 7 µA
~10x improvement
* Ref STM32L4
**Accelerometer low-power mode @ ODR 26 Hz
life.augmented
12

Future intelligent sensors

Future Intelligent Sensors: More adaptable and autonomous

Intelligent sensors will become more autonomous and adaptable. Sensor would be able to adjust their sensing and operating parameters and behaviors based on changing conditions

- This adaptability will improve their performance in dynamic environments and enable them to meet specific application needs more effectively

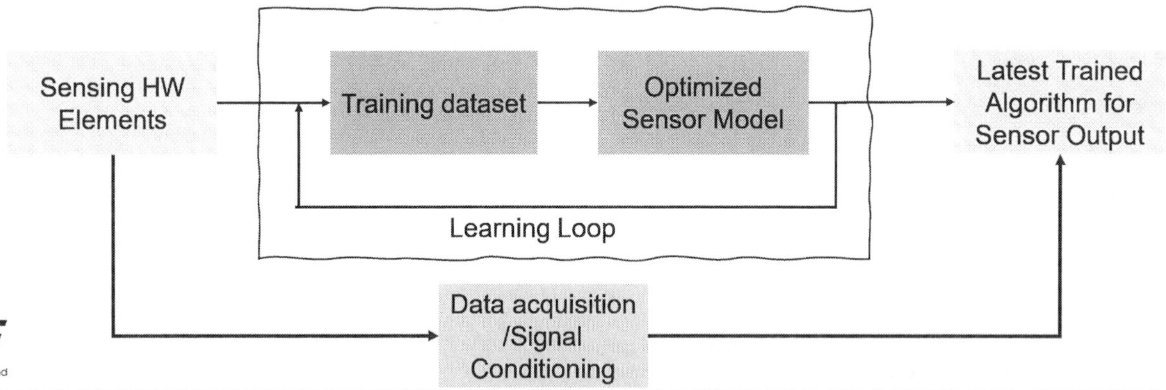

14

Future Intelligent Sensors:
More computational power

- Intelligent sensors will incorporate more computational power and onboard artificial intelligence capabilities
- This trend is driven by the need for faster processing and decision-making at the edge of networks, reducing latency and reliance on cloud-based systems

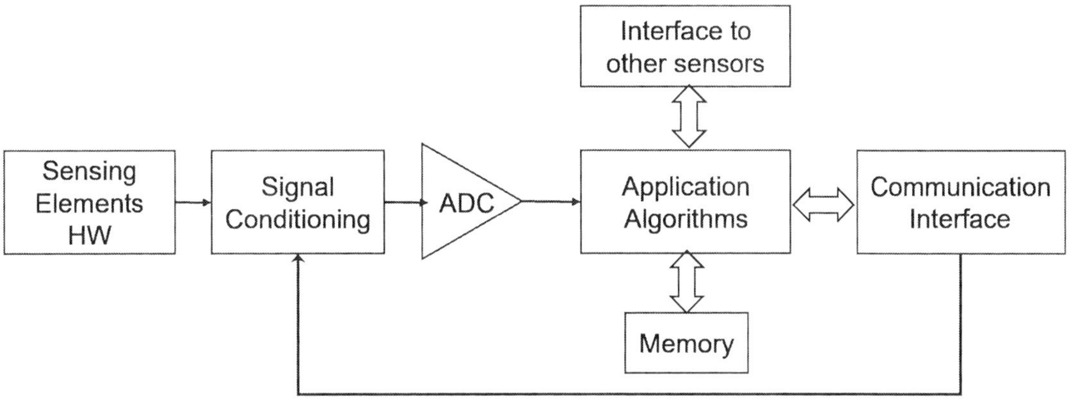

life.augmented

15

Future Intelligent Sensor:
Improved energy efficiency

Longer battery life, reduced power consumption, and potentially the integration of energy harvesting technologies will be utilized to power the sensors

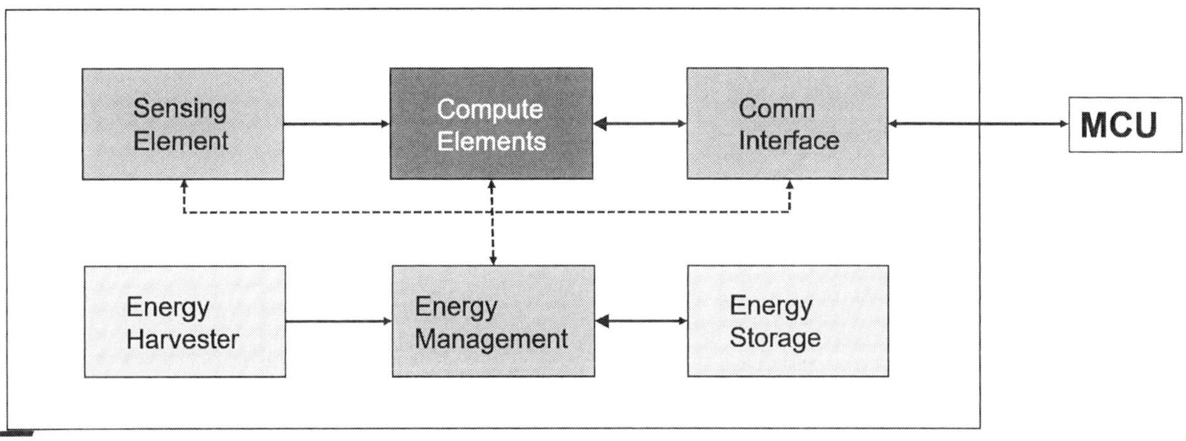

life.augmented

16

Future Intelligent Sensor: Increased contextual awareness

- Future intelligent sensors will have the ability to understand and interpret the context in which they operate
- These sensors will gather data also from external sources to maintain and provide a comprehensive view of environment
  - Environmental factors
  - Spatial awareness
  - Temporal context
  - User context
  - Networked context
  - Task context

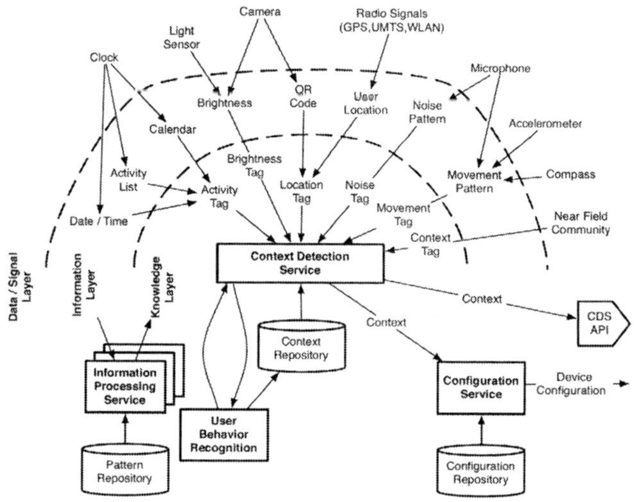

life.augmented

Takeaways

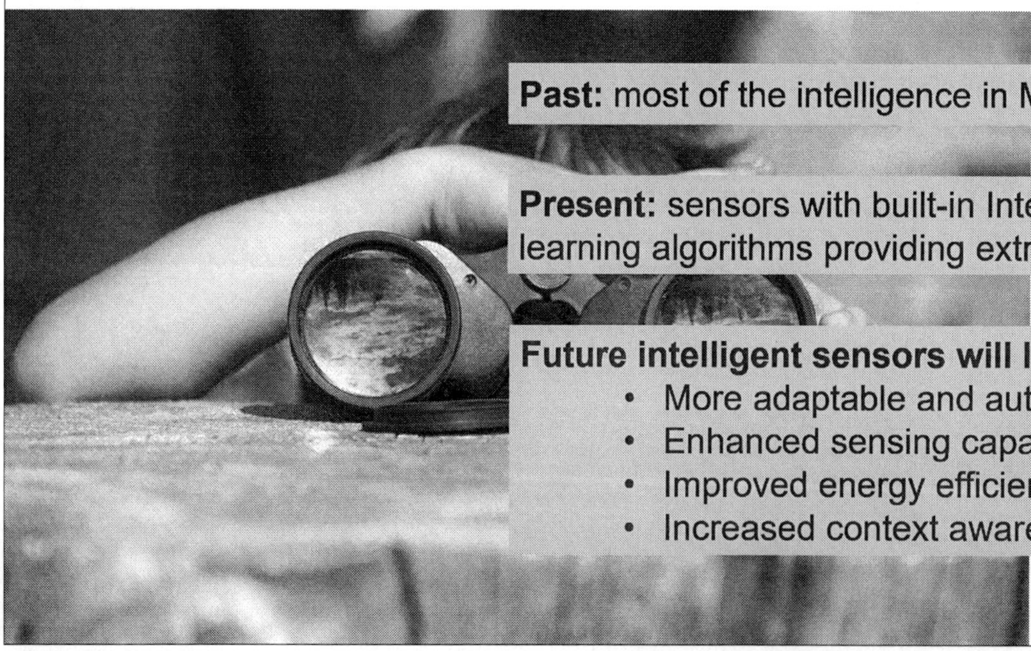

Past: most of the intelligence in MCU or cloud

Present: sensors with built-in Intelligence run machine learning algorithms providing extreme power efficiency

Future intelligent sensors will likely have:
- More adaptable and autonomous capabilities
- Enhanced sensing capabilities through fusion
- Improved energy efficiency
- Increased context awareness

Our technology
starts with You
Find out more at www.st.com/MEMS
© STMicroelectronics - All rights reserved.
ST logo is a trademark or a registered trademark of STMicroelectronics International NV or its affiliates in the EU and/or other countries.
For additional information about ST trademarks, please refer to www.st.com/trademarks.
All other product or service names are the property of their respective owners.
life.augmented

Making Sense of Atmospheric Carbon Dioxide Measurements with Low-Cost Sensors

Tyler Boyle
National Institute of Standards and Technology (NIST)
6/21/2023
tyler.boyle@nist.gov

*References are made to certain commercially available products in this presentation to adequately specify the experimental procedures involved. Such identification does not imply recommendation or endorsement by NIST, nor does it imply that these products are the best for the purpose specified.

NIST NATIONAL INSTITUTE OF STANDARDS AND TECHNOLOGY U.S. DEPARTMENT OF COMMERCE 1 Sensors Converge

NIST's Greenhouse Gas Measurement Program

Purpose: Develop internationally recognized, greenhouse gas emissions measurements and standards for reliable and accurate mapping of urban to regional greenhouse gas emissions that inform timely and effective mitigation actions and science-based policy decisions.

Components:

- Urban GHG Measurements Testbed System, Tools, and Methods
- Stationary or Point Source Emission Metrology (advances in smokestack Continuous Emissions Monitoring (CEMs) technology)
- Measurement Tools, Standards and Reference Data
- Satellite Calibration and Atmospheric Carbonaceous Aerosols Measurements & Standards
- International Documentary Standards Development for Urban GHG Flux Measurements

https://www.nist.gov/spo/greenhouse-gas-measurements-program

Slide courtesy of Israel Lopez-Coto

NIST NATIONAL INSTITUTE OF STANDARDS AND TECHNOLOGY U.S. DEPARTMENT OF COMMERCE 2 Sensors Converge

Measuring Atmospheric CO_2

- Why measure atmospheric CO_2 concentrations?
  - CO_2 is emitted when burning fossil fuels
  - CO_2 and other greenhouse gases (GHGs) build up in the upper atmosphere, contributing to climate change
  - Measuring CO_2 over time allows us to monitor pollution emissions and target efforts to reduce emissions
  - Typical atmospheric CO_2 range: 400-700 ppm
- Techniques for measuring atmospheric CO_2:
  - Satellites (OCO-2, Carbon Mapper)
  - Aircraft-based analyzers (NASA DC-8)
  - Ground or near-ground (*in-situ)* analyzers
- NIST and other research organizations typically measure *in-situ* atmospheric CO_2 with cavity ring-down (CRDS) spectrometers
  - Many deploy CRDS instruments in networks
  - Instruments are highly precise and accurate (can measure CO_2 within 0.1 ppm)
  - Instruments are expensive (~ $100K, typically mounted to cell towers, requiring additional support infrastructure)

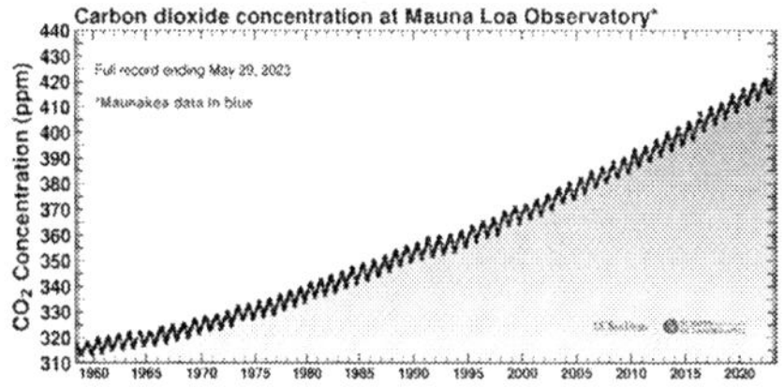

Keeling Curve, showing increase in atmospheric CO_2. CO_2 can vary by ~6 ppm between summer and winter. Figure courtesy of scripps.ucsd.edu

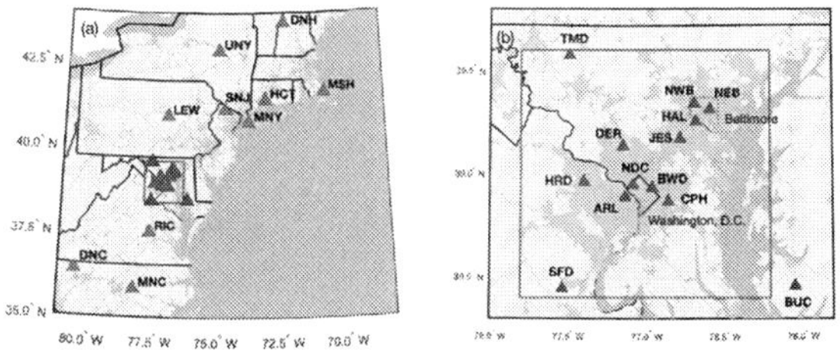

a) Northeast Corridor (NEC) Urban Test Bed
b) Zoomed-in Baltimore/Washington portion of NEC Urban Test Bed

Picarro 2401 CRDS analyzer, courtesy of picarro.com

Cost-Effective CO_2 Measurement Techniques

- Large number of commercially-available low-cost GHG sensors have become available in recent years
  - Small size (often credit card size or smaller)
  - Low cost ($10 - $500)
- Most sensors designed for consumer market use
  - Typically designed for indoor air quality CO_2 ranges: 400 – 3000 ppm (K96) or 400 – 10000 ppm (SCD30)
  - Some claim sensitivity ~ 0.1 ppm (K96), or accuracies at $\pm 30\ ppm \pm 3\%$ (K30)
- Challenges when using for research applications:
  - Measurements are less accurate/precise than CRDS measurements
  - Sensors are susceptible to long-term (temporal) drift
  - Many sensors require custom solutions/approaches for calibrating
- Despite challenges, research shows that low-cost sensor measurements can be beneficial when coupled with CRDS urban measurement networks (Lopez-Coto et al. 2017)
- NIST's Low-Cost Sensors Project Goals:
  - Characterize low-cost sensor uncertainties over ideal conditions
  - Develop and deploy a network supporting ~50 low-cost GHG sensor stations in Baltimore/Washington region to augment measurements from high-accuracy analyzers

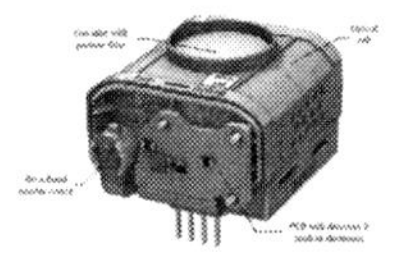

Senseair Prototype K96 (courtesy of Wastine et. al, 2022)

Sensirion SCD30 (courtesy of sensirion.com)

Senseair K30 (courtesy of senseair.com)

2nd generation low-cost sensor station deployed on campus at NIST

Characterizing Sensor Performance

- Methods for validating sensor measurements
  - Co-location with calibrated reference instrumentation
  - Calibration with known reference gases
- Low-cost sensor validation experiment
  - Deployed a low-cost sensor payload with 3 sensors outside of a building at NIST **(Verify System Design)**
  - Deployed sensor payload alongside a Picarro 2301 CRDS analyzer **(Characterize Sensor Performance)**
  - Automatically calibrated sensors with 400 and 600 ppm reference gases every 12 hours **(Simulate In-Field Calibration)**

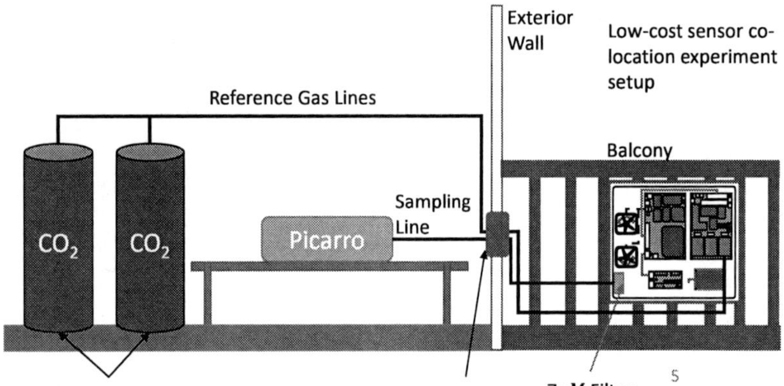

Prototype K96 with custom calibration cap

Sensors Converge

Sensor Validation: Correcting Initial Measurements

- Previous research suggests low-cost sensors are susceptible to temperature/pressure/humidity impacts (C. Martin et al., 2017, Shusterman et al., 2016, Arzoumanian et al, 2019)
- After variety of testing, established a preliminary correction process:
  - Select a fit window with varying P/T/RH/CO_2 conditions (see supplementary slides for details)
  - "Profile" each sensor by calculating coefficients for 2 multiple linear regressions (MLRs) to correct P/T/RH dependencies
  - Use a two-point calibration to correct temporal drift
- Low-cost sensor target measurement accuracy/precision:
  - Mean diff. ~ 0 ppm
  - S. dev ≤ 2 ppm
- Will explore performance through a 2-month deployment outside at NIST

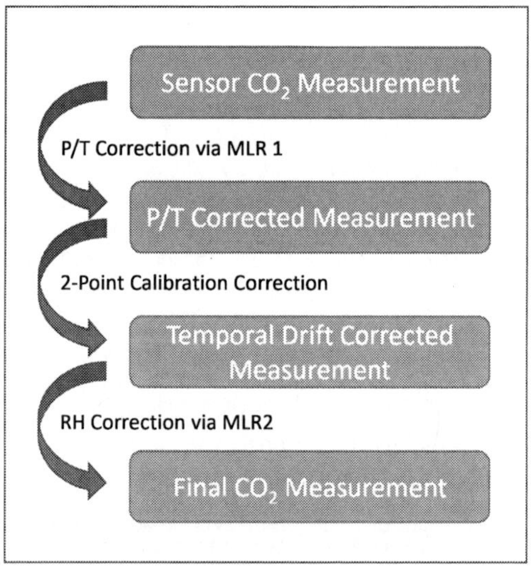

CO_2 Correction Process

NIST NATIONAL INSTITUTE OF STANDARDS AND TECHNOLOGY U.S. DEPARTMENT OF COMMERCE

Sensors Converge

Initial Sensor-Derived CO_2 Measurements

- Large offsets between CRDS and low-cost sensor measurements
- Large offsets between low-cost sensors
- Low-cost sensor sensitivities are within manufacturer specifications, but further corrections needed for our research application

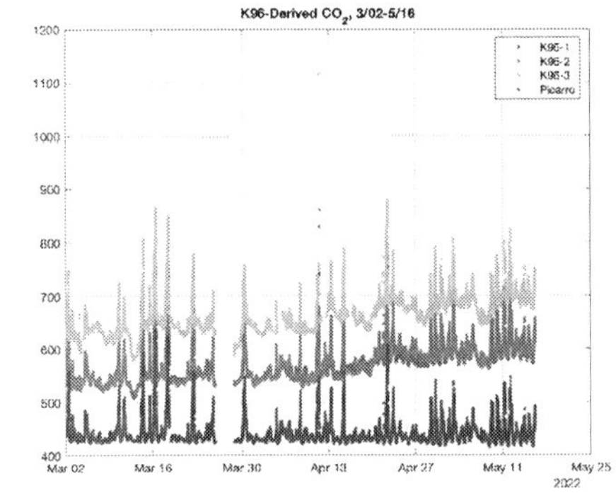

Timeseries of sensor-derived CO_2 measurements

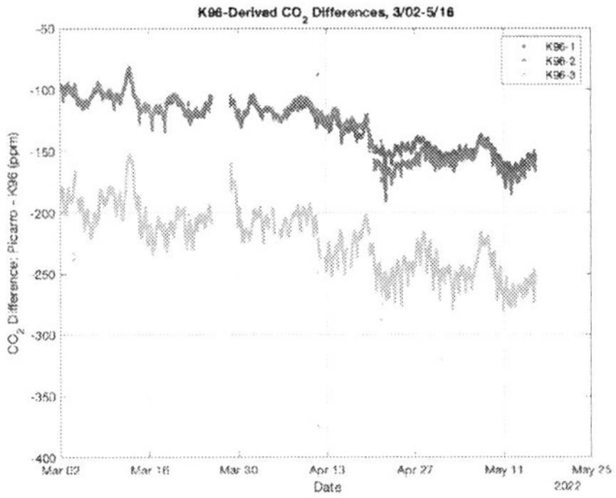

Difference between CRDS sensor-derived CO_2 measurements.

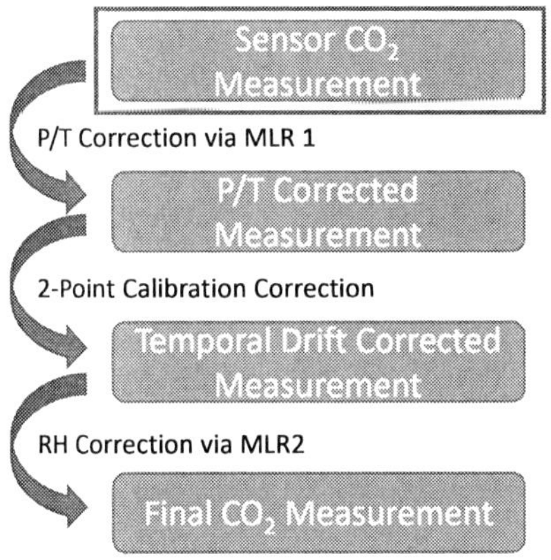

Sensor	Mean (ppm)	S.dev (ppm)
K96-1	-128.84	19.7
K96-2	-129.97	23.82
K96-3	-222.11	25.89

Sensor-derived concentration statistics

Note: mean and standard deviation calculated for entire timeseries window

NIST National Institute of Standards and Technology, U.S. Department of Commerce

7

Sensors Converge

Final Corrected CO_2 Measurements

- Applying correction process reduced standard deviation below 2 ppm!
- Mean difference ~ 0 for sensors 1 and 3

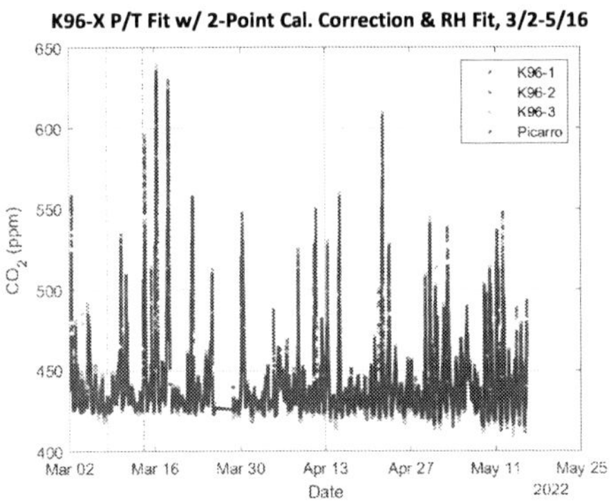

Timeseries of P/T/RH/drift corrected CO_2 measurements

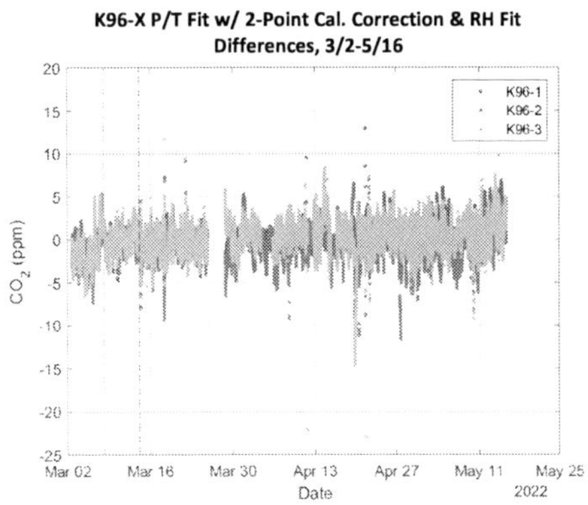

Difference between CRDS and P/T/RH/drift corrected CO_2 measurements.

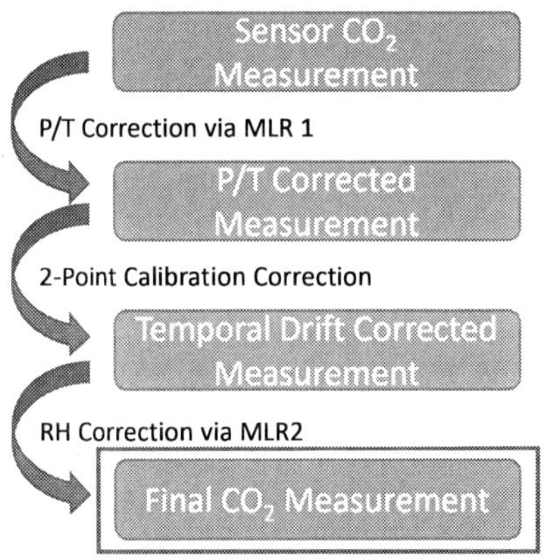

Sensor	Mean (ppm)	S.dev (ppm)
K96-1	0.19	1.79
K96-2	-0.5	1.81
K96-3	0.08	1.92

P/T/RH/drift corrected concentration statistics

Note: mean and standard deviation calculated for entire timeseries window

NIST National Institute of Standards and Technology, U.S. Department of Commerce

8

Sensors Converge

Experiment Takeaways and Next Steps

- Experiment Takeaways:
  - Sensors performed within manufacturer specifications!
  - Further measurement corrections needed if used for research applications
  - Applying measurement corrections reduced mean and s. dev. within target goals!
  - Current technique for profiling sensors not feasible for large scale deployment
- Next Steps:
  - Revise system to support more sensors **(Completed)**
  - Utilize environmental chamber with T/RH control to simulate wide range of environmental conditions **(Completed)**
  - Redeploy system outside at NIST with CRDS and reference gases to test env. chamber MLR coefficients **(In Progress)**

Profiling station placed inside environmental chamber

Detailed view of profiling station inside the environmental chamber

NIST NATIONAL INSTITUTE OF STANDARDS AND TECHNOLOGY U.S. DEPARTMENT OF COMMERCE

9

Sensors Converge

Final Conclusion and Closing Thoughts

- Consumer-grade low-cost sensors can be useful for scientific research applications if used properly
- Considerations when selecting low-cost sensors for scientific research applications:
  - How important is accuracy? Do sensors need to be calibrated before/during use?
  - Is the target measurement range within sensor specifications?
  - Will all sensors perform similarly?
- Making consumer-grade low-cost sensors feasible for research applications:
  - Providing the ability for users to calibrate their sensors
  - Documenting internal sensor measurement processes - are measurements being corrected internally? Is there access to raw measurements?

*References are made to certain commercially available products in this presentation to adequately specify the experimental procedures involved. Such identification does not imply recommendation or endorsement by NIST, nor does it imply that these products are the best for the purpose specified.

NIST NATIONAL INSTITUTE OF STANDARDS AND TECHNOLOGY U.S. DEPARTMENT OF COMMERCE

10

Sensors Converge

Extra Slides

11

References

- Lopez-Coto I. Ghosh S. Prasad K. & Whetstone J. (2017). Tower-based greenhouse gas measurement network design—the national institute of standards and technology north east corridor testbed. *Advances in Atmospheric Sciences* 1095–1105. https://doi.org/10.1007/s00376-017-6094-6
- Benoit W. Christine H. Maksym B. Henrik R. Hans M. & Stephan S. (2022). Compact non-dispersive infrared multi-gas sensing platform for large scale deployment with sub-ppm resolution 1789–1789. https://doi.org/10.3390/atmos13111789
- C R. N Z. A K. R R. X R. B N. & K J. (2017). Evaluation and environmental correction of ambient co2 measurements from a low-cost ndir sensor. *Atmospheric Measurement Techniques* 2383–2395. https://doi.org/10.5194/amt-10-2383-2017
- A A. V E. A J. C N. J K. & R C. (2016). The berkeley atmospheric co2 observation network: initial evaluation. *Atmospheric Chemistry and Physics* 13449–13463. https://doi.org/10.5194/acp-16-13449-2016
- E A. F R. A B. B G. O L. M R. & P C. (2019). Characterization of a commercial lower-cost medium-precision non-dispersive infrared sensor for atmospheric co2 monitoring in urban areas. *Atmospheric Measurement Techniques* 2665–2677. https://doi.org/10.5194/amt-12-2665-2019

NIST NATIONAL INSTITUTE OF STANDARDS AND TECHNOLOGY U.S. DEPARTMENT OF COMMERCE

12

Sensors Converge

Collaborators

NIST:
Kevin Cossel, David Long, David Allen, Julia Marrs, Aaron Johnson, Rodney Bryant, David F. Plusquellic, Antonio Possolo, and many more...

Other institutions:
Paul B. Shepson, Colm Sweeney, Eric Kort, Xinrong Ren, Brian McDonald, Russell R. Dickerson, Charles Miller, Riley Duren, Kenneth Davis, Kevin R Gurney, Phillip Decola, Jocelyn Turnbull, Ray Weiss, Ralph Keeling, Alan Brewer, Ariel Stein, Christopher Loughner, Lucy Hutyra, and many more...

NIST
National Institute of Standards and Technology
U.S. Department of Commerce

Stony Brook University · University of Maryland · Purdue University · PennState · University of Michigan · NAU Northern Arizona University

NOAA · NASA · JPL Jet Propulsion Laboratory, California Institute of Technology · Scripps Institution of Oceanography, UC San Diego · GNS Science

2

Slide courtesy of Israel Lopez-Coto

Low-Cost CO_2 Station Design

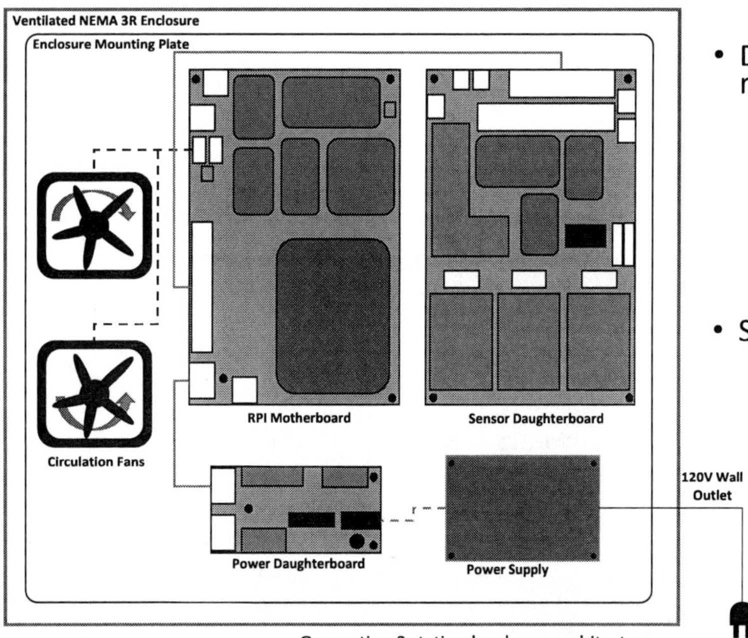

Generation 3 station hardware architecture

- Design considerations, sampling packages must be:
  - Standardized
  - Compatible with off-the-shelf sensors and microcontrollers
  - Modular
  - Low power
  - Compatible with reference standards for in-field calibration
- System must allow for redundant sensors

K96 with custom calibration cap

NIST National Institute of Standards and Technology, U.S. Department of Commerce

14

Sensors Converge

Sensor Package: Supporting Network Infrastructure

- Custom-designed network supporting:
  - Secure real-time data collection from stations to centralized servers
  - Remote accessibility to stations
  - Ability to consolidate measurements from different instruments (Picarro, etc.)
  - Support for real-time calibrations with reference standards
  - An interactive dashboard for data visualization
- Infrastructure designed to be scalable/modular, allowing:
  - Easy addition of new sensor measurements to the database
  - Simple deployment of new stations to the network
- System uses open-source software and protocols in accordance with industry standards

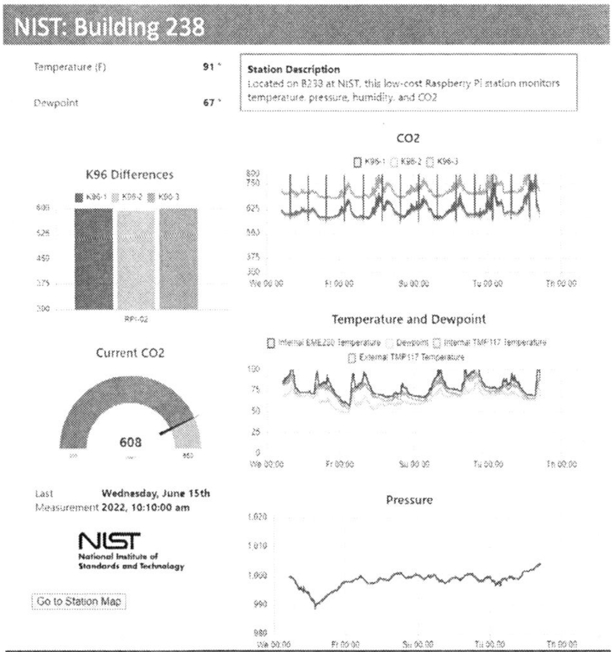

Screenshot of online station dashboard

Sensor Package: Network Architecture

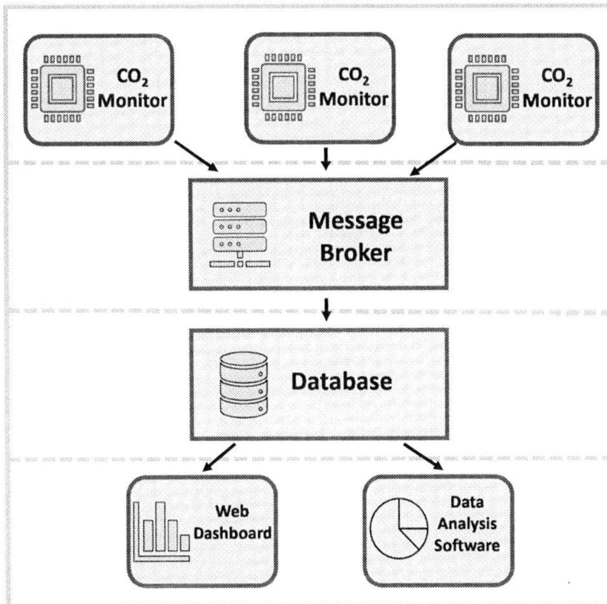

Device Layer	Queries sensors and processes real-time measurements using custom modular shell and python scripts
Messaging Layer	Sends measurements through Mosquitto, an open-source messaging platform that implements the MQTT protocol (mosquitto.org)
Data Storage Layer	Stores measurements using MongoDB, an open-source No-SQL database
Data Presentation Layer	Presents measurements to end-user through platforms like Node-Red or Grafana

Note: images courtesy of PowerPoint

Sensor Package: Device Layer Architecture

Sensor Reading Component `k96.py, readTMP117.py, etc.`	Queries sensors every 3 seconds	K96 Diagram, courtesy of Wastine et. al, 2022
Data Logging Component `sensor_to_redis.sh`	Logs messages to Redis open-source, in-memory database (redis.io)	Redis logo, courtesy of redis.io
Data Processing Component `redis_to_json.py`	Queries Redis, calculates 1-minute averages, outputs a properly-formatted JSON message	Abbreviated JSON packet
Message Output Component `json_to_mqtt.sh`	Uses Mosquitto and MQTT to send a JSON message to the messaging layer	Mosquitto logo, courtesy of mosquitto.org

{"start_epoch": 1676221133, "co2": 450 … }

mosquitto

NIST NATIONAL INSTITUTE OF STANDARDS AND TECHNOLOGY U.S. DEPARTMENT OF COMMERCE

Sensors Converge

Initial Sensor-Derived CO_2 Measurements

- Large offsets between CRDS and sensor measurements
- Large offset between sensor 3 and sensors 1 and 2
- Precision measurements are within manufacturer specifications, but further corrections needed for research applications

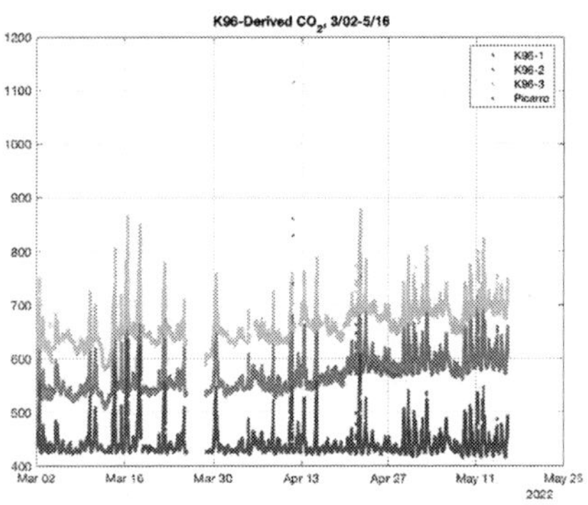

Timeseries of sensor-derived CO_2 measurements

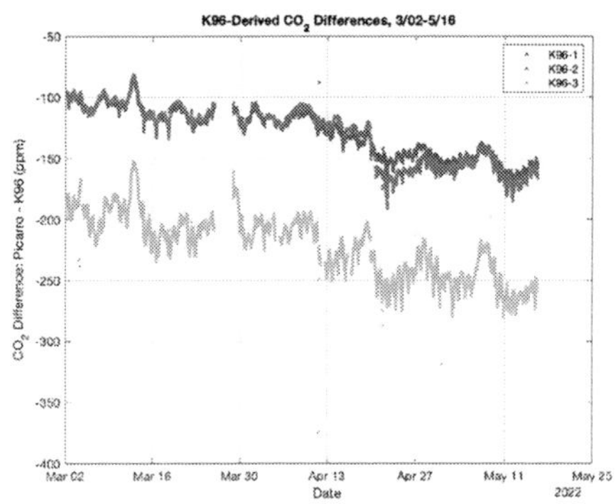

Difference between CRDS and sensor-derived CO_2 measurements.

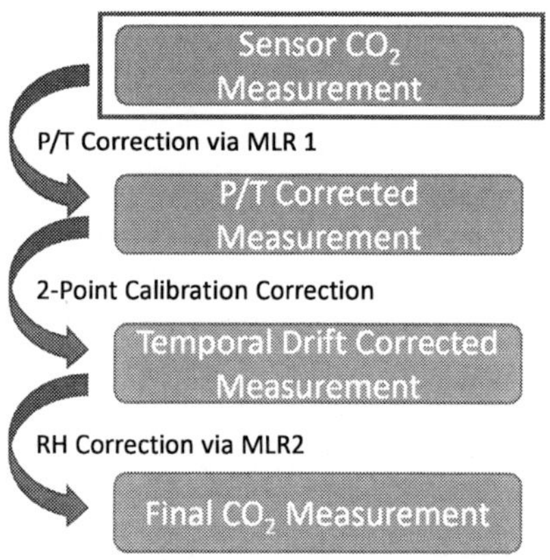

Sensor	Mean (ppm)	S. dev (ppm)
K96-1	-128.84	19.7
K96-2	-129.97	23.82
K96-3	-222.11	25.89

Sensor-derived concentration statistics

Note: mean and standard deviation calculated for entire timeseries window

NIST NATIONAL INSTITUTE OF STANDARDS AND TECHNOLOGY U.S. DEPARTMENT OF COMMERCE

Sensors Converge

Correcting P/T Impacts

- MLR groups low-cost sensor concentrations together, but further corrections needed to remove temporal drift

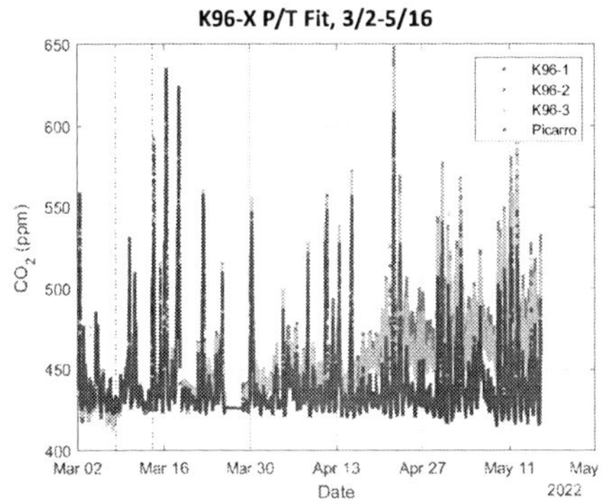

Timeseries of P/T corrected CO_2 measurements from 3/2-5/16

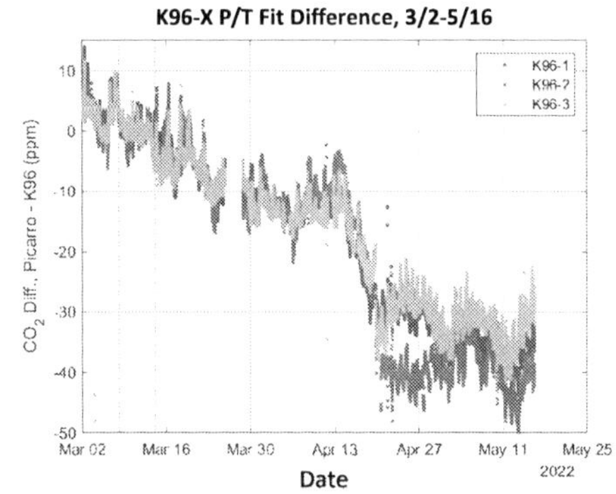

Difference between CRDS and low-cost sensor CO_2 measurements. Temporal drift present throughout timeseries

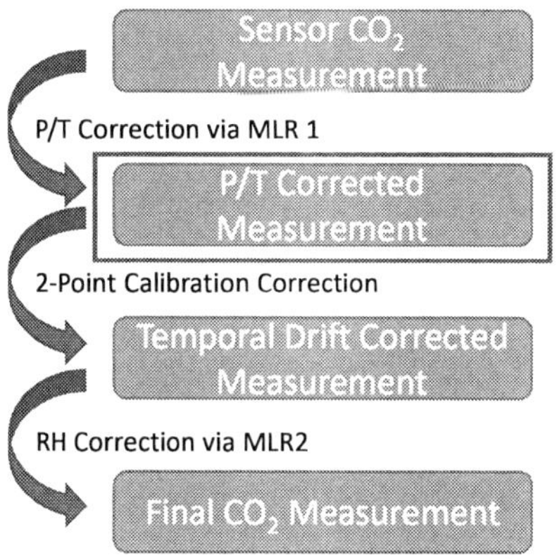

Note: mean and standard deviation calculated for entire timeseries window

Sensor	Mean (ppm)	S. dev (ppm)
K96-1	-17.1	14.26
K96-2	-18.88	16.94
K96-3	-16.92	13.11

Table 3: P/T corrected concentration statistics

NIST NATIONAL INSTITUTE OF STANDARDS AND TECHNOLOGY U.S. DEPARTMENT OF COMMERCE

19

Sensors Converge

Applying a 2-Point Calibration

- 2-Point calibration removes temporal drift, but standard deviations are larger than desired

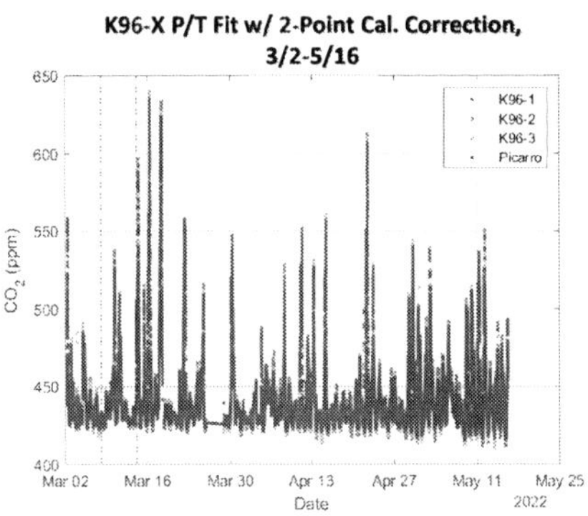

Timeseries of P/T/drift corrected CO_2 measurements from 3/2-5/16

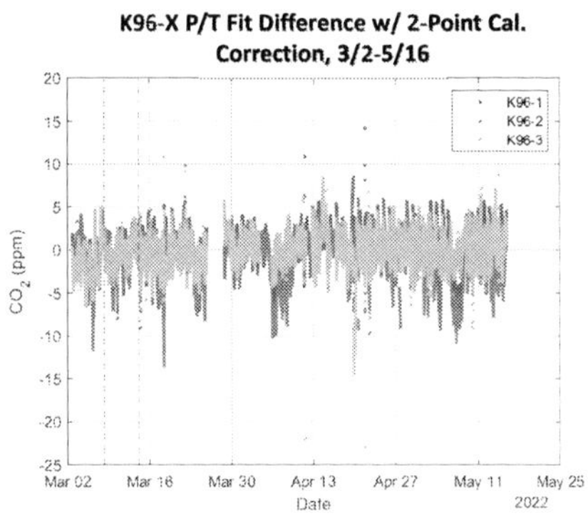

Difference between CRDS and P/T/drift corrected low-cost sensor CO_2 measurements.

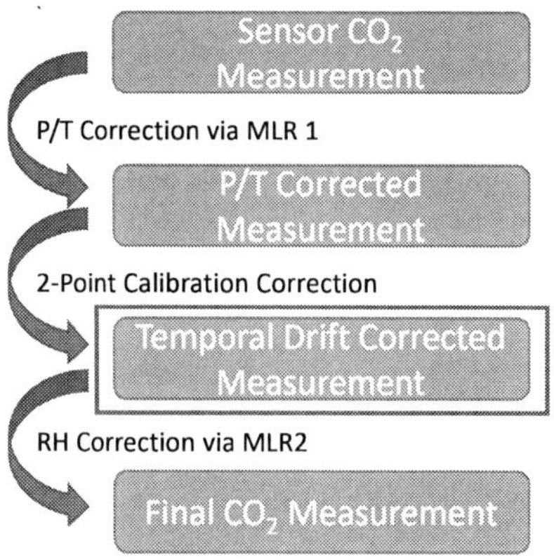

Note: mean and standard deviation calculated for entire timeseries window

Sensor	Mean (ppm)	S. dev (ppm)
K96-1	-0.15	2.54
K96-2	-0.57	2.88
K96-3	-0.33	1.92

2-Point calibrated P/T corrected concentration statistics

NIST NATIONAL INSTITUTE OF STANDARDS AND TECHNOLOGY U.S. DEPARTMENT OF COMMERCE

20

Sensors Converge

Final Corrected CO_2 Measurements

- Applying correction process reduced standard deviation below 2 ppm!
- Mean difference ~ 0 for sensors 1 and 3

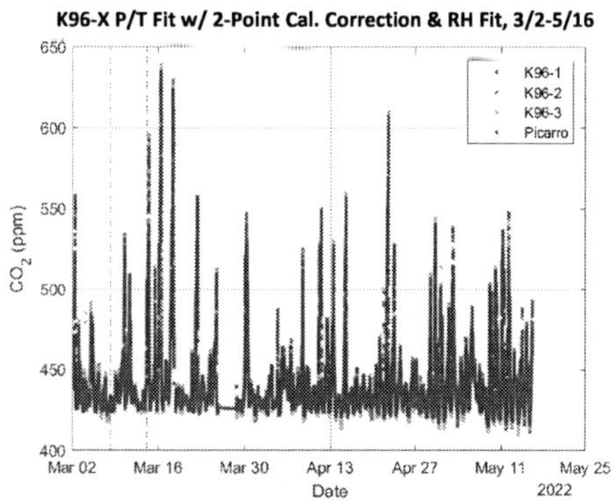

Timeseries of RH corrected CO_2 measurements

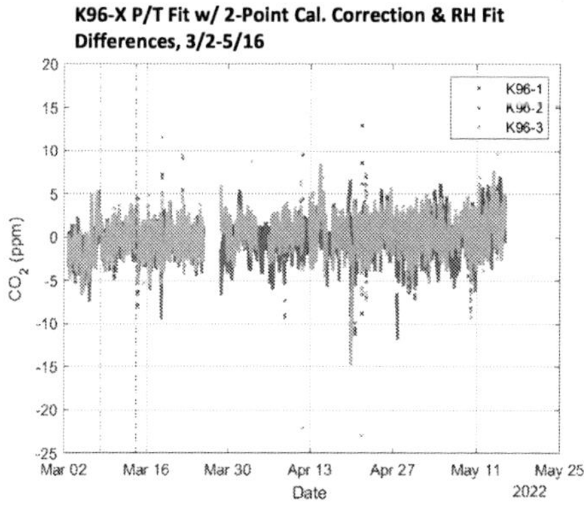

Difference between CRDS and RH corrected low-cost sensor CO_2 measurements.

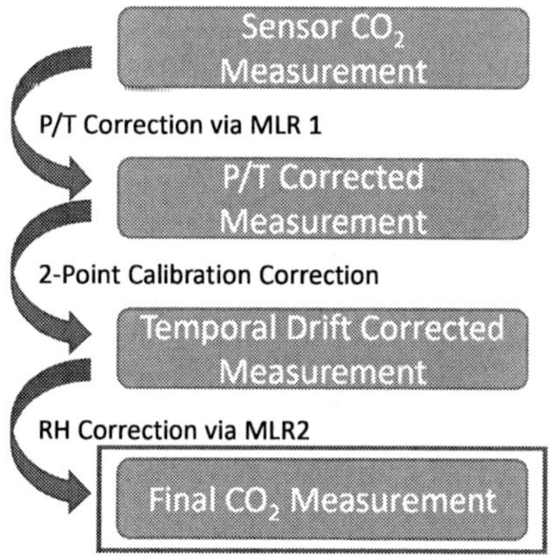

Sensor	Mean (ppm)	S. dev (ppm)
K96-1	0.19	1.79
K96-2	-0.5	1.81
K96-3	0.08	1.92

P/T/RH/drift corrected concentration statistics

Note: mean and standard deviation calculated for entire timeseries window

NIST NATIONAL INSTITUTE OF STANDARDS AND TECHNOLOGY U.S. DEPARTMENT OF COMMERCE

21

Sensors Converge

Fitting Window

- CO_2, P, T, and RH conditions varied throughout the experiment
- For MLRs, a training window with varying conditions was selected (3/8/22 - 3/14/22)

Parameter	Min	Max
Temp (C)	0.69	25.28
Pres (hPa)	983.1	1012
RH (%)	18.88	52.29
CO_2 (ppm)	424.3	531.3

Training window statistics

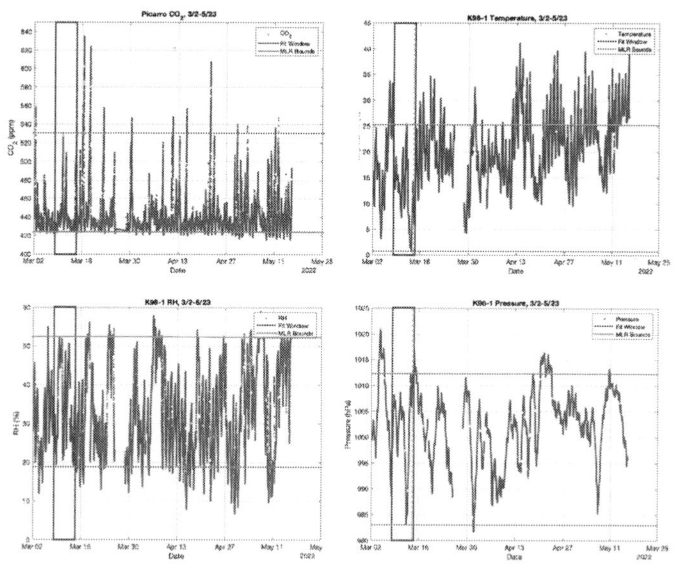

CO_2/T/RH/P timeseries throughout experiment

NIST NATIONAL INSTITUTE OF STANDARDS AND TECHNOLOGY U.S. DEPARTMENT OF COMMERCE

22

Sensors Converge

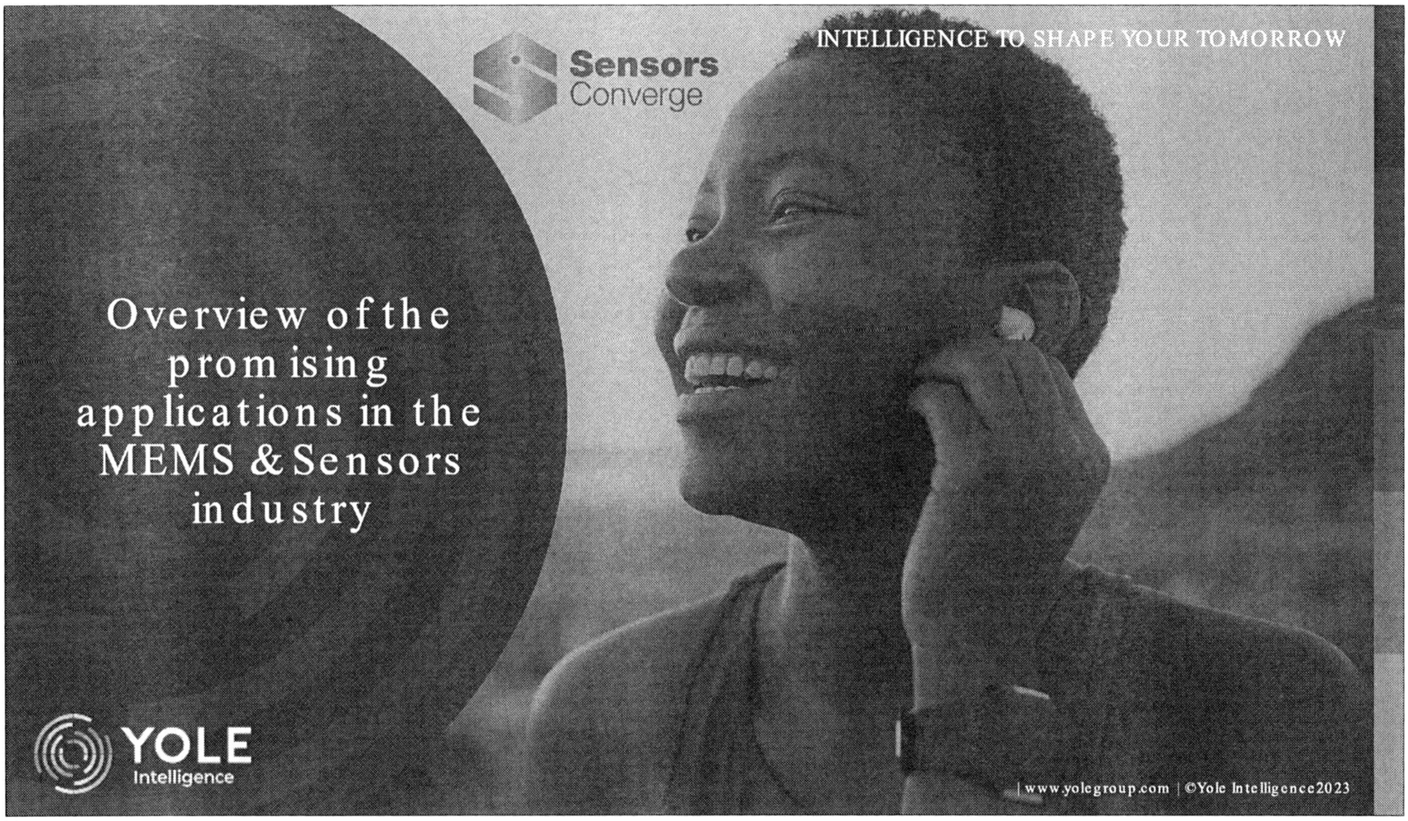

AGENDA

- Yole Group presentation
- Context, market overview and examples of promising applications for:
  - Wearables
  - Automotive
- MEMS & Sensors market shares
- Takeaway

YOLE GROUP PRESENTATION

YOLE Intelligence

YOLE GROUP'S MAJOR ACTIVITIES PER ENTITY

Market, technology, and strategy consulting

M&A and evaluation of companies

Direct acces to the analysts

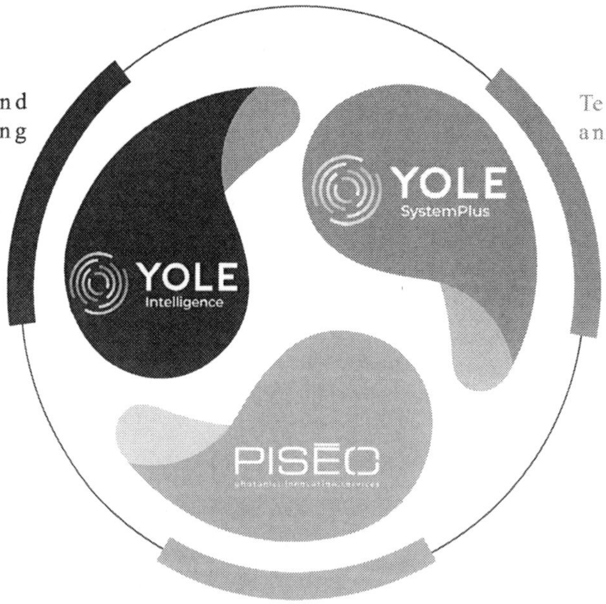

Technology, process & cost analysis

Teardown and reverse engineering

Comparative analysis

Characterization of electro-optical performances and risks

Specification, design and industrialization of systems

YOLE Intelligence

FIELDS OF EXPERTISE COVERING THE SEMICONDUCTOR INDUSTRY

- Photonics & Lighting
- Imaging
- Sensing & Actuating
- Display

- Semiconductor Packaging
- Semiconductor Manufacturing
- Memory
- Computing and Software

YOLE Group

- Radio Frequency
- Compound Semiconductors
- Power Electronics
- Batteries

- Electronic Systems
- Emerging Technologies

WEARABLES

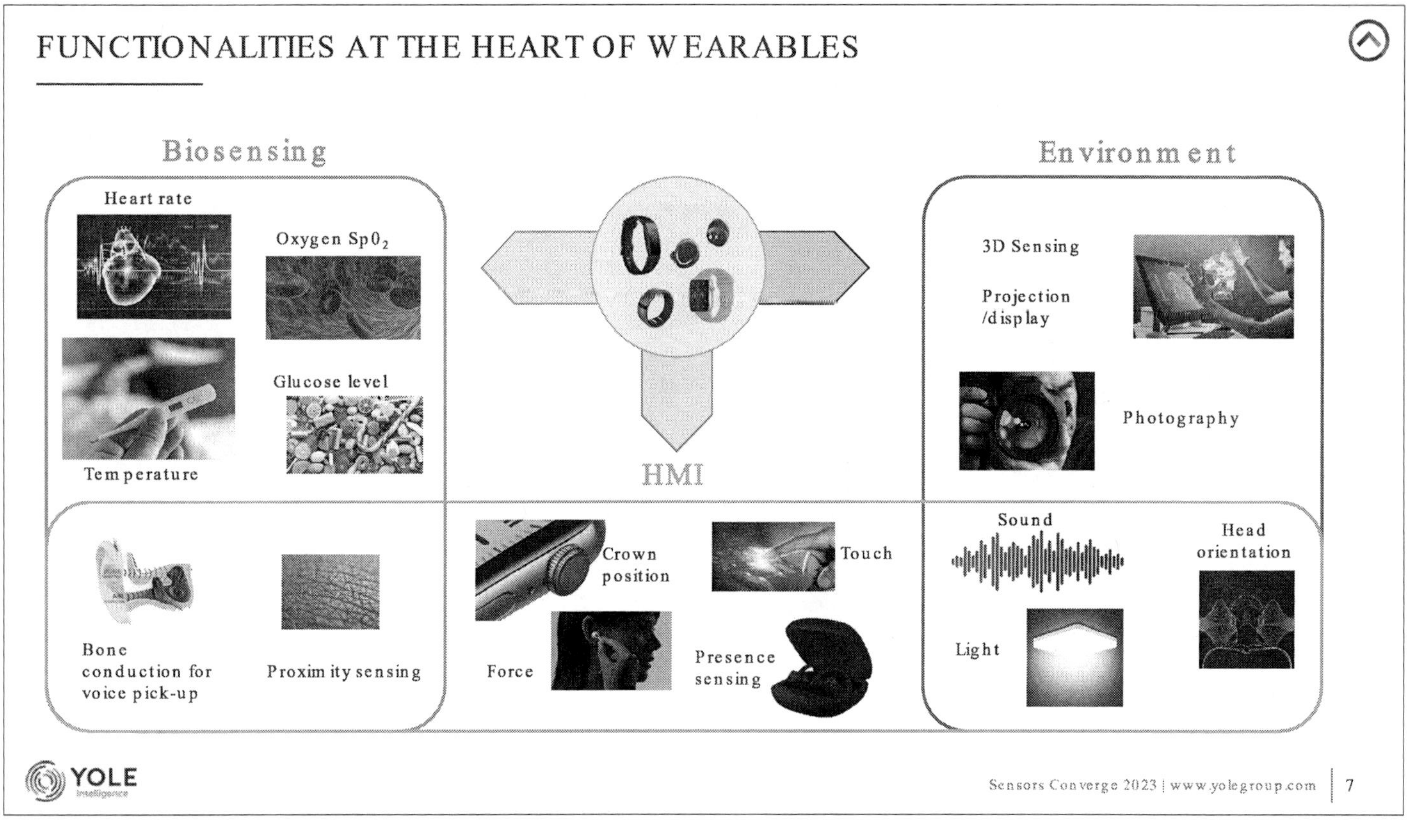
FUNCTIONALITIES AT THE HEART OF WEARABLES
Biosensing
Heart rate
Oxygen Sp0$_2$
Glucose level
Temperature
Environment
3D Sensing
Projection /display
Photography
HMI
Bone conduction for voice pick-up
Proximity sensing
Crown position
Touch
Force
Presence sensing
Sound
Head orientation
Light
YOLE Intelligence
Sensors Converge 2023 | www.yolegroup.com
7

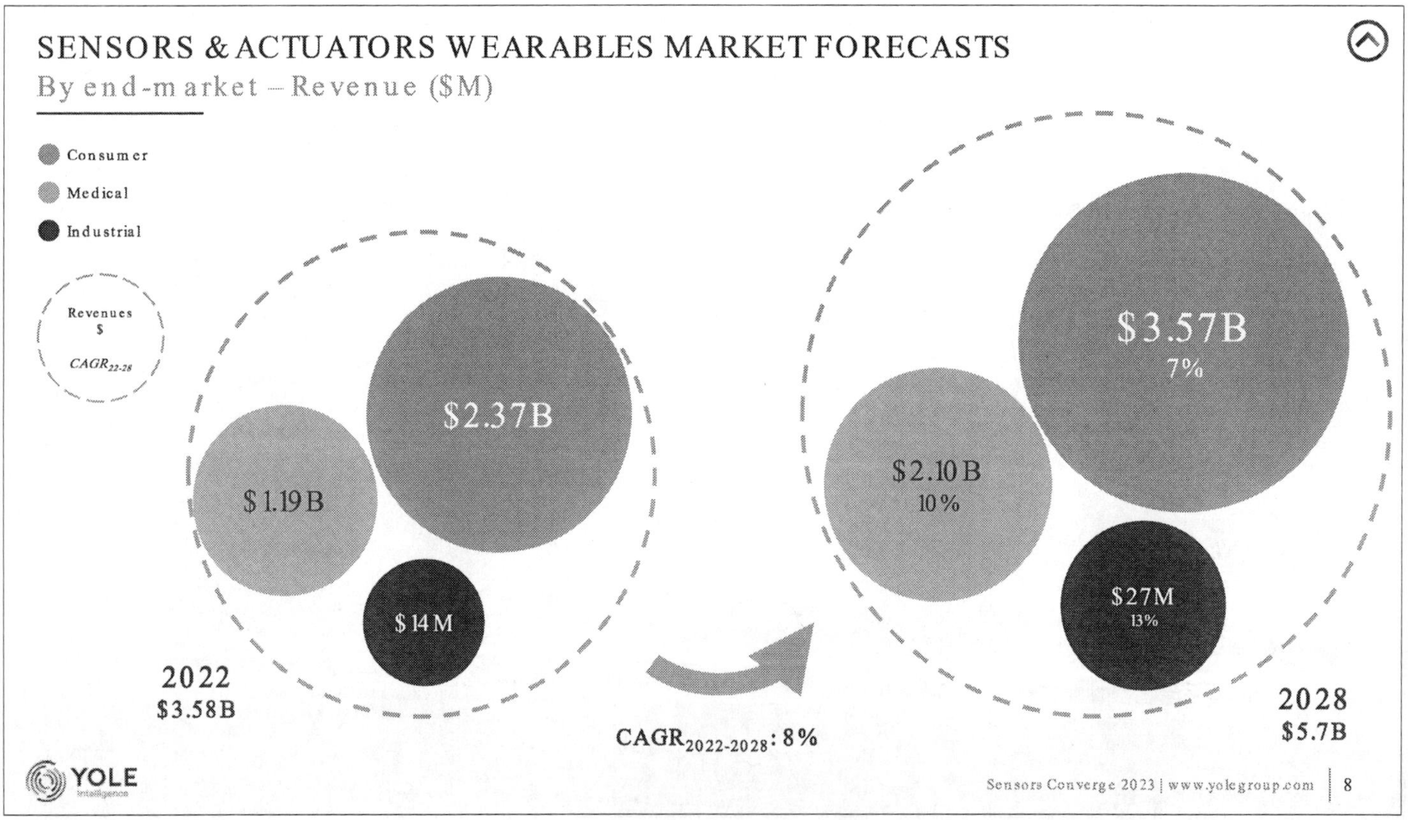
SENSORS & ACTUATORS WEARABLES MARKET FORECASTS
By end-market – Revenue ($M)
Consumer
Medical
Industrial
Revenues $
CAGR$_{22-28}$
$2.37B
$1.19B
$14M
2022
$3.58B
$3.57B
7%
$2.10B
10%
$27M
13%
2028
$5.7B
CAGR$_{2022-2028}$: 8%
YOLE Intelligence
Sensors Converge 2023 | www.yolegroup.com
8

SENSORS & ACTUATORS FOR WEARABLES MARKET SHARES

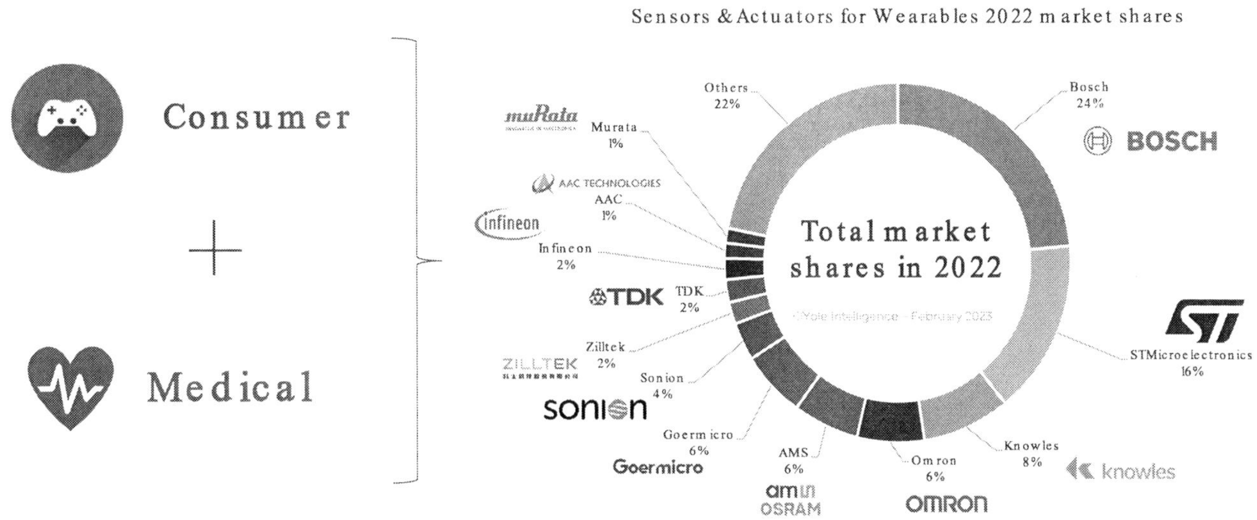

EXAMPLE OF SMART WEARABLE

Apple Watch and the evolution of the sensing requirements

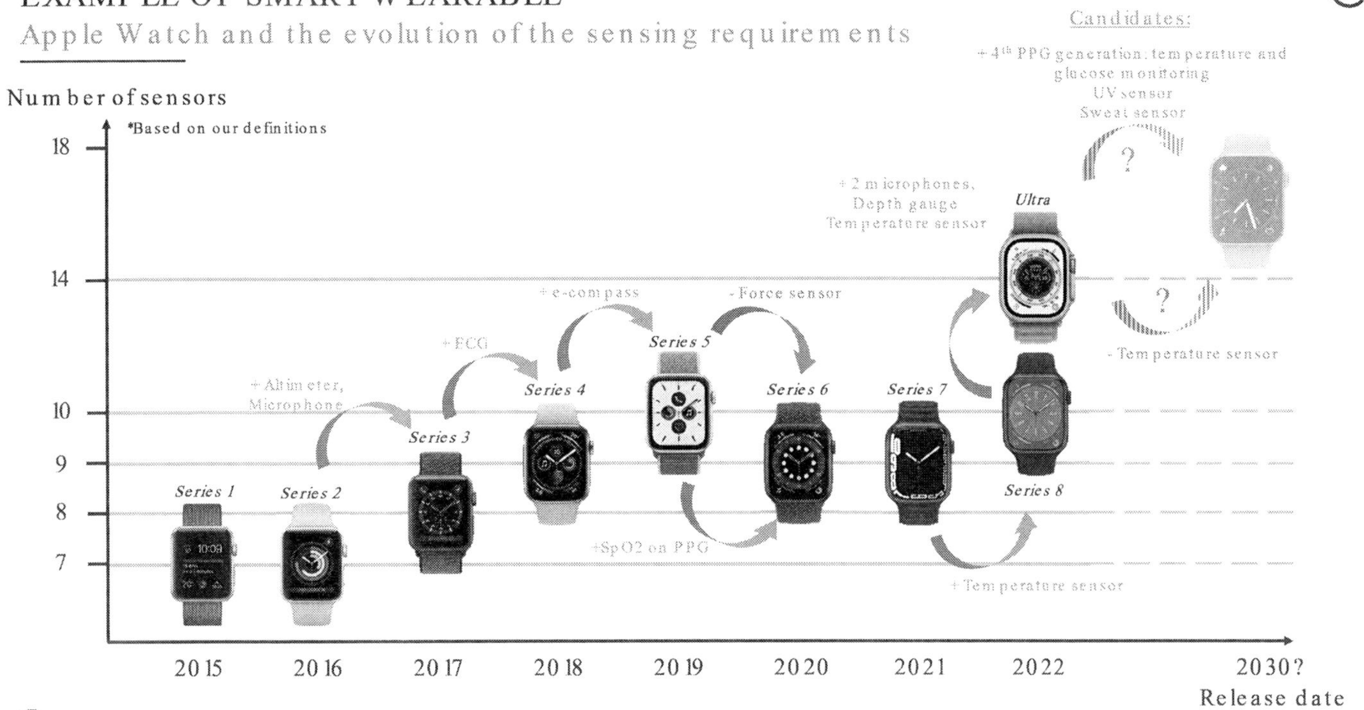

EXAMPLE OF SMART WEARABLE

Hearing aids and the advent of OTC

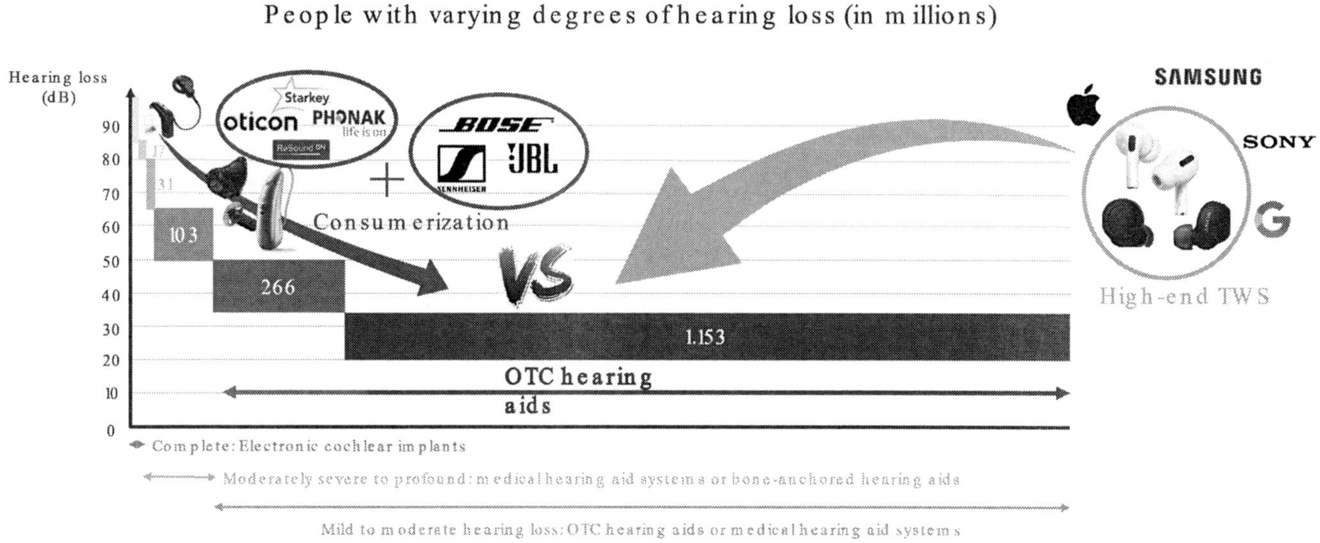

CONSUMER AND MEDICAL END-MARKETS ARE COMING CLOSER AND CLOSER

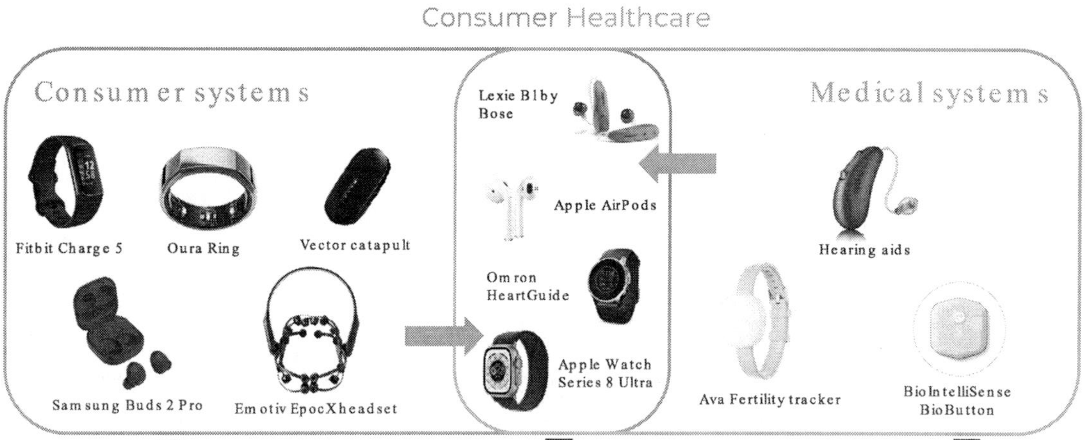

Fitness and well-being applications
No approval
From 10k to a million units
Retail stores

Consumer healthcare (OTC)
Approval, or function approved by a health organization
From thousands to millions of units
Over the counter

Medical device
Approval from health organization
From thousands to 100k units
Prescription mandatory

AUTOMOTIVE
YOLE
Intelligence
Sensors Converge 2023 | www.yolegroup.com
13

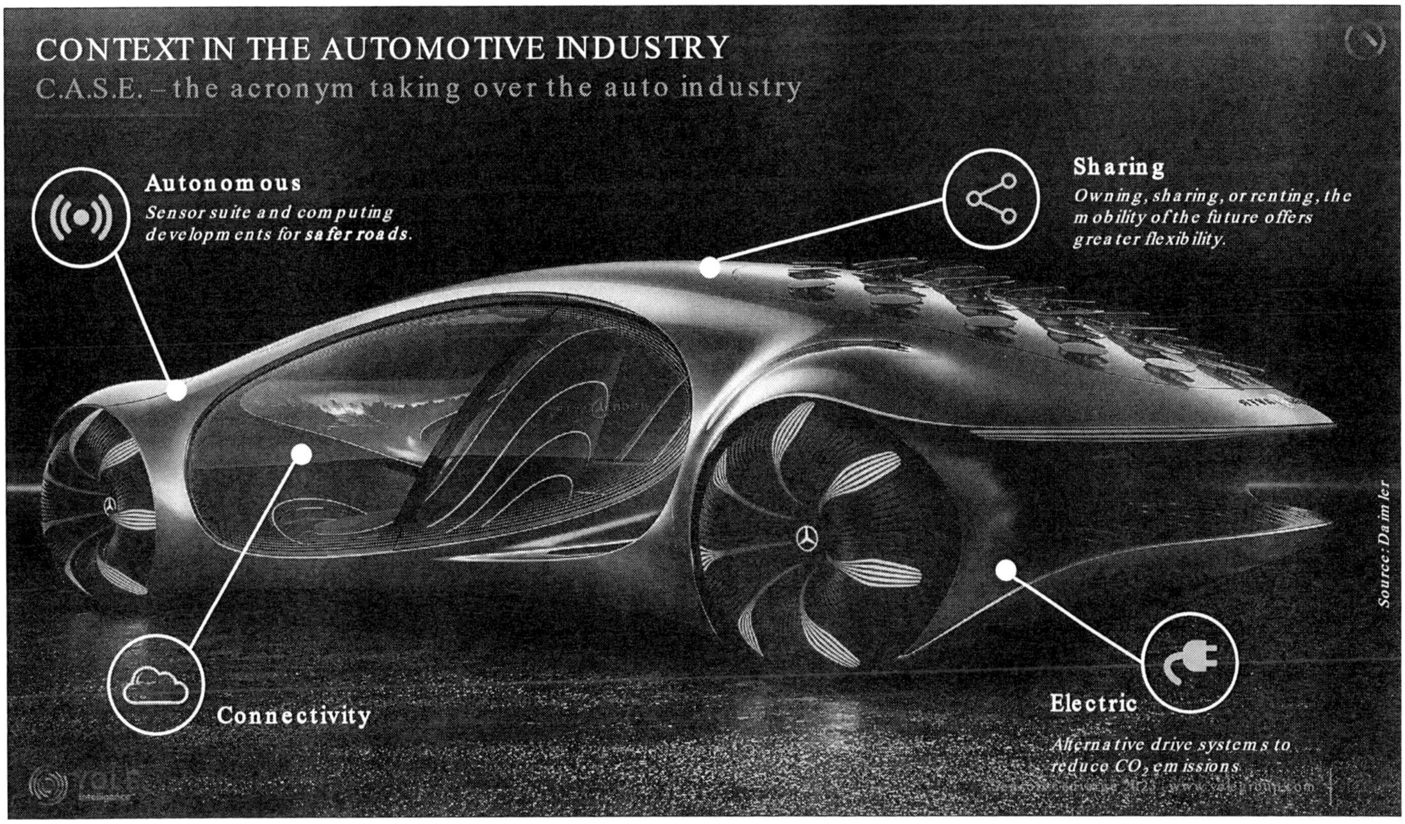
CONTEXT IN THE AUTOMOTIVE INDUSTRY
C.A.S.E. – the acronym taking over the auto industry
Autonomous
Sensor suite and computing developments for safer roads.
Sharing
Owning, sharing, or renting, the mobility of the future offers greater flexibility.
Connectivity
Electric
Alternative drive systems to reduce CO_2 emissions
Source: Daimler

2022-28 SENSOR MARKET* FOR AUTOMOTIVE APPLICATIONS BY DOMAIN

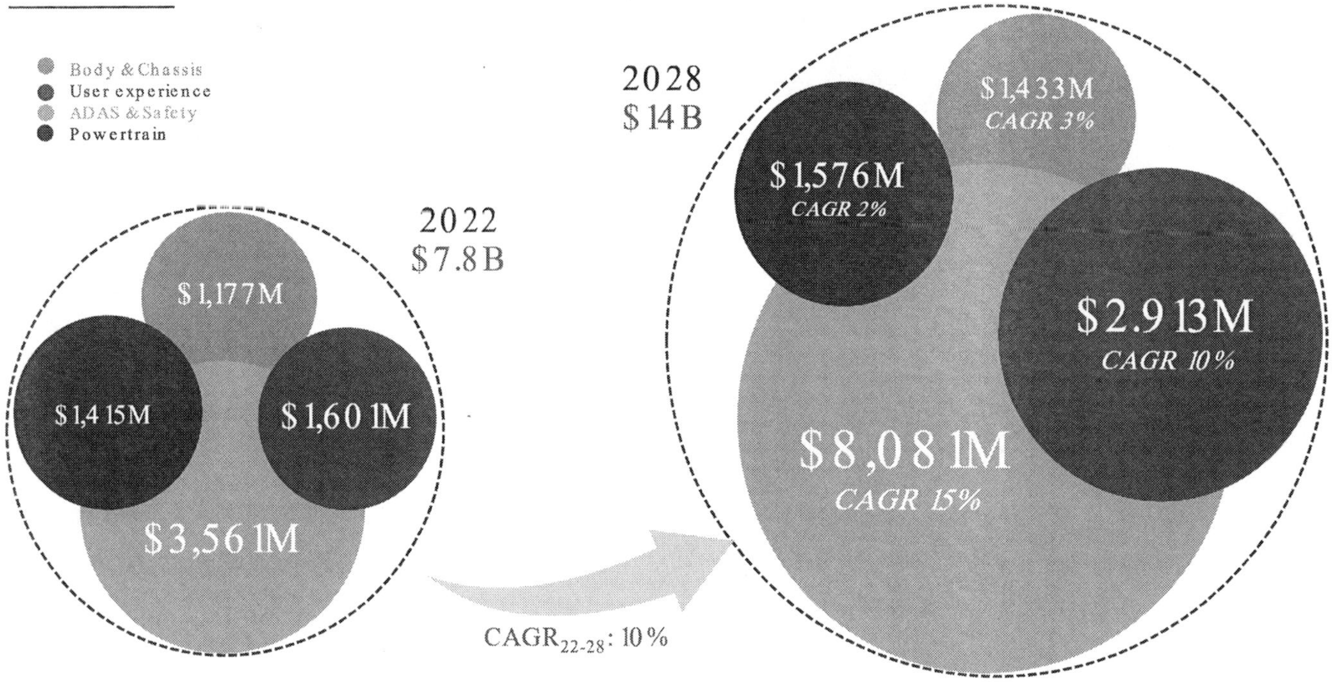

SENSORS FOR AUTOMOTIVE SUPPLY CHAIN

Global semiconductor sensor market shares

Bosch is the player having the highest market share, with 16% of the market that represent $1.2B in revenue.

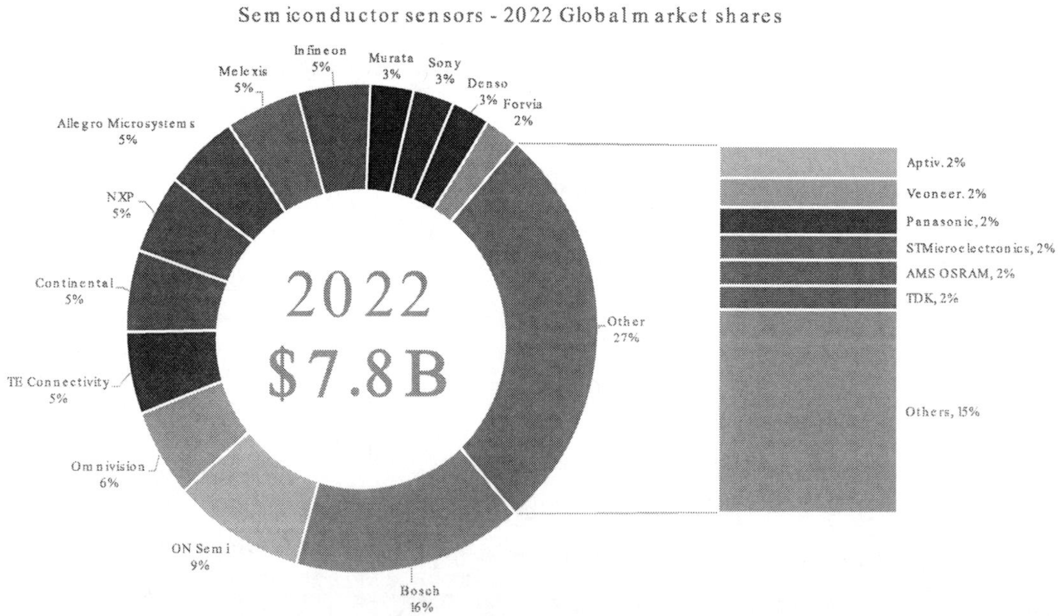

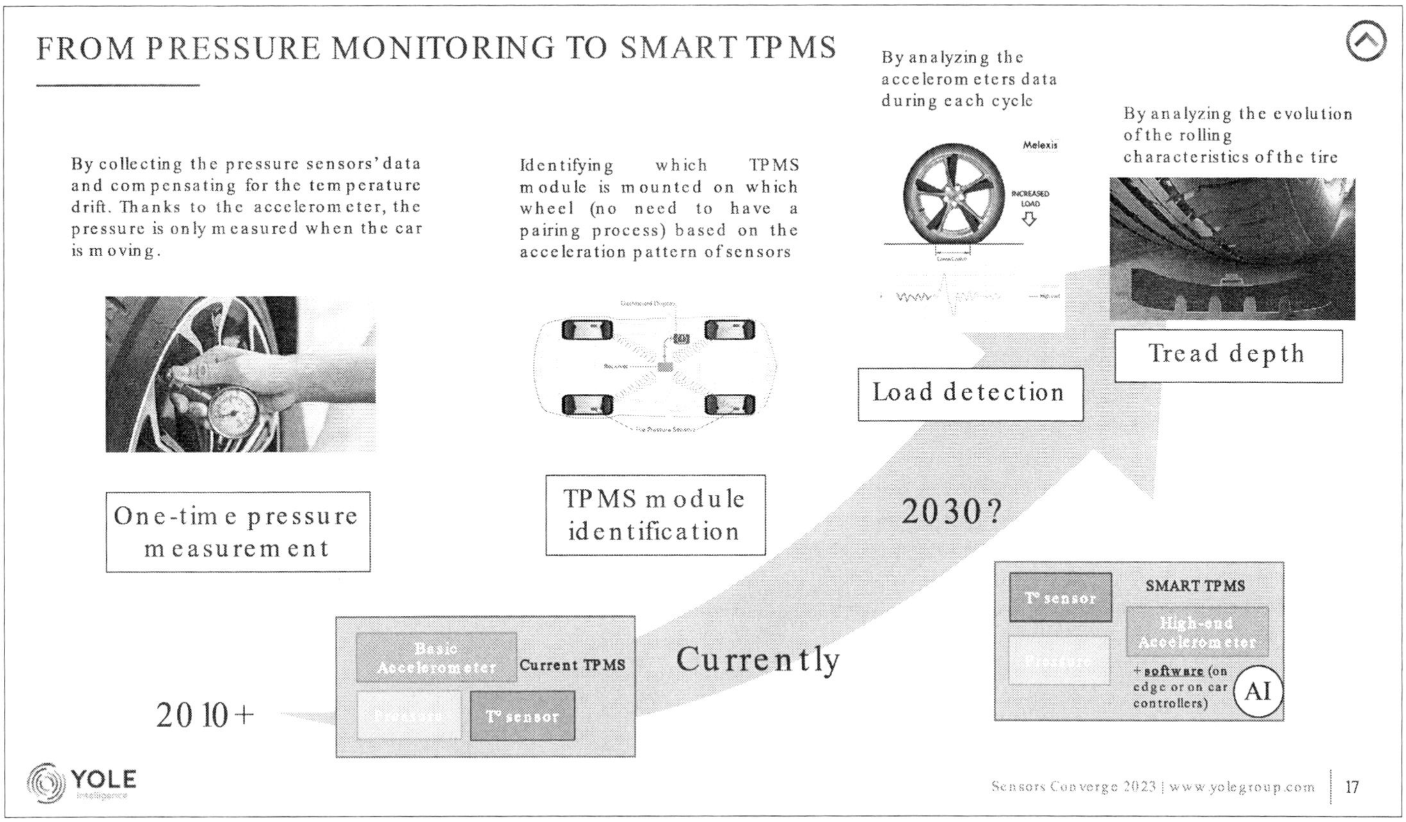
FROM PRESSURE MONITORING TO SMART TPMS
By collecting the pressure sensors' data and compensating for the temperature drift. Thanks to the accelerometer, the pressure is only measured when the car is moving.
Identifying which TPMS module is mounted on which wheel (no need to have a pairing process) based on the acceleration pattern of sensors
By analyzing the accelerometers data during each cycle
By analyzing the evolution of the rolling characteristics of the tire
Melexis
INCREASED LOAD
One-time pressure measurement
TPMS module identification
Load detection
Tread depth
2030?
2010+
Basic Accelerometer
Current TPMS
Pressure
T° sensor
Currently
SMART TPMS
T° sensor
High-end Accelerometer
Pressure
+ software (on edge or on car controllers)
AI
YOLE Intelligence
Sensors Converge 2023 | www.yolegroup.com
17

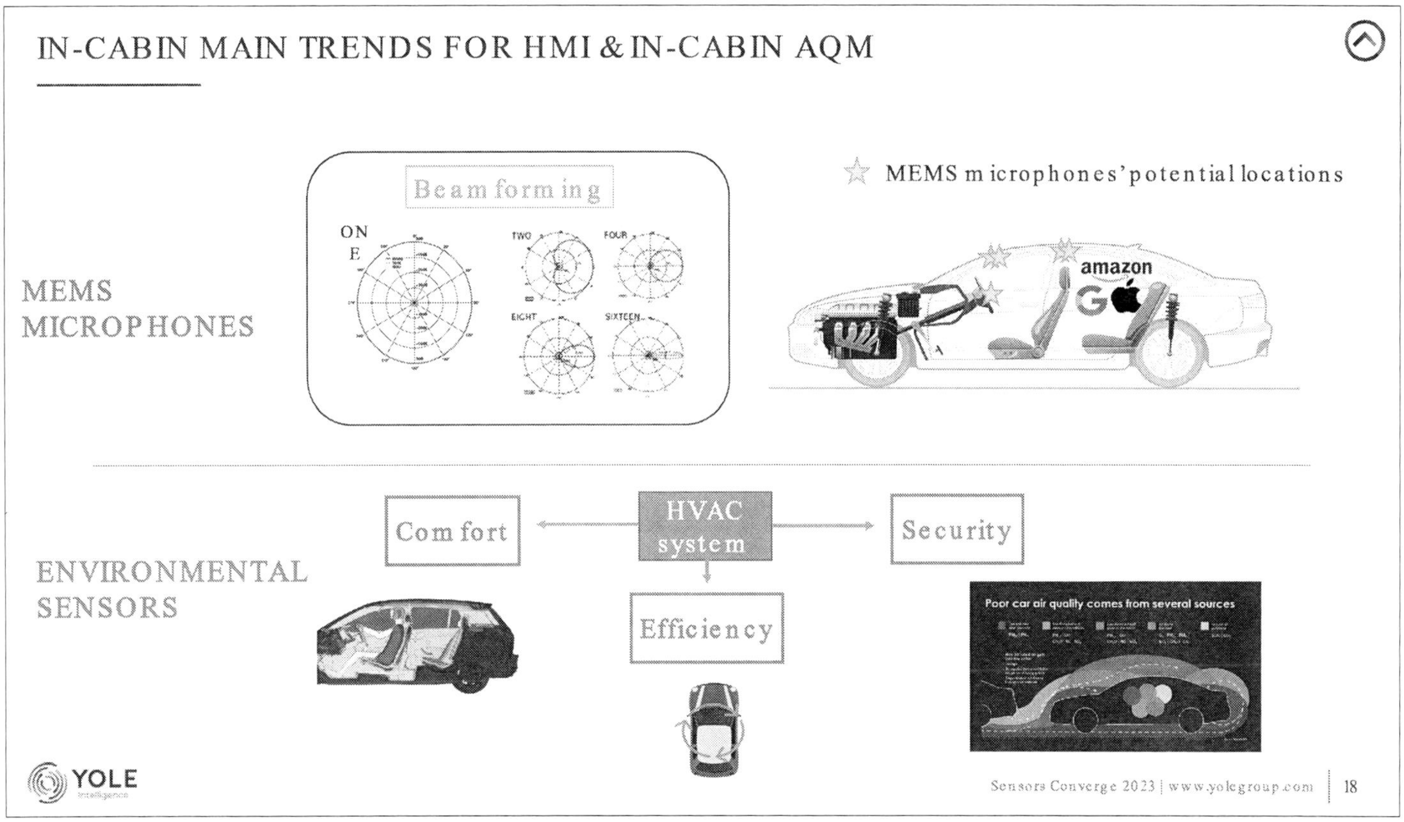
IN-CABIN MAIN TRENDS FOR HMI & IN-CABIN AQM
MEMS MICROPHONES
Beamforming
ONE
TWO
FOUR
EIGHT
SIXTEEN
MEMS microphones' potential locations
amazon
ENVIRONMENTAL SENSORS
Comfort
HVAC system
Security
Efficiency
Poor car air quality comes from several sources
YOLE Intelligence
Sensors Converge 2023 | www.yolegroup.com
18

INFOTAINMENT – ROAD ACTIVE NOISE CANCELING

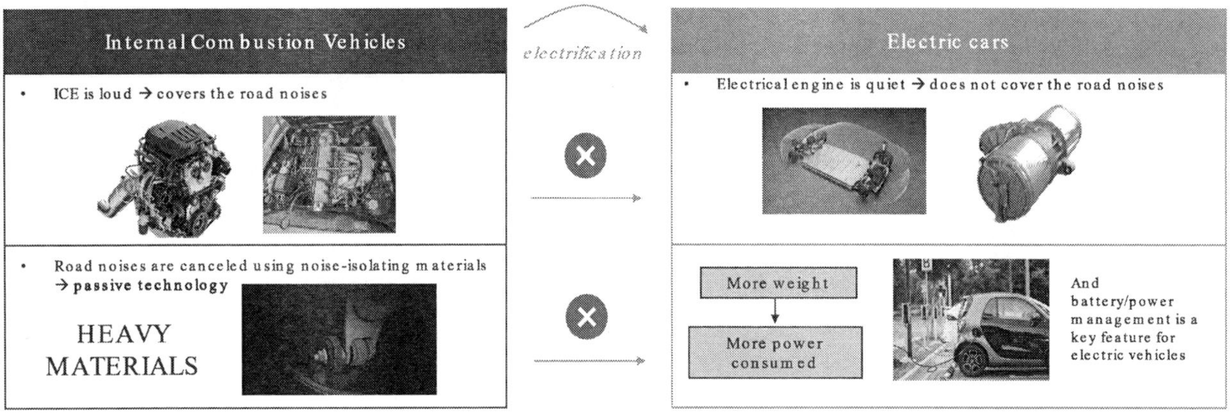

- MEMS Accelerometers: detects the vibrations of the road
- Microspeakers (probably **not** MEMS as you need a high sound pressure levels) to offset the road-induced vibrations
- MEMS microphones: providing feedback data to the controller to adjust the signal

TAKEAWAY

TAKEAWAY

Pushed by mega-trends like the:

- Increasing interest in biosensing functionalities
- Sensorization of end-systems for more enjoyable experiences

} Wearables

- Electrification of cars
- Autonomous driving
- Improved HMI & in-cabin comfort

} Automotive

we expect MEMS & Sensors to remain mandatory in the coming years.

Key new applications are on their way to nurture this multi $B industry!

THANK YOU FOR LISTENING

Sensors & Actuators for Wearables 2023

Semiconductor Sensors for Automotive 2023

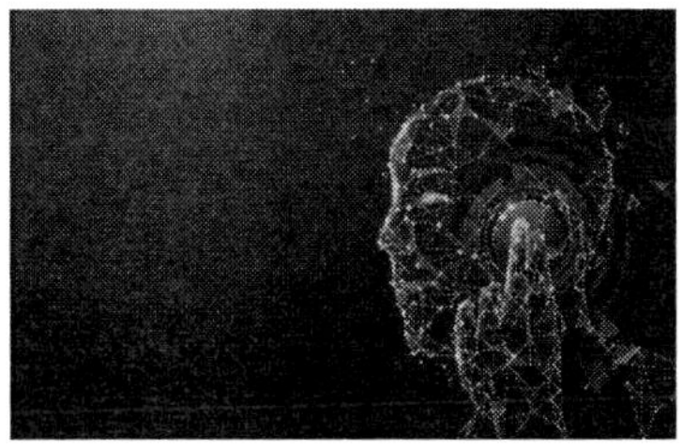

Status of the MEMS Industry 2022 (2023 edition planned for July)

Thanks for listening, and if you have any question on the presentation or on related topics, don't hesitate to contact me:

pierre.delbos@yolegroup.com

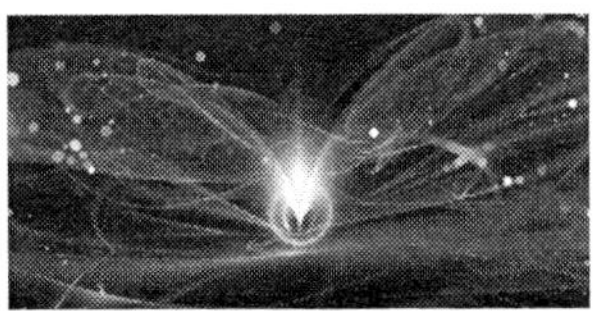

Magnetic Sensor 2022

Gas & Particle Sensors 2021 (2023 edition planned for October)

Sensors Converge

ANALOG DEVICES

AHEAD OF WHAT'S POSSIBLE™

Intelligent Industrial Edge

June 20–22, 2023 | Santa Clara, CA

#SensorsConverge

Agenda

- Concept of "Industrial Edge"
- Why Industrial Edges needs to be intelligent
- How it saves tremendous amount of resources (sustainability)
- How it enables flexible manufacturing and increases productivity
- ADI Solutions for flexible manufacturing

#SensorsConverge

Sensors Converge

Concept of the "Industrial Edge"

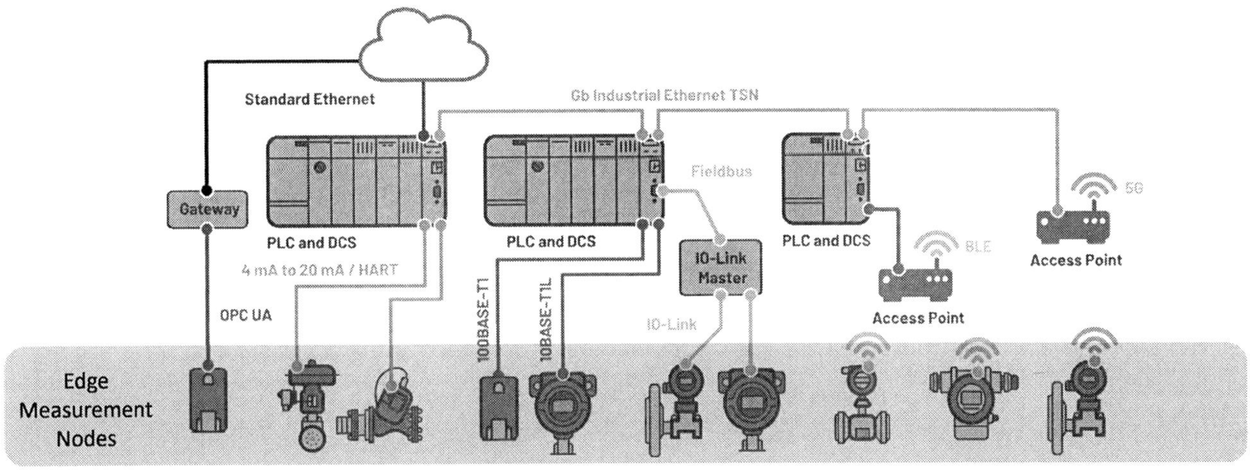

Wide range of sensing modality and connectivity options

#SensorsConverge

Sensors Converge

Legacy Industrial Edges

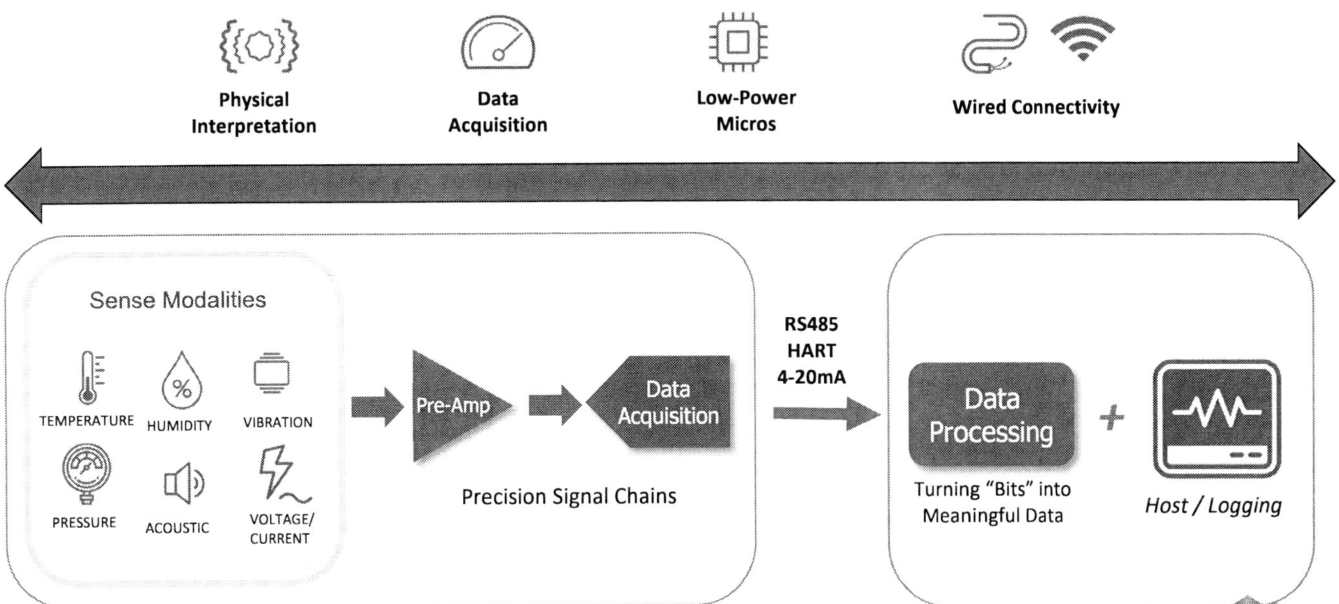

#SensorsConverge

Sensors Converge

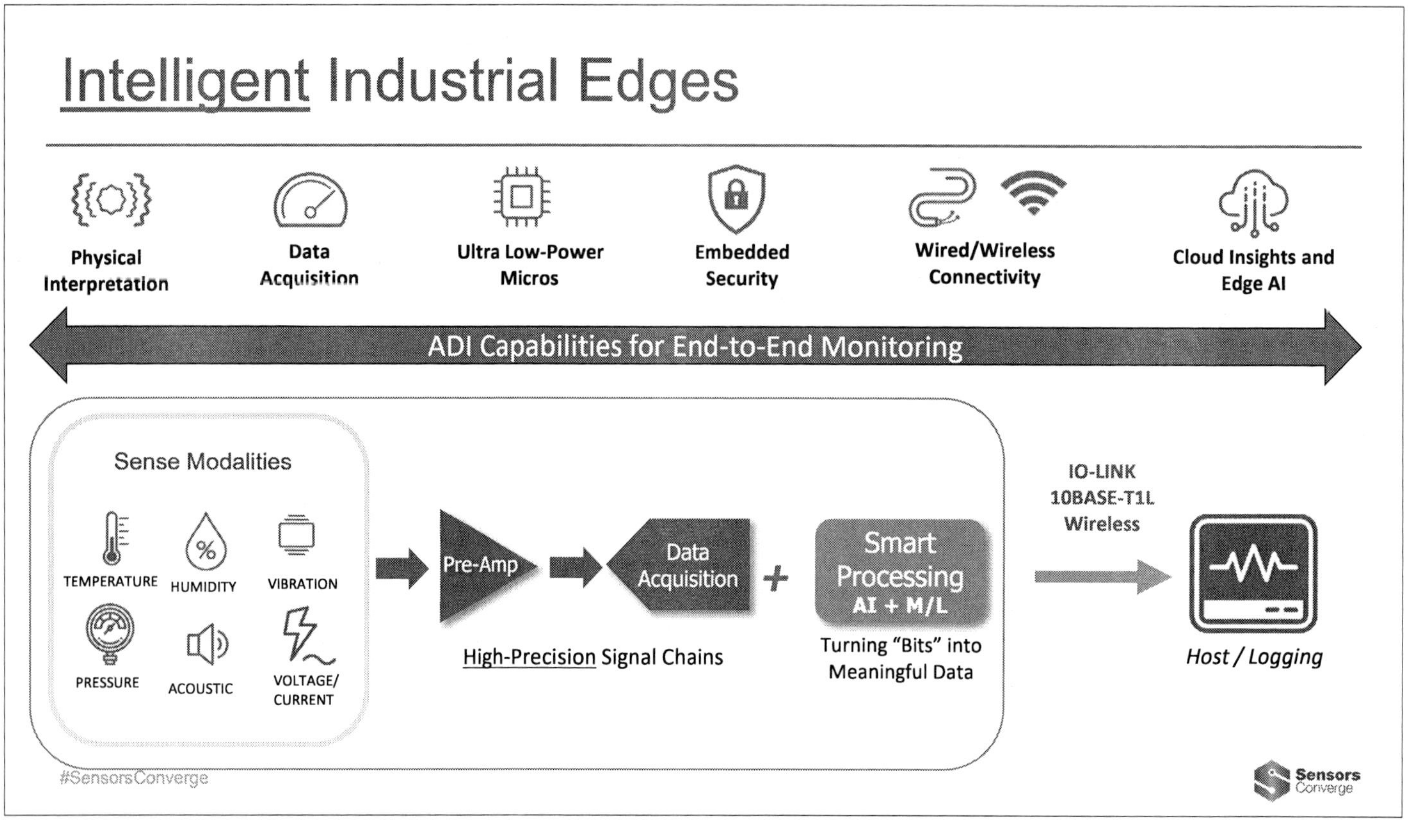
Intelligent Industrial Edges
Physical Interpretation
Data Acquisition
Ultra Low-Power Micros
Embedded Security
Wired/Wireless Connectivity
Cloud Insights and Edge AI
ADI Capabilities for End-to-End Monitoring
Sense Modalities
TEMPERATURE
HUMIDITY
VIBRATION
PRESSURE
ACOUSTIC
VOLTAGE/ CURRENT
Pre-Amp
Data Acquisition
+
Smart Processing
AI + M/L
High-Precision Signal Chains
Turning "Bits" into Meaningful Data
IO-LINK
10BASE-T1L
Wireless
Host / Logging
#SensorsConverge
Sensors Converge

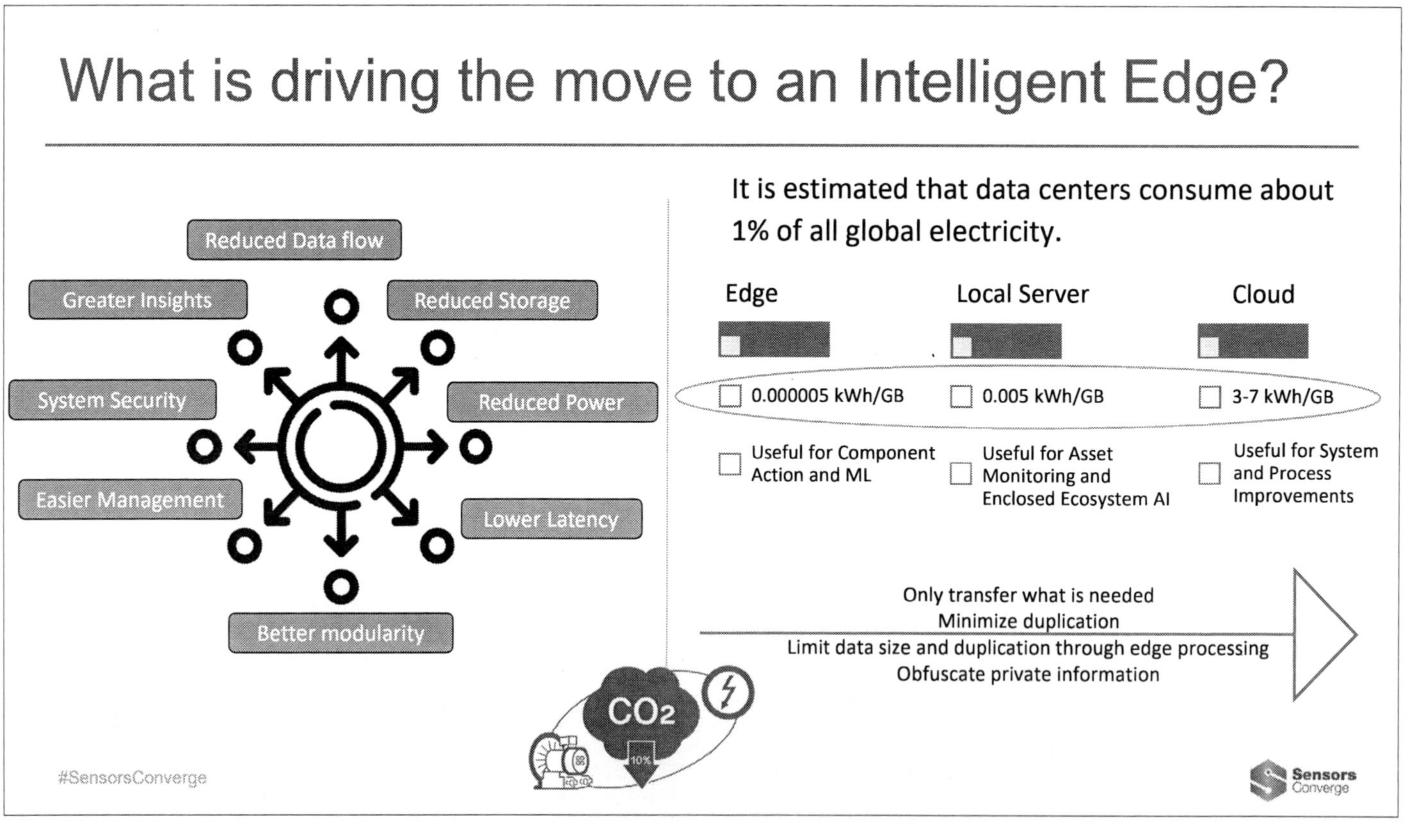
What is driving the move to an Intelligent Edge?
Reduced Data flow
Greater Insights
Reduced Storage
System Security
Reduced Power
Easier Management
Lower Latency
Better modularity
It is estimated that data centers consume about 1% of all global electricity.
Edge
Local Server
Cloud
0.000005 kWh/GB
0.005 kWh/GB
3-7 kWh/GB
Useful for Component Action and ML
Useful for Asset Monitoring and Enclosed Ecosystem AI
Useful for System and Process Improvements
Only transfer what is needed
Minimize duplication
Limit data size and duplication through edge processing
Obfuscate private information
CO2
#SensorsConverge
Sensors Converge

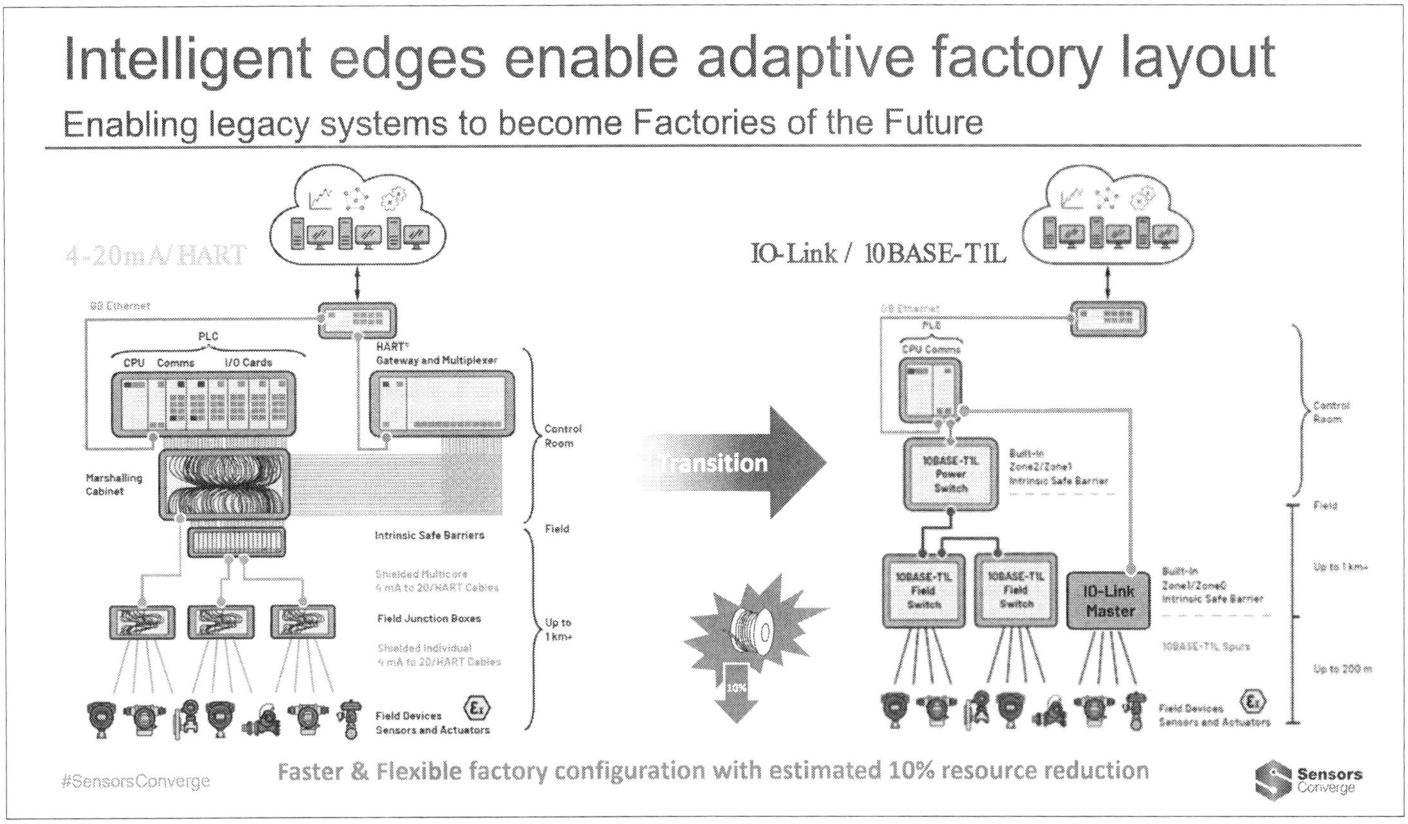
Intelligent edges enable adaptive factory layout
Enabling legacy systems to become Factories of the Future
4-20mA/HART
IO-Link / 10BASE-T1L
PLC
CPU Comms I/O Cards
HART
Gateway and Multiplexer
Control Room
Marshalling Cabinet
Intrinsic Safe Barriers
Field
Field Junction Boxes
Up to 1km+
Field Devices Sensors and Actuators
Transition
10%
10BASE-T1L Power Switch
10BASE-T1L Field Switch
10BASE-T1L Field Switch
IO-Link Master
Field Devices Sensors and Actuators
#SensorsConverge
Faster & Flexible factory configuration with estimated 10% resource reduction
Sensors Converge

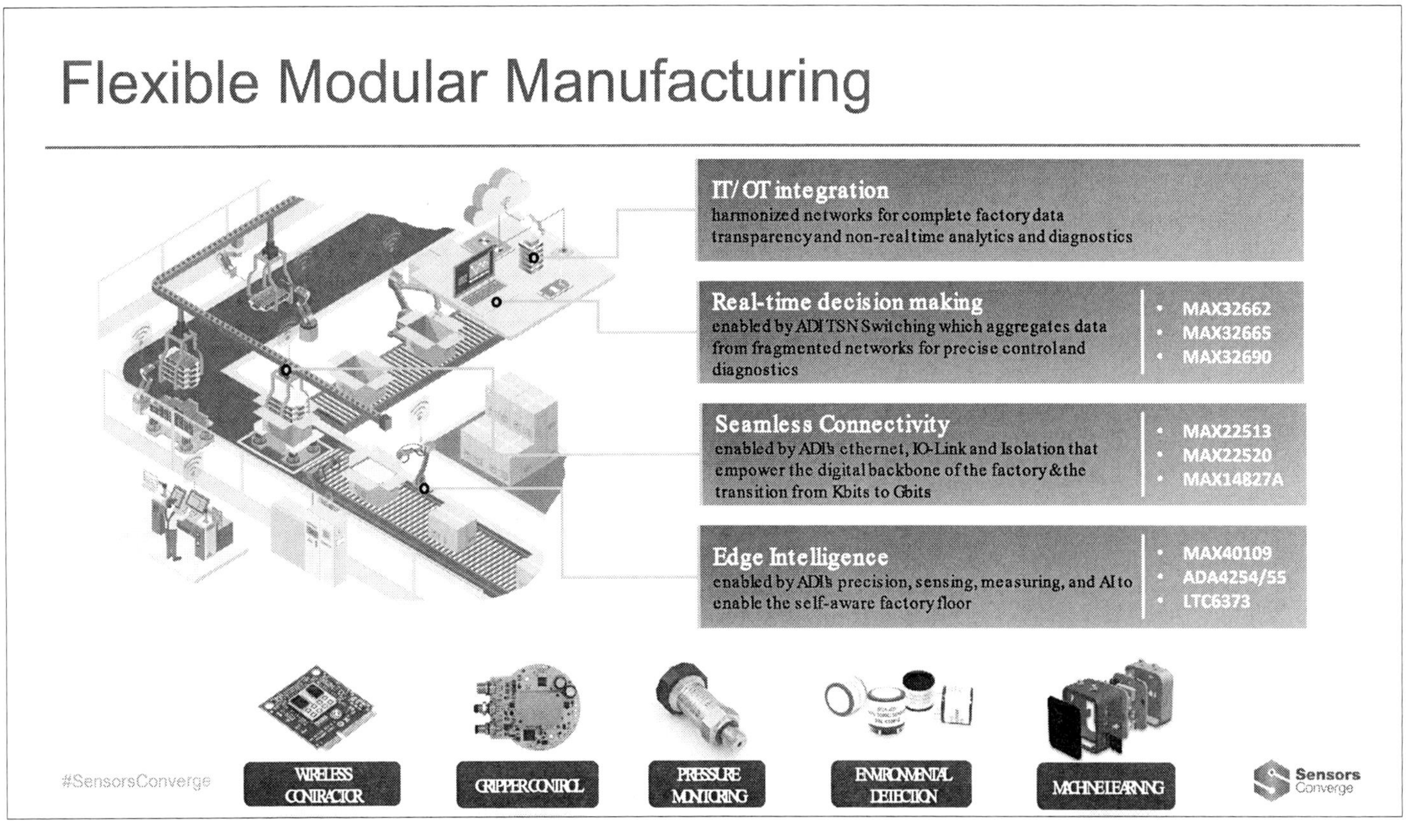
Flexible Modular Manufacturing
IT/OT integration
harmonized networks for complete factory data transparency and non-realtime analytics and diagnostics
Real-time decision making
enabled by ADI TSN Switching which aggregates data from fragmented networks for precise control and diagnostics
MAX32662
MAX32665
MAX32690
Seamless Connectivity
enabled by ADI's ethernet, IO-Link and Isolation that empower the digital backbone of the factory & the transition from Kbits to Gbits
MAX22513
MAX22520
MAX14827A
Edge Intelligence
enabled by ADI's precision, sensing, measuring, and AI to enable the self-aware factory floor
MAX40109
ADA4254/55
LTC6373
WIRELESS CONTRACTOR
GRIPPER CONTROL
PRESSURE MONITORING
ENVIRONMENTAL DETECTION
MACHINE LEARNING
#SensorsConverge
Sensors Converge

Sensors
Converge
June 20 -22, 2023
Santa Clara Convention Center
ANALOG
DEVICES
AHEAD OF WHAT'S POSSIBLE™
"ADI Technology enables Digital Factory"
Thank You #ADIahead
Visit Booth #1034
@ADI_News
@analogdevices
@AnalogDevicesInc
Analog Devices

Sensors Converge

Accurate Soil Moisture Sensing

Accurate soil sensing using changing magnetic properties with moisture

Bruce Borden farm(x)

June 20–22, 2023 | Santa Clara, CA

#SensorsConverge

Soil Moisture Sensing for Precision AgTech

Example use case:

Soil moisture sensing on a commercial farm to determine needed irrigation in an orchard

Determining percolation rate and water usage using soil moisture sensing

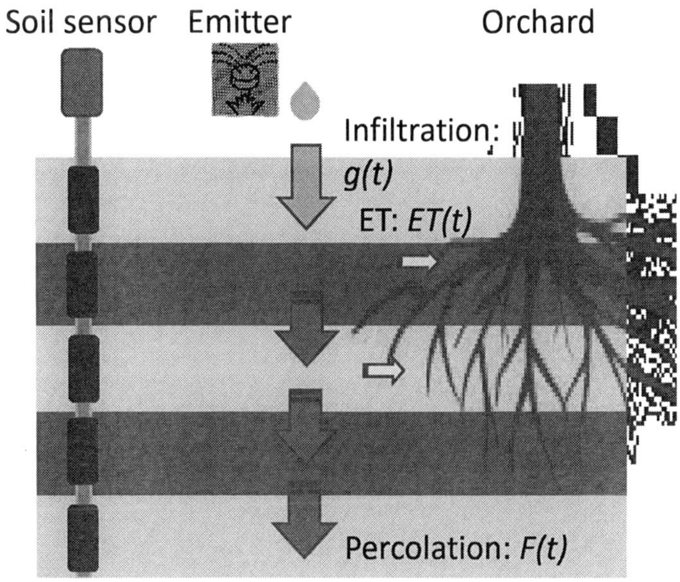

#SensorsConverge farm(x) Sensors Converge

Soil Moisture Sensor Evolution

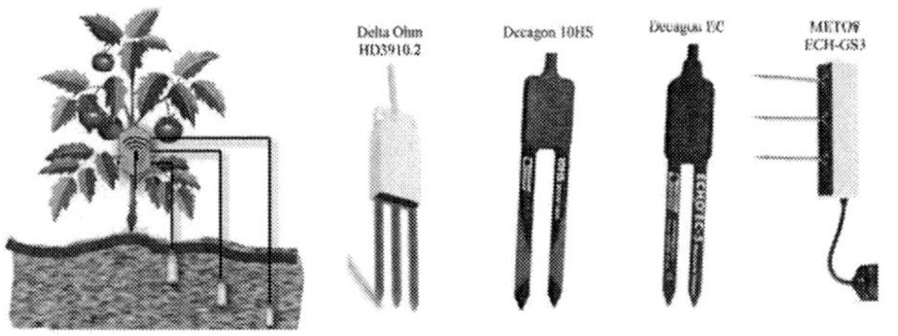

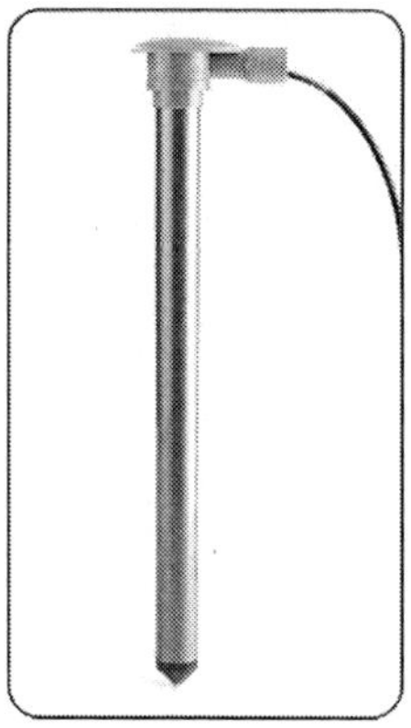

Fork Sensing
Single-level
Capacitive Sensing
Circa 2000

Drill and Drop
Multi-level
Capacitive Sensing
Circa 2010

Drill and Drop
Multi-level
Magnetic Sensing
Circa 2020

#SensorsConverge

farm(x)

Sensors Converge

Range of Capacitive vs. Magnetic Comparison

Capacitive

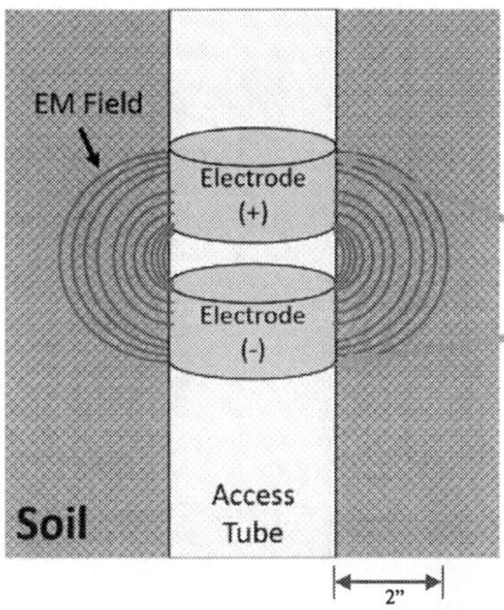

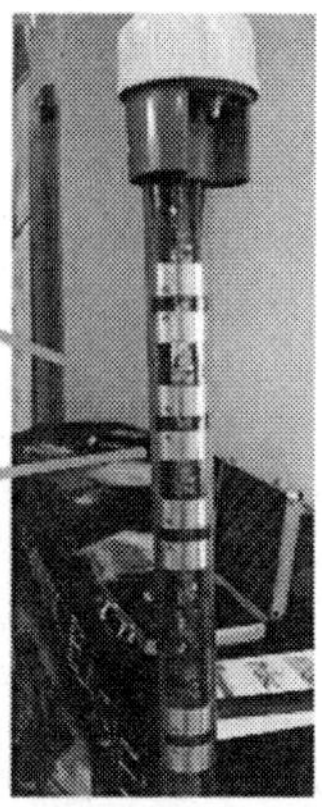

Most of the water measured is sensed within 1" of tube. Heavily influenced by water running down tube outside wall.

Magnetic Sensing

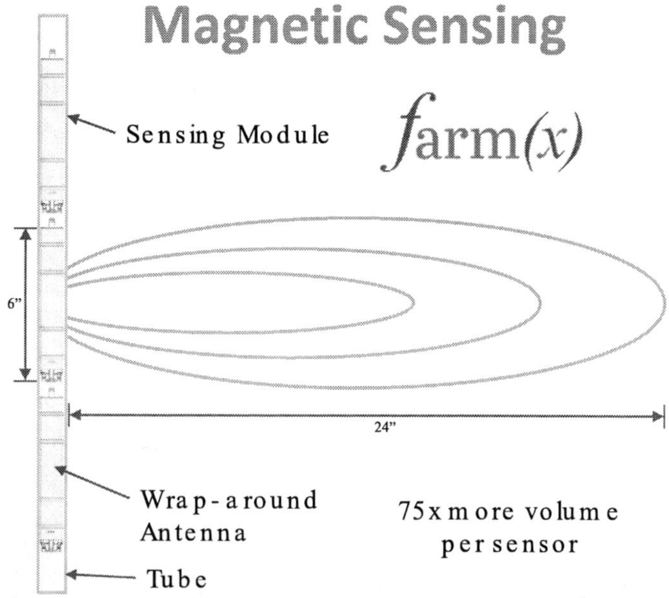

#SensorsConverge

farm(x)

Sensors Converge

Magnetic Permeability changes with moisture

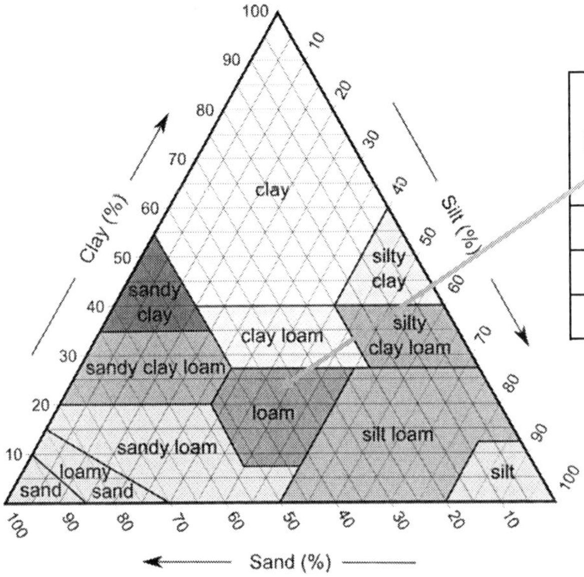

Loam Soil Moisture (VWC)	μ_r@120 MHz
2.5%	0.94
8.2%	0.95
25.6%	0.97

Values of Relative Permeability (μ_r) taken from soil measurements made under supervision of Sandia National Laboratories, see:
https://inis.iaea.org/collection/NCLCollectionStore/_Public/27/040/27040410.pdf

#SensorsConverge farm(x) Sensors Converge

Detecting shift in magnetism in the sensor

Variable Core Inductor

Inductance shifts with moisture by detecting change in magnetic permeability

- The sensor's antenna acts as a "variable core inductor" when coupled to soil
- The magnetic permeability of the "variable core inductor" changes as the soil varies from dry to wet. This shifts the inductance in an oscillator tank circuit, which we measure.
- Inductance of the variable core inductor is proportional to the magnetic permeability
- Example inductances as moisture changes:
  - Dry Conditions has an inductance of 1304 nH
  - 50% Wet Conditions has an inductance of 1324 nH
  - 100% Wet Conditions has an inductance of 1344 nH
- Not a perfect model as there are small losses in the enclosure and packaging

#SensorsConverge farm(x) Sensors Converge

Example sensing element electronics

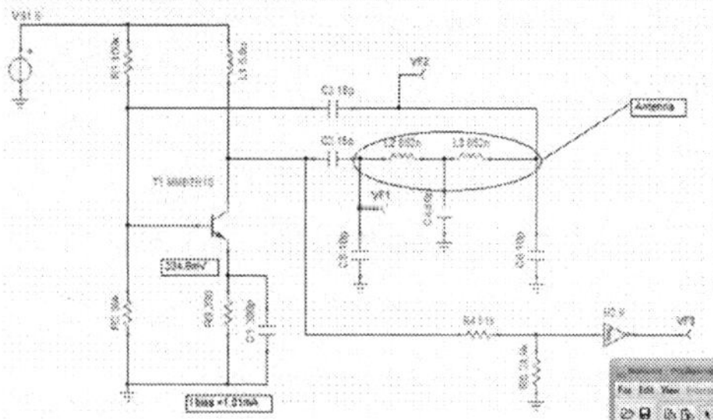

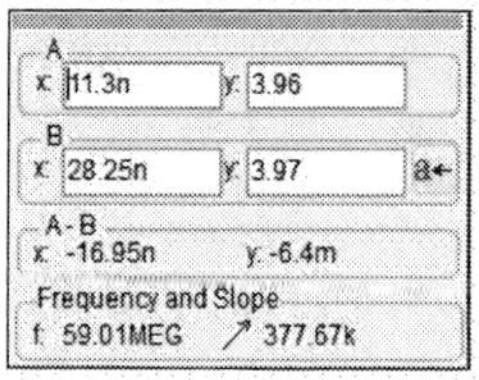

In simulations, the VF2 sine wave is "flatter" than the VF1 sine wave. This is achieved by the transistor bias. This flattening of the spectrum for VF2 induces both a 1st and 2nd harmonic, as shown by a Spectrum Analyzer measurement in Air. Need nominally 120 MHz for sampling soil moisture (2nd harmonic), which is seen with this trace:

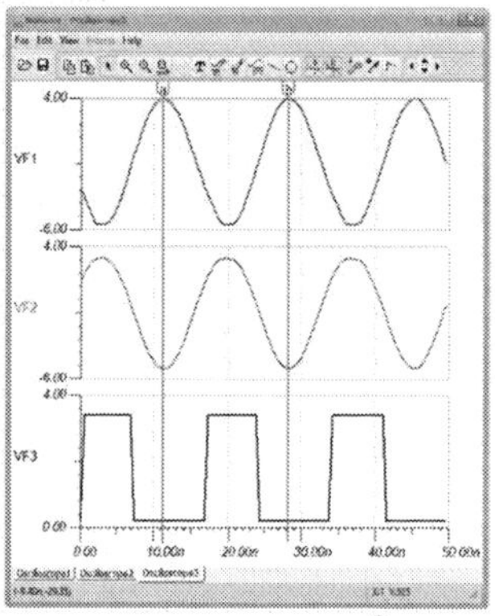

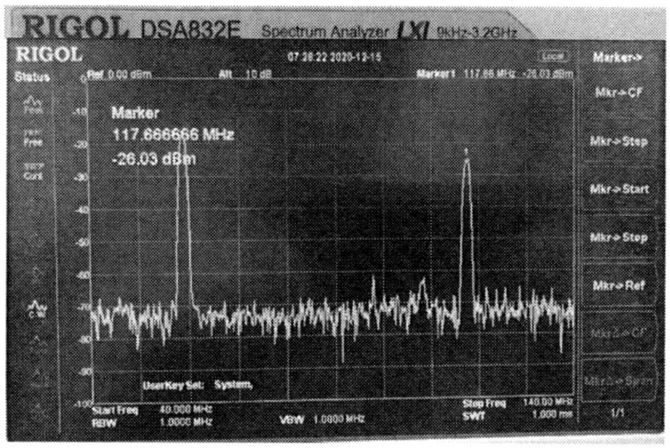

<u>Simulation of Full Dry</u>

Antenna Inductance is 1304 nH
Primary Frequency: 59.01MHz
2nd Harmonic: 118.02 MHz

#SensorsConverge farm(x) Sensors Converge

Sensing element with it's antenna

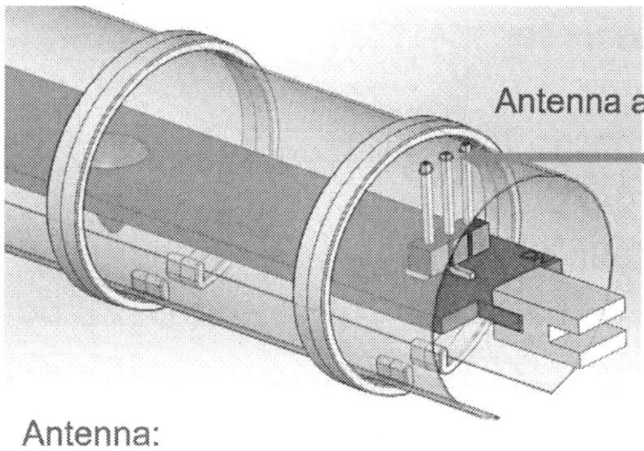

Antenna attached to PCBA

Top view of a Single Sided Flex Circuit
80 mil traces
Center tap antenna
2.6 inches by 5.5 inches

Antenna:
- Wraps on outside of a clamshell
- Secured in place with clips
- Soldered to a header on the PCB assembly that has the oscillator circuit on it

PCBA with antenna is enclosed in a waterproof outer pipe during final assembly

#SensorsConverge farm(x) Sensors Converge

Field Results: Magnetic vs. Capacitive Sensing

Magnetic Sensing | **Capacitive Sensing**

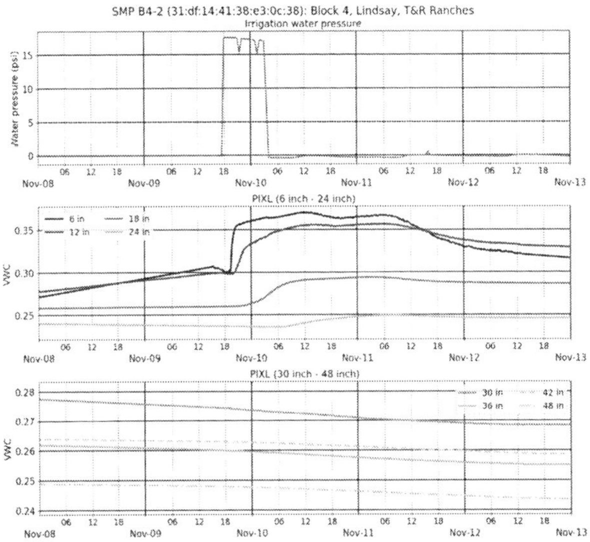

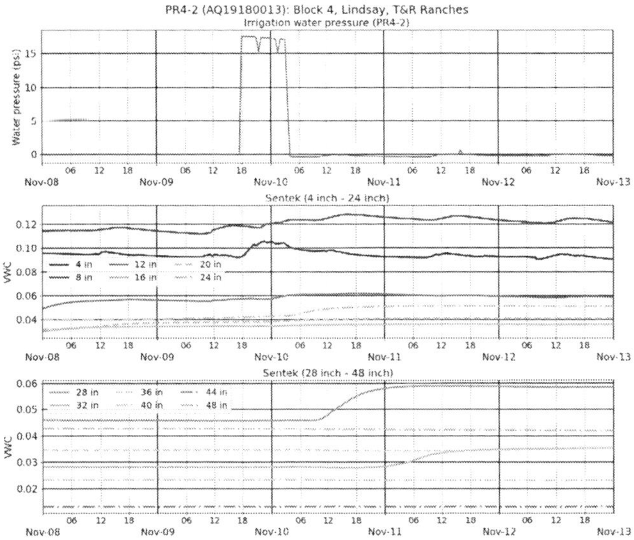

#SensorsConverge

farm(x)

Sensors Converge

Benefits of larger sensing volume of soil moisture

Benefits of larger sensing volume:

- Hydrostatic -- moisture. Hydrodynamics - speed of water
- We measure moisture flow over time
- Continuous sensing volume not slices at sensed depths enables soil water flow through root zone monitoring by sensing directional flow, both up and down
- Larger sampling volume reduces anomalous readings from rocks and cracks

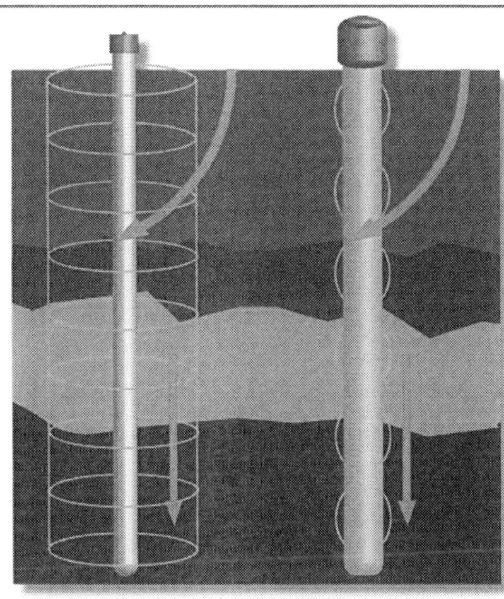

Magnetic Sensing | Capacitive Sensing

#SensorsConverge

farm(x)

Sensors Converge

Conclusion

- Soil moisture sensing is critical for improving cost effectiveness of irrigation for commercial farming
- A new generation of soil sensing is possible by measuring the shift in the magnetic properties of soil when it changes its moisture content
- The implementation of a sensor is cost effective and low power, which enables commercialization of this technology
- Growing food effectively is possible with better utilization of resources, enabled by sensing farm conditions, including it's soil moisture content during irrigation

#SensorsConverge farm(x) Sensors Converge

Sensors Converge

Accelerating Sensor Development with Digital Twins

Dr. Leyla Mirmomen, CEO, Optimuos
Dr. Pirouz Kavehpour, Chief Scientist, Optimuos

#SensorsConverge

Optimuos

Simulating Excellence Through The Integration of Physics & Data, Digital Prototyping/Twinning

Leyla@optimuos.com
www.optimuos.com

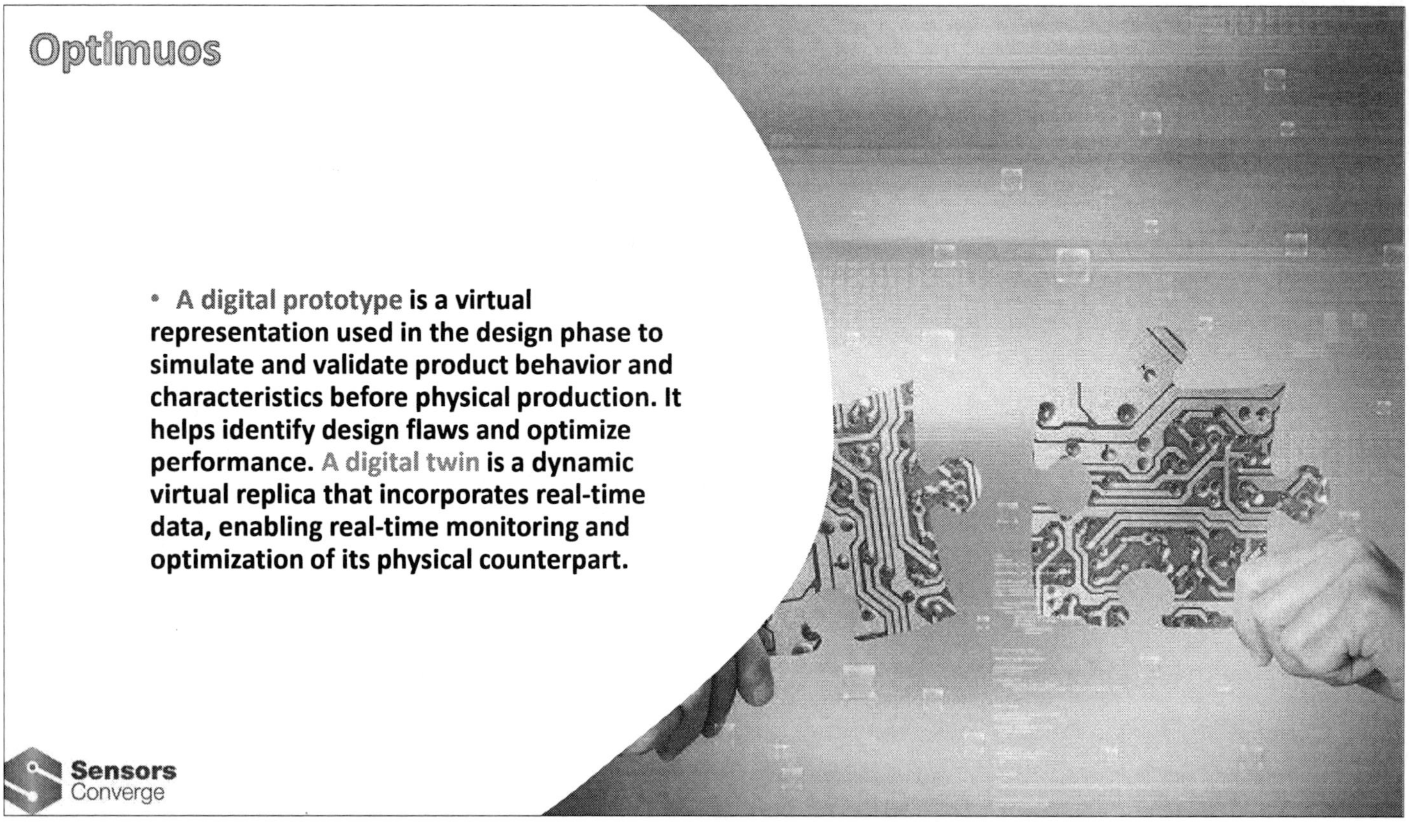
Optimuos
• A digital prototype is a virtual representation used in the design phase to simulate and validate product behavior and characteristics before physical production. It helps identify design flaws and optimize performance. A digital twin is a dynamic virtual replica that incorporates real-time data, enabling real-time monitoring and optimization of its physical counterpart.
Sensors Converge

Optimuos
• In our presentation, we will showcase the transformative potential of high-fidelity simulation, data fusion, and digital twinning in revolutionizing sensor development. By leveraging these cutting-edge technologies, we can gain a deeper understanding of sensor behavior and optimize their performance through virtual replicas. Through the integration of data fusion techniques, we can enhance sensitivity, accuracy, and calibration while identifying optimal sensor placement. This approach accelerates iterations, reduces costs, and delivers feasible solutions. Our case studies will demonstrate the tangible benefits of this innovative approach, highlighting its potential to reshape the landscape of sensor development and calibration.
Sensors Converge

Optimuos

Leveraging digital twin technology, data-driven physics-based simulation, and data fusion techniques we can address:

Industry Challenges:

1. Performance Optimization:

Current Challenge: Achieving reliable long-range communication while operating on low power.

Current Approach: Iterative testing and optimization based on empirical data and limited simulation.

2. Power Consumption and Battery Life:

Current Challenge: Achieving low-power operation for extended battery life.

Current Approach: Power management techniques, hardware optimization, and limited simulation.

3. Sensitivity and Accuracy:

Current Challenge: Ensuring accurate sensing for reliable data collection and analysis.

Current Approach: Calibration techniques, empirical testing, and limited simulation.

4. Cost Optimization:

Current Challenge: Developing low-cost sensor solutions without compromising performance.

Current Approach: Component selection, manufacturing optimization, and limited simulation.

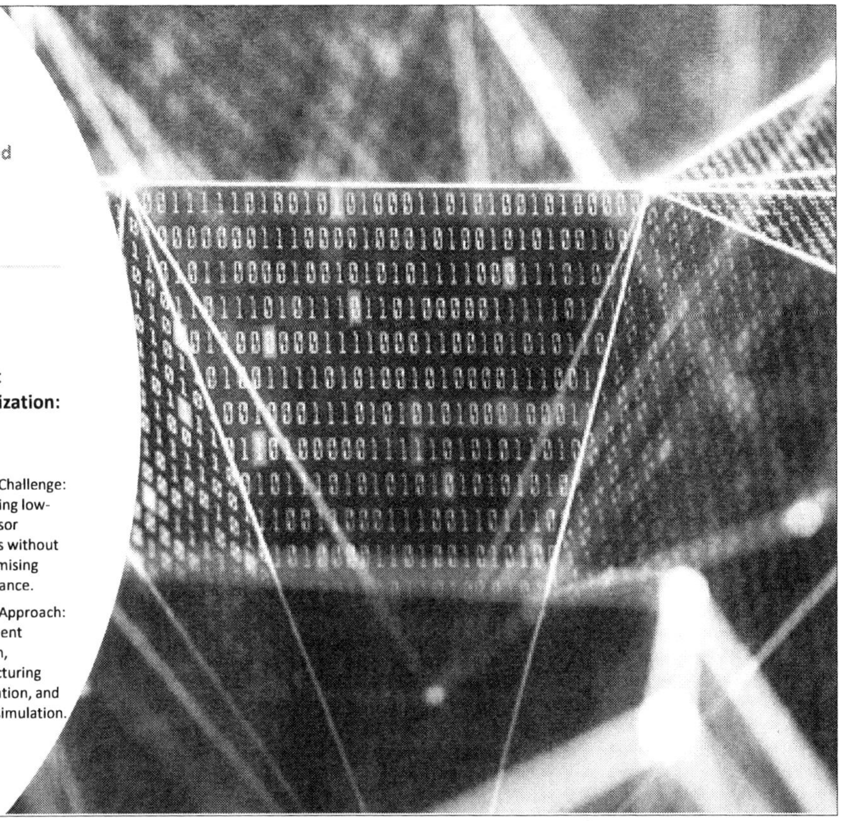

Sensors Converge

Optimuos

- **The Road Map** to Digital Twin **begins with building the core block of data-driven physics-based simulation, which serves as the foundation for developing a robust digital prototype. By integrating real-time data streams and advanced analytics, we can enhance the prototype's capabilities and evolve it into a comprehensive digital twin, enabling continuous monitoring, analysis, and optimization of the physical system for enhanced performance and informed decision-making.**

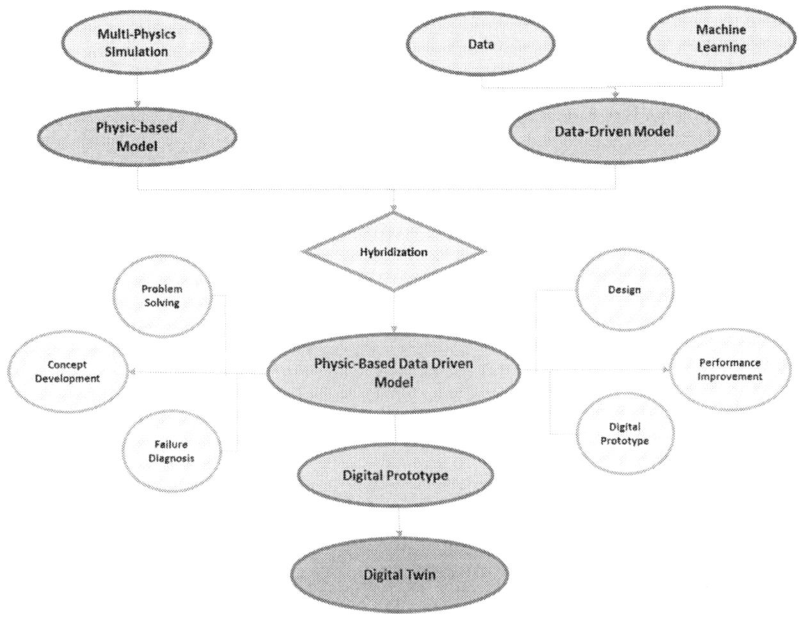

Sensors Converge

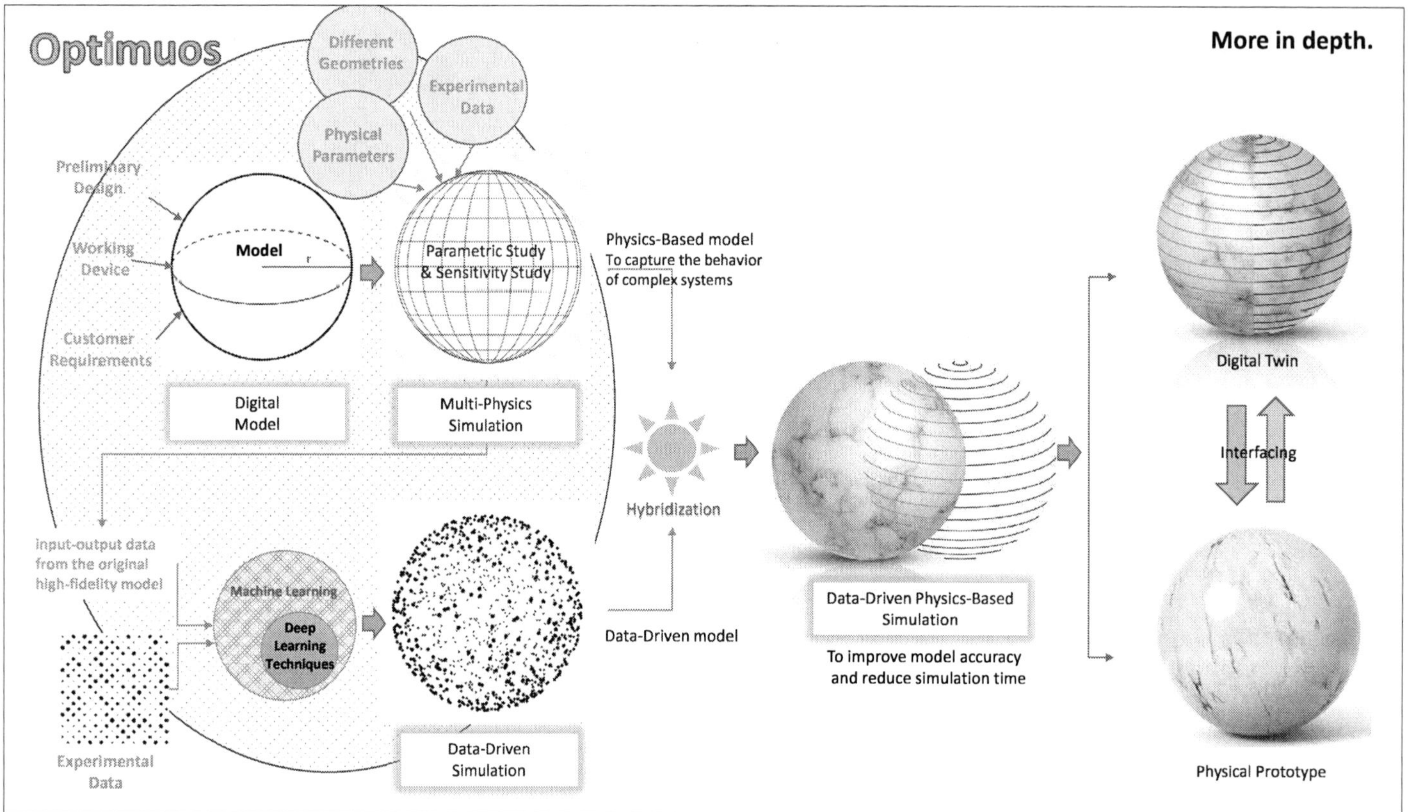

Optimuos

How to Leverage our method for Design and Optimization

Multi-Fidelity Physics-Based ROM Construction (MFP-ROM)

- Allows for efficient and accurate modeling of complex systems with large numbers of variables.
- Integrates physics-based simulation and experimental data to create a more accurate and reliable model.
- Enables faster design iterations and optimization of system components and processes.
- Provides a cost-effective alternative to traditional high-fidelity simulations.
- Enables real-time monitoring and control of system behavior.

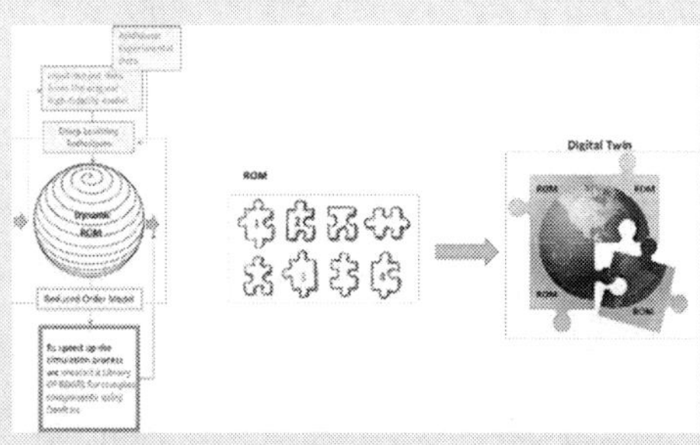

Physics-Informed Neural Networks (PINNs)

- To combine noisy data and mathematical models using neural networks.
- PINNs can solve problems that cannot be solved by existing algorithms due to noisy data, complex mesh generation, or high-dimensional problems governed by parameterized PDEs.
- PINNs can solve expensive inverse problems with hidden physics that require different formulations and elaborate computer codes.
- PINNs can design specialized network architectures that automatically satisfy physical invariants for better accuracy, faster training, and improved generalization.
- PINNs have been successfully used to solve Burgers' equation as an example of their capabilities.

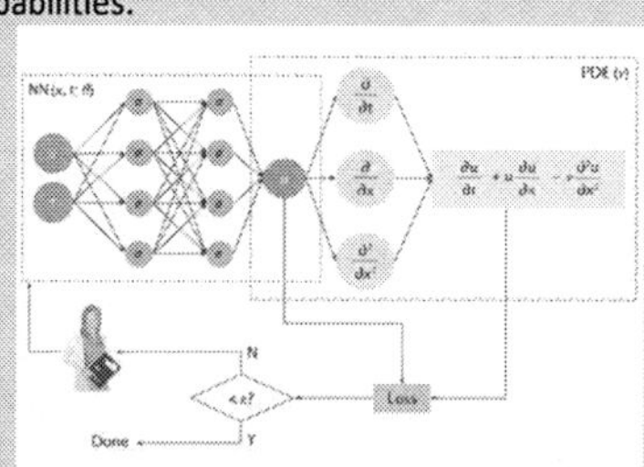

Physics-based modeling

- can be used to develop a digital twin that accurately represents the physical behavior of a system or process in real-time.
- By integrating physics-based models with data-driven models, we can leverage the benefits of both approaches to improve accuracy and reduce uncertainty.
- Physics-based modeling can be used to simulate different scenarios and predict system behavior under various conditions, which can help in decision-making and optimization.
- With a digital twin, we can monitor and analyze system performance in real-time and identify potential issues before they become critical, enabling proactive maintenance and reducing downtime.
- The digital twin can be used to design and test control strategies, allowing for optimization and improvement of system performance.

Optimuos

Case Studies

Sensors Converge

Optimuos Why Incorporating Data Is Essential

- Example: Surface-Machined Accelerometer
  - Multi-Physics: Solid Mechanics, Electrostatics
  - Moving Mesh
  - Small components (sub millimeter)
- Simulations for 5 cases take 20 min
  - Ideal cases
  - No transient behavior captured
  - Only provides general behavior
- By hybridization with experiments data, high fidelity model can be achieved.

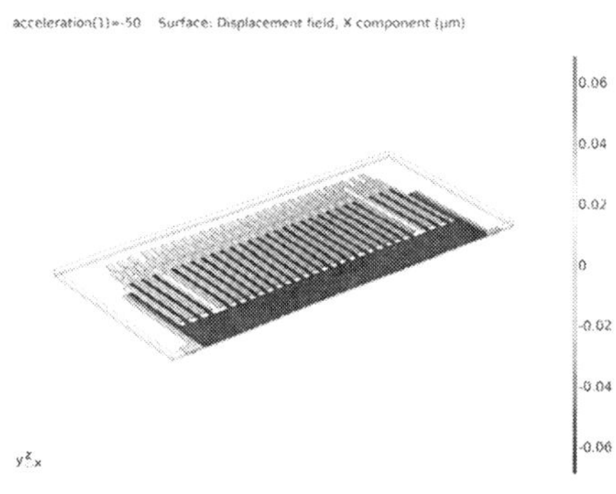

Optimuos Sensor Arrangement Optimization

Case study: Implementation of data science on thermal sensors location and output.

- Aluminum Plate
  - 10 cm x 20 cm x 0.5 cm
- Heater size: 0.5 cm x 0.5 cm x 0.5 cm
  - Heater location can vary within the plate
  - Heat generation can also vary
- 4 Thermocouples placed in plate:

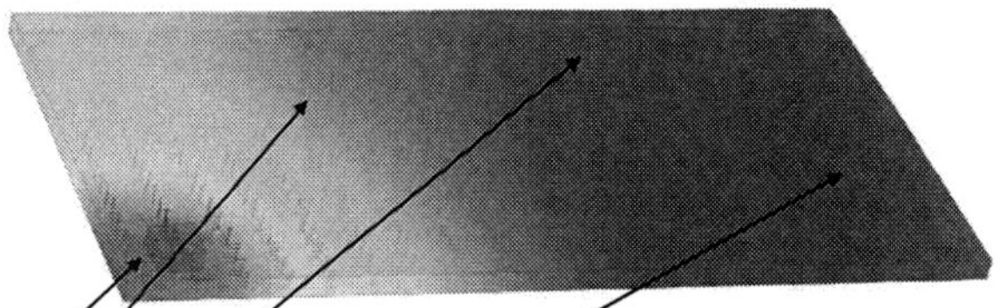

Locations	x	y	z
T1	0.5	0.5	0.1
T2	6	7	0.2
T3	14	9	0.3
T4	18	3	0.4

Using data science and AI to detect the value power generation and location of heat source in a plate using thermocouples.

Optimuos Sensor Arrangement Optimization

Data Fusion by combining DoE data and experimental data

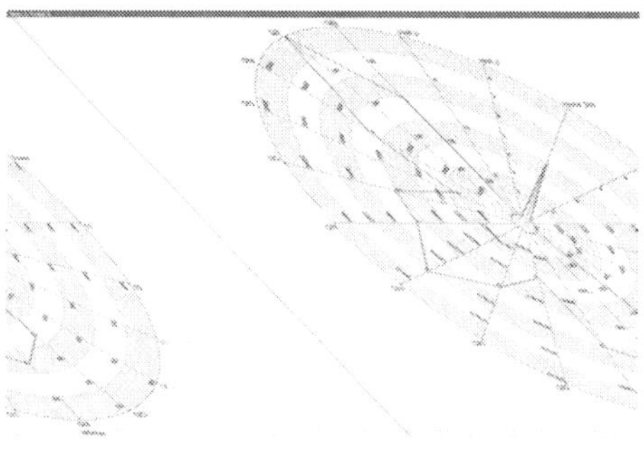

Using DoE to generate data for the Neural Network (500 different cases)

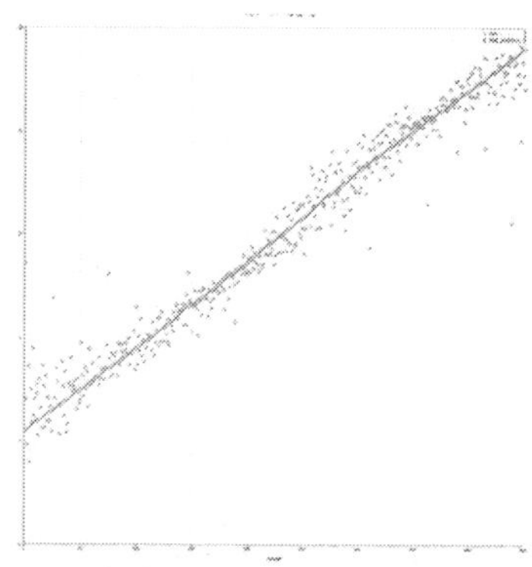

When input 4 measured values of temperature, power and location of the heat source is found within 99% accuracy.

Optimuos Sensor Calibration Using Digital Twin

Case study: Heat flux sensor calibration using digital twin

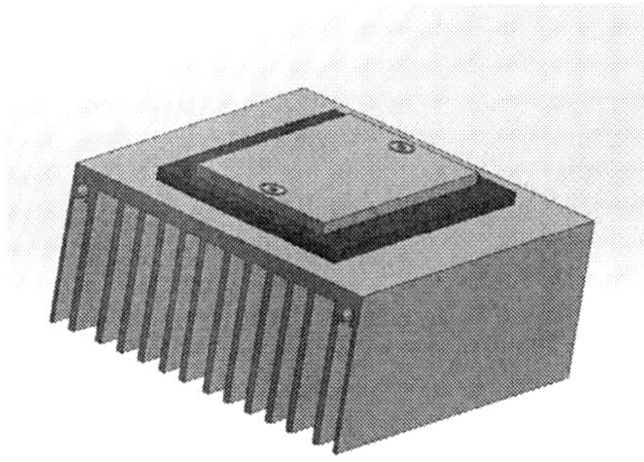

Hardware
- Components:
  - Aluminum Heat Sin
  - Peltier Plate
  - Insulation
  - Fan
  - Aluminum top plate
- Sensors
  - Temperature sensors at top plate and air
  - Heat flux sensor between Peltier plate and top plate

Creating digital twin by combining simulation and data to accurately calibrate heat flux sensor.

Optimuos Sensor Calibration Using Digital Twin

- Reduced Order Models (ROMs) of each component are built using hybridization technique.
- Digital twin first generation is fabricated.
- Digital twin was trained by set of data from experiments.
- Digital twin next generation behave identical to the system.
- Digital twin provides accurate heat flux calibration.

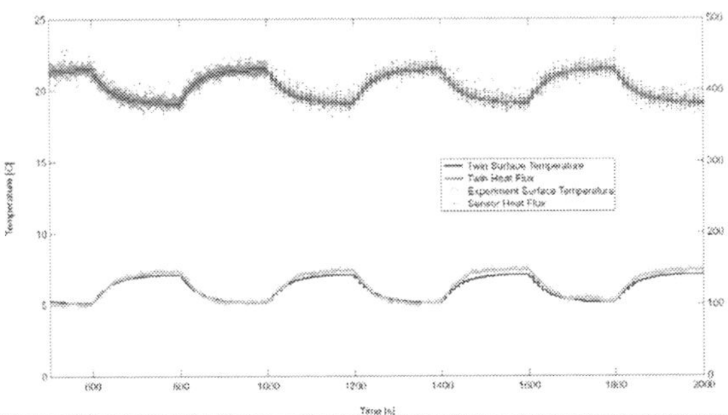

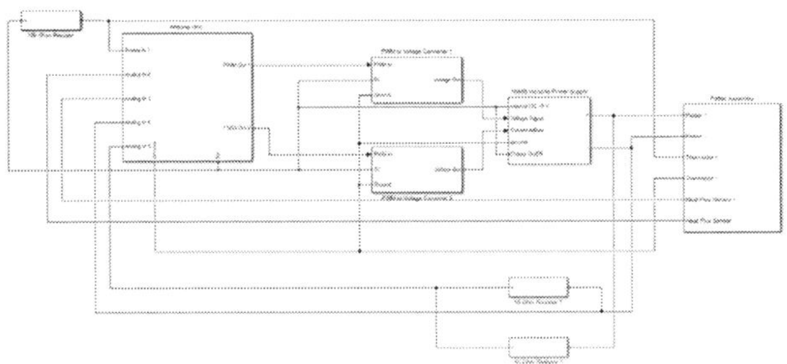

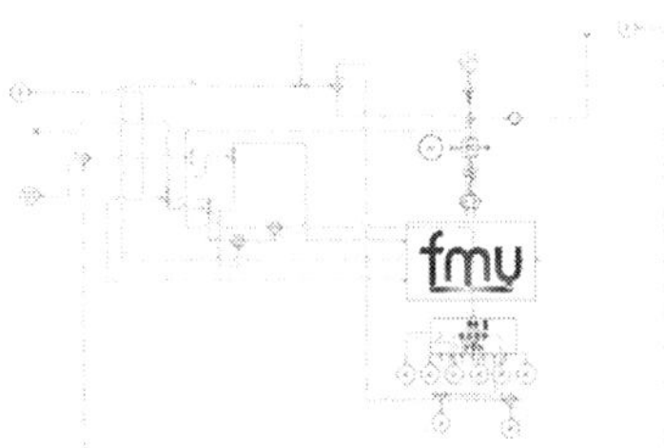

Using data science and AI to detect the value power generation and location of heat source in a plate using thermocouples.

Optimuos

Who We Are

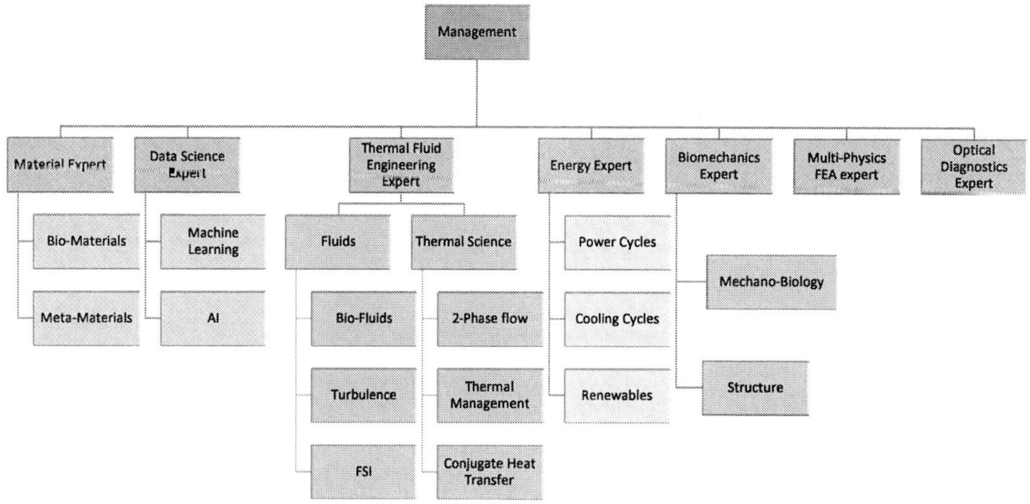

Optimuos

Thank You

Optimuos

Case Study

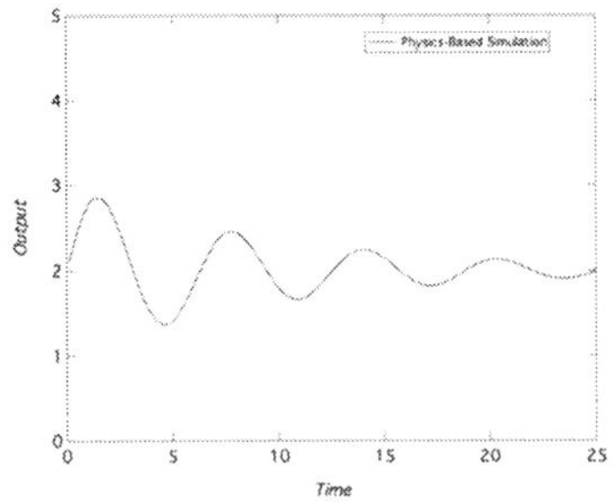

Drift in experimental data

Off-set of model vs. data

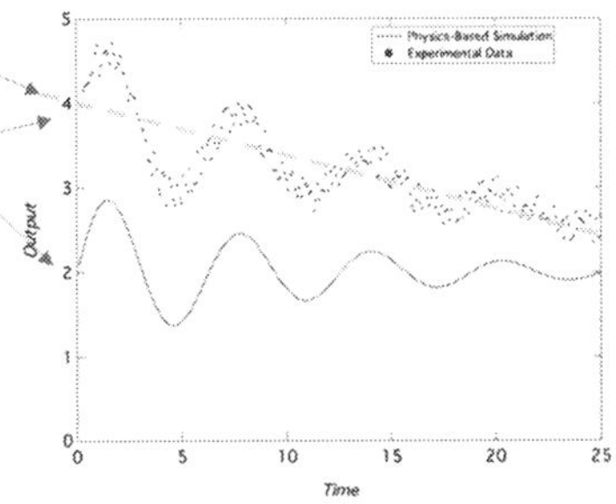

- Physics-based simulation can't capture the actual boundary and initial conditions
- Physics-based simulation can't capture behaviors that are not incorporated in the simulation either due to lack of knowledge or complexity.

Hybridization

Data- Driven Physics-informed simulation
- High-fidelity simulation
- Includes complexities and dynamic response

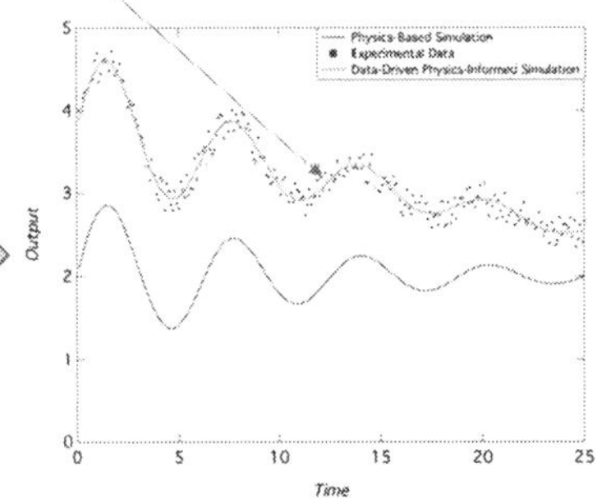

Reduced Order Model of the component

High-fidelity, low computation time of overall system model

Automation Within Automation removes human error and the time needed for human inspection and subjectiveness of the supervisor.

Sensors Converge

Grow Sensor Adoption with Standard JavaScript Drivers

June 20–22, 2023 | Santa Clara, CA

#SensorsConverge

Who am I?

moddable

Andy Carle, PhD

Co-Founder, Moddable Tech, Inc.
Member, Ecma International Technical Committee 53
Contributor to the ECMA-419 ECMAScript embedded systems API specification

#SensorsConverge

Sensors Converge

Why Do Sensor Drivers Matter?

The availability of high-quality, easy-to-use, full-featured drivers is a crucial consideration when selecting which sensor to use in an IoT product.

Basic sample code showing how to use a component in a generic context is not enough. Fully-realized, production-ready drivers that are portable across silicon solutions are a massive competitive advantage for securing design wins in IoT product development.

Sensor Manufacturers

Must provide these drivers and make them easily discovered by designers who are selecting component to secure design wins.

IoT Product Developers

Seek these drivers while selecting components and building initial prototypes.

#SensorsConverge

Sensors Converge

Why JavaScript for Embedded Systems?

- **JavaScript is rapidly becoming the *lingua franca* of product development across all platforms**
- **JavaScript-based products are:**
  - simple to write and maintain
  - easily ported across silicon solutions
  - inherently reliable & secure
  - built on open standards
  - a natural fit for products with cloud connectivity and/or displays
- **The JavaScript ecosystem accommodates developers with many different needs and skills:**
  - TypeScript
  - Node-RED / Node-RED MCU Edition
- **The Moddable SDK is an open source platform for IoT product development with hundreds of useful examples and modules for building product firmware**

#SensorsConverge

Sensors Converge

ECMA-419: ECMAScript embedded systems API specification

A JavaScript standard for resource-constrained microcontrollers and other embedded systems.

Includes standard APIs for:

- Interacting with MCU I/O
- Configuring and sampling generic sensors
- Working with dozens of specific sensor types
- Controlling peripherals & displays
- Networking connections & protocols

https://419.ecma-international.org/

#SensorsConverge

Sensor Class Pattern

- **A JavaScript API with 3 fundamental methods, an error-handling callback, and supporting details**
- **Methods:**
  - constructor
  - configure
  - sample
- **Callback:**
  - onError
- **The entire Sensor Class Pattern is only about a page long**
- **Compatible with the W3C Generic Sensors API for the web**

```
import APDS9301 from "embedded:sensor/AmbientLight/APDS9301";
import config from "mc/config";

let sensor = new APDS9301({
    sensor: {
        ...device.I2C.default,
        io: device.io.SMBus
    },
    alert: {
        pin: config.interrupt_pin,
        io: device.io.Digital
    },
    onAlert: () => {
        const sample = sensor.sample();
        trace(`Alert! ${JSON.stringify(sample)}\n`);
    }
});

sensor.configure({
    thresholdLow: 500,
    thresholdHigh: 15_000,
    thresholdPersistence: 4
});

trace(`Sensor configuration is: ${JSON.stringify(sensor.configuration)}\n`);
trace(`Sensor identification is: ${JSON.stringify(sensor.identification)}\n`);
```

#SensorsConverge

Sensor Classes

- **Define common sensor capabilities for specific sensor categories**
- **Sensor capabilities not supported by the Sensor Class may be added in well-defined ways**

Proximity

The `Proximity` class implements access to a proximity sensor or range finder.

See Annex A for the formal algorithms of the `Proximity` sensor class.

Properties of a sample object

These properties are compatible with the attributes of the same name in the W3C Proximity Sensor draft.

Property	Description
`near`	A boolean that indicates if a proximate object is detected. This property is required.
`distance`	A number that represents the distance to the nearest sensed object in centimeters or `null` if no object is detected. This property is optional: some proximity sensors can only provide the `near` property.
`max`	A number that represents the maximum sensing range of the sensor in centimeters.

#SensorsConverge

Sensors Converge

Why Build & Use Conformant Sensor Drivers?

Sensor drivers that implement an ECMA-419 Sensor Class can be efficiently integrated into product prototypes and easily interchanged, while still exposing product-specific features.

Sensor Manufacturers

Create a plug-and-play sensor driver to open the door to design wins at the prototyping stage. Exceptional hardware features can be easily used by developers and can help prototyping wins carry through to production.

IoT Product Developers

Can rapidly prototype with many different, interchangeable components to experiment with each part's strengths and weaknesses, including accuracy, reliability, and special features.

Can more easily change components later to adjust to supply constraints.

#SensorsConverge

Sensors Converge

Class Specifications for Embedded Hardware Components

A publicly-available, royalty-free repository of ECMAScript class definitions for specific embedded hardware components.

spec / docs / Hardware Components / sensors /

- Accelerometer-Gyroscope-InvenSense-MPU6050.md
- Accelerometer-Gyroscope-InvenSense-MPU9250.md
- Accelerometer-Gyroscope-Senodia-SH200Q.md
- Accelerometer-Magnetometer-STMicroelectronics-LSM303DLHC.md
- Accelerometer-STMicroelectronics-LIS3DH.md
- AirQuality-ScioSense-CCS811.md
- AmbientLight-Proximity-STMicroelectronics-VL6180.md
- AtmosphericPressure-Temperature-Bosch-BMP180.md
- AtmosphericPressure-Temperature-Bosch-BMP280.md
- Gyroscope-STMicroelectronics-L3GD20.md
- Humidity-Temperature-Aosong-AHT10.md
- Humidity-Temperature-Aosong-AM2320.md
- Humidity-Temperature-MeasurementSpecialties-HTU21D.md
- Humidity-Temperature-Sensirion-SHT3x.md

#SensorsConverge

Sensors Converge

Class Specifications for Embedded Hardware Components

A publicly-available, royalty-free repository of ECMAScript class definitions for specific embedded hardware components.

spec / docs / Hardware Components / sensors /

- Humidity-Temperature-Sensirion-SHTC3.md
- Humidity-Temperature-SiliconLabs-SI7020.md
- Magnetometer-AsahiKasei-AK8963.md
- Magnetometer-Honeywell-HMC5883.md
- Moisture-Capacitive-DFRobot-SEN0193.md
- Moisture-SmartPrototyping-ZioQwiicSoilMoisture.md
- Proximity-Temperature-DFRobot-URM09.md
- Temperature-Melexis-MLX90614.md
- Temperature-NTC_Thermistor.md
- Temperature-NXP-LM75.md
- Temperature-TexasInstruments-TMP102.md
- Temperature-TexasInstruments-TMP117.md
- Touch-FocalTech-FT6x06.md

#SensorsConverge

Sensors Converge

Class Specifications for Embedded Hardware Components

Sensor Class for Bosch BMP280 Atmospheric Pressure and Temperature sensor

1 Scope

This document defines the ECMAScript class supporting the BMP280 atmospheric pressure and temperature sensor from Bosch.

2 Conformance

This class specification conforms to the Barometer and Temperature Sensor Classes of ECMA-419, ECMAScript® Embedded Systems API Specification.

3 Normative References

- Bosch BMP280 data sheet
- ECMA-419, ECMAScript® Embedded Systems API Specification

#SensorsConverge

Sensors Converge

Class Specifications for Embedded Hardware Components

A publicly-available, royalty-free repository of ECMAScript class definitions for specific embedded hardware components.

Sensor Manufacturers

Contribute sensor driver documentation to the repository to make sensor driver modules easily discovered and aid in the integration of sensor drivers into product prototypes.

IoT Product Developers

Browse the repository to find sensor drivers that fit product design needs and conform to the relevant ECMA-419 Sensor Class.

https://github.com/EcmaTC53/spec/tree/master/docs/Hardware%20Components

#SensorsConverge

Sensors Converge

Get Involved: Sensor Manufacturers

1. **Design a sensor class API for your sensor that conforms with application ECMA-419 classes**
   - Browsing the Hardware Components repository to see examples will ease this process
2. Develop a JavaScript sensor driver module for your component
   - Start from existing sensor driver implementations in the Moddable SDK to inherit reliable development patterns
3. **Agree to the Ecma International Policy on Submission, Inclusion and Licensing of Software**
   - https://www.ecma-international.org/wp-content/uploads/Ecma_Policy_on_Submission_Inclusion_and_Licensing_of_Software.pdf
4. **Open a Pull Request on the EcmaTC53/Spec repository to publish your document and link to your implementation**
   - https://github.com/EcmaTC53/spec/pulls

Bonus: Join Ecma International & TC53 to help shape the future of sensors for Embedded JavaScript

#SensorsConverge

Sensors Converge

Get Involved: Product Developers

moddable

Node-RED MCU Edition

Conventional Developers

1. Download a JavaScript runtime for embedded, such as the Moddable SDK

Low-Code Developers

1. Download Node-RED MCU Edition

2. Experiment with basic sensor-based examples on the microcontroller of your choice
3. Browse the Class Specifications for Embedded Hardware Components to find a sensor that matches your product needs
4. Order hardware samples and experiment with the open source sensor driver using the real component
5. Freely change components using the same application code by simply swapping sensor drivers

#SensorsConverge

Sensors Converge

Case Study: Spraying Systems Sustainability Monitor

- **Interchangeable ECMA-419-conformant sensors**
- **Beautiful touchscreen interface**
- **Cloud connectivity**

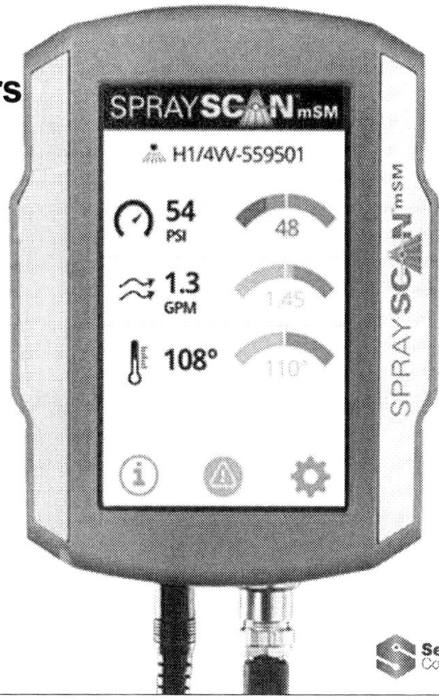

#SensorsConverge

Sensors Converge

Conclusion

- Providing real, portable, production-ready drivers for sensors is a massive competitive advantage for securing IoT design wins at the prototyping stage
- Working in the JavaScript ecosystem provides access to a large developer pool and diverse tools:
  - Moddable SDK: https://www.moddable.com/
  - Node-RED MCU Edition: https://github.com/phoddie/node-red-mcu
  - TypeScript for enterprise development: https://www.typescriptlang.org/
- The ECMA-419 Specification provides a target for driver development that allows a component to be easily "dropped in" to a product prototype while still exposing unique features of the component
  - https://419.ecma-international.org/
- The Class Specifications for Embedded Hardware Components repository is a marketplace for components and drivers that can be used for new IoT product designs
  - https://github.com/EcmaTC53/spec/tree/master/docs/Hardware%20Components

Come chat with me in Booth 802 to learn more!

#SensorsConverge

Sensors Converge

Sensors Converge

IoT and IoB in Safety, Security, and Risk Assessment of Critical Infrastructures

June 20–22, 2023 | Santa Clara, CA

#SensorsConverge

Presentation Outline

- Connected World
- Exponential Technologies and the Internet of Things (IoTs)
- Cyber Physical Systems
- Small and Connected World and Critical Infrastructure (CIS)
- Internet of Behaviors (IoBs)
- Existing Applications of IoBs
- IoTs and IoBs
- Dual Use Technologies
- Opportunities and Challenges
- Recommendations

#SensorsConverge

Sensors Converge

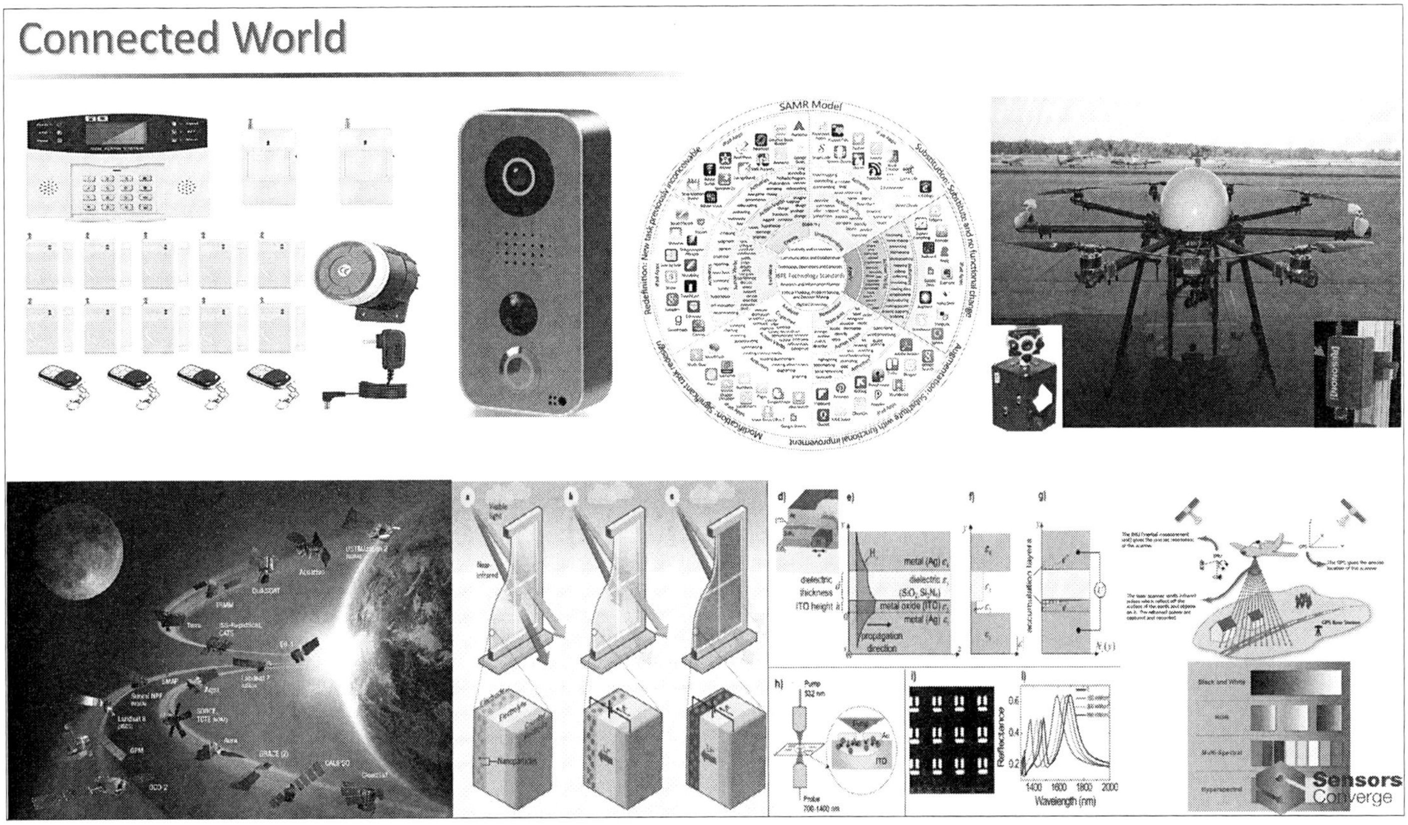
Connected World
SAMR Model
Sensors Converge

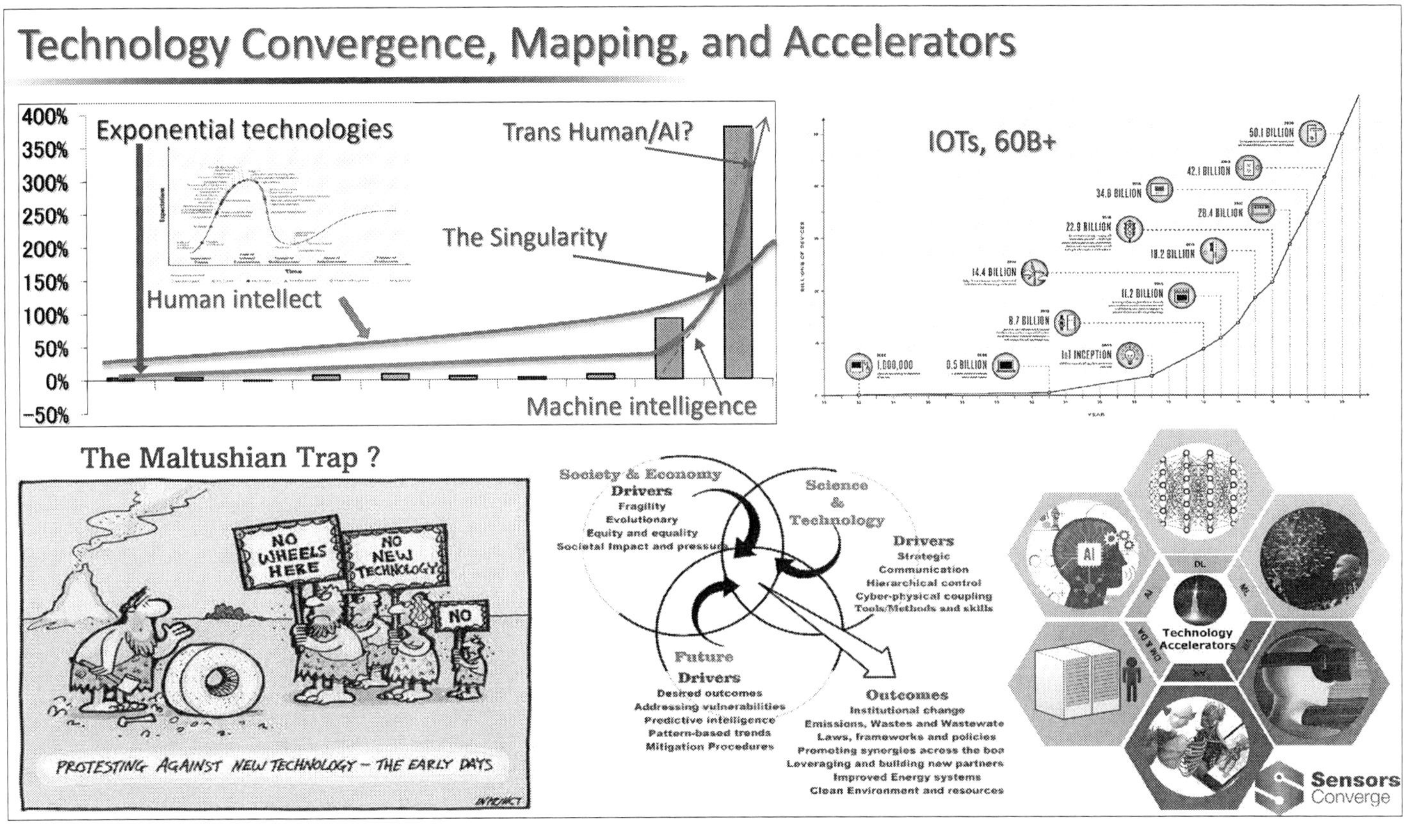
Technology Convergence, Mapping, and Accelerators
Exponential technologies
Trans Human/AI?
The Singularity
Human intellect
Machine intelligence
400%
350%
300%
250%
200%
150%
100%
50%
0%
-50%
IOTs, 60B+
50.1 BILLION
42.1 BILLION
34.8 BILLION
28.4 BILLION
22.9 BILLION
18.2 BILLION
14.4 BILLION
11.2 BILLION
8.7 BILLION
1st INCEPTION
1,000,000
0.5 BILLION
The Maltushian Trap ?
NO WHEELS HERE
NO NEW TECHNOLOGY
NO
PROTESTING AGAINST NEW TECHNOLOGY – THE EARLY DAYS
Society & Economy
Drivers
Fragility
Evolutionary
Equity and equality
Societal Impact and pressure
Science & Technology
Drivers
Strategic
Communication
Hierarchical control
Cyber-physical coupling
Tools/Methods and skills
Future
Drivers
Desired outcomes
Addressing vulnerabilities
Predictive intelligence
Pattern-based trends
Mitigation Procedures
Outcomes
Institutional change
Emissions, Wastes and Wastewate
Laws, frameworks and policies
Promoting synergies across the boa
Leveraging and building new partners
Improved Energy systems
Clean Environment and resources
AI
DL
Technology Accelerators
Sensors Converge

Cyber-physical systems – Concept

- Cyber-Physical systems (CPS) is a multidisciplinary engineering discipline that is focused on technology with a strong foundation in mathematical abstractions.
- CPS integrates the dynamics of the physical processes with the software and networking, providing abstractions and modeling, design, and analysis techniques.
- Cyber-Physical domain consists of integrated and networked system-of-systems where physical processes are controlled or monitored by computer-based algorithms.
- The physical and software components are operating on different spatial and temporal scales, exhibiting multiple, yet distinct behavioral modalities, and interacting with each other in ways that change with context, within a domain of interest (DOI).
- Embedded computers and networks monitor and control the physical processes, with feedback loops where physical processes affect computations and vice versa.
- Challenge: is to conjoin abstractions that have evolved over centuries for modeling physical processes (differential equations, stochastic processes, etc.) with abstractions that have evolved over decades in computer science (algorithms and programs, which provide a "procedural epistemology".
- In the Security Arena – in addition to monitoring and surveillance – the use of CPS is to map human behavior by algorithmic estimation of various parameters.

Sensors Converge

Cyber Physical systems – Mission Space

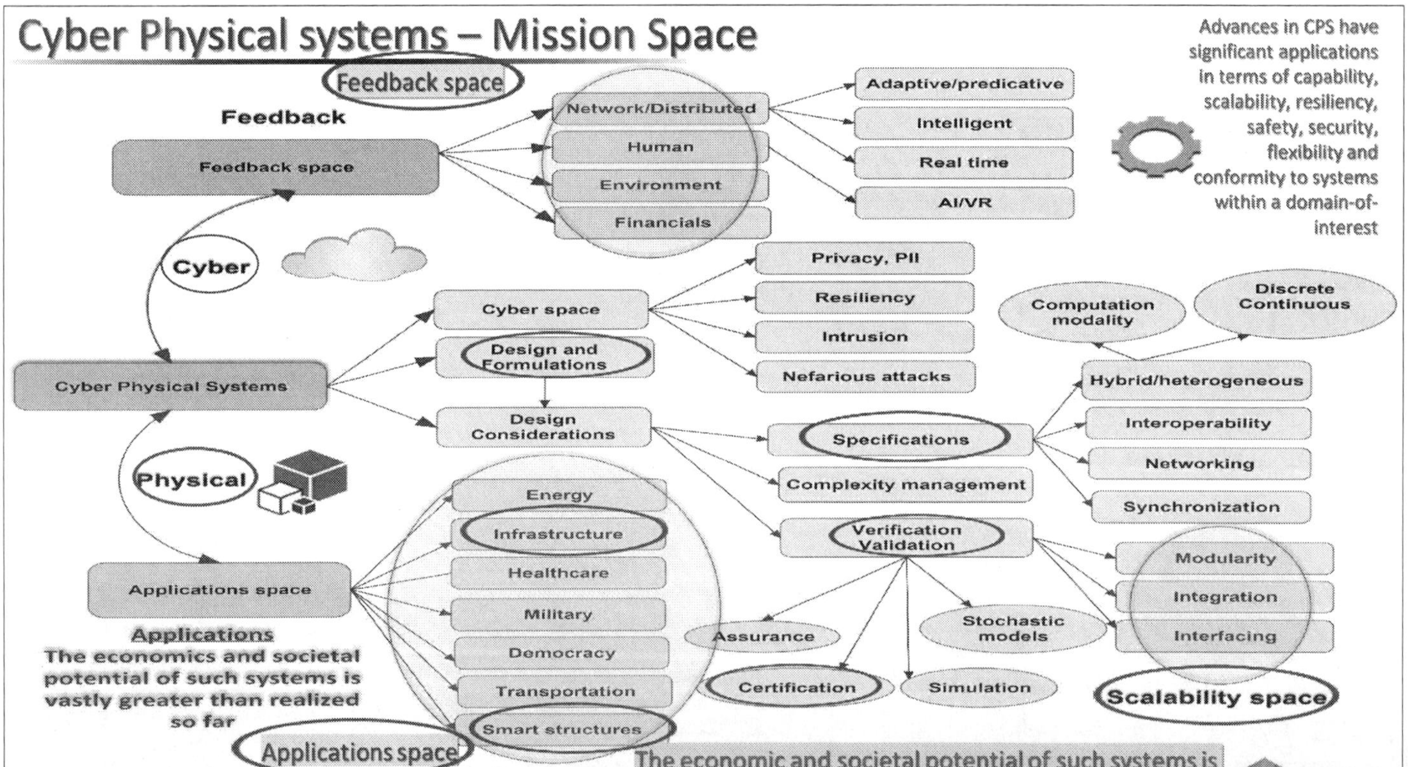

The economic and societal potential of such systems is vastly greater than what has been realized.

Sensors Converge

Cyber-Physical Systems – Components and Architectures

Information and Management flows

- ❑ SCADA
- ❑ Building Control Systems
- ❑ Process Control Systems
- ❑ Industrial Automation Networks

Physical sensing and control

- ❑ PLC
- ❑ Smart Controllers
- ❑ Industrial IoT
- ❑ Remote Terminal Units

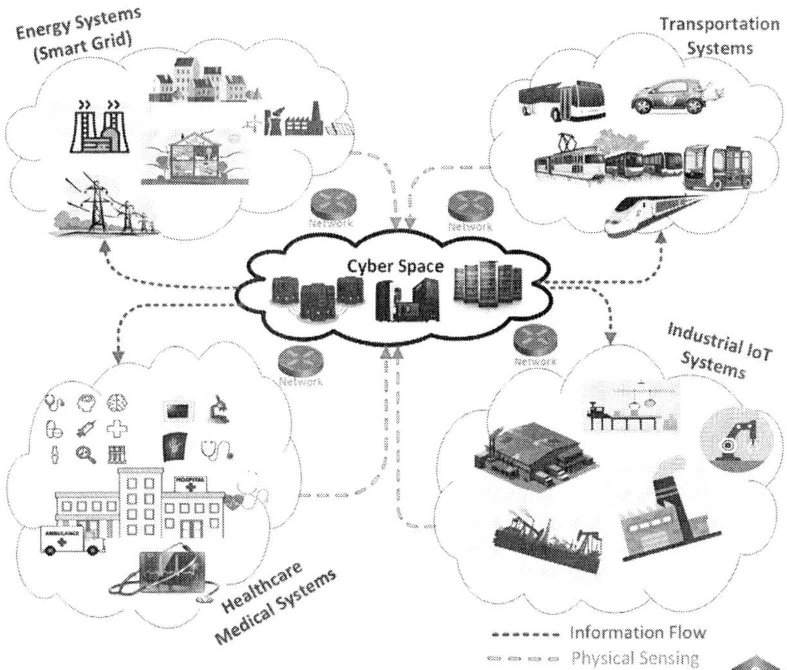

Sensors Converge

Cyber-Physical Systems – Vulnerabilities and Mitigation Controls

- ❑ Designed around the availability and safety
- ❑ Cybersecurity features were not part of the original design
- ❑ "Security by obscurity"

Top 10 attack vectors

- Zero-Day
- Brute Force
- DDoS
- Compromised Credentials
- Malicious Insiders
- Missing or Poor Encryption
- Misconfiguration
- Ransomware
- Phishing
- Trust Relationships

Top 10 Mitigation Controls

Sensors Converge

Critical Infrastructure (CIS)

Critical Infrastructure is the body of systems and networks – physical or virtual assets - that are essential such that their continued operation is required to ensure the security of the state, nation, its economy, and the public's health and/or safety.

Any physical or virtual information system that controls, processes, transmits, receives, or stores electronic information in any form that is vital to the functioning of a society's economy, public health, and safety, security, or any combination of the above, including the food and agriculture sectors, transportation systems, energy and water supply, financial services, telecommunications & broadband internet, defense, and more.

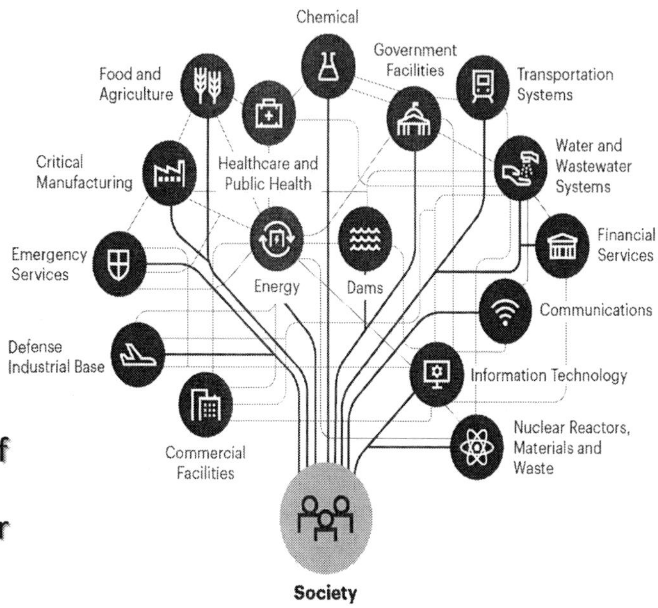

Sensors Converge

CIS Assets, Vulnerabilities, and Resilience

The CIS Assets encompass industrial control systems (ICS), including supervisory control and data acquisition (SCADA) systems, which are used to automate industrial processes.

The threat of crippling cyberattacks against industrial control systems has severe security, financial, and supply-chain implications as the attackers are increasingly going after CIS and operational technology (OT) while improving their penetration capabilities – as vulnerabilities.

Infrastructure resilience is the ability to withstand, adapt to changing conditions, and recover positively from shocks and stresses. This applies to physical infrastructure assets and the wider system of which these assets are part, including the natural environment, the organizations that own and operate these systems, and the humans who make decisions across the value chains.

Sensors Converge

Smart and Connected Communities - Vision

- Communities around the world are entering a new era of transformation in which residents and their surrounding environments are increasingly connected through rapidly changing intelligent technologies.
- This transformation offers great promise for improved well-being and prosperity, however, poses significant challenges at the complex intersection of technology and society.
- The goal of the Smart and Connected Communities program is to accelerate the creation of the scientific and engineering foundations (with Advanced Nanomaterials and nanotechnologies) that will enable connected systems and societies to bring about new levels of;
  - Economic opportunity, prosperity, and growth,
  - Safety and security,
  - Health and wellness, and
  - Improve overall quality of life.

Sensors Converge

Internet of Behaviors

- Internet of Behavior, also known as IoB, refers to the behavioral data analysis gathered from the Internet of Things and other sources and then attempts to make effective use of that data for specific applications. IoB is a relatively new topic when used in the context of IoT. Although in a different context, it has existed for quite some time. (Examples – next slides)
- Due to the ubiquitous nature of IoT, this evolving trend has very useful applications and at the same time poses security risks. This data is amassed through wearable technologies, individual online activities, household electrical devices, and vehicles. When added with biometrics, facial recognition patterns, location tracking, AI, and data analytics – it unleashes a potential that we have not yet considered.
- Studying behavior has been in existence for some time, as most financial institutions use it and so do online retailers – like Amazon. IoB normally refers to personalization, service effectiveness, and adaptability to behaviors. However, accessing behaviors through IoT along with personal physiological data presents challenges.
- We anticipate that almost everyone will likely be exposed to IoB going forward. Examples: Future workforce, lessons from COVID – should we have another pandemic, education, elections, surveys, predictive intelligence tools, and security, ... just to name a few.

Sensors Converge

IoT & IoB and its Implications in CIS Risk Assessment

IoB Examples

- IoB in location tracking
- IoB for the healthcare industry
- IoB in Travel Recommendations
- IoB For E-commerce
- IoB For Logistic Industry
- IoB in Tracking Citizen Behavior For Credit Score
- IoB in improving care insurance pricing

Teachers in Denmark are using apps to audit their students' moods
Companies say the software can help improve well-being, but some experts worry it could have the opposite effect. MIT Tech Review: April 17, 2023

Present objective: Safety and Security of Critical Infrastructures

Sensors Converge

Dual-use Paradigm

The term "dual-use" traditionally has been used to describe technologies that could have both civilian and military usage. Initially used in the context of Nuclear and later in biology (synthetic), the term has, at least, three different dimensions that pose a dilemma for modern technologies and its possible misuse for hostile purposes:

- Ostensibly civilian facilities that are in fact intended for the military – terrorists/bad actors may use;
- Equipment, (information), and agents that could be misappropriated and misused; and
- The generation and dissemination of scientific knowledge that could be misapplied or misused.

Sensors Converge

Information Technology and Dual Use Paradigm

- **Selected aspects**
  - Information vs. misinformation/disinformation
  - Social media – Information sharing vs. recruitment by bad actors
  - Enhanced Knowledge vs. distraction
  - Email vs. spam, (Distributed) DoS attacks
  - Cyber security vs. cyber-warfare
  - Critical infrastructure vs. Ransomware (Colonial Pipeline)
  - Automated Health Records vs. Intrusion of Privacy
  - Artificial Intelligence vs. Privacy
  - Machine learning vs. Privacy
  - Foresight vs. Disillusion

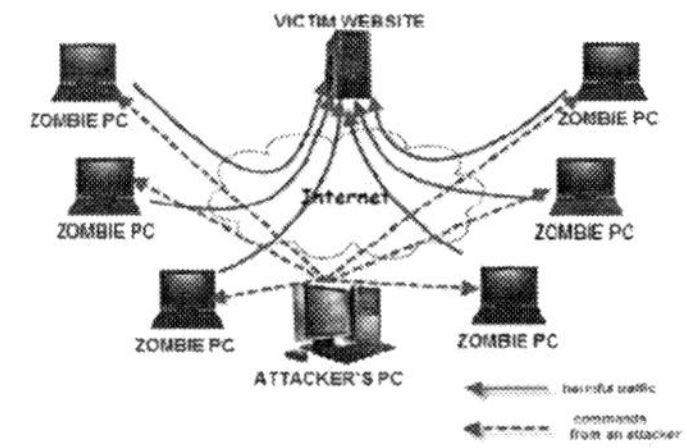

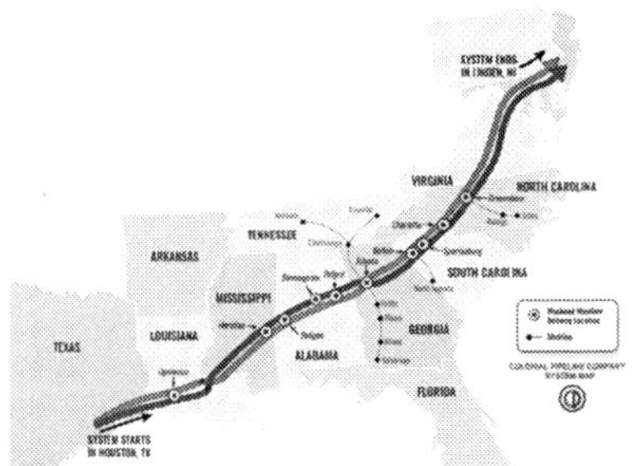

Resilience of Critical Infrastructure Systems to Hybrid Threats with Information Disruption
Helmir Thorisson, Fabrizio Balardi, David G. Angeler, Kuldar Taveter, Ashok Vaseashta, Paul D. Rowe, Wojciech Piotrowicz, Thomas L. Polmateer, James H. Lambert, Igor Linkov.
DOI: 10.3233/NICSP190017

Sensors Converge

Cyber Risk

- Breach is an uncertain incident (event) created as a result of a system malfunction that severely impacts organizational assets and business objectives.
- Risk - is defined as the potential for harm to an organization's resources when a vulnerability is exploited - loss of privacy, financial loss, legal complications, etc. Hence, the overall risk of the CPS is assessed by analyzing the vulnerability, exposure, and threat of different entities in the critical infrastructure.
- Risk analysis - The process of identifying risks, determining their probability and impact, and identifying areas needing safeguards.
- Risk measurement - A process to determine the likelihood of an adverse event or threat occurring and the potential impact of such an event on the institution. The result of risk measurement leads to the prioritization of potential risks based on severity and likelihood of occurrence.
- Risk assessment - A prioritization of potential business disruptions based on severity and likelihood of occurrence. The risk assessment includes an analysis of threats based on the impact on the institution, its customers, and financial markets, rather than the nature of the threat.

Sensors Converge

Risk Measures

How to show results?
We need guidelines and scales.

One scale for assessing likelihood
(ex: "Very Likely", "Likely", "Possible", "Unlikely", "Very Unlikely")

And

One for severity
(ex: "Severe," "Significant," "Moderate," "Minor," and "Negligible")

Impact →

Likelihood	Negligible	Minor	Moderate	Significant	Severe
Very Likely	Low Med	Medium	Med Hi	High	High
Likely	Low	Low Med	Medium	Med Hi	High
Possible	Low	Low Med	Medium	Med Hi	Med Hi
Unlikely	Low	Low Med	Low Med	Medium	Med Hi
Very Unlikely	Low	Low	Low Med	Medium	Medium

These scales can easily be converted into numbers and plugged into equations for assessing inherent and residual risk.
For example,
"Very Likely" and "Severe" can be assigned as 5
"Very Unlikely" and "Negligible" can be as 1.

Inherent risk

Inherent risk scores represent the level of risk an institution would face if there weren't controls to mitigate it.

Inherent risk = [Impact of an event] * Probability

Residual risk

Residual risk is the risk that remains after controls are taken into account.

Residual risk = [Inherent risk] * Control effectiveness

Residual risk is greatest when the inherent risk is high and the controls for mitigating the risk aren't effective. It decreases when controls are effective.

Sensors Converge

Risk Assessment in Critical Infrastructures

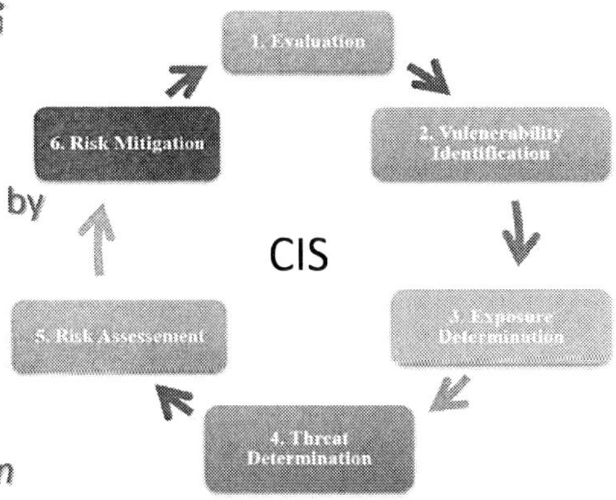

A risk assessment evaluates both likelihood and impact.

Impact. The impact is an estimate of the harm that could be caused by an event. *For example, a cyber breach could have a catastrophic impact.*

Likelihood. The likelihood of how probable it is that an event will occur. *For example, a cyber breach seems a very likely occurrence when there is no firewalls, endpoint protection software, or intrusion detection software to prevent it.*

The more likely or severe an event, the greater the risk.

- **IoT and IoB** – both are an integral part of many systems around us.
- **Current focus**: IoT and IoB in safety and security in Critical Infrastructures

IoT and IoB: Opportunities

Connected home solutions and personal devices

- Security cameras and door locks with face recognition capabilities
- Voice-controlled smart home devices
- Automatic pill dispensers
- Hearing aids
- Indoor navigation systems for the visually impaired
- In-home remote monitoring systems for the elderly and patients with chronic conditions

Fitness devices

- Wearable physical activity trackers, including innovative accessories
- Fitness mirrors with computer vision functionality
- Connected fabrics and apparel
- Training and weight measuring equipment enhanced with sensors

Wellness technology

- Baby tech solutions: camera and sensor-based monitors, smart cribs, intelligent baby formula makers, and connected body temperature thermometers and nebulizers
- Femtech products: smart pads, tampons, and menstruation cups; connected bras and breast cups, hardware-based fertility trackers, pelvic floor training tools
- Vitals monitoring devices: wearables for heart rate, blood pressure, and oxygen monitoring
- Diabetes management systems: smart glucose meters, wearable insulin pumps, and sensor-infused medication storage devices.

IoT and IoB: Opportunities

Smart hospital solutions

- Biometric-based identification systems for patients and hospital staff
- Connected hospital beds with vitals monitoring functionality
- Point-of-care testing equipment
- Stationary medication dispensers
- Integrated IoT systems for inpatient, outpatient, and remote patient care

Implantable and ingestible devices

- Organ systems: heart implants, artificial pancreas systems, smart stents, cochlear implants for individuals with hearing loss, artificial retina implants
- IoT-based prosthetic limb systems
- Neurological IoB solutions: brain-computer interfaces (BCI) with implantable sensors, deep brain stimulation solutions, seizure monitors
- Digital pills for non-invasive diagnostic procedures and medication intake monitoring

Advantages

- 24/7 patient monitoring
- Non-invasive diagnostics
- Improved QoL
- Precision medicine
- Personalized health plans.

Sensors Converge

IoT and IoB: Challenges

Privacy: collecting, analyzing, and using physiological, behavioral, and biometric data

- IoT devices can track body parameters – walking, working, cardiac, sleep, menstrual cycle, etc. Implication related to accessing these data poses a serious challenge.
- Biometric devices – data from devices such as at the airport, implantable cardiac devices, fingerprint pattern readers, and arm motion trackers (especially for warehouse workers).

Security

- IoB devices have the same security vulnerability as IoTs. The IP-based cameras have been hacked and have fallen victim to malware attacks. vulnerabilities may span cumbersome software updates installation processes, hard-coded and easy-to-guess passwords, the use of insecure or outdated software and hardware components, and a failure to encrypt data. Personal and biometrics data breach through IoTs needs better security. Also, a comprehensive IoB cybersecurity framework needs to be implemented by NIST and FDA.

Ethics

- Without proper regulations, the IoBs might, inadvertently, monitor other people surrounding the user, which violates their privacy. Also, healthcare providers and insurance companies may (or already) incorporate wearable data into treatment plans and health coverage.

Sensors Converge

Algorithmic Machine Learning

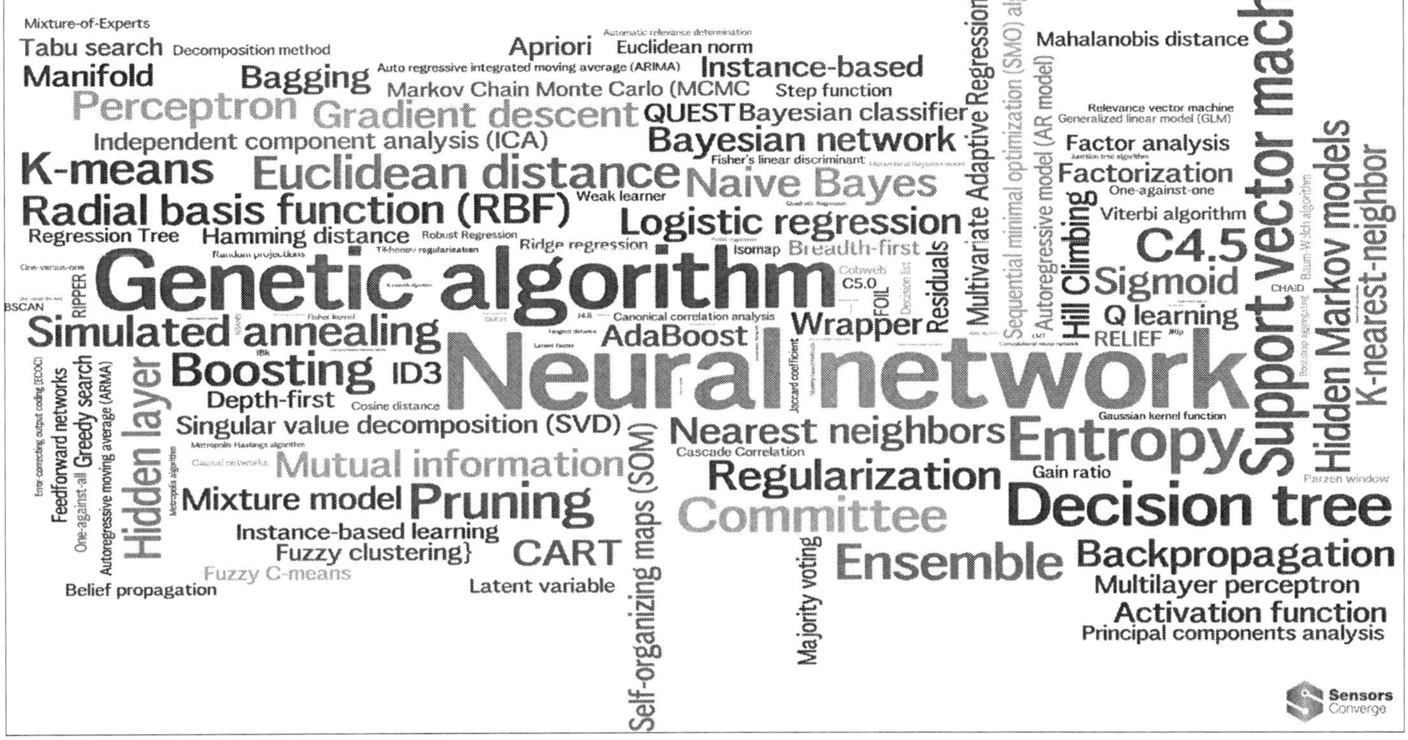

Sensors Converge

Algorithmic Data Analysis and Interpretation – AI, ML, DI, VR

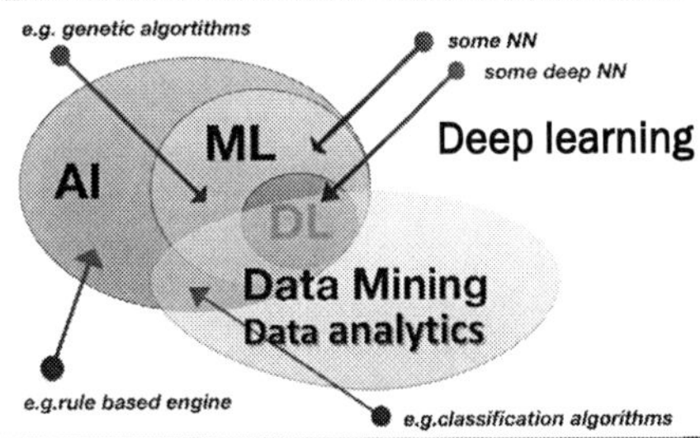

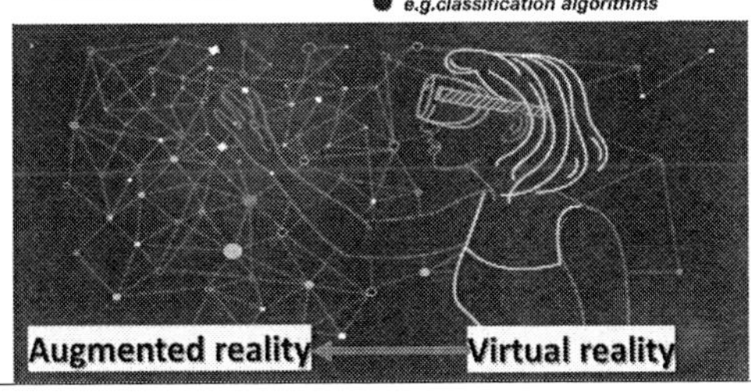

Artificial intelligence holds the potential to transform how brands market their data across networks, such as - Facebook, Instagram, Twitter, and LinkedIn. It can automate many tedious tasks related to social media management, and it can even do social media monitoring at large scale.

Automation – AI takes up the role of delivering your content to your customers. Some of the tasks undertaken are social engagement, scheduling, analytical tracking, etc.

Performance Measurement – AI technology helps marketers review their performances. Be it their social media reach, customer engagement, or social insights, it can collect data to help you review your performance. For example, Hootsuite, an AI technology, allows you to gain insight into your customer preferences.

Optimized Content – Since AI technology can optimize social media content with machine learning, it optimizes and displays the content according to your preference pattern.

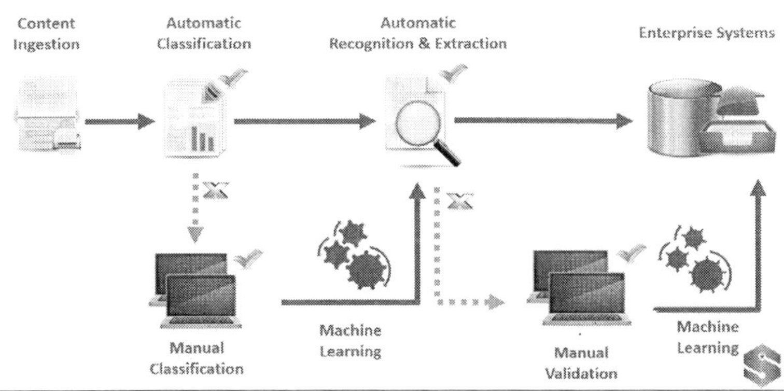

Sensors Converge

Application of AI, DL, ML in Defense

- Animal research that translates to operational readiness
- Human performance optimization – predictive intelligence for over-training/overreaching
  - Apps in TBI, muscle failure during endurance (bonking), infection, sleep, nutrition, and behavior
- Use of AI in how outside entities work within secure environments
- AI in surgery in the austere environment
- TBI – use of neuro optometry and neuro radiology – Intrepid emergency center
- Biomarkers/physiological response
- Quantum computing in Data security.
- AI in OODA loop

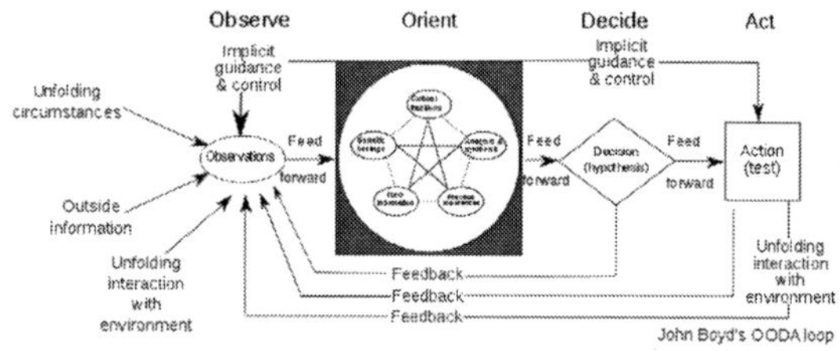

Notes taken on 09/29/2021

Sensors Converge

Use of UAVSP in Power Grid, Transport, Hydrology etc.

- ❑ Railroads
- ➢ Track alignment
- ➢ Track surface integrity
- ➢ Track wear and tear
- ➢ Bridge inspection
- ➢ Telecommunication antenna
- ➢ Corridor vegetation encroachment
- ➢ Physical and mechanical threat security
- ➢ Air quality monitoring
- ➢ Spill and Environment monitoring
- ➢ Facilities management
- ➢ Construction progress reporting
- ❑ Power Grid
- ➢ Many examples
- ❑ Hydrology
- ➢ Many Examples

Sensors Converge

Use of UAVSP in Public Infrastructure

- Cases: Bridges, Dams, Tunnels, Highways, more...
  - Corrosion
  - Roadbed wear
  - Weather and flooding damage
  - Spillway cracks
  - Geologic site conditions
  - Hydrology
  - Emergence Preparedness documentation
  - Structural Stability
  - Vegetation encroachment
- Examples
  - Embedded sensor systems for load testing
  - Surface deflection
  - Environmental parameters
  - License Plate Readers
  - Cell phone tower ping recording
  - IR cameras (thermal imaging)
  - Real-Time Beyond Visual Line-of-Sight (BLOS)
  - Vehicle Reconnaissance System (VRS)
  - Black Hornet Personal Reconnaissance System (PRS

Oblique & NADIR Aerial Imagery

Wireless Sensor Network

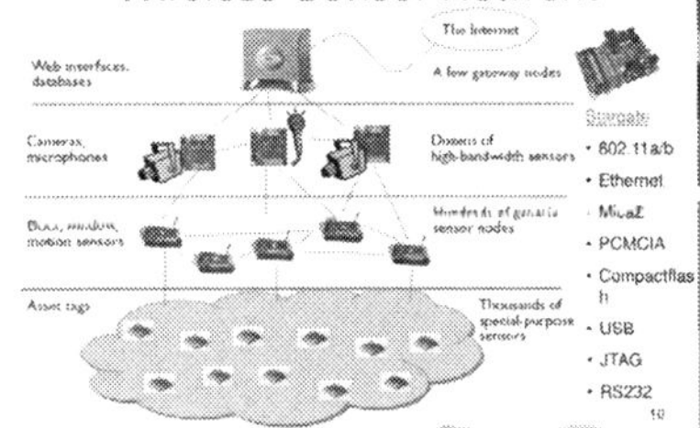

Sensors Converge

Rapid Risk Assessment/Verification Research

PC-based rapid risk assessment tool: TechFARM, ADAMS, NESTTS

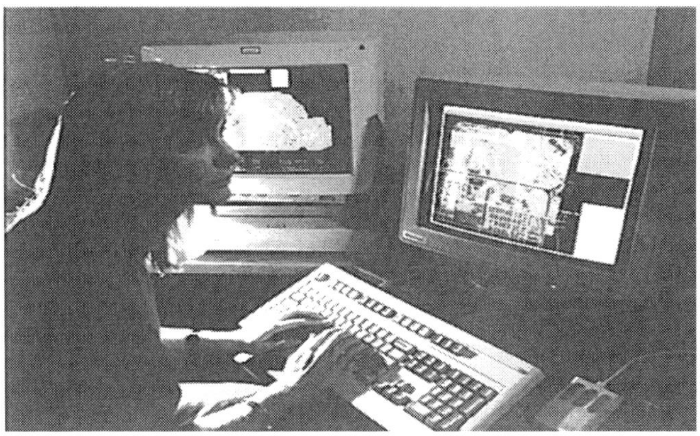

Verification center

- Online monitoring
- Water treatment
- Decontamination/filtration
- Water Management

ETV

- Threat scenario simulations and screening level risk analyses - TTX/FTX
- Threat Assessment
- Disease surveillance

Sensors Converge

Conclusions and Path Forward

- Paradigm shift using nexus of technological innovations
- Convergence of interdisciplinary fields to monitor risks in the structural integrity
- Smart and Connected Systems to enhance situational awareness
- Integration of new platforms, IoT & IoB
- Creation of new opportunities
- New challenges
  - ➢ privacy vs security
  - ➢ Licensing requirements – RPIC
  - ➢ Bandwidth – needs different frequency bandwidth and its integration with L3, G4, or G5.
  - ➢ Weight vs battery lifetime
  - ➢ Civil applications vs law enforcement
  - ➢ Medical Emergencies - jurisdiction

Sensors Converge

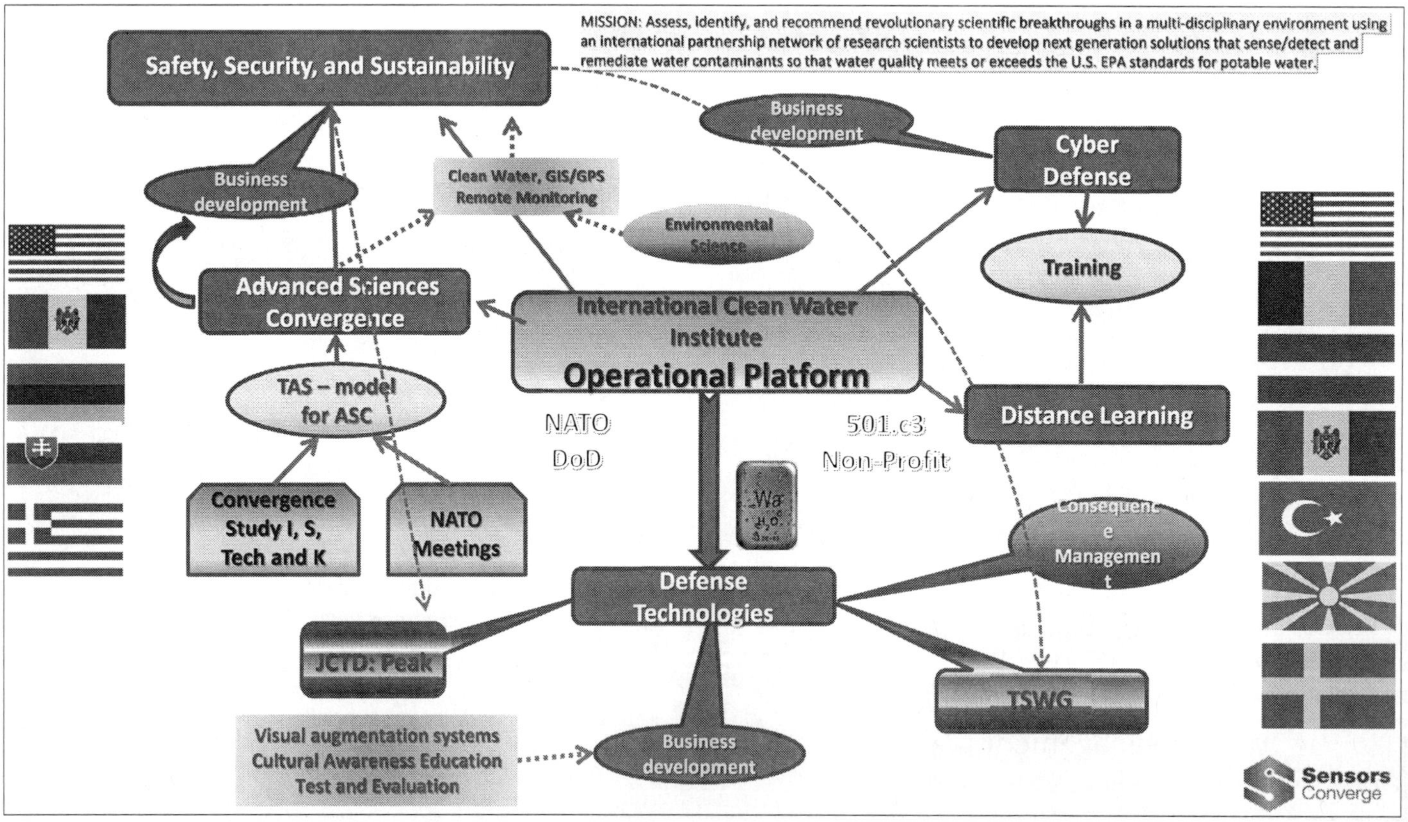

Contact

Ashok Vaseashta, Prof. Dr. Acad.

International Clean Water Institute, Manassas, VA USA

Transylvania University of Brasov, Brasov, ROMANIA

Ghitu Institute of the Electronic Engineering & Nanotechnologies, Chisinau, MOLDOVA

Email: prof.vaseashta@ieee.org

#SensorsConverge

Sensors Converge

LVR, a new linear sensor for use in extremes of temperature, radiation, chemical and other harsh environments, better performance than an LVDT and it's output is stable to <3 ppm/degree C.

Sensors Converge

LVR, a Temperature Independent Alternative to LVDT's in Harsh Environments

June 20–22, 2022 | Santa Clara, CA

#SensorsConverge

Current method for measurements in Harsh Environment

LVDT (Linear Variable Differential Transformer

History of 200 years and Michael Faraday

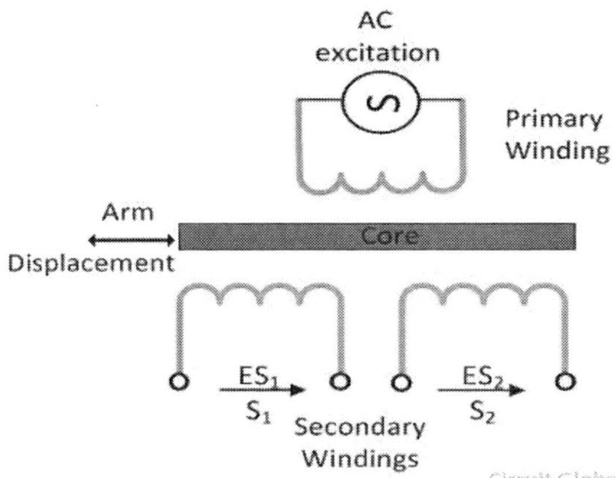

#SensorsConverge

Sensors Converge

Electronics is located away from Harsh Environment Requires 6 wires, 2 for each coil

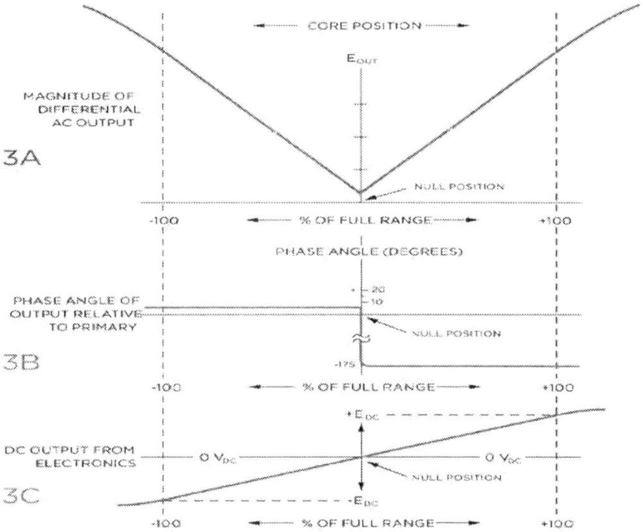

#SensorsConverge

Sensors Converge

Performance Specs for LVDT

- Accuracy at Null Point: 0.25% Full Scale
- Resolution at Null Point : 0.1% Full Scale
- Temperature stability at Null Point : 50ppm/Degree C
- Operational temperature -55 to 200 C

#SensorsConverge

Sensors Converge

LVR (Linear Variable Resonance) Sensor Electronics located outside Harsh Environment

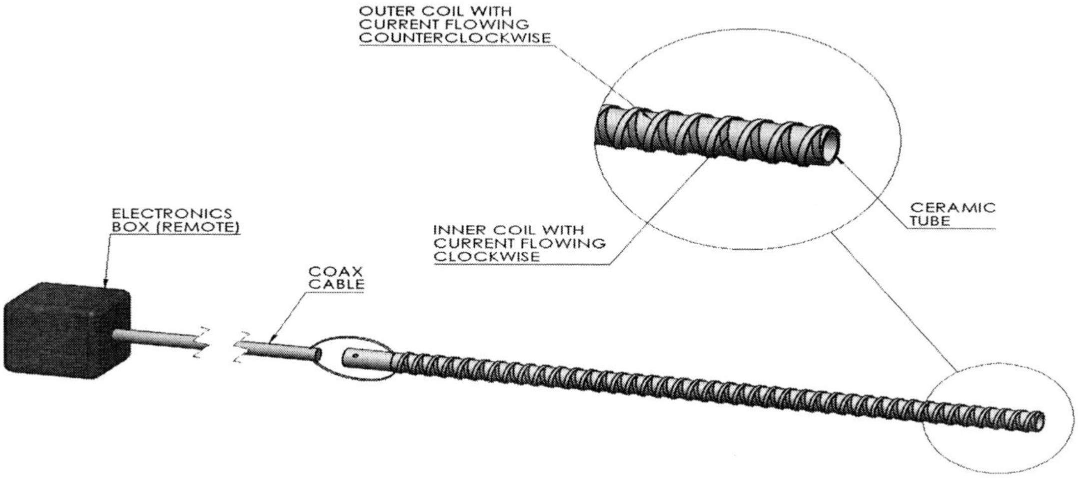

#SensorsConverge

Sensors Converge

X axis is magnetic field
Z axis is electric field
Curled fingers are direction of current flow
Magnetic fields of the two coils cancel but Electric fields add

Right Hand Rule

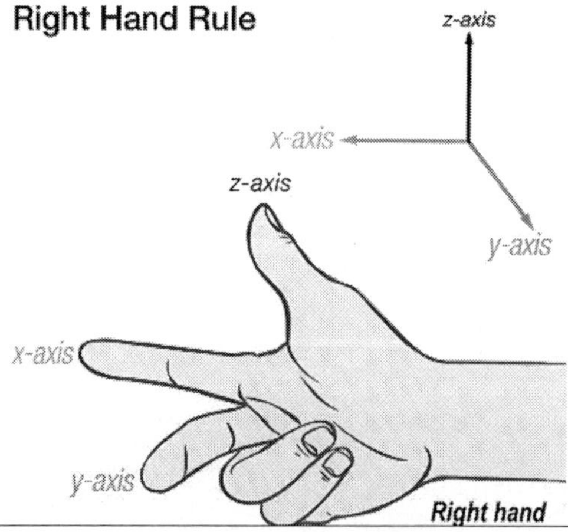

#SensorsConverge

Sensors Converge

200 refers to the coax cables between the coil and the electronic box

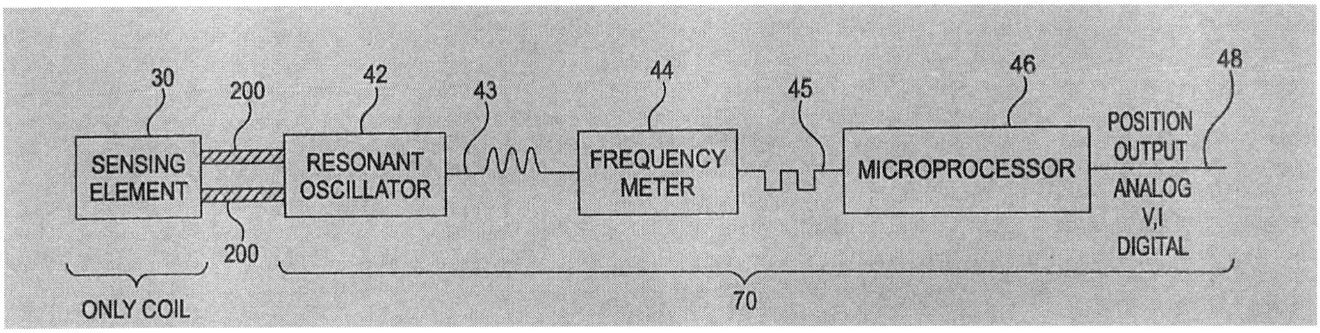

#SensorsConverge

Sensors Converge

Frequency formula depends on inductance (L) and capacitance (C) but not Resistance

Signal amplitude does change with temperature and could be a rough temperature sensor

Signal output is digital not analog

Resonant Frequency Formula

$$f = \frac{1}{2 \cdot \pi \cdot \sqrt{L \cdot C}}$$

where 'f' = frequency in hertz
'L' = inductance in henrys
'C' = capacitance in farads

#SensorsConverge

Sensors Converge

Electric Fields are short range

The long range magnetic fields are cancelled. Only short range remains.

#SensorsConverge

Sensors Converge

Frequency output is mapped against a calibrated source producing the results below

Perfect quadratic fit allows full calibration with only three data points
Note the large change in easily measured frequency

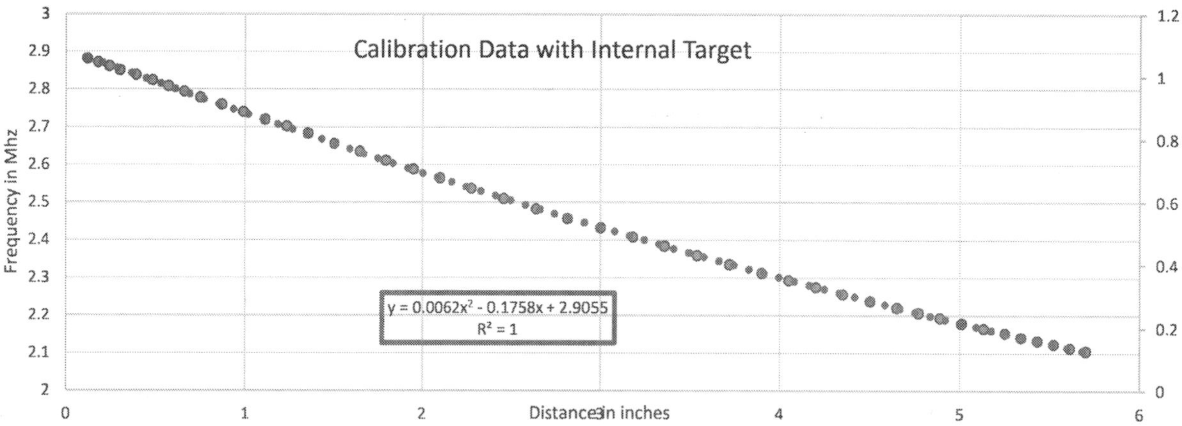

#SensorsConverge

Sensors Converge

Frequency change is measured by a frequency meter with a 1 hertz resolution out of a minimum change of 500 Khz

Accuracy is currently 0.1% FS will improve to 0.01%

Resolution is 0.01% FS will improve to 0.001%

Temperature range -70 C to 200 C

rated for 450 C but are awaiting new oven to test

Using Refractory metals could raise rating to >1000 C

Remaining small temperature effect is due to mechanical expansion (or contraction) of physical components

#SensorsConverge

Sensors Converge

Gap change between coil and target rod does change frequency and gives small temperature effect.

This is basis for use as a gap sensor.
This effect is eliminated with choice of Titanium for the target rod.

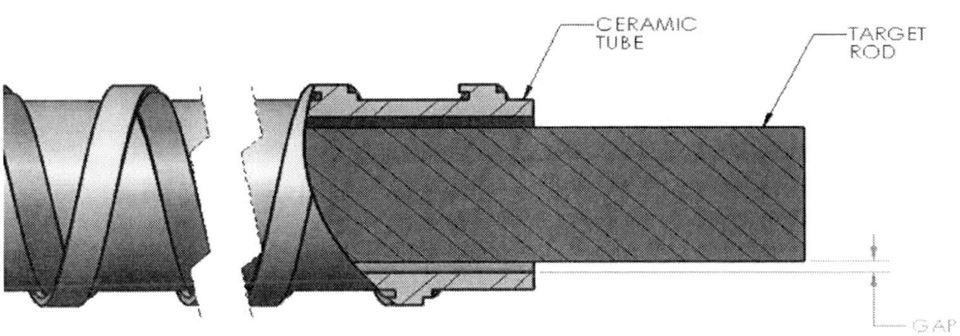

#SensorsConverge

Sensors Converge

- The position measurement changes by les than 0.1% FS over full range.
- This is equivalent to 3 ppm/degree C
- This data taken with a sensor that had only 0.1% FS accuracy

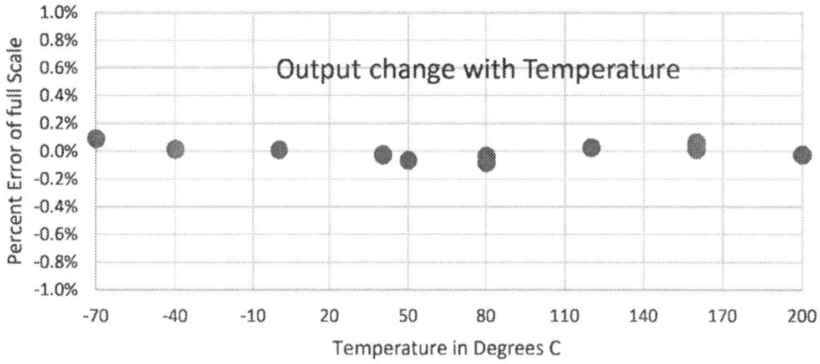

#SensorsConverge

Sensors Converge

Ti

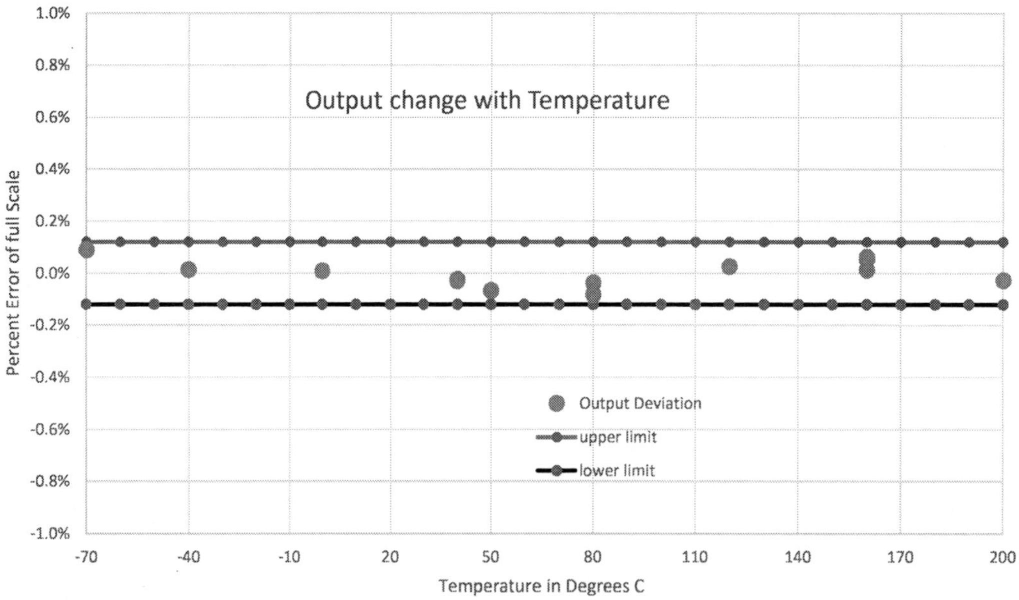

#Sens

Sensors Converge

Comparison of LVR to LVDT

	LVR	LVDT
Fundamental Output Signal	Digital	Analog
Operating Temperature Range (°C)	-70 to 200 C Optional to 450 C Possible to >1000 C	-55 to 200 C
Stroke to Length Maximum Length	2:1 > 8 feet	3:1 1-2 feet
Resolutionand	.001% FS	.1% FS
# of Wires to Electronics	2	6
Accuracy (Full-scale)	0.01% FS	0.25%FS
Temperature Sensitivity	<3ppm C	>50 ppm C
Requires Shielding from External Magnetic Fields	No	Yes

- LVR can also be used as a rotary sensor, a gap sensor and liquid level sensor

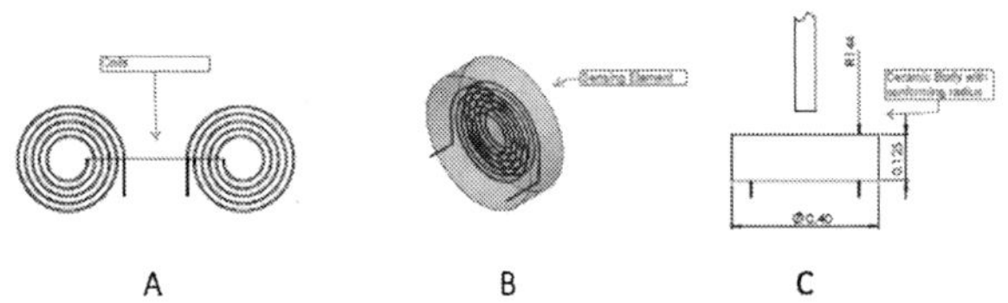

A. Diagram of windings of conductive coils
B. Sensing element of stacked conductive coils encased in ceramic body
C. Sensing element encased in jet engine wall with compressor blade in proximity

#SensorsConverge

Sensors Converge

Deviation of output from Linear

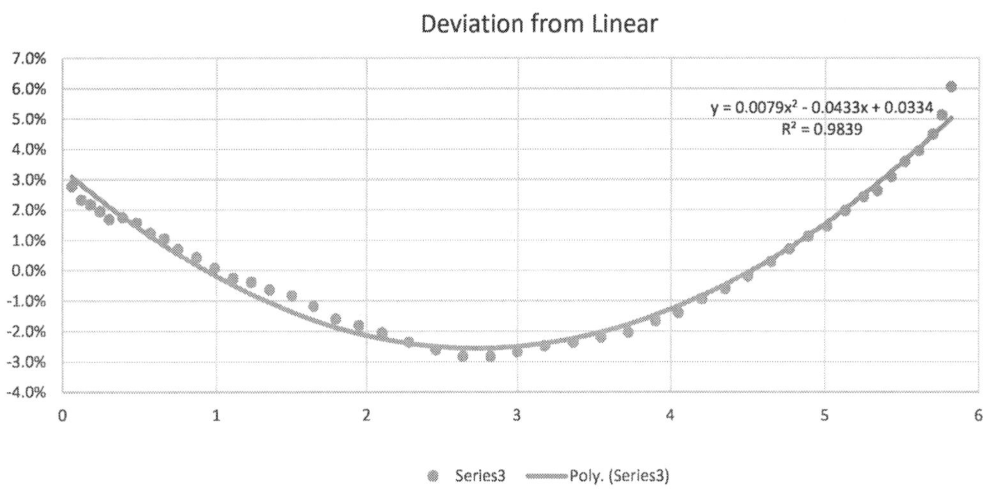

#SensorsConverge

Sensors Converge

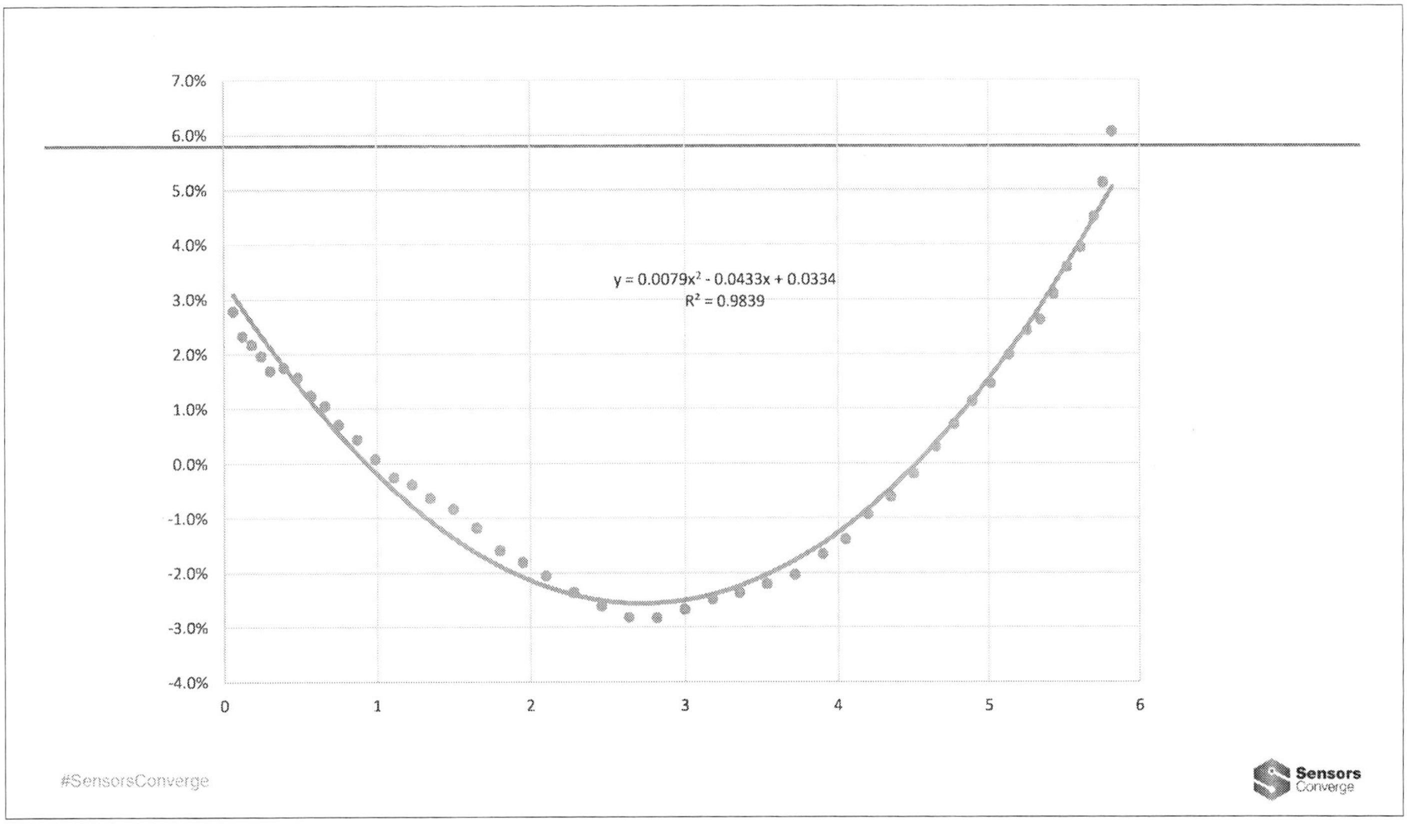
7.0%
6.0%
5.0%
4.0%
3.0%
2.0%
1.0%
0.0%
-1.0%
-2.0%
-3.0%
-4.0%
0
1
2
3
4
5
6
y = 0.0079x² - 0.0433x + 0.0334
R² = 0.9839
#SensorsConverge
Sensors Converge

Sensors Converge

June 20-22, 2023
Santa Clara, CA

www.sensorsconverge.com
#SensorsConverge

Interoperability & Standards

Smart Sensor and Actuator Standards and Interoperability for IoT, IIoT & CPS

Eugene Song, PhD
Electronics Engineer of the Internet of Things (IoT)
Devices and Infrastructure Group
National Institute of Standards and Technology

Smart Sensor & Actuator Standards and Interoperability for IoT/IIoT/CPS

1. **Sensors & Actuators Are Used Everywhere in IoT/IIoT/CPS Applications**
2. **What Are IoT/IIoT/CPS Requirements for Sensors and Actuators?**
3. **What Are Smart Sensors and Actuators?**
4. **IEEE 1451 Interface Standards for Smart Sensors & Actuators, and Networks**
5. **Key Takeaways**

1. Sensors & Actuators Are Used Everywhere

Aerospace

Automobile

Global Warming & Environmental Monitoring

Smart Cities

Sensors and Actuators Are Used Everywhere In IoT/IIoT/CPS Applications

Health Care

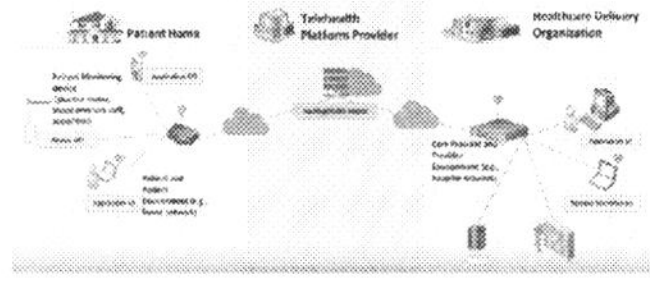

Smart Grid

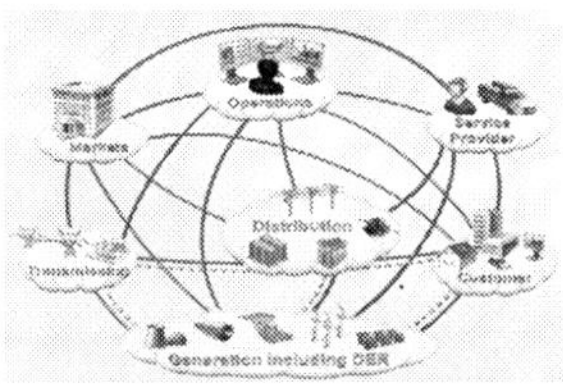

Smart Home and Building

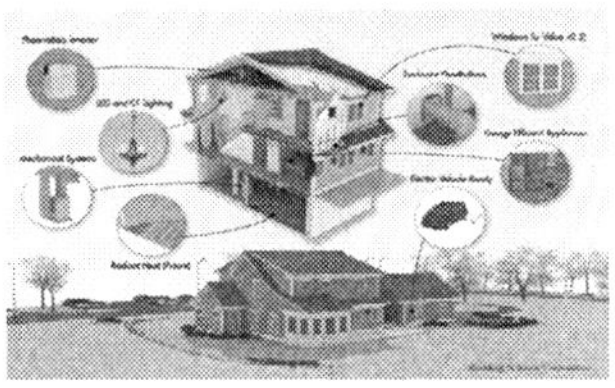

Industrial Automation/Manufacturing

#SensorsConverge

Sensors Converge

2. What Are IoT/IIoT/CPS Requirements for Sensors & Actuators?

IoT/IIoT/CPS Requirements for Sensors and Actuators:

- **Sensing/actuation capability**
- **Uniquely and globally identified**
- **Internet or network access**
- **Security and Privacy**
- **Time-aware & synchronization**
- **Location-awareness**
- **Self-description/identification**
- **Edge computing with AI**
- **Network communication protocols and interfaces to achieve interoperability**

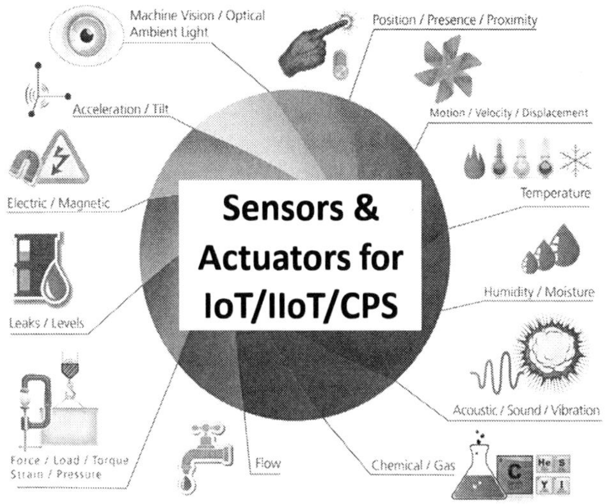

Source: https://www.postscapes.com/wp-content/uploads/2018/05/sensors.jpg

#SensorsConverge

Sensors Converge

2. What Are IoT/IIoT/CPS Requirements for Sensors & Actuators? (Cont'd)

Sensors and Actuators:

- Should be smart and intelligent enough using edge computing and AI
- Should adopt various standards:
  - Global identity
  - Security
  - Time synchronization
  - Network communication protocols and interfaces to achieve interoperability and plug & play.

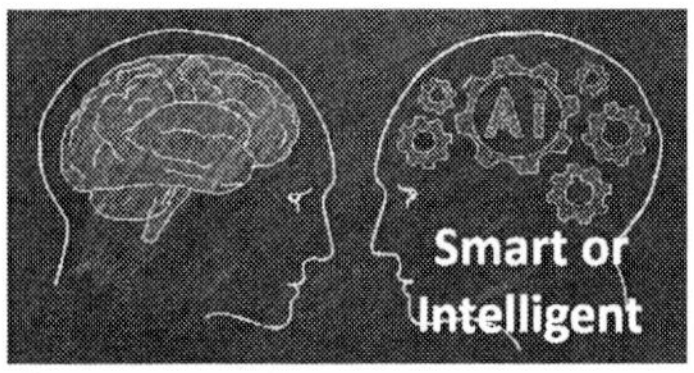

Source: https://www.industryweek.com/operations/continuous-improvement/article/21170962/dumb-smart-or-intelligent-whats-really-relevant-in-the-factory

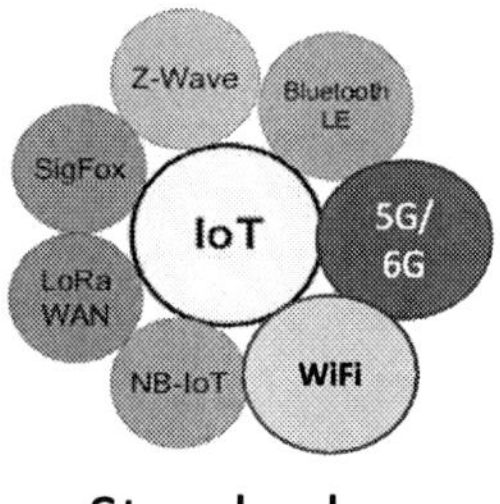

Standards

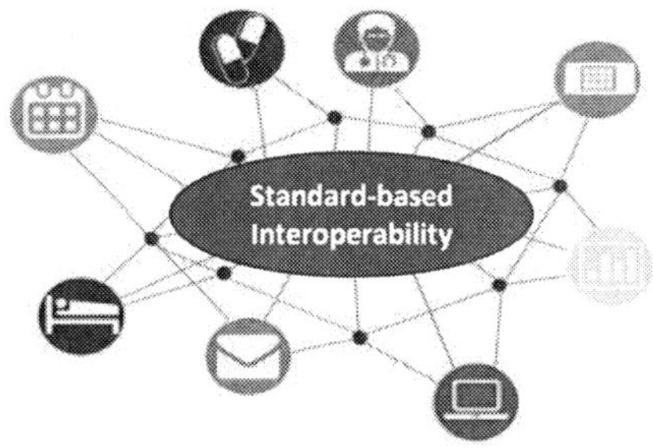

Plug & Play

#SensorsConverge

Sensors Converge

3. What Are Smart Sensors and Actuators?

What Is A Smart Sensor?

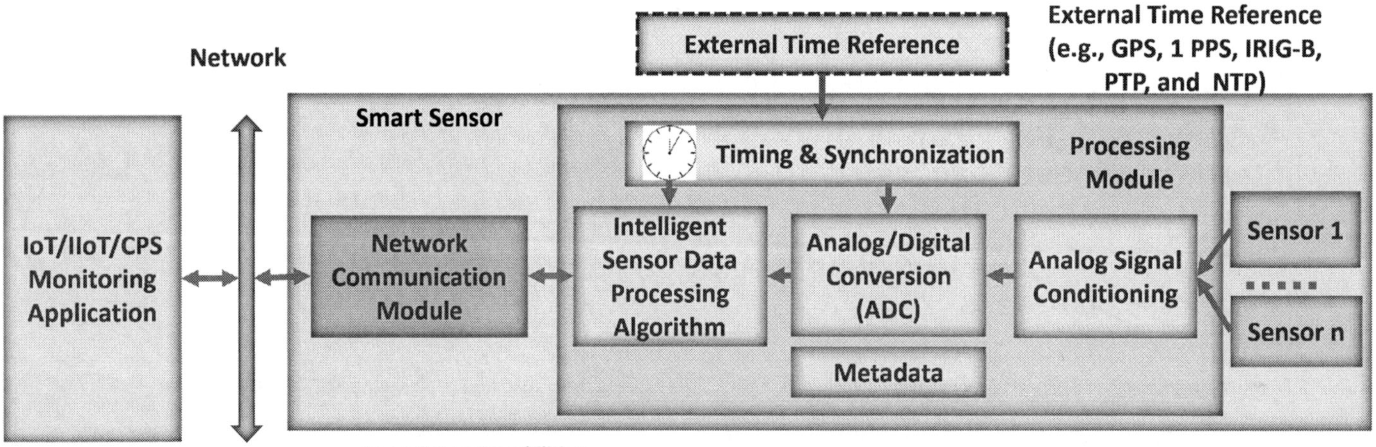

Smart Sensor Capabilities:

- Sensing
- Signal/Data Processing & Conversion
- Time & Synchronization
- Metadata
- Network Communication

#SensorsConverge

Sensors Converge

3. What Are Smart Sensors and Actuators? (Cont'd)

What Is A Smart Transducer (Sensors and/or Actuators)?

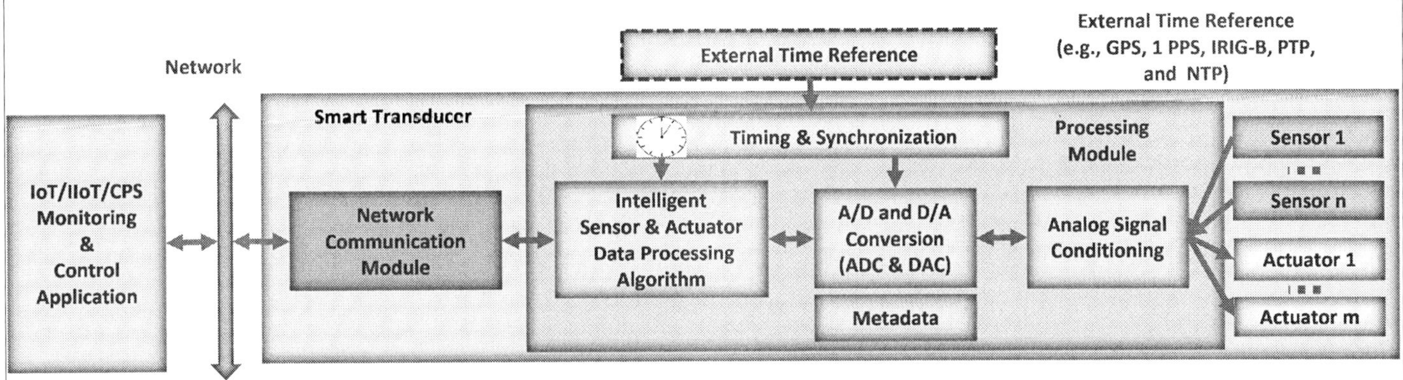

Smart Transducer (Sensor and/or Actuator) Capabilities:

- Sensing and/or Actuation
- Signal/Data Processing & Conversion
- Time & Synchronization
- Metadata
- Network Communication via Network Interface

4. IEEE 1451 Interfaces Standards for Smart Transducer (Sensor & Actuator) Networks

IEEE 1451-based Smart Sensor Networks

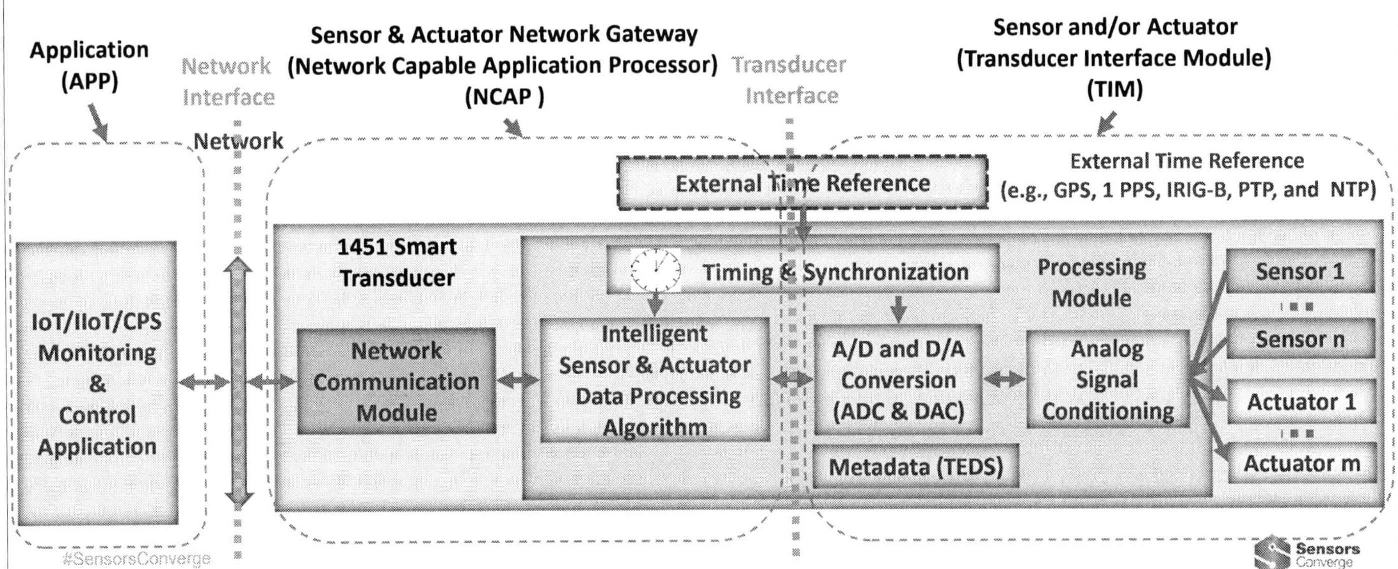

4. IEEE 1451 Interfaces Standards for Smart Transducer (Sensor & Actuator) Networks (Cont'd)

Reference Architecture for the Family of IEEE 1451 Standards

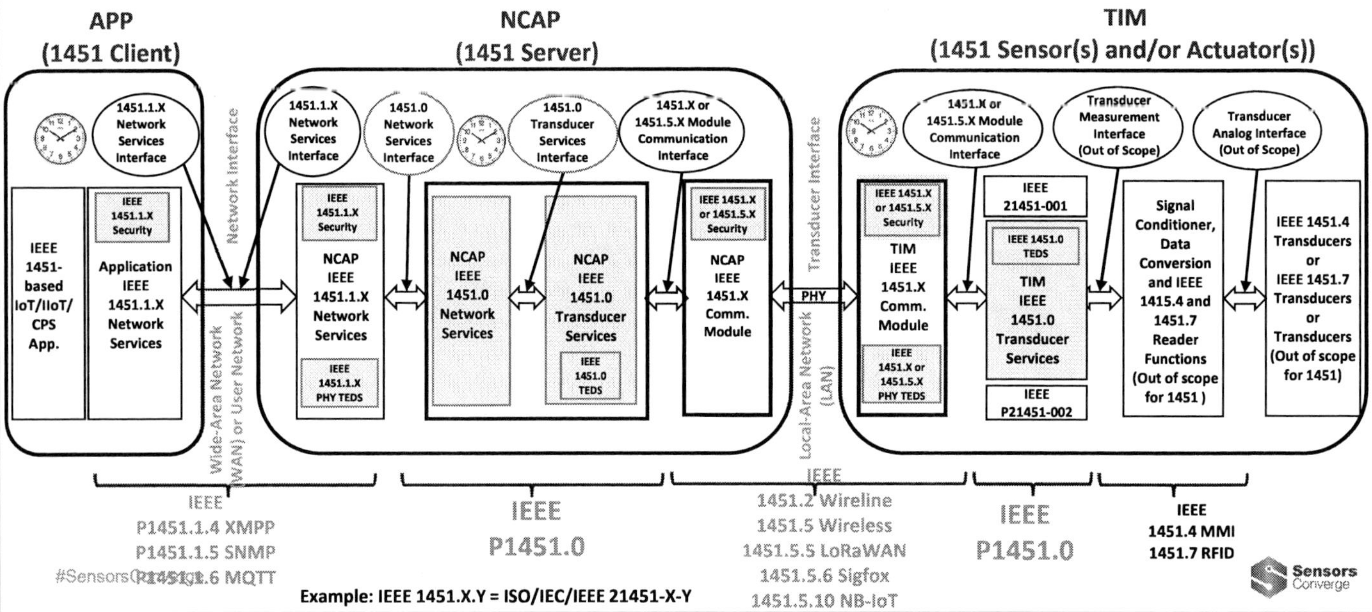

#SensorsConverge

Example: IEEE 1451.X.Y = ISO/IEC/IEEE 21451-X-Y

Sensors Converge

4. IEEE 1451 Interfaces Standards for Smart Transducer (Sensor & Actuator) Networks (Cont'd)

IEEE P1451.0 Standard Defines:

- Three devices: **APP, NCAP, and TIM**
- Network services command and reply messages **between APPs and NCAPs**
- Transducer services command and reply messages between NCAPs and TIMs
- Universal Unique Identification **(UUID)** for `appId`, `ncapId`, and `timId`
- Transducer Electronic Data Sheet (TEDS)
- Security foe WAN, LAN & WLAN
- Time Synchronization for WAN, LAN & WLAN

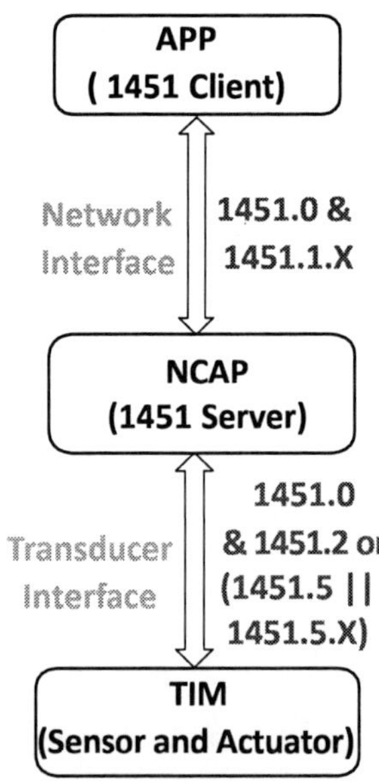

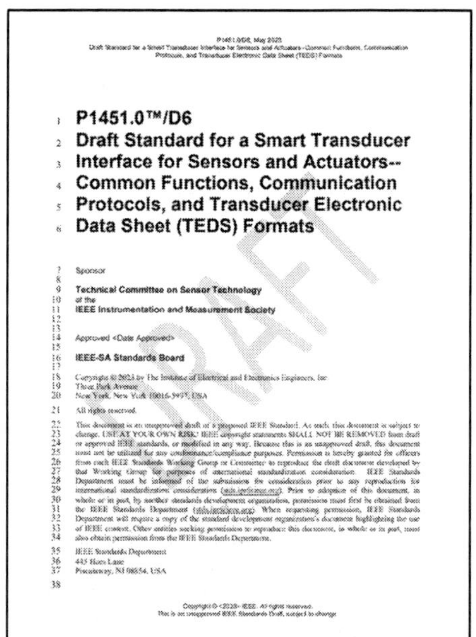
P1451.0™/D6
Draft Standard for a Smart Transducer Interface for Sensors and Actuators-- Common Functions, Communication Protocols, and Transducer Electronic Data Sheet (TEDS) Formats

Sponsor

Technical Committee on Sensor Technology
of the
IEEE Instrumentation and Measurement Society

Approved <Date Approved>

IEEE-SA Standards Board

#SensorsConverge

4. IEEE 1451 Interfaces Standards for Smart Transducer (Sensor & Actuator) Networks (Cont'd)

Universal Unique Identification (UUID)

- **The UUID establishes uniqueness by assembling an identification number comprising of manufacturer location and specific information, year and time of manufacture.**
- **UUID for APP (`appId`), NCAP (`ncapId`) and TIM (`timId`)**

Smart Sensor with UUID

```
struct UUID   {// 16 bytes      (128 bits)
OctetArray    geolocation;      //  6 bytes  (48 bits)
OctetArray    manufacturer;     //  3 bytes  (24 bits)
UInt16        year;             //  2 bytes  (16 bits)
OctetArray    time;             //  5 bytes  (40 Bits)
};
```

#SensorsConverge

Sensors Converge

4. IEEE 1451 Interfaces Standards for Smart Transducer (Sensor & Actuator) Networks (Cont'd)

- **Transducer Electronic Datasheet (TEDS):** a memory device attached to the transducer in a TIM, stores **transducer identification, measurement range, calibration, location, user and manufacture-related information**.
- **Self-description and Self-identification**

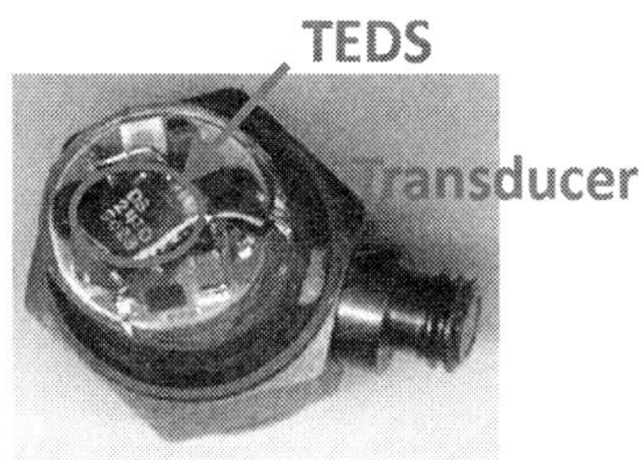

IEEE P1451.0 TEDS Classification:

Mandatory:
- Meta TEDS
- TransducerChannel TEDS

Optional:
- User's transducer name TEDS
- PHY TEDS
- Calibration TEDS
- Frequency Response TEDS
- Transfer Function TEDS
- Text based TEDS
- End user application specific TEDS
- Manufacturer-defined TEDS

Text based TEDS:
- Meta-Identification TEDS
- TransducerChannel Identification TEDS
- Calibration-Identification TEDS
- Commands TEDS
- Location and Title TEDS
- Geographic Location TEDS
- Security TEDS
- Time Synchronization TEDS


```
<?xml version="1.0" encoding="UTF-8"?>
<xs:schema
xmlns:stml="http://grouper.ieee.org/groups/1451/0/1451HTTPAPI"
xmlns:xs="http://www.w3.org/2001/XMLSchema"
targetNamespace="http://grouper.ieee.org/groups/1451/0/1451HTTPAPI"
elementFormDefault="qualified" attributeFormDefault="unqualified">
   <xs:include schemaLocation="SmartTransducerDataModel.xsd"/>
   <xs:element name="MetaIdTEDSDataBlock">
      <xs:annotation>
         <xs:documentation>This is the schema for the contents of the
data block for the Meta Identification TEDS</xs:documentation>
      </xs:annotation>
      <xs:complexType>
         <xs:sequence>
            <xs:element name="manufacturerid" type="stml:_String"
minOccurs="0"/>
            <xs:element name="ModelNo" type="stml:_String"
minOccurs="0"/>
            <xs:element name="ProductDescription" type="stml:_String"
minOccurs="0"/>
            <xs:element name="serialNo" type="stml:_String"
minOccurs="0"/>
            <xs:element name="dateCode" type="stml:_String"
minOccurs="0"/>
            <xs:element name="versionCode" type="stml:_String"
minOccurs="0"/>
         </xs:sequence>
      </xs:complexType>
   </xs:element>
</xs:schema>
```


#SensorsConverge

Sensors Converge

4. IEEE 1451 Interfaces Standards for Smart Transducer (Sensor & Actuator) Networks (Cont'd)

Security & Security TEDS for IEEE 1451.0-based Sensor Networks

Security Policy:

- Encryption
- Authentication
- Authorization

Define Six Levels of Security:

N: none
A: Encry
B: Authen
C: Encry + Authen
D: Authen + Author
E: Encry + Authen + Author

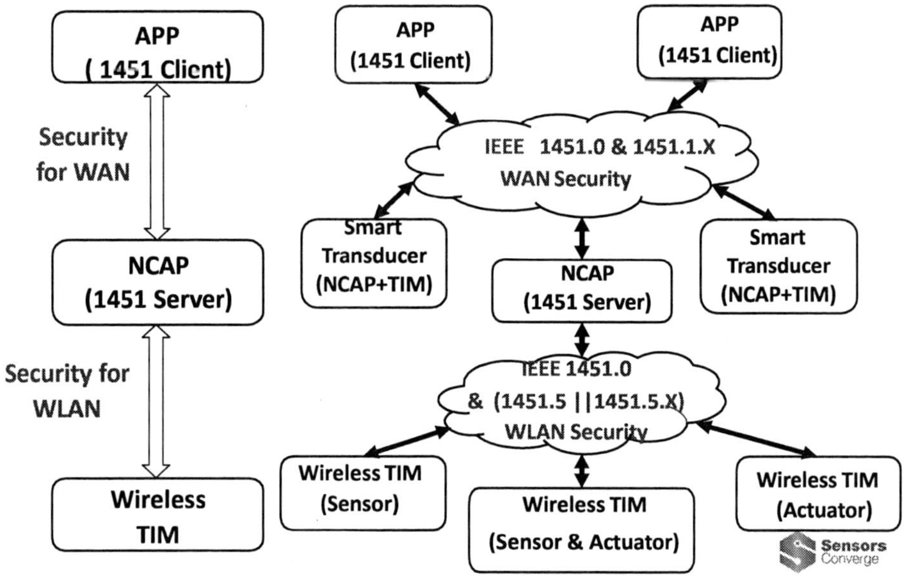

#SensorsConverge

Sensors Converge

4. IEEE 1451 Interfaces Standards for Smart Transducer (Sensor & Actuator) Networks (Cont'd)

Time Synchronization and TimeSync TEDS for IEEE 1451.0-based Sensor Networks

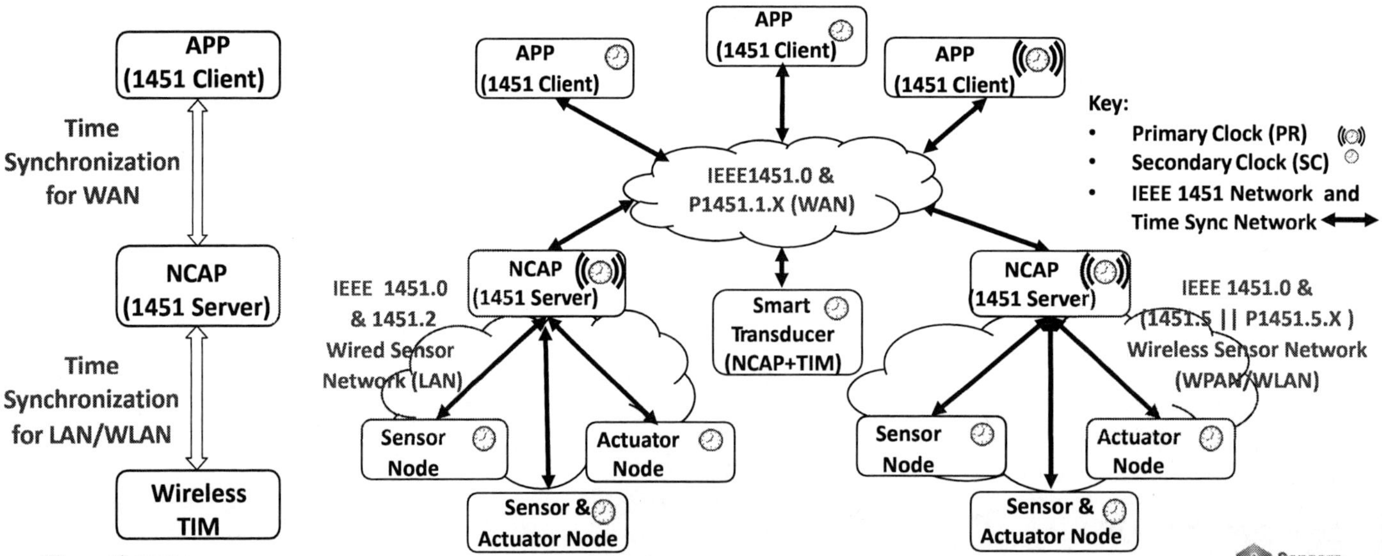

#SensorsConverge

Sensors Converge

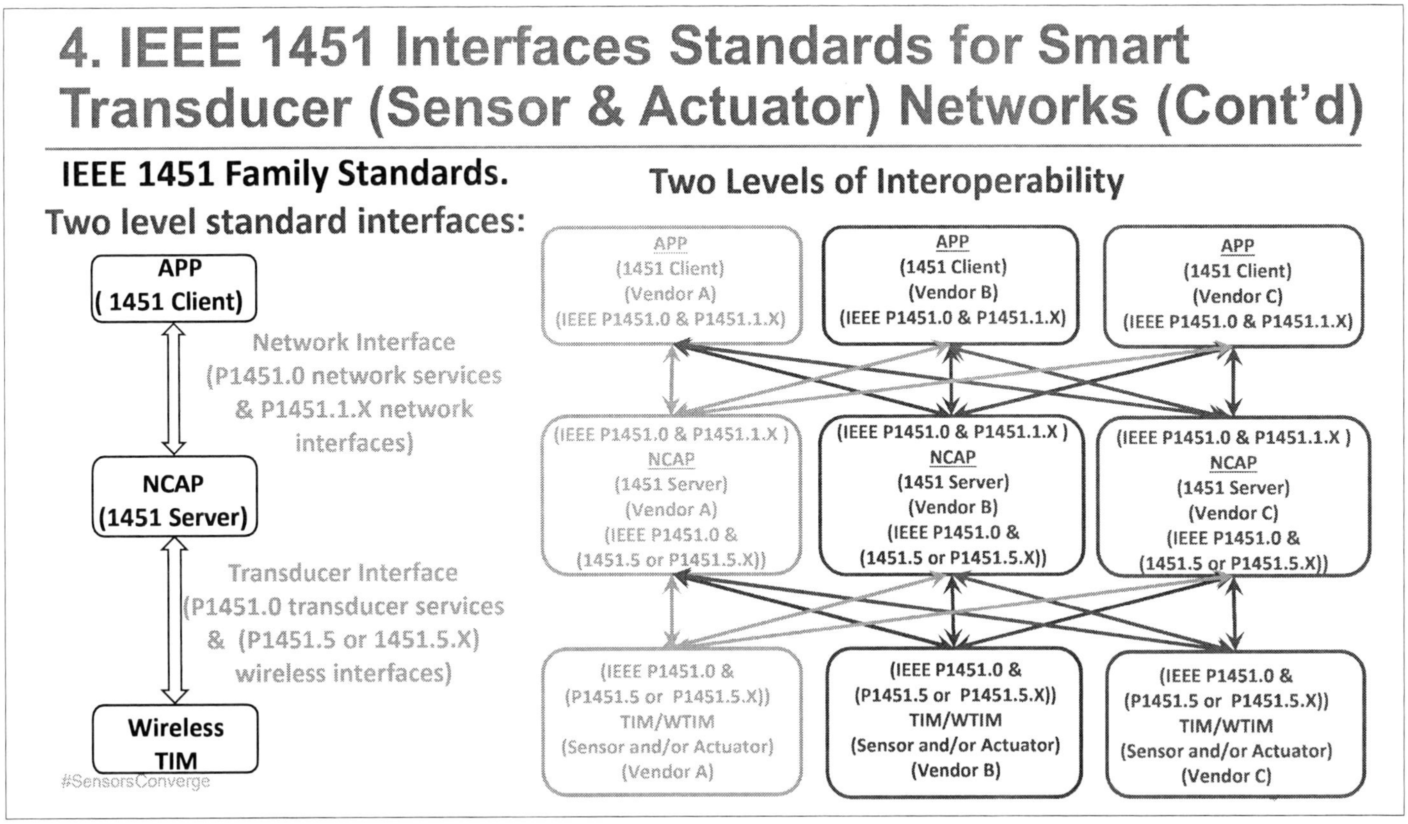
4. IEEE 1451 Interfaces Standards for Smart Transducer (Sensor & Actuator) Networks (Cont'd)
IEEE 1451 Family Standards.
Two level standard interfaces:
APP (1451 Client)
Network Interface (P1451.0 network services & P1451.1.X network interfaces)
NCAP (1451 Server)
Transducer Interface (P1451.0 transducer services & (P1451.5 or 1451.5.X) wireless interfaces)
Wireless TIM
#SensorsConverge
Two Levels of Interoperability
APP (1451 Client) (Vendor A) (IEEE P1451.0 & P1451.1.X)
APP (1451 Client) (Vendor B) (IEEE P1451.0 & P1451.1.X)
APP (1451 Client) (Vendor C) (IEEE P1451.0 & P1451.1.X)
(IEEE P1451.0 & P1451.1.X) NCAP (1451 Server) (Vendor A) (IEEE P1451.0 & (1451.5 or P1451.5.X))
(IEEE P1451.0 & P1451.1.X) NCAP (1451 Server) (Vendor B) (IEEE P1451.0 & (1451.5 or P1451.5.X))
(IEEE P1451.0 & P1451.1.X) NCAP (1451 Server) (Vendor C) (IEEE P1451.0 & (1451.5 or P1451.5.X))
(IEEE P1451.0 & (P1451.5 or P1451.5.X)) TIM/WTIM (Sensor and/or Actuator) (Vendor A)
(IEEE P1451.0 & (P1451.5 or P1451.5.X)) TIM/WTIM (Sensor and/or Actuator) (Vendor B)
(IEEE P1451.0 & (P1451.5 or P1451.5.X)) TIM/WTIM (Sensor and/or Actuator) (Vendor C)

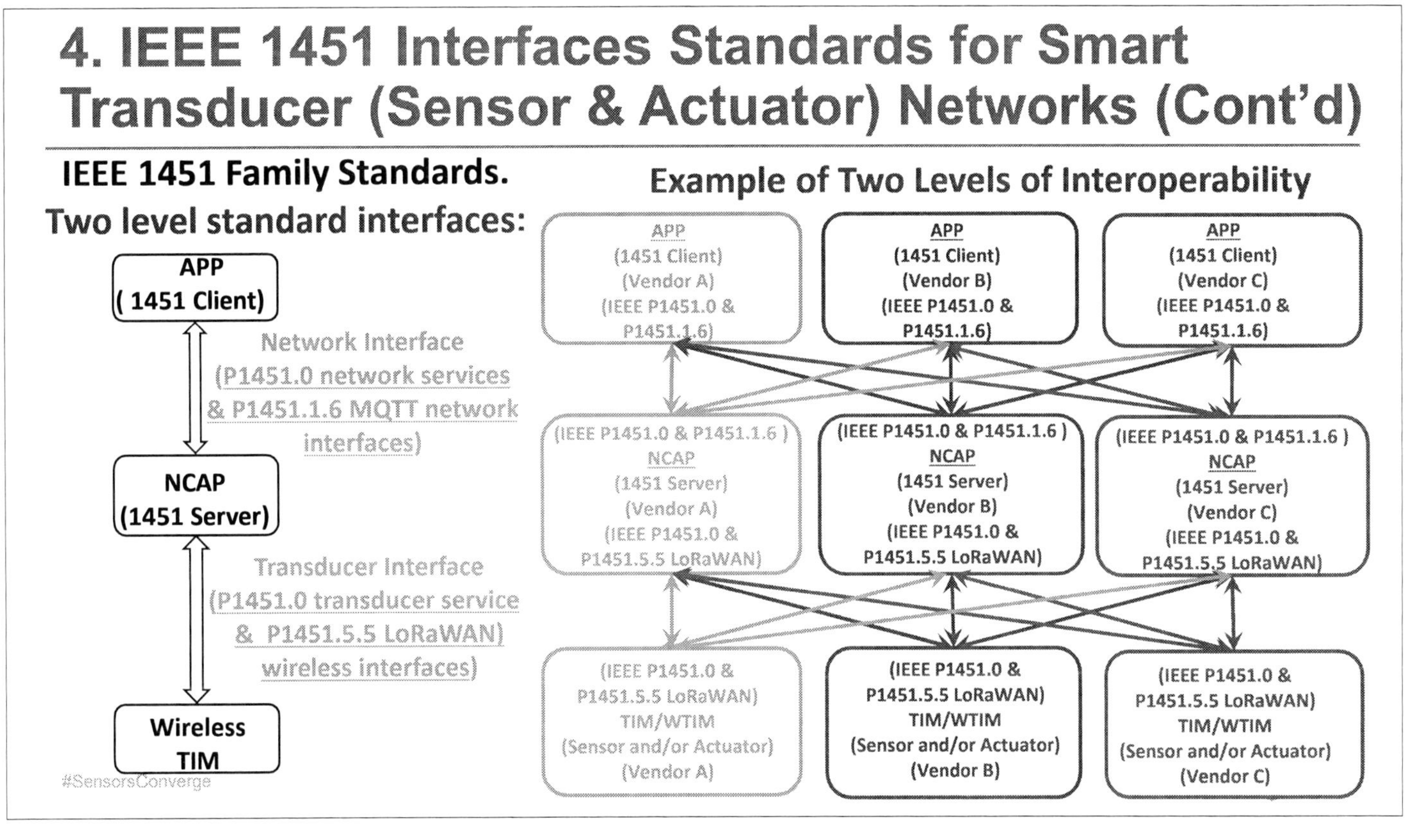
4. IEEE 1451 Interfaces Standards for Smart Transducer (Sensor & Actuator) Networks (Cont'd)
IEEE 1451 Family Standards.
Two level standard interfaces:
APP (1451 Client)
Network Interface (P1451.0 network services & P1451.1.6 MQTT network interfaces)
NCAP (1451 Server)
Transducer Interface (P1451.0 transducer service & P1451.5.5 LoRaWAN) wireless interfaces)
Wireless TIM
#SensorsConverge
Example of Two Levels of Interoperability
APP (1451 Client) (Vendor A) (IEEE P1451.0 & P1451.1.6)
APP (1451 Client) (Vendor B) (IEEE P1451.0 & P1451.1.6)
APP (1451 Client) (Vendor C) (IEEE P1451.0 & P1451.1.6)
(IEEE P1451.0 & P1451.1.6) NCAP (1451 Server) (Vendor A) (IEEE P1451.0 & P1451.5.5 LoRaWAN)
(IEEE P1451.0 & P1451.1.6) NCAP (1451 Server) (Vendor B) (IEEE P1451.0 & P1451.5.5 LoRaWAN)
(IEEE P1451.0 & P1451.1.6) NCAP (1451 Server) (Vendor C) (IEEE P1451.0 & P1451.5.5 LoRaWAN)
(IEEE P1451.0 & P1451.5.5 LoRaWAN) TIM/WTIM (Sensor and/or Actuator) (Vendor A)
(IEEE P1451.0 & P1451.5.5 LoRaWAN) TIM/WTIM (Sensor and/or Actuator) (Vendor B)
(IEEE P1451.0 & P1451.5.5 LoRaWAN) TIM/WTIM (Sensor and/or Actuator) (Vendor C)

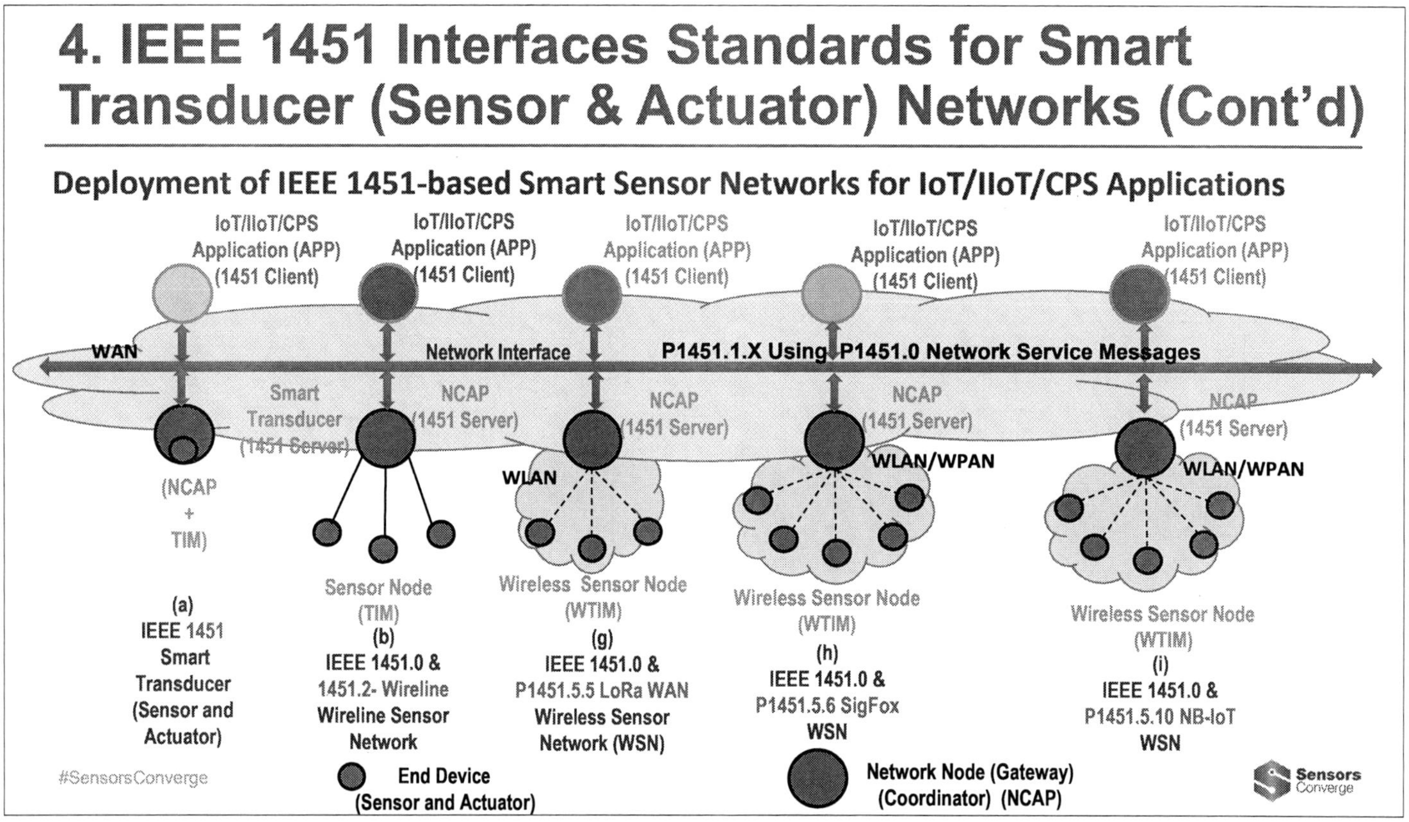
4. IEEE 1451 Interfaces Standards for Smart Transducer (Sensor & Actuator) Networks (Cont'd)
Deployment of IEEE 1451-based Smart Sensor Networks for IoT/IIoT/CPS Applications
IoT/IIoT/CPS Application (APP) (1451 Client)
WAN
Network Interface
P1451.1.X Using P1451.0 Network Service Messages
Smart Transducer (1451 Server)
NCAP (1451 Server)
(NCAP + TIM)
WLAN
WLAN/WPAN
Sensor Node (TIM)
Wireless Sensor Node (WTIM)
(a) IEEE 1451 Smart Transducer (Sensor and Actuator)
(b) IEEE 1451.0 & 1451.2- Wireline Wireline Sensor Network
(g) IEEE 1451.0 & P1451.5.5 LoRa WAN Wireless Sensor Network (WSN)
(h) IEEE 1451.0 & P1451.5.6 SigFox WSN
(i) IEEE 1451.0 & P1451.5.10 NB-IoT WSN
#SensorsConverge
End Device (Sensor and Actuator)
Network Node (Gateway) (Coordinator) (NCAP)
Sensors Converge

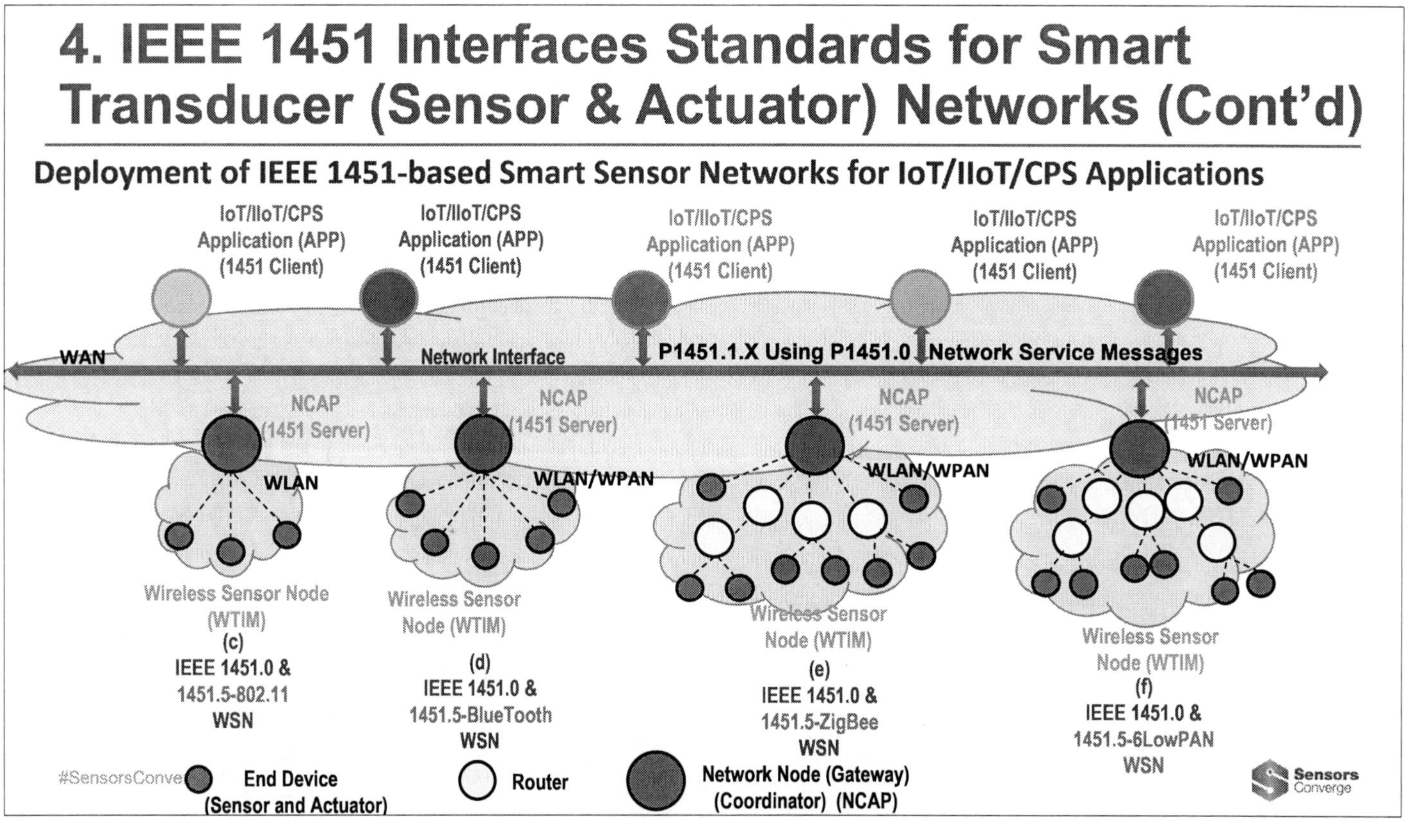
4. IEEE 1451 Interfaces Standards for Smart Transducer (Sensor & Actuator) Networks (Cont'd)
Deployment of IEEE 1451-based Smart Sensor Networks for IoT/IIoT/CPS Applications
IoT/IIoT/CPS Application (APP) (1451 Client)
WAN
Network Interface
P1451.1.X Using P1451.0 Network Service Messages
NCAP (1451 Server)
WLAN
WLAN/WPAN
Wireless Sensor Node (WTIM)
(c) IEEE 1451.0 & 1451.5-802.11 WSN
(d) IEEE 1451.0 & 1451.5-BlueTooth WSN
(e) IEEE 1451.0 & 1451.5-ZigBee WSN
(f) IEEE 1451.0 & 1451.5-6LowPAN WSN
#SensorsConve
End Device (Sensor and Actuator)
Router
Network Node (Gateway) (Coordinator) (NCAP)
Sensors Converge

4. IEEE 1451 Interfaces Standards for Smart Transducer (Sensor & Actuator) Networks (Cont'd)

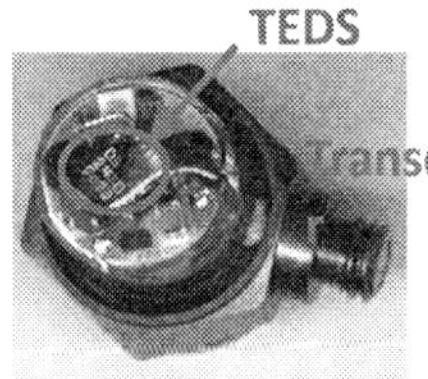

Benefits of IEEE P1451.0 to Manufacturers and End Users

Benefits of IEEE 1451 :

- Sensor data interoperability **(network and sensor levels) and** plug-and-play
- Global Identification **using UUID**
- Self-description **&** self-identification **of sensors or actuators based on TEDS & UUID**
- Security for WAN (network interface), Wireless LAN (WLAN) (transducer interface)
- Time synchronization for WAN, LAN & WLAN
- Long-term self-documentation **based on TEDS**
- Reduce human errors **(no need to enter data manually)**
- Ease field installation, upgrade, and maintenance **based on TEDS, Plug & Play**
- Reduce the total–life cycle costs **of sensor networks**
- ...

#SensorsConverge

Sensors Converge

5. Key Takeaways

IEEE 1451 Standards Support:

✓UUID for APP, NCAP, and TIM
✓TEDS (Metadata)
✓Network services (messages) and transducer services (messages)
✓Security for WAN, and WLAN
✓Time synchronization for WAN, and LAN & WLAN
✓Sensing and actuation functions for IoT, IIoT and CPS
✓Wireline and wireless sensor networks for IoT/IIoT/CPS
✓Standards-based sensor data interoperability and plug & play

A strong business case for using IEEE 1451 standards:

✓Reduce human errors **by using TEDS**
✓Improve (enhance) and maintain sensor measurement accuracy **by using calibration TEDS data**
✓Ease field installation, upgrade, and maintenance **(by plug & play)**
✓Reduce the total life-cycle costs **of sensor networks**

#SensorsConverge

Sensors Converge

Questions?

Contact Info:
Eugene Song Ph.D.
Electronics Engineer
Chair of IEEE P1451.0 WG
email: eugene.song@nist.gov

Kang Lee
Chair of IEEE I&M TC9, IEEE 1451 Family Standards
email: kang.lee@nist.gov

#SensorsConverge

Sensors Converge

Backup Slides

#SensorsConverge

Sensors Converge

What Is Interoperability?

Interoperability (according to IEEE):
The ability of two or more systems or components to exchange information and to use the information that has been exchanged.

Interoperability :
The ability of two or more systems to exchange information and to use the information that has been exchanged through a standard communication protocol in order to achieve the specific functions or goals.

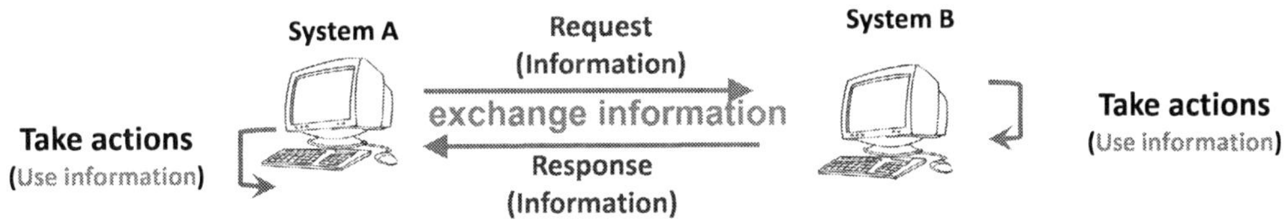

#SensorsConverge

Sensors Converge

What Are Challenges of Sensors & Actuators in IoT/IIoT/CPS Applications?

- **Various wireline and wireless connectivity**
- **Wireless network performances (e.g., bandwidth, latency, packet loss)**
- **Spectrum coverage, sharing, and interference**
- **Cybersecurity and privacy**
- **Scalability**
- **Power consumption/energy efficiency**
- **Time synchronization**
- **Standardization & interoperability**

#SensorsConverge

Sensors Converge

What Are Challenges of Sensors & Actuators in IoT/IIoT/CPS Applications?

Standardization & Interoperability

1. **Heterogeneity of standards and protocols**
2. **The lack of standard implementation**
   - **Limited resources to implement standards**
   - **Lack of implementing standards for some emerging technologies and new applications**
3. **Lack of standards harmonization**
4. **Interoperability test and plugfest**
5. **Lack of fundamental methodologies and software tools**
   - **Interoperability modeling**
   - **Interoperability measurement and assessment**

#SensorsConverge

Sensors Converge

Sensors & Actuators Are Used Everywhere

Internet of Things (IoT) is a network that connects uniquely identifiable "Things" to the Internet. (IEEE)

IEEE IoT Architecture

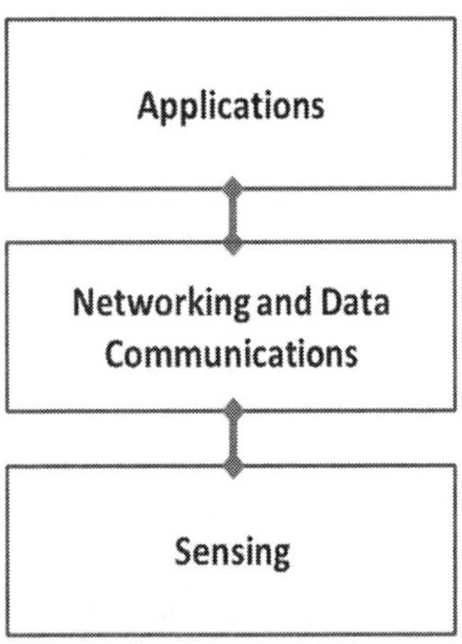

Source: https://iot.ieee.org/images/files/pdf/IEEE_IoT_Towards_Definition_Internet_of_Things_Revision1_27MAY15.pdf

IoT vs CPS:

- IoT is mainly **concerned about unique identification, connecting with the Internet and accessibility of "things."**
- CPS is mainly concerned about the **collaborative activities between cyber and physical system through sensing and actuation**
- **CPS uses IoT systems** to achieve the collaborative work of the distributed systems.

Cyber-physical systems (CPS) are smart systems that include engineered interacting networks of physical and computational components. (NIST)

NIST CPS Conceptual Model

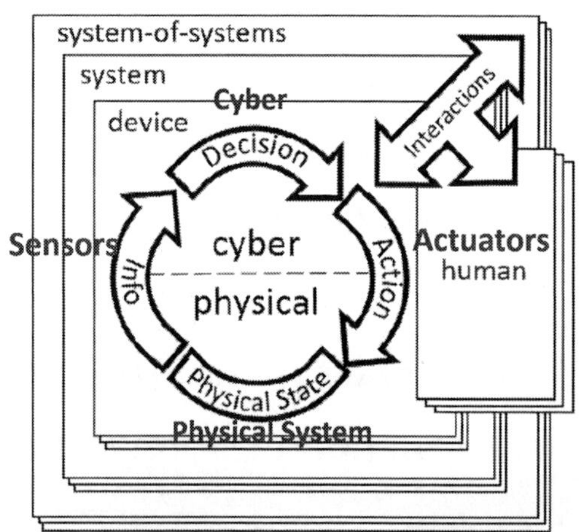

Source: https://pages.nist.gov/cpspwg/

#SensorsConverge 26

Sensors Converge

IEEE 1451 Interfaces Standards for Smart Transducer (Sensor & Actuator) Networks

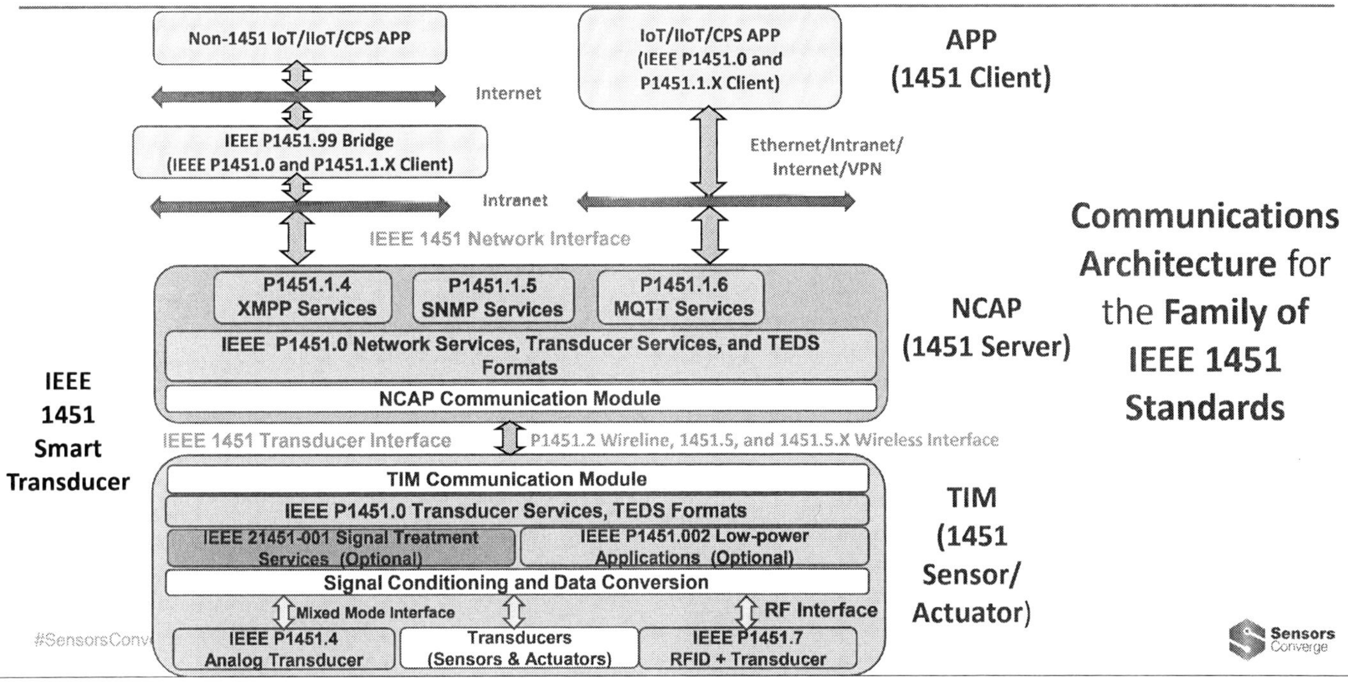

IEEE 1451 Interfaces Standards for Smart Transducer (Sensor & Actuator) Networks

IEEE 1451.0 Client-Server Communication Model

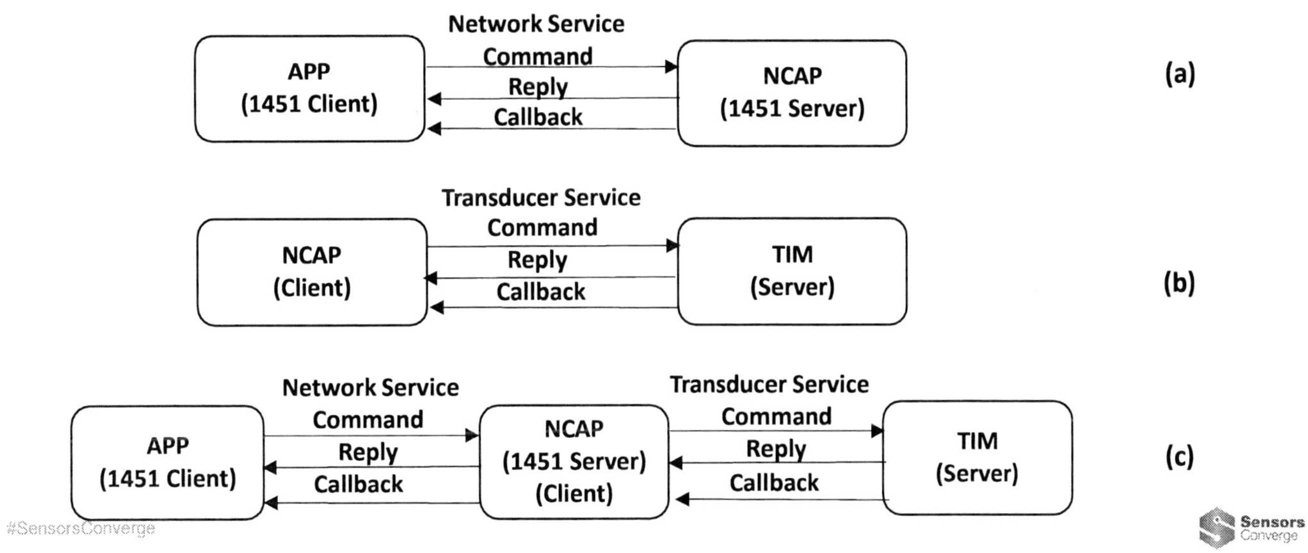

IEEE 1451 Interfaces Standards for Smart Transducer (Sensor & Actuator) Networks

IEEE 1451.0 Publish-Subscribe Communication Model

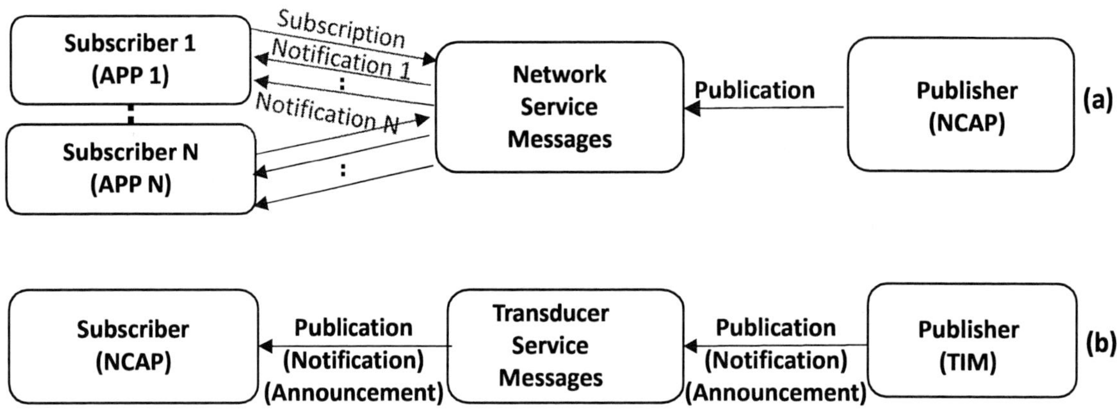

#SensorsConverge

Sensors Converge

IEEE 1451 Interfaces Standards for Smart Transducer (Sensor & Actuator) Networks

IEEE 1451.0 Publish-Subscribe Communication Model

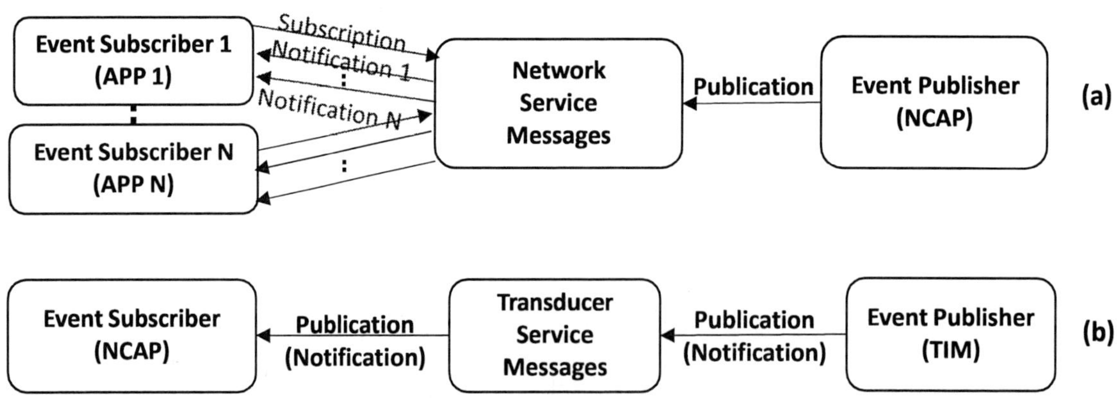

#SensorsConverge

Sensors Converge

IEEE 1451 Interfaces Standards for Smart Transducer (Sensor & Actuator) Networks

IEEE P1451.0 Network Services & APIs

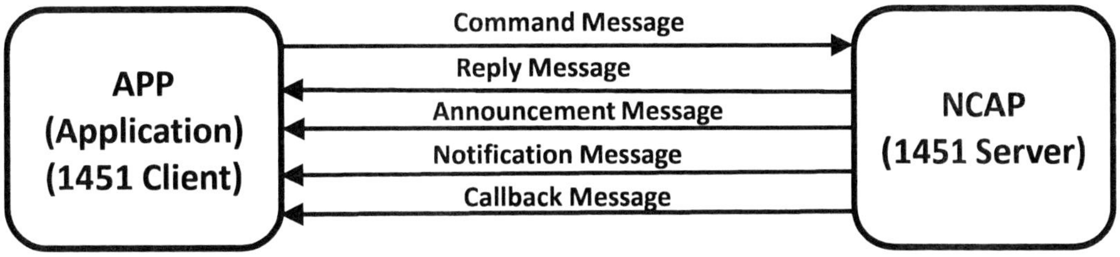

Network Service Type Name (Meaning)	Network Service Type (Enumeration)
Reserved	0
Discovery services	1
Transducer access services	2
TEDS access services	3
Event notification services	4

Message Type Name (Meaning)	Message Type (Enumeration)
Reserved	0
Command	1
Reply	2
Announcement	3
Notification	4
Callback	5

	1-Octet							
	7	6	5	4	3	2	1	0
Message Header	Network Service Type (1,2,3, and 4)							
	Network Service ID (1,2,3,… N))							
	Message Type (1, 2, 3, 4, 5)							
	Length (most significant octet)							
	Length (least significant octet)							
Message Body	Message Body …							

#SensorsConverge

Sensors Converge

IEEE 1451 Interfaces Standards for Smart Transducer (Sensor & Actuator) Networks

IEEE P1451.0 Transducer Services & APIs

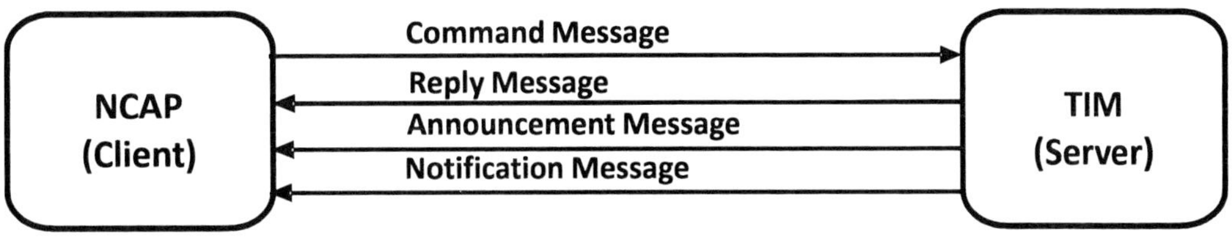

Transduce Message Type (Meaning)	XdcrMsgType (Enumeration)
Command	1
Reply	2
TIM Announcement	3
TIM Notification	4
Reserved	5-127
Open to Manufacturer	128-255

Message Section	1-Octet							
	7	6	5	4	3	2	1	0
Message Header	**Command class Id (1)**							
	Command function Id							
	Transducer Message type							
	Length (most significant octet)							
	Length (least significant octet)							
Message Body	• UUID: timId • Destination or Source TransducerChannel Number (UInt16) • Message type-dependent information. (Message class, function, msg type-dependent octets) …							

#SensorsConverge

Sensors Converge

muRata
INNOVATOR IN ELECTRONICS

Tech Talk
June 22, 2023

Explore the latest connectivity innovations for IoT sensor applications

Tony Garcia
Senior Business Development Manager

Design Challenges

muRata
INNOVATOR IN ELECTRONICS

What are your major challenges when deciding on a Wireless Technology to add to your design?

- Technology
- Regulatory
- Availability
- Cost

 20 June 2023 2

Communication Protocol

muRata
INNOVATOR IN ELECTRONICS

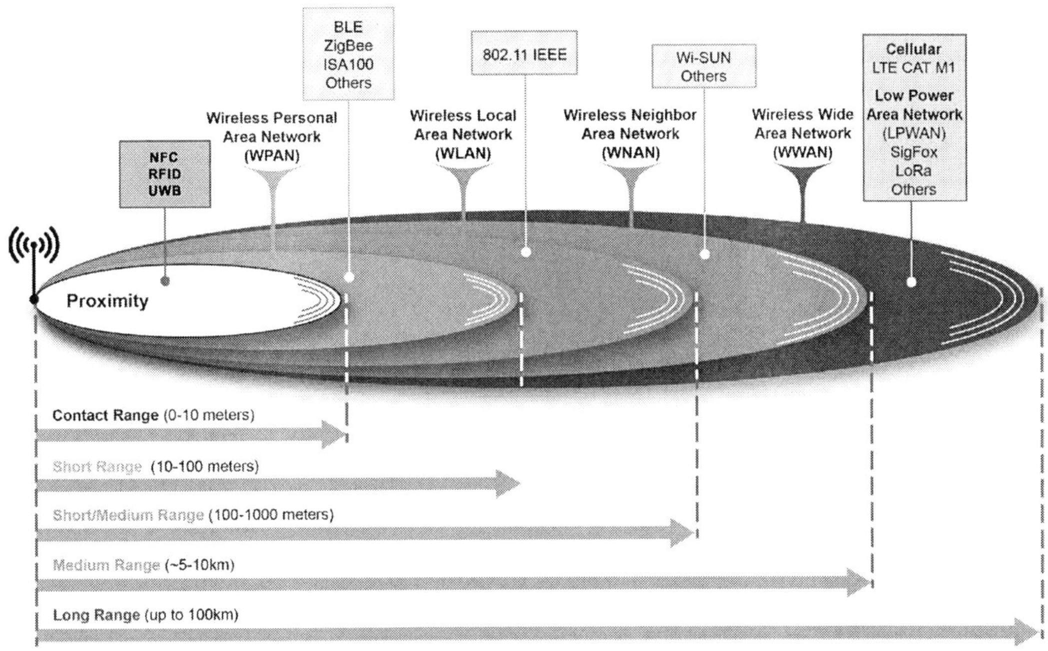

 20 June 2023 3

Wireless Technologies

muRata
INNOVATOR IN ELECTRONICS

When it comes to wireless technologies and sensor applications many things should be considered.

- Range & throughput are major considerations. Another important consideration would be regulatory certifications required.
- Which technology will best serve your design needs?
- LTE (Long Term Evolution)
- LoRa (Long Range)
- Wireless LAN (2.4GHz, 5 GHz, 6GHz)
- Bluetooth®
- 802.15.4
- UWB (Ultra Wide Band)
- GNSS (Global Navigation Satellite System)
- Others (NFC/RFID)

 20 June 2023 4

LTE and LoRa

- LTE and LoRa have the longest ranges however there through-put is lower but very usable in long distance sensor monitoring that does not require high through-put.
- One example would be to monitor a simple state such as on or off. LTE relies on carrier availability or a private network. LTE may require carrier certifications.
- LoRa can be used with a Network operator, or you can build your own gateway system.

Applications:
Agricultural monitors such as moister sensing or animal monitoring
Meter applications (Water, gas, electric)

 20 June 2023 5

Wireless LAN (Wi-Fi®)

Wireless LAN has some of the highest through-put.

- **Wi-Fi 7 – 802.11be** (under development)
- **Wi-Fi 6 – 802.11ax** (6E support 6GHz band) hundreds of Mbps to Gbps
- **Wi-Fi 5 – 802.11ac** (2.4GHz and 5GHz) Mbps to low hundreds of Mbps
- **Wi-Fi 4 – 802.11n** (2.4GHz) Mbps to low hundreds of Mbps

Data rates can vary depending on if the device is SISO (single in single out / 1 antenna) and MIMO (multiple in multiple out, 2x2, 3x3….).

Other determining factors to the through-put would be the processor and operating system.

For example, a 2x2 MIMO device connected to an ARM 9 processor over PCIe running Linux would run faster than a SISO device connected the same way.

Matter – using a tri-band radio (Wi-Fi, BT, 802.15.4)

 20 June 2023 6

Bluetooth®

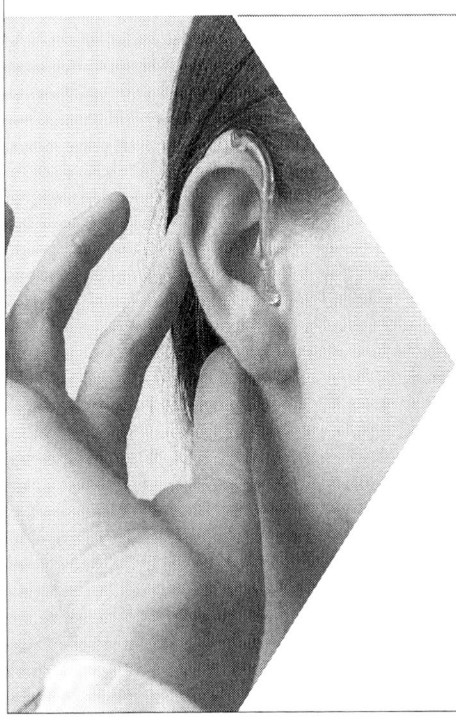

- Bluetooth Classic or Bluetooth Low Energy operate in the 2.4GHz ISM band. With the advances in Bluetooth Low Energy, it can be used for more and more applications and has lower power consumption than Bluetooth Classic.
- Bluetooth Classic has 79, one MHz channels while Bluetooth Low Energy has 40, two MHz channels.
- Bluetooth can be used for multiple applications such as provisioning, mesh networks, positioning [AoA (angle of arrival), AoD (angle of departure), RTLS]. The newer Bluetooth Low Energy can be used for hearing aid applications.

 20 June 2023 7

802.15.4

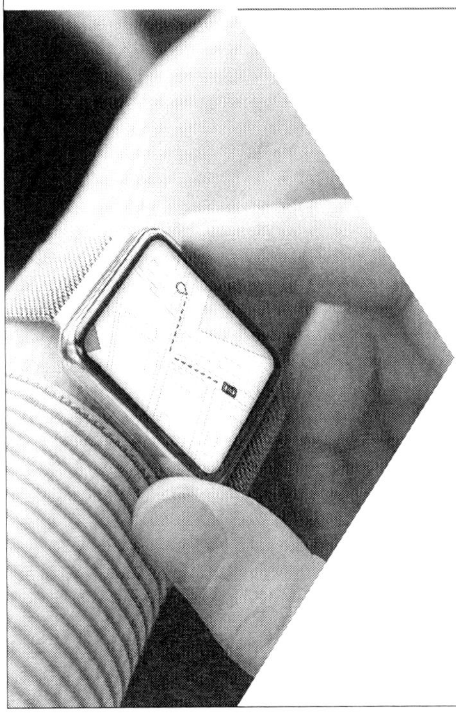

- The 802.15.4 is being included in more combination chipsets. There are many stand alone 802.15.4 enabled devices that are often tied together with gateways and then the data was sent over another network such as Wi-Fi or others.
- The Wi-Fi IC manufacturers are now including 802.15.4 in tri-band radios which include Wi-Fi, Bluetooth® and 802.15.4.

 20 June 2023 8

UWB

- Ultra-wide (UWB) band has been around for many years and this technology is being used for many applications. With this technology now being included with some smart phones use cases are increasing.
- This technology is being used for tracking and proximity applications.
- For tracking applications, you will need to use UWB anchors for best results.

 20 June 2023 9

GNSS

- Global Navigation Satellite System can be combined with other wireless technologies to report location activity.
- Imagine very expensive equipment on a construction jobsite, if you want to make sure the equipment is on the jobsite you may want to track it.

 20 June 2023 10

75+ Years of Innovation

muRata
INNOVATOR IN ELECTRONICS

From 1 to 80,000 employees worldwide

The Murata story began in 1944, when Akira Murata (1921-2006) started Murata Manufacturing as a personal venture in Nakagyo-ku, Kyoto-shi. A small factory of 150 square meters was opened in the center of Kyoto City starting the production of titanium-oxide ceramic capacitors with heterodyne radios being the primary application for these products.

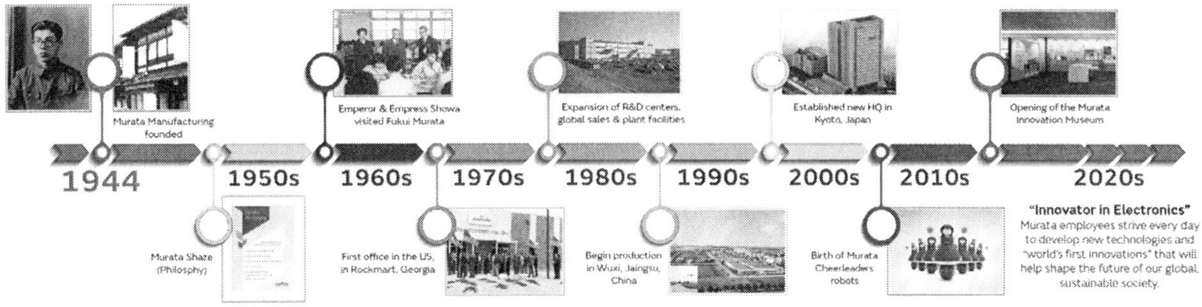

"Innovator in Electronics"
Murata employees strive every day to develop new technologies and "world's first innovations" that will help shape the future of our global, sustainable society.

Global Organization: Our Footprint

muRata
INNOVATOR IN ELECTRONICS

Murata's strength lies in our expansive footprint that allows us to deliver high-quality solutions, unsurpassed service, and a vast global network.

Subsidiaries outside of Japan: 59
Subsidiaries in Japan: 30
Employees outside of Japan: 45.3K
Employees in Japan: 32.3K

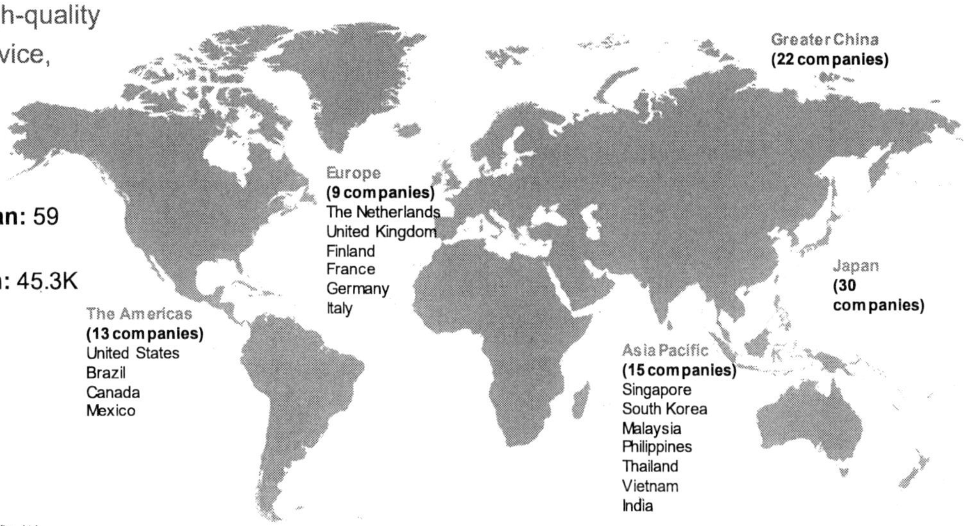

Murata value report(integrated report) | Murata Manufacturing Co., Ltd.

![muRata INNOVATOR IN ELECTRONICS]

Why choose Murata?

- Long historic ability to focus on global market pricing requirements
- Competitive pricing focus for : Connectivity , Healthcare , Industrial , Mobility and more
- Attractive pricing models to support channel sales (distribution) and EMS markets
- High volume pricing models to support Tier 1 customers

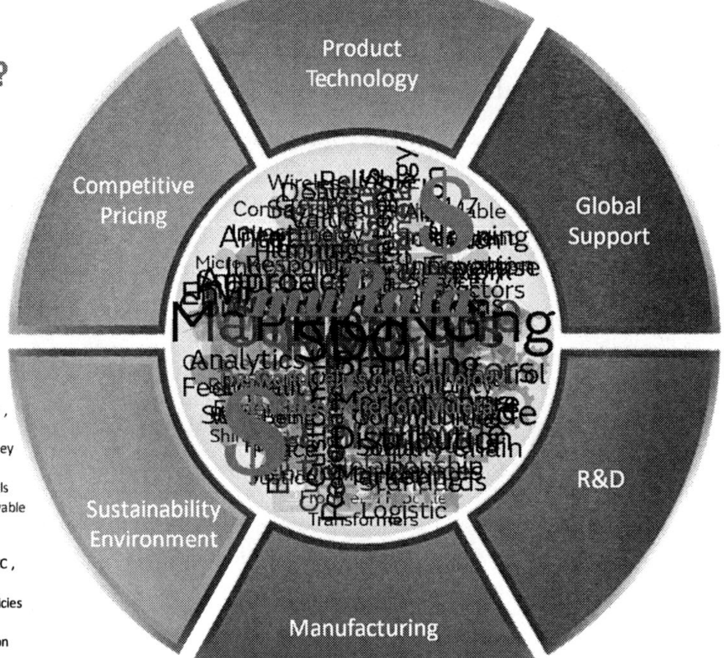

- Over 75 years of class-leading ceramic technologies expertise
- Broad product portfolio – over 25 different electronic technologies
- Leader in advanced materials technology processing
- Murata has over 75,000 employees globally
- Extensive sales, engineering, and customer service support network
- Authority in Solution Technologies (Healthcare, Mobility, Connectivity, Industrial)
- Long history in effective channel sales support (distribution)
- Global leader in components / modules miniaturization
- Expertise in key markets served (connectivity, mobility, healthcare, industrial)
- Partners with top IC Manufacturers
- Global #1 market share leader in several product technologies
- Provider of innovative online solutions for Engineering and software tools
- Innovation (first to develop Gigafil, Switch Connectors, Three Terminal Capacitors)
- Global EDI capabilities to support customer purchasing and delivery requirements

- [illegible] locations, 190 subsidiaries Matrix
- Vertical integration … Human Rights … control key components of manufacturing
- Advances in materials & development … materials technology being developed (renewable energy …)
- Global leader … and miniaturization
- Carbon Neutral initiatives
- Advanced material processing capabilities (LTCC, …)
- … sanitation policies
- Large manufacturing and production capacities offer improved availability
- Continues road map plans for adding production capacity and building new plants

- 10% of Murata gross income re-invested back into R&D yearly
- Global leader in the number of electronic components & modules patents
- R&D expertise in front end , product and back-end materials technologies
- Expansion of three (3) new R&D facilities in Japan
- Expertise to address future forecasts and solutions for the electronics market

 20 June 2023 13

![muRata INNOVATOR IN ELECTRONICS]

Q & A ?

14 20 June 2023

muRata
INNOVATOR IN ELECTRONICS
Visit us in Booth 916
Community Forum >
Contact Info >
Inquiries >
Design Tools >
Thank you for joining!

Central Gateway operation with The Things Stack and Atsign

Setting up a single gateway is a challenge.

But *very* rewarding when it's done!

LoRaWAN setup in my well house

atsign

2

Colin Constable
Co-founder & CTO

atsign

Managing gateways at scale is a drag...

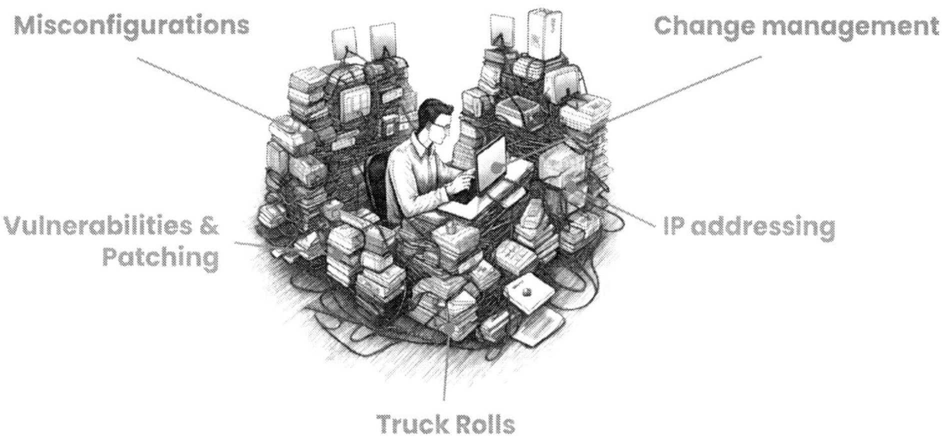

atsign

4

..until now.

atsign

5

Efficiently and securely manage LoRaWAN gateways at scale with

Atsign

A control plane built for Scale

atsign

6

IP Addresses

Yes we need them

But we do not have to know them

@lw_gateway01

atsign

7

NAT/1918/Firewall Rules/Mangles/IPTables

No one wants to manage them

So let's not worry about them

Deny All Inbound

atsign

9

VPNs

No one wants to manage them either

So let's not worry about them

End to End Data Encryption + TLS v1.3

atsign

11

Management GUI's

No one wants a GUI at scale or to trust an API

So let's have a

Global Network Control Plane

atsign

13

Standards + Tools

No one wants to be locked in

So let's not worry about either

OpenBSD 3 license fully extendable

atsign

15

Atsign ecosystem

Software	Hardware	Our SDKs
android	X86	Dart
	arm	Flutter
	RISC-V	Java
	ESP32	
	ARDUINO	

16

Sound interesting?

atsign

17

Want to get involved ?

Yay!

atsign

18

Colin@atsign.com

See more demos and peek into the code.

atsign

19

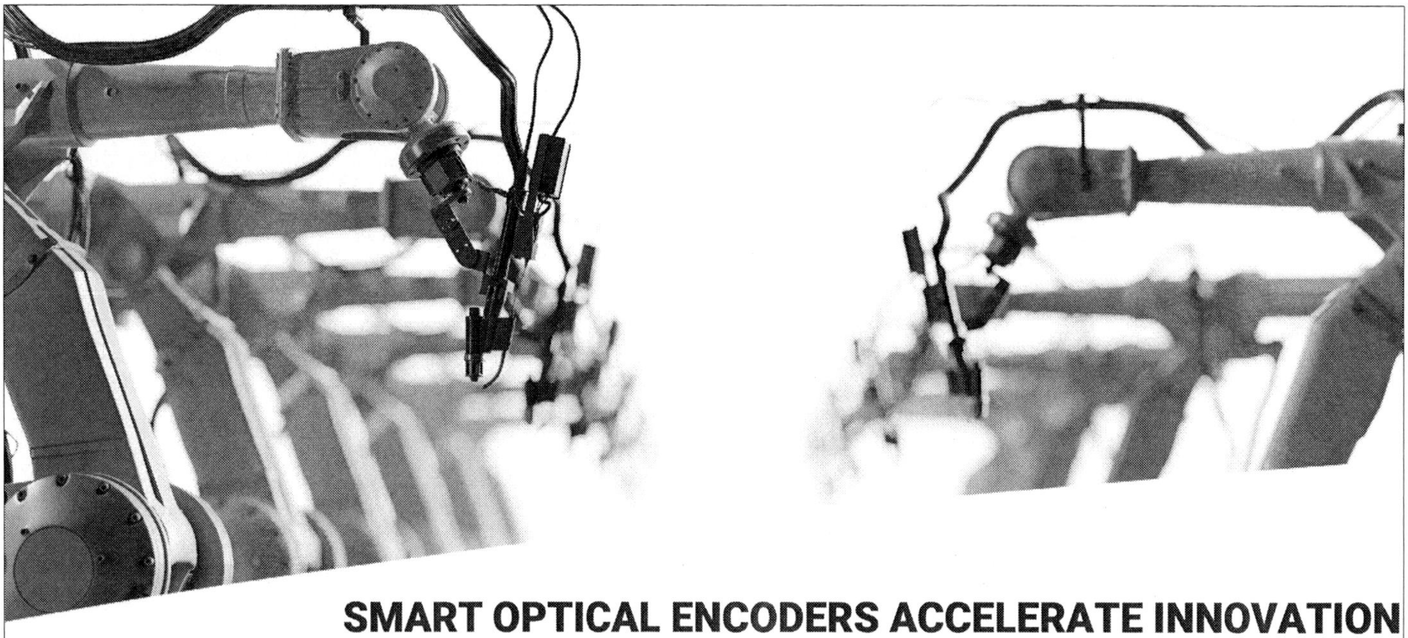

SMART OPTICAL ENCODERS ACCELERATE INNOVATION
IN AUTOMATION AND ROBOTICS FOR INDUSTRY 4.0

TT Electronics

Sergey Komarov, Business Development Engineer

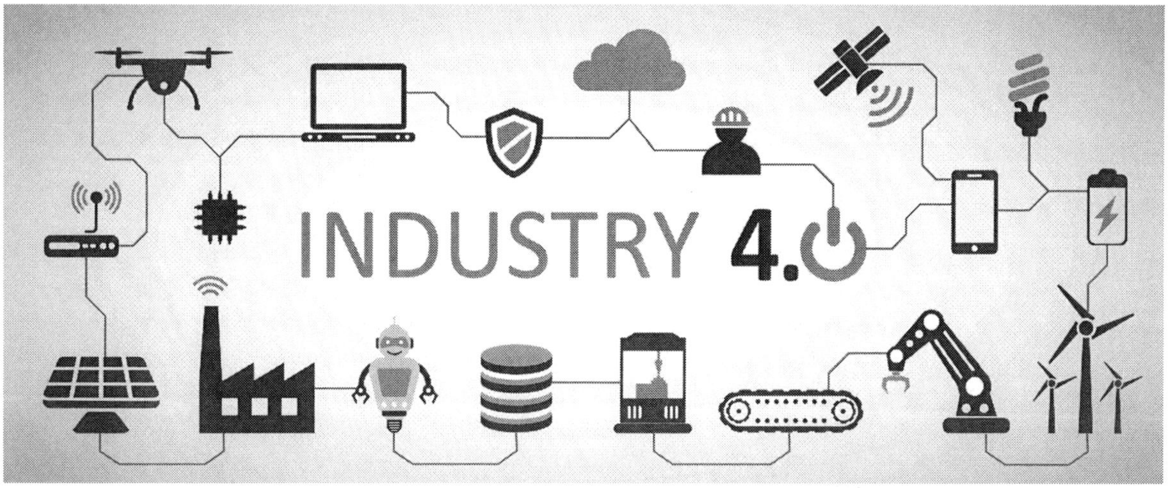

Industry 4.0 relies on smart sensors which enable manufacturing processes and predictive maintenance with minimal downtime, maximum efficiency and sustainable throughput.

This precise level of control, data collection and processing is guaranteed by a new generation of highly integrated, multi-functional smart optical sensors.

ENCODERS 101

Low-cost control electronics are trending up, allowing more industrial segments to automate. This has led to the widespread use of encoders.

Encoders automatically detect shaft rotation or linear displacement. This information is fed back into a computer or control mechanism for controlling velocity or shaft position. The main applications are motor feedback, robots and numerical control machine tools (CNC machines).

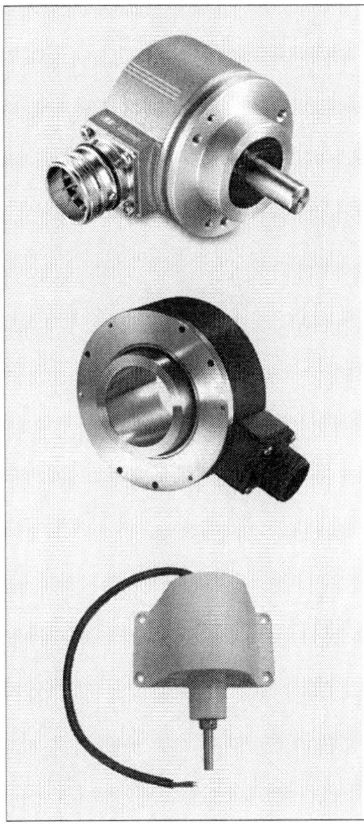

ENCODERS

Encoders can generally be categorized into 3 types:

- Optical
- Magnetic
- Mechanical-Contact

There are two basic types:

- Linear
- Rotary

While the principles behind them are similar, their specific applications most often are not.

LINEAR ENCODERS

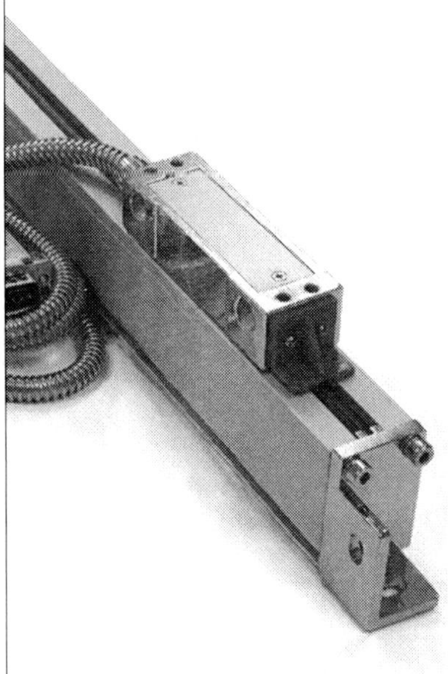

- Operates on photoelectric scanning principle (like rotary encoders)
- Linear scale = straight construction
- Output signals are interpolated (digitized differently in a direct manner)
- Linear feedback systems achieve resolutions in the submicron range (required in semiconductor industry and in ultra-precision machining)

 5

LINEAR ENCODERS

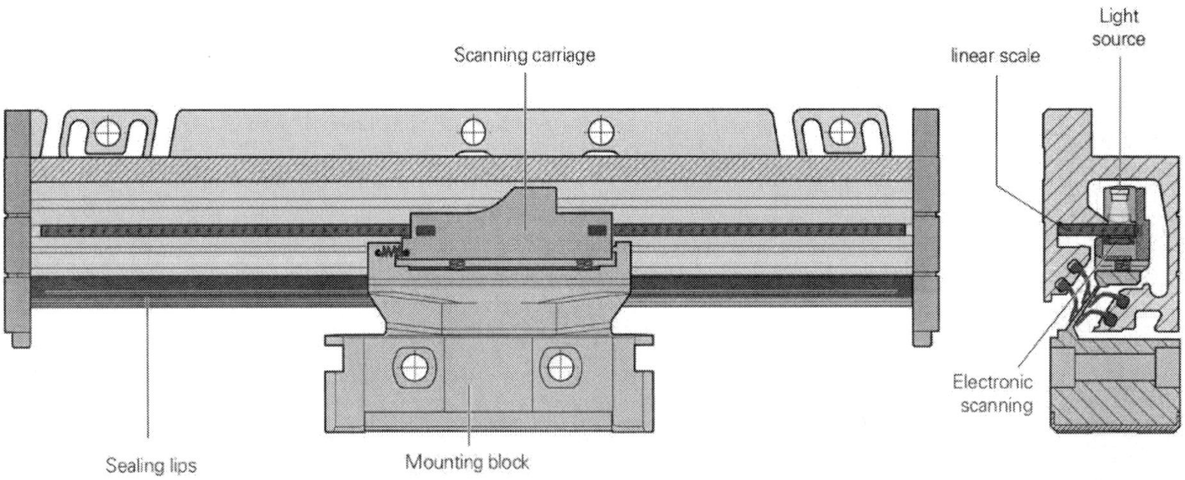

 6

LINEAR ENCODERS

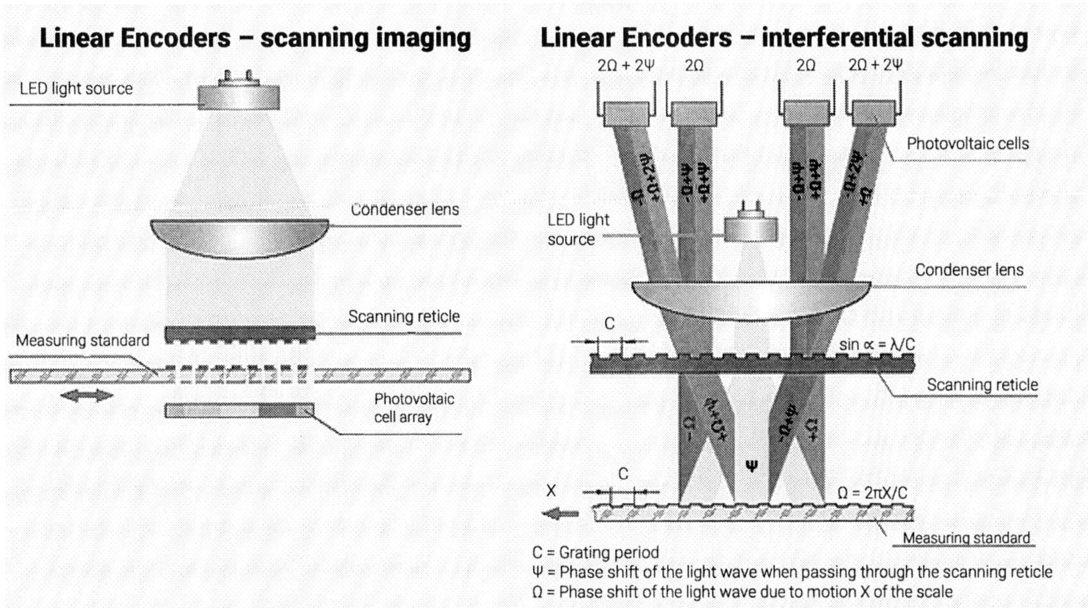

© TT Electronics 7

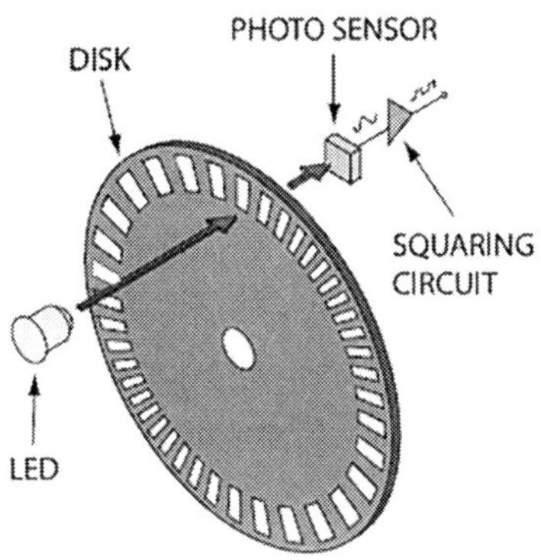

Of all optical rotary encoders being used today

ROTARY ENCODERS

The code "tracks" on an incremental encoder. It consists of evenly spaced opaque lines that act as "shutters" that alternately open and close to allow light from the light source to the photodetector.

The output signals are evaluated by an electronic counter. The measured value is determined by counting increments.

© TT Electronics 8

ROTARY ENCODERS

Types:

- Incremental for measuring angles
- Incremental for measuring linear positions (used in conjunction with measuring ball screws or rack/pinion)
- Absolute for one rotation (single-turn rotary encoders for measurement of angles)
- Absolute for several rotations (multi-turn rotary encoders)

ROTARY ENCODER UNIT

- Light source
- Condenser lens for collimating the beam
- Scanning reticle
- Encoder disk
- Silicon photosensors
- Amplification circuitry to "square-up" the photodetector outputs
- Analog and digital signal processing (e.g. interpolation)

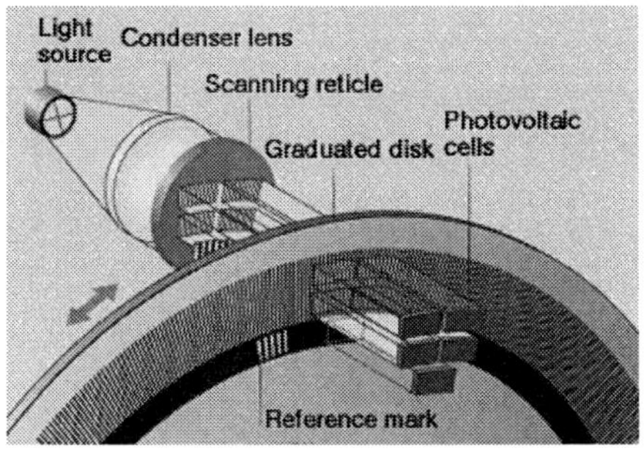

 9

3 FORMS OF ENCODER RESOLUTION

Native resolution is determined by the number of lines on the disk.

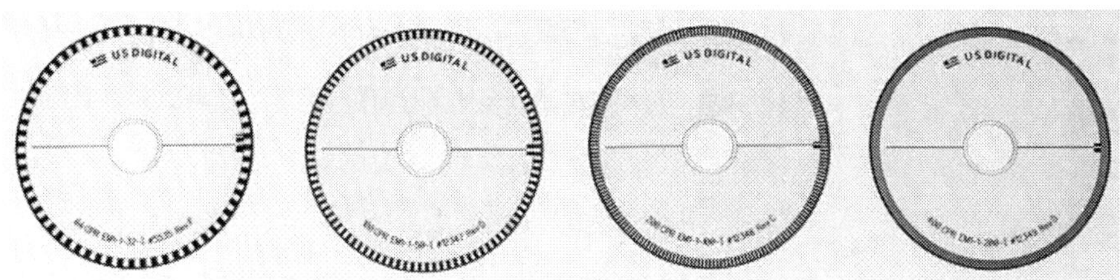

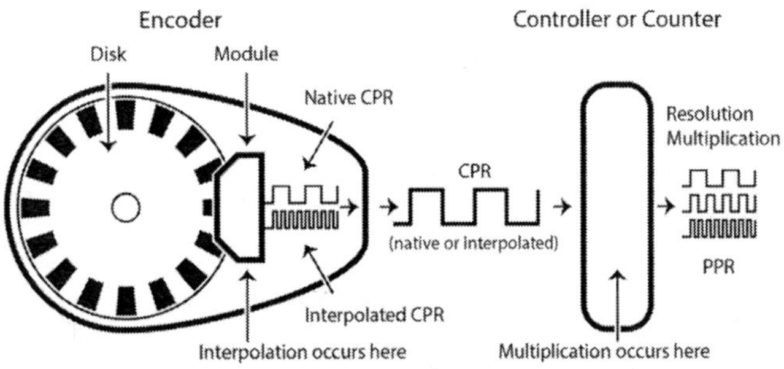

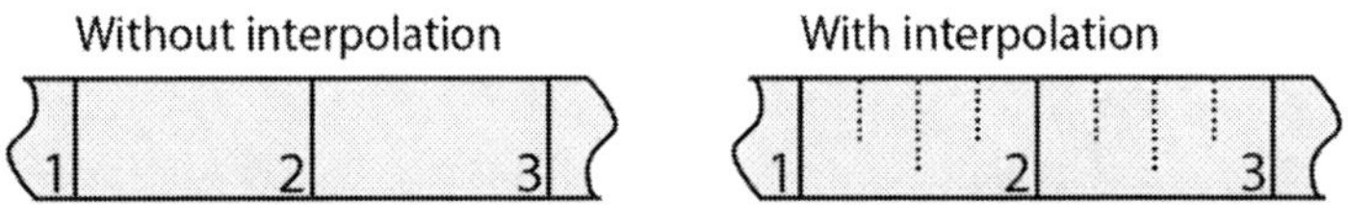

Interpolated measurements produce higher resolution, without the need for more lines.

 10

QUADRATURE SIGNALS

Quadrature signals are produced by using two photo-sensors – one positioned precisely one half a slot width from the other.

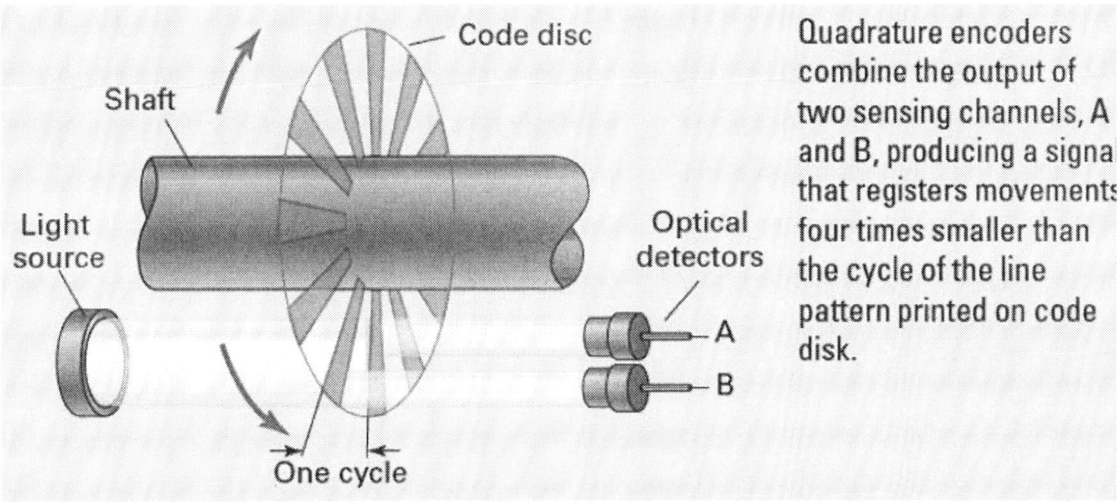

© TT Electronics 11

QUADRATURE SIGNALS

These encoders also provide an additional single marker on the disk used to produce a reference pulse. By properly decoding and counting these signals, the direction of motion, speed, and relative position of the encoder can be determined.

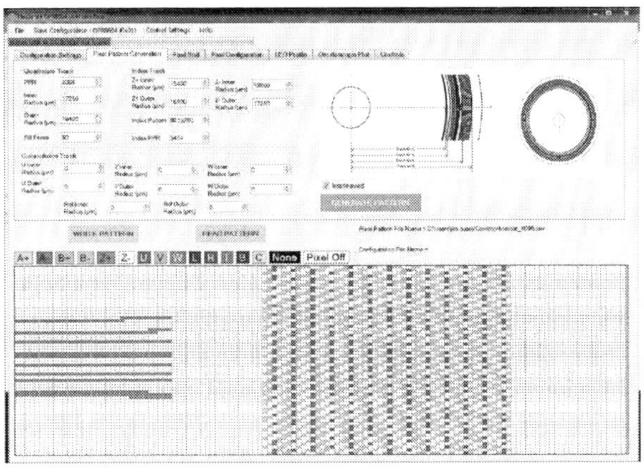

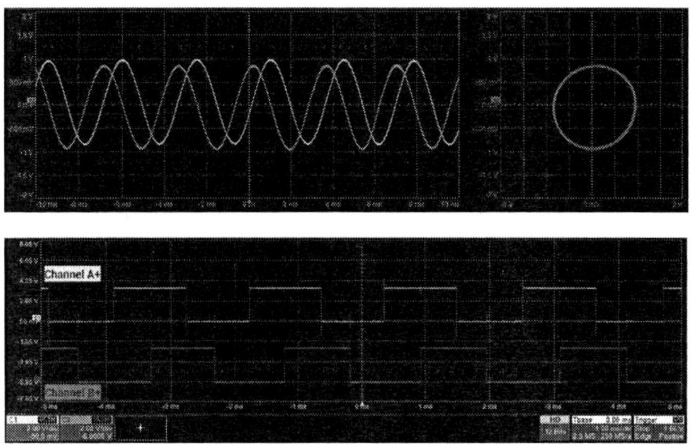

The direction of the rotation can be detected by monitoring the relative phase of both signals. For example, if Channel A leads Channel B, then CCW movement could be indicated. Conversely, if Channel B leads Channel A, CW rotation could be indicated. The shorter the signal period, the smaller the measuring step.

© TT Electronics 12

INTRODUCING FLEXSENSE™

A patented optical sensor array that can be programmed for a wide range of code-wheel diameters and resolutions.

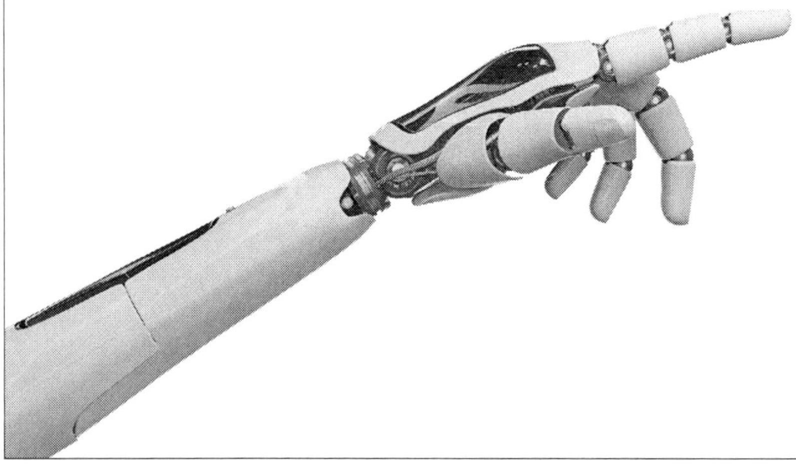

FS210

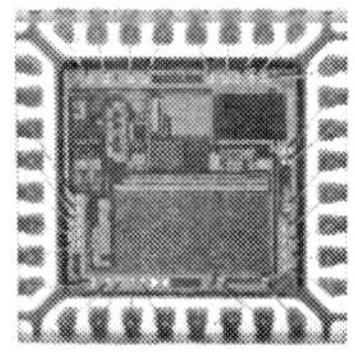

FS310

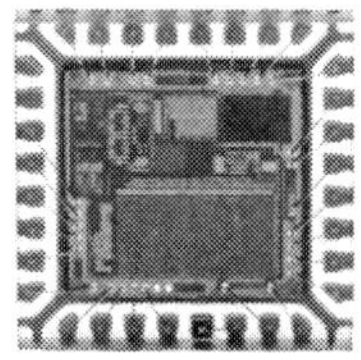

© TT Electronics 13

AVAILABLE IN TRANSMISSIVE AND RELFECTIVE

FS210 **TRANSMISSIVE SENSOR**

FS310 **REFLECTIVE SENSOR**

© TT Electronics 14

FLEXSENSE CODE WHEEL

- Incremental optical encoder sensor
- 2 quadrature, 1 index, 3 commutation tracks
- User-programmable photosensor pattern
- 10-40mm code-wheel radii compatibility
- 500-6k PPR resolution compatibility

FLEXSENSE FEATURES

Innovative user-programmable sensor pattern with included software GUI

Complete system-on-chip, includes integrated LED driver, up to 8x interpolation, divide down up to 2048 and I2C communication

Compact, low profile 32-pin 5mm x 5mm x 0.65mm Opto QFN package

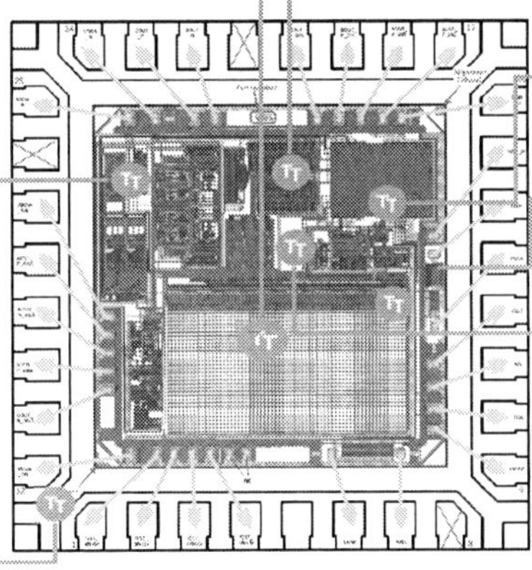

On-chip amplification and adjustment to detect multiple wavelengths including 460nm, 640nm and 850nm

High quality analog sine / cosine signals with less than 1% THD

High-speed, high-resolution signal at native 400kHz frequency

Predictive maintenance signals and interrupt alerts:

- Temperature output proportional to absolute chip temperature with interrupt signal
- LED-drive control loop with alert and interrupt signal
- Wobble detect sin^2 + cos^2 = 1

TARGET END APPLICATIONS

Factory Automation

- Motor control
- Robotics

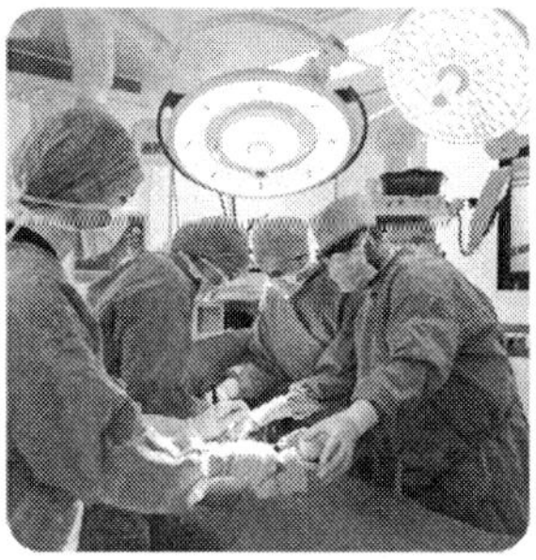

Medical

- Medical imaging

Oil and Gas

- Drill motors
- Top drives
- Rotary tables
- Mud pumps

Alternative Energy

- Wind power plants
- Wind turbines

WHY FLEXSENSE?

Accelerate time-to-market with programmable sensor pattern and auto alignment

Reduce system cost and design complexity with next generation reflective encoder

Predictive maintenance alerts to **minimize downtime disruption**

FLEXSENSE AND INDUSTRY 4.0

By utilizing smart encoder options such as FlexSense sensors paired with data analytics and sophisticated AI strategy, industrial operations can gain access to the intelligence needed to transform and sustain business value.

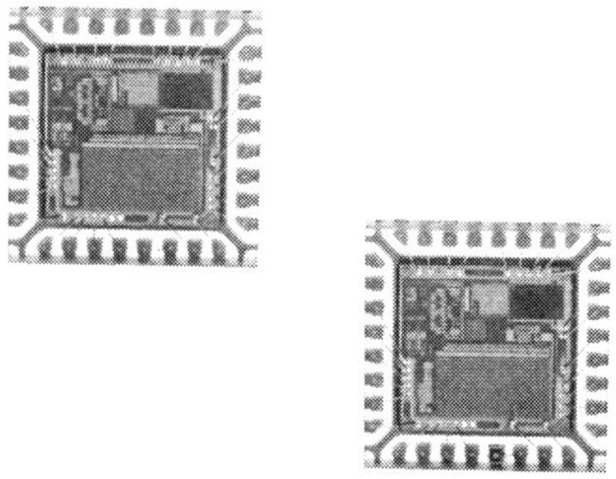

Interested in learning more about how FlexSense™ can optimize your encoder applications?

COME SEE US AT BOOTH #722

Or visit us at www.ttelectronics.com/flexsense

TT Electronics

THANK YOU!

Sergey Komarov

Business Development Engineer

Phone: 214-490-3439

Email: sergey.komarov@ttelectronics.com

www.ttelectronics.com

life.augmented
STMicroelectronics SubGHz SoC's Spirit, STM32WL
Tim Nakonsut
Product Marketing, Microcontrollers
SPIRIT
STM32WL

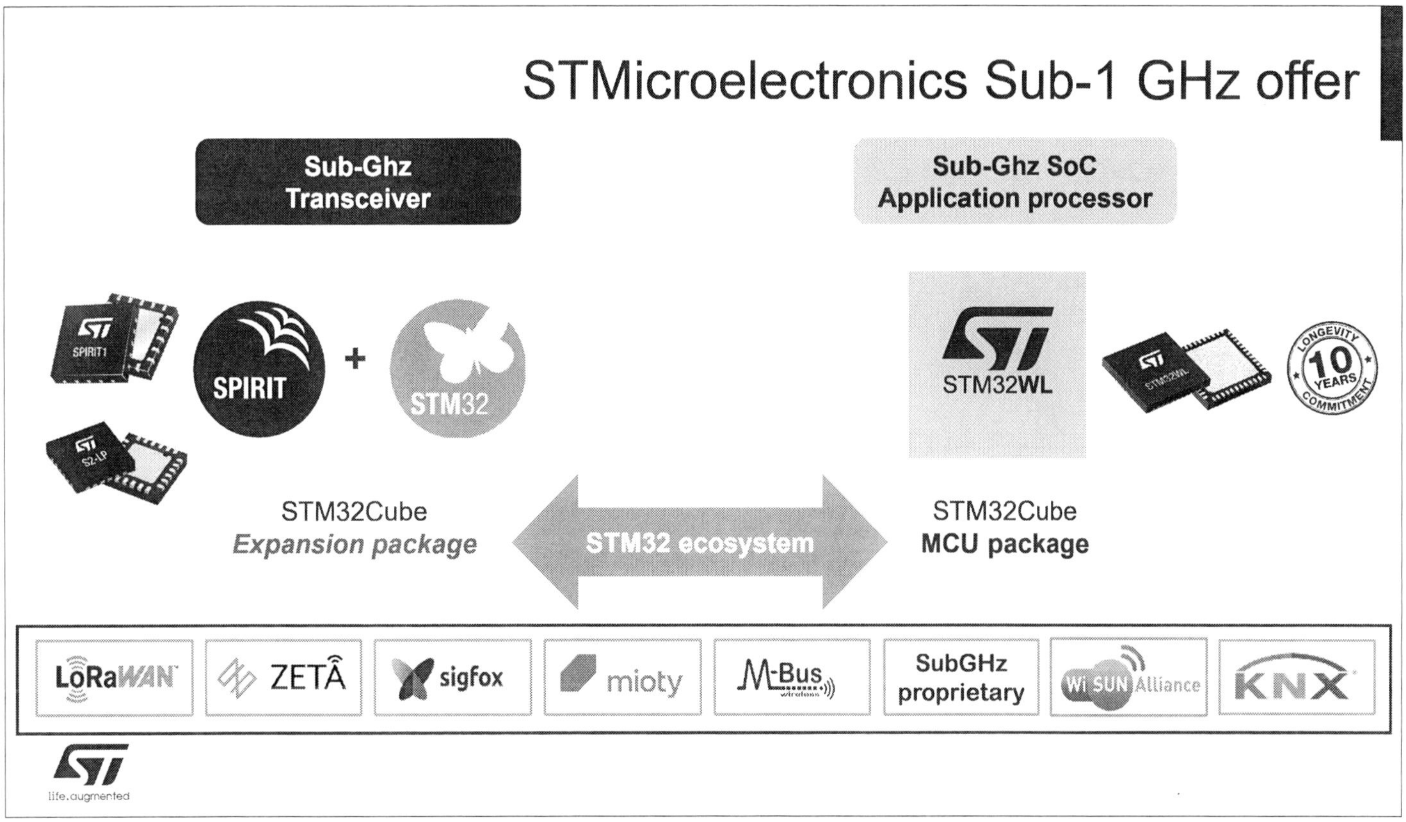

STMicroelectronics Sub-1 GHz offer
Sub-Ghz Transceiver
Sub-Ghz SoC Application processor
SPIRIT1
S2-LP
SPIRIT
+
STM32
STM32WL
LONGEVITY 10 YEARS COMMITMENT
STM32Cube Expansion package
STM32 ecosystem
STM32Cube MCU package
LoRaWAN
ZETA
sigfox
mioty
M-Bus
SubGHz proprietary
Wi SUN Alliance
KNX
life.augmented

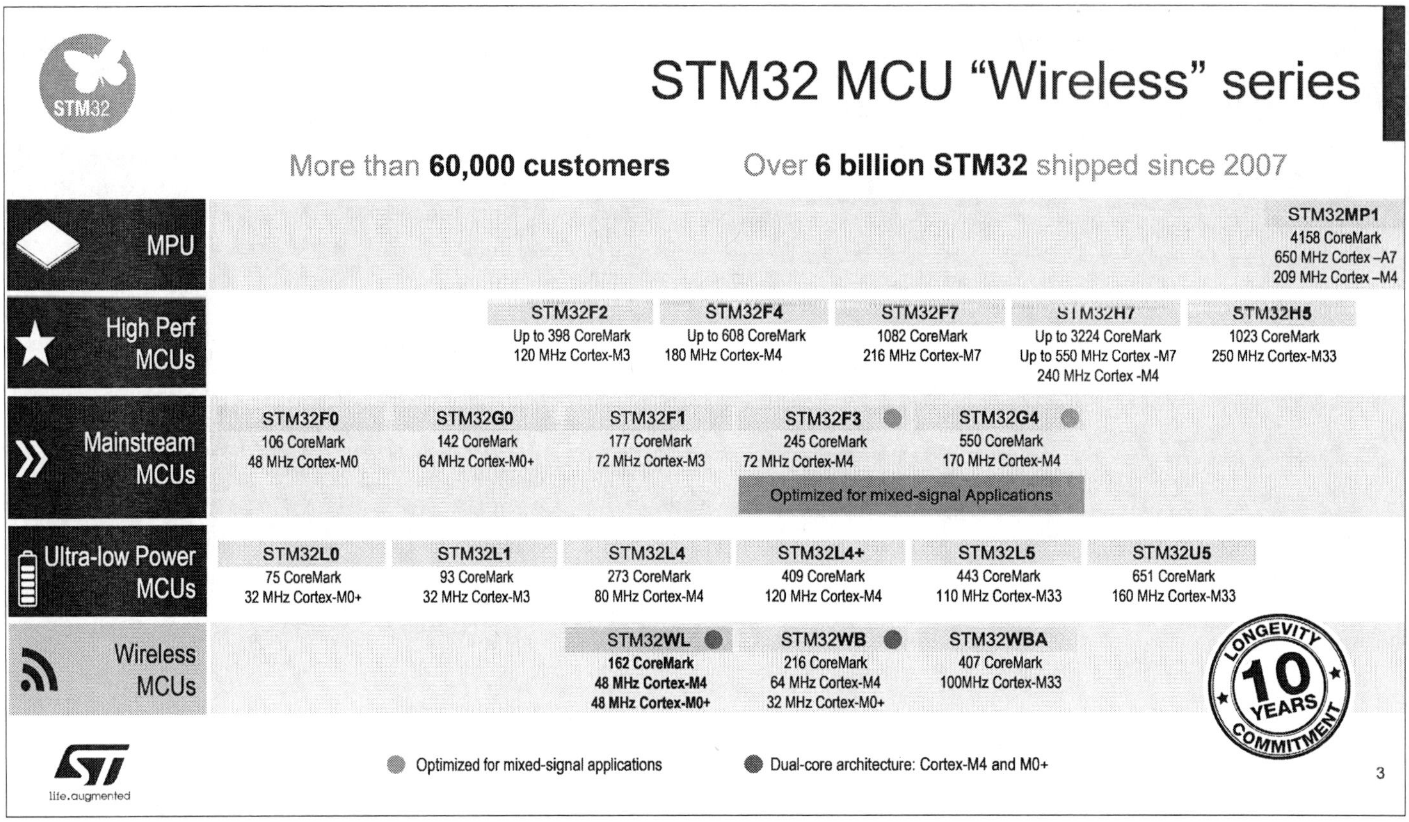
STM32 MCU "Wireless" series
More than 60,000 customers
Over 6 billion STM32 shipped since 2007
MPU
STM32MP1
4158 CoreMark
650 MHz Cortex –A7
209 MHz Cortex –M4
High Perf MCUs
STM32F2
Up to 398 CoreMark
120 MHz Cortex-M3
STM32F4
Up to 608 CoreMark
180 MHz Cortex-M4
STM32F7
1082 CoreMark
216 MHz Cortex-M7
STM32H7
Up to 3224 CoreMark
Up to 550 MHz Cortex -M7
240 MHz Cortex -M4
STM32H5
1023 CoreMark
250 MHz Cortex-M33
Mainstream MCUs
STM32F0
106 CoreMark
48 MHz Cortex-M0
STM32G0
142 CoreMark
64 MHz Cortex-M0+
STM32F1
177 CoreMark
72 MHz Cortex-M3
STM32F3
245 CoreMark
72 MHz Cortex-M4
STM32G4
550 CoreMark
170 MHz Cortex-M4
Optimized for mixed-signal Applications
Ultra-low Power MCUs
STM32L0
75 CoreMark
32 MHz Cortex-M0+
STM32L1
93 CoreMark
32 MHz Cortex-M3
STM32L4
273 CoreMark
80 MHz Cortex-M4
STM32L4+
409 CoreMark
120 MHz Cortex-M4
STM32L5
443 CoreMark
110 MHz Cortex-M33
STM32U5
651 CoreMark
160 MHz Cortex-M33
Wireless MCUs
STM32WL
162 CoreMark
48 MHz Cortex-M4
48 MHz Cortex-M0+
STM32WB
216 CoreMark
64 MHz Cortex-M4
32 MHz Cortex-M0+
STM32WBA
407 CoreMark
100MHz Cortex-M33
LONGEVITY 10 YEARS COMMITMENT
Optimized for mixed-signal applications
Dual-core architecture: Cortex-M4 and M0+
life.augmented
3

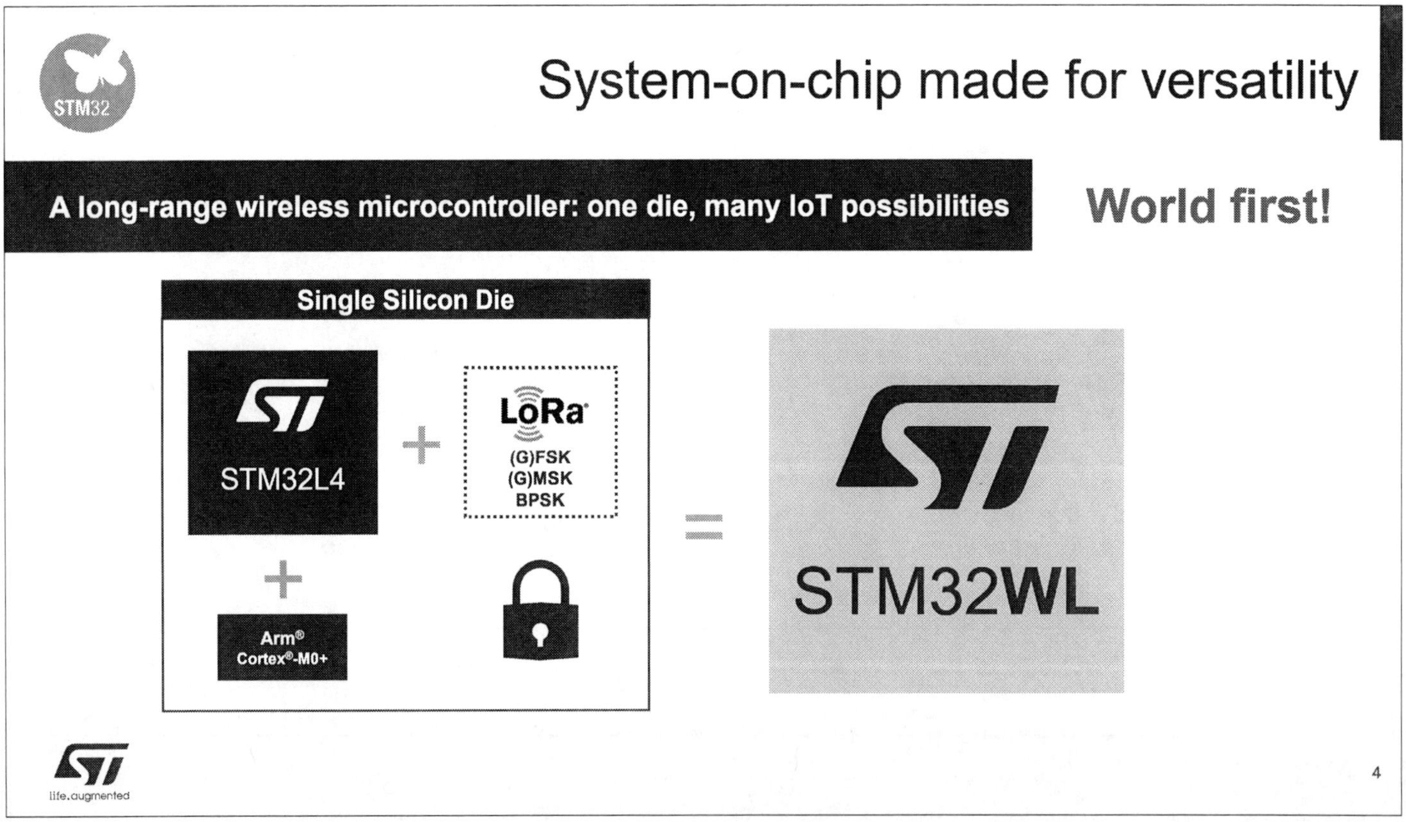
System-on-chip made for versatility
A long-range wireless microcontroller: one die, many IoT possibilities
World first!
Single Silicon Die
STM32L4
LoRa
(G)FSK
(G)MSK
BPSK
Arm®
Cortex®-M0+
STM32WL
life.augmented
4

STM32 SubGHz Portfolio

STM32WL | SPIRIT

SubGhz SoC Dual Core

STM32WL5x

SubGhz SoC Single Core

STM32WL3x*
(ex- SPIRIT3)
Comming soon

STM32WLEx

SubGhz Transceiver

1st Generation
SPIRIT1

General Purpose Sub-1GHz radio

2nd Generation
S2LP

Ultra Low Power Sub-1GHz radio

SPIRIT1	S2LP / STM32WL3x	STM32WL5x / STM32WLEx
2 (G)FSK	2/4 (G)FSK	2 (G)FSK
(G)MSK	(G)MSK	(G)MSK
-	BPSK (Sigfox)	BPSK (Sigfox)
OOK	OOK	-
ASK	ASK	-
-	*DSSS on WL3	LoRa (WLx5 P/N)

life.augmented

STM32WL5x Line - a rich feature set
Dual-core and enhanced security

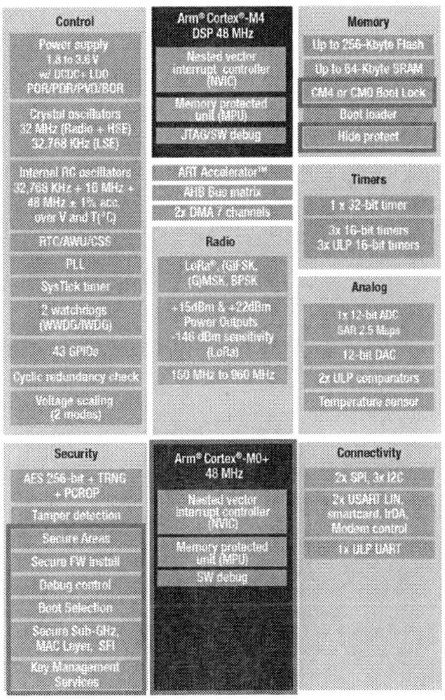

KEY FEATURES

- Arm® Cortex®-M4 & DSP up to 48 MHz
- Up to 256 KB Flash and 64 KB SRAM
- Arm® Cortex®-M0+ up to 48 MHz

- **Sub-GHz Radio**
  - Multi-modulation: LoRa, (G)FSK, (G)MSK, BPSK
  - 2 embedded power amplifiers:
    - 1 output up to +15 dBm
    - 1 output up to +22 dBm
  - LoRa RX sensitivity: -148 dBm (SF12, BW=10.4kHz)
  - RX: 4.82mA and TX: 15mA (at 10dBm) / 87mA (at 20dBm) [3.3V]

- **Ultra-Low Power consumption**
  - < 71µA/MHz Active mode (3V - RF OFF)
  - 1 µA Stop2 mode with RAM retention
  - 390 nA Standby mode with RTC
  - 31 nA Shutdown mode

- **Peripherals**
  - 3xI²C, 2xUSART, 1xLP-UART, 2xSPI
  - 7x timers + 2x ULP Comparators

- **Advanced security features**

- 1.8 to 3.6V voltage range (DC/DC, LDO)
- -40 to up to +105°C temperature range

-> Packages: QFN48, BGA73

6

Flexible power scheme FlexPowerControl

Typ with LDO @ V_{DD} = 3 V @ 25 °C

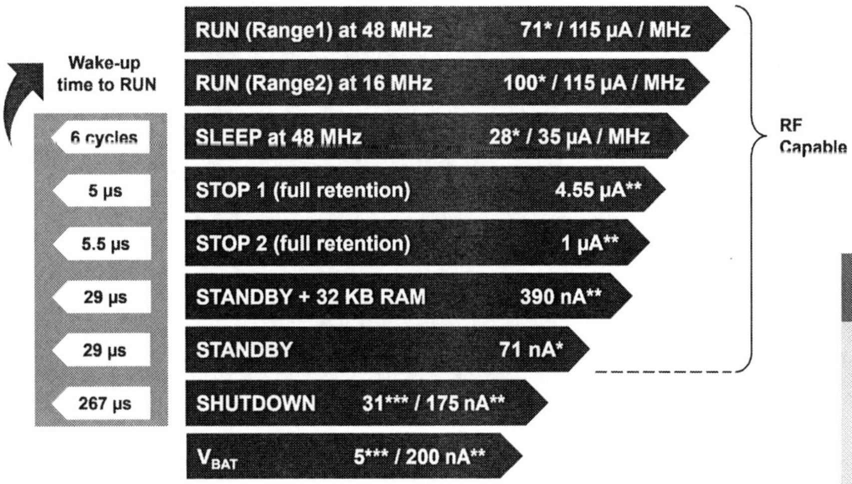

* Typical values with SMPS, **RF OFF**
** with RTC on LSE Bypass
*** All OFF

Benchmark scores

- High Efficiency
  - ➔ CoreMark score = 162
- Ultra Low-Power Platform
  - ➔ ULPBbench score ≈ 204

life.augmented

7

4 modulations - many protocols

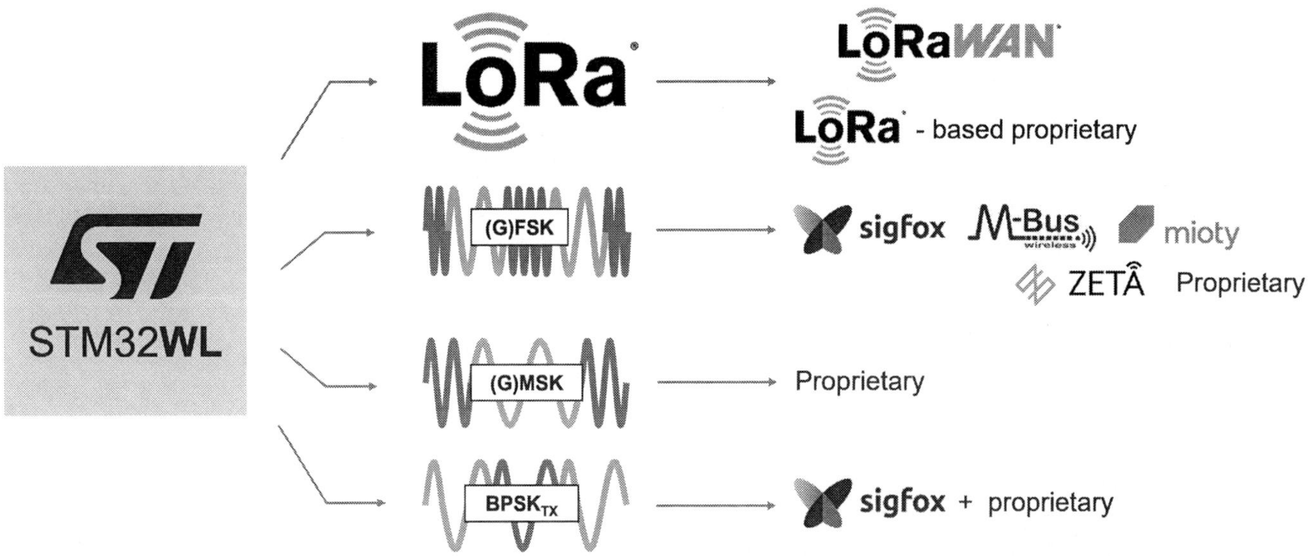

life.augmented

8

STM32WL - safety and security

Secure your application with embedded safety & security

Safety

- Back-up clock circuitry
- Supply monitoring
- Dual watchdog
- Flash memory with ECC (address status register)
- SRAM Parity check
- Cyclic Redundancy Check
- Brown-out reset in all modes
- Clock Security System
- Backup byte registers

STM32**WL**

Security

- Tamper detection
- Read & Write protection
- Memory Protection Unit (MPU)
- Software IP Protection
- True Random Number Generator
- AES and Public Key Accelerator
- Unique IDs (64- and 96-bit)
- Boot-Lock in user Flash

- Secure hardware isolation between CM4 / CM0
- Boot selection
- Secure Boot code protection
- Debug control
- Secure Firmware Install
- Secure Boot Secure Firmware Update*
- Key Management Services*
- Crypto Library*

Available on STM32WL5x dual-core versions

** Software downloadable on st.com*

life.augmented

9

Bring more security to your LoRaWAN apps

Your implementation, your choice

STM32WL

USER FLASH

- User Application
- LoRaWAN stack
- User boot

SYSTEM FLASH

- Bootloader

Standard Implementation

STM32WL

- User Application

Isolation

- **LoRaWAN stack**
- **Secure Key Management Services**
- **Secure Firmware Update**
- **FUOTA capability**
- **Secure Boot**

Secure Implementation

life.augmented

10

Flexible power implementation

Tailor STM32WL to the requirements of IoT applications

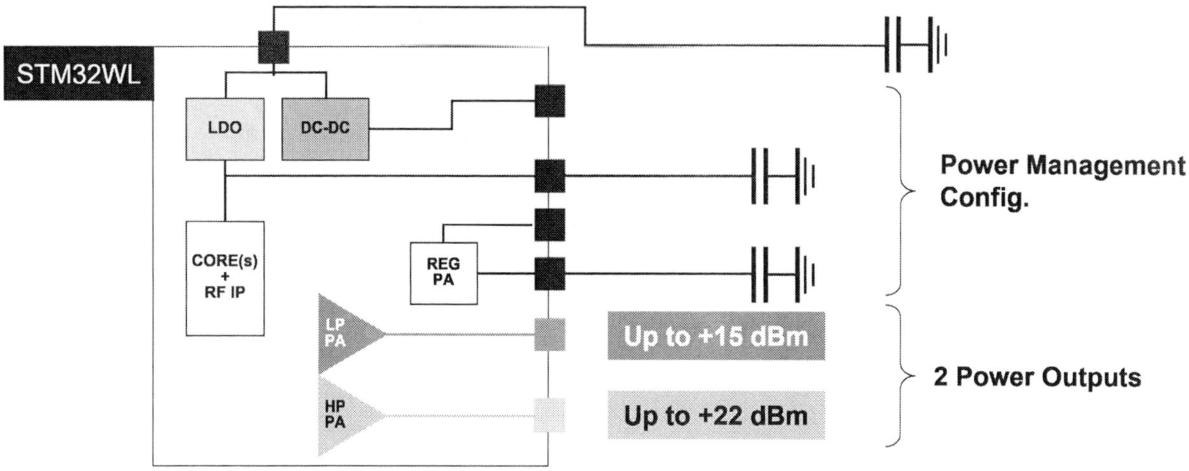

life.augmented

11

NEW

STM32WL IPD Integrated Passive Device

STM32WL RF Front end in a 1.2mm²

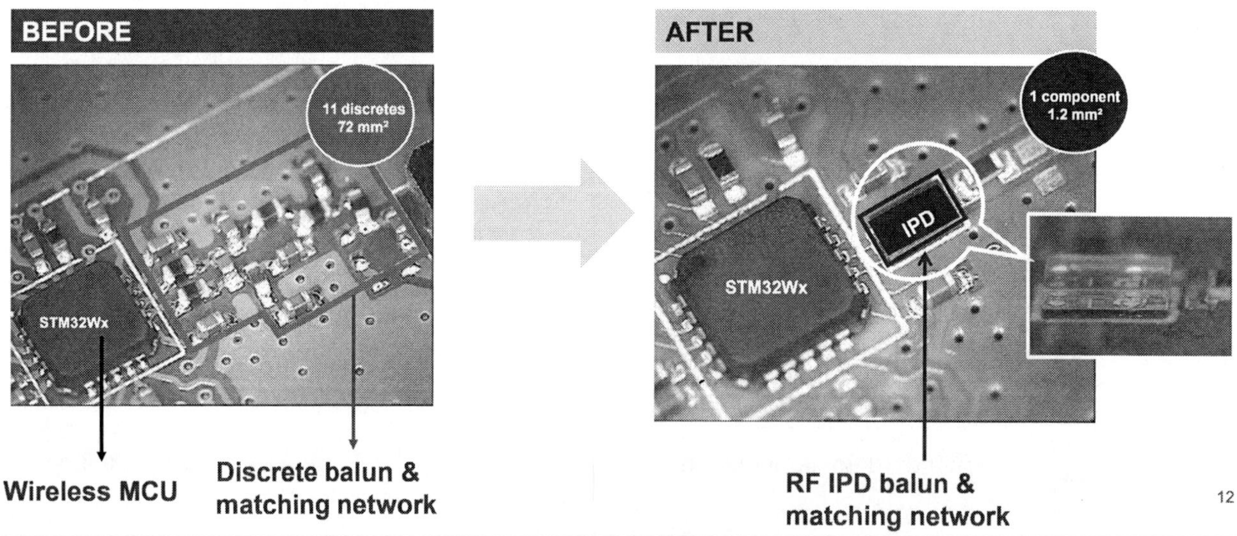

life.augmented

12

STM32W Sub-GHz – large portfolio

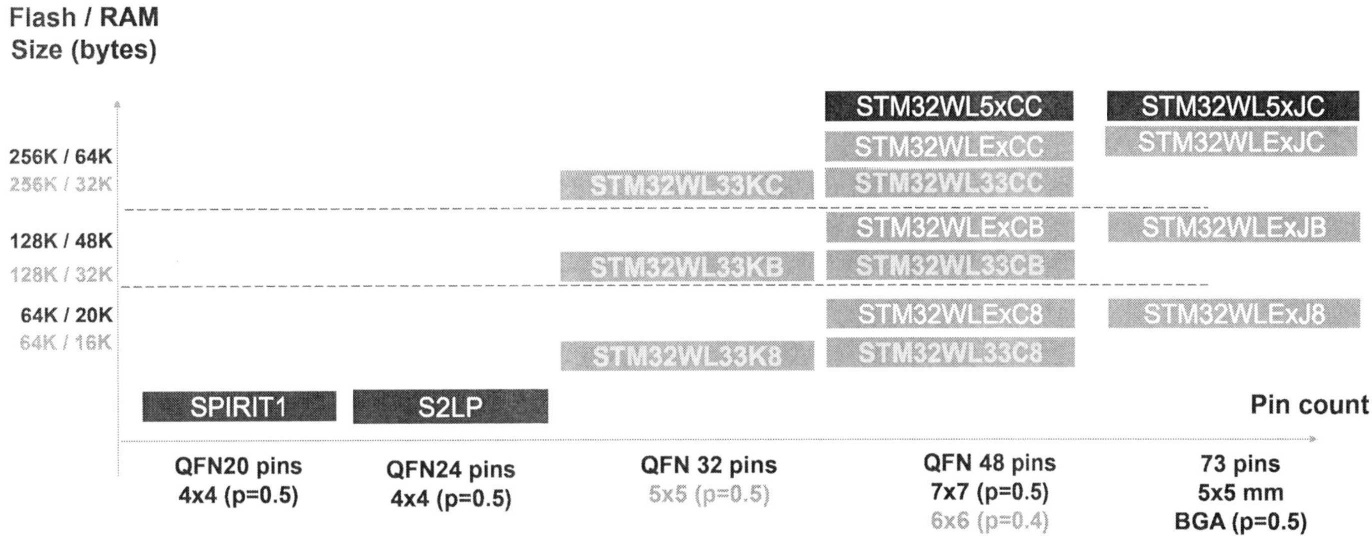

Transceiver only | Single Cortex-M0+ | Single Cortex-M4 | Dual core: CM4 & CM0+

life.augmented

13

The STM32WL Nucleo-64 at a glance

Main Features

NUCLEO-WL55JC1

868/915/923 MHz

NUCLEO-WL55JC2

433/470 MHz

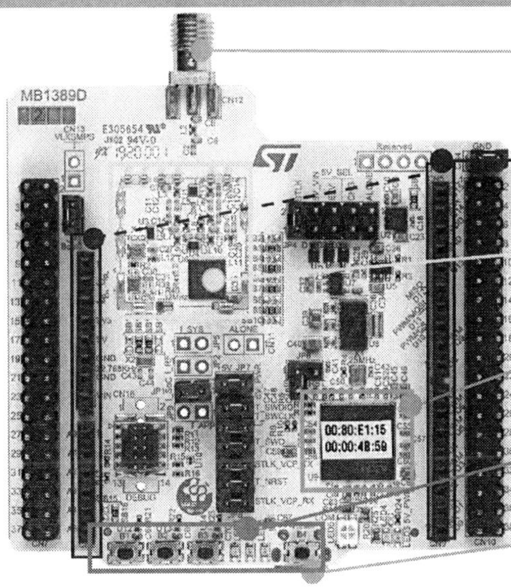

SMA Antenna connector

Arduino™ extension connectors : easy access to add-ons

STM32WL
(under a metallic shield)

Integrated ST-LINK/V3: mass storage device flash programming

4 push buttons, 3 color LEDs, Jumper settings

Flexible board power supply : through USB or external source

life.augmented

14

S2-LP transceiver overview

SPIRIT

Performance

S2-LP / S2-LPCB

Sub 1GHz

- 413-479MHz / 826-958MHz
- 452-527 MHz / 904-1055 MHz
- -40°C to +105°C
- QFN24 4x4x1

Radio performance

- 100bps to 500kbps
- -130dBm @ 0.3kbps
- +16dBm output power

Ultra low-power consumption

- Sleep / Shutdown: 700nA / 2.5nA
- Rx peak: 7mA
- Tx peak: 10mA @+10dBm

Protocols

sigfox

6LoWPAN
IPv6-based Low-power Wireless Personal Area Networks

M-Bus wireless

KNX

Wi SUN

Markets

- Remote metering
- Smart living
- Alarm & surveillance
- Smart home
- Smart utilities
- Healthcare & assistance
- Smart parking
- Smart agriculture

life.augmented

15

S2-LPTX overview
S2-LP based radio transmitter

SPIRIT

S2-LPTX

Sub 1GHz

- 413-479MHz / 826-958MHz
- Pin to Pin compatible with S2-LP
  - **No need for a new Sigfox certification!**
- QFN24 4x4x1

sigfox

M-Bus wireless

Radio performance

- 100bps to 500kbps
- +16 dBm output power

Ultra low-power consumption

- Sleep / Shutdown: 700 nA / 2.5 nA
- Tx peak current: 10 mA @ +10 dBm

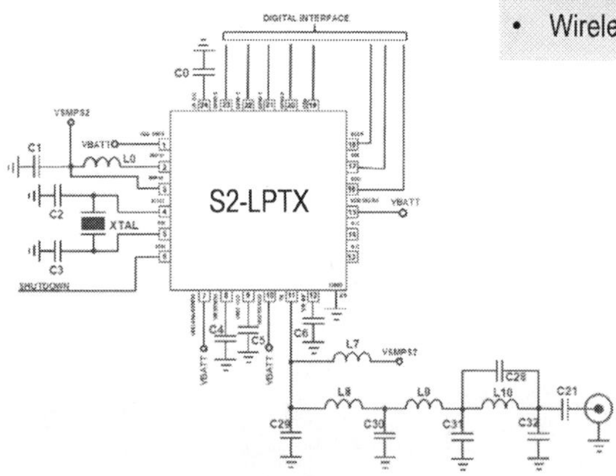

Applications

- Asset Tracking
- Alarm System
- Home and Building Automation
- Remote key entry
- Wireless Sensor Networks

LONGEVITY 10 YEARS COMMITMENT

life.augmented

16

STM32WL – ecosystem overview

Fully integrated into the rich and market-proven STM32 ecosystem

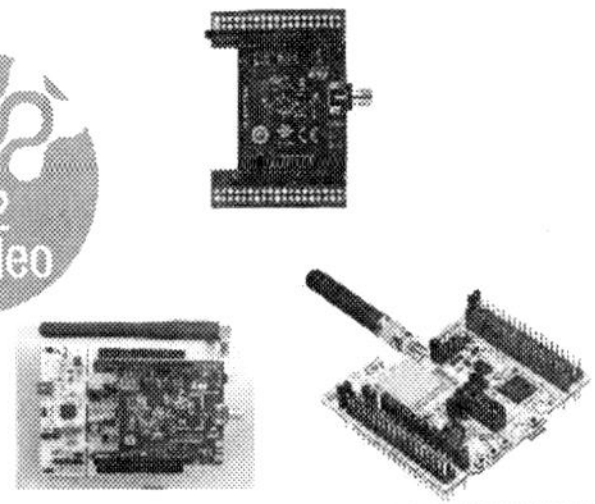

STM32 Nucleo

STM32CubeMX STM32CubeProgrammer STM32CubeIDE STM32CubeMonitor STM32 Cube

STM32 Open Development Environment · IAR SYSTEMS · arm KEIL

LoRaWAN · Wi SUN Alliance · mioty · M-Bus wireless · sigfox · ZETA Alliance

STM32 Nucleo-64	Dev tools	Stacks
NUCLEO-WL55JC1/2 X-NUCLEO-S2868/915A1 STEVAL-FKI915V1	STM32CubeMX STM32CubeWL STM32CubeMonitor STM32CubeProg X-CUBE-SUBG2 STSW-S2LP-DK STM32CubeIDE + Partners IDEs	LoRaWAN (ST) Sigfox (ST) Wireless-MBUS / Mioty (Stackforce) ZETA (Zifisense) WiSUN (3rd Party License)

life.augmented

17

Releasing your creativity

STM32

/STM32

@ST_World

community.st.com

https://www.st.com/en/wireless-connectivity

wiki.st.com/stm32mcu

github.com/stm32-hotspot

www.st.com/stm32-mcu-developer-zone

life.augmented

18

Sensors Converge

AI and machine learning: A must-have for 5G/6G wireless connectivity and sensor design

June 20–22, 2023 | Santa Clara, CA

#SensorsConverge

Agenda

- Introduction
- Wireless sensor design
- 5G/6G, Wi-Fi perspective
- Challenges of sensor networks
- AI/ML for wireless sensing
- Wireless sensing/detection example
- Summary

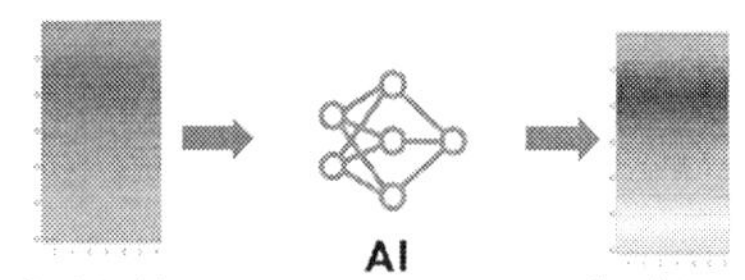

#SensorsConverge

Sensors Converge

Digital Twin: Authoring multi-domain wireless sensor scenarios

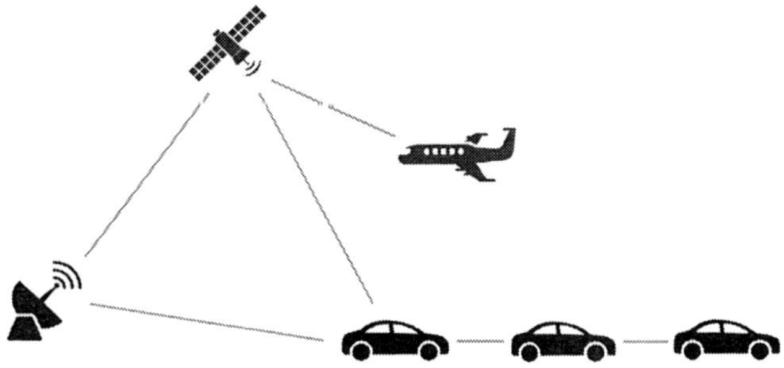

Multi-domain for actors: mixes different types of actors, e.g., land-, sea-, air-, or space-based

Multi-domain for sensors: mixes different types of sensor systems, e.g., radar, comms, lidar, navigation, sonar

#SensorsConverge

Urban & Terrestrial Outdoor Scenes

Urban

Terrestrial / aerial (UAV)

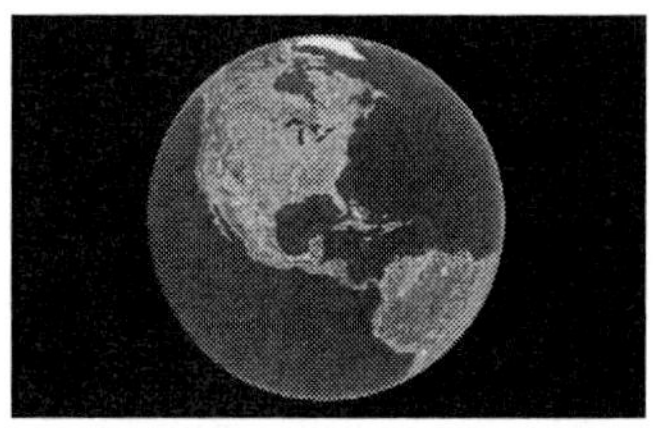

Space (Satellite)

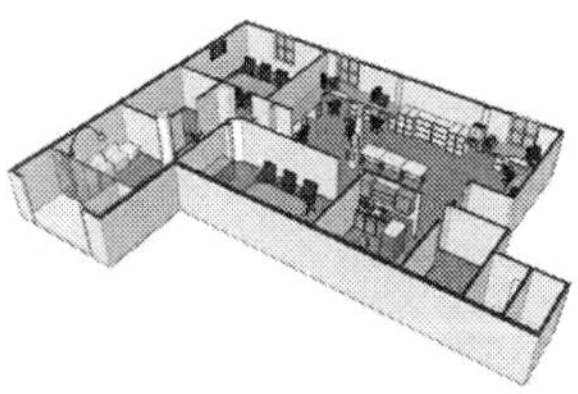

Indoor

Hybrid outdoor/indoor

Underwater

Space (Non-Earth)

#SensorsConverge

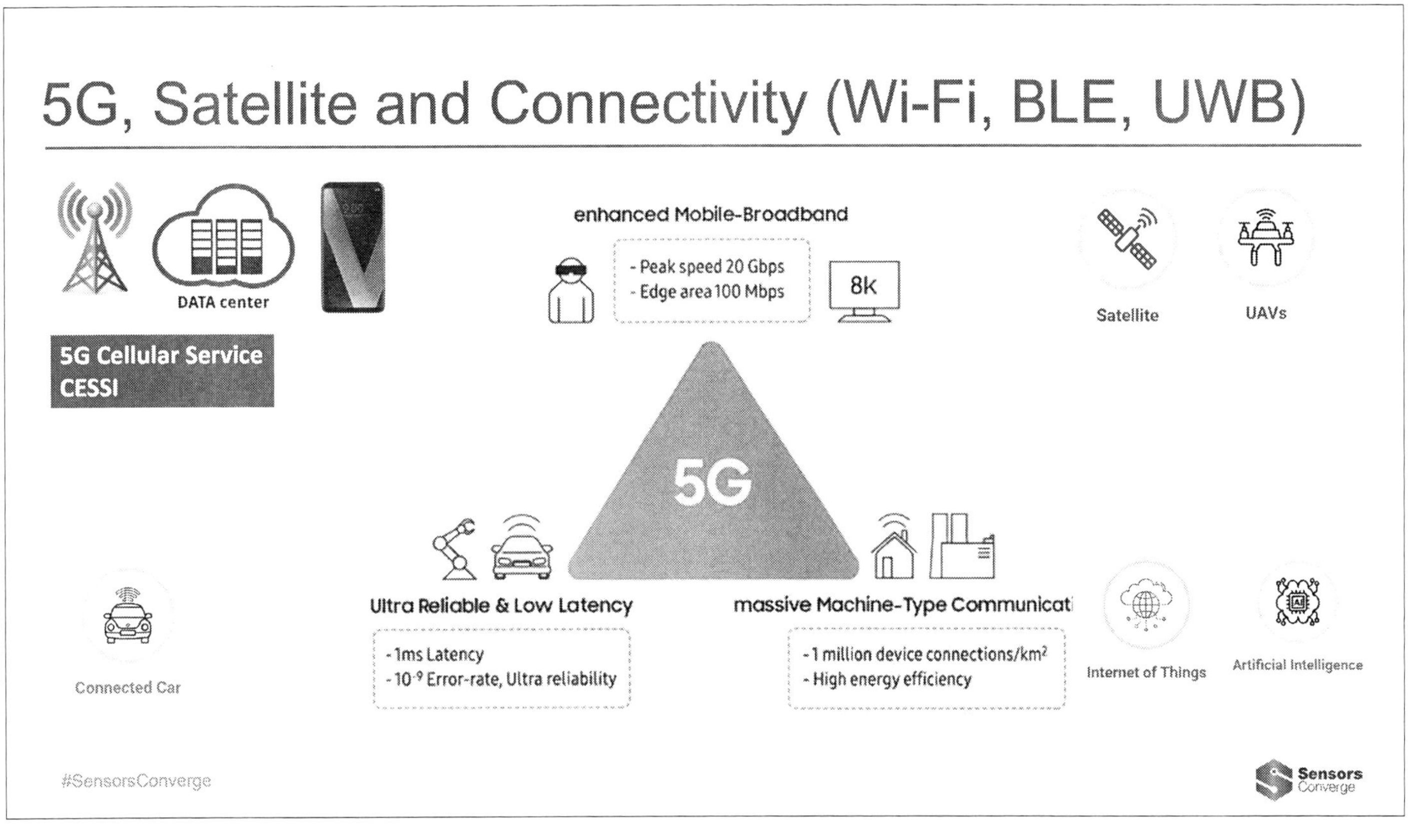
5G, Satellite and Connectivity (Wi-Fi, BLE, UWB)
DATA center
5G Cellular Service CESSI
enhanced Mobile-Broadband
- Peak speed 20 Gbps
- Edge area 100 Mbps
8k
Satellite
UAVs
5G
Ultra Reliable & Low Latency
- 1ms Latency
- 10-9 Error-rate, Ultra reliability
massive Machine-Type Communicati
- 1 million device connections/km2
- High energy efficiency
Connected Car
Internet of Things
Artificial Intelligence
#SensorsConverge
Sensors Converge

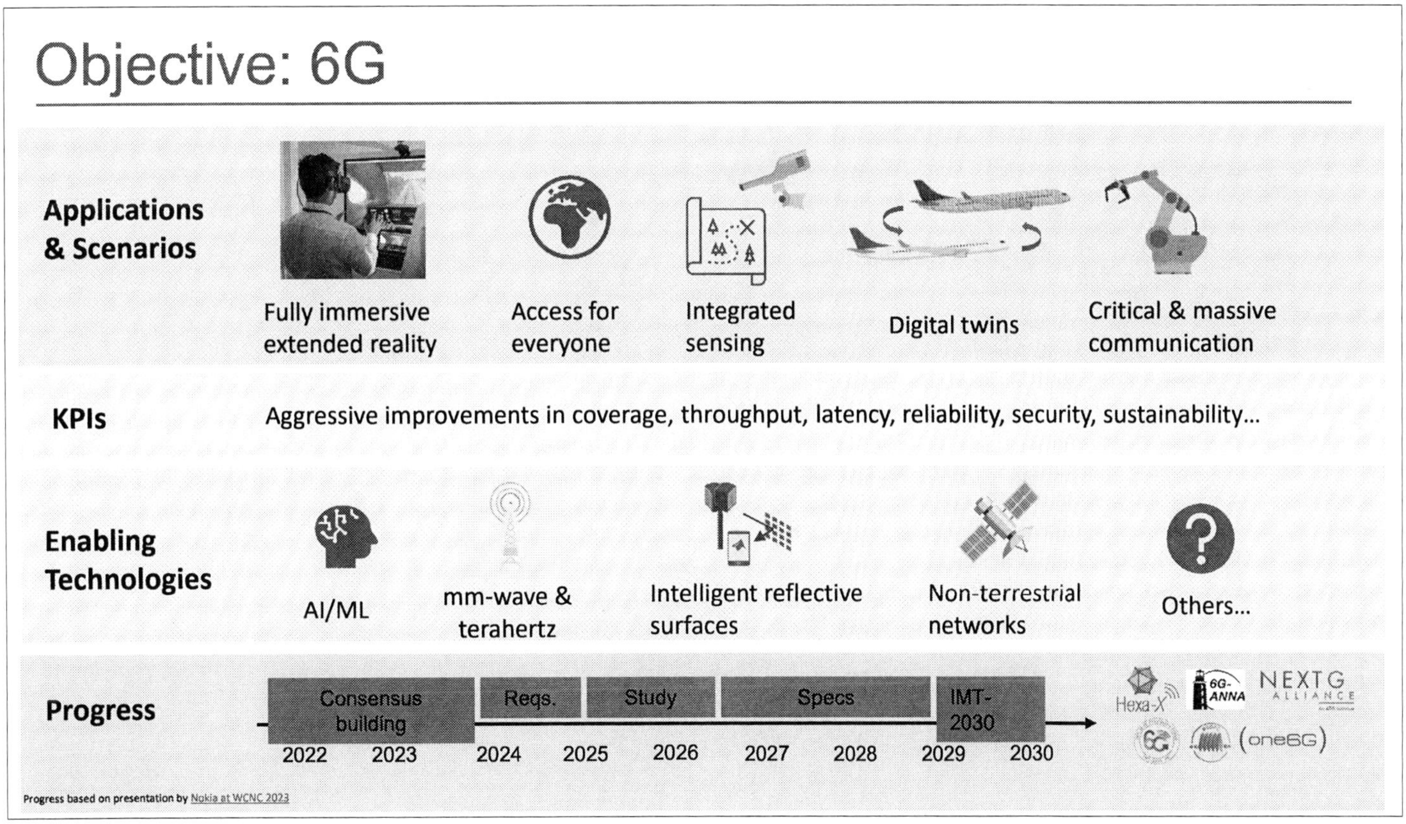
Objective: 6G
Applications & Scenarios
Fully immersive extended reality
Access for everyone
Integrated sensing
Digital twins
Critical & massive communication
KPIs
Aggressive improvements in coverage, throughput, latency, reliability, security, sustainability...
Enabling Technologies
AI/ML
mm-wave & terahertz
Intelligent reflective surfaces
Non-terrestrial networks
Others...
Progress
Consensus building
Reqs.
Study
Specs
IMT-2030
2022
2023
2024
2025
2026
2027
2028
2029
2030
Hexa-X
6G-ANNA
NEXTG ALLIANCE
(one6G)
Progress based on presentation by Nokia at WCNC 2023

Emerging WLAN standards

- **802.11be** – Extremely high throughput
  (Wi-Fi 7)
- **802.11bf** – Wireless sensing
- **802.11bn** – Ultra-high reliability
  (Wi-Fi 8)
- **TG-AIML** – Topic Interest Group for Artificial Intelligence and Machine Learning

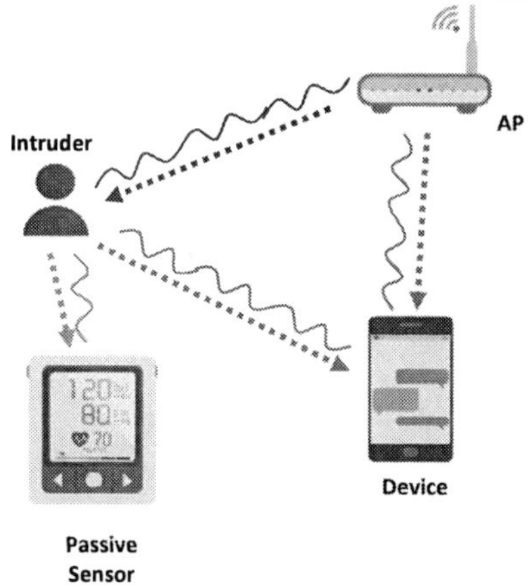

Leverage AI/ML

#SensorsConverge

Sensors Converge

Challenges: RF Propagation, Scenario Modeling & Visualizations

Antenna Pattern

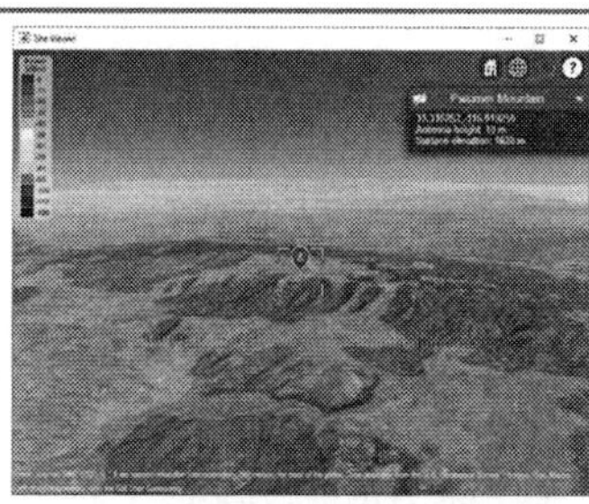

Coverage Map

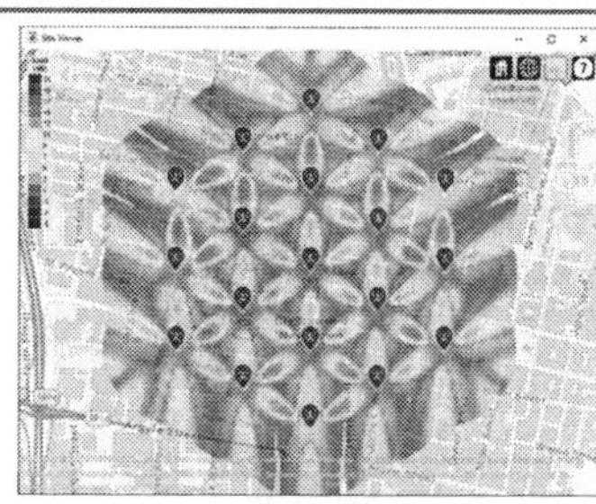

SINR Map

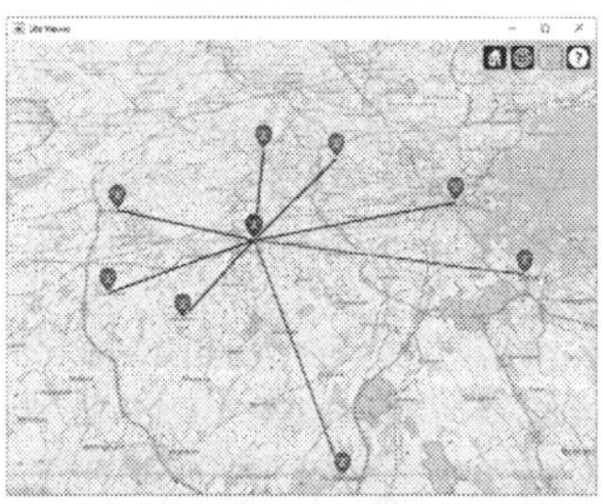

Comm Link

Line-of-Sight

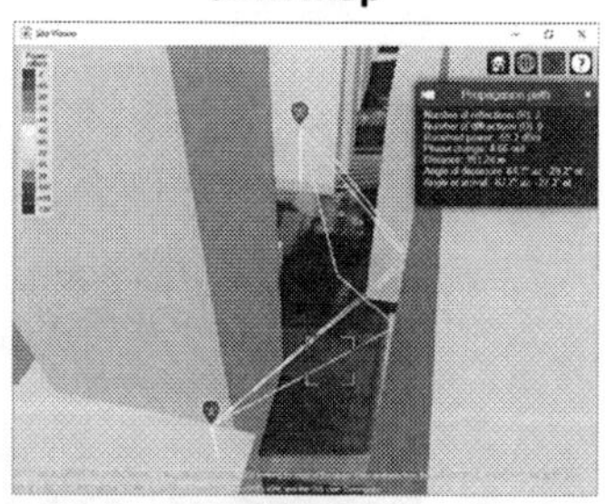

Ray Tracing

#SensorsConverge

Sensors Converge

Urban Environment for Ray Tracing

- You can download data from OpenStreetMap
  - Free, open, crowd-sourced database
- Import buildings from OpenStreetMap file in Site Viewer

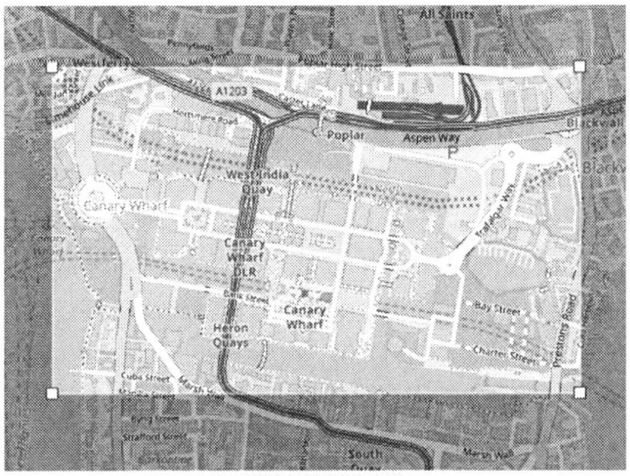

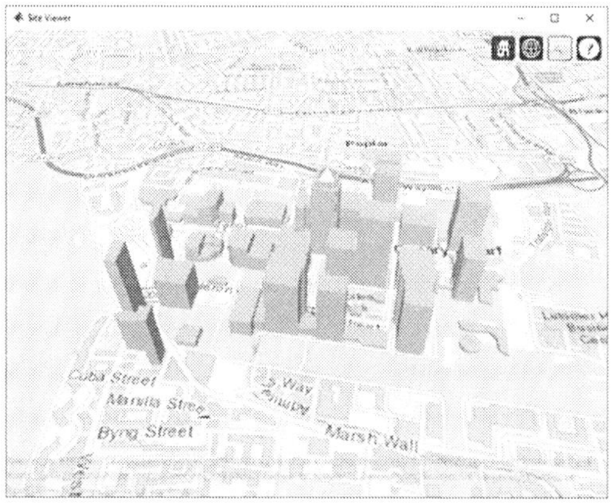

OpenStreetMap

```
siteviewer("Basemap","topographic", ...
           "Buildings","canarywharf.osm");
```

#SensorsConverge

Sensors Converge

Programmatic Access to Rays

- Returned ray object contains properties for geometry and RF Propagation values
- Use rays to:
  - Re-compute path loss with different materials using raypl
  - Compute Phased Array beam steering vectors
  - Configure channel models

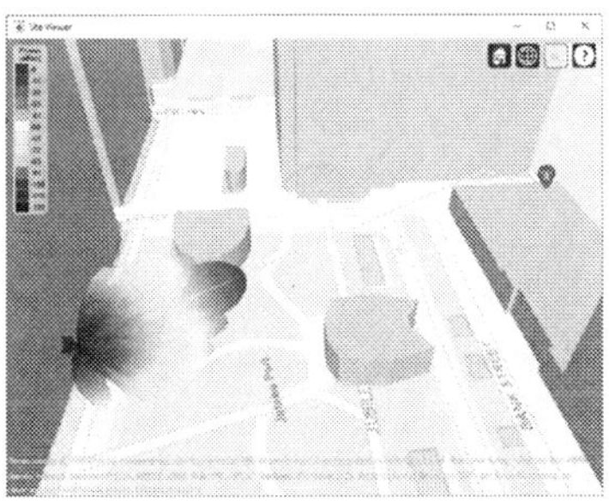

```
rays = raytrace(tx,rx);
disp(rays{1}(1))
```

```
  Ray with properties:

      PathSpecification: 'Locations'
       CoordinateSystem: 'Geographic'
    TransmitterLocation: [3×1 double]
       ReceiverLocation: [3×1 double]
            LineOfSight: 0
           Interactions: [1×1 struct]
              Frequency: 2.8000e+10
         PathLossSource: 'Custom'
               PathLoss: 115.4896
             PhaseShift: 4.0976

  Read-only properties:
       PropagationDelay: 6.6488e-07
    PropagationDistance: 199.3261
       AngleOfDeparture: [2×1 double]
         AngleOfArrival: [2×1 double]
        NumInteractions: 1
```

#SensorsConverge

Sensors Converge

Site Viewer Map Data Layers

RF Propagation Environment

```
siteviewer("Terrain","gmted2010", ...
           "Buildings","hongkong.osm");
```

Building Geometries

Basemap Imagery

Terrain Elevation

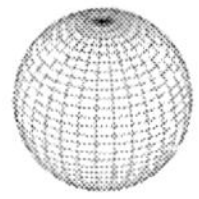

Earth Ellipsoid (WGS84)

#SensorsConverge

Sensors Converge

Effect of Environment/Material on Sensor Connectivity

- Support building materials specified in OpenStreetMap file
  - Technology leverage: 3D Geometry Library (material attributes on scene mesh)
- MATLAB API to import & edit buildings

```
% Read OSM buildings into table (Mapping Toolbox required)
bldgs = readgeotable("manhattan.osm",Layer="buildings");

% Update building materials, colors, or geometries
bldgs(1,:).Material = "glass";
bldgs(2,:).Material = "metal";
bldgs(3,:).Material = "concrete";

% Pass buildings to Site Viewer
sv  = siteviewer(Buildings=bldgs);
```

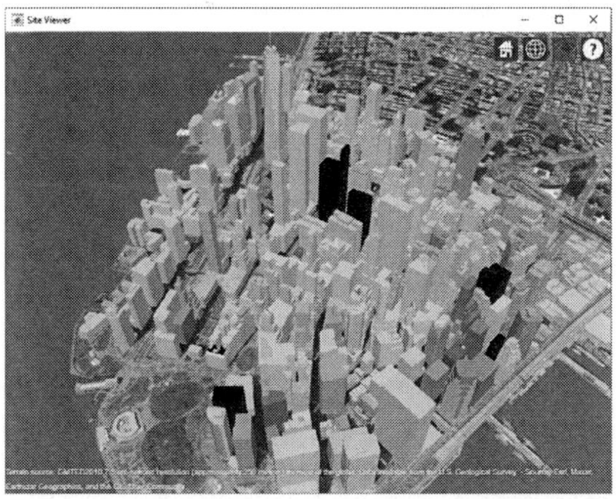

#SensorsConverge

Sensors Converge

Artificial Intelligence (AI)

MOTIVATIONS FOR AI IN WIRELESS

- Success of AI in other application areas (image processing, NLP)
- Hardware and computation power advancements

→ Improve performance using data-driven vs model-based approaches

→ Reduce algorithm complexity

→ Facilitate joint optimization of network and device operations

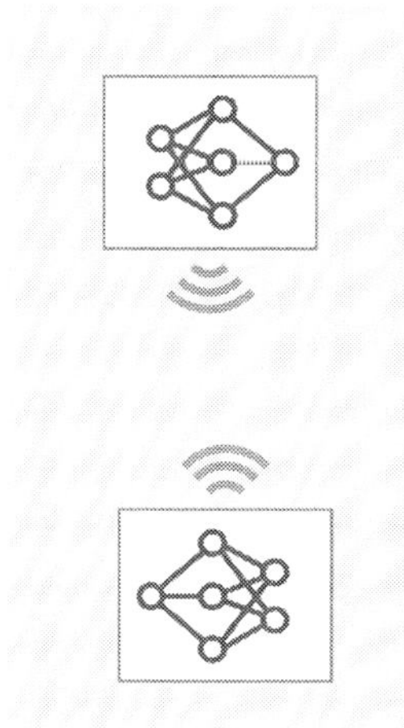

#SensorsConverge

Sensor Converge

Workflow of AI-driven Wireless System Design

Data Preparation	AI Modeling	Simulation & Test	Deployment
Data cleansing and preparation	Model design and tuning	Integration with complex systems	Embedded devices
Human insight	Hardware accelerated training	System simulation	Enterprise systems
Simulation-generated data	Interoperability	System verification and validation	Edge, cloud, desktop

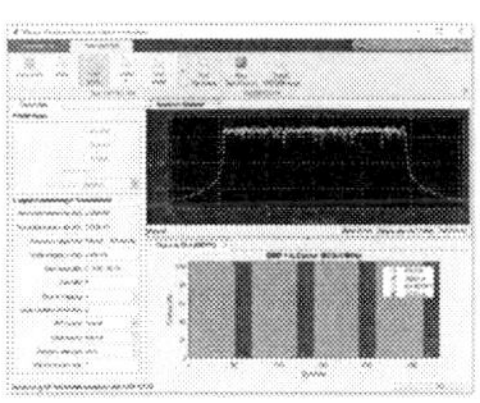

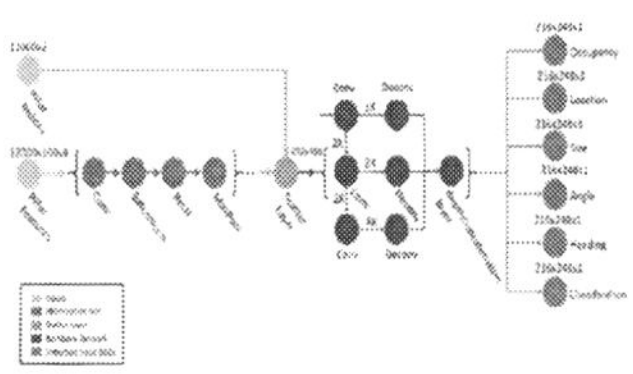

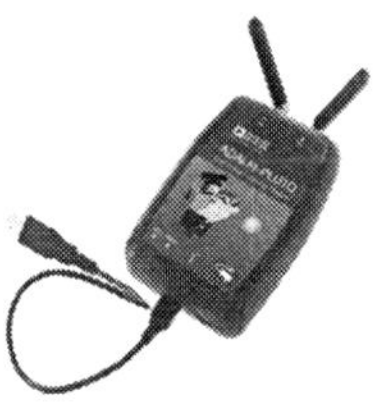

14

Reinforcement Learning

Training a self-driving car

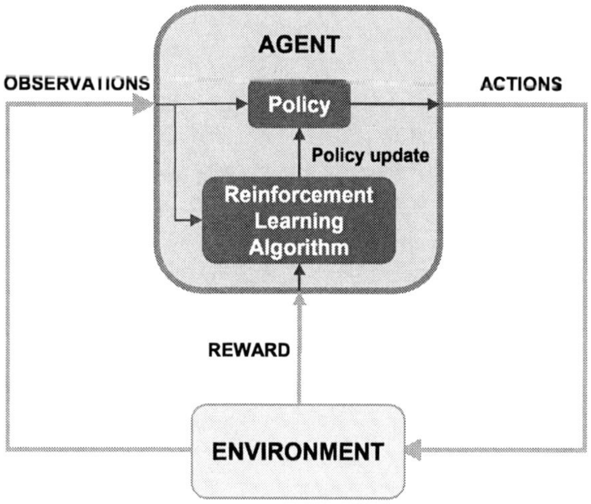

- Vehicle's computer... (**agent**)
- is reading sensor measurements from LIDAR, cameras... (**observations**)
- that represent road conditions, vehicle position... (**environment**)
- and generates steering, braking, throttle commands... (**action**)
- based on an internal state-to-action mapping... (**policy**)
- that tries to optimize, e.g., lap time & fuel efficiency... (**reward**)
- The policy is updated through repeated trial-and-error by a **reinforcement learning algorithm**

#SensorsConverge

Sensors Converge

AI for 6G – How MATLAB Can Help

Ready-to-use AI Workflows for Wireless

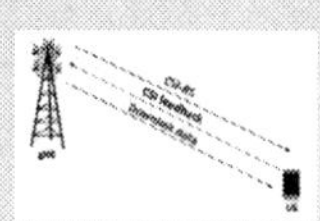

CSI Feedback with Autoencoders

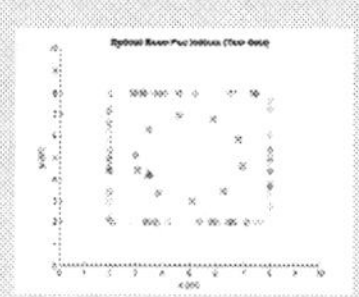

Neural Networks for Beam Selection

Neural Networks for Digital Predistortion

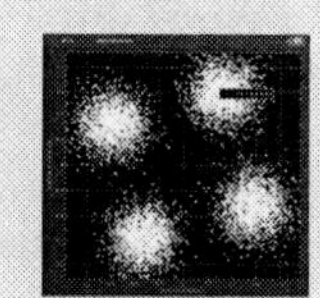

E2E Comms Systems with Autoencoders

Interoperate and Exchange Models with Python and other Frameworks

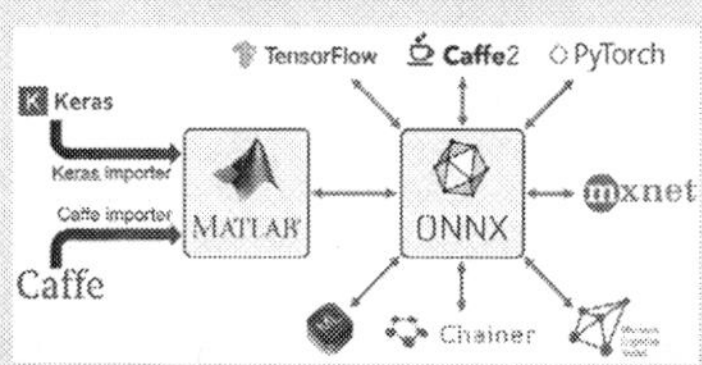

Capture Over the Air Signals to Train AI Models

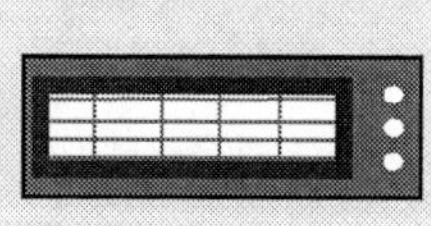

Test and Measurement Devices

Software-Defined Radios

#SensorsConverge

Sensors Converge

Presence Detection Using Wireless Sensing

R2023a

Use Wi-Fi channel state information to detect the presence of people in a room

- Capture Wi-Fi beacon CSI with SDR and WLAN Toolbox with and without movement to create a data set or use downloaded 3P data set
- Train a neural network to classify presence

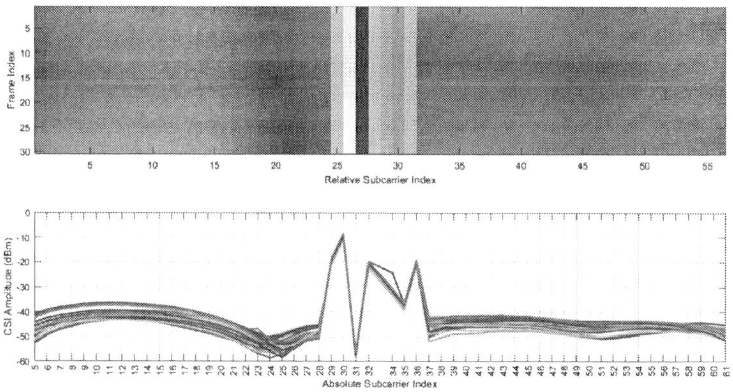

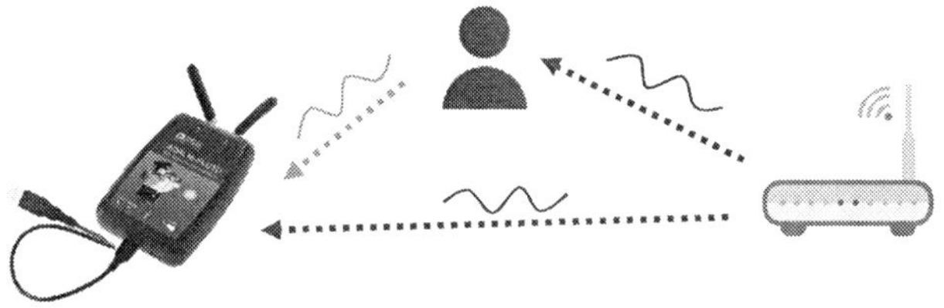

#SensorsConverge

Summary

- Operation of sensor networks rely heavily on "situational awareness" and "Localization and Positioning" of sensors in use
- 5G/6G and Wi-Fi evolution requires modeling the channel models and their real-time dynamics
- Joint wireless communications and sensing combines spatial awareness, link analysis and channel modeling
- MATLAB tools in RF propagation, Ray tracing and Reinforcement leaning can jointly optimize Digital, RF and Antenna parts of your sensor network design.

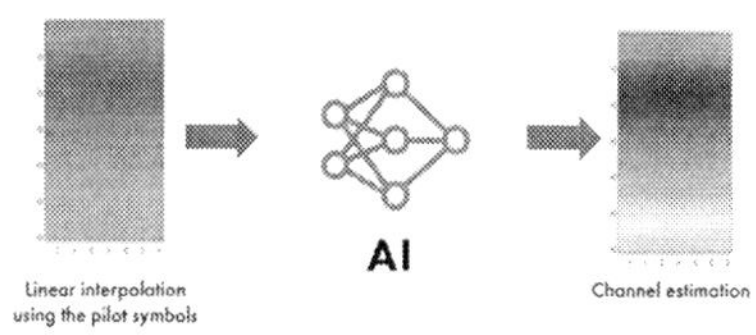

#SensorsConverge

AGENDA

- Smart Manufacturing
- Data Maturity Model
- Challenges in data collection in Manufacturing
- Industrial Data Flow
- Industry 4.0 Reference Architecture
- Introduction to HiveMQ
- Success Stories
- Next Steps

Smart Manufacturing?

HIVEMQ

Global Trends & Challenges in Manufacturing

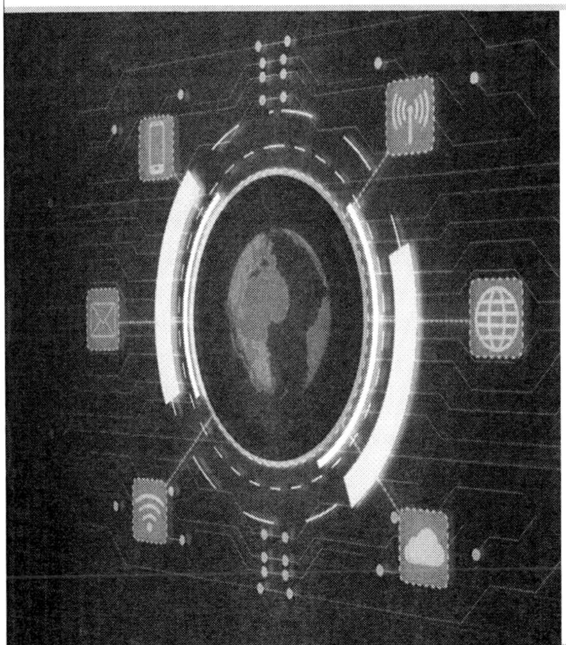

- **Material shortage** leads to reduced output and difficult planning
- **Carbon Footprint & Energy Cost** has increasing impact on profit margins
- **Security Vulnerabilities** become major business risk
- **Global Supply Chains** are more fragile than imagined
- **Demographic & Society Changes** lead to skills shortage & lack of young talent
- **Regulations & Bureaucracy** becomes an increasing burden

7

Components of Smart Manufacturing

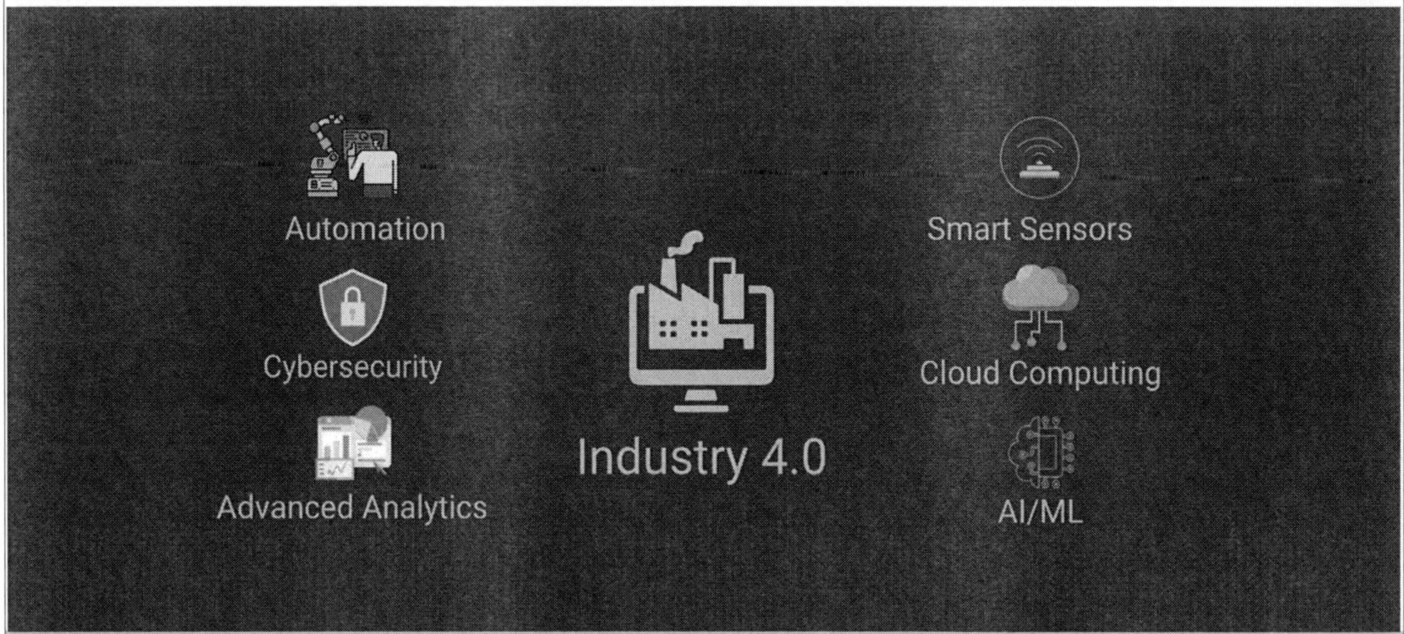

 8

Power of Smart Manufacturing through I4.0, IIoT & AI

McKinsey Report: Capturing the true value of Industry 4.0

- 30-50% reductions in machine downtime
- 10-30% increases in throughput
- 15-30% improvements in labor productivity
- 85% more accurate forecasting

IIoT enables AI to learn from your production process by connecting it to your physical assets & to automatically adjust & optimize it

 9

Short & Long Term Impact on Business

- **Automation** → reduce workforce, eliminate repetitive / unhealthy work & be the most attractive employer
- **Operational efficiency** → increased productivity with higher margins
- **Shorter and more optimized supply chains** → strategic flexibility to mitigate globalization risks
- **Secure communication between plants, data center & cloud** → eliminate business interruption risk
- Enable **new product innovation** through further adoption

Data Maturity Model

HIVEMQ

Data Maturity Model for Industry 4.0

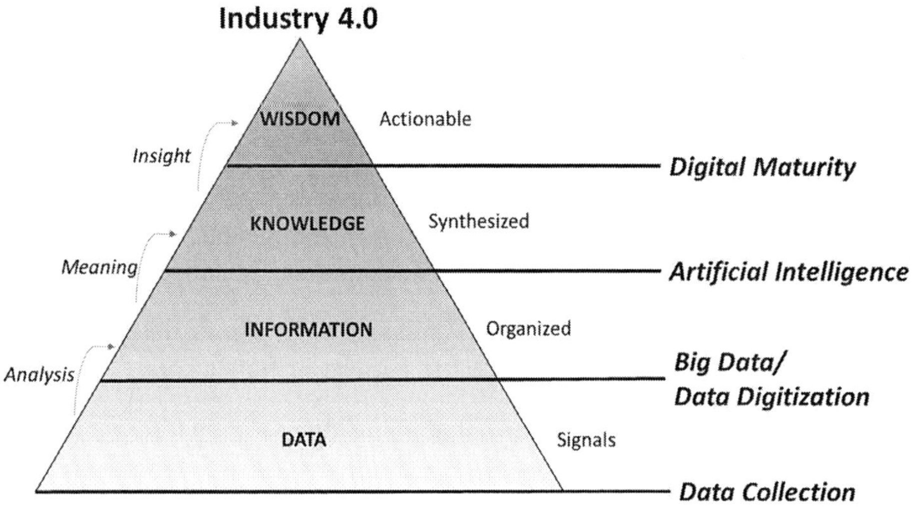

Challenges in data collection in Manufacturing

- Working to solve complex issues like **heterogeneous devices, protocols, vendor solutions** on the shop floor
- **Data silos** with the various machines, processes and applications on the shop floor and between different sites
- **Unreliable connectivity** on the factory networks
- **Legacy architectures** that lack bi-directional data connectivity
- **Limited bandwidth** for communication

Data Collection Value Creation Loop

Gather

Gather data and signals from the field

Analyze

Analyze on Edge or Cloud

Share

Share with enterprise systems

Control

Control and manage the endpoints in the field

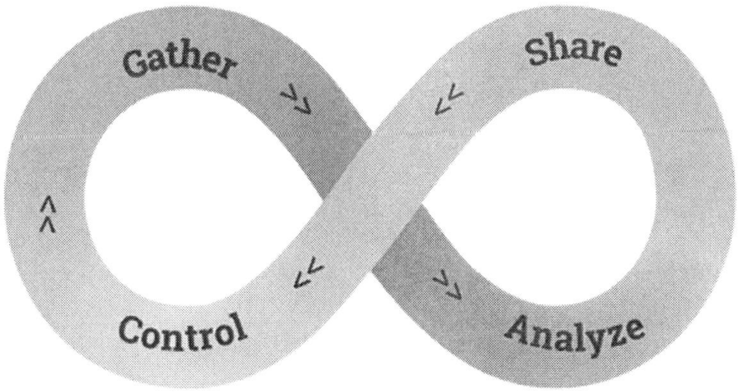

Manufacturing Data Flow

HIVEMQ

Data Flow prior to Enterprise data set up

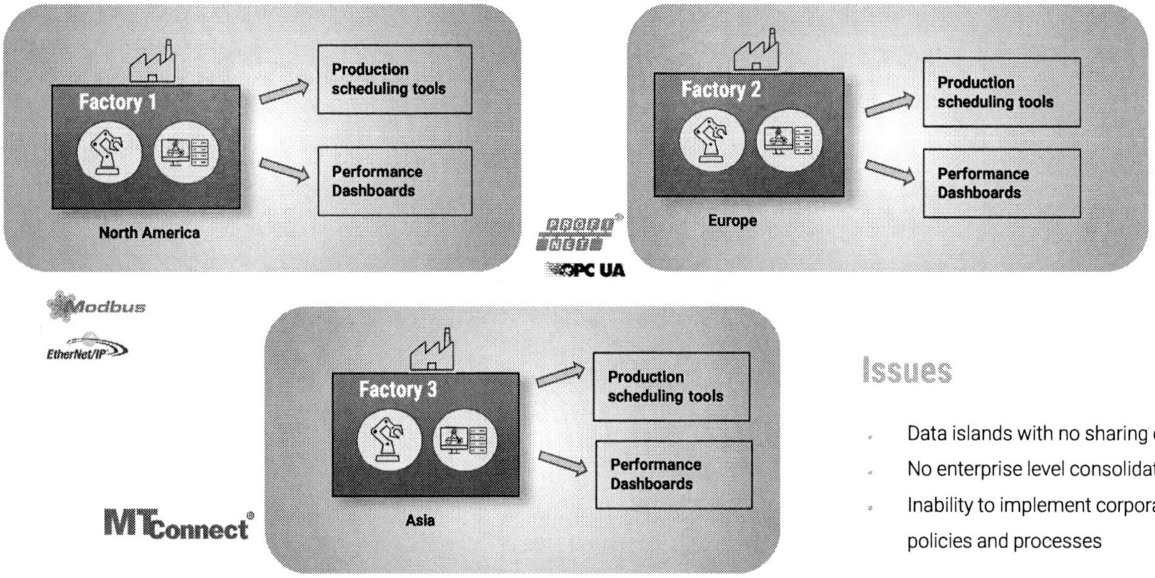

Issues

- Data islands with no sharing of best practices
- No enterprise level consolidation of data
- Inability to implement corporate level data policies and processes

What is MQTT?

- A standard binary publish-subscribe messaging protocol designed for fast and reliable data transport between devices especially under very constrained conditions
- Constraints include unreliable network connectivity, limited bandwidth, limited battery power, and so on
- Built on top of TCP/IP
- Ideal for the Industrial Internet of Things

MQTT

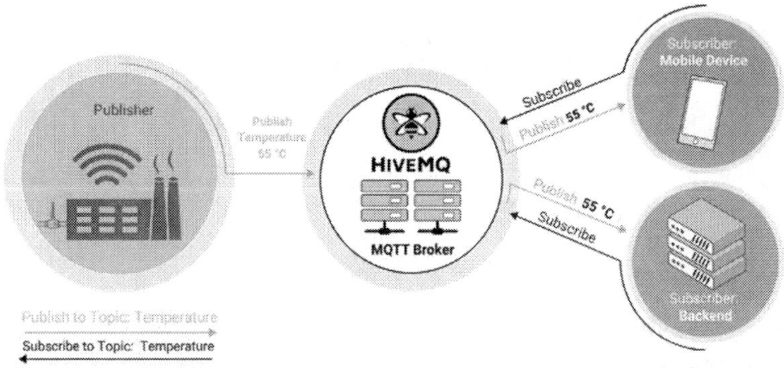

Data Flow After Enterprise Data Set up with MQTT

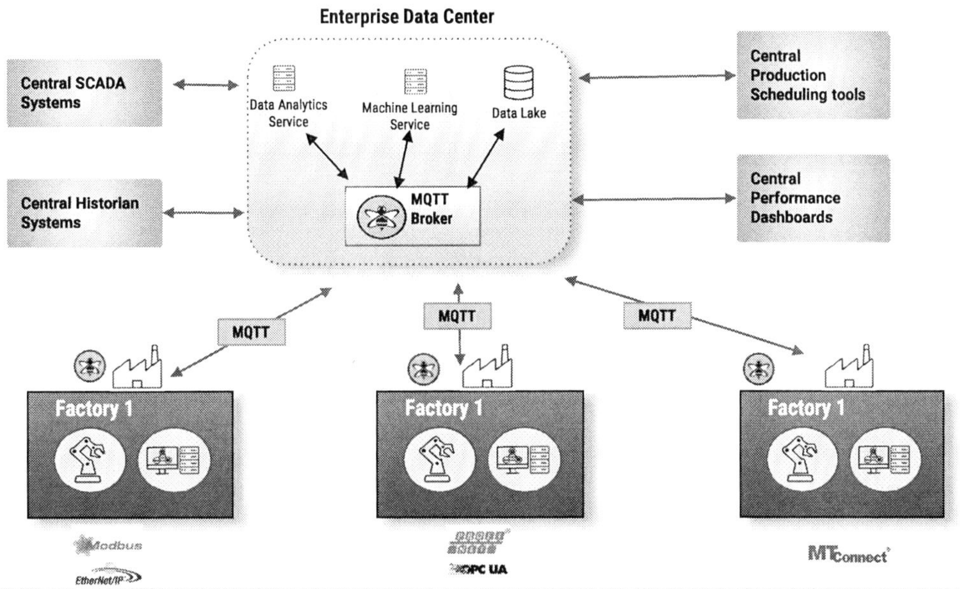

Benefits

- Secure open standard based communication over public Internet
- Scalability & Hyperconnectivity on enterprise or cloud
- No data silos
- Enterprise level insights & optimization

 18

Connecting Factory systems using MQTT

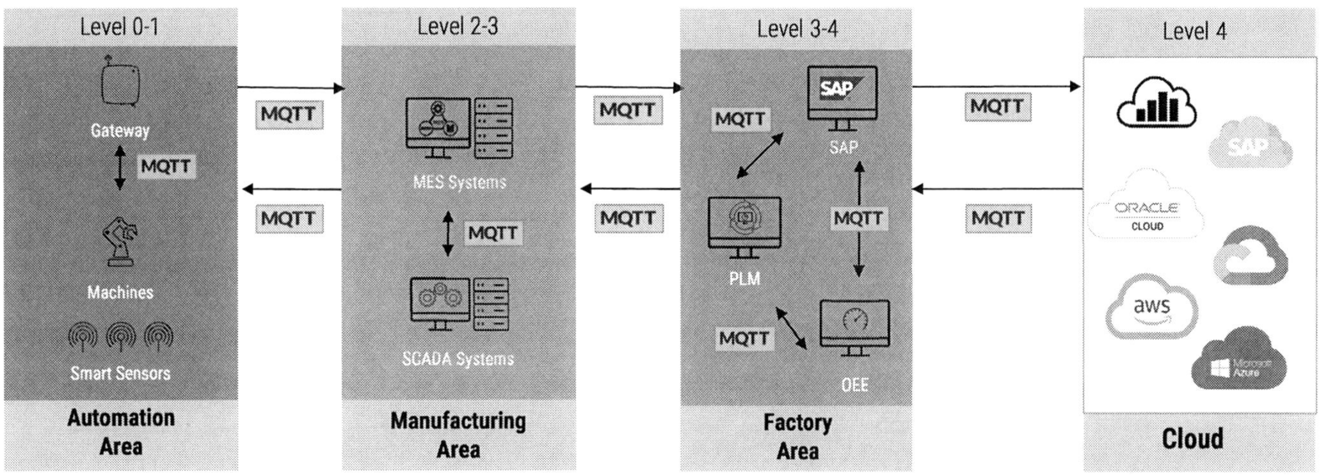

Which of the following protocols do you consider strategic to fulfill your IIoT strategy?

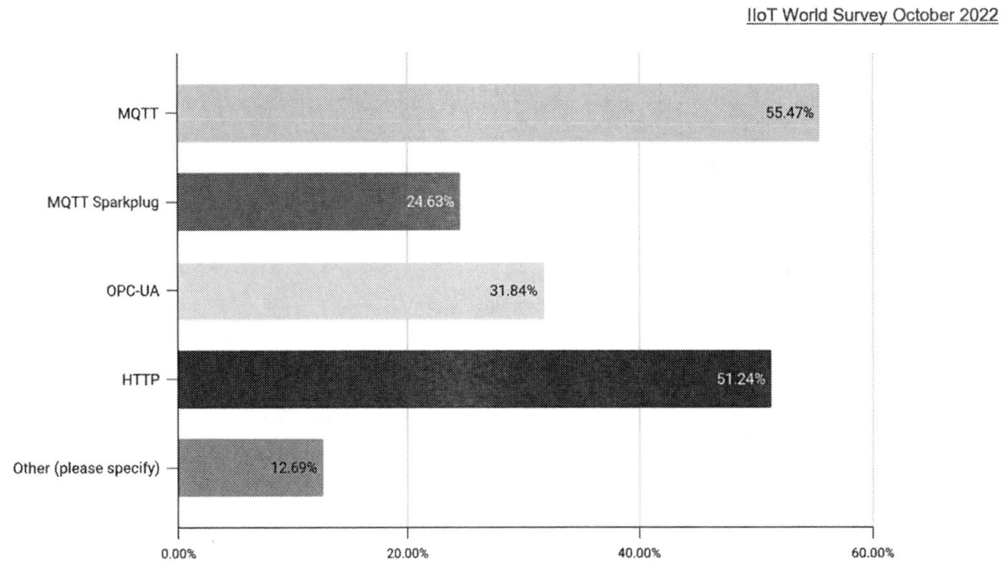

 20

Industry 4.0 Reference Architecture with Unified Namespace

HIVEMQ

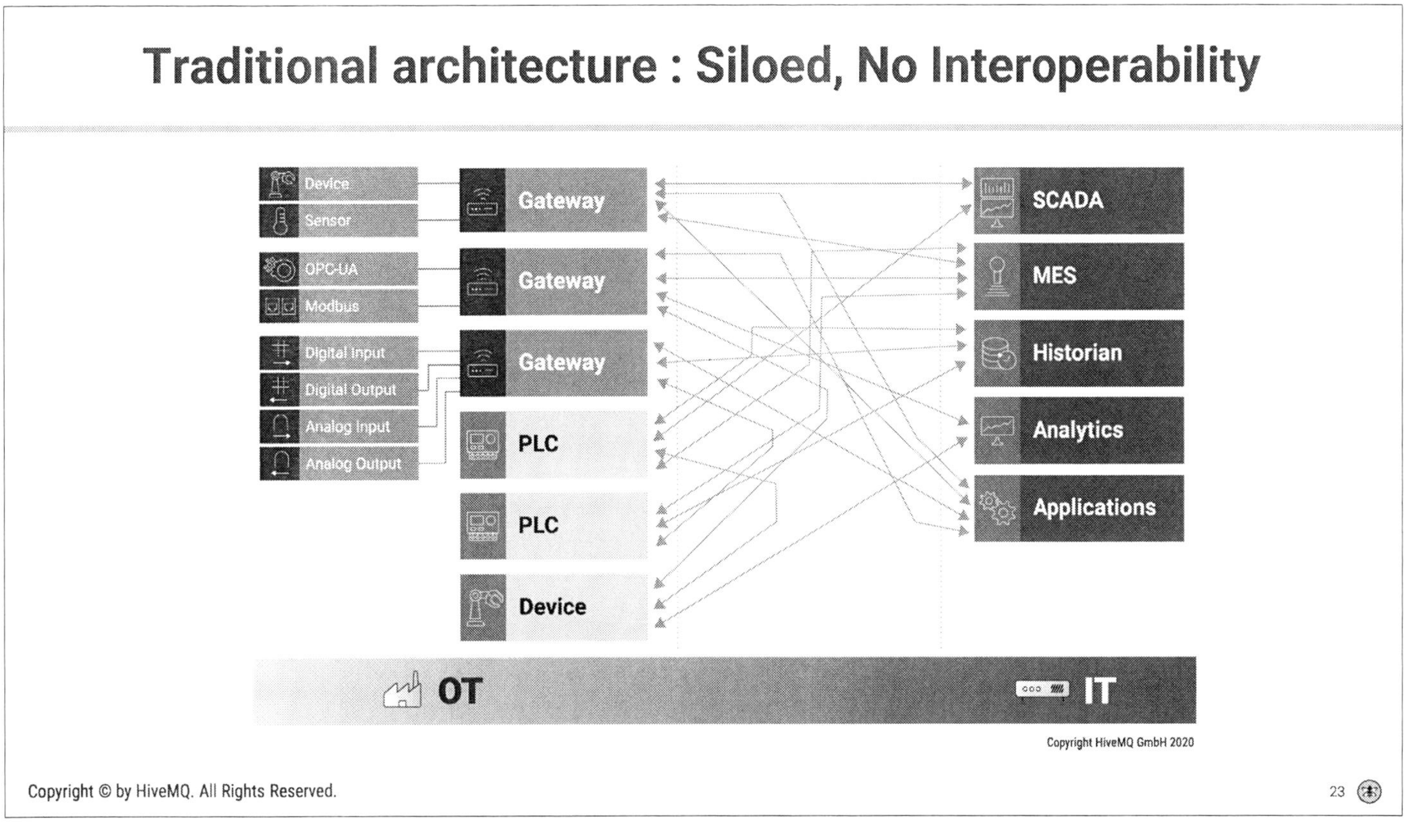
Traditional architecture : Siloed, No Interoperability
Device
Sensor
OPC-UA
Modbus
Digital Input
Digital Output
Analog Input
Analog Output
Gateway
Gateway
Gateway
PLC
PLC
Device
SCADA
MES
Historian
Analytics
Applications
OT
IT
Copyright HiveMQ GmbH 2020
Copyright © by HiveMQ. All Rights Reserved.
23

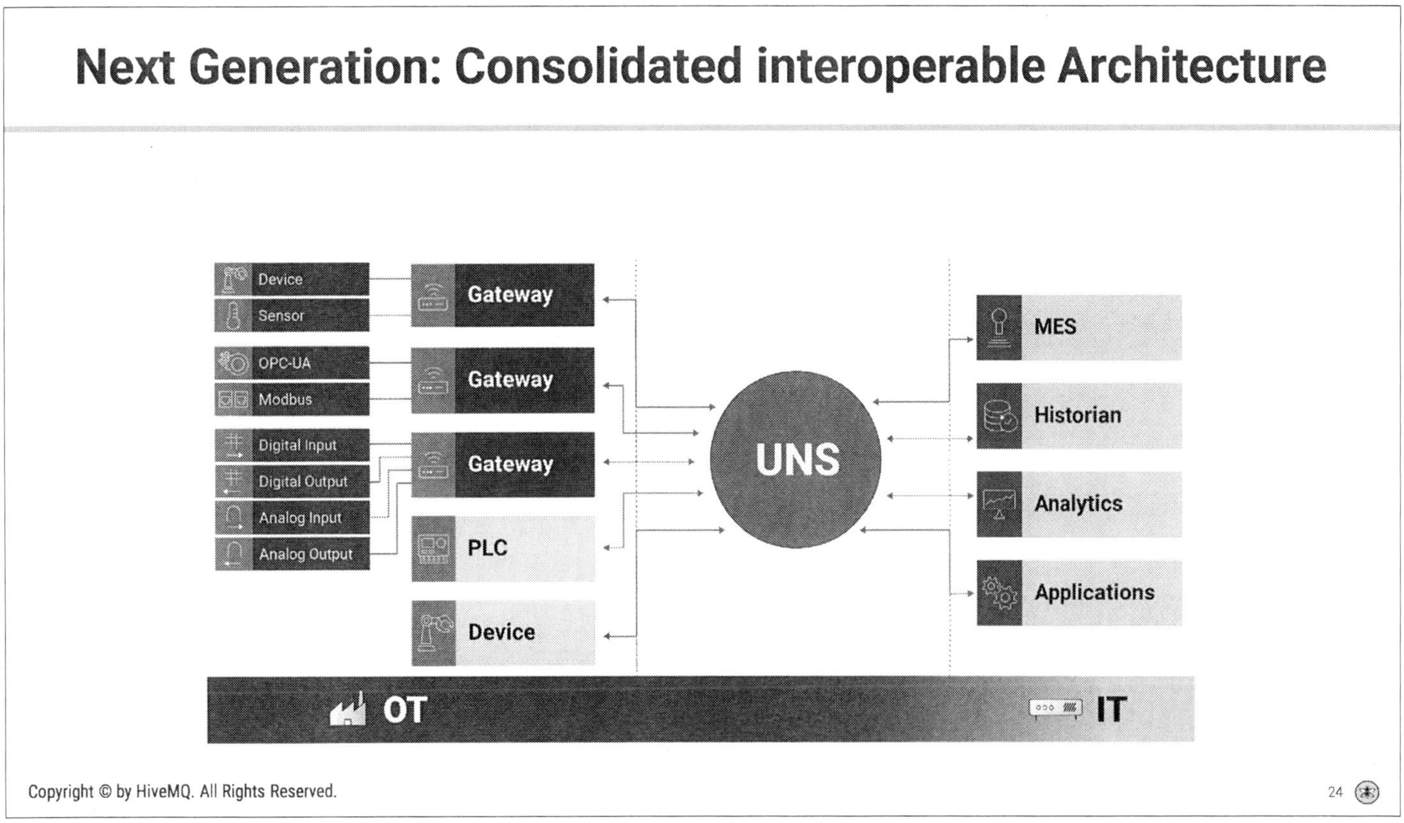
Next Generation: Consolidated interoperable Architecture
Device
Sensor
OPC-UA
Modbus
Digital Input
Digital Output
Analog Input
Analog Output
Gateway
Gateway
Gateway
PLC
Device
UNS
MES
Historian
Analytics
Applications
OT
IT
Copyright © by HiveMQ. All Rights Reserved.
24

Reference architecture with MQTT Sparkplug

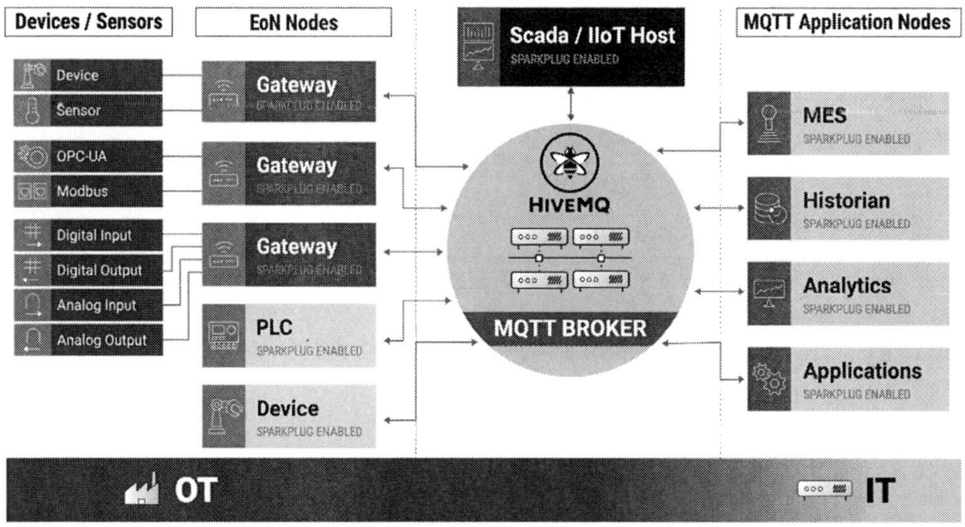

Introducing HiveMQ

HIVEMQ

Introduction to HiveMQ

- **Founded in 2012**, based outside of Munich
- HiveMQ helps **move data to and from connected devices** in an **efficient**, **fast** and **reliable** manner
- 160+ employees
- **180+ customers** with production IoT applications

MOST INNOVATIVE IoT
GERMAN ACCELERATOR
50 Technology Fast 50 2018

Audi SIEMENS LIBERTY GLOBAL

MQTT.ORG
OASIS MQTT TC
Helped standardize IoT Standard

Sparkplug

iot eclipse.org
Eclipse IoT working group
Member

Enterprise MQTT Platform

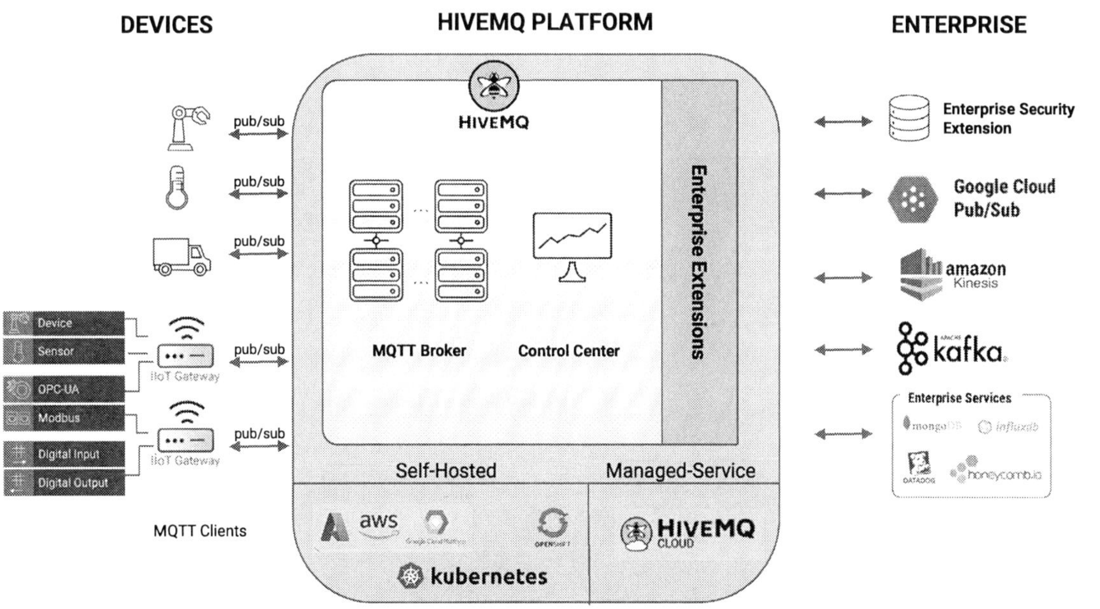

- Scalable
- Highly Available
- Reliable
- Robust
- Secure
- Observable
- Interoperable
- Integrates anything
- Runs anywhere

HiveMQ Extension Overview

HIVEMQ
EXTENSION
FOR KAFKA

Seamlessly integrates MQTT messages into the Kafka messaging flow

HIVEMQ
Enterprise Security
Extension

Enable crucial security features for safe and secure enterprise IT and OT deployments

HIVEMQ
ENTERPRISE BRIDGE
EXTENSION

A Scalable & Secure solution that bridges a HiveMQ cluster with any other MQTT broker

HIVEMQ
ENTERPRISE EXTENSION
FOR GOOGLE CLOUD PUB/SUB

Seamlessly integrates the HiveMQ platform with Google Cloud, enabling MQTT data transmission at hyper-scale

HIVEMQ
DISTRIBUTED TRACING
EXTENSION

Trace MQTT data end-to-end, using OpenTelemetry and monitor 1,500+ metrics via your APM solution

NEW

HIVEMQ
ENTERPRISE EXTENSION
FOR AMAZON KINESIS

Quickly move your MQTT data from the broker directly into AWS via Amazon Kinesis Data Streams

 29

Our Enterprise Customers

HIVEMQ

Automotive Manufacturing

Benz Vehicle Diagnostics System (VDS)

- VDS is critical part of manufacturing process and can not go down
- If VDS goes down for >10 min, assembly line may stop
- Requires reliable messaging platform for factory to cloud connectivity

HiveMQ Solution

- Each instance of VDS includes multiple test devices on factory floor, connected with a HiveMQ broker located in factory
- Ensures a test device continues to behave properly if network connection is dropped and reconnected
- Fast, efficient and easy way to share information between factory floor and enterprise IT systems

Result
- Rolled out to 24 factories around the world
- 10,000 testing devices connected
- Generating 470 million messages/month

31

Media Streaming

Customer can control set-up box with phone in the same way as with the remote

- Handle more than 5 million simultaneous connected devices
- Instant switching between screens (main screen, mobile, etc.)
- Consistent response time as customers move between devices

LIBERTY GLOBAL

HiveMQ solution

- HiveMQ is reliable, always-on and can scale easily
- Lightweight nature of MQTT allow low network latency
- HiveMQ delivers millisecond latency
- HiveMQ monitoring provides observability for operations team

Result
- Customer satisfaction scores very high
- 1.5 million connected in 2019
- global rollout to 2.5 million devices is planned

32

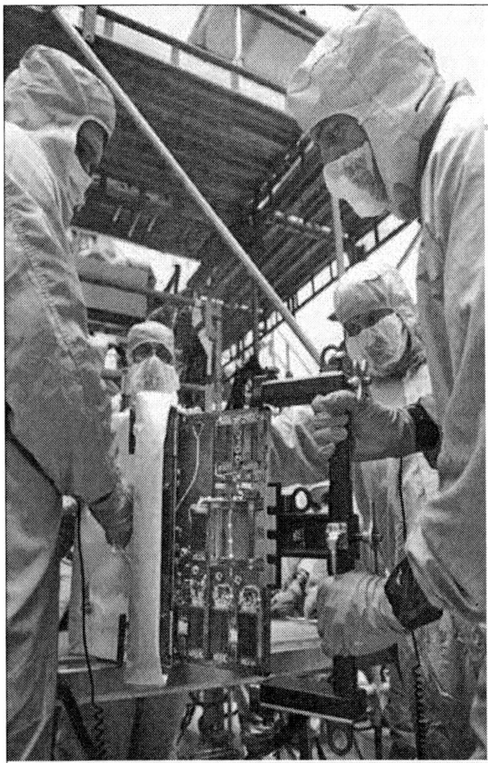

Pharma Manufacturing

Company's global manufacturing business drivers

- Make data driven business decisions across the enterprise
- Automate regulatory reports and flag any quality issues as early as possible
- **Drive efficiency and productivity by 30%**

Corporate Goal and measure of success:

- **$ 1.5 billion productivity goal by 2024** in their 15 factories globally (100 Million per site)

HiveMQ Solution

- Installed in 6 factories with a goal to be expanded to 15
- Connected all strategic assets on factory floor to a HiveMQ broker located in factory
- Fast, efficient and easy way to share information between brokers in different factory locations to a centralized enterprise HiveMQ broker that provides a single pane of glass
- Enable bi-direction movement of data to and from cloud platform for reporting, dashboarding and analytics

 33

Connected Cars

Mobile app using SMS/HTTP took up to 30 secs to unlock door

HiveMQ solution

- Always-on connectivity for all devices
- HiveMQ runs on expandable Kubernetes cluster
- MQTT is designed for network low latency and Push communication
- HiveMQ implements all quality of service levels to guarantee delivery
- MQTT saves
  - 34% network bandwidth per message
  - Up to 80% if more than 100 messages

Result	• Sub-second response time for key capabilities like unlock car • Core communication infrastructure of the most popular car sharing app of Germany

 34

HiveMQ: Trusted by more than 180 Brands

- Building new digital products
- Improving customer experience
- Creating more efficient operations

...and more

THANK YOU

HIVEMQ

Key HiveMQ Assets

Blog on MQTT Sparkplug Enables Smart Manufacturing Blog

New to MQTT Sparkplug? Get the MQTT Sparkplug Essentials eBook

HIVEMQ

Get started with HiveMQ today: https://www.hivemq.com/downloads/

Manufacturing White Paper: Modernizing the Smart Manufacturing Industry with MQTT

Voler SYSTEMS

What Does 5G Do for IoT and Wearable Devices?

Sensors Converge June 22, 2023

The Promise of 5G

- **Higher bandwidth, ultra-reliable, low-latency**
- **Addresses three key problems for the wireless infrastructure:**
  - **Enhanced data throughput** – astounding amount of data
  - **Always on** – ability for devices to always be connected
  - **Reduced latency** – enable additional types of solutions (i.e. healthcare, manufacturing and automotive applications)

But these are not important for most IoT applications.

2

Voler SYSTEMS

5G Spectrum Within Three Key Frequency Bands

Similar to 4G Coverage and capacity — *New with 5G*

BELOW 1 GHZ

Low-band spectrum

- Will support widespread coverage across urban, suburban and rural areas
- Good in-building coverage
- Peak data speeds up to 100 Mbps
- Used by carriers in the U.S. for LTE
- Bandwidth is nearly depleted

1-6 GHZ

Mid-band spectrum

- Good mixture of coverage and capacity benefits.
- Peak data speeds reach as high as 400 Mbps
- Faster speeds and lower latency than lower band
- Does not penetrate buildings as well as low-band

6 GHz – 86 GHz

High-band spectrum

- *Above 6 GHz needed for ultra-high broadband speeds. 28 GHz to 39 GHz bands identified in the USA*
- *Up to 2 Gbps*
- *Often referred to as mmWave*
- ***Major weaknesses:** low coverage area and poor building penetration*
- *Blocked by walls, windows, cars, trees, rain, or snow*

3

Voler SYSTEMS

5G Coverage, Bandwidth, and Latency

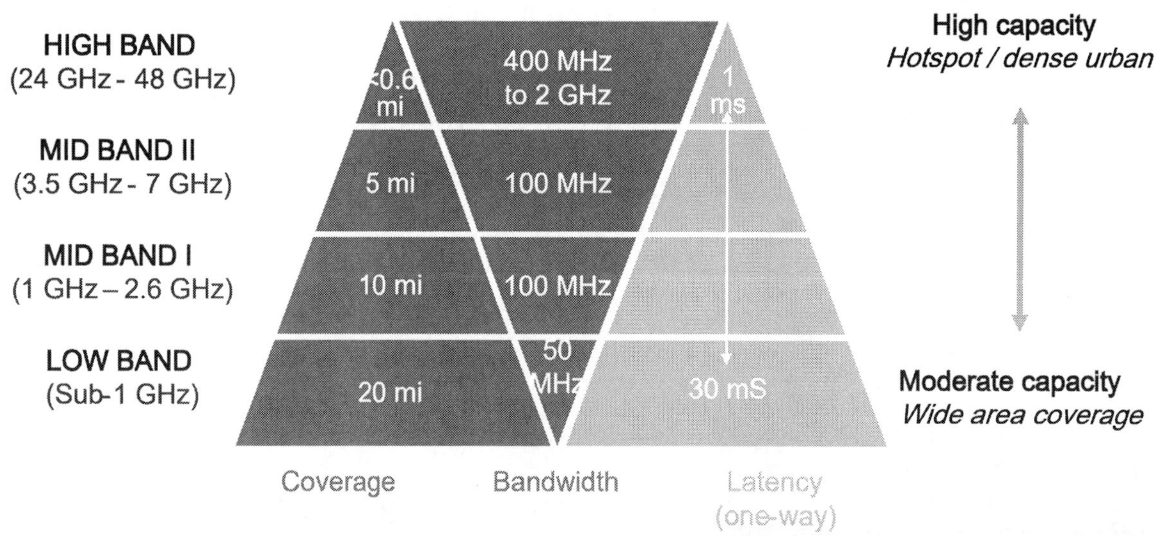

4

Source: SCTE•ISBE and NCTA and others

Voler SYSTEMS

The 5G Service Classes

eMBB
Enhanced mobile broadband
Very high data rates
Very High traffic capacity

CHARACTERISTIC
High peak data rates | High speed mobility | down to 4 ms of air latency

USE CASES
Smart phones, tablets, home/enterprise/venues applications, UHD TV (4K and 8K) broadcast, and virtual reality/augmented reality

5G

mMTC
Massive machine-type communications
Massive number of devices
Very low device cost
Very low energy consumption

CHARACTERISTIC
Will support massive IoT deployments

USE CASES
Smart buildings, logistics, tracking, fleet management, wearable devices, and smart meters

URLLC
Ultra-reliable and low-latency communications
Very low latency
Ultra high reliability and availability

CHARACTERISTIC
As low as 1 ms air latency

USE CASES
Traffic safety and control, remote surgery, and industrial control

5 Source: ITU-R SGO5 Voler SYSTEMS

URLLC Service Class - Mostly On-Premise

Scenario	End-to-end latency	Reliability	User experienced data rate	Traffic density	Service area dimension
Discrete automation – motion control	1 ms	99.9999%	1 Mbps up to 10 Mbps	1 Tbps /km^2	100 x 100 x 30 m
Process automation – remote control	50 ms	99.9999%	1 Mbps up to 100 Mbps	100 Gbps /km^2	300 x 300 x 50 m
Electricity distribution – high voltage	5 ms	99.9999%	10 Mbps	100 Gbps /km^2	200 km along power line
Intelligent transport systems – infrastructure backhaul	10 ms	99.9999%	10 Mbps	10 Gbps /km^2	2 km along a road

6 Source: NOKIA 2018 Voler SYSTEMS

URLLC Limitations

Mostly On-Premise uses

- No wide area coverage
- Equipment typically installed by the user
- Not for public service

Latency is one way from transmitter to receiver

- Local termination reduces network latency that is up to 100 mS in 4G
- Does not include the delay in the backbone of the network in latency figures

Highly reliable communication

- Much better than 4G

7

Voler SYSTEMS

mMTC (IoT) Service Class

- **Low-power Wide-area (LPWA)**
- **160 bits/sec (up to 10 Kb/sec)**
- **1 million devices / km^2**
- **Round trip latency of 10 seconds with 20-byte payload**
- **Low cost hardware**
- **Not available now in 5G**

8

Voler SYSTEMS

Current State of mMTC

- 5G mMTC standards are being worked on
- Current 5G not optimized for packet size, short sessions
- Inefficient control signaling – 100 bytes of signaling to send 10 bytes of data
- Present channel coding schemes are inefficient with small data packets
- 5G uses higher power than 4G
- LTE services have been adopted as part of 5G

Voler SYSTEMS

Other Issues with 5G

mmWave signals are blocked by walls, windows, trees, cars, people, rain, or snow

mmWave signals don't transmit very far
- C-net Reported best coverage is line of sight 100 to 300 ft from base station

Phones use higher power for mmWave band
- Phone switches to lower band or 4G at high ambient temperature

Base stations use 3 times the power of LTE – not green

Concern about health effects of mmWave signals

Interference with weather satellites by mmWave frequencies

10

Voler SYSTEMS

LTE (4G) is being expanded for IoT Services

NB-IoT

NB-IoT and LTE-M (also called CAT-M)

- Coverage in the U.S. is good.
- 50,000 devices per cell
- NB-IoT and LTE-M will coexist with 5G for years into the future
- Now part of 5G mMTC spec
- NB-IoT not suitable for mobile – lack automatic zone switching

Non-cellular services are not included in 5G, but will still work

- LoRa, Sigfox and others
- Use unlicensed spectrum – lower cost air-time
- Not available most places

11

Voler SYSTEMS

Comparison of Existing IoT Wireless Standards

	NB-IoT NB1	NB-IoT NB2	CAT-M1 LTE-M	CAT-M2 LTE-M	LoRa	Sigfox
Range	1-50 km	1-50 km	1-50 km	1-50 km	2-50 km	10-50 km
Data rate	26-66 Kbits/s	120-150 Kbits/s	1 Mbits/s	4-7 Mbit/s	200-50K bits/s	300 bits/s
Supports Voice	No	No	Yes	Yes	No	No
Network	Public	Public	Public	Public	Public or Private	Public
Available	Good coverage	Good coverage	Good coverage	Good coverage	Yes Limited public	30% of US population

12

Voler SYSTEMS

The 5G Service Classes

Not for IoT

eMBB
Enhanced mobile broadband
Very high data rates
Very High traffic capacity

Uses LTE services

5G

mMTC
Massive machine-type communications
Massive number of devices
Very low device cost
Very low energy consumption

High speed on-premise IoT

URLLC
Ultra-reliable and low-latency communications
Very low latency
Ultra high reliability and availability

13

Voler SYSTEMS

NB-IoT Coverage by T-Mobile, June 2021

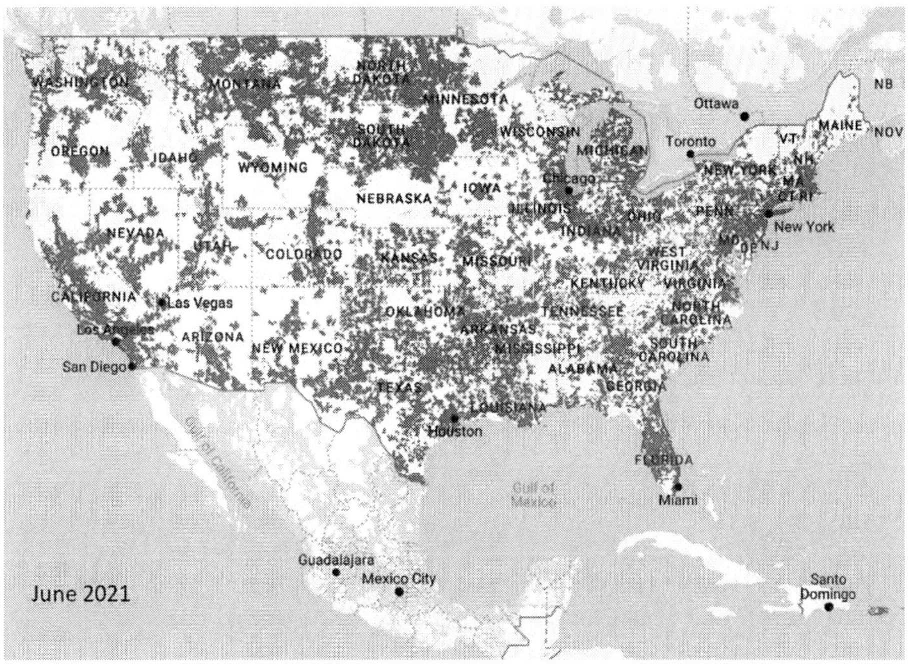

14

Voler SYSTEMS

NB-IoT and LTE-M Deployment

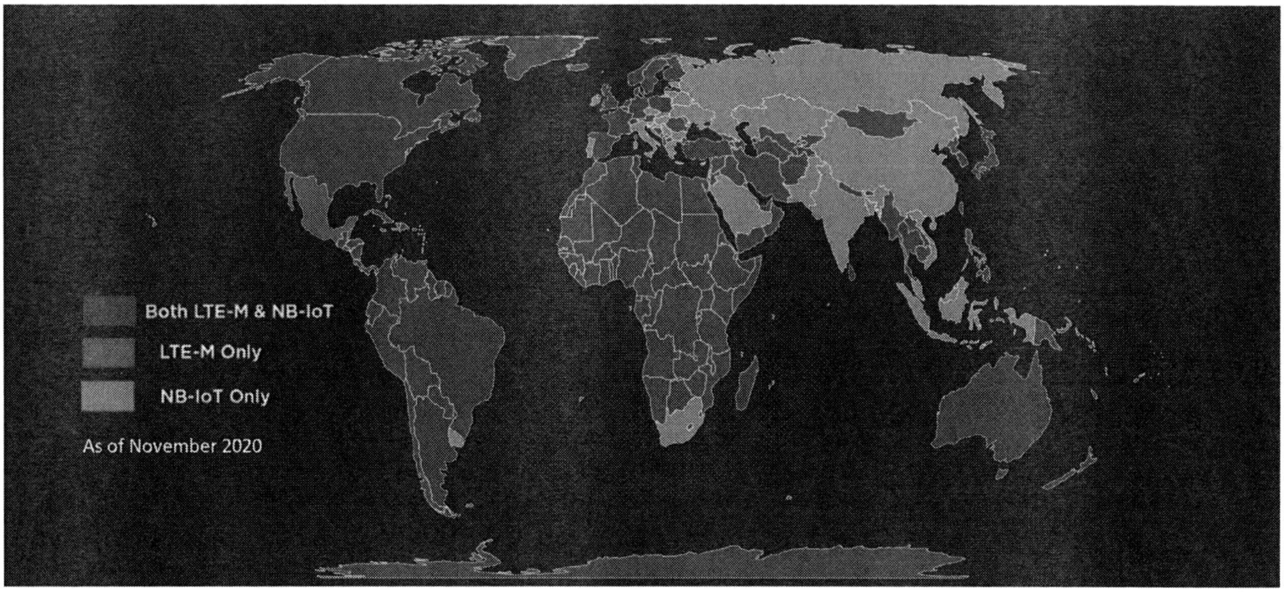

15

Voler SYSTEMS

LPWAN (IoT) Compared to Others
Power – How much? How far?

	100 bps		10K bps		40K bps	
1 m	BLE4/Zigbee	**0.15**	BLE4/Zigbee	**7.5**	Zigbee	**30**
	BLE Mesh	**0.15**	BLE Mesh	**7.5**	LoRa	**20**
	LoRa	**0.5**	LoRa	**10**	NB-IoT	**50**
	Sigfox	**0.5**	NB-IoT	**20**	CAT-M1	**50**
	NB-IoT	**0.5**	CAT-M1	**20**		
	CAT-M1	**0.5**				
50 m	Zigbee	**20**	Zigbee	**30**	NB-IoT	**100**
	LoRa	**0.5**	LoRa	**20**	CAT-M1	**100**
	Sigfox	**0.5**	NB-IoT	**30**		
	NB-IoT	**1.0**	CAT-M1	**30**		
	CAT-M1	**1.0**				
1 km	LoRa	**20**	NB-IoT	**100**	NB-IoT	**500**
	Sigfox	**20**	CAT-M1	**100**	CAT-M1	**500**
	NB-IoT	**20**				
	CAT-M1	**20**				

Units: mW

Voler SYSTEMS

< Slide 17 >

What should be considered for tradeoffs?

- Data rate
- Transmission distance
- Power Consumption
- Cost
- Licensed vs unlicensed spectrum
- Carrier deployed vs customer deployed
- Availability of technology
- Density of end devices
- Where it gets deployed
- Firmware updates
- Drivers for your OS
- Component/ module selection
- Antennas

Voler SYSTEMS

Let Voler Help You Succeed!

Voler designs IoT and wearable devices with expertise in wireless communication and sensors

Walt Maclay, Voler Systems
Walt@volersystems.com
408-245-9844 ext 101

Quality Electronic Design & Software
Wearable Devices | Sensor Interfaces | Wireless | Medical Devices

Slides will be at www.volersystems.com

Voler SYSTEMS

Sensors Converge

Case Study: Evaluating an Automotive User Interface Design

June 20–22, 2023 | Santa Clara, CA

#SensorsConverge

Agenda

- **Overview**
- **Mechanical Switch Basics**
  - Typical operation
  - Failure modes
  - Maintenance
- **Design Goal**
- **Push-button Knob**
  - Sensor replacement
  - Simulation
  - CORDIC
- **Turn Indicator**
  - Sensor replacement
  - Simulation
  - Vector Angles
- **Test Results**
- **Demonstration**
- **Summary**

Steering column stalk module

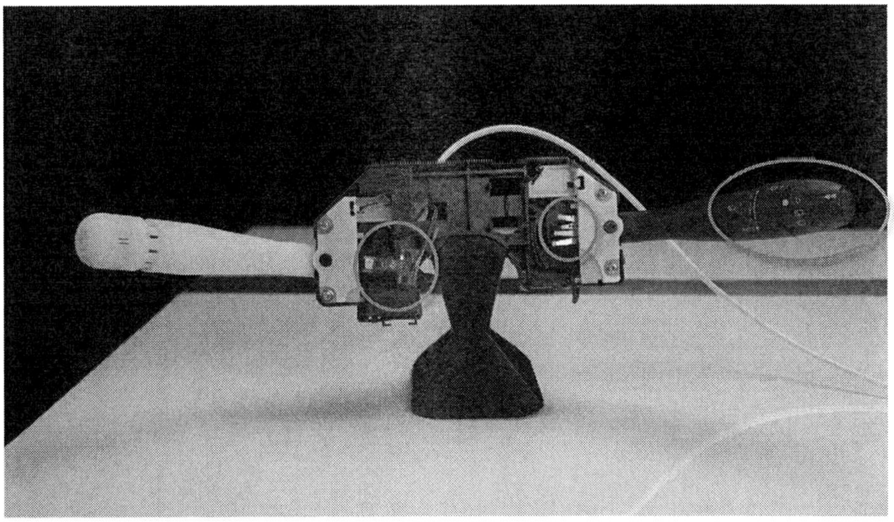

Mechanical wiper contact basics

- Wiper controls slide across a resistive surface and create a changing voltage divider

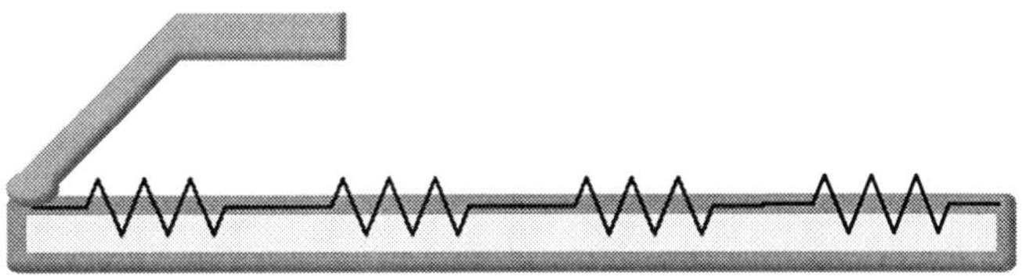

- Cantilevered throws toggle between open and closed positions to change electrical path

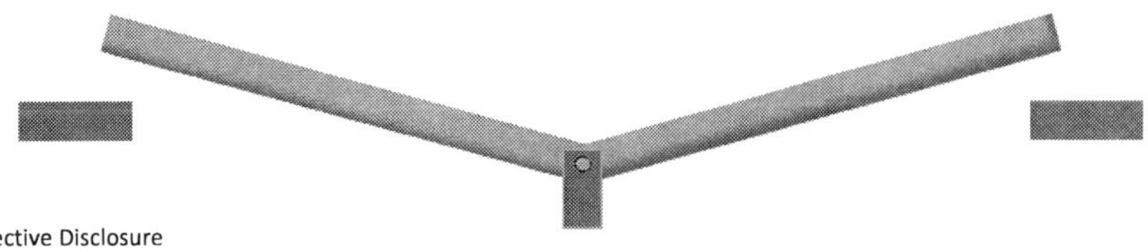

Mechanical wiper challenges

- Mechanical wear can result in slippage

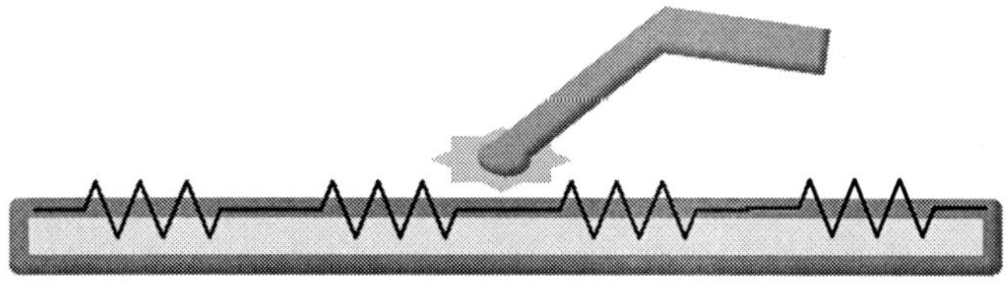

- Oxidation and corrosion can prevent good contact or result in stuck relays

Wetting current and diagnostics

Wetting current: 1-15 mA

Wetting current adjustment resistor

Blocking diodes to prevent current back flow in shared ECU implementation

Input capacitor for ESD protection

FET + resistors for wetting current timing control

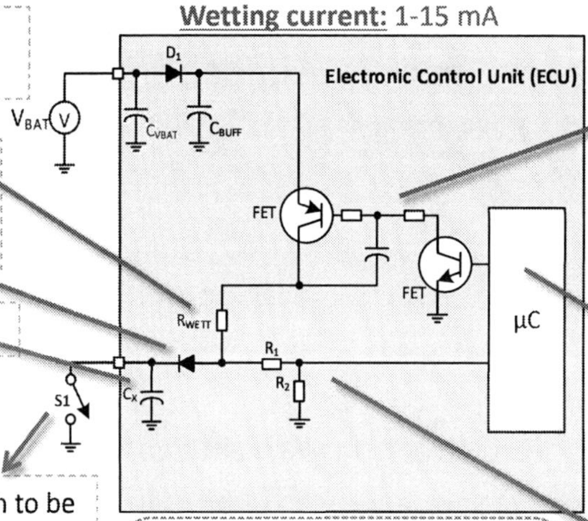

1 µC GPIO for every switch to be monitored

Switch to be monitored

Components required to support each switch channel:

- 5 resistors
- 2 capacitors
- 1 diodes
- 2 FETs

Resistor divider to scale down the input voltage for the µC to sample

7

Three dimensional sensors

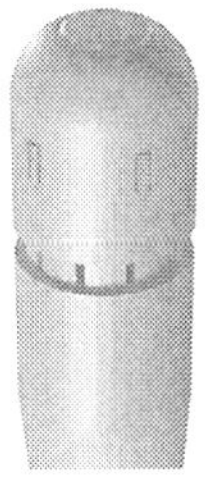

Push-button Knob: Potentiometer contact

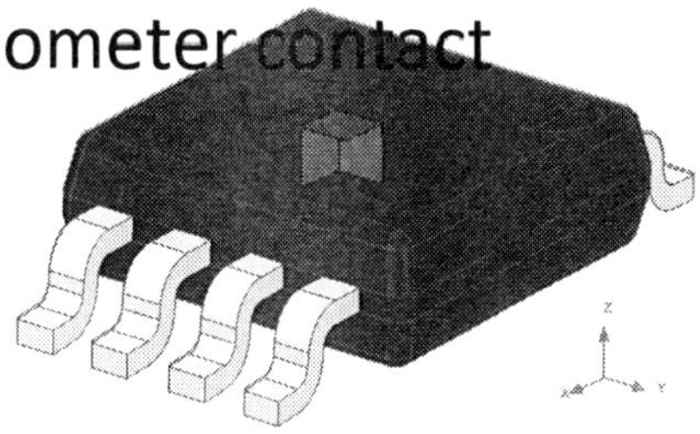

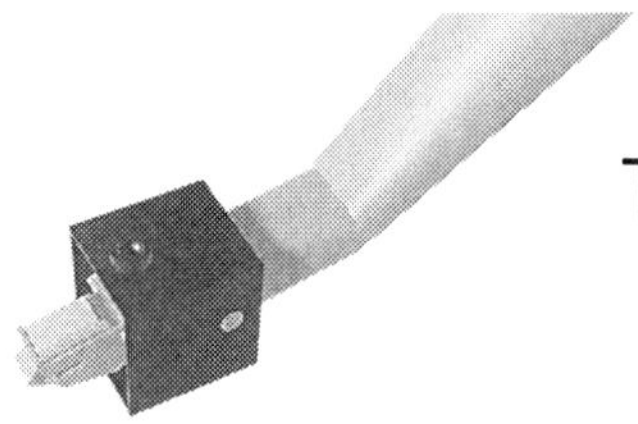

Turn Indicator: Multi-position relay contact

Push-button knob function

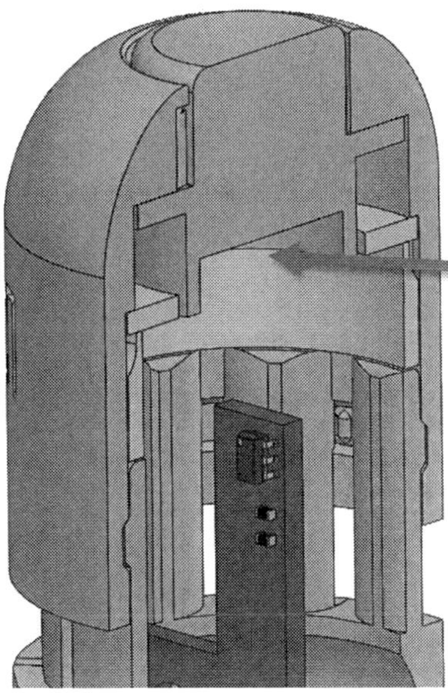

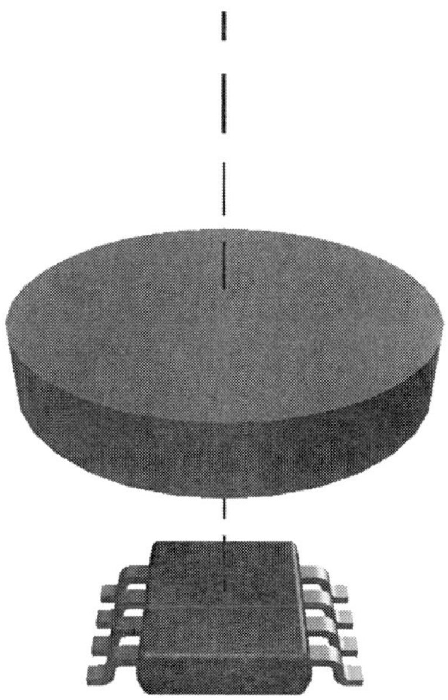

Unpressed Knob Simulation

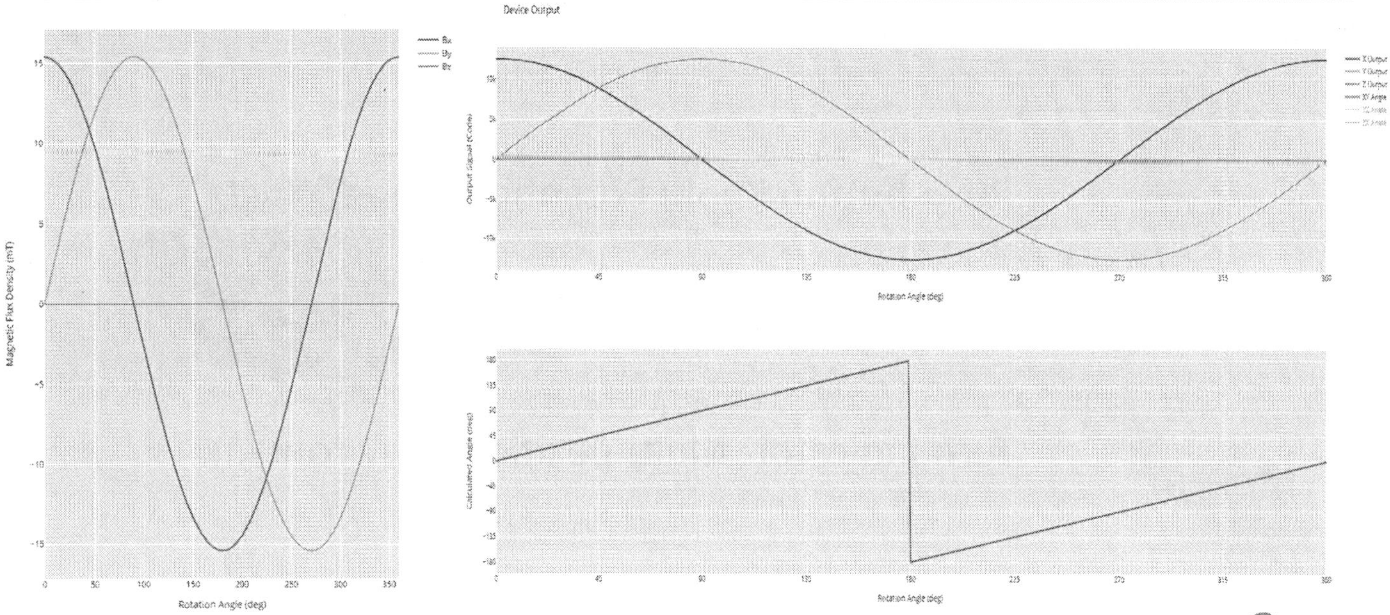

#SensorsConverge TI Information – Selective Disclosure

Sensors Converge

CORDIC algorithm

Coordinate

Rotation

Digital

Computer

Error = 49.5°
- 45°
- 26.56°
+ 14.04°
+ 7.13°
+ 3.58°
- 1.79°
- 0.90°
≅ 0°

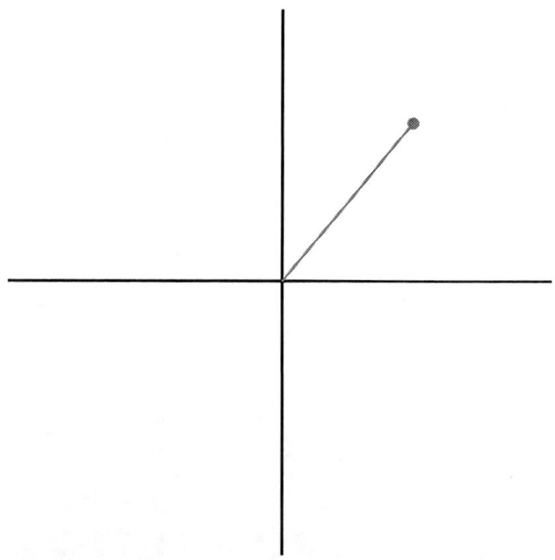

#SensorsConverge TI Information – Selective Disclosure

Sensors Converge

Turn indicator function

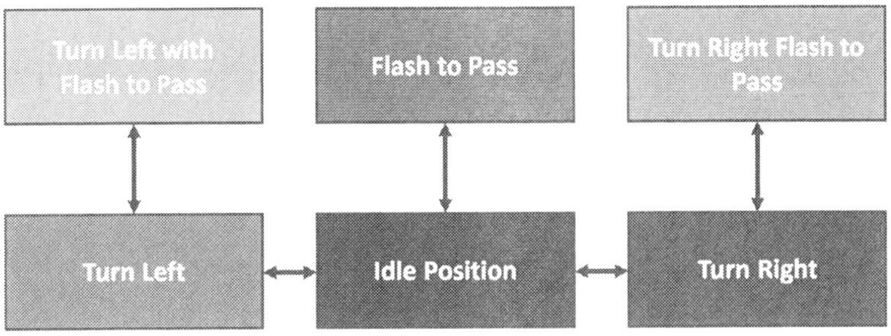

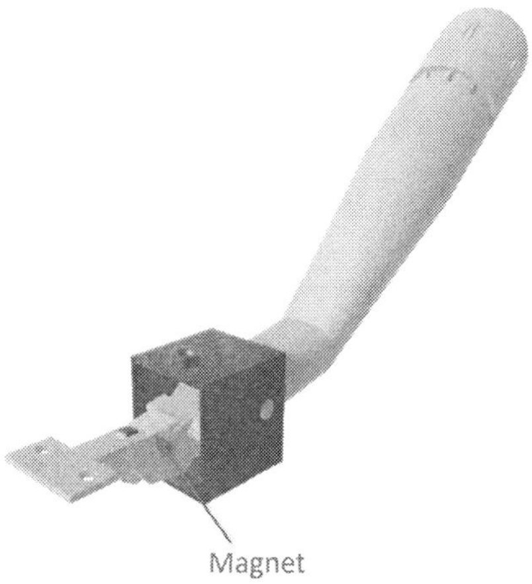

Turn indicator simulation

- Motion parameters
  - Lock into 3 horizontal positions: -8, 0, +8 degrees
- Magnet Selection:
  - N52
  - 12.7mm x 6.35 mm x 3.175 mm
    - (0.5 in x 0.25 in x 0.125 in)
  - Default tilt at 5 degrees
  - Magnet Center 30 mm from fulcrum
- Sensor placement
  - Tilted 10 degrees on bracket align to magnet
  - 34 mm from fulcrum

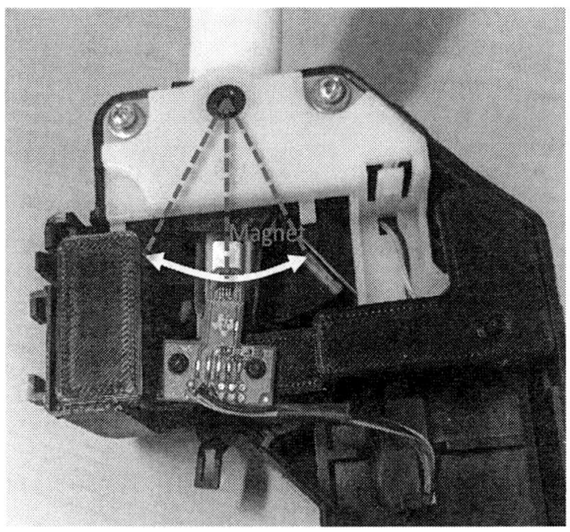

Turn indicator simulation

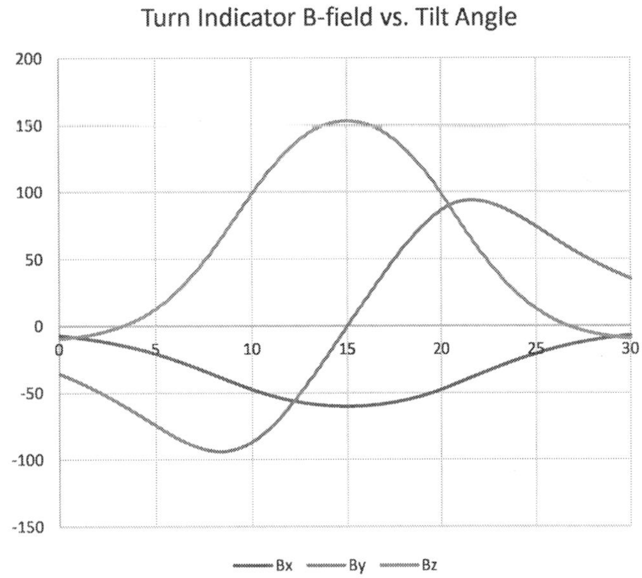

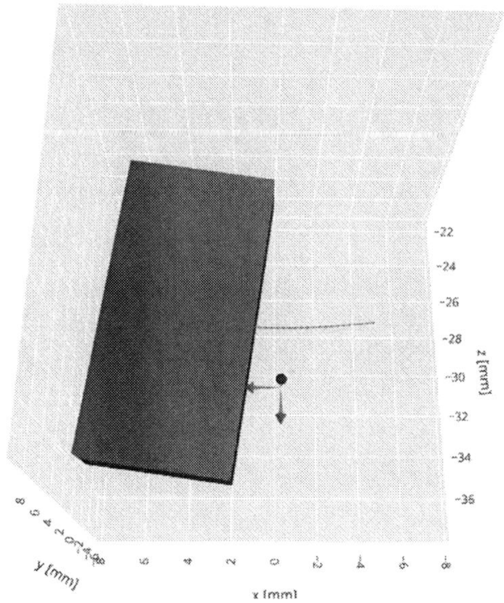

#SensorsConverge TI Information – Selective Disclosure

Sensors Converge

Alpha and Beta angles

$$\alpha = \text{atan}\left(\frac{\sqrt{{B_z}^2 + {B_x}^2}}{B_y}\right)$$

$$\beta = \text{atan}\left(\frac{\sqrt{{B_z}^2 + {B_y}^2}}{B_x}\right)$$

$$magnitude = \sqrt{{B_x}^2 + {B_y}^2 + {B_z}^2}$$

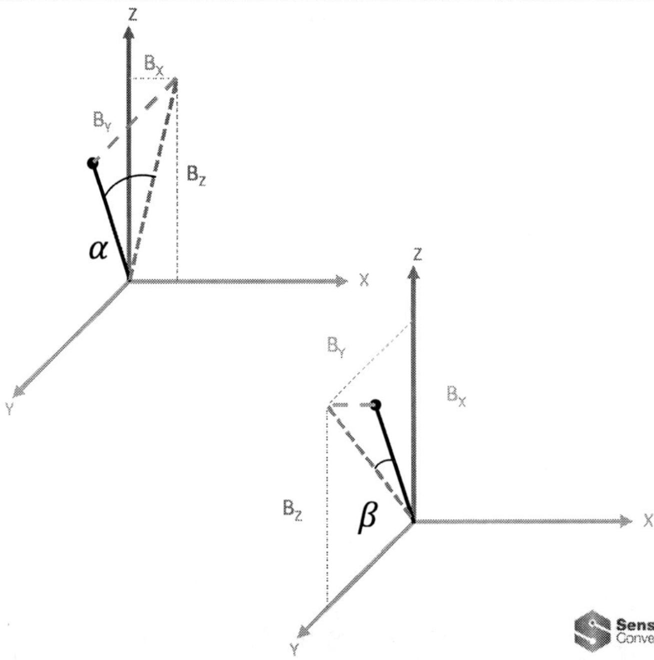

#SensorsConverge TI Information – Selective Disclosure

Sensors Converge

Test data

Push-button Headlamp / Wiper Speed Control Knob

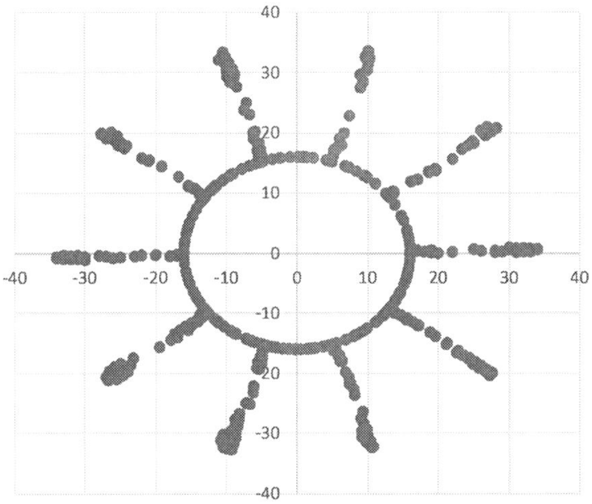

Steering Column Stalk Position

Functional demonstration

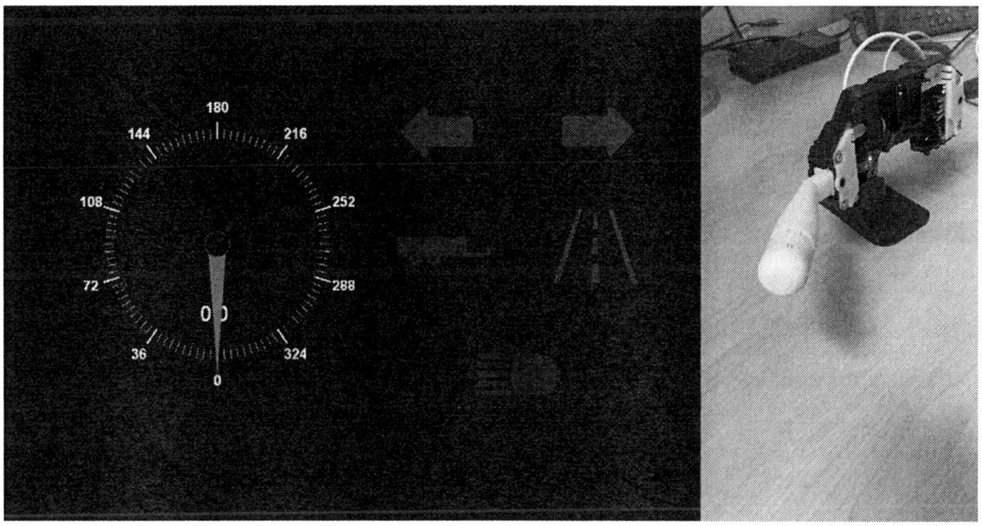

Summary of results

- 3D Magnetic Hall-effect sensors track angular position for magnets in both lever and knob controls
- Integrated diagnostics reduced additional circuitry
- Contact free form factor eliminates need to maintain contact using wetting current
- Measurements are primarily limited by mechanical tolerances
- Invalid data can be used to indicate a mechanical fault in the system
- Integrated angle calculations using CORDIC algorithm can free up microcontroller instructions

Questions ?

#SensorsConverge TI Information – Selective Disclosure Sensors Converge

Sensors Converge

Thermal Interface Materials (TIMs) and Their Role in the Automotive Semiconductor Space

Nikhil Jani
Zeon Specialty Materials-Electronic Materials Divsion
June 20–22, 2023 | Santa Clara, CA

#SensorsConverge

ZEON

Agenda

- Overview of Automotive Semiconductors
- Trends in Sensorization
- Why are Thermal Interface Materials Important
- Current Solutions and their Shortcomings
- Ideal TIM for Automotive Applications

ZEON

Overview of Automotive Semiconductors

Requirements from the Automotive Industry

- High reliability requirements
- Wide temperature operating range
- Smaller packages
- Quick on/off cycling
- Cost

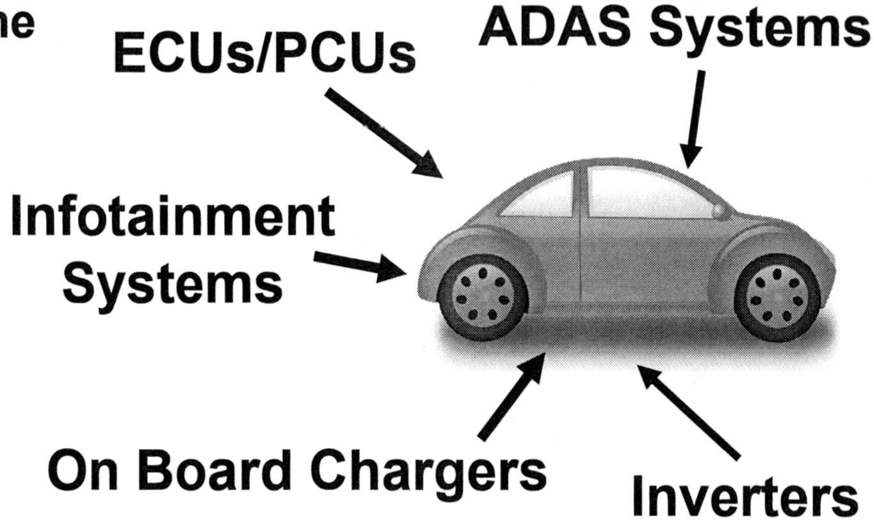

3 Electronics Materials Division

ZEON

Trends in Sensorization

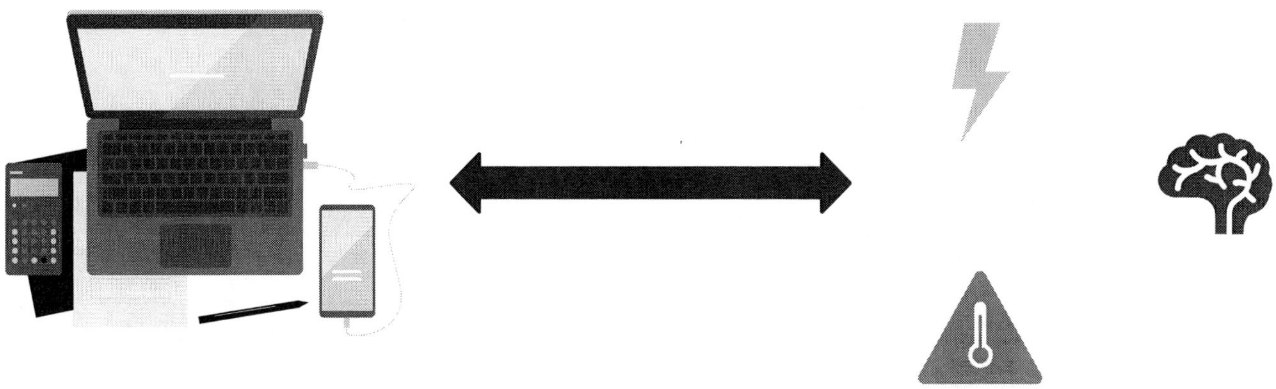

The demands of the general market are requiring electronics to shrink while also demanding higher processing requirement

4 Electronics Materials Division

ZEON

Importance of Thermal Interface Materials

TIM is a material used to fill the gap between parts that generate heat (i.e. IC chips) and parts that dissipate them (i.e. heat sinks) in order to let the heat transfer and dissipate efficiently.

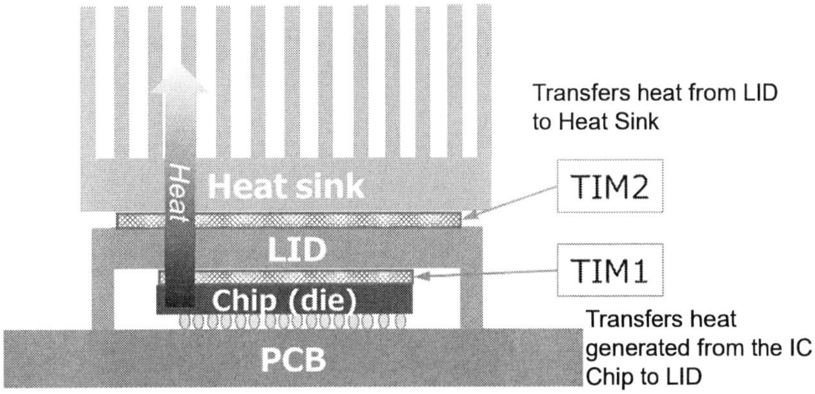

ZEON

Current Solutions

TIM	Pros	Cons	Acceptable in the Automotive Industry
Thermal Grease	• Low bond line thickness • Low cost • Easy application	• Low thermal performance • Risk of physical and thermal degradation during cycling • Risk of pump out	✗
Phase Change Material	• High thermal conductivity • High cycling reliability • Good conformability	• Limited thermal operating range (roughly 50 C per material type) • Expensive	✗
Metal TIMs (Solders)	• High thermal conductivity • Easy application	• Expensive • Risk of cracking due to CTE mismatch during cycling	✗
Gap Pad	• Low cost • Good mechanical properties • Good adhesion	• High bond line thicknesses • Low thermal performance • Low thermal operating range	✗

ZEON

What is the Ideal TIM?

- High temperature polymer
- Good mechanical properties
- Easy application
- Low cost

- High thermal conductivity
- High cycling reliability
- Wide temperature operating range

7 Electronics Materials Division

ZEON

Questions?

Nikhil Jani l Business Development Specialist
Zeon Specialty Materials Inc.
25 Metro Drive, Suite 238 l San Jose, CA 95110 l USA
Mobile: +1.502.656.5089 l Nikhil.Jani@zeonsmi.com

8 Electronics Materials Division

Sensors Converge

Charging the Future of IoT

Cesar Johnston, Energous

June 20–22, 2023 | Santa Clara, CA

#SensorsConverge

Forward Looking Statements

This presentation contains "forward-looking statements" within the meaning of Section 27A of the Securities Act of 1933, as amended, and Section 21E of the Securities Exchange Act of 1934, as amended, that are intended to be covered by the "safe harbor" created by those sections, including statements regarding our future performance, ability to enter into future partnerships, future portfolio and ability to obtain future regulatory approval.

All statements in this presentation that are not based on historical fact are forward-looking statements. Forward-looking statements can generally be identified by the use of forward-looking terms such as "believe," "expect," "may," "will," "should," "could," "seek," "intend," "plan," "estimate," "anticipate" or other comparable terms. While management has based any forward-looking statements on its current expectations, the information on which such expectations are based may change. Forward-looking statements involve inherent risks and uncertainties which could cause actual results to differ materially from those in the forward-looking statements, as a result of various factors including those risks and uncertainties described in the risk factors and management's discussion and analysis of financial condition and results of operations sections of our most recent annual report on Form 10-K and any subsequent quarterly reports on Form 10-Q. We urge you to consider those risks and uncertainties in evaluating our forward-looking statements. We caution readers not to place undue reliance upon any such forward-looking statements, which speak only as of the date hereof. Except as otherwise required by the federal securities laws, we disclaim any obligation or undertaking to publicly release any updates or revisions to any forward-looking statement contained herein (or elsewhere) to reflect any change in our expectations with regard thereto or any change in events, conditions or circumstances on which any such statement is based.

In this document, we refer to information based on studies, publications, surveys, and other data obtained from third-party sources. We believe that all such information is correct as of the date of this presentation and has been obtained from reliable sources that are customarily relied upon by companies in our industry. However, we have not independently verified and make no representation as to the adequacy, fairness, accuracy, or completeness of any such information.

This presentation includes certain financial measures not presented in accordance with generally accepted accounting principles in the United States ("GAAP"), which are used by management in making operating decisions, allocating financial resources, and internal planning, and forecasting, and for business strategy purposes, have certain limitations, and should not be construed as alternatives to financial measures determined in accordance with GAAP. The non-GAAP measures as defined by us may not be comparable to similar non-GAAP measures presented by other companies. Presentation of such measures, which may include adjustments to exclude unusual or non-recurring items, should not be construed as an inference that our future results will be unaffected by other unusual or non-recurring items. A reconciliation is provided elsewhere in this presentation for each non-GAAP financial measure to the most directly comparable financial measure stated in accordance with GAAP.

#SensorsConverge

Sensors Converge

Unleashing The Full Potential Of IoT Through Wireless Power Networks

Agenda

- IoT Market Trend
- Current and Future Deployment challenges
- Wireless Power Network Solutions
- Product Safety
- Design and Deployment Considerations
- Energous at a glance
- Q&A

IoT Ecosystem is Rapidly Expanding

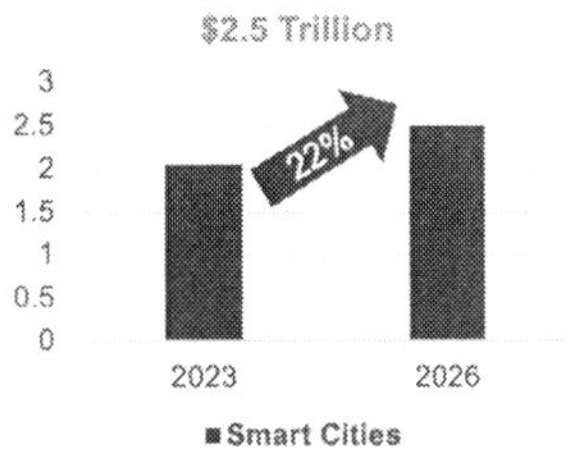

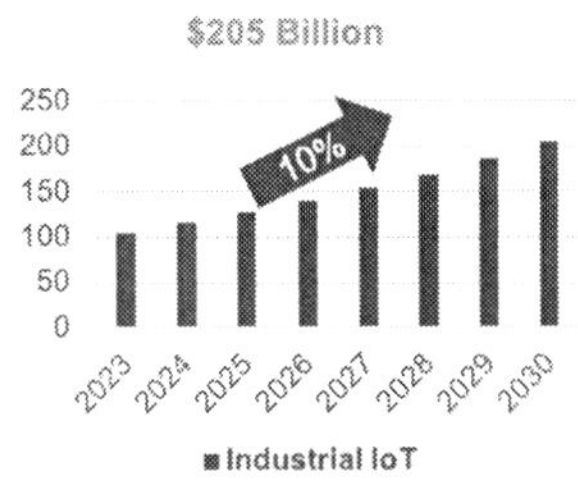

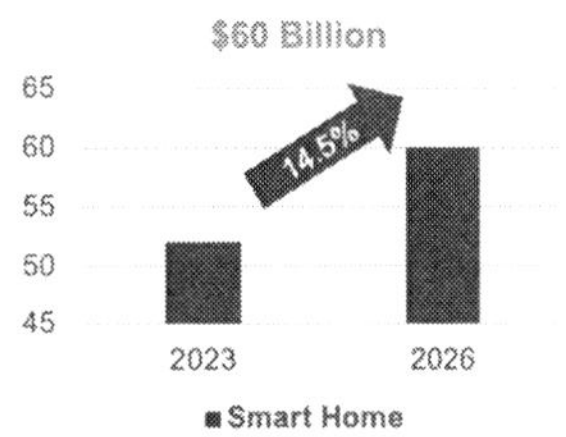

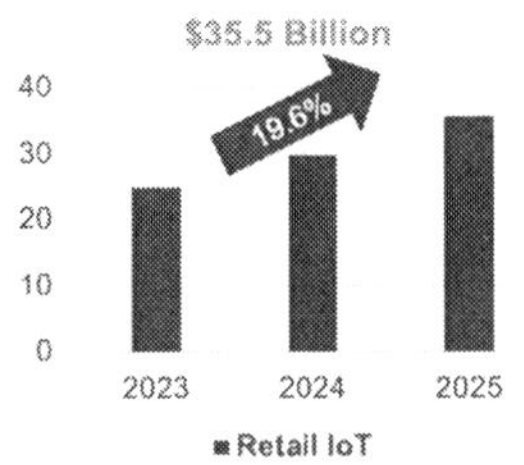

12B IoT DEVICES 2021

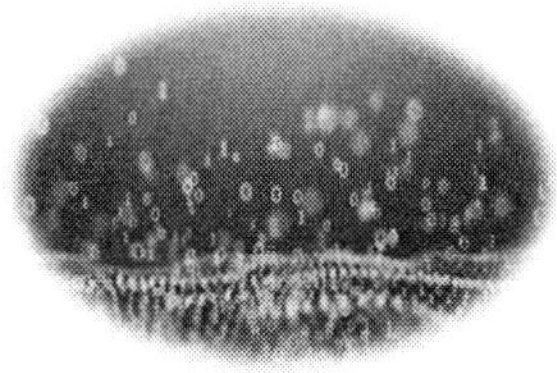

Massive Amounts of Data Being Generated as IoT Device Deployments are Rapidly Increasing.

#SensorsConverge

Sensors Converge

Current & Future IoT Deployment Challenges

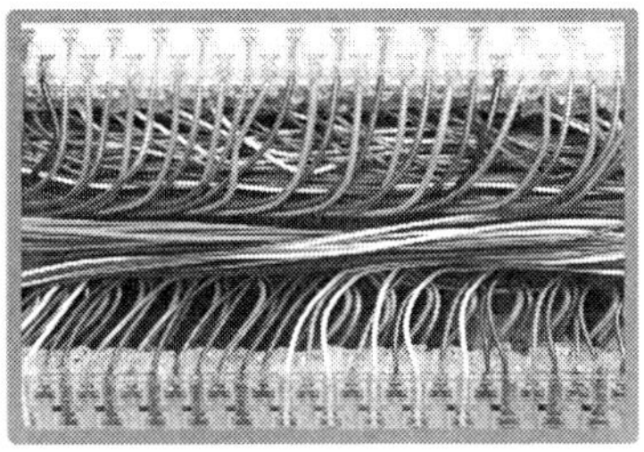

BATTERIES

- Capacity limits new features
- Toxic waste/landfill issues
- Labor intensive and cost prohibitive servicing
- Limited usage in challenging environments and access

WIRES/CABLES

- Limited or no mobility/flexibility
- High installation cost
- Location limitation
- Limited movement
- Extended downtime

DATA OVERLOAD

- Data overload
- Limits usable devices
- Maintenance cost
- Reduced communications efficiency

#SensorsConverge

Sensors Converge

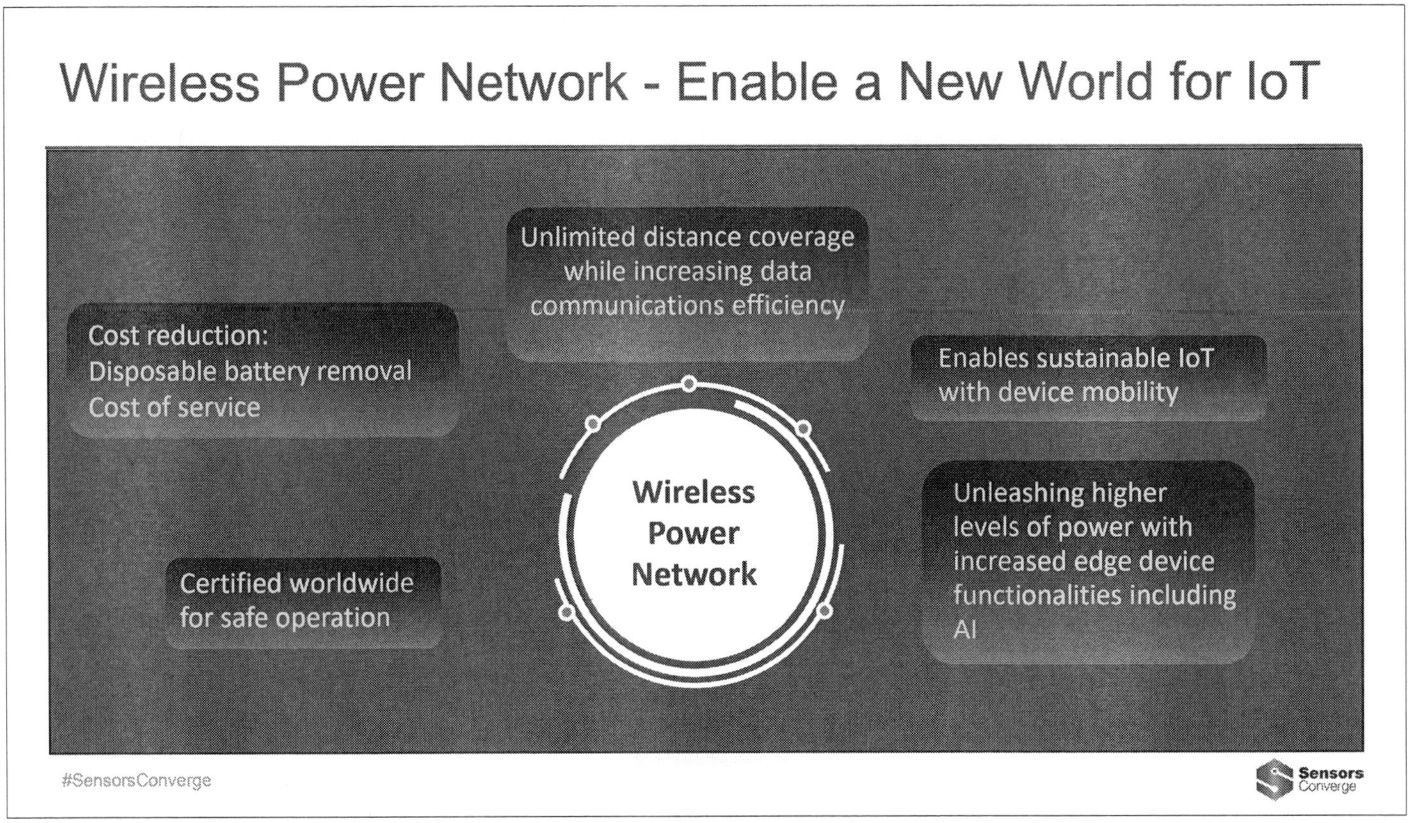
Wireless Power Network - Enable a New World for IoT
Unlimited distance coverage while increasing data communications efficiency
Cost reduction:
Disposable battery removal
Cost of service
Enables sustainable IoT with device mobility
Wireless Power Network
Unleashing higher levels of power with increased edge device functionalities including AI
Certified worldwide for safe operation
#SensorsConverge
Sensors Converge

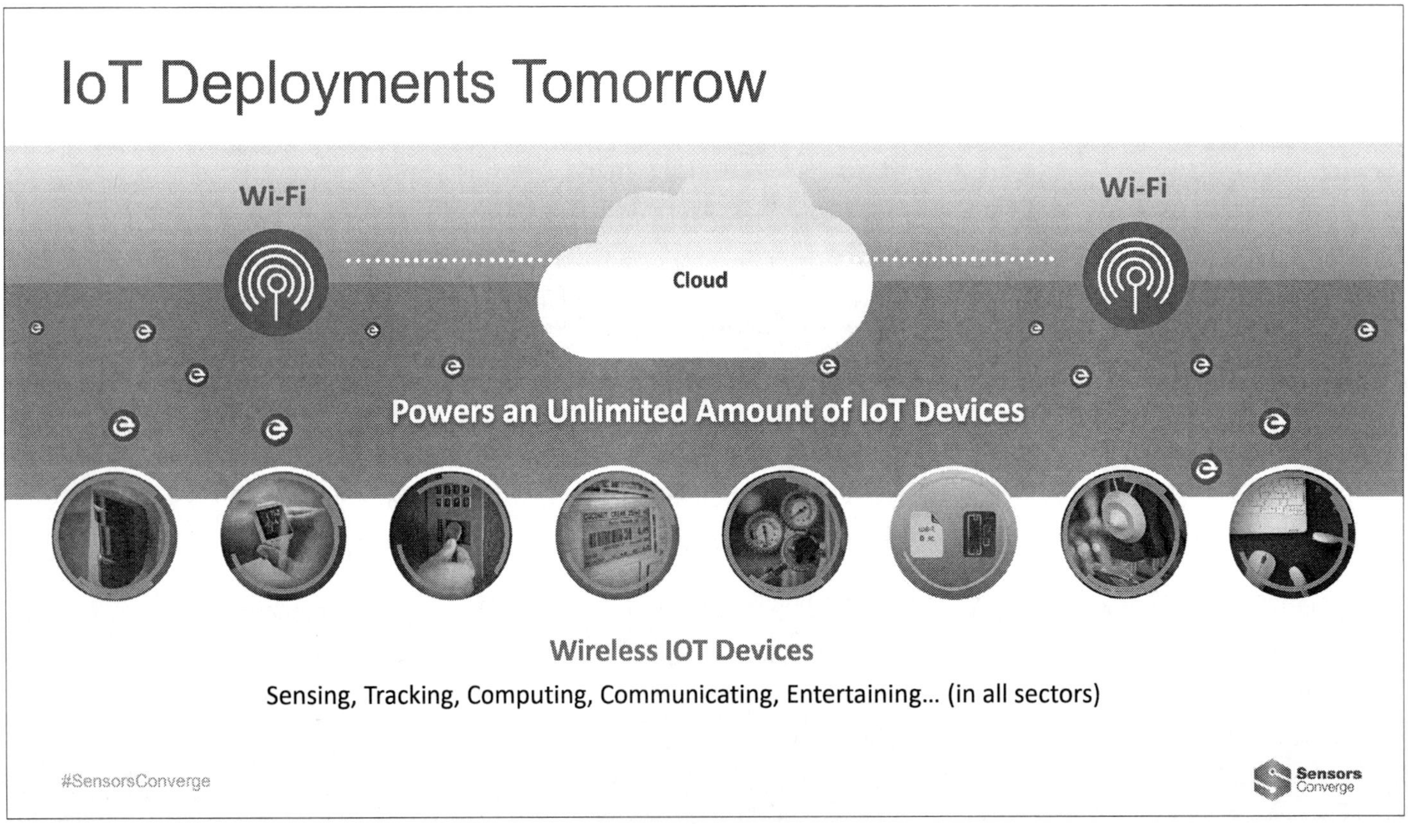
IoT Deployments Tomorrow
Wi-Fi
Cloud
Wi-Fi
Powers an Unlimited Amount of IoT Devices
Wireless IOT Devices
Sensing, Tracking, Computing, Communicating, Entertaining... (in all sectors)
#SensorsConverge
Sensors Converge

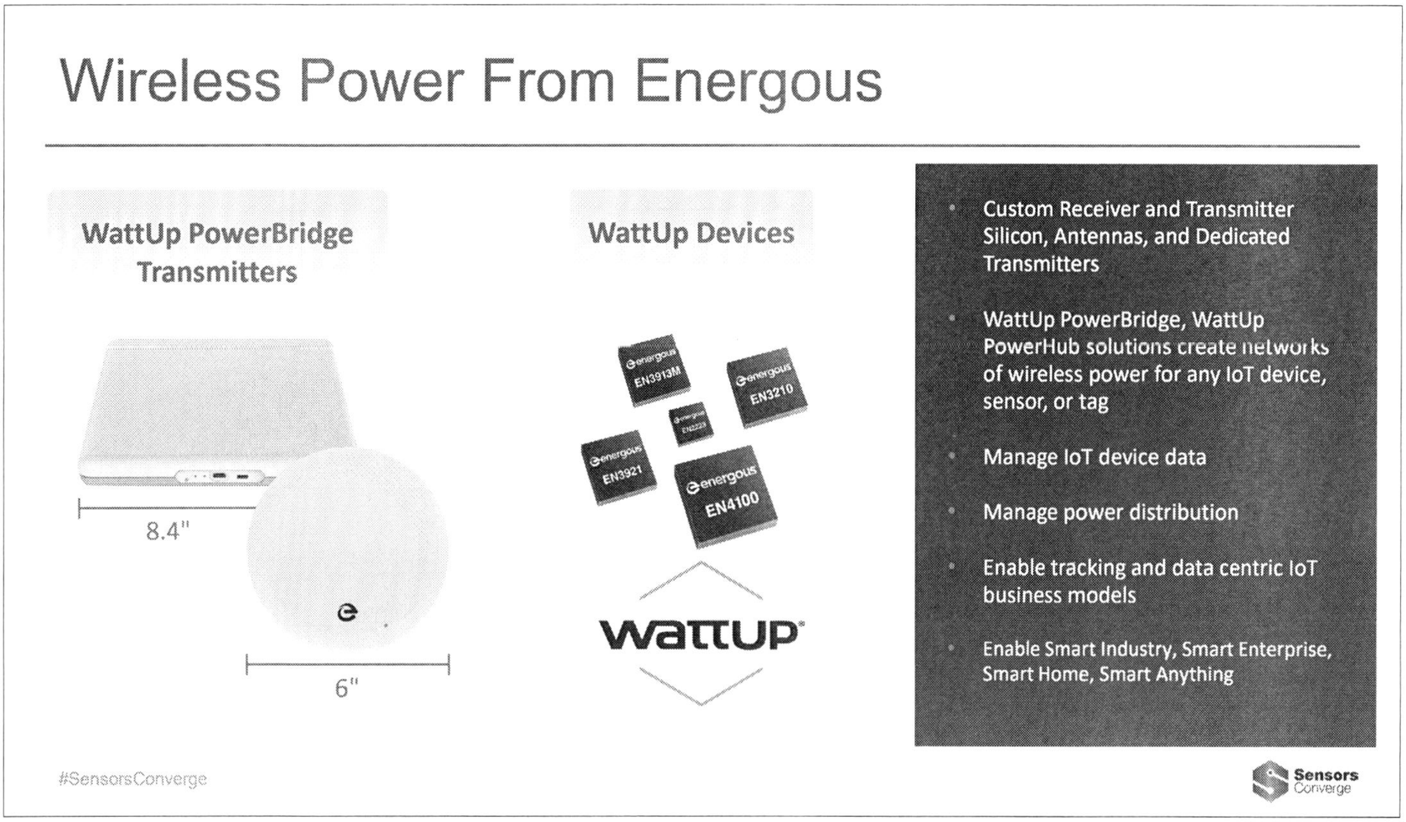

Wireless Power From Energous
WattUp PowerBridge Transmitters
WattUp Devices
8.4"
6"
EN3913M
EN3210
EN3921
EN4100
WattUp
Custom Receiver and Transmitter Silicon, Antennas, and Dedicated Transmitters
WattUp PowerBridge, WattUp PowerHub solutions create networks of wireless power for any IoT device, sensor, or tag
Manage IoT device data
Manage power distribution
Enable tracking and data centric IoT business models
Enable Smart Industry, Smart Enterprise, Smart Home, Smart Anything
#SensorsConverge
Sensors Converge

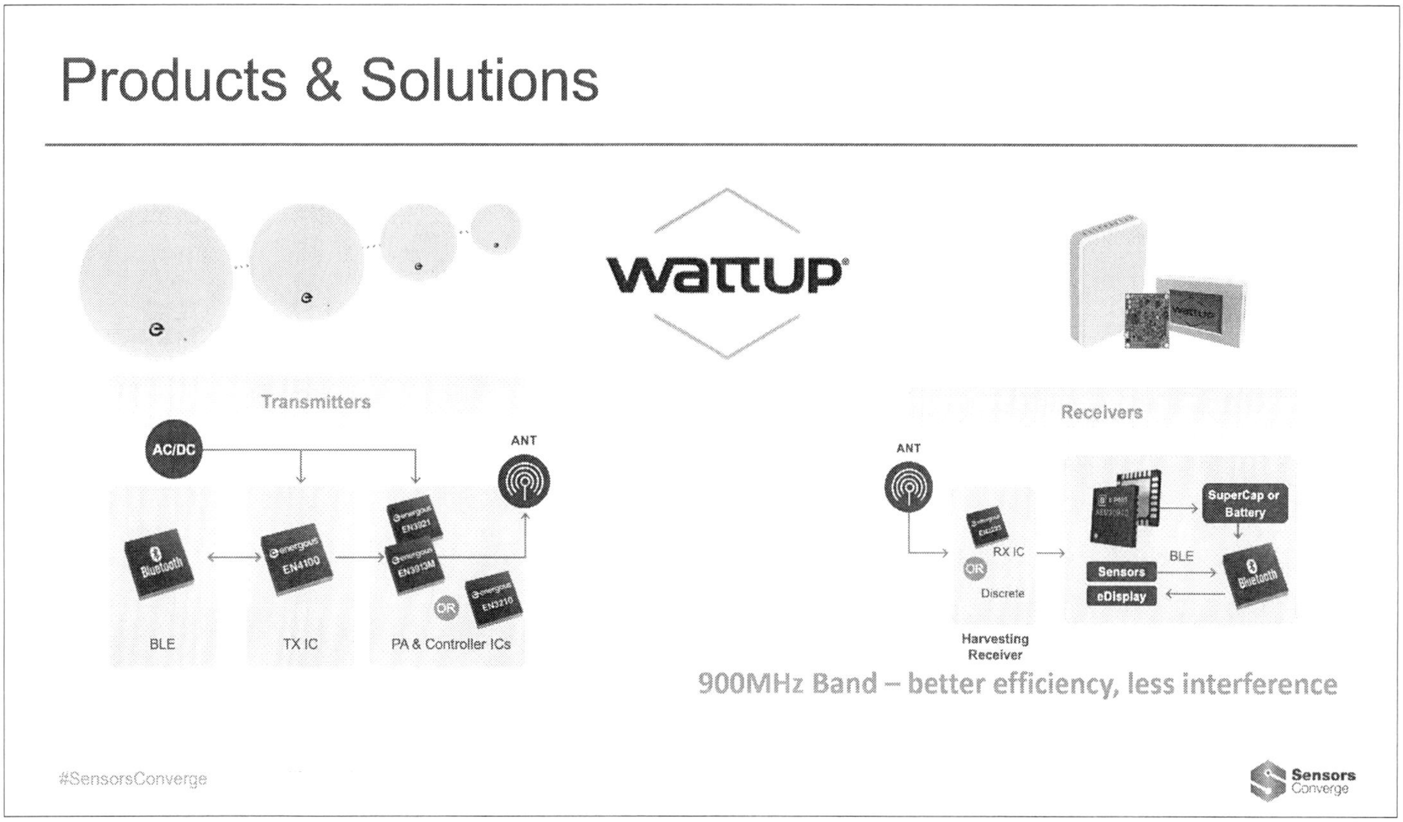

Products & Solutions
WattUp
Transmitters
AC/DC
ANT
BLE
TX IC
PA & Controller ICs
OR
Receivers
ANT
RX IC
OR
Discrete
Harvesting Receiver
SuperCap or Battery
BLE
Sensors
eDisplay
900MHz Band – better efficiency, less interference
#SensorsConverge
Sensors Converge

Interoperability

Energous co-defined the AirFuel standard

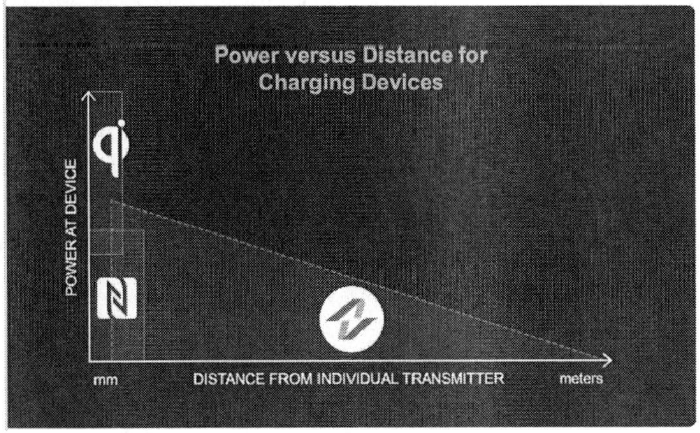

AirFuel™ Alliance

The only wireless power standard that covers power at a distance

Enables a large variety of (small) IOT devices over a broad range of power levels and distances

WattUp from Energous is an AirFuel interoperable solution

#SensorsConverge

Sensors Converge

Regulatory Certified In World's Largest Markets

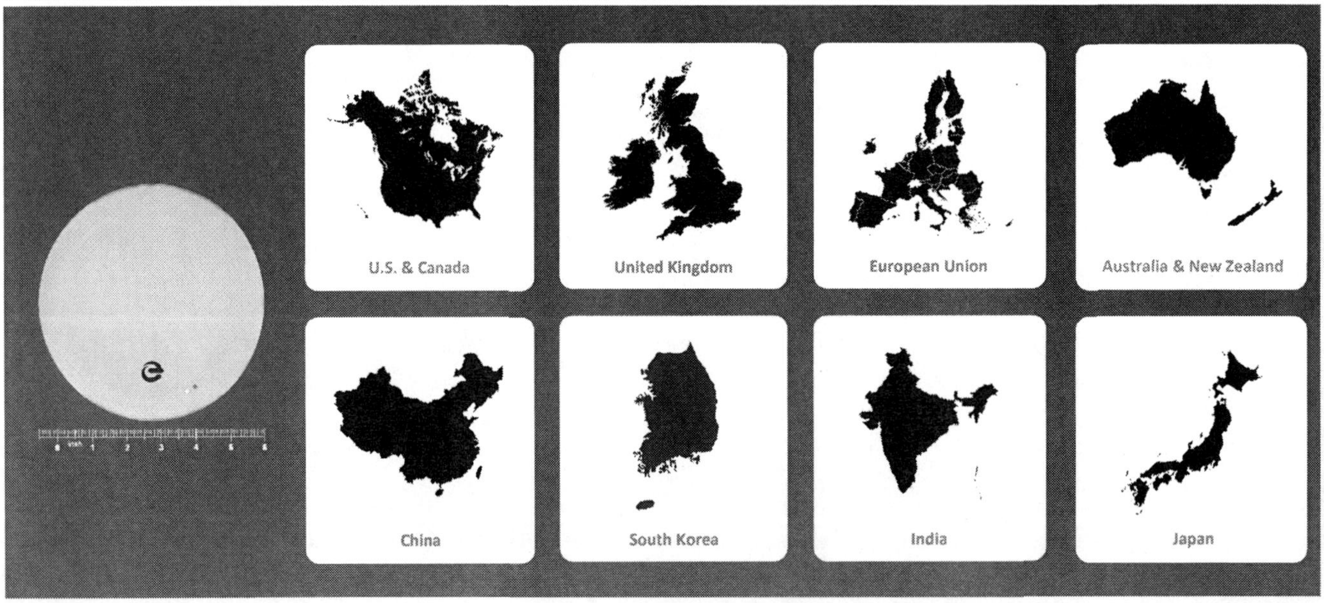

#SensorsConverge

Sensors Converge

Prioritizing Product Safety

Low SAR Levels

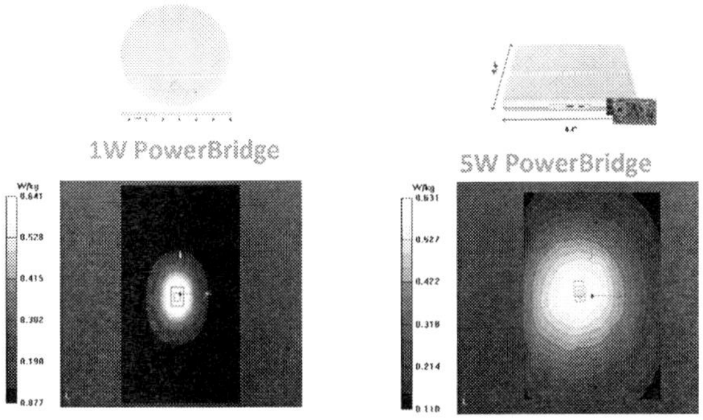

SAR(1g) = 0.608 W/kg at 5cm

SAR(1g) = 0.586 W/kg at 20cm

FCC Limit is 1.6W/kg

All products comply with Intl. RF Safety(SAR) limits

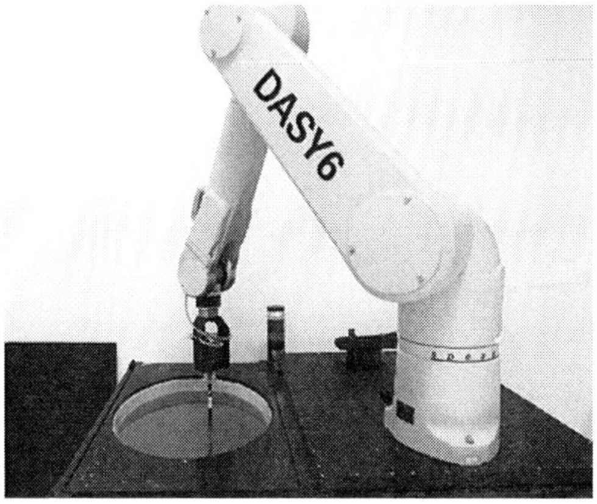

#SensorsConverge

Sensors Converge

Focus IoT Market Applications

END-TO-END DEVICE TRACKING

RF Tags enabled for real-time charging, tracking and management of products through their entire supply chain

In partnership with

Wiliot

ELECTRONIC SHELF LABELS & DIGITAL INFORMATION DISPLAY

Movable digital displays provide dynamic pricing, alerts, notifications and instructions wherever located

In partnership with

Eink

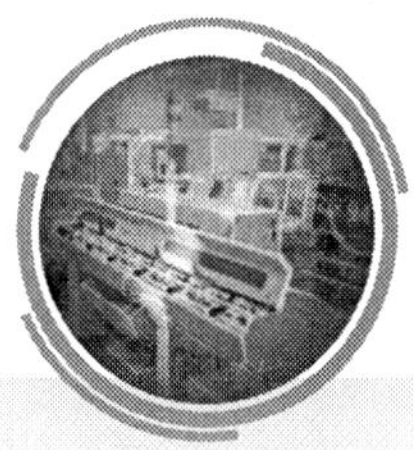

IOT SENSORS

IoT sensors detect, respond and report changes in an environment. Input can come from a variety of sources such as light, temperature, motion, humidity and more

In partnership with

SENSIRION ams OSRAM

#SensorsConverge

Sensors Converge

IoT Market Opportunities

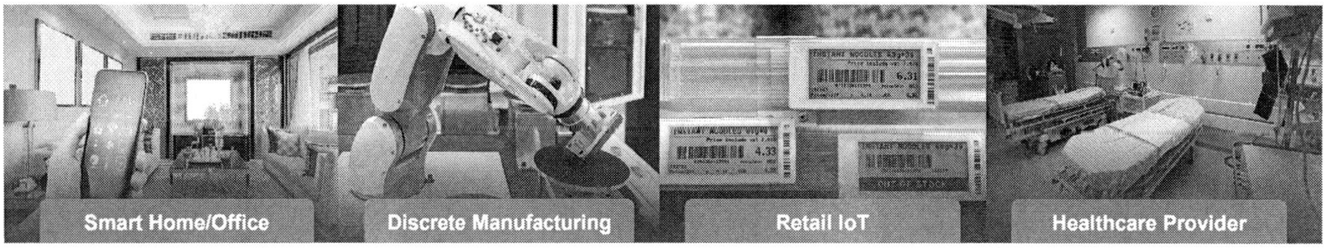

Smart Home/Office

- Smoke/Co2 Detectors
- Smart Thermostat
- Home/Office Security
- Window/Door Sensors
- Motion Detectors
- Smart Bathrooms

Discrete Manufacturing

- ESL - Industrial
- Robotics
- Fault Prevention Sensors
- Floor Security
- Work Safety Chemical/ Gas/Water Leak Sensor
- Air Quality/Co2 Monitor
- Warehouse Operation IOT

Retail IoT

- ESL - Retail
- Occupancy Sensors
- Smart Shopping Carts
- Temperature/ Humidity Sensors

Healthcare Provider

- ESL - Healthcare
- Asset Trackers
- Vaccinations/Drugs Storage Monitor
- Patient Trackers
- Window/Door Sensors

#SensorsConverge

Sensors Converge

Partner Ecosystem

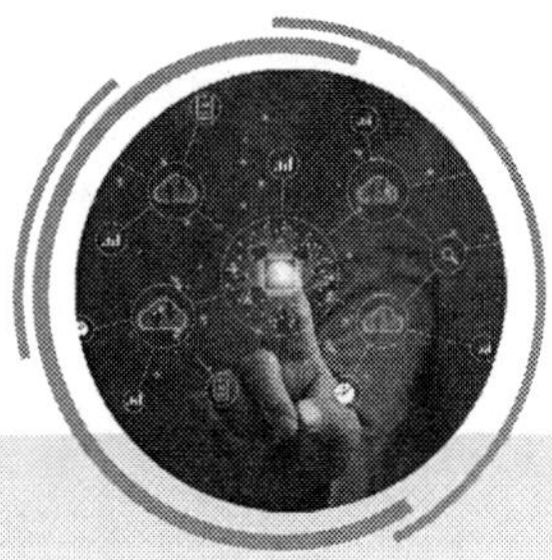

TECHNOLOGY PARTNERS

Juniper driven by Mist AI, e-peas, NGK Insulators, E Ink, Wiliot, Atmosic, Catapult, LIXIL, ams, OSRAM, Sensirion, Syntiant, SATO Powered On Site/, CAP-XX Supercapacitors

SYSTEM INTEGRATORS

SATO Powered On Site/, thinaer, Flagship, InnoTractor

DISTRIBUTION PARTNERS

CISPER

世强硬创平台 www.sekorm.com

#SensorsConverge

Sensors Converge

Award-Winning Technology

2020

Global Technology Innovation Award by Frost & Sullivan

2021

Golden Bridge Awards: Gold Winner in Technology - Wireless

2022

IOT Breakthrough Award: Partnership with e-peas

2022

CES Honoree: Embedded Technology Eco-Design Smart Energy

2023

CES Honoree: Embedded Technology

#SensorsConverge

Sensors Converge

Logistics Application Example

Requirements

- Tracking assets at 250 sq meter
- 60 pallets should be tracked
- In/out dock door detection

#SensorsConverge

Sensors Converge

Logistics Application Example

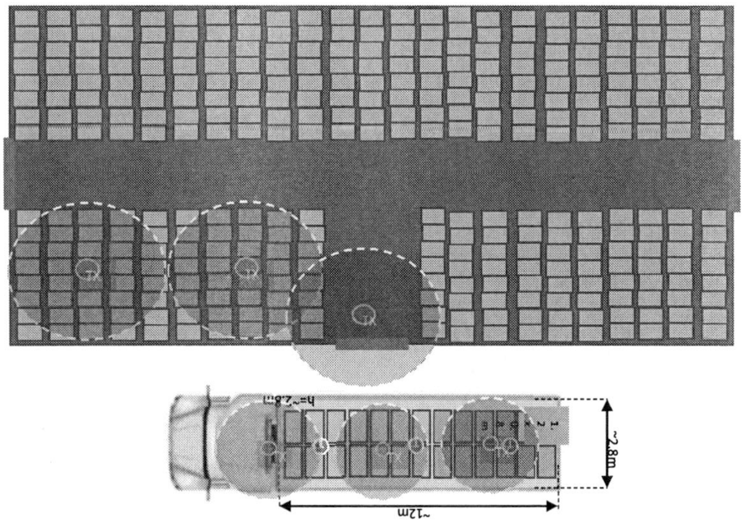

Requirements

- Tracking assets at 250 sq meter
- 60 pallets should be tracked
- In/out dock door detection

Solution

- ✓ Energous Transmitters
- ✓ 99% read
- ✓ No cable
- ✓ No dock door gate needed
- ✓ Information available on mobile devices

#SensorsConverge

Sensors Converge

Second Successful Retail Deployment Flagship

Thousands of Wiliot Pixel RF-tags in an Academy Brand store energized by multiple 1W WattUp PowerBridge transmitters.

2nd Retail Deployment Announced with Flagship

First deployment was announced on August 1, 2022

Instant and Automatic Inventory Counts

Of stores, storerooms and warehouse allowing staff to focus their time on the customer experience.

Loss prevention insights

Keep track of inventory and reduce theft and shrinkage.

Fitting room sessions

Better understand what items customers are trying on, what sizes and what they ultimately purchase.

Replenishment requirements

Get an accurate end of day stock count for each store indicating which items need to be replenished from the stockroom.

Actionable Merchandising Insights

Know how customers are engaging with products for ultimate floor merchandising, including items tried on, items tried on together and highest converting items.

#SensorsConverge

Sensors Converge

IoT Sensing Proof of Concept Deployment - SATO

SATO IoT sensing mat energized by 1W WattUp® PowerBridge transmitter

Out of stock prevention

Helping customers and distributor to have direct access to product inventory

Detection of in-store inventory

Of stores, storerooms and warehouse allowing staff to focus their time on the customer experience.

Measuring promotion campaigns

Understand price promotion effectiveness

Improve operational quality

Ensure product availability

#SensorsConverge

Sensors Converge

Smart Football Deployment – Catapult

College football energized by WattUp® transmitter

Multiple deployment announced in college football

Boston College and University of Nevada

Real time analytics viewed by coaching staff and broadcast

Localization, speed, and velocity

Football localization

UWB technology to detect ball's exact location

Assess player performance

Sensor technology to assess player performance and readiness

#SensorsConverge

Sensors Converge

Thank You

Sensors Converge

Simplifying your design with Hall-effect sensors

June 20–22, 2023 | Santa Clara, CA

#SensorsConverge

Agenda

- Hall-effect Sensor Types
- Design Options
  - Linear Displacement
  - Hinged Rotation
  - Axial Rotation
  - Joystick
- Free Tools
  - FEMM
  - MagPyLib
  - Magnetic Sense Enhanced Proximity Tool

Hall-effect sensor types

Switch

- Operate and Release thresholds
- Omni-polar or uni-polar

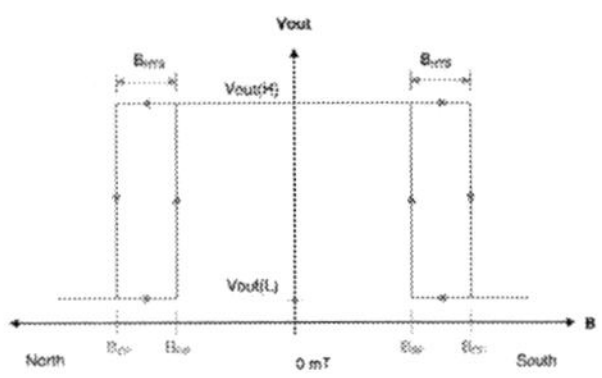

- Limit Detection

Latch

- Symmetric operate and release thresholds for alternating fields

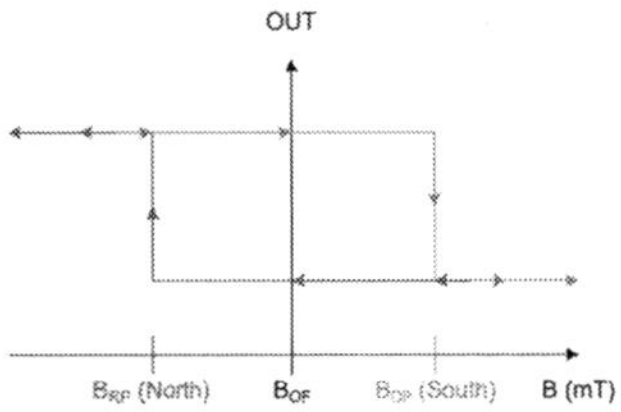

- Speed and Direction
- Motor Commutation

Analog linear

- Produce a linear output voltage with changing magnetic fields

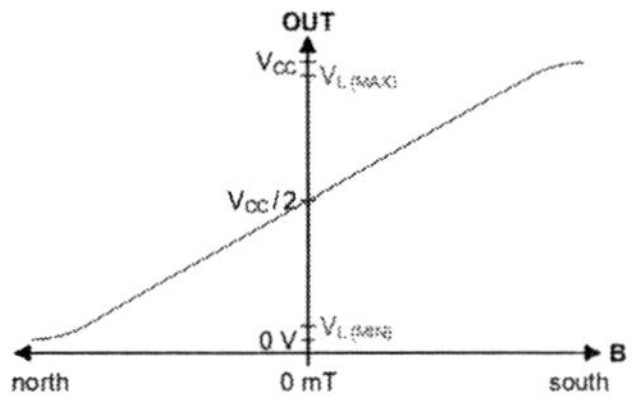

- Linear Arrays
- Angle

Digital linear

- Integrated ADC and digital interface for programable sensors
- Support 3D sensor configurations

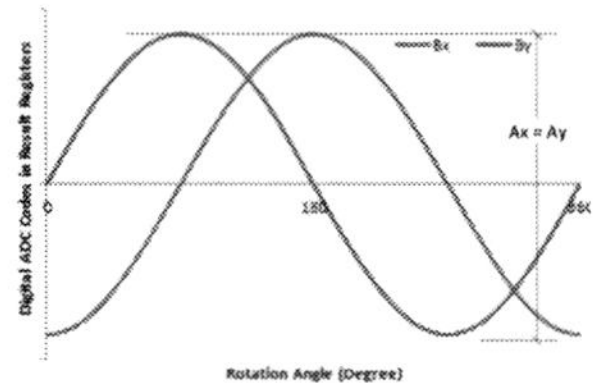

- Absolute Field
- Tamper detect
- Angle

#SensorsConverge TI Information – Selective Disclosure

Sensors Converge

Hinged rotation

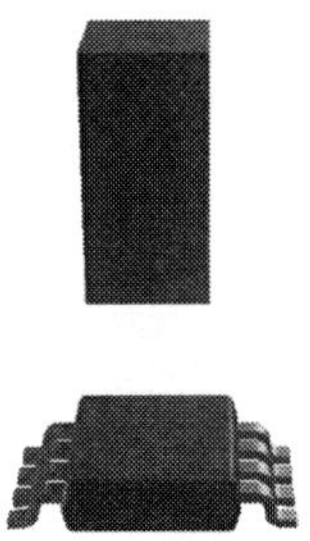

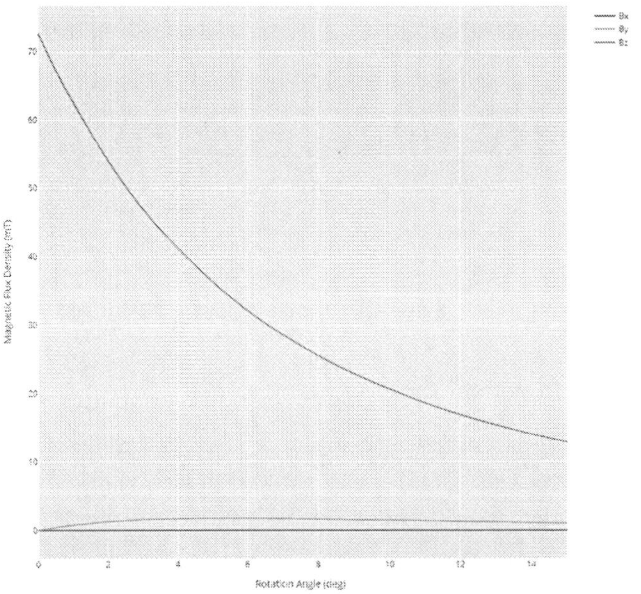

- Exponential decay closely resembling the head-on equation

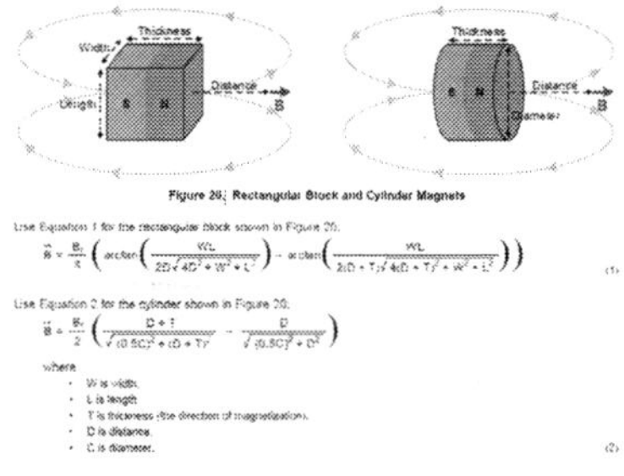

- Design for B_{OP} max and B_{RP} min for robust design

#SensorsConverge TI Information – Selective Disclosure

Sensors Converge

Linear displacement

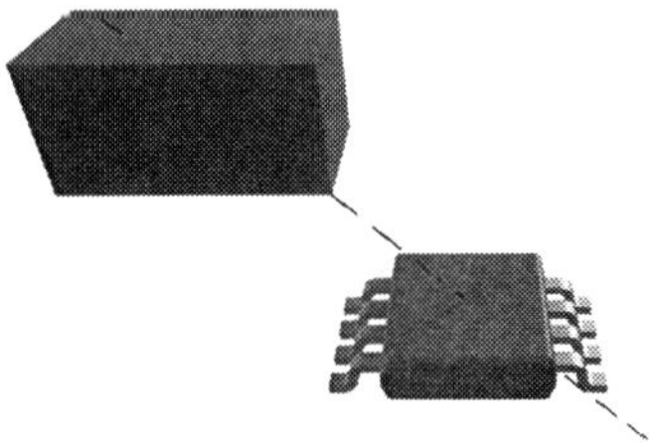

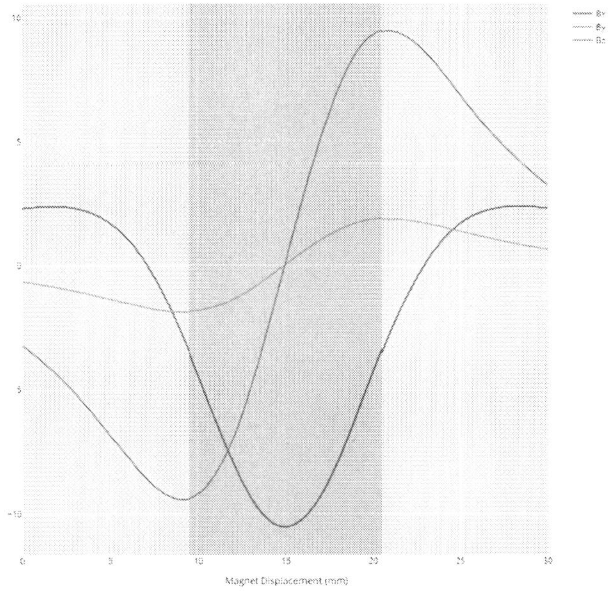

- Linear region ≈ magnet length
- 1D sensors can only be used for the linear region
- 3D sensors can expand range by using full vector

#SensorsConverge TI Information – Selective Disclosure

Sensors Converge

Axial rotation

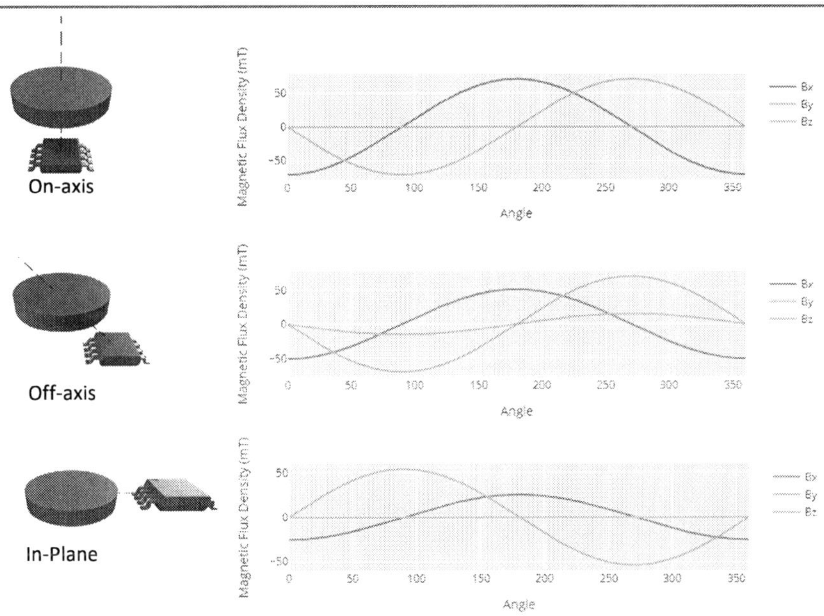

- Field components are naturally 90 degrees separated in phase
- Arctangent can be used to calculate absolute angle
- Amplitude mismatch will result in non-linearity.
  - This error can be corrected using scalar amplitude correction.

#SensorsConverge TI Information – Selective Disclosure

Sensors Converge

Joystick tilt

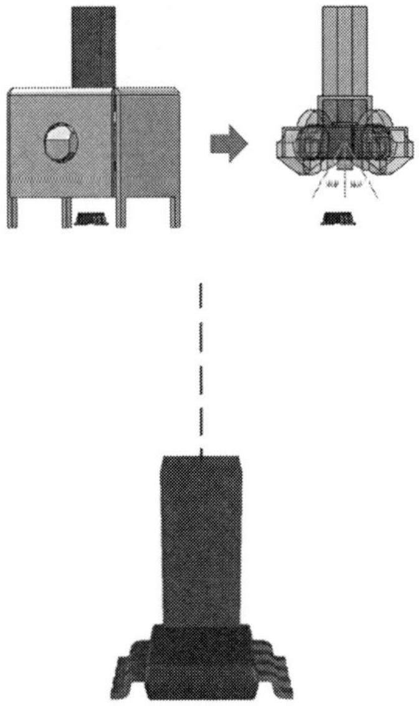

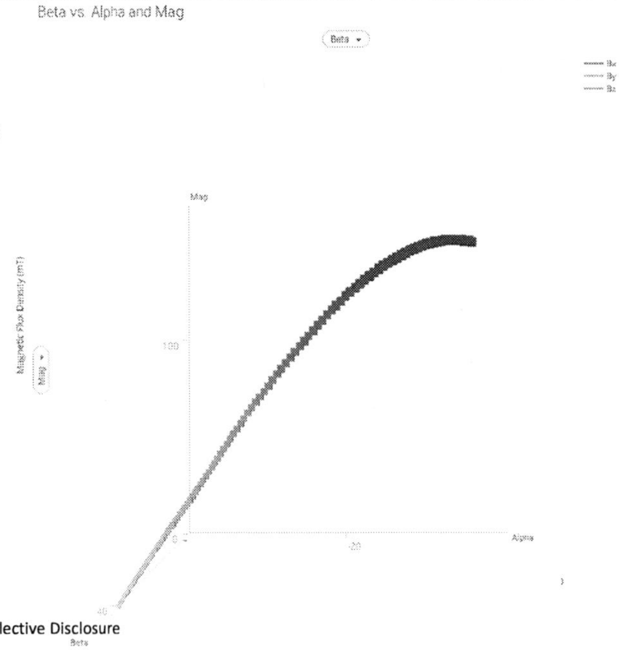

- Similar profile to slide-by example in linear displacement
- Commonly tracked using Alpha and Beta angles:

$$\alpha = \text{atan}\left(\frac{\sqrt{{B_z}^2 + {B_x}^2}}{B_y}\right)$$

$$\beta = \text{atan}\left(\frac{\sqrt{{B_z}^2 + {B_y}^2}}{B_x}\right)$$

$$magnitude = \sqrt{{B_x}^2 + {B_y}^2 + {B_z}^2}$$

#SensorsConverge TI Information – Selective Disclosure

Sensors Converge

Design options

Solve using Equations

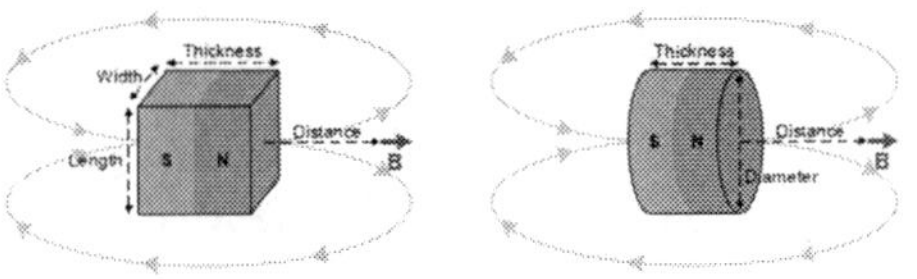

Figure 20. Rectangular Block and Cylinder Magnets

Use Equation 1 for the rectangular block shown in Figure 20:

$$\vec{B} = \frac{B_r}{\pi}\left(\arctan\left(\frac{WL}{2D\sqrt{4D^2 + W^2 + L^2}}\right) - \arctan\left(\frac{WL}{2(D+T)\sqrt{4(D+T)^2 + W^2 + L^2}}\right)\right) \quad (1)$$

Use Equation 2 for the cylinder shown in Figure 20:

$$\vec{B} = \frac{B_r}{2}\left(\frac{D+T}{\sqrt{(0.5C)^2 + (D+T)^2}} - \frac{D}{\sqrt{(0.5C)^2 + D^2}}\right) \quad (2)$$

where

- W is width.
- L is length.
- T is thickness (the direction of magnetization).
- D is distance.
- C is diameter.

Time consuming and difficult

Iterate Prototypes

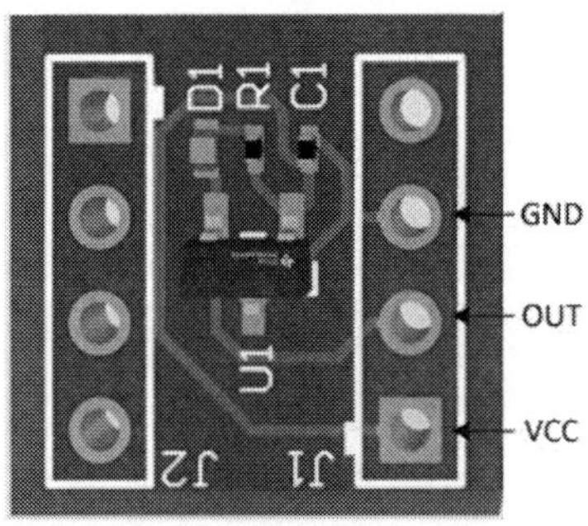

Immediate feedback on design, but expensive to iterate

Simulations and Tools

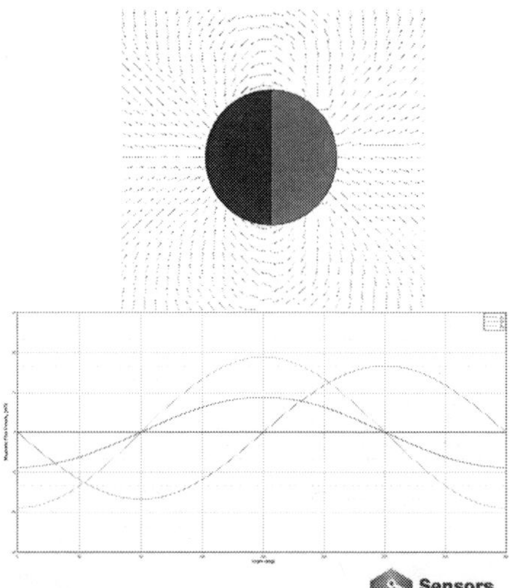

#SensorsConverge TI Information – Selective Disclosure

Sensors Converge

FEMM – Finite Element Method Magnetics

- Free to download and Open Source
- Simulates in 2D, either assuming radial symmetry or infinite length
- Doesn't support all magnet shapes, but runs quickly with a mesh based algorithm

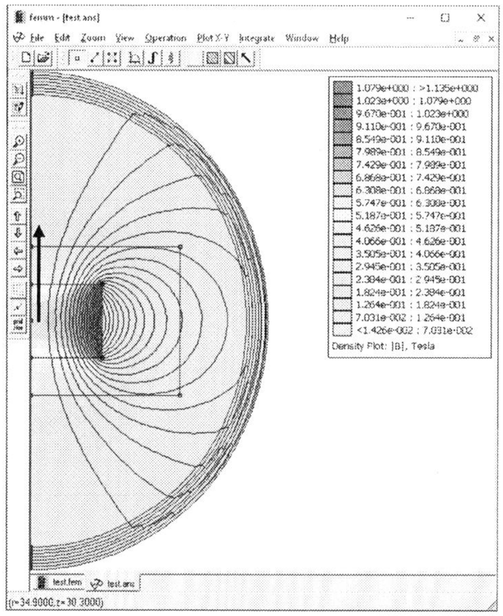

MagPy Lib

- Free to download and Open Source
- Equation based algorithm that supports a variety of magnet shapes and pole arrangements using superposition
- Full 3D Support
- Runs extremely fast and comparable to industry standard tools
- Does not support materials that interact with magnetic fields (i.e. Steel, Nickel, Chrome)

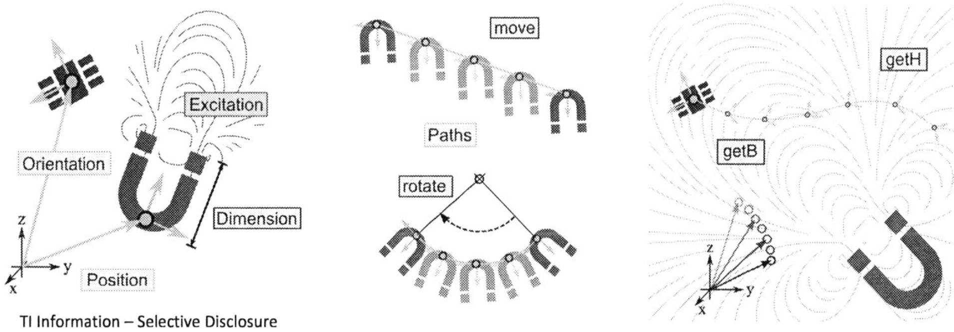

Magnetic Sense Enhanced Proximity Tool

- Free downloadable
  - Webtool format (TIMSS) deploying in June 2023
- Built using the MagPyLib tool
- Supports all the motion types discussed
- Includes device output emulation for rapid system verification
- Runs many times faster than mesh algorithms for quick evaluation

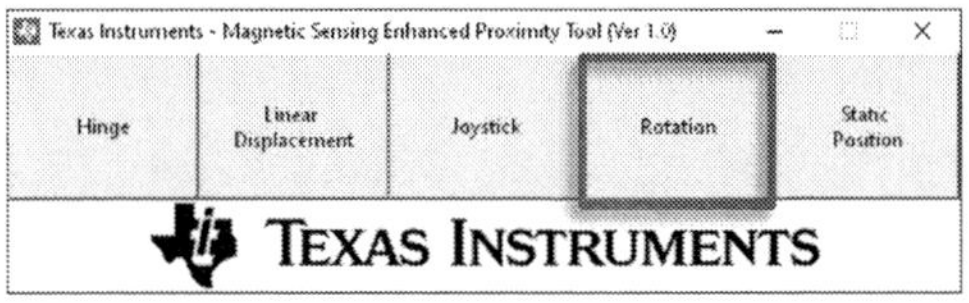

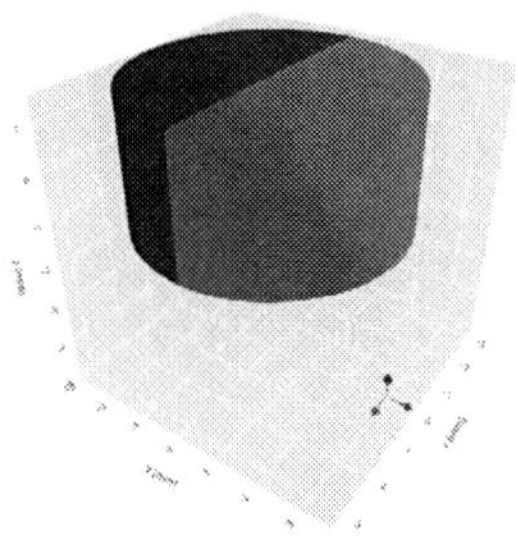

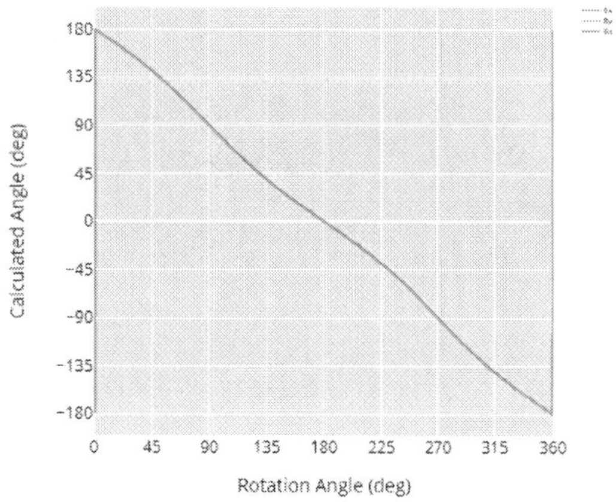

Resources

- FEMM: https://www.femm.info/wiki/HomePage
- MagPyLib: https://magpylib.readthedocs.io/en/latest/
- Magnetic Sense Enhanced Proximity Tool: https://www.ti.com/tool/download/MAGNETIC-SENSE-ENHANCED-PROXIMITY/1.0
- Equation Based Articles:
  - https://pubs.aip.org/aapt/ajp/article/78/3/229/1058297/Cylindrical-magnets-and-ideal-solenoids
  - https://www.jpier.org/issues/reader.html?pid=11112606
  - https://ieeexplore.ieee.org/abstract/document/6392436
  - https://hal.science/hal-01011497/

Questions?

#SensorsConverge

Sensors Converge

Lightning Talks: Low Power Design

Cutting the Cords and Batteries from Sensor Networks Strengthens AI

June 20–22, 2023 | Santa Clara, CA

#SensorsConverge

Feed your AI!

- AI decision-making requires data and lots of it
- Sensors, sensors, sensors!
- A big challenge: wiring all the sensors is not realistic
- Batteries must last the life of the system to avoid maintenance
- Low power design enables:
  a. Battery-free energy harvesting sensors
  b. Lifetime Power® battery-powered sensors

#SensorsConverge

Sensors Converge

Battery-Free Sensor Example

AI Network

PCT100 RFID Sensor Tag
Or BLE Sensor Tag

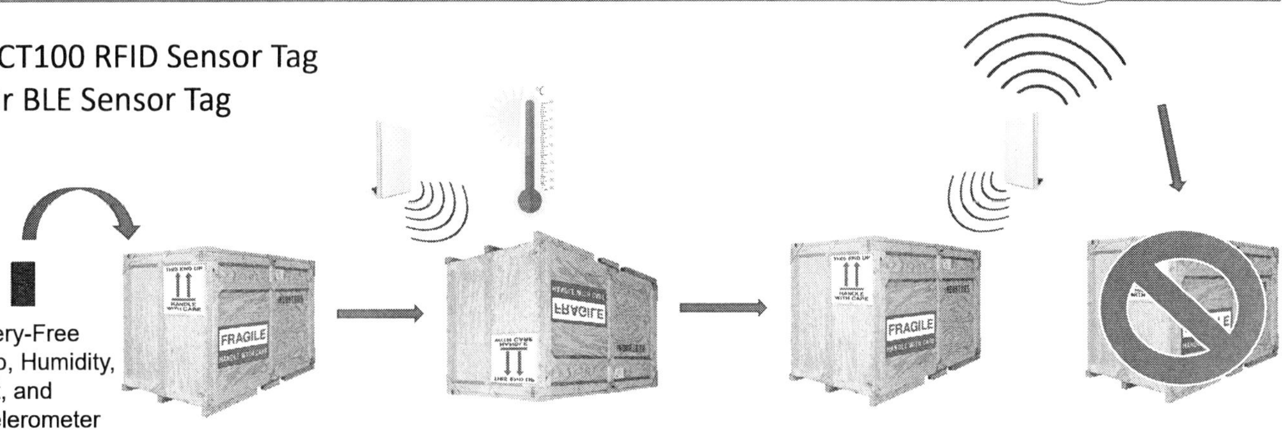

Battery-Free Temp, Humidity, Light, and Accelerometer Sensor

- **How it works**
  - Powered by an RFID reader or other transmitter
  - Charge and fire – capacitor based
  - Max distance 120ft

#SensorsConverge

Sensors Converge

25-Year Lifetime Power Battery Example

- **HVAC and Lighting Control**
  - Light, Motion, Security, Heating & Cooling Sensors
  - Warehouses, Offices, Stadiums
  - Easy to implement and retrofit
  - Can harvest energy from the environment – RF, Solar, etc.

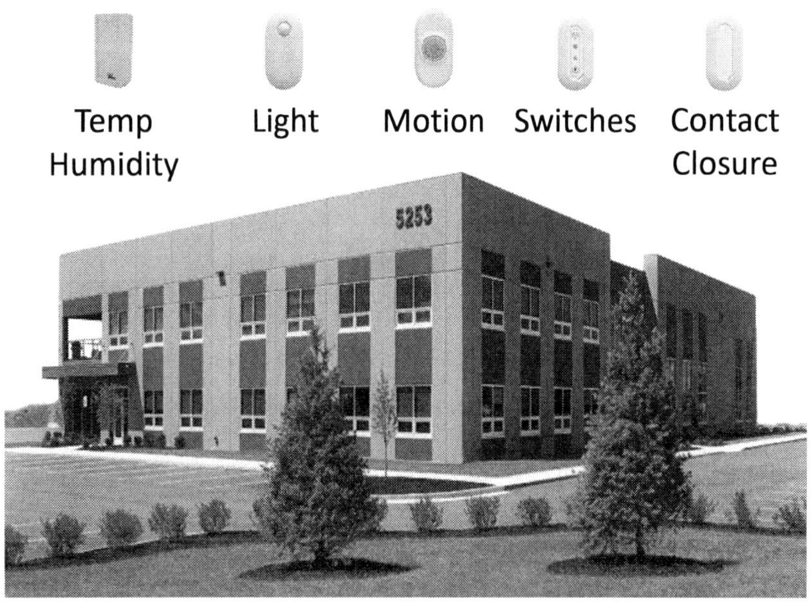

#SensorsConverge

Sensors Converge

Sensors that last for 25 Years?

Design considerations:

- Stable battery chemistry
- Soldered in batteries
- Minimize leakage currents
- Conformal coating on PCBA to avoid leakage paths from future contaminants

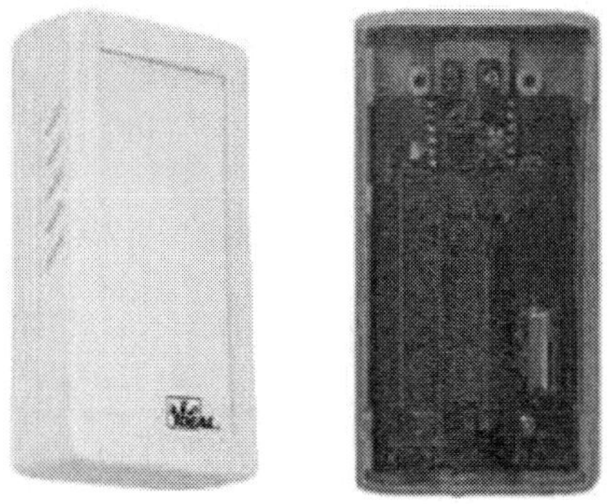

Can be integrated with building systems and AI to optimize energy conservation automatically.

#SensorsConverge

Sensors Converge

Enabled by Wireless Power and Energy Harvesting

The upcoming AI revolution will need more data than is currently available. Next-generation sensors will have to be:

- Low/No Maintenance
- Ultra low power
- Sustainable and Reliable
- "Always-on" and Ubiquitous; able to be placed on, or in places easily without wires or battery maintenance

#SensorsConverge

Sensors Converge

Sensors Converge

Jump Start Your Low-Power IoT Sensors Application Development

June 20–22, 2023 | Santa Clara, CA

#SensorsConverge

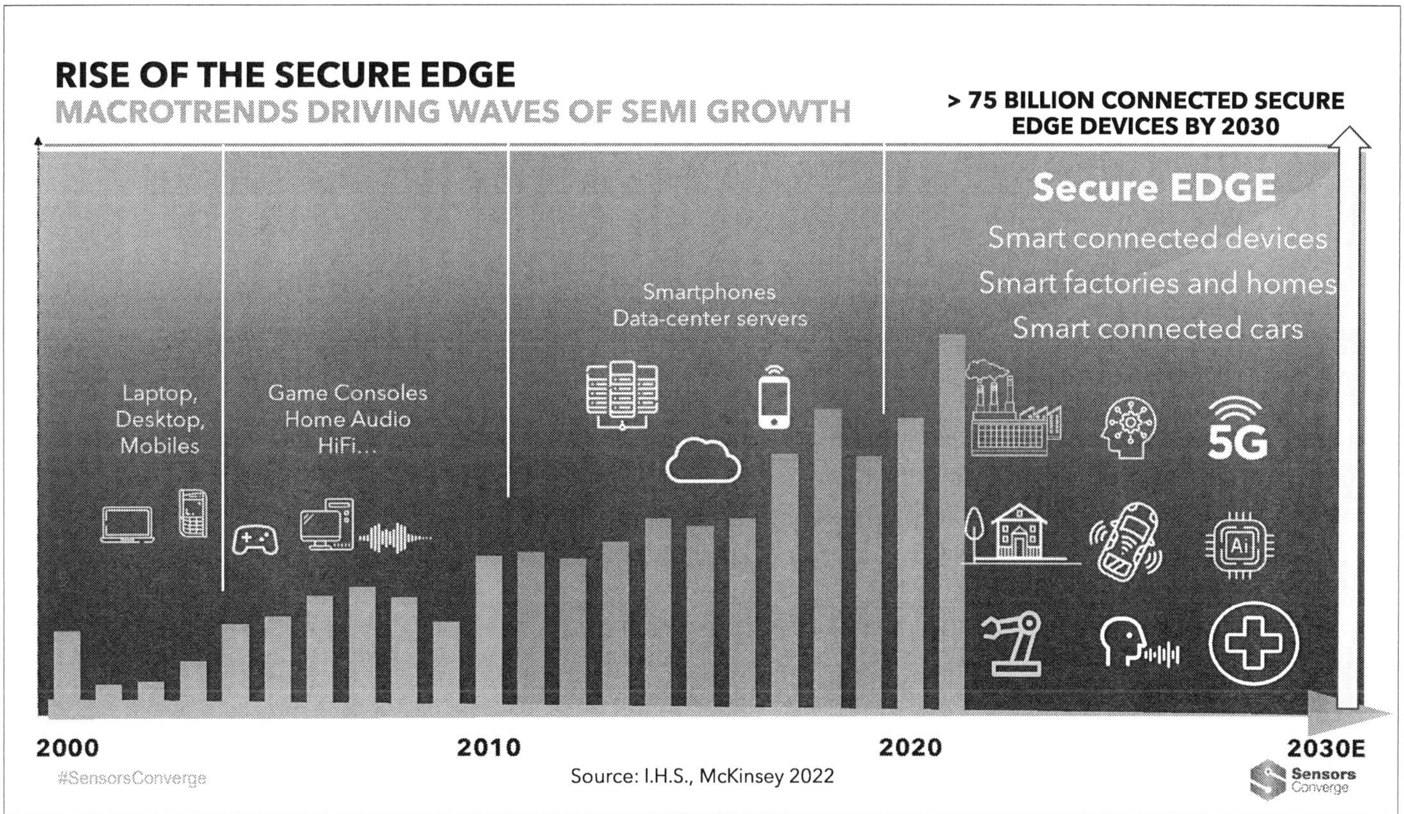

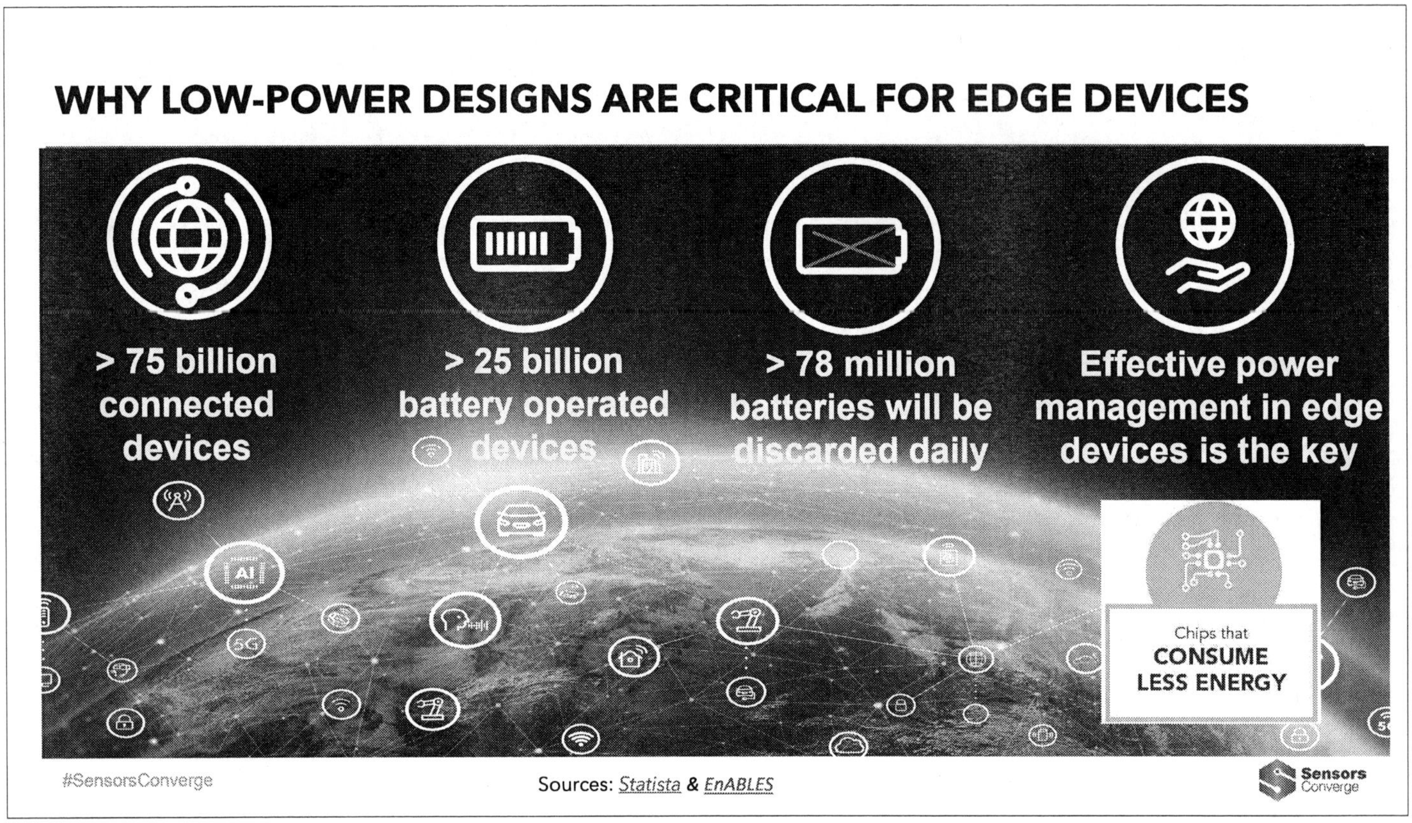
WHY LOW-POWER DESIGNS ARE CRITICAL FOR EDGE DEVICES
> 75 billion connected devices
> 25 billion battery operated devices
> 78 million batteries will be discarded daily
Effective power management in edge devices is the key
AI
5G
Chips that CONSUME LESS ENERGY
#SensorsConverge
Sources: Statista & EnABLES
Sensors Converge

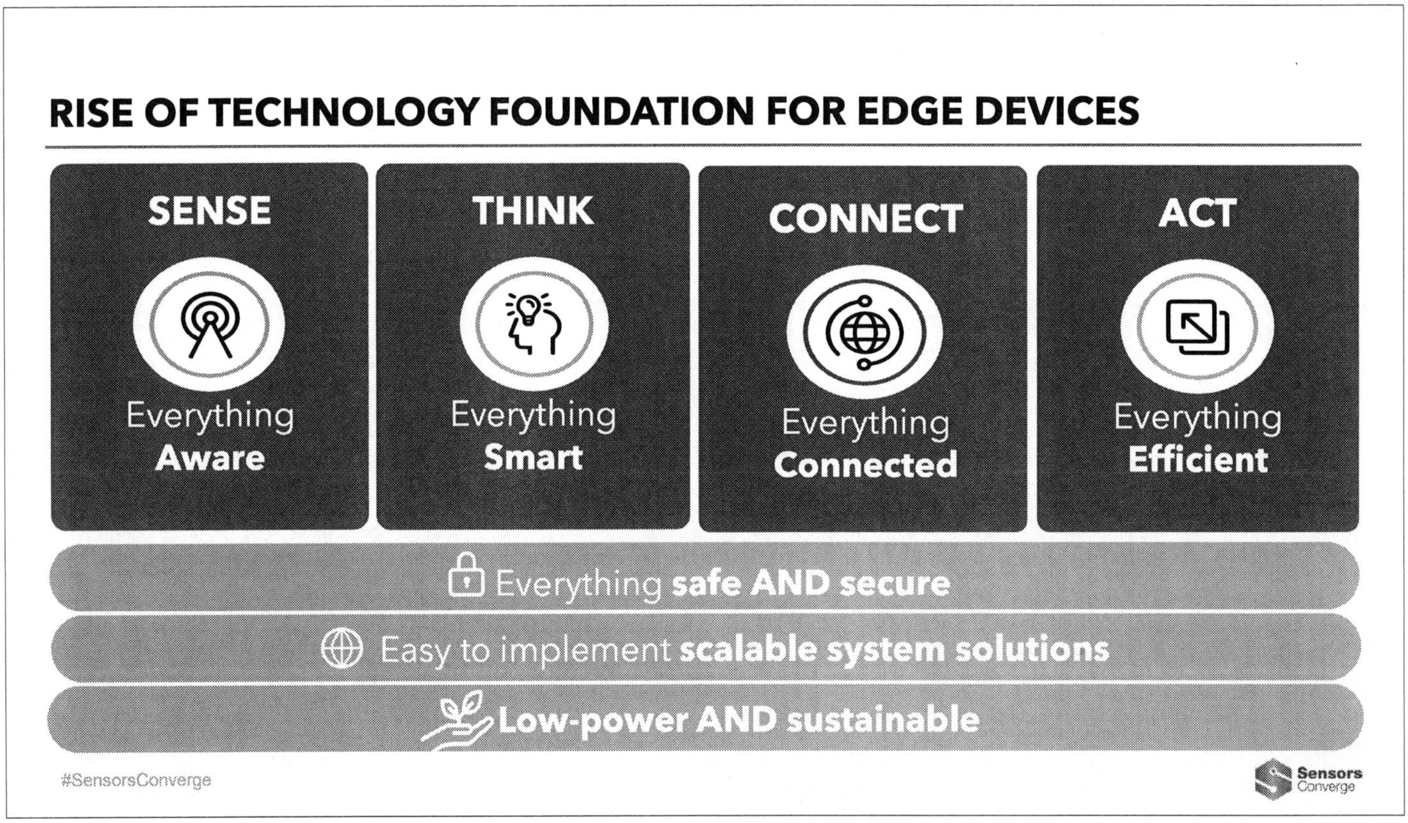
RISE OF TECHNOLOGY FOUNDATION FOR EDGE DEVICES
SENSE
Everything Aware
THINK
Everything Smart
CONNECT
Everything Connected
ACT
Everything Efficient
Everything safe AND secure
Easy to implement scalable system solutions
Low-power AND sustainable
#SensorsConverge
Sensors Converge

KEY CONSIDERATIONS FOR LOW-POWER IOT APPLICATIONS

Low-Power Operation:

- ❑ Integrated PMU
- ❑ Reduced power modes
  - Sleep, Deep-Sleep, Power Down, Deep-Power Down modes
- ❑ Configurable wake-up options
- ❑ Low-power consumption (nAmp to uAmp)
- ❑ Quick wake-up time (transition to active mode)

Embedded Functions:

- ❑ Fully configurable, completely autonomous solution
- ❑ Programmable thresholds, timers
- ❑ Reduces bandwidth, latency and computational requirements
- ❑ Interrupt mode
- ❑ No complex algorithm, low-code, low-memory

#SensorsConverge

Sensors Converge

KEY CONSIDERATIONS FOR LOW-POWER IOT APPLICATIONS

Enablement Ecosystem:

- ❑ Hardware & software enablement ecosystem with rapid development kits
- ❑ Helps in improving ease-of-use and quick evaluation.
- ❑ Accelerate end user development
- ❑ Improve OOBE (Out Of Box Experience)

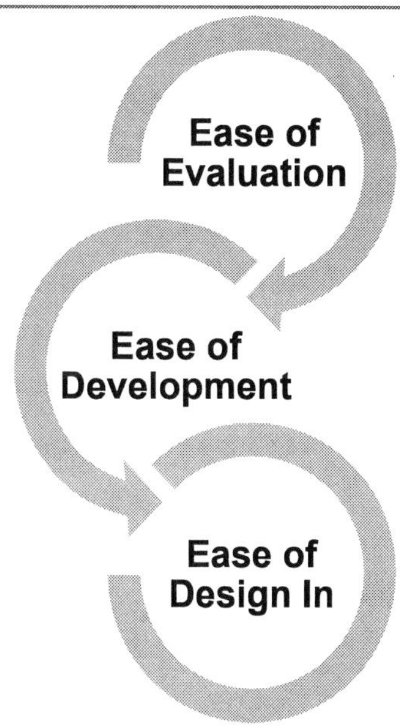

Key Takeaways

- ✓ Ease of evaluation, development and design prototyping.
- ✓ Reference out-of-box examples showcasing low-power operation.
- ✓ Increase customer's confidence, help jump-start their development.

#SensorsConverge

Sensors Converge

ENABLEMENT ECOSYSTEM

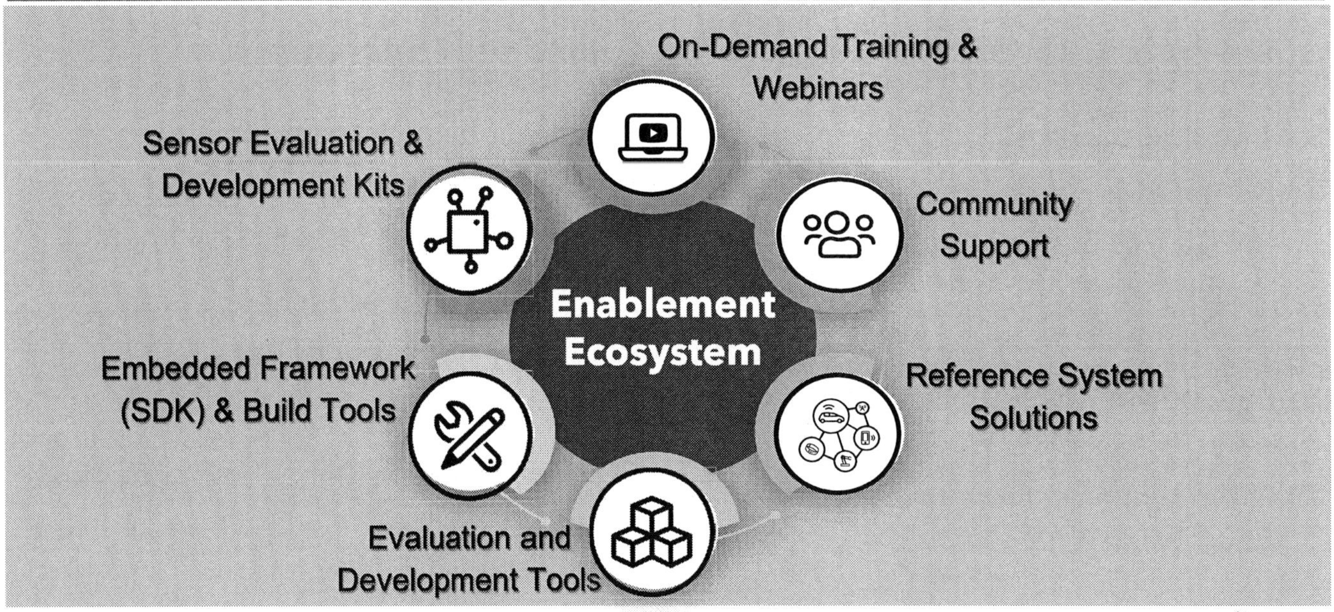

#SensorsConverge

Sensors Converge

RAPID DEVELOPMENT KITS

Demo Kit (Shield + MCU)

Complete Solution for 'Out of Box' sensor demonstration, evaluation and development

Shield Board

Evaluation Boards, pin compatible with most Arduino and FRDM development boards

Breakout/Click Board

Boards for product prototyping, can be easily wired to host MCU

Demonstration Kit (Shield + MCU)

- Officially supported combination of a Sensor Shield board and an Arduino® development MCU board.

Shield Board

- Pin compatible across most Arduino® development MCU boards.
- Pins available as test points for evaluating pin signals such as VDD, GND, I^2C, SPI, INT etc.

Breakout/Click Board

- Small form factor design or mikroBUS™ based design, ideal for product prototyping.

#SensorsConverge

Sensors Converge

EMBEDDED FRAMEWORK AND BUILD TOOLS

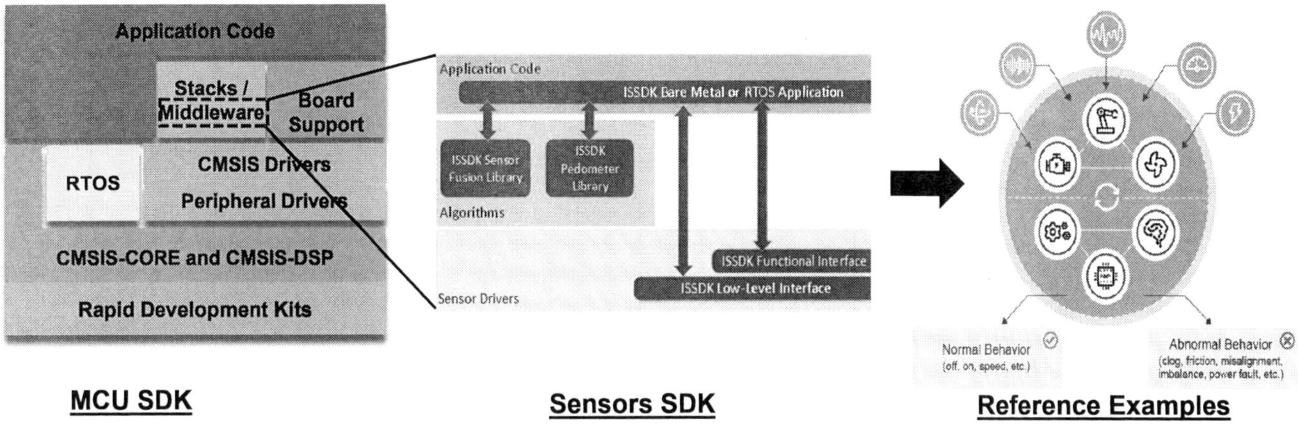

Key Benefits to End Users:

- ❑ Open Source: Sources are released under BSD-3 clause open source.
- ❑ Portability: CMSIS compliance enabling easy porting across broad range of Arm® Cortex®-M core based MCUs.
- ❑ Quality: Production-grade quality, reference out-of-box examples.
- ❑ Tools Integration: Integrated with SW & Tools for quality user experience.

#SensorsConverge

Sensors Converge

EVALUATION AND DEVELOPMENT TOOLS

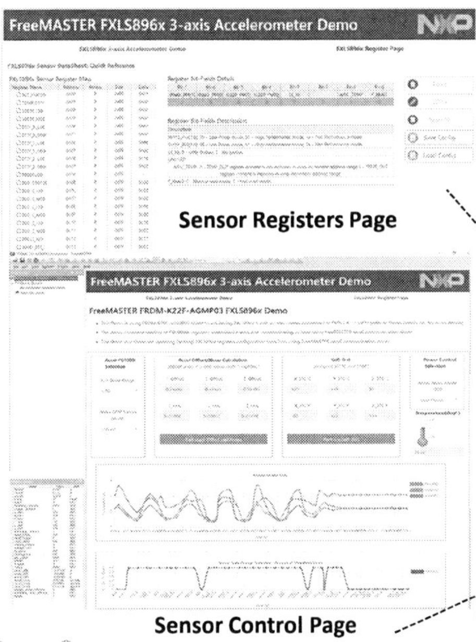

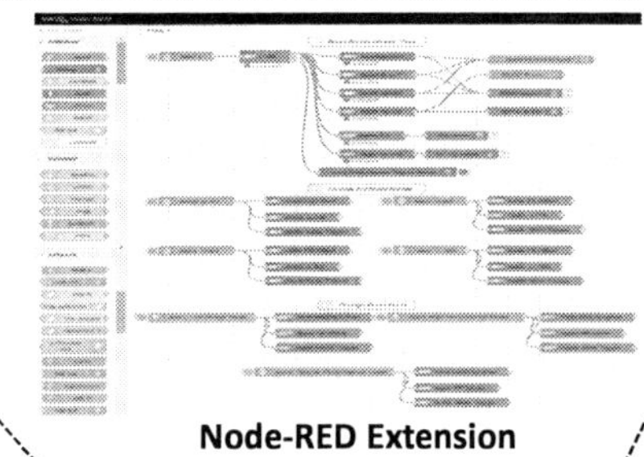

Key Benefits to End Users:

- ❑ Plug & Play Tool
- ❑ Enables Quick Evaluation
- ❑ Register bit-fields read/write
- ❑ Real-time control & monitoring

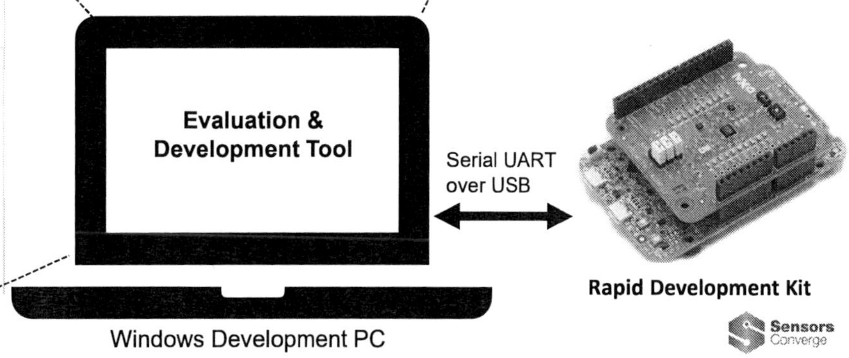

#SensorsConverge

Sensors Converge

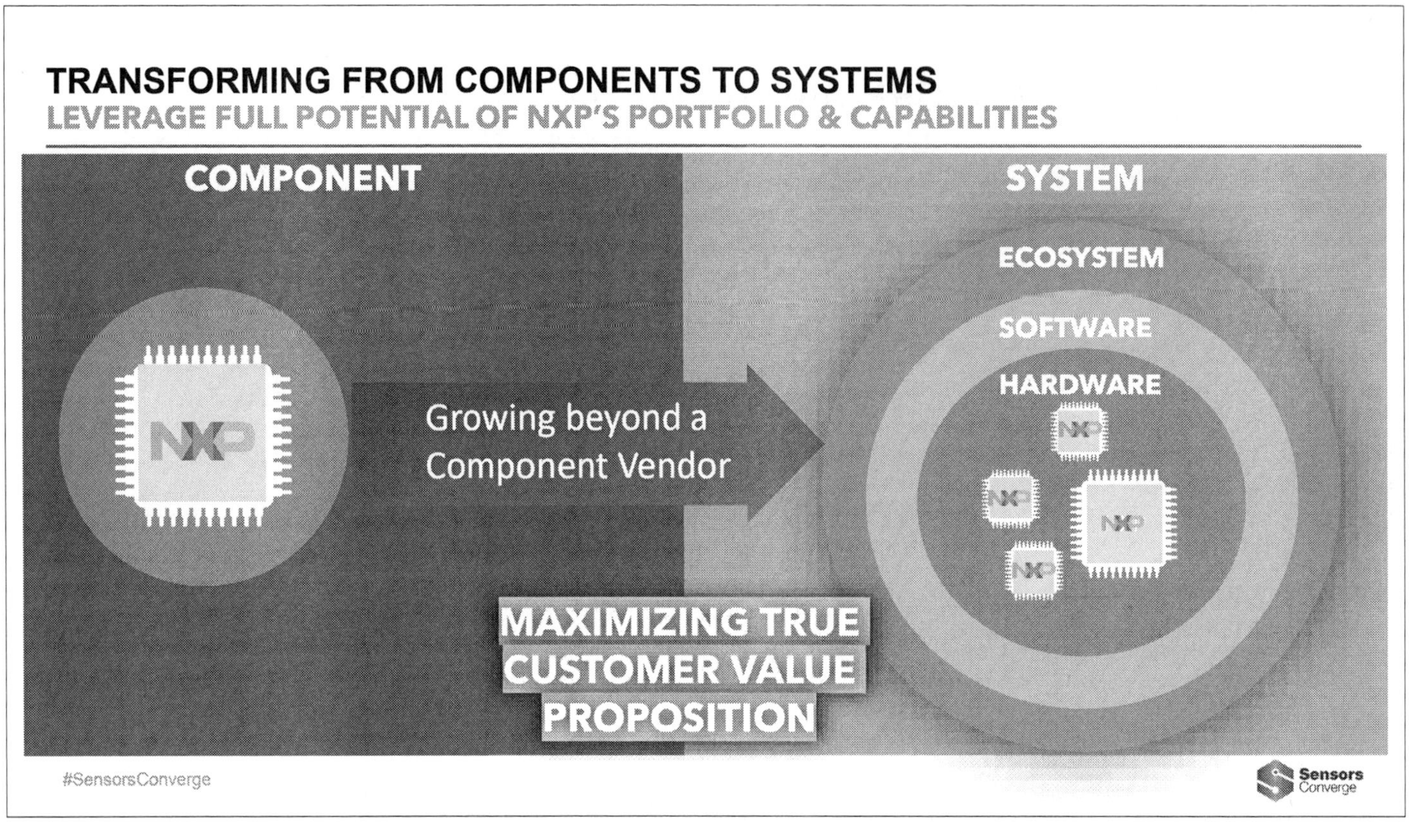
TRANSFORMING FROM COMPONENTS TO SYSTEMS
LEVERAGE FULL POTENTIAL OF NXP'S PORTFOLIO & CAPABILITIES
COMPONENT
SYSTEM
ECOSYSTEM
SOFTWARE
HARDWARE
Growing beyond a Component Vendor
MAXIMIZING TRUE CUSTOMER VALUE PROPOSITION
#SensorsConverge
Sensors Converge

Sensors Converge
Q & A
#SensorsConverge

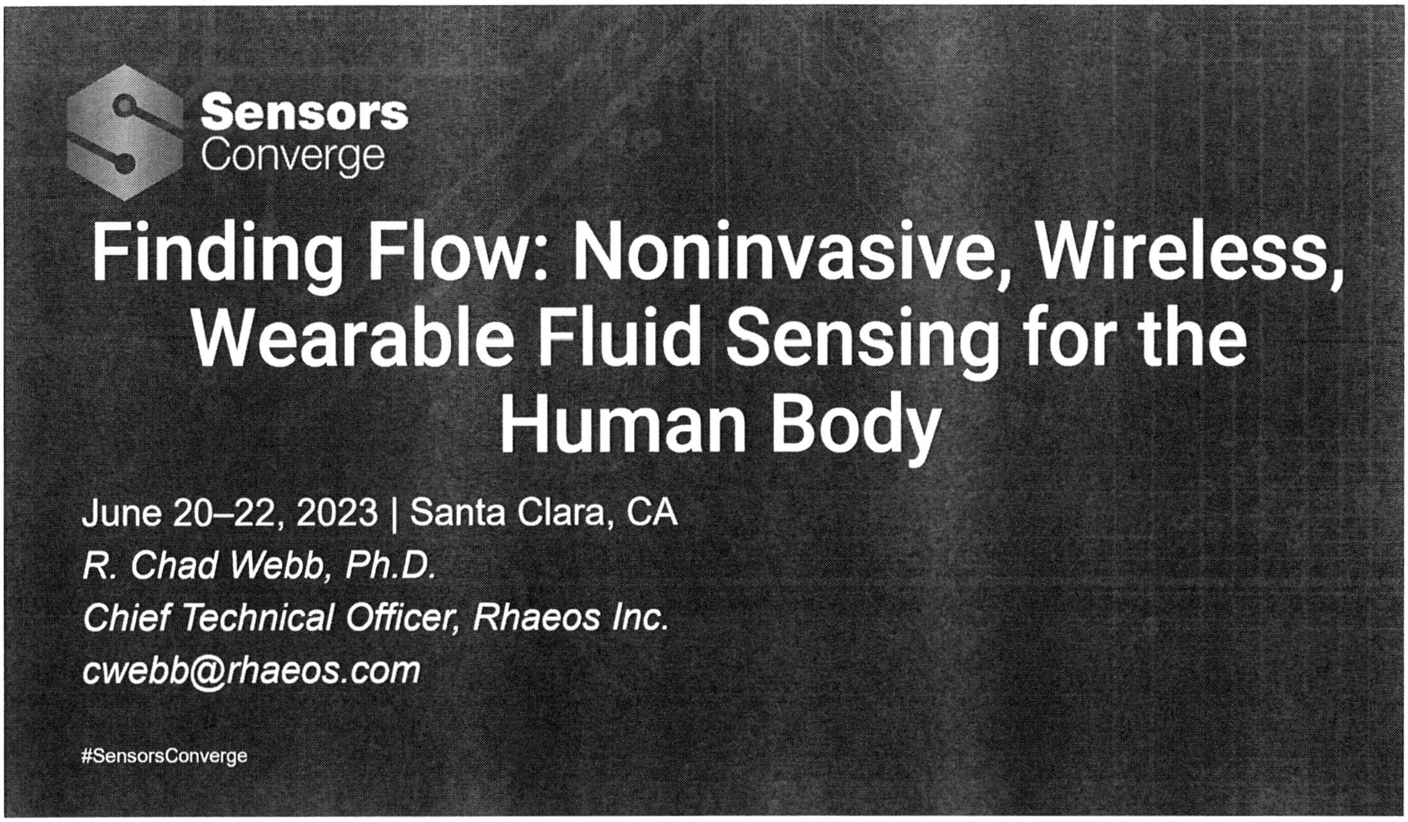
Sensors
Converge
Finding Flow: Noninvasive, Wireless, Wearable Fluid Sensing for the Human Body
June 20–22, 2023 | Santa Clara, CA
R. Chad Webb, Ph.D.
Chief Technical Officer, Rhaeos Inc.
cwebb@rhaeos.com
#SensorsConverge

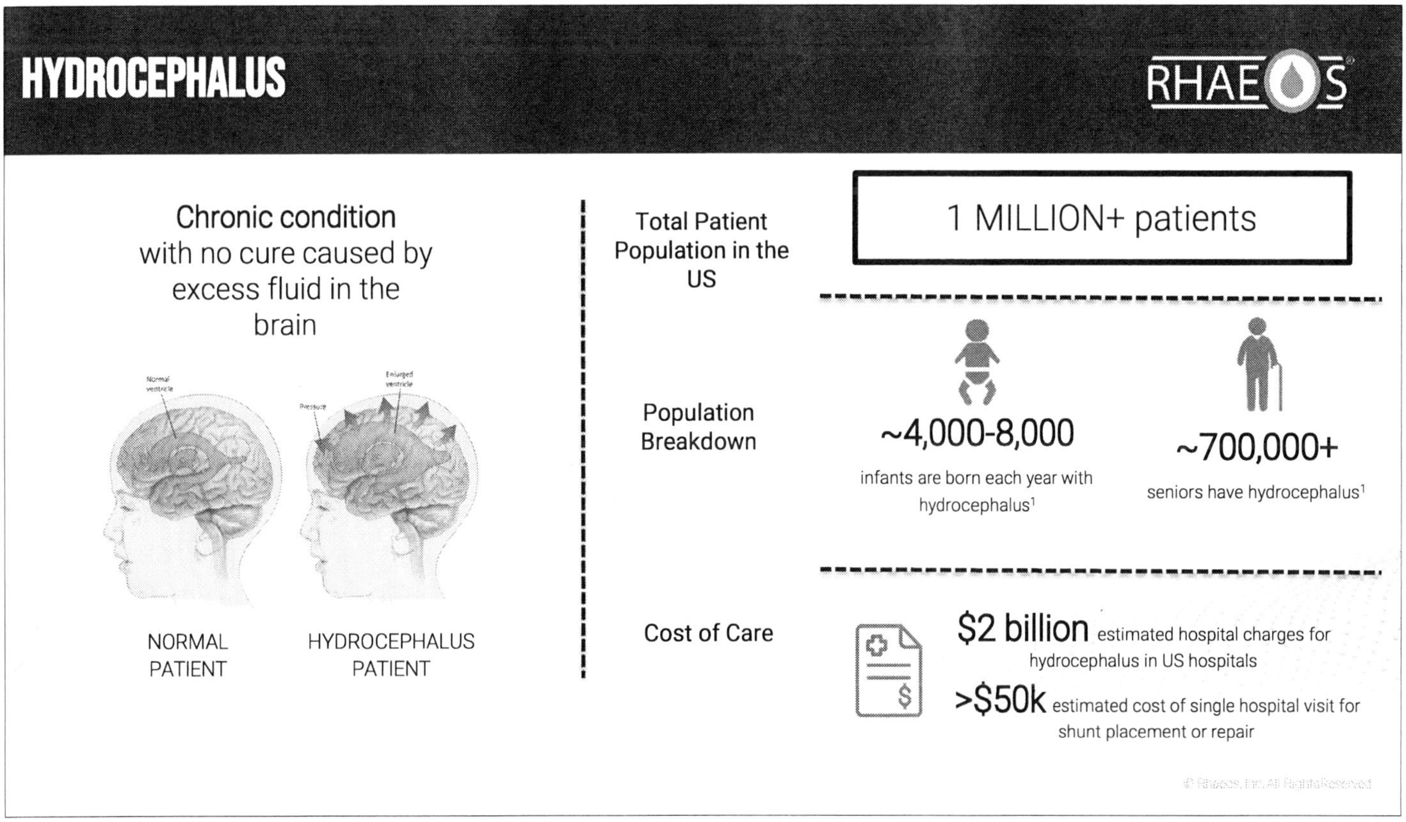
HYDROCEPHALUS
RHAEOS
Chronic condition with no cure caused by excess fluid in the brain
Normal ventricle
Enlarged ventricle
Pressure
NORMAL PATIENT
HYDROCEPHALUS PATIENT
Total Patient Population in the US
1 MILLION+ patients
Population Breakdown
~4,000-8,000
infants are born each year with hydrocephalus[1]
~700,000+
seniors have hydrocephalus[1]
Cost of Care
$2 billion estimated hospital charges for hydrocephalus in US hospitals
>$50k estimated cost of single hospital visit for shunt placement or repair
© Rhaeos, Inc. All Rights Reserved

HYDROCEPHALUS

RHAEOS®

Standard treatment

Shunts = tubing that "drains the brain" of excess fluid

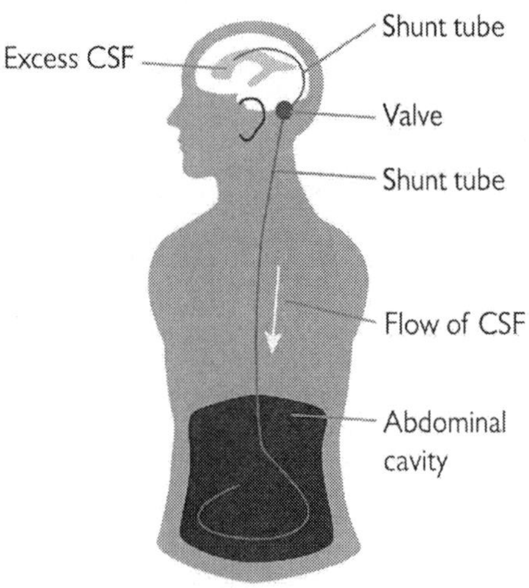

Shunt Problems

- **50%** of shunts fail within **2 years**
- Fail due to infection, obstruction, & disconnection
- Symptoms are non-specific: headache, lethargy, nausea, etc.
- Need to be revised = another neurosurgery
- High clinical costs for shunted patients

CHALLENGE: DIFFICULT SHUNT FUNCTION DIAGNOSTICS

RHAEOS®

Shunted patient presents w/ non-specific symptoms → **Need: Diagnosis of shunt malfunction**

Malfunction?

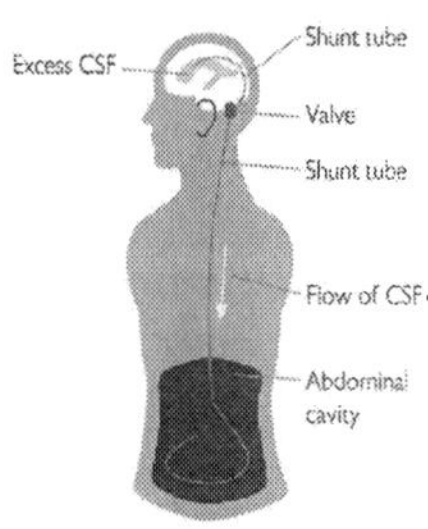

No Good Options Today
No Direct Measure of Shunt Flow or Pressure

Option	Sens./Spec.	Drawbacks
CT Scan	*65%/84% Sens./Spec.*	*Radiation; Capital Equipment Scheduling; Need Specialist*
Shunt Tap	*31%/89% Sens./Spec.*	*Invasive; OR Scheduling; Need Specialist*
Shunt Series	*18%/97% Sens./Spec.*	*Radiation; Capital Equipment Scheduling; Need Specialist*
MRI	*51%/89% Sens./Spec.*	*Capital Equipment Scheduling; Need Specialist*

Boyle (2014) Pediatrics
Boyle (2017) PAS
Desai (2007) Pediatric Radiology
Griffey (2007) Radiology
Lehnert (2011) Emergency Radiology
Mater (2008) CJEM
Vassilyadi (2010) J Neurosurgery Pediatrics
Zorc (2002) Pediatric Emergency Care

HOW DO WE GET A MORE DIRECT MEASURE OF IMPLANTED SHUNT PATENCY?

RHAEOS

Intracranial Pressure

- Direct measure of pressure buildup
- Invasive (probe into brain)
- Ongoing research into implantable and noninvasive wearable solutions (some traction out of Brazil).

Natus Camino® 1104L Catheter

Ultrasound

- Normal CSF lacks natural Doppler scatterers
- Some research into exciting bubbles to support ultrasound use.

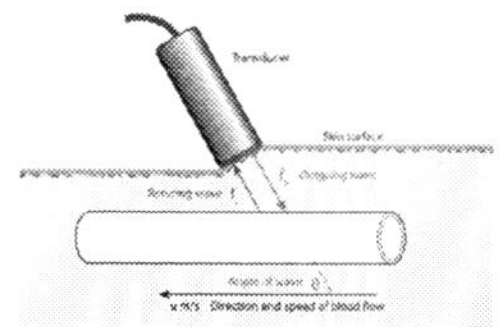

Direct Flow From Within the Shunt

- Implant flow sensor directly into shunt catheter ("smart shunt")
- Ongoing research – needs to work reliably as permanent implant
- Long regulatory path

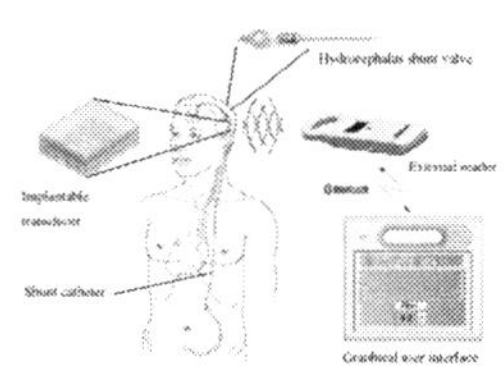

Noninvasive Thermal Flow Sensing

- Doesn't require scatterer
- Can be applied as wearable to surface of skin over shunt
- Rhaeos FlowSense® currently in clinical trials for FDA clearance
- Must manage other physiological and environmental thermal signals

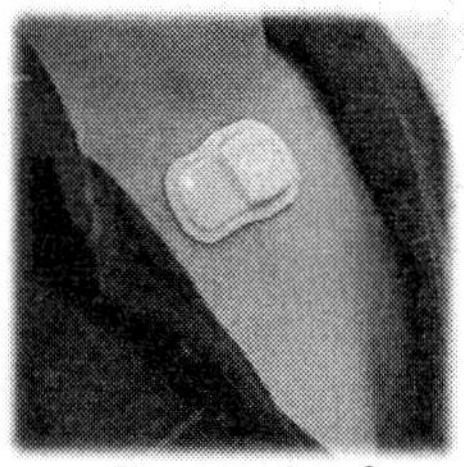

Rhaeos FlowSense®

LEVERAGING PRECISION THERMAL TRANSPORT

RHAEOS

Commercial Examples of thermal flow measurements

Mass-Flow Controllers

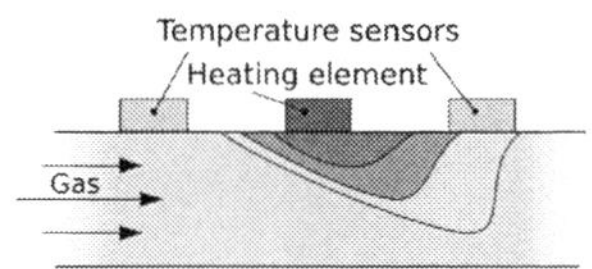

Wikimedia commons

Swan-Ganz Thermodilution Catheter

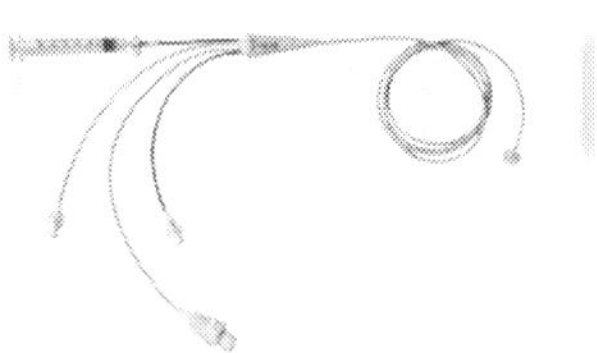

Edwards Life Sciences

Side View

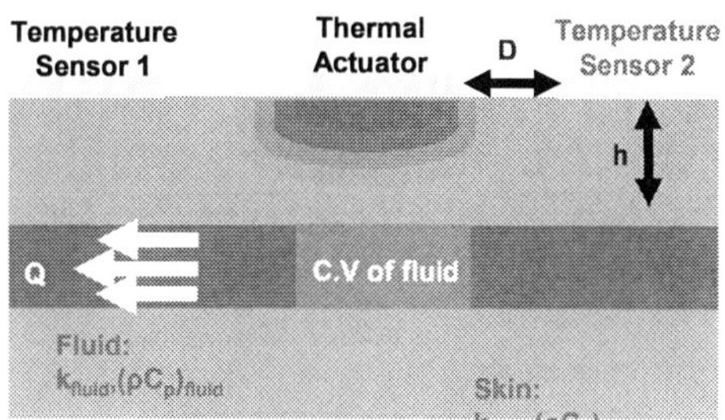

Front View

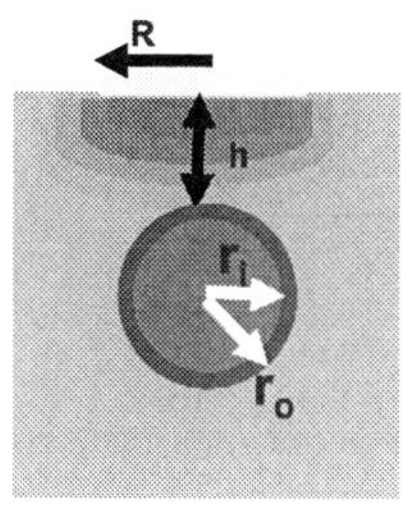

Flow parameter:

$\Delta T_{sensors}/T_{actuator} \equiv \alpha$

$\alpha = \alpha(Q, P, D, h, r_i, r_o, R, k_{skin}, (\rho C_p)_{skin}, k_{fluid}, (\rho C_p)_{fluid})$

Geometrical parameters (D, h, r_i, r_o, R); Thermal parameters (k_{skin}, $(\rho C_p)_{skin}$, k_{fluid}, $(\rho C_p)_{fluid}$)

Diffusion through skin: $h \sim \sqrt{\frac{k_{skin} t}{(\rho C_p)_{skin}}}$

Thermal mass of flowing fluid: $C_{th} \sim \dot{m} C_p$

LEVERAGING PRECISION THERMAL TRANSPORT

RHAEOS

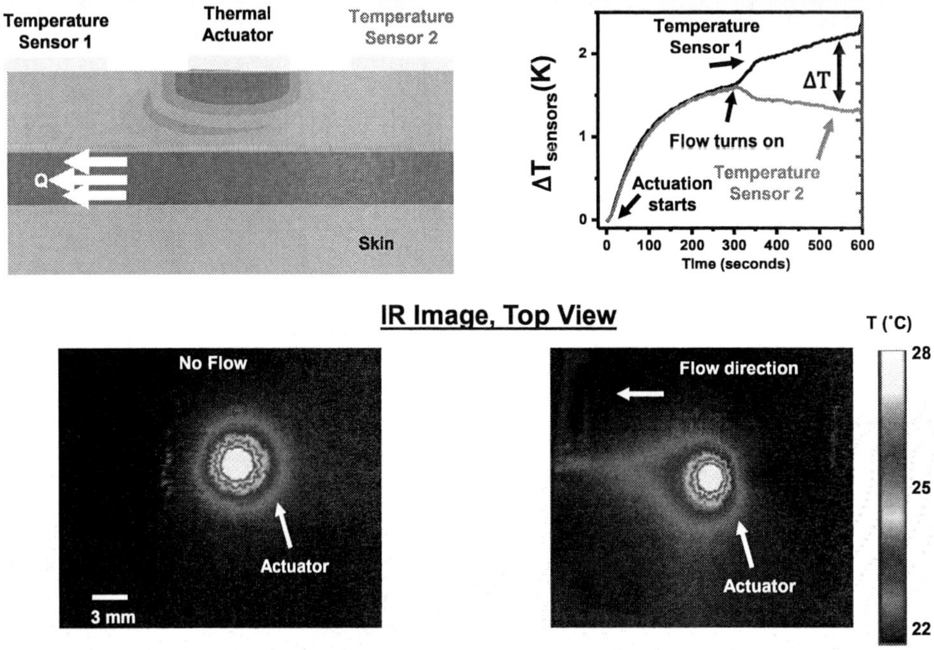

APPLICATIONS TO SHUNTS

RHAEOS

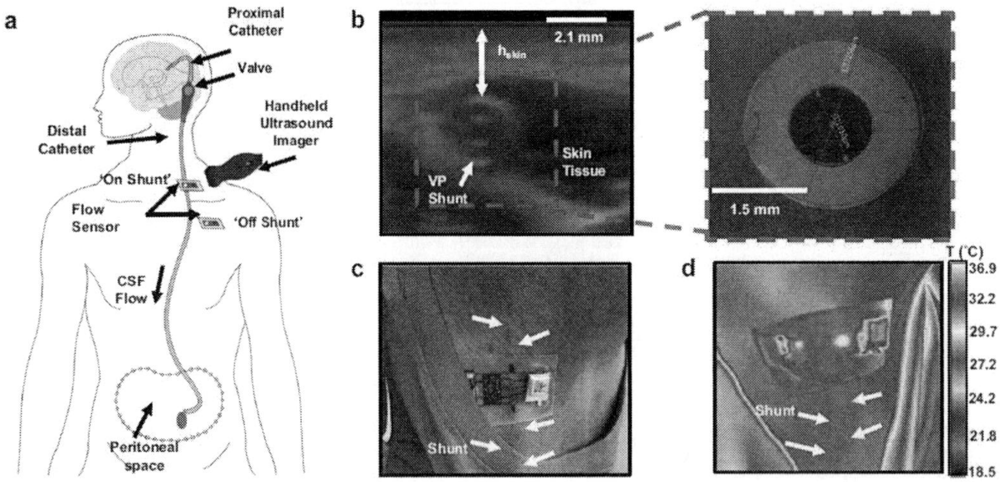

Krishnan, et. al., npj Digital Medicine (2020).

EARLY SHUNT FLOW DATA

RHAEOS

Early Flow Measurements

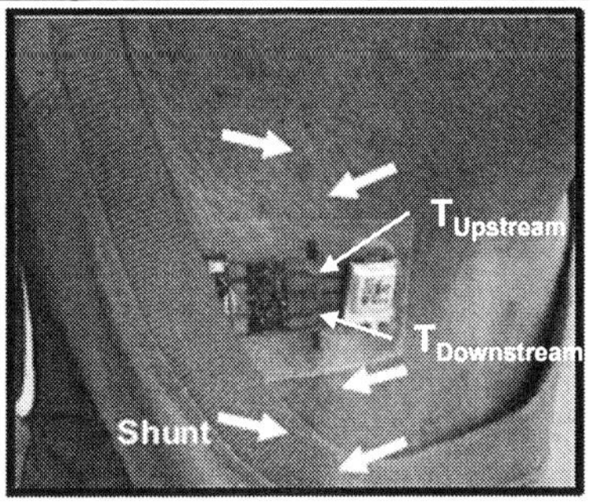

No Flow

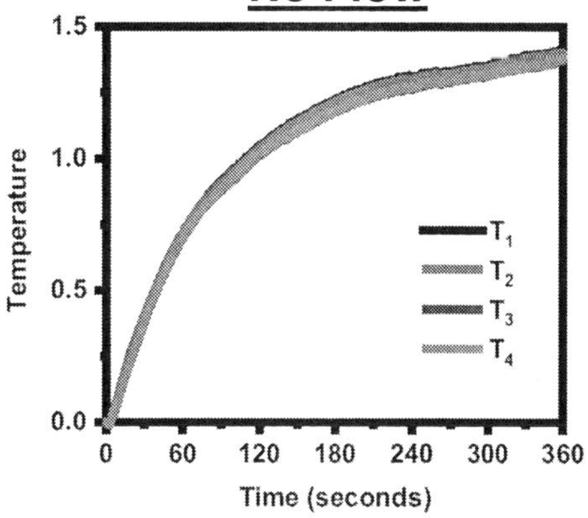

CSF Flow

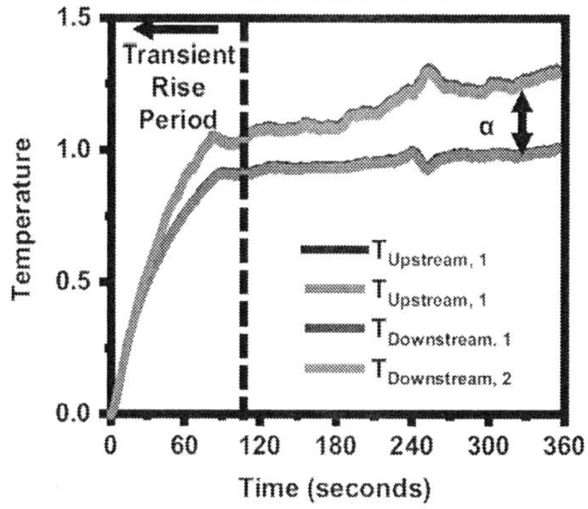

Krishnan, et. al., npj Digital Medicine (2020).

EARLY SHUNT FLOW DATA

RHAEOS

Noninvasively assessing presence of flow in implanted CSF shunts

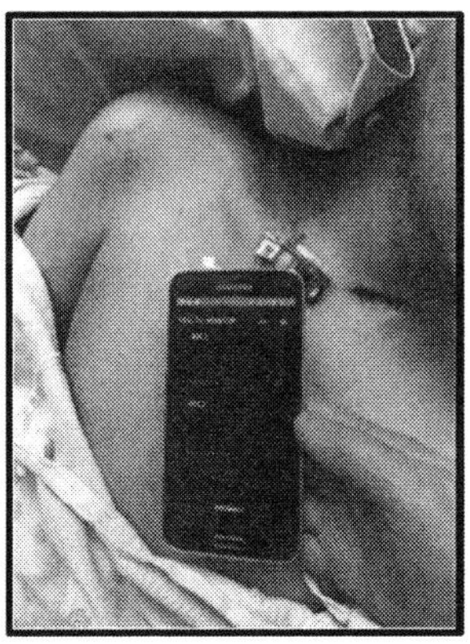

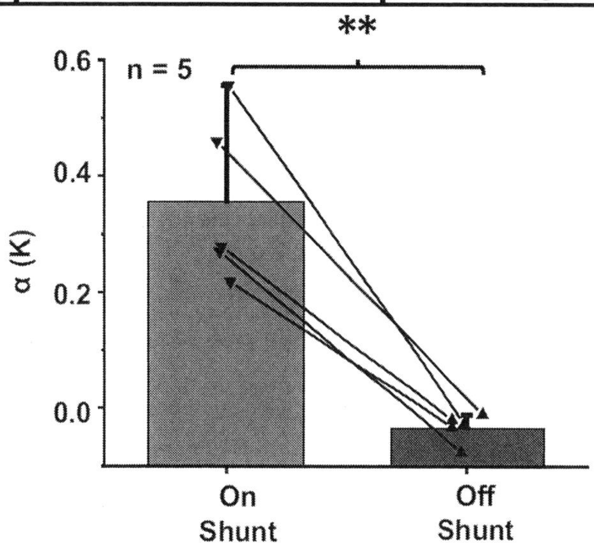

Krishnan, et. al., npj Digital Medicine (2020).

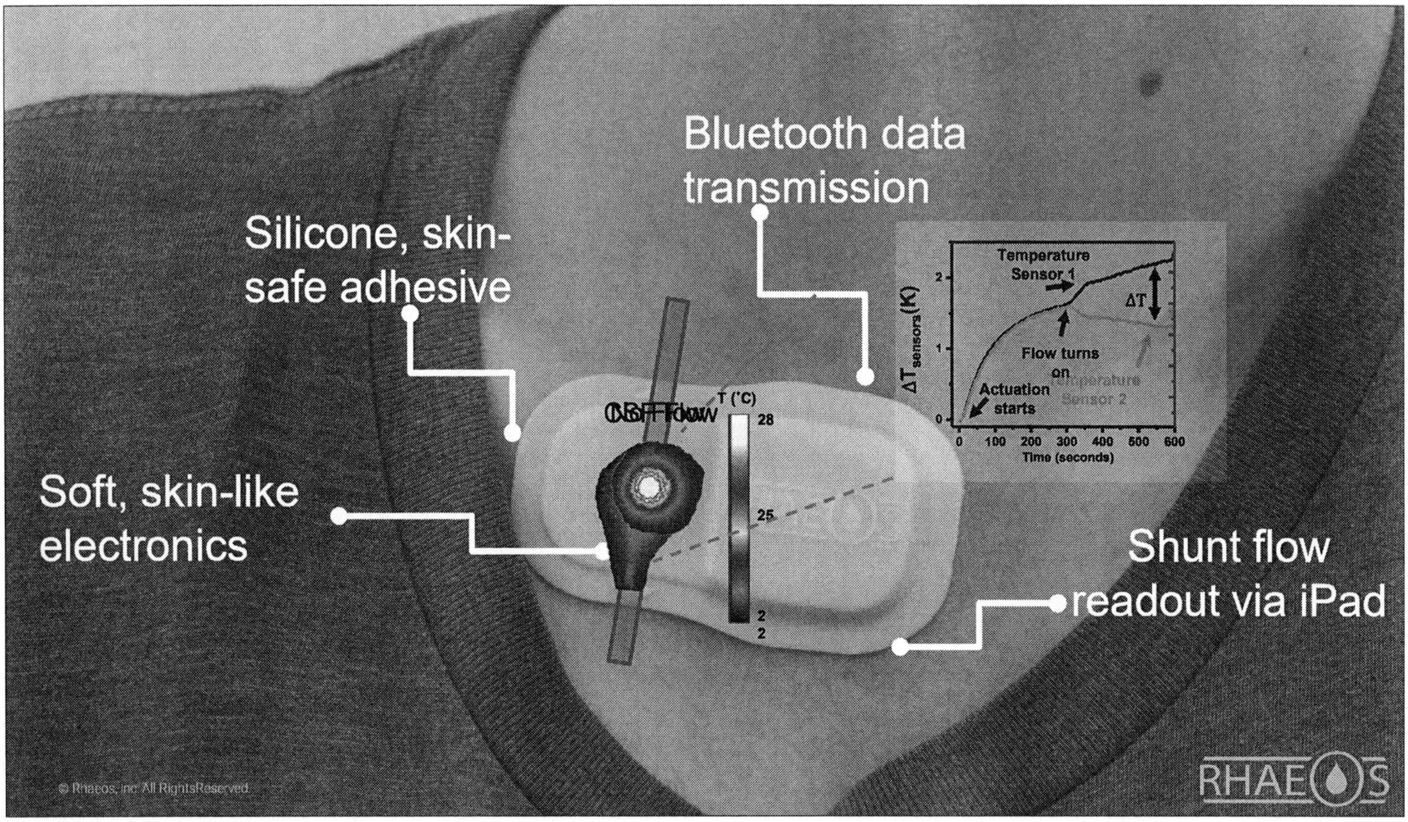

FLEX ELECTRONICS FOR CONFORMAL CONTACT

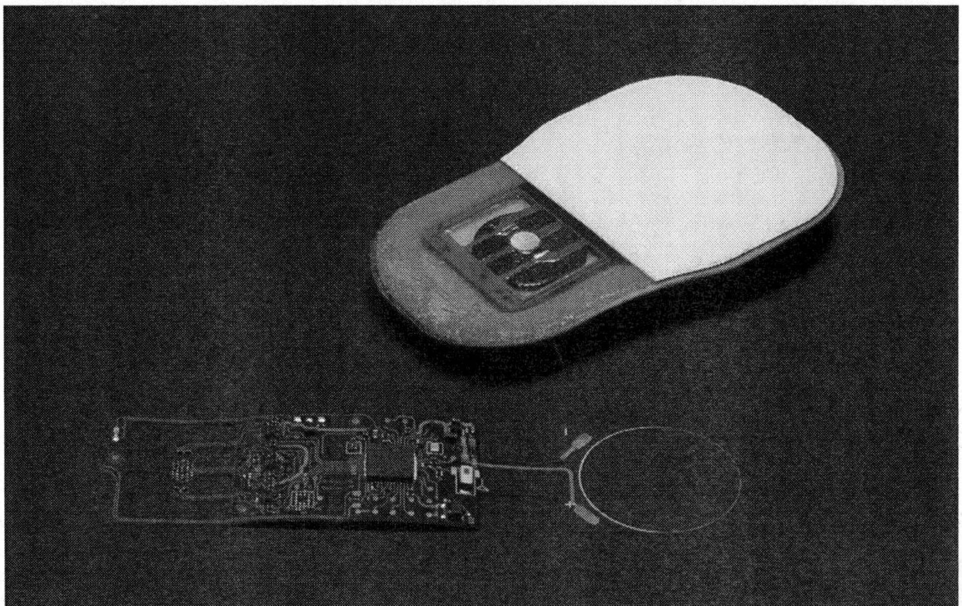

BENEFITS OF NONINVASIVE SHUNT ASSESSMENTS

RHAEOS®

Patients
>50% imaging reduction
>$500 reduction in out-of-pocket expenses

REDUCED
ER visit length
radiation exposure
diagnostic testing
unnecessary surgeries
readmissions

Providers
Saves >1hr of diagnostic testing time

Payors
>30% reduction in diagnostic testing
>40% reduction in unnecessary admission

Hospitals
Readmissions: up to $200K/pt

*Numerical assumptions are based on US healthcare data

SUMMARY

RHAEOS®

- Leverage thermal physics + wearable mechanics for noninvasive fluid flow sensing
- Enables new generation of diagnostics for conditions which impact near surface biological fluid flow
- Applications across numerous biological fluids
- Clinical studies in progress for applications in hydrocephalus shunts

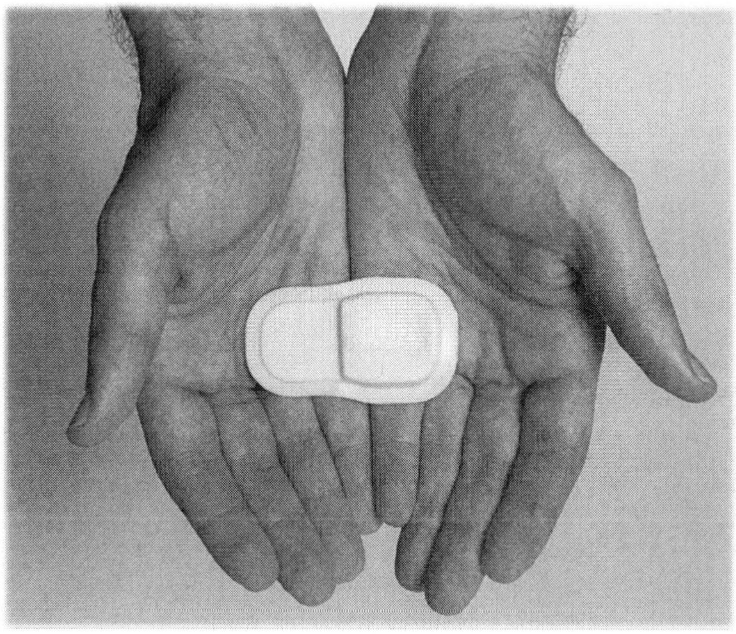

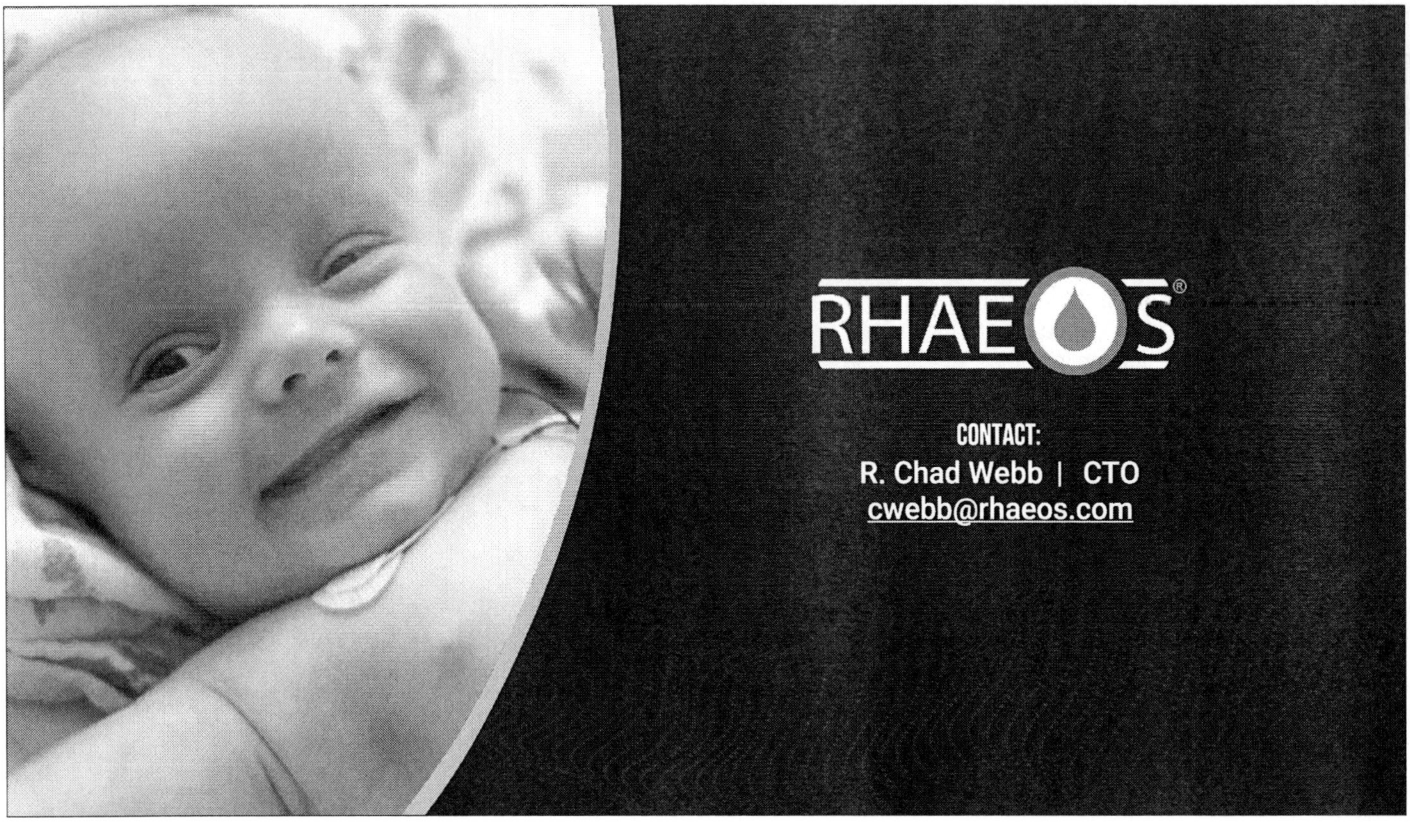
RHAEOS®
CONTACT:
R. Chad Webb | CTO
cwebb@rhaeos.com

Sensors Converge

Sensor Innovations for the Next Generation of Wearables

June 20–22, 2023 | Santa Clara, CA

Dr. Tess Skyrme, Technology Analyst, t.skyrme@IDTechEx.com

#SensorsConverge

Talk Agenda

1. **Twenty years of wearables in 5 minutes**
2. **Sensor Innovations for the:**
   - **Healthcare Market**
   - **Consumer Market**
   - **Deep-Tech**
3. **Closing Remarks/ Q&A**

__Dr. Tess Skyrme__ is a Technology Analyst supporting the company's research and consulting within sensor technology and electronics. Prior to IDTechEx, she was a PhD researcher in the Quantum Sensors group at Cambridge University from which she also obtained an MRes in Sensor Technology.

#SensorsConverge

Sensors Converge

The value proposition of wearables

The Value Proposition of Wearable Technology IDTechEx Research

EFFICIENT	CONTINOUS
Access to technology is easier	Access to technology is uninterrupted

#SensorsConverge

Sensors Converge

The value proposition of wearables

The Role of Wearable Technology IDTechEx Research

SENSING

- Biometrics
- Neural Signals
- Motion
- Location
- Strain
- Temperature
- Air-quality
- Force

DISPLAYING

- Time
- Messages
- Notifications
- Entertainment
- Augmented reality
- Virtual reality
- Warnings
- Lighting

ACTUATING

- Audio
- Heating
- Lighting
- Haptic vibrations
- Electrical stimulation
- Photo-biomodulation
- Electro-magnetic stimulation

COMMUNICATING

- Bluetooth
- Wifi/5G
- Cellular
- LoRa
- Smart-phones
- Implantables
- Internet of Things
- Central databases

#SensorsConverge

Sensors Converge

Wearable technology – historic and future trends

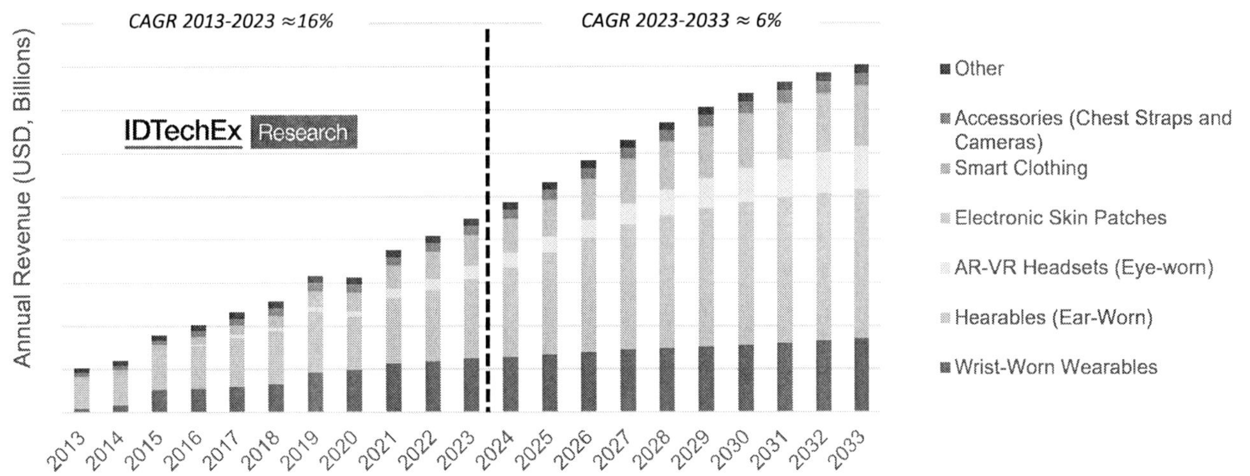

#SensorsConverge

Sensors Converge

The outlook for the wearables market at a glance

Wrist-worn device market-share to shrink with maturity

Electronic Skin Patch market share stabilized by CGM adoption

Hearable market to remain the largest

AR-VR technology has emerged from obscurity

Smart Clothing market share in decline

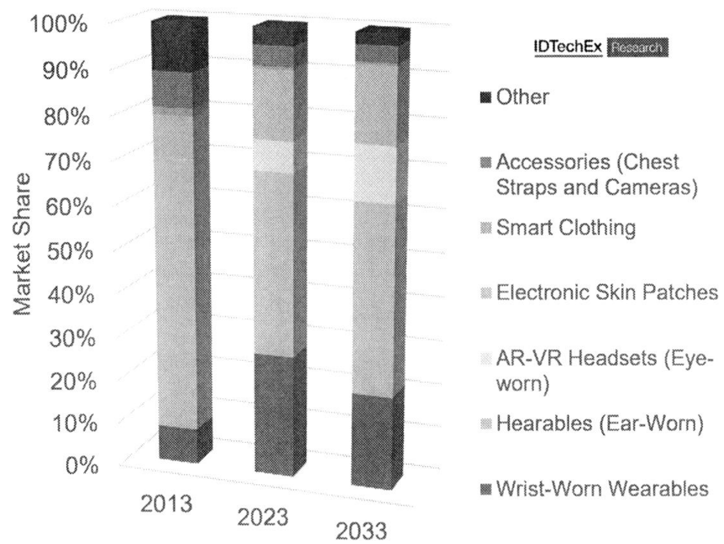

#SensorsConverge

Sensors Converge

Which sensor technologies are emerging?

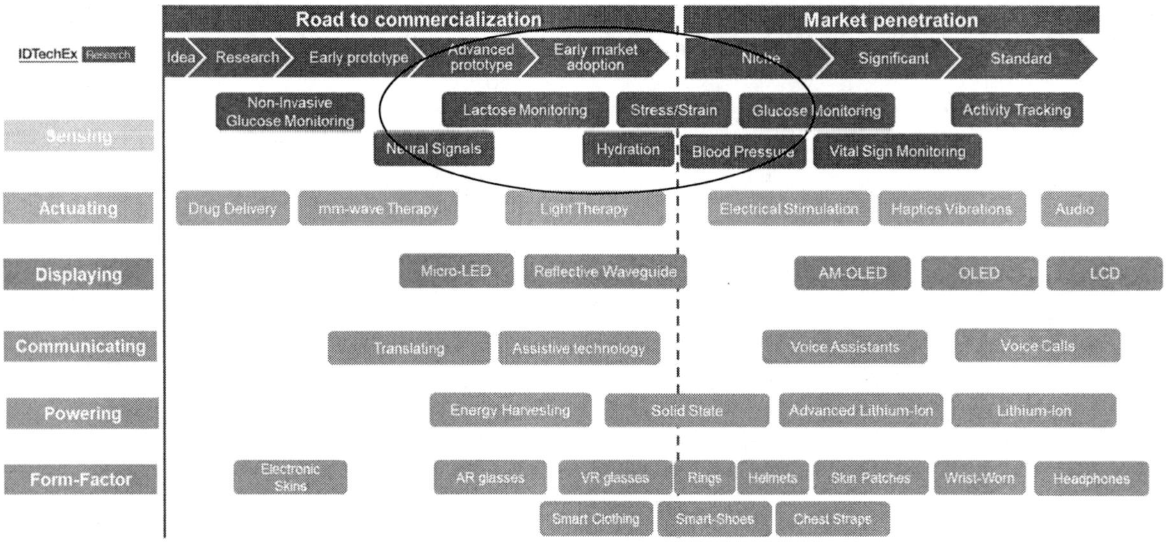

#SensorsConverge

Sensors Converge

Where is the growth potential?

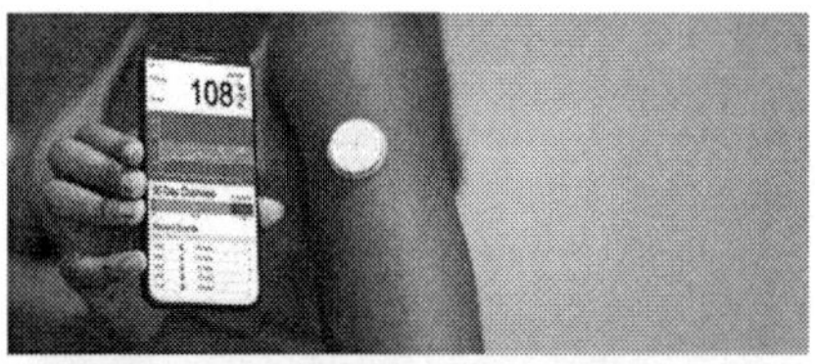

Healthcare Market: Chronic Disease Management

Consumer Market: Immersive Experiences

Deep-Tech: Quantum Technology

#SensorsConverge

Sensors Converge

Healthcare Market: Chronic Disease Management

Megatrends driving healthcare reforms

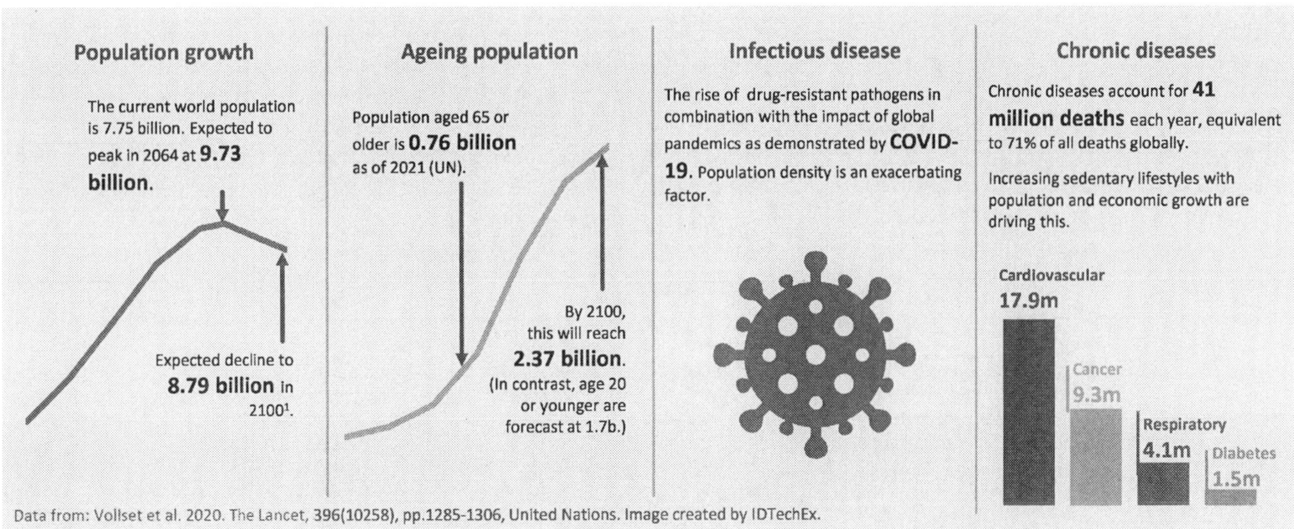

#SensorsConverge

Sensors Converge

Wearable devices are playing a growing role in remote patient monitoring programmes

Remote patient monitoring programs focus on key chronic diseases accounting for 90% of patients:

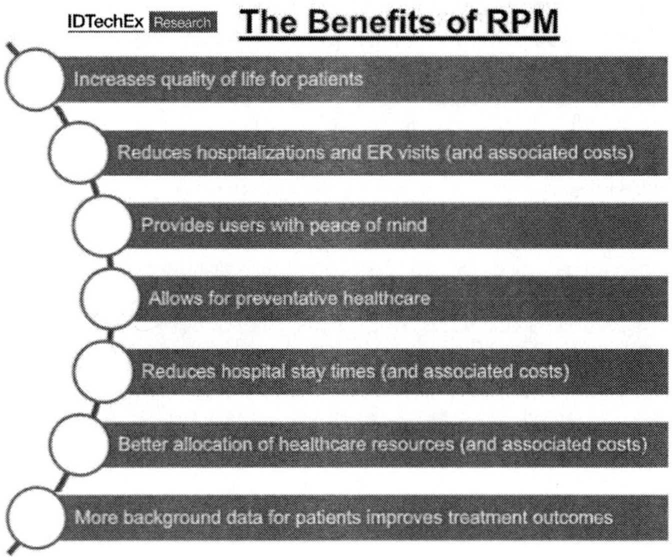

#SensorsConverge

Converge

Future RPM programmes are expected to be more dependent on new wearable technology

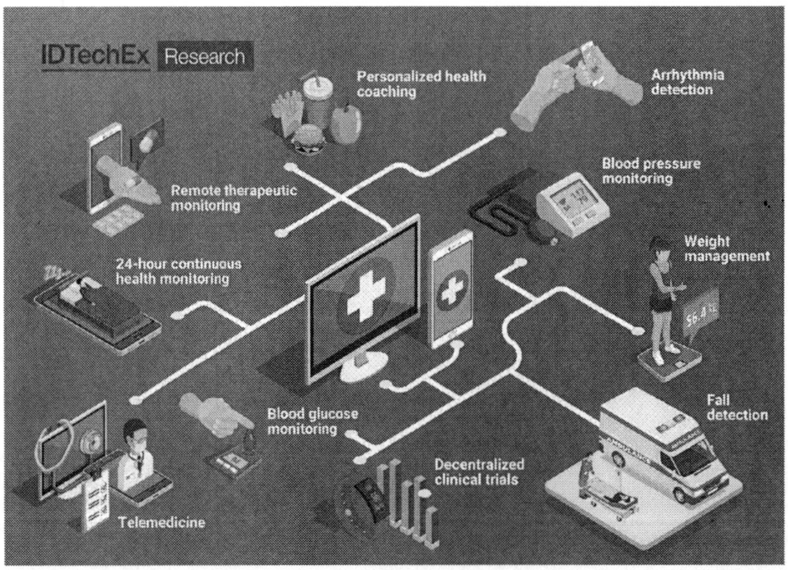

#SensorsConverge *Image Sources: Omron, Teledoc Health*

Sensors Converge

Future RPM programmes are expected to be more dependent on new wearable technology

VitalSight
Remote Patient Monitoring
By
OMRON

Blood Pressure Monitor | Body Weight Scale | Data Hub

Teladoc HEALTH

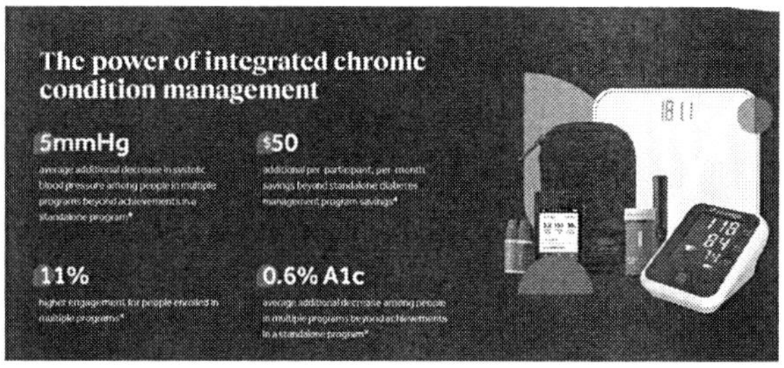

#SensorsConverge *Image Sources: Omron, Teledoc Health*

Sensors Converge

Future RPM programmes are expected to be more dependent on new wearable technology

*There is a need for **mass screening and early detection** in developed nations where hypertension may affect up to one in two adults.; hundreds of heart attacks and strokes can be prevented via early detection and management – Dr.Nadia Tsao, IDTechEx*

#SensorsConverge

Sensors Converge

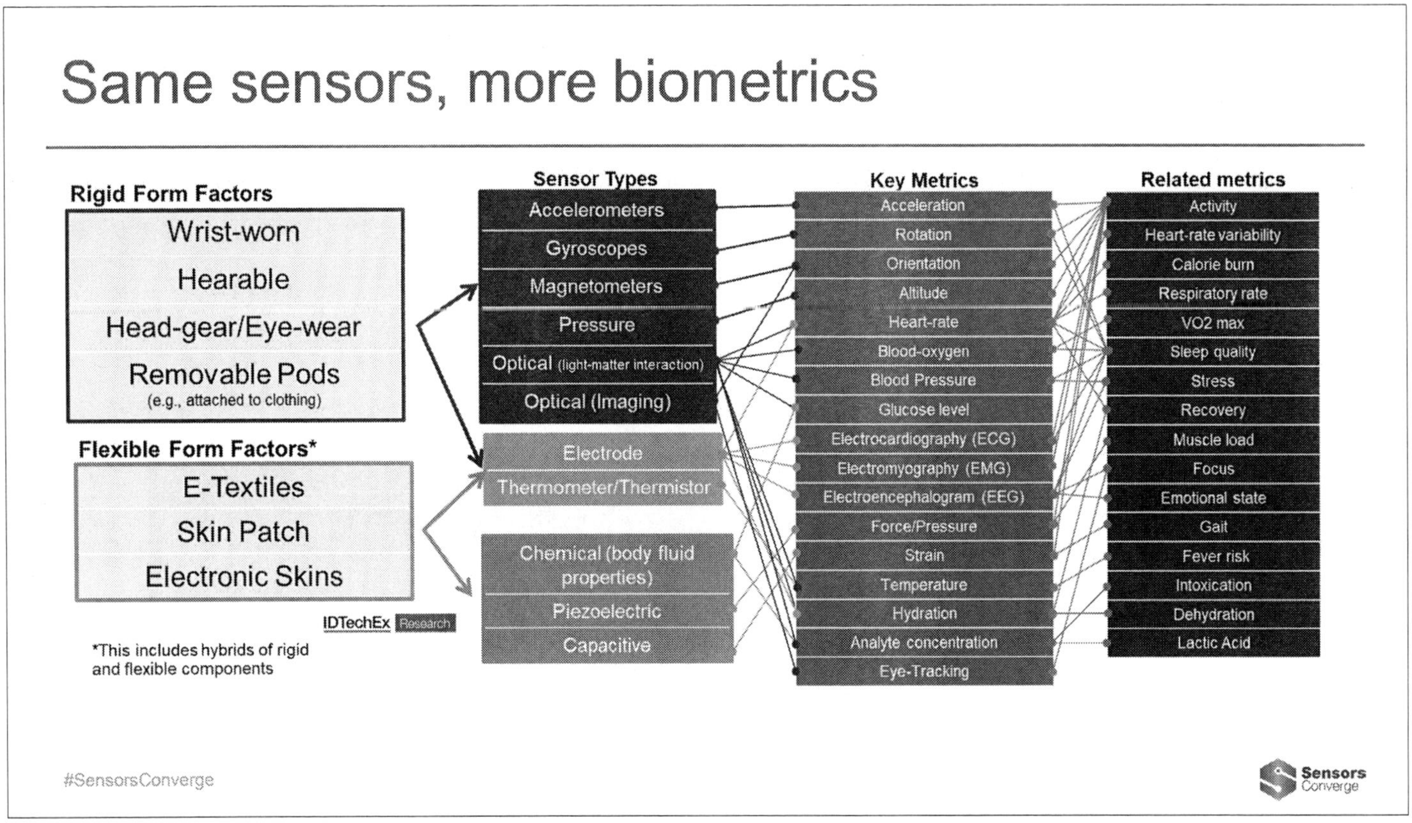
Same sensors, more biometrics
Rigid Form Factors
Wrist-worn
Hearable
Head-gear/Eye-wear
Removable Pods
(e.g., attached to clothing)
Flexible Form Factors*
E-Textiles
Skin Patch
Electronic Skins
IDTechEx Research
*This includes hybrids of rigid and flexible components
Sensor Types
Accelerometers
Gyroscopes
Magnetometers
Pressure
Optical (light-matter interaction)
Optical (Imaging)
Electrode
Thermometer/Thermistor
Chemical (body fluid properties)
Piezoelectric
Capacitive
Key Metrics
Acceleration
Rotation
Orientation
Altitude
Heart-rate
Blood-oxygen
Blood Pressure
Glucose level
Electrocardiography (ECG)
Electromyography (EMG)
Electroencephalogram (EEG)
Force/Pressure
Strain
Temperature
Hydration
Analyte concentration
Eye-Tracking
Related metrics
Activity
Heart-rate variability
Calorie burn
Respiratory rate
VO2 max
Sleep quality
Stress
Recovery
Muscle load
Focus
Emotional state
Gait
Fever risk
Intoxication
Dehydration
Lactic Acid
#SensorsConverge
Sensors Converge

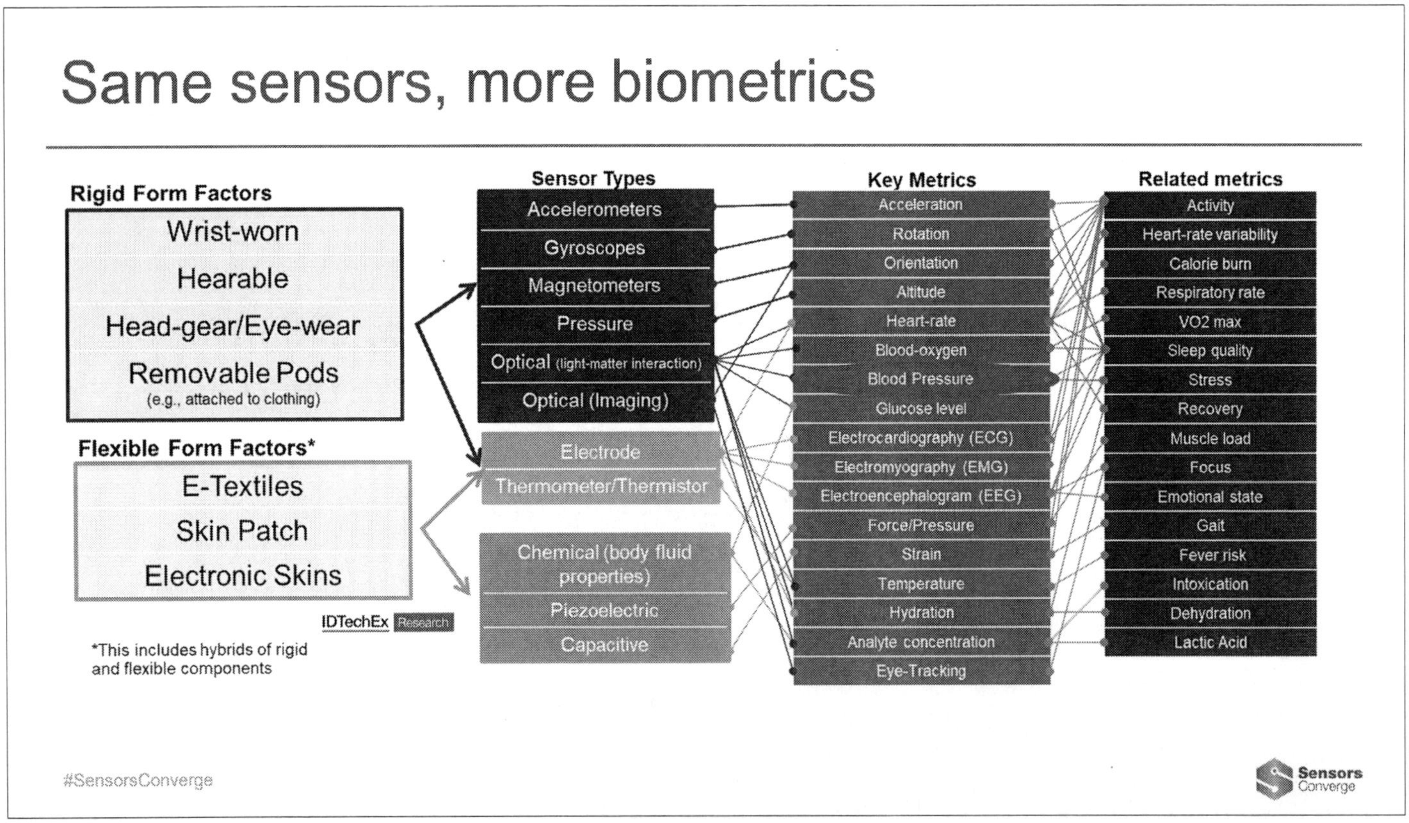
Same sensors, more biometrics
Rigid Form Factors
Wrist-worn
Hearable
Head-gear/Eye-wear
Removable Pods
(e.g., attached to clothing)
Flexible Form Factors*
E-Textiles
Skin Patch
Electronic Skins
IDTechEx Research
*This includes hybrids of rigid and flexible components
Sensor Types
Accelerometers
Gyroscopes
Magnetometers
Pressure
Optical (light-matter interaction)
Optical (Imaging)
Electrode
Thermometer/Thermistor
Chemical (body fluid properties)
Piezoelectric
Capacitive
Key Metrics
Acceleration
Rotation
Orientation
Altitude
Heart-rate
Blood-oxygen
Blood Pressure
Glucose level
Electrocardiography (ECG)
Electromyography (EMG)
Electroencephalogram (EEG)
Force/Pressure
Strain
Temperature
Hydration
Analyte concentration
Eye-Tracking
Related metrics
Activity
Heart-rate variability
Calorie burn
Respiratory rate
VO2 max
Sleep quality
Stress
Recovery
Muscle load
Focus
Emotional state
Gait
Fever risk
Intoxication
Dehydration
Lactic Acid
#SensorsConverge
Sensors Converge

A growing number of OEMs recognize the value in wearable blood pressure sensing

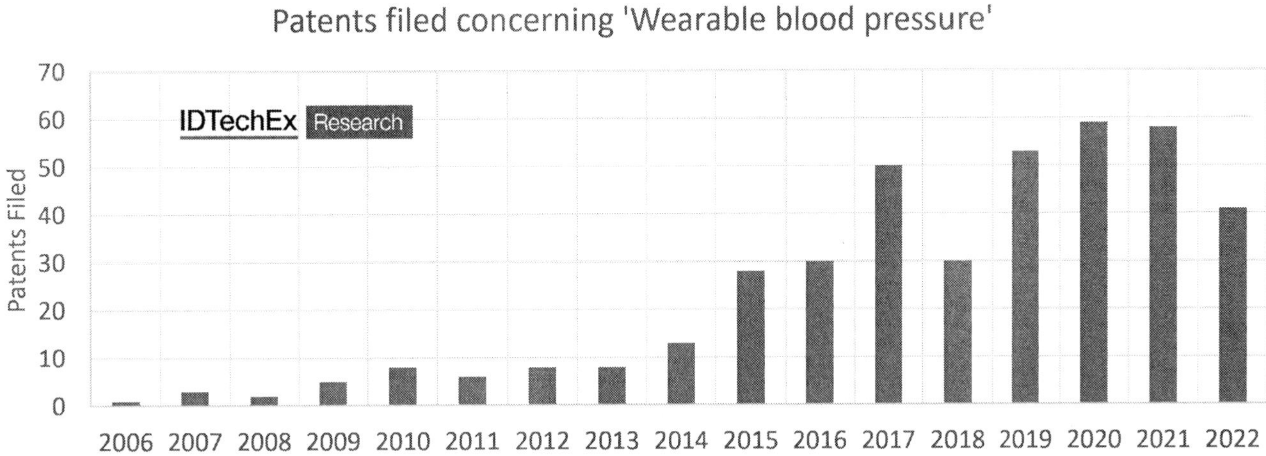

#SensorsConverge

Sensors Converge

Calibration and noise mitigation solutions are key in unlocking the potential of the wearable blood pressure market

VALENCELL

"The crux of the issue in data collection is a trade-off between the ease of data collection versus noise in the data" – Valencell, 2020

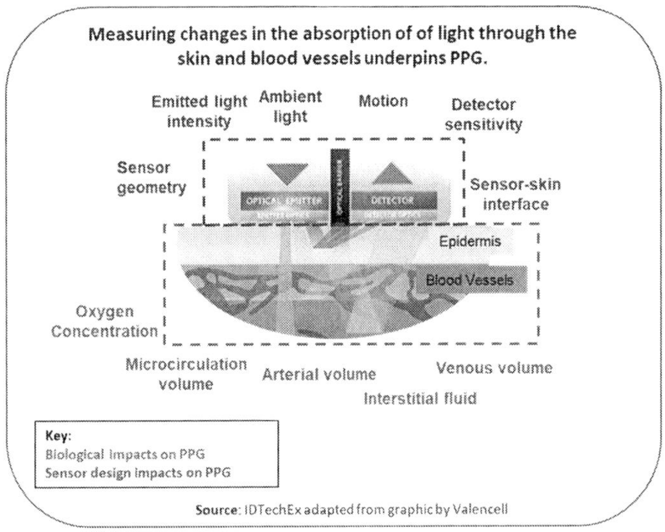

#SensorsConverge

Sensors Converge

Calibration and noise mitigation solutions are key in unlocking the potential of the wearable blood pressure market

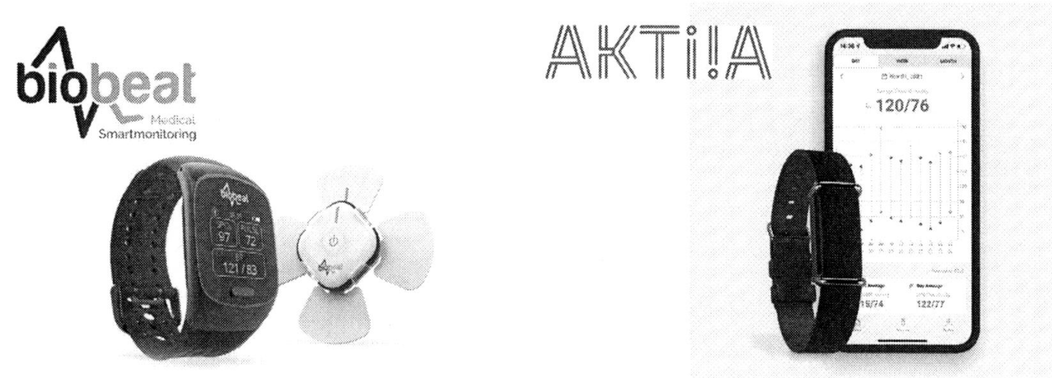

Aktiia Bracelet G1 is a non-invasive blood pressure (BP) monitor intended to measure optical Photoplethysmography (PPG) ***signals on the user's wrist*** *and to calculate blood pressure values using a Pulse Wave Analysis (PWA) technique,* ***following a calibration process using an oscillometric blood pressure monitor***

#SensorsConverge *Image Sources: Aktiia, Biobeat*

Sensors Converge

Calibration and noise mitigation solutions are key in unlocking the potential of the wearable blood pressure market

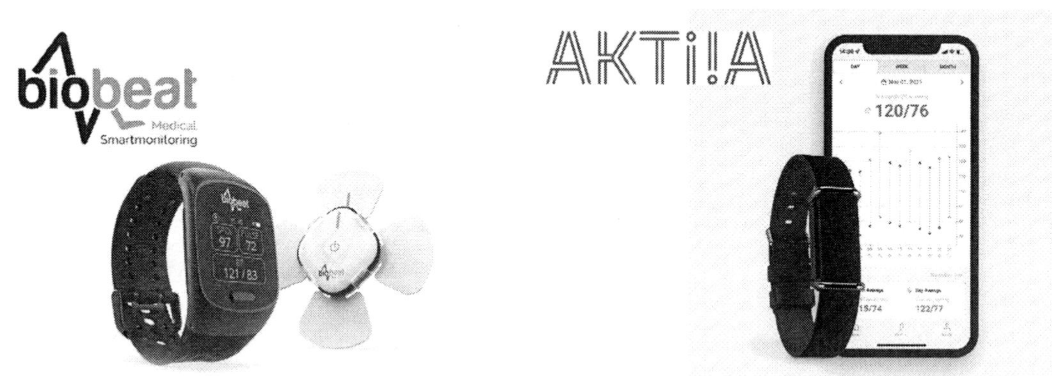

The Biobeat Platform tracks changes in blood pressure based on Pulse Wave Transit Time (PWTT) which is obtained utilizing pulse measurements from the integrated SpO2 sensor, ***following a calibration process using an FDA-cleared oscillometric blood pressure monitor****.*

#SensorsConverge *Image Sources: Aktiia, Biobeat*

Sensors Converge

Outlook for wearable blood pressure technology in the healthcare market?

IDTechEx Research

Practical proxys

- Encouraging increased blood pressure monitoring with calibrated wearables will still play a key role hyper-tension management with RPM.

The promise of ML

- Machine learning, and the rapid advancements in AI could overcome the challenges in relating cuff-less, cal-free wearable data proxys to a 'gold-standard' BP measuremen

Regulatory influences

- Essential, slow, and not a guarantee of medical adoption.

#SensorsConverge

Sensors Converge

Consumer Market: Immersive Experiences

Mega-trends driving demand for 'immersive experiences'

Escapism and Play

Escapism during play may be more valuable with the backdrop of global pressures

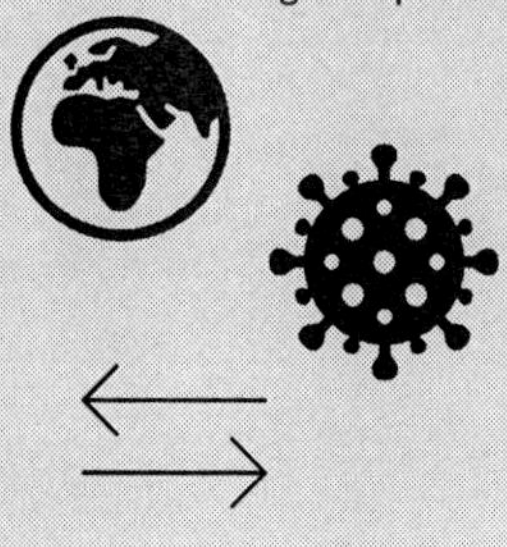

Efficiency and Convenience

User experience improvements from existing consumer hardware is plateauing

Remote Working

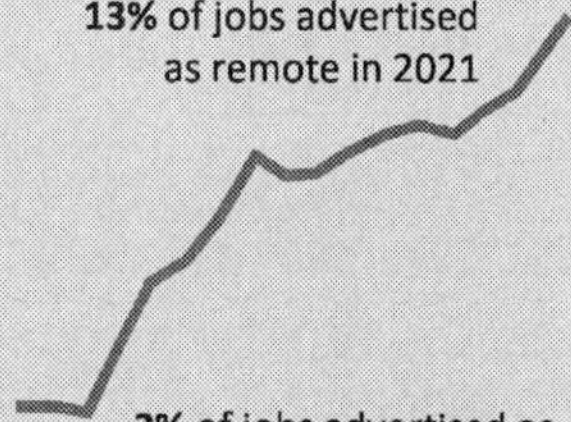

The number of jobs advertised as remote rose from2%-13% between 2020 and 2021

Customer Engagement

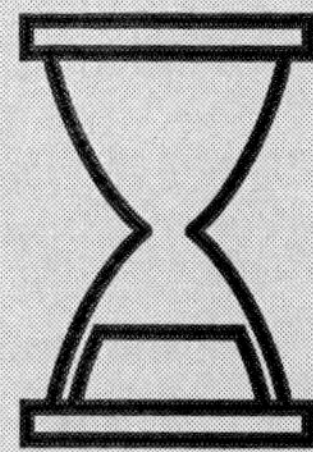

More immersive experiences can increase customer engagement time, increase memorability and ease interfacing with online retailers

Data from:LinkedIn.

#SensorsConverge

Sensors Converge

Established applications in VR and AR

Gaming

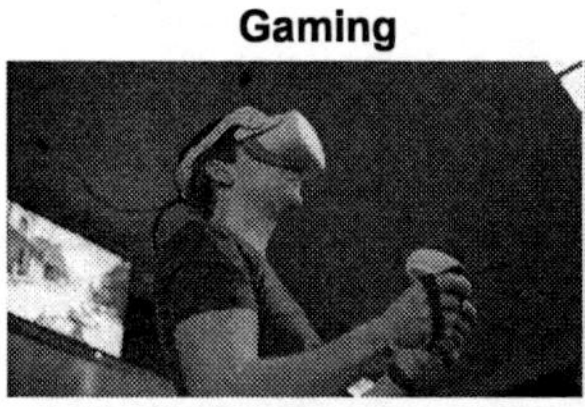

Education

Visualisation

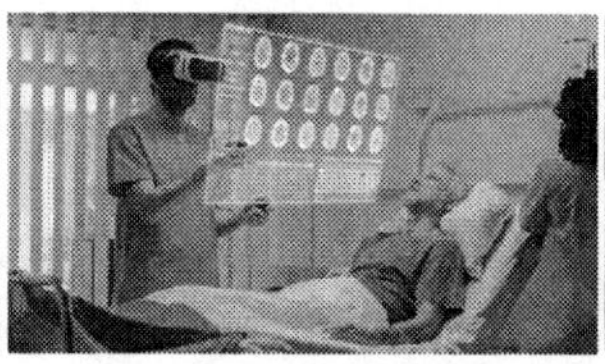

Retail

Design

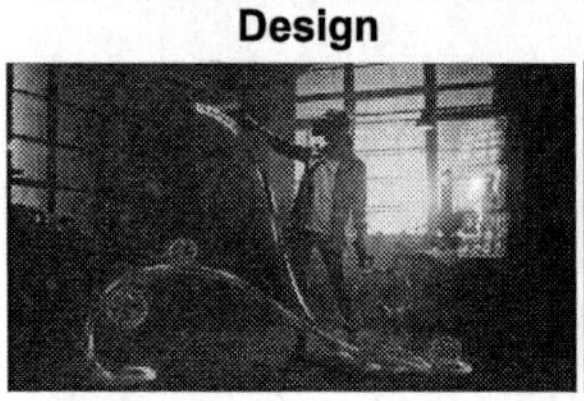

Training

Productivity

Industrial

Image sources: shutterstock

#SensorsConverge

Sensors Converge

Controllers and sensing connect AR and VR devices to the environment and the user

Growing immersion →

- Head tracking: what direction is the user looking?
- Tracking hand location/ direction: where is the user pointing?
- Positional tracking: where is the user in the environment?
- Full hand tracking: how are the user's hands interacting with the virtual environment?
- Eye tracking: where exactly is the user looking?
  Note that a key additional use of eye tracking is enabling foveated rendering.
- Face tracking: what is the user's facial expression?
- Full body tracking: how exactly is the user interacting with the environment?

#SensorsConverge

Sensors Converge

Consumer trends: smart-straps could take control in AR/VR

Motion Sensing

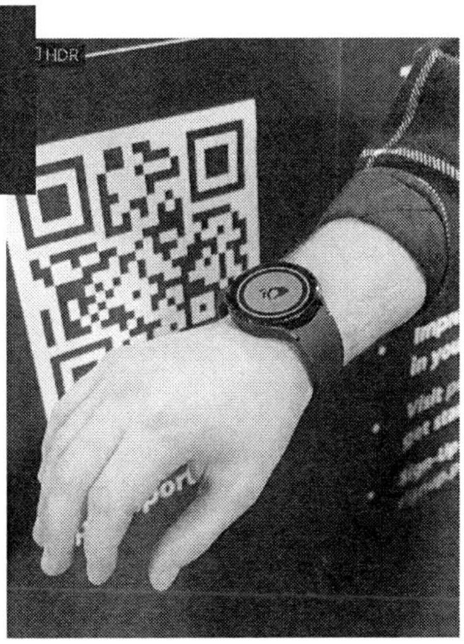

Port 6 demoing their detection of the 'pinch' gesture measured with standard smart-watch sensors (IMUs and optical). IDTechEx photo.

'Surface Nerve Conductance'

WEARABLE DEVICES

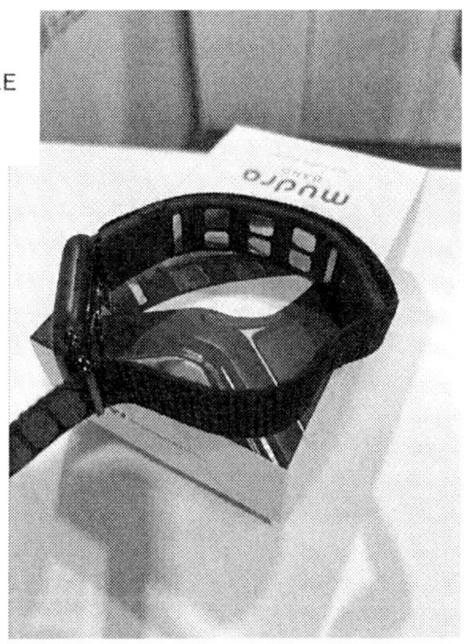

Mudra band brain computer interfacing using a combination of bipotential sensing, including 'surface nerve conductance'. IDTechEx photo.

#SensorsConverge

Sensors Converge

Electrode innovations for improved neural signal measurements

'Dryode' Technology

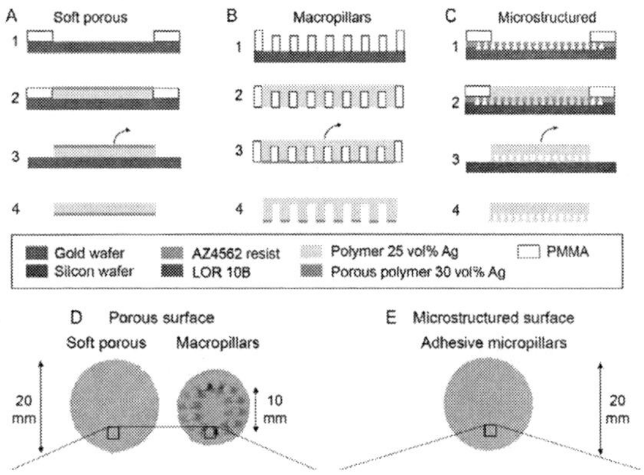

Image Source: Skin Conformal Polymer Electrodes for Clinical ECG and EEG Recordings (2018) *Flurin Stauffer et al.*

IDUN Technologies

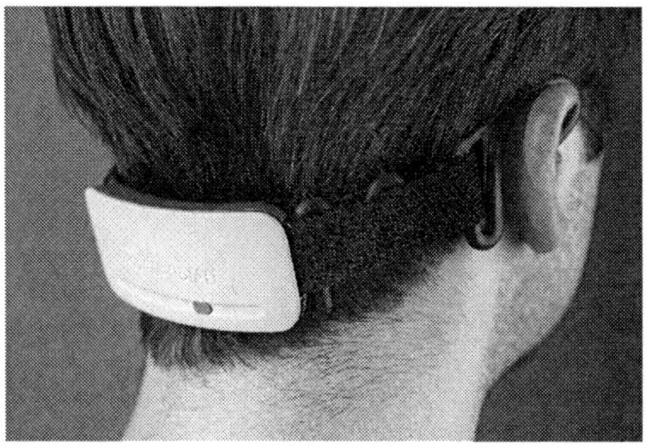

Image Source: IDUN Guardian

#SensorsConverge

Sensors Converge

Wearables sensors as assistive technology

EarSwitch

EarSwitch showing their in-ear device controlling a gaze-controlled keyboard. Example of a new operating principle, using established hardware
Image source: EarSwitch; Strap Tech

Strap tech

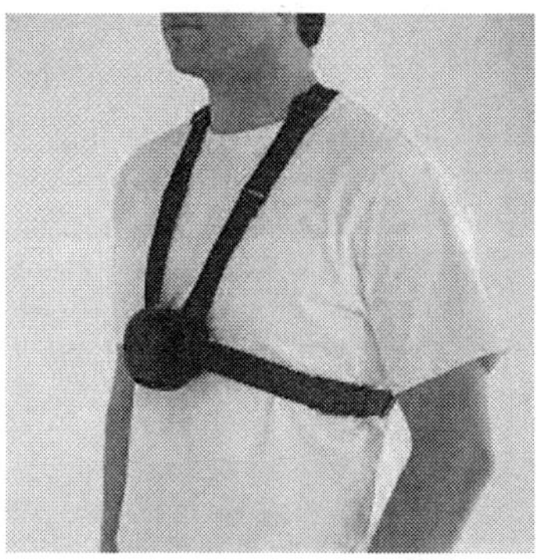

Strap-tech uses lidar within a chest-strap to improve navigational experiences for the visually impaired.

#SensorsConverge

Sensors Converge

Outlook for sensor technology in the consumer market?

IDTechEx Research

Wearable sensors could be key for human machine interfacing

- As AR/VR head-set adoption rises, so will the need for gesture control and hand-tracking. Different use-cases will require some combination of in-bult cameras, hand-held controllers or wearables.

The value sensors enabling 'immersive experiences' will rise

- Those sensors able to maintain and improve immersion will rise in value. For example, wearable control systems could offer a less clunky user experience than controllers – as well as offering that crucial value proposition of efficient and continuous access.

Dry electrode technology could bring brain-computer interfacing to the mass-market

- Interfacing with neural signals via dry electrodes is better suited to the consumer market than wet-electrodes or implants. Improving the signal to noise achievable is a key technological challenge many players are now tackling.

#SensorsConverge

Sensors Converge

Deep-Tech (Quantum)

The quantum technology industry is growing

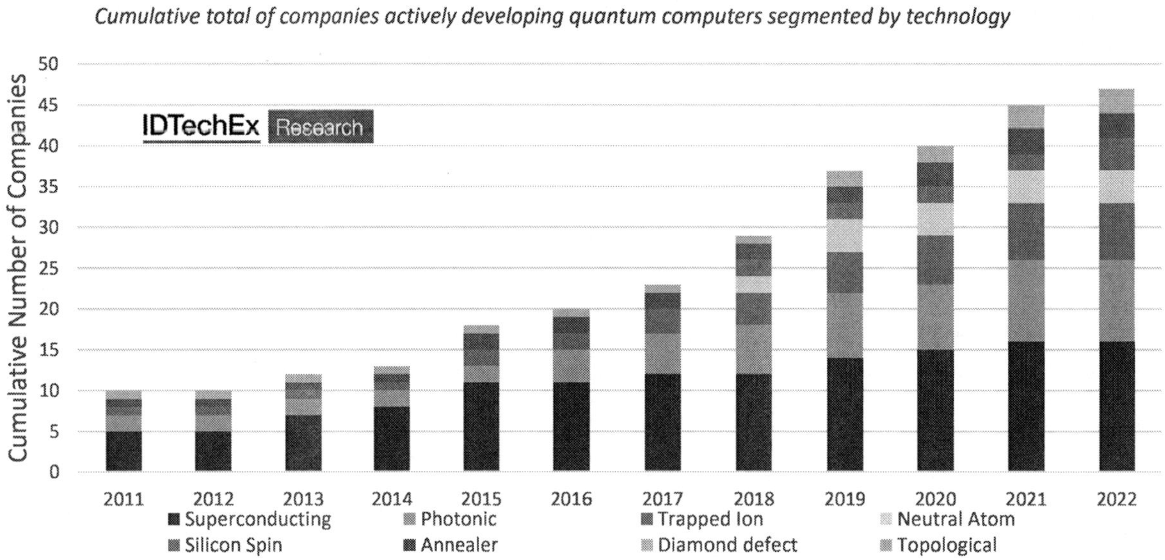

#SensorsConverge

Sensors Converge

Government investment in sensing and imaging rivals computing

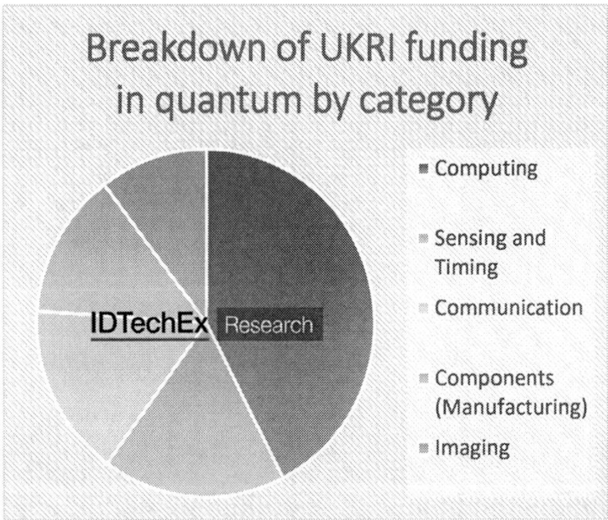

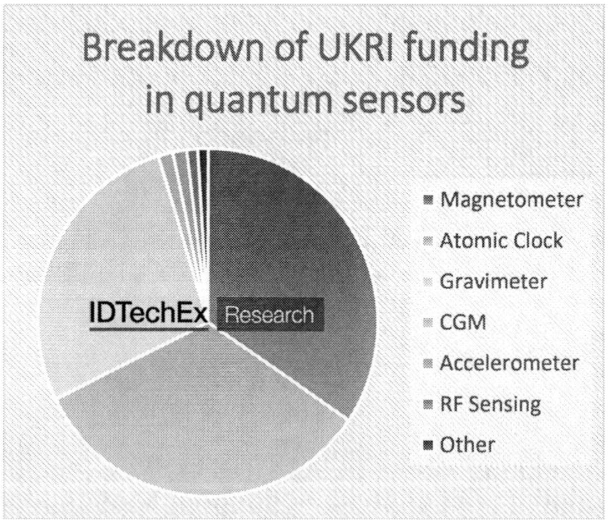

#SensorsConverge

Sensors Converge

The trend towards chip-scale quantum sensors

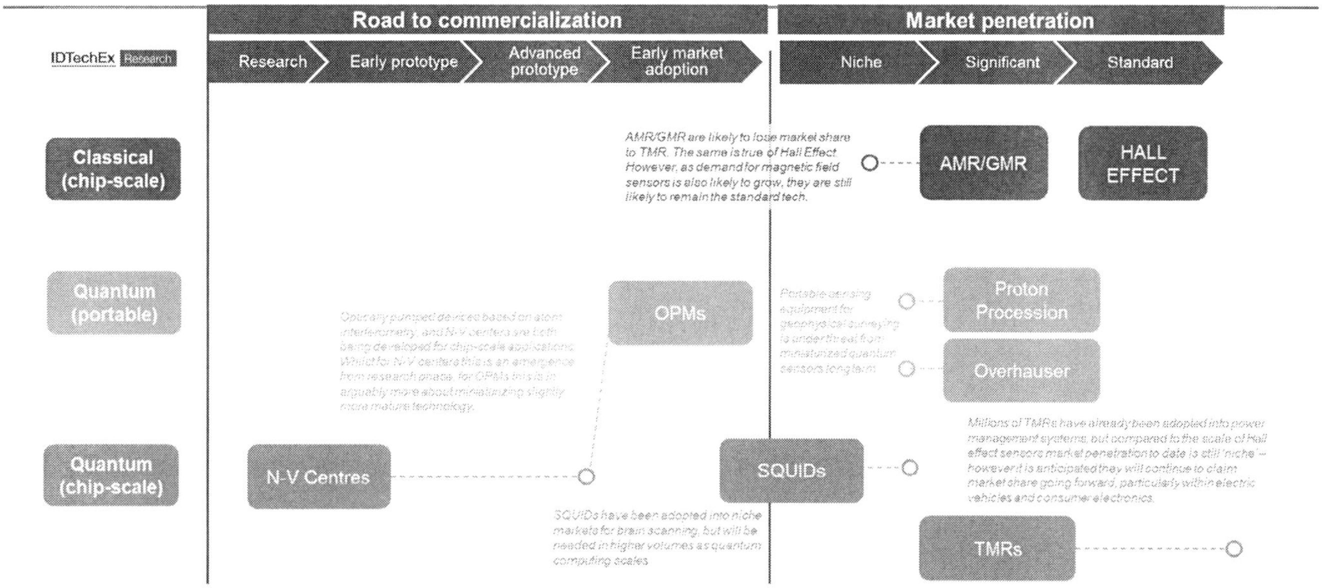

#SensorsConverge

Sensors Converge

Long-term opportunities for wearable quantum sensors

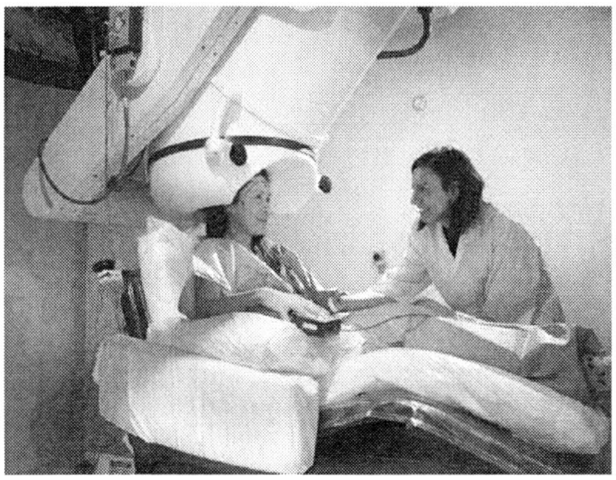

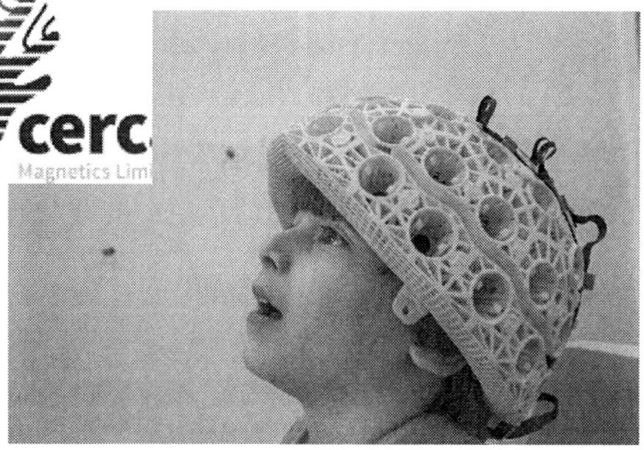

Image Source: Cerca Magnetics

Miniaturized quantum magnetic field sensors for biomagnetic imaging

#SensorsConverge

Sensors Converge

Long-term opportunities for wearable quantum sensors

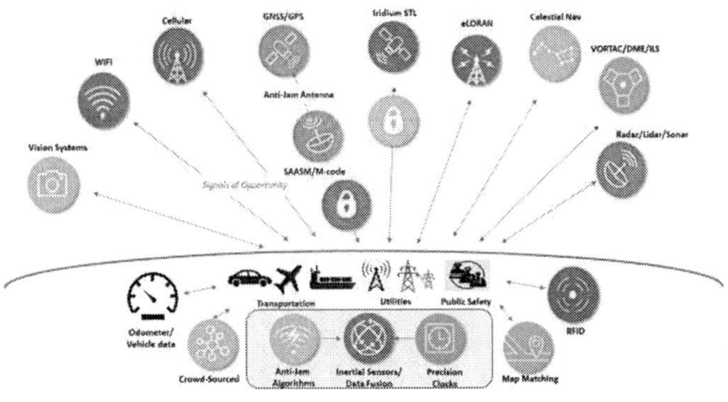

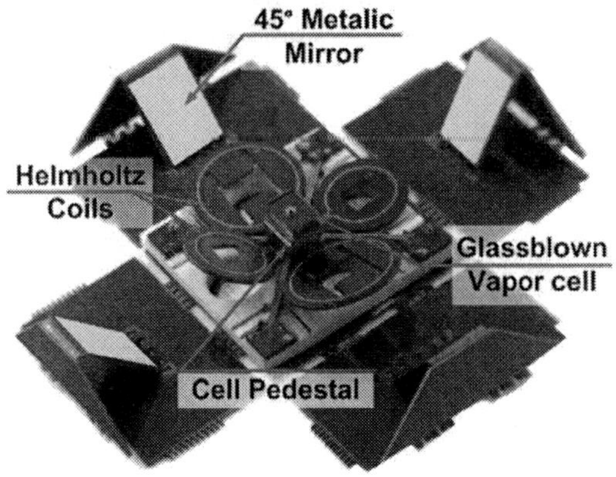

MEMS manufacturing for alkali vapor-based quantum sensors could offer more sensitivity, and less drift, valued for navigation in GPS denied environments.

#SensorsConverge

Image Sources: R. M. Noor et al., in Proceeding of 2017 IEEE International Symposium on Inertial Sensors and Systems (INERTIAL) (2017), pp. 156-159. , Orolia

Sensors Converge

Outlook for sensor technology in the consumer market?

IDTechEx Research

- Quantum technology is rapidly commercializing and miniaturizing
- Quantum sensing is likely a higher volume hardware opportunity than computing
- Wearable quantum sensors could impact both the healthcare and consumer market

#SensorsConverge

Sensors Converge

Closing remarks

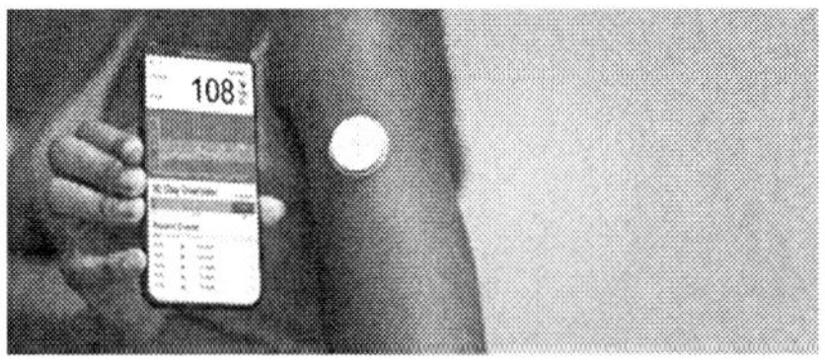

Healthcare Market: **Chronic Disease Management**

- Technical challenges overcoming calibration and noise
- Opportunity for ML

Consumer Market: **Immersive Experiences**

- Sensors can add value in immersive control systems for AR/VR
- Immersion can add value through escapism or inclusivity

Deep-Tech: **Quantum Technology**

- Quantum sensor technology is being miniaturized to the chip-scale
- There are opportunities for wearable quantum sensors in the consumer and healthcare markets long-term

#SensorsConverge

Sensors Converge

Q & A

IDTechEx.com/wearables

IDTechEx.com/quantumcomputing

#SensorsConverge

Sensors Converge

AUTHOR INDEX

Questex Media Group, Inc.
275 Grove Street, Suite 2-130
Newton, Massachusetts 02466
USA

ISBN 979-8-3313-0064-7

CURRAN ASSOCIATES INC.
proceedings.com